THE MIDDLE EAST AND SOUTH ASIA

ELISABETH YARBAKHSH

THE WORLD TODAY SERIES®

2020-2022

54TH EDITION

Elisabeth Yarbakhsh

A researcher at the Centre for Arab and Islamic Studies (the Middle East and Central Asia) at the Australian National University (ANU), Canberra, Australia, Dr. Yarbakhsh completed her PhD in 2017. She has a Bachelor of Arts (Honors), majoring in anthropology and development studies, and a Bachelor of Asian Studies, majoring in Urdu/Persian and contemporary Asian societies, both from ANU. Dr. Yarbakhsh was the recipient of the Australian National University's University Medal for Anthropology in 2012. Her research interests include contemporary Iran, refugees and migration in the Middle East and South Asia, and the intersection of Islam and politics in modern-day society.

Adapted, rewritten and revised annually from a book entitled *The Middle East and South Asia 1967*, published in 1967 and succeeding years by

Rowman & Littlefield
An imprint of The Rowman & Littlefield Publishing Group, Inc.
4501 Forbes Blvd., Suite 200, Lanham, MD 20706
www.rowman.com

Library of Congress Control Number Available

ISBN 978-1-4758-5645-3 (pbk. : alk. paper)
ISBN 978-1-4758-5646-0 (electronic)

Cover design by Sarah Marizan

Cartography by William L. Nelson

Typography by Barton Matheson Willse & Worthington

The World Today Series has thousands of subscribers across the U.S. and Canada. A sample list of users who annually rely on this most up-to-date material includes:

Public library systems
Universities and colleges
High schools
Federal and state agencies
All branches of the armed forces & war colleges
National Geographic Society
National Democratic Institute
Agricultural Education Foundation
ExxonMobil Corporation
Chevron Corporation
CNN

CONTENTS

**Door to the *Ka'aba*, the sacred shrine
of the Great Mosque in Mecca**

The Middle East and South Asia Today

The deadly convulsion of violence that gripped Israel and Palestine in April 2021, brought a timely and devastating reminder that the issues and tensions historically shaping the region have by no means receded, even as the world's attention has understandably been focused on the rapid global spread of Covid-19. Two years on from the publication of the 53rd volume of The Middle East and South Asia, the world is, in some respects, a very different place. India, today, is in the grip of a national tragedy of epic proportions, as the novel coronavirus sweeps through its population leaving a wake of death and destruction. Iran has struggled to bring Covid-19 under control since the first case was reported in February 2020. Shortages of critical equipment and a severely damaged health infrastructure continue to put tens of thousands of lives at risk in Syria. Countries across the regions of the Middle East and South Asia are once again re-entering strict lockdowns as cases spike and new variants of the virus circulate. Amidst the gloom there are some rare success stories: while Bangladesh teeters on the cusp of disaster, only weeks ago the populous nation was being held up as an example of a country that had successfully implemented a multi-pronged policy response to the Covid threat; today, the wealthy Gulf monarchies are leveraging the advantages of strong economies and small populations to roll out rapid vaccination programs and are cautiously re-opening borders; Bhutan has vaccinated almost its entire adult population; and Israel has lifted restrictions after declaring itself "Covid-free."

What has become increasingly clear over the past year, is that Covid is as much a social and political event as it is a health crisis. Domestic, regional and global disparities have been exposed by the virus. Existing fault lines have, in many cases, been significantly exacerbated. Authoritarian modes of government across the region have been strengthened and the virus has, not infrequently, provided convenient cover for crackdowns on opposition groups and for the suppression of legitimate protest. Ethnic and religious minorities have found themselves blamed for outbreaks of the virus and targeted in vicious attacks. Migrants and refugees have faced new restrictions on movement and involuntary repatriations on the pretext that they pose an epidemiological threat to citizens. War has hampered a coordinated response to the pandemic and some populations have been denied timely access to vaccines in the context of conflict. This volume provides an important reminder of the forces that have shaped and continue to shape the Middle East and South Asia. It touches on an array of topics from history to geography, and from politics to the economy, in an effort to provide a broad view and pique the interest of a wide readership. It is the expectation that this will be just the starting point to a deeper exploration of themes and countries of specific interest.

Together, the Middle East and South Asia comprise a fascinating region. It is a region that stretches from the desert sands of the Arabian Peninsula, to the Sundarbans mangrove forests in the Bengal Delta. The region's highest point is in the perennially snow-covered Himalayas, while its lowest is the Dead Sea, many hundreds of meters below sea level. The region encompasses extremes: from the glittering urban centers of the hyper-modern Arab Gulf, to the mist-shrouded traditions of Bhutan's "Land of the Thunder Dragon." Importantly, this diversity extends beyond mere features of landscape. Hundreds of ethnic groups, dozens of languages, and five major world religions—in addition to numerous local traditions and practices—make up the 24 states of the Middle East and South Asia.

If we focus solely on diversity, however, we may overlook some of the ways in which the region can productively be viewed as a cohesive whole. The countries of the Middle East and South Asia have a long history of cultural, political, and economic ties. Islam, from its origins in the Hijaz on the Red Sea, has profoundly shaped an area stretching from the Mediterranean to the Bay of Bengal. Indian Ocean trade routes historically connected India to the Middle East; long pre-dating European control of sea routes, traders from Arabia and India's west coast made use of seasonal monsoon winds to travel vast ocean distances. European colonialism brought a different kind of shared experience, and was very often the crucible in which nationalisms—and thus the modern states of the region—were forged.

In the past two years, the borders between states of the region have become less permeable, as governments imposed unprecedented restriction on movement in an effort to stem the spread of disease. No longer could young Saudis venture along the King Fahd Causeway to briefly enjoy the relative freedom of Bahrain; Iranian pilgrims have been unable to make their way to the holy sites of Karbala and Najaf in Iraq; and traders from India's northeast are being turned back on the Bhutanese border. The world has fragmented with surprising speed, yet at the same time the sense of global interconnectedness has rarely felt greater, or more threatening. A cough in Tehran brought a deadly outbreak of disease threatening lives and livelihoods in Kabul; tourists visiting the Egyptian city of Luxor in Egypt, returned home to Europe and North America carrying the potentially deadly coronavirus in their lungs. The long-term economic impact of the virus will be felt across the region and recovery will almost certainly depend on cooperation between states that have not found common ground in the past. In the meantime, many of the ongoing issues of concern in the region, can now be viewed through the lens of the Covid-19 pandemic.

This book is divided into two broad sections. The first draws on some of the major topics and themes that have shaped the region historically and to the present day. These themes include the struggles of ordinary people of the Middle East and South Asia to achieve democratic rights; the role of oil in shaping economies and societies; burgeoning environmental threats; and the emergence of IS across the region. It provides a broad historical overview, focusing on the major civilizations that have shaped the Middle East and South Asia to the present. The second section gives detailed information about the politics, economies, and societies of 24 states, a small number of disputed territories, and the main regional organizations. The 54th edition of The Middle East and South Asia builds on previous editions, while offering the most up-to-date information. Important events of the past 12 months are examined in detail, revealing the extraordinary dynamism of the region, while detailing regional responses to the coronavirus pandemic.

The consistent goal of The World Today series is an appreciation of peoples and states from their own perspectives, lightly moderated by the views of the author. In the following pages, I shine a light on conflicting claims and charges to help the general reader understand recent and past developments. This approach perhaps inevitably risks accusations of partiality, however it is an approach driven, above all else, by a sincere respect for the peoples and places represented. I hope that readers will come to share a similar appreciation for these peoples and places.

Technicalities: Arabic sounds are transliterated into English by a variety of systems, such that multiple spellings are common. In general, this volume retains the common English spellings for well-known personalities but otherwise adopts specialized spellings, minus diacritical markings for ease of reading. Thus, King Hussein rules Jordan; his great-grandfather was Sharif Husayn of Mecca. Outside the Arab world, the national transliteration of Muslim names applies, the founder of Bangladesh being Mujibur Rahman, not Mujib al-Rahman.

Figures provided for country GDP and GDP per capita are real U.S. dollar amounts, not Purchasing Power Parity (PPP). Per capita refers to all residents of a country, not just citizens. This is particularly important to note in countries such as the Gulf Arab states that have a high ratio of non-citizens to citizens.

Few countries in the region have conducted recent population censuses. Lebanon, for example, for political reasons has not conducted an official nation-wide census since 1932. Other countries have experienced extreme demographic fluctuations in recent years. As many as 9 million people have left Syria since the outbreak of hostilities in 2011, swelling the populations of neighboring states. In this volume, population statistics are latest estimates based on U.N. figures and projections.

Elisabeth Yarbakhsh
Canberra, Australia
June 2021

The State of Democracy: Seasons of Hope and Despair

For many political analysts, the state of democracy globally can be described as one of worrying retreat. Many of the gains made between the collapse of the Berlin Wall and the early 2000s have now been rolled back or are under serious threat. Around the world, democratic institutions have come under sustained attack, even in nations with a long history of robust democracy. A number of democratic norms—from freedom of expression, to the upholding of the rights of migrants and refugees—have suffered unprecedented setbacks. Two trends are cause for particular concern.

The first is the rise of ethnic cleansing and forced demographic change, a phenomenon that defined the 1990s but is now making a disturbing comeback. As the Syrian civil war sputters to its likely conclusion, the full horror of ethnic cleansing, as undertaken by various actors including the Assad regime and the Islamic State (IS), is being exposed. In South Asia, Bangladesh has struggled to cope with the mass-influx of Muslim Rohingya refugees from neighboring Myanmar. Efforts to repatriate the Rohingya have been frustrated by ongoing atrocities committed by the Myanmar military and armed ethnic groups.

More subtle efforts to alter a population's ethnic or religious composition are also underway. In Bahrain, the Sunni monarchy has implemented policies to erode the state's Shi'a majority. The citizenship of hundreds of Shi'a Bahraini has been revoked, often on the flimsiest of grounds. Shi'a political groups have, in some cases, been banned or their activities severely curtailed. In East Jerusalem, Israel has actively worked to reduce the Palestinian population vis-à-vis Jewish Israelis. Discriminatory housing policies, demolitions, over-policing of Palestinian communities, under-allocation of municipal services, and the imposition of Israeli culture, has coincided with increased Israeli settlement and the deliberate isolation of East Jerusalem from the remainder of the West Bank. A new law introduced in 2018, allows the interior minister to revoke the residency of Jerusalem-based Palestinians for, among other things, breaches of "loyalty" to Israel.

The second trend of concern is the propensity of some countries to act extra-territorially in targeting dissidents and critics. The most high-profile incident of 2018 was the shocking and brutal murder of journalist Jamal Khashoggi inside Saudi Arabia's consulate in Turkey. Saudi Arabia has aggressively pursued its critics across international borders. It is not alone in doing so. In the Gulf region, Bahrain and Iran have pursued exiled opponents, engaging in tactics of harassment, propaganda campaigns, targeting of family members,

extradition requests, and abductions. Turkey has systematically targeted hundreds of dissidents living abroad, transferring its increasingly authoritarian domestic policies to the global arena.

For the time being, democracy in South Asia has remained on a relatively stable course, democratic setbacks in some areas, and in some countries, have been offset by gains in others. In the Middle East prospects for democracy are far bleaker. The optimism of the Arab Spring has been replaced with the unhappy realisation that authoritarian regimes, at least in the short-term, are here to stay. Democracy, however, has enduring appeal. It provides the foundation upon which conditions for a better life, for ordinary citizens, can be built. The ballot box continues to be viewed as the best way to hold leaders accountable. Demands for democracy, at the grassroots, are likely to be undimmed.

NEW HOPE IN SOUTH ASIA

India is often described as "the world's largest democracy." With a population of 1.37 billion and a flourishing democracy that has rarely faltered in the seven decades since independence, India has every claim to that impressive status. Some Indians—with far less evidence—suggest that India is also the *oldest* democracy, with democratic institutions that pre-date Athens. While such matters may be of interest to historians (and Indian nationalists) more pressing is the question of why democracy emerged (or re-emerged) in India in 1950 and why it has remained so robust, in a region where democracy's roots are generally shallow and where authoritarianism, both benign and malign, has dominated. While India has at various points in time been the *only* peaceful democracy in South Asia, recent years have seen a new flourishing of openness. By many measures, South Asia today is more stable and democratic than it has been in decades.

If this is reason for hope, it is tempered by the reality that democracy in many parts of South Asia remains fragile and the return to authoritarianism may, in some cases, be no further away than an unforeseen political crisis or a single electoral cycle. The vulnerability of democracy is perhaps best illustrated in the tumultuous Maldivian experience of authoritarian rule and democratic flourishing in the decade from 2008 to 2018.

In the Maldives, President Maumoon Abdul Gayoom initiated political reform, following protests sparked by the 2003 death in custody of a young Maldivian man, brutally killed by soldiers during a prison riot. Political opponents of the president were able to skilfully wield public discontent; forcing Gayoom to hold free

elections. In 2008, Gayoom relinquished a three-decade hold on power, handing the reins of government to the opposition in a surprisingly peaceful electoral process. The Maldives had made an important political transition, and while its democracy lacked depth, the country appeared—for the first time in its history—to be set on a path towards full democracy. This democratic trajectory was abruptly halted in 2012, when President Nasheed was forced from office, ostensibly at gunpoint. Following the 2013 elections that brought Abdulla Yameen Gayoom to power, many commenters gloomily concluded that the embryonic democracy of the Maldives had been killed-off.

Over five years Yameen systematically jailed or forced into exile the entire opposition leadership. Journalists were murdered or disappeared and the government seized control of institutions such as the judiciary and the electoral commission. An al-Jazeera investigation traced a billion-dollar money-laundering operation directly back to the president. In this environment, it was widely assumed that elections would be rigged in Yameen's favor. The international community was surprised therefore, not only by the opposition's win at the ballot box, but also Yameen's willingness, in the event, to relinquish power.

The results of the 2018 election put the Maldives back on the path of democracy. However, there remains some cause for concern. The ruling coalition includes Islamist parties and others who are not necessarily sympathetic to the imposition of democratic norms on Maldivian society. Anti-corruption efforts may be hampered by the self-interest of those in government, and attempts to reform the judiciary face considerable hurdles.

One democracy of South Asia that teeters on the verge of authoritarianism is Sri Lanka. Victory over the separatist Liberation Tigers of Tamil Eelam (the Tamil Tigers) emboldened democratically elected President Mahinda Rajapaksa to become increasingly authoritarian. By 2013, many were despairing of Sri Lankan democracy. The defeat of Rajapaksa in both presidential and parliamentary elections of 2015, surprised pundits and boosted democratic prospects in Sri Lanka. Unfortunately, recent events show that a strand of authoritarianism remains dominant. In late 2018, President Maithripala Sirisena unilaterally and unconstitutionally dismissed Prime Minister Ranil Wickremesinghe from office, replacing him with Rajapaksa, presumably seeking to forestall a bid for power from the former president. When Wickremesinghe refused to accept the dismissal, Sirisena dissolved parliament, an act overturned by the Supreme Court within a matter of weeks.

The State of Democracy: Seasons of Hope and Despair

While democracy continues to function in Sri Lanka, it is most seriously threatened by those who are expected to uphold it—democratically elected office-holders. In June 2019, Sirisena caused consternation by declaring that the 19th Amendment to the Constitution should be repealed. The 19th Amendment was introduced by Sirisena, himself, in 2015, as a way of diluting the president's considerable power and bolstering the nation's democracy.

There is still ample opportunity for Sri Lanka to pull back from the brink of authoritarianism. Like India, Sri Lanka has a long history of conducting regular elections. This history will likely stand Sri Lanka in good stead. However, events in Sri Lankan politics over the past several years expose the importance of remaining vigilant against creeping efforts to undermine democratic rule.

Confirming the consolidation of democracy, a new government took office in Nepal in 2018, following the first elections in the country since the abolition of the monarchy in 2008 and the promulgation of the 2015 Constitution that designated Nepal a federal republic and instituted a range of democratic norms and rights.

The small country of Bhutan, located between the emerging superpowers of democratic India and authoritarian China, has experienced a similar maturing of democracy. The elections of 2018 were the third consecutive peaceful transition of power in Bhutan, within a democratic electoral system. They also marked ten years since Bhutan's former king unilaterally decreed democracy, a somewhat novel case of democracy granted from above rather than demanded from below.

Almost two decades on from the U.S. invasion of Afghanistan, and notwithstanding the holding of regular elections and the (relatively) peaceful transfer of power from President Karzai to the National Unity Government (NUG) of President Ahraf Ghani and Abdullah Abdullah, robust democracy is yet to take root in Afghanistan. Elections continue to be marred by allegations of corruption, vote rigging, multiple voting, ballot box stuffing, and the intimidation of voters. While Afghans brave violence to take part in voting, high levels of poverty, rampant corruption, and frequent terrorist attacks inhibit the flourishing of democracy. Afghans have clearly been failed not only by their own governments but, more importantly, by the U.S. and its allies who have promised and failed to deliver the necessary conditions for democratic reform to the country.

The three countries of the former British Raj have a shared colonial history, but vastly different political experiences post-independence. Volumes have been written, in an effort to explain why democracy has flourished in India, even as it has struggled (and for the most part, failed) to take hold in Pakistan and Bangladesh. Some of the reasons for this, can be identified in the events surrounding Partition. India drew on the institutions established under the British Raj, handily supported by stability in the upper echelons of government (India's first prime minister, Jawaharlal Nehru, won four consecutive general elections). By way of contrast, Pakistan (then comprised of East and West Pakistan) had no such institutional foundation to draw on and its governor-general and champion of an independent Pakistan, Muhammad Ali Jinnah, died just a year after Partition. Bangladesh, meanwhile, emerged out of a bloody civil war, that rent apart the two non-contiguous elements of Pakistan. For much of their history both Bangladesh and Pakistan have experienced intermittent military coups. However, both countries today are enjoying periods of stable civilian rule and in 2018 Pakistan celebrated only the second democratic transfer of power between civilian governments in its seventy-year history.

In 2018, elections in Bangladesh saw the incumbent Awami League claim victory with an unlikely 80%. While most pundits agree that the Awami League could have won in a fair vote, the election was anything but fair. In the lead up to the polls police harassed opposition politicians and imprisoned opponents or forced them into exile. Violence and voter intimidation were widespread. Globally, criticism has been relatively muted. With per capita incomes increasing in Bangladesh and real poverty halved, it seems the international community is willing to trade the democratic aspirations, and human rights, of ordinary Bangladeshis for economic prosperity. Whether, in the long-run, the citizens of Bangladesh will be willing to accept the same trade-off is unclear.

In Pakistan, civilian rule has not necessarily greatly diminished the role of the military in politics. While Prime Minister Imran Khan claims the moral authority of a democratically elected leader, the backing he enjoys of Pakistan's powerful generals is no secret.

The consolidating victory of Narendra Modi's Bharatiya Janata Party (BJP) in India's 2019 elections shows two potentially disturbing trends in Indian democracy. The first is the rise of a cult of personality around the figure of Prime Minister Modi, an unexpected turn of events in India's parliamentary system. The second is the retreat of India's secular politics in the context of a majoritarian nationalism espoused by the BJP.

If India, with its long electoral history and its founding commitments to secularism and democracy can fall prey to the sort of ethnic and religious nationalism promoted by the BJP, the long-term prospects for democracy in the broader region may need to be re-assessed.

ARAB EXCEPTIONALISM AND THE PERSISTENCE OF AUTHORITARIANISM

Democracy and liberty spread almost worldwide in the 1980s and 1990s. One great exception was the Middle East, and for nearly two decades political scientists, historians, and commentators sought to explain why authoritarian regimes continued to dominate that region. Their analyses often concluded that Arab societies and politics were similar to one another, but very different from the rest of the world. Certain scholars came to use the term "Arab exceptionalism."

Some theories explained the region's stable authoritarianism with reference to the past, particularly Islamic culture and the legacies of colonialism. Other theories emphasized the present—U.S. and European support maintained rulers if they adopted desired foreign policies. Others argued that oil wealth was key. Whatever the causes, though, there was consensus that Arab countries had proven remarkably resistant to democracy. Arab populations were perceived (incorrectly, as it would transpire) to be uniquely content with authoritarian rule.

The Arab Spring

In early 2011, the Arab world convulsed as demonstrators in their thousands and even hundreds of thousands defied their governments and filled public squares to demand "Irhal!" ("Go!"). What had so inflamed public opinion, and created citizens brave enough to risk arrest, torture, and possible death by publicly demanding their rulers' ouster?

The economic conditions for revolution had long existed in those countries that were most affected by the Arab Spring. In countries such as Egypt and Syria unemployment rates were high and entrenched poverty and economic inequality prevailed. Male university graduates in their twenties were commonly unable to obtain jobs paying well enough to start a home and family, thus finding themselves shut out from the possibility of marriage.

This was equally true for women. Although Arab cultures have traditionally depicted a woman's place as in the home, the Egyptian TV program "I Want to Get Married" portrayed the resulting anguish and humor from a woman's point of view. It became a hit. Its political significance, largely overlooked, was the existence of a large pool of university graduates, either poorly employed or jobless, with time, the

The State of Democracy: Seasons of Hope and Despair

Tank crews ordered into Tahrir Square wait outside the Egyptian Museum. Egypt's military identified its interests with the national good, not President Mubarak's.

Photo courtesy of Jim Neergaard

internet, social media, and dissatisfaction on their hands.

Moreover, economies that had adopted free-market doctrines and opened to international trade proved defenseless when global prices rose sharply. Popular opinion often blamed the International Monetary Fund (IMF) and leaders sympathetic to it. Social distress also rose in other respects. Inadequate low-income housing, insufficient public transportation, and poor government services made daily life difficult for the lower classes.

Nevertheless, simple socio-economic distress fails to fully explain the protests. The revolution began in Tunisia, statistically one of the better-off countries. In Egypt, unemployment was a problem but not to the point where it might have provoked the overthrow President Mubarak. When the "Arab Spring" formally began the slogans and signs in Tunisia and Egypt's Tahrir Square were not about the price of bread. Clearly, there was more to the explosion than economic distress.

Given the fawning government media so dominant in the region, it seems plausible to conclude that protests occurred partly because electronic communication—al-Jazeera on television, and the social media quartet of Facebook, YouTube, texting and, Twitter—told truths and provided images about societies that governments could not control.

Repression, corruption and nepotism had become endemic; now the public could visualize them, sometimes with graphic pictures of victims of police torture. This was not new, of course. Indeed, images from Iran's post-election demonstrations in 2009 had already shown what influence new media could have on grassroots activism.

For a brief window of time, it appeared that media innovations were moving faster than government efforts to censor or restrict access. In 2011, social media enabled a small number of young organizers—inspired by a desire for social freedoms and political rights—to call for demonstrations in ways the regimes could not easily repress.

Calls to protest, whether on social media or otherwise, resonated because the organizers combined a simple message about change with issues of human rights; avoiding the complexities of constitutional reform. At least in Egypt, this was initially a middle class revolution, as evidenced by the clothing worn by many demonstrators. Avoiding the extreme mantras of Islamists and the radical economic demands of leftists, the protest organizers publicized a patriotic movement that could unite ordinary citizens.

President Hosni Mubarak resigned after just 18 days of public demonstrations (see Egypt: history). In February 2011, the Arab Spring seemed powerful enough

	Population (millions)	Median Age	Jobless Rate	Below Poverty Line (%)	Internet Users (m)
Egypt	80.5	24.0	9.6%	20.0%	20.0
Jordan	6.4	21.8	13.4%	14.2%	1.6
Lebanon	4.09	29.4	na	28.0%	1.0
Saudi Arabia	25.7	24.9	10.8%	na	9.6
Syria	22.1	21.5	8.3%	11.9%	4.4
Palestinian Territories	2.5	20.9	16.5%	46.0%	1.3
Yemen	23.4	17.9	35.0%	45.2%	2.2

Table I. Social Indicators Suggesting Popular Distress in 2011

Sources: BBC, IMF, CIA Factbook

The State of Democracy: Seasons of Hope and Despair

First sparked by technology-savvy young activists, individuals from many walks of life and socio-economic classes often joined the protests. Note the variety of clothing styles, later an indication of profession, lifestyle and attitude.

to overthrow other authoritarian Arab rulers. Elsewhere, however, opposition protests often ended in violence and reinvigorated state repression. The patterns of revolutionary success and failure are complex, and demonstrate the old slogan that all politics is local.

Almost a decade later, the euphoria of February 2011 seems somewhat naïve, and sadly misplaced. Although Mubarak himself fell from power, and was imprisoned on charges of inciting the murder of hundreds of protestors, the dominance of the Egyptian military was ultimately undiminished. Today, democracy is on retreat in Egypt and the hopes of Tahrir Square have been dashed.

In other Arab countries of the Middle East, the Arab Spring has likewise had no discernable impact on the short-term stability of authoritarian regimes. In Bahrain, activists from the Haqq Movement for Liberty and Democracy and the Bahrain Center for Human Rights drew on a history of confrontation over reforms and experience with election boycotts. Inspired by events in Cairo, they held marches and eventually assembled crowds at the Pearl Roundabout, the capital's most prominent traffic circle. Initially hesitant, the Sunni royal family and ruling elite eventually ordered the security forces to crush the demonstrators, many of them of the island's Shi'a majority. Armed soldiers

subsequently killed a number of protestors. As the situation deteriorated and other Gulf rulers pressed for action, the government blamed Iranian instigators and called in Saudi troops.

Because the government alienated the protest movement, later promises of reform largely failed. The largest legal opposition societies, *al-Wifaq* and *Wa'ad*, found it difficult to accept the Crown Prince's call for national dialogue, especially given their small representation at the talks. Although the regime enjoys significant support from Sunnis and wealthier members of society (including secular Shi'a families), the activists and opposition political groups—not all of whom are Shi'a—almost certainly represent a majority of the population.

The only other Gulf state where significant protest activity occurred was Oman. Sultan Qabus responded with financial benefits and the dismissal of allegedly corrupt and ineffective officials. These swift responses seemed to dampen the fervor of the Omani opposition, and there were no calls for the overthrow of the sultan. Indeed, the personal charism and prestige of the sultan has effectively masked the lack of democracy and violations of human rights.

In other Gulf Arab countries, leaders combined harsh repression of dissent with the announcement of new benefits and

subsidies, essentially bribing their populations into acquiescence as populations across the Middle East and North Africa rose up against their governments.

The regime of President Ali Abdullah Salih in Yemen had already met many characteristics of a failed state, with the region's worst poverty, simmering rebellions in the north and south, and an active resident terrorist group, al-Qaeda in the Arabian Peninsula. Initially, Salih fended off the domestic protesters—including women and traditional tribal rivals—with false promises, manipulation, and military force exercised by a presidential guard commanded by his son. In the short run, an attempted Arab Spring revolution halted when an elite military unit turned its weapons on its own unarmed citizens, but eventually an autocrat was forced from power. The resulting instability and political turmoil set the stage for what has now become a civil war in Yemen. Houthi rebels once based in the north today hold sway over the capital, Sana'a. President Abd Rabbuh Mansur Hadi, who replaced President Salih, briefly went into exile in Riyadh in 2015. He has since returned to Yemen with the help of Saudi Arabia, an external player in the country's civil war.

The Arab Spring came relatively late to Syria. Only in March 2011, did the use of fatal violence against protesters in Dar'a ignite widespread demonstrations.

The State of Democracy: Seasons of Hope and Despair

Bashar al-Assad's regime claimed to support reform by offering some concessions like ending the decades'-old emergency laws. Simultaneously, it portrayed the demonstrations as an armed insurrection by foreign Islamic extremists and others. After military units and pro-regime thugs descended on town after town, government media duly displayed the bodies or funerals of dead soldiers and police as evidence. Activists and their pictures told a different, darker story: unprovoked shootings of demonstrators by the security forces and the Shabiha militia, followed sometimes by the executions of soldiers who refused to shoot civilians.

The ensuing civil war has continued for eight long years, devastating Syria and seeing the emergence of new threats such as the Islamic State (IS). Half a million people have been killed, half the population displaced, and an estimate of the total cost of reconstruction is $400 billion. The long-term social costs are incalculable; repairing a society rent by ethnic and sectarian conflict is a task that may well take generations.

In contrast to the bloodshed in so many countries, Jordan's police initially responded to protesters by handing out bottles of water. Even before the events in Tahrir Square, economic protests and riots had shaken the regime's southern heartland. In response, however, King Abdullah's security forces avoided creating martyrs. Instead, the king sacked his prime minister and promised reforms. A bizarre attack on police by Jordan's own *Salafist* extremists no doubt reinforced the king's argument that stability depended on the monarchy. While King Abdullah remains in power, in the face of popular demands he has voiced support for reforms that if implemented should make Jordan increasingly democratic.

Years after it began, pessimism about the Arab Spring has settled in. Measured by actual changes at the head of government, popular demands in 2011 overthrew four dictators (Ben Ali in Tunisia, Mubarak in Egypt, Qaddafi in Libya, and Salih in Yemen). Of these, only Tunisia, today, has anything resembling a democratic system. Other autocrats have seemingly been strengthened by events of the Arab Spring. No Arab monarchy was overthrown. Either, Arab citizens accepted traditional, hereditary authorities that made few claims of democracy better than they did those who presented the sham of pseudo-democratic republics, or such governments were able to better wield the apparatus of state against opposition.

But it is fair to say, autocracies do not last forever. The Arab Spring dramatically portrays a cultural region—the Arab world—in the throes of epochal changes that will

The bloodstained clothing of martyrs—the men and women slain while demonstrating—provided evidence of their willingness to risk life for political reform and social change
Photo courtesy of Jim Neergaard

affect kings and emirs as well. The legitimacy of autocratic rule has been broken, and old ideas have been discredited.

Rulers may continue to suppress popular demands and deny aspirations for freedom and human dignity, but they are running against a tide of real and popular desires for constitutions that define the state and protect civil liberties.

While ruling minorities in Bahrain and Syria may hang on, the repression they exercised after 2011 renders them more dependent than ever on simple brute force and, significantly, the support of outside powers.

Moreover, those months of demonstrations throughout the region frequently saw young women play activist roles that went far beyond the area's cultural experiences. That alone may prove one of the most long-lasting impacts, notwithstanding the rise of Islamist politics.

In the short run, Egypt's Muslim Brotherhood and similar groups benefitted from their hard-won reputations for opposition to the dictators and their superior organization compared to secular political groups. Arab Muslims clearly esteem the ideals, dedication, and accomplishments of Islamic organizations. Banned as political parties, some became social agencies to provide services to the poor and victims of natural disasters.

Voters knew them, and initially trusted them. In Tunisia, the moderately Islamist Ennahda won a plurality, while in Egyptian parliamentary elections, the Freedom and Justice Party of the Muslim Brotherhood won a strong plurality, with the ultra-conservative Salafist Al-Nour Party second. In a democracy, parties with such popular support eventually form a government, alone or in a coalition. That said, elections often draw candidates to the center, in search of votes. The Brotherhood's Mohammad Morsi did exactly that when as a presidential candidate he promised that Copts would have their rights and women would not be forced to wear the headscarf. Unfortunately for all concerned—Egypt, the Copts, Morsi, and the Brotherhood itself—Morsi failed to keep these promises. Following the 2013 overthrow of Morsi, Egypt has experienced a return to what is essentially military rule under former general Abdel Fattah el-Sisi.

Power tends to transform idealists, even when it does not corrupt them. Citizen demands for jobs, schools, sanitation, water, and other urgent needs force governments to address popular needs. Consequently, in a democracy, many Islamist parties are likely to become less rigidly ideological, and more apt to compromise. It was a failure to compromise that undermined Morsi's government. Given his ouster after only a year in office, however, the Brotherhood and its supporters are likely to claim they never had the chance. One great danger of Egypt's experience, then,

The State of Democracy: Seasons of Hope and Despair

In Egypt, both the youthful activists and the Muslim Brotherhood proclaimed the unity of the two major religious groups, evidenced by the joined symbols.

Photo courtesy of Jim Neergaard

is the possibility that Islamist parties will have learned that their suspicions of the democratic process were justified.

Another longer-run result of the Arab Spring is the changed dynamics of the Is-raeli–Palestinian conflict. From Egypt to Bahrain, the slogans rarely addressed such matters. Palestinian rights, once the issue that ignited Arab passions, became second in priority to human rights within one's own nation. Governments, therefore, find it far more difficult to manipulate Palestinian issues for regime legitimacy while posing no direct threat to Israel. Syria portrayed itself as the heart of Arab resistance for decades, but it only challenged Israel through proxies in Lebanon and Palestine.

Faced with demonstrations in 2011, al-Assad's regime cynically attempted to create a confrontation with Israel through a civilian Palestinian crossing of the Jewish state's truce lines. This resulted in the deaths of more than a dozen Palestinians, but it failed to accomplish the primary goal: reuniting the Syrian people with their ruler against an outside enemy. In fact, the gesture provoked a backlash among young Palestinians who resented the manipulation.

The old politics of blaming Israel for so many of the problems in the Arab world may thus begin to fade. However, without major progress towards peace—and an equitable and sustainable solution for Palestinians—the Jewish state's regional isolation will likely remain firmly entrenched.

Arab and Islamic cultures have traditionally valued human rights, but on their own terms and often differently than the more secular West. One hopes that in the future, looking back, the most long-lasting impact of the Arab Spring will be its emphasis on human dignity, women's rights, freedom, justice, and democracy—all elements characterized by the aspirational early days of the uprisings. If so, the upheaval will have extended beyond politics; its martyrs will have transformed not just regimes but societies. Prospects for that outcome remain highly uncertain, however, and the road in that direction remains long.

UNEVEN DEMOCRACY IN THE NON-ARAB MIDDLE EAST

If democracy is simply absent in the Arab Middle East, the picture in the non-Arab Middle East (Iran, Israel, and Turkey) is

more nuanced. All three countries have at least some democratic institutions, while also facing various constraints on democracy. These constraints can be considered severe in the case of Iran, where a theocratic system curtails the development of electoral democracy into something that offers its citizens any sort of genuine democratic rights. The Iranian experience shows that presidential elections—even when the polls are conducted with relative legitimacy (the 2009 elections being a possible exception)—is not enough to grant democratic status to a country. Iranians vote for their president, and for members of the legislature—and credible accusations of vote-rigging are rare. However, it is Iran's two-tiered system of government, in which an unelected body approves all candidates for office and the Supreme Leader retains ultimate authority, that most dramatically curtails democratic flourishing in Iran. In the uneasy relationship between the Islamic and republican strands within Iranian politics, democracy has clearly lost out.

Conversely, democracy in Israel can be described as resilient. Established as an ethnically Jewish state—simultaneously instituting democracy and secularism as founding values—Israel is often described as "the only democracy in the Middle East." Certainly the democratic features that were instituted at the establishment of Israel only act to emphasise the authoritarianism of the broader region. However, it is fair to say that Israel's democracy is maintained, at least in part, by the denial of democratic rights to Arabs in the Occupied Territories. Furthermore, Israel has often benefitted from the persistence of authoritarianism in neighboring states. By some measures, Israel's 2018 Basic Law, which downgraded the status of Arabic and introduced the principle that only the Jewish people have the right to exercise self-determination in the country, represents a significant escalation of nationalism and, therefore, a threat to Israel's democratic credentials. Managing the dual strands of democratic and Jewish identity is a long-term issue for Israel and one that is dramatically complicated by the continuing occupation of the Palestinian Territories.

In recent years, Turkey has come to be counted amongst a growing number of countries that have experienced significant democratic declines. Determinedly secular since its inception in 1923, and considered a beacon of democracy in the region since 1945, the advent of Islamist politics in Turkey under President Recep Erdoğan's Justice and Development Party (AKP) was heralded as long-sought evidence of the compatibility of Islam and democracy. That assessment has been drastically revised, as authoritarianism

The State of Democracy: Seasons of Hope and Despair

In Egypt, activists frisk those joining a demonstration; protesters regularly chanted the slogan "silmiyya"—"non-violent"— and where possible chose peaceful methods

Photo courtesy of Jim Neergaard

came to define the AKP's rule. An attempted coup in 2015 was the justification for a broad crackdown on human rights and the consolidation of unprecedented power to the president. Turkey, today, has the dubious accolade of being the world's foremost jailer of professional journalists.

In April 2019, Erdoğan dramatically ordered a re-run of the Istanbul mayoral election, when a political opponent of the AKP claimed victory. Few conceded that there were any credible legal grounds

for holding a second election and critics, both within Turkey and among the international community, feared that Erdoğan would somehow engineer the election, set for June 23, in the AKP's favor. However, the outcome of the second election was an even more convincing victory, with a wider margin, for the opposition candidate. The outcome was viewed as a clear rebuke of Erdoğan's authoritarianism, with tens of thousands of Turkish citizens flooding on to the streets of Istanbul to

celebrate the apparent reinvigoration of Turkish democracy.

What is clear from the above is that democracy in the Middle East and South Asia should neither be taken for granted, not be too hastily dismissed. While there is clear reason for concern, as authoritarian regimes consolidate power and make new gains (in some cases) and democracies experience setbacks (in others), the desire for democratic rights, amongst ordinary citizens, is undiminished.

Black Gold or Resource Curse? The Impact of Oil on the Middle East and Beyond

Petroleum refining involves precision engineering and extensive equipment

Courtesy: Royal Embassy of Saudi Arabia

The countries of the Middle East and South Asia enjoy few natural riches, and most of the famed mineral deposits of antiquity have been exhausted for centuries. The great exception, of course, is petroleum. Perhaps 60% of the world's proven and probable oil deposits lie in the sedimentary basin between central Arabia and the mountains of Iran. From northern Iraq to the Strait of Hormuz, crude oil often occurs in large fields relatively near the surface. Cheap to extract, with lower financial and environmental costs than drilling in deep waters or Arctic tundra, the oil is piped short distances to coastal terminals, loaded onto tankers, and shipped to refineries worldwide.

So abundant is the oil, and so efficient its production, refining and transportation, that Saudi oil probably costs under U.S. $ 0.50 per gallon to pump, refine, and transport, but it may sell for $6–$10 per gallon in Europe and $2–$3 in the United States. Governments and companies manage to extract enough taxes and profits from consumers to boost prices as high as other energy sources. The special physical qualities that make oil a desirable fuel also generate great wealth for those able to manipulate its price.

The Search for Oil in the Middle East

The ancients knew something about oil. Asphalt seeped to the surface in Mesopotamia. Tar paved the streets of Babylon, calked seams, and mortared bricks. Mysterious fires there and in Persia burned indefinitely, without consuming any known fuel.

Petroleum's role remained largely unchanged until the industrial revolution. By the 19th century, the new factories in Europe and the United States required great quantities of oil, for light and to lubricate moving parts. Inventors and entrepreneurs in Europe and North America dug the first wells to obtain petroleum, and after 1900 the popularity of gasoline-powered automobiles spurred demand for oil tremendously.

An integrated industry developed rapidly. The search for petroleum deposits spread to the Middle East, where prospecting began first in Iraq and Iran (Persia), where the English entrepreneur William D'Arcy negotiated a concession from the Shah of Persia in 1901. After five years of disappointments, in 1908 his drillers struck the first commercial well in the Middle East, at Masjid-i Suleiman, in what is now the Khuzestan Province of western Iran.

D'Arcy moved rapidly to exploit the find. He organized the Anglo-Persian Oil Company, which laid a pipeline to the coast and gained permission from a local chief to construct a refinery on Abadan Island at the head of the Gulf. On the eve of World War I, with the Royal Navy switching from coal to oil for fuel, Winston Churchill arranged for the British government to purchase a majority share in the company, known today as British Petroleum.

After World War I, the concessions for oil prospecting in Iraq fell to British, French, and American firms who in the late 1920s formed the Iraq Petroleum Company (IPC). In the 1920s and 1930s, geologists discovered vast oil fields elsewhere in the Middle East, first in Bahrain. In 1938, an American company exploring in Saudi Arabia struck commercial quantities with its seventh well. Geologists eventually recognized that quite distant

Black Gold or Resource Curse?

oil strikes really tapped parts of one vast field, the Ghawar. Some 160 miles long, it ranks as the largest in the world, even surpassing Kuwait's Burgan field. Oil production in Qatar, the United Arab Emirates, and Oman became significant only in the 1950s and 1960s.

In contrast to plantation agriculture or modern industry, petroleum requires a relatively small but highly skilled workforce, after the initial construction of pipelines, storage facilities, loading terminals, and perhaps a refinery. Although they employed relatively few workers, the oil companies greatly affected local society. They established training programs and schools. Roads, towns, shops, medical facilities, and models of new lifestyles often resulted—at least for some of the population. Another major impact was financial. Royalties, taxes, and profit-sharing flowed to the rulers, and exports supplied foreign exchange, normally scarce in developing countries.

Countries and Companies Clash over Profits

In the Middle East, land ownership of untilled areas traditionally belonged to the government and, as a result, oil companies negotiated agreements, or concessions, from governments. These stipulated the territorial limits of company operations and specified payments to the ruler.

Companies initially bargained from strength and the rulers from weakness, because the rulers needed money and neither side knew what oil wealth existed, or if it would flow in profitable quantities. The oil industry was dominated by just a few companies—sometimes called the "Seven Sisters"—which kept prices high and maintained large reserve capacities, so their negotiations for concessions reflected corporate strengths.

In contrast, governments badly needed money and preferred large initial payments for prospecting rights, while accepting low royalties on output that might never occur. Thus, in 1931 Iraq agreed to royalties of only four gold shillings per ton, about twelve cents per barrel. Saudi Arabia accepted the same figure two years later. Some oil companies earned remarkable profits on productive investments, but other investments proved complete losses despite years of exploration.

Middle East nations soon felt they deserved better, that their original concessions provided too generously for the companies and failed to reflect the changed circumstances after oil was discovered. Being sovereign, they could demand revisions in what the companies considered legally binding contracts. The first important changes came with Reza Shah Pahlavi's Iran in 1933. Thereafter,

Offshore drilling requires large platforms, here arriving in the Gulf
Courtesy: Royal Embassy of Saudi Arabia

governments repeatedly pressed for greater revenues and for minimum annual payments. By 1950, agreements often fixed payments as 50% of gross income less production expenses. However, income was difficult to determine when oil was sold to another subsidiary of the same company. Eventually, both sides accepted artificial "posted prices" to calculate the profits to be divided.

Iran's attempt to gain control of its oil in 1951 highlighted the limits that countries faced in their continuing struggles to gain greater benefits from oil. After Prime Minister Mohammad Mossadeq nationalized operations of the Anglo-Iranian Oil Company, the company increased output in Kuwait and diverted its tankers to other sources. The Anglo-Iranian Oil Company halted payments to the government, and its lawyers prevented sales of Iranian oil in Western Europe.

Most consequentially, Mossadeq's nationalization of Iranian oil cost him his position as Prime Minister. In 1953 a coup d'état masterminded by the United

States and backed by Britain expelled the democratically-elected leader from office. With more amenable leadership in Iran, the two sides eventually agreed that a consortium of companies would operate the oil fields for the National Iranian Oil Company. The lessons were clear: governments depended for their very survival on the tax revenues from oil, but the "majors" maintained sufficient excess capacity to meet their customers' needs without the exports of any one nation, and would lend oil to each other. Therefore, a single country lacked the power to force a major oil company to accept its terms. More profoundly, ordinary citizens across the Middle East recognized that oil had the capacity to empower (and enrichen) authoritarian leaders, at a cost to democratic representation and the regional promotion of human rights. The U.S., having positioned itself as a beacon of democracy in the post-World War II era (not least against the backdrop of British empire), was reputationally damaged in the Mossadeq saga. It had become clear, to the peoples (and

Black Gold or Resource Curse?

rulers) of the Middle East, that economics would trump democracy.

In 1959, with world oil supplies plentiful and market prices soft, the major oil companies announced—rather than negotiated—a lower posted price for crude oil and thus reduced their payments to governments. In response, representatives of Iran, Iraq, Kuwait, Saudi Arabia, and Venezuela met in Baghdad and established the Organization of Oil Exporting Countries (OPEC). From its inception in 1960, OPEC's goals have concerned export prices, royalties, and the taxation of profits.

Until the late 1950s, international oil companies treated Middle Eastern supplies as supplemental and set prices based on the U.S. market, thus keeping prices high in the U.S. Around 1970, however, American production peaked and soon began to decline, while U.S., European, and Japanese demand continued to grow rapidly. The increase could only be met from the Middle East. Its oil, hitherto excluded from the United States on grounds of "national security," became increasingly necessary for the world's largest economy.

Against this background, specific events gained disproportionate importance. The Suez Canal remained closed after the 1967 war, straining oil tanker capacity. A puncture in 1970 shut down the Saudi pipeline to the Mediterranean, and Libya simultaneously acted against some small oil companies for violating terms. Fears of worldwide oil shortages created the opportunity for OPEC to demand higher revenues.

The resulting 1971 Tehran Agreement between OPEC nations and the companies increased posted prices immediately and set them at $5 per barrel by the late 1970s. Hailed at the time as a major victory for the oil exporters, the Tehran Agreement raised revenues to the countries by 25%, enabling these nations to limit production and still pay their bills. The countries no longer needed to produce more: they discovered that at current conditions, they could reduce production and raise prices. Future increases in demand would also allow them to force further price increases on the companies and consumers.

The Curse of Oil: Since the 1970s, a number of scholars have argued that the absence of democracy in the Middle East can be attributed to the presence of oil. Indeed, for decades governments of the Middle East have had the luxury of using oil wealth to fund a system of patronage. For more than half a century, Middle Eastern governments have used oil wealth to fund a system of economic patronage. The notion of a resource curse is linked to

"rentier state theory." A rentier state is one in which governments derive a substantial portion of their revenue from selling off national resources or bargaining for foreign backing, rather than extracting taxes from citizens. In some countries, such as Saudi Arabia and the United Arab Emirates (UAE), the revenue has come from the sale of domestic oil resources; in others, such as Egypt and Jordan, they have come in the form of transfers from regional patrons with oil wealth. Throughout the Middle East, governments have used oil resources to fund stable jobs, education, and health care, and in return, populations have remained politically quietist. This theory hold that while oil has brought an abundance of wealth to the region it is not an unmitigated social good.

Oil in the Global Market: During the October 1973 War between Israel and the Arab nations of Egypt and Syria, hostility to the U.S. rose in the Arab world. King Faisal of Saudi Arabia won wide approval when he embargoed oil exports to the United States. To make the policy effective he also decreed a 10% cut in all exports.

Sensing their power, the Gulf oil exporters then broke the previous pattern of negotiated prices and set export prices without consulting oil companies. Fears of shortages seized consumers worldwide, and prices on the spot market rose to $15 per barrel. Gas lines appeared across the U.S., service stations closed on Sundays, and rationing was implemented. In 1974, President Nixon introduced a national maximum speed limit of 55 miles per hour (under 90 kilometers per hour) in an effort to reduce consumption.

Some of the long-term impacts of the 1970s oil crisis included the development of alternative energy sources including renewable energy, nuclear power, and domestic fossil fuels. In 1975, the Brazilian government implemented its *proálcool* project, mixing ethanol with gasoline for automotive fuel. In Israel, a solar energy industry began to develop. The oil crisis saw the production of smaller, more compact vehicles, a trend that greatly benefited Japan's automotive industry vis-à-vis that of the U.S.

Recognizing the opportunity, OPEC met in December 1973 and raised the price countries would pay to $11.65 per barrel. Great transfers of wealth followed the 1973 price increase. Prices doubled again during shortages created by the Iranian Revolution in 1979–80, bringing inconceivable riches. Iran's revenues, for instance, rose almost seven-fold between 1973–74 and 1977–78. In 1981, Saudi Arabia received roughly $120 billion for its oil, over $12,000 per inhabitant. Massive purchases of foreign goods clogged ports

throughout the Middle East. However, in just a few years conservation measures by consumers, cheating by OPEC members, and increased production outside OPEC brought prices down by about 50%.

Price Fluctuations in the 1990s

The rise of oil futures markets in the 1980s meant that OPEC members could not set world prices, but they could influence them. Given consumers' desires and non-OPEC production, OPEC members might collectively produce just enough to balance supply and demand at a target price. By the late 1980s, however, the cartel could not enforce the discipline. Kuwait and the United Arab Emirates over-produced, arguing that fairness should link the size of the quota to oil export capacity, rather than to population or poverty. Consumers benefited worldwide from the lower prices, but revenues plummeted. Iraq, in financial desperation when prices plunged to $14 per barrel, invaded Kuwait in 1990 (see Iraq: history).

After seizing Kuwait, Iraq controlled the sources of roughly 20% of OPEC's exports. When U.N. sanctions on Iraq and occupied Kuwait blocked their export of oil, fears rose of oil shortages, and crude oil prices rapidly doubled. Industrial nations headed for recession, but despite Iraqi threats, OPEC approved extra output, and with help from oil in storage, a worldwide shortfall was averted.

By the mid-1990s, global use of oil had expanded, particularly in East Asia, while supplies from non-OPEC producers grew slowly during a decade of lower prices. Prices rose well above $20, and OPEC nations found that they could cheat at their quotas and enjoy higher prices at the same time. However, Saudi Arabia persuaded the cartel's members to increase the total OPEC quota from 23.833 million barrels per day (m b/d) to 26.185 m b/d (without Iraq) just as East Asia suffered economic recession. When market speculators realized that some nations, particularly Venezuela, Nigeria, and Qatar, exceeded even the larger quotas, prices dropped immediately and rapidly, to levels last seen in 1973. Some experts proclaimed the death of OPEC, and argued that the rational policy for Gulf producers was to earn money from volume production, even if prices reached $5 per barrel. Such prices, after all, would render oil from Alaska and the North Sea too expensive to be profitable.

After losing billions of dollars in exports and revenues, OPEC cut quotas in 1998 and 1999. Moreover, sympathetic nations outside OPEC, including Mexico, Norway, Russia, and Oman also agreed to cut exports. After several months, the cuts persuaded the markets, and every American

Black Gold or Resource Curse?

Small vessels play important roles in supply and security
Courtesy of the Royal Embassy of Saudi Arabia

driver witnessed the result. Oil prices soared, gasoline prices climbed, and regular gasoline prices exceeded $2 per gallon in parts of California. So often proclaimed dead, OPEC had again revived.

High Prices after 2004

Oil prices rose modestly during the U.S. invasion of Iraq in 2003. This was predictable: the conflict halted Iraqi production and exports. Most strategists expected a rapid resumption of Iraqi exports, increasing world supplies and thus reducing prices. Instead, annual average prices climbed rapidly in 2004–05, in 2007 surpassed the 1980s peak of $85 in today's prices, and in mid-2008 refineries began to pay more than $150 per barrel. There are a number of reasons for this, as outlined below.

World oil consumption rose 11%, insensitive to price:

The annual price of crude oil climbed from a very low average of $12.50 in 1998 to $68 in 2007, a rise of over 400%. Economic theory suggests that consumers who face such increases would attempt to reduce consumption, but during that decade U.S. consumers increased their consumption by almost 10%, or 1.75 million barrels per day. With the rapid spread of

automobiles in China, its oil consumption rose by 84%, or nearly 3.5 million barrels per day, and other rapidly-growing Asian nations and the rest of the developing world added another 5.8 million barrels per day of consumption.

Outside OPEC, only Russia significantly increased production:

Despite the high prices, U.S. crude oil output actually fell slightly, and major declines occurred in Britain (41%), Norway (18%), and several smaller producers. As a group, however, non-OPEC producers increased crude output by nearly 13%. Nearly all the increase came from territories of the former Soviet Union, and 63% came from Russia alone, as it modernized production and in 2009 overtook Saudi Arabia as the world's largest producer.

Speculative money flooded into oil futures:

Seeking high returns when stock markets and housing loans offered modest profits, after 2000 hedge fund managers and others speculated in many raw materials, including crude oil. Given the tight global supply, and the possibility that political unrest, terrorism, natural disaster, or simply bad luck could reduce that supply, speculators found many

reasons to bid up prices, and little reason to fear a downward spiral.

Oil economies in Transition

Despite the incredible run up in the price of oil in the first 8 years of the 2000s, the price crash that came in the second half of 2008 was just as dramatic. By January 2009, oil was trading at approximately $46 per barrel, down from more than $150 in June of 2008. Over the course of just six months, the price of oil had dropped nearly 70%.

From that early 2009 low, oil began its climb back to $100 per barrel, crossing that threshold on February 1, 2011. From that point, price was fairly consistent for the next three years, never swinging more than $20 per barrel in either direction.

In June 2014, however, another reverse began. Prices began to slip; then they began to fall more freely. By January of 2015, oil was trading below $50 per barrel. A year later, in January 2016, the price of a barrel had fallen to $29, since then price movement has gradually shifted upwards. At May 2019 the per barrel price of crude stands at just under $67.

Why has the market seen so much volatility? A combination of factors can help to make sense of this. First, countries around the world, but the United States in particular, are going through what some have called a "Shale Revolution." Using a relatively new (and often controversial) technology called hydraulic fracturing, or "fracking," the U.S. and others are increasingly able to tap sources of energy that were previously inaccessible. This technology involves drilling and the injection of high-pressure liquid—a mixture of water, sand, and chemicals—into shale (a kind of sedentary rock below the earth's surface). This high-pressure liquid forces natural gas out of the rock and to the head of the well, where it can be collected.

As oil prices increased during the early and mid-2000s, it became relatively less expensive to exploit energy in this new way. The consequence was that a bigger supply of natural gas in particular hit the global market, creating oversupply, and eventually energy prices began to fall.

What happened next was counterintuitive for some. Despite the oversupply, OPEC countries began to pump more gas. The objective here was to drive the price of energy so low that higher cost producers would be forced out of the market entirely. On some level this worked: shale revenue declined by more than 30% in 2015, and a number of alternative energy producers filed for bankruptcy.

The bigger shale companies, though, seem to have weathered the storm, and in 2019 shale production is predicted to

Black Gold or Resource Curse?

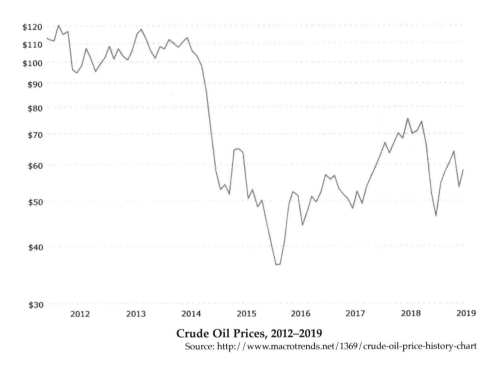

Crude Oil Prices, 2012–2019

Source: http://www.macrotrends.net/1369/crude-oil-price-history-chart

emitting greenhouse gases. Analysts agree that the U.S. shale oil bonanza is calamitous to global efforts at addressing climate change. A key criticism is that investment in hydraulic fracturing, a long-term venture if it is to be in any way economically viable, has drastically disrupted attempts to shift to renewable sources of energy.

Despite these setbacks, there is a clear trajectory towards increased investment in alternative and renewable forms of energy. Some of the key oil producing states of the Middle East are, at 2019, beginning to invest in a sector that is rapidly proving its economic value. There is clearly potential for a productive renewables sector in the Middle East. Abundant sunshine lends itself to solar farming, while Egypt, Iran, Israel, Jordan, and Kuwait have all invested in wind farms. The United Arab Emirates leads the region in investment in renewable energy. Saudi Arabia, in the meantime, has implemented its 2030 Vision, involving a diversification of the economy away from oil, with renewables part of the mix. Globally, the transition to non-fossil fuels is likely to occur sooner than the oil runs out. If countries in the Middle East fail to make the requisite changes to their economies over the longer term, the subsequent economic, political, and social shocks are likely to be profound.

increase with growth rates of 16% for the full year. While oil shale has the potential to allow North America to achieve energy independence—and, in fact, the United States is now the world's largest oil producer—it has significant drawbacks. In addition to the impacts of surface mining on the landscape, and the problem of induce seismic activity, most energy intensive extraction processes use a significant quantity of water and introduce pollutants to both the air and surface water, as well as

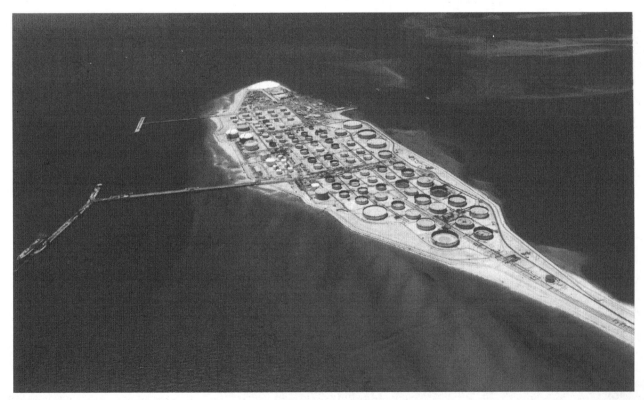

Off-shore loading saves time, but requires vast tank farms

Courtesy of the Royal Embassy of Saudi Arabia

An Uncertain Climate: Regional Environment Challenges

From North Africa to western India, the lands of the Middle East and South Asia receive sparse rainfall, usually far less annually than the 16–20 inches (40–50 centimeters) essential for cultivation. With few cloudy days and the sun blazing directly overhead most of the year, hot temperatures quickly dry the landscape even when rain has fallen. Early human settlements clustered around rivers because water was always scarce. Now, the Middle East faces a worsening crisis as a changing climate brings new challenges and individual countries attempt to claim insufficient common resources. By contrast, in the Indian sub-continent seasonal floods take hundreds of lives annually and rivers inundate productive fields, carrying their valuable silt to the sea.

The environment is emerging as a key issue of concern across the Middle East and South Asia. While some predict that climate change will exacerbate conflict, others see the potential for new forms of cooperation in the context of an emerging threat to livelihoods and, indeed, to human life.

When Will the Taps Go Dry?: For thousands of years people living in the region adapted to desert and near-desert conditions. They farmed fertile lands beside rivers, some irrigating with water from mountains hundreds or even thousands of miles away, benefiting from seasonal floods that soaked the soil and deposited nourishing silt. Drier lands were used to graze livestock, particularly camels, goats, and sheep.

Desert societies established water rights over the scarce flow of oasis wells and springs to irrigate crops and water livestock. For transport, travelers and nomads depend on the camel, with its legendary survival with minimal water. Their days surrounded by barren desert, nomads dreamed of rivers and greenery, even seeing them in the form of occasional mirages. Both Judaism and Islam portrayed heaven as filled with trees and water. An Arab proverb states that water, like bread, comes from God.

The modern era brought sharp changes. The technology and energy of the 20th century brought the façade of abundant water. Homes enjoyed taps and sewer connections; carefully irrigated trees lined boulevards in desert cities; and industries developed. Urban water use increased rapidly, for example, doubling in arid Saudi Arabia between 1980 and 1985. But most of all, agriculture based on irrigation fed desert nations and even provided exports of tomatoes, oranges, wheat, and other irrigated crops. The desert truly seemed to bloom.

Many Middle Eastern countries literally began to run out of water by the 1990s.

Some of the world's fastest-growing populations, rising standards of living, and increasing agricultural production left Israel, Jordan, and Egypt facing difficult choices between conservation and development. In the 21st century, water scarcity threatens bitter conflicts within and between the region's nations. Cooperation, by contrast, offers a chance to postpone water shortages and bring peace to a region too long troubled by violent conflict.

Water Resources as Threats to Peace
Nowhere in the region is the issue of water rights more contentious than in the Jordan basin. The Jordan River looms large in popular imagination. However, visitors to the Biblical "holy lands," are often disappointed to find that the river in which Jesus is said to have been baptized, is no more than a narrow, salty stream, dangerously contaminated by sewage. The Dead Sea, deprived of the normal flow of Jordan River water, is drying up. Historically subject to climate-induced periods of shrinkage and growth, human activity is likely to significantly speed up what may well be the complete disappearance of the lake.

Attempts to establish national water rights began in the 1950s, when U.S. President Eisenhower sent a special ambassador to negotiate the shares of the Jordan basin countries. At the technical level, his findings established reasonable national shares, but politically his mission failed. No international agreement yet apportions the river's waters.

With dreams of making the desert bloom, in the 1960s Israel constructed the National Water Carrier, a pipeline almost 10 feet in diameter, to bring water from the Sea of Galilee to the coastal plain and the Negev desert. The water was vital. Arab threats to the project, by attempting to divert the Jordan's headwaters in Lebanon and Syria from flowing into Israel played a major role in the crises that led to the 1967 Arab-Israeli war. Israel's conquest of the Golan Heights and the West Bank ensured its unilateral use of the Jordan River.

Almost immediately, water from the Jordan proved to be insufficient for Israel's purposes. Along the coast and in the desert, Israeli farmers used two-thirds of the nation's water for farming. To supply their fields as well as thirsty homes and factories, Israel had long pumped the Mediterranean coastal aquifer, a layer of porous rock that trapped water slowly seeping toward the sea.

When the volume of water pumped out began to exceed the rainwater trickling down into the aquifer, water levels and pressures began to fall. Salty seawater started to seep into the aquifer, reducing its water quality. By 1990, about 10% of the water pumped from this resource

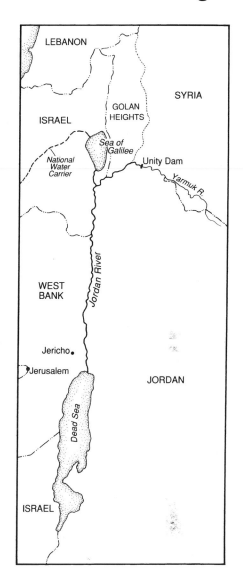

exceeded the national limit for chloride salt. In addition, pollution increased as nitrates from fertilizers leached into the aquifer. During the winter, the Water Authority now pumps surplus Jordan River water down into coastal wells, hoping to replenish the aquifer.

The first Israeli desalination plant, completed in 2005, produces 100 million cubic meters of fresh water annually, less than 5% of the water used.

Israel's thirst also drains the separate Yarkon/Tannim aquifer. Known as the "mountain aquifer," it collects rain falling on the hilly West Bank. A few points of the aquifer extend into the 1967 boundaries, and Israel currently pumps about 20% of its water from this source. This vastly exceeds the pumping permitted the West Bank Palestinians, whose land supplies the rainfall that annually renews this resource. In addition, the more than 400,000 Israeli settlers in the West Bank consume about as much water as the 2.9

An Uncertain Climate: Regional Environment Challenges

million Arabs, whose drilling is restricted in several ways. Water further exacerbates tensions between Palestinians and Israeli settlers in the Occupied Territories.

Any future creation of a Palestinian state threatens Israel's total control of the mountain aquifer. Fears of future water shortages may influence political opinion against granting concessions. The figures themselves show few alternatives: against average rainfall of 1.7 billion cubic meters, current water use reaches 1.9 billion cubic meters. Israelis consume five times as much per capita as residents of neighboring Arab nations. Because of this, the shallow wells of dozens of Palestinian West Bank villages no longer reach water. In the Gaza Strip, the contamination of water supplies has reached critical proportions. The denial of water to Palestinians living under Israeli occupation is a matter that Israel must urgently confront.

The Wahda Dam on the Yarmuk River, completed in 2011, captures the flow of the Jordan's last underused tributary. The Yarmuk flows between Syria and Jordan, joining the Jordan just below the Sea of Galilee. With water resources far smaller than Israel's or Syria's, Jordan decades ago proposed building a "Unity Dam" at Maqarin to trap winter flood waters for summer use by farms, homes, and industry. Israel threatened to destroy any such dam, as it benefited by capturing some of the flow in the Sea of Galilee. However, its 1994 peace treaty with Jordan removed that threat.

Jordan eventually gained Syrian approval for a combined-purpose dam to provide water to Jordan and electricity to Syria, and the foundation stone was laid in 2003. However, rainfall in the Yarmuk basin falls mostly in Syria, and that country favors smaller, upstream projects within its boundaries. Such projects capture most of the run-off, and as a result, by 2005 the river's flow had fallen below the agreed level. In years of low rainfall, the national populations that share rights to the Jordan River all find themselves critically short of water, a deficit that is projected to approach about 600 million cubic meters annually even with average rainfall. With climate change models predicting extreme regional temperatures and possible reduced rainfall, this situation is likely to become increasingly dire over the coming decades.

The countries of the Levant—Israel, Jordan, Lebanon, Syria, and the Palestinian Territories— face questions of water use so difficult that one of them may attempt to settle issues by force. Indeed, recently Israel threatened Lebanon with war because it pumped modest amounts for local irrigation from a tributary of the Jordan.

One hope to relieve the water shortages is the proposed Red Sea–Dead Sea canal

or pipeline. Advocates believe water from the Gulf of Aqaba would prevent the Dead Sea from drying up, generate electricity, and provide, via desalination plants, millions of cubic meters of fresh water annually. The engineering has been possible for decades, but politics and finances proved prohibitive.

A 2014 agreement between Israel and Jordan would see water brought from the Red Sea to a desalination plant in Jordan; with the brine byproduct piped 125 miles (200 kilometers) north to replenish the Dead Sea. Implementation of the project has been delayed by political tensions, including the stalled Israeli–Palestinian peace process. In 2019, Israel reiterated its commitment to the project as an important act of regional cooperation. A feasibility study found that failure to take action would have a profound and devastating on the Dead Sea.

The Nile

The world's longest river, stretching nearly 4,200 miles (approximately 6,800 kilometers), drains mountainous central Africa and the Ethiopian highlands of about 84 billion cubic meters each year, making Egypt "The Gift of the Nile." For that country and northern Sudan, no other renewable water supply exists. Survival depends on the Nile River.

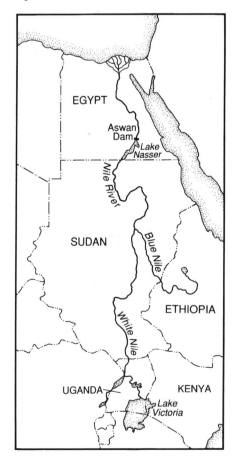

Throughout the 19th and 20th centuries, the potential for conflict over Nile River waters was very low. Ever since ancient times, Egyptian farmers had practiced "basin agriculture." Crops flourished in fields saturated with moisture from the annual summer flood and were nourished with silt that the Blue Nile had carried out of Ethiopia. Egypt's desire to capture more of the flow for year-round irrigation was reflected in the construction of barrages and small dams from the 19th century onwards. Negotiations to establish water rights followed; the first Nile Waters Agreement was signed with Sudan in 1929. Renegotiated in the 1950s before construction of the Aswan High Dam (see Egypt, economy), the agreement presently provides Egypt 55 billion cubic meters yearly, three times the amount allowed Sudan.

By the 1980s, severe water shortages appeared when years of drought in Ethiopia reduced the flow of the Blue Nile. Behind the High Dam, Lake Nasser dwindled. Conserving water for irrigation reduced the release of water for hydroelectric power and some years cut drastically the almost 40% of national electricity produced at Aswan.

The crisis, brought to an end when rains restored the Nile's flow, highlighted the inevitable future shortage of water in Egypt. Accurate figures are difficult to obtain, but one study suggested that the nation actually uses 70 billion cubic meters each year. With the population growing by one million mouths annually and the government attempting to extend cultivation, water demand will naturally increase. But Egypt's present use is only possible because Sudan fails to consume its full allotment.

Despite these dire threats, millions are not yet dying of thirst. Agriculture claims more than 80% of available water and opportunities exist for conservation. The *fellah* (farmer) typically obtains his water free, from unlined canals, and channels it to soak his fields. Free water makes sense for these poor people, whose yearly income is only a few hundred dollars; water-saving drip irrigation systems remain beyond their purchasing power. Thus, conservation will not be painless, and will impose costs, if not on very poor people, upon the government. It may also mean abandoning some lands to the insistent demands of the desert.

Until recently, it was commonly accepted that international disputes over Nile water were unlikely to end in violence. Decades of negotiation established rights and precedents. Egypt's determination to receive its historic and vital flow is firmly advertised and well-recognized by Sudan. However, the less-powerful nations upstream seem increasingly dissatisfied

An Uncertain Climate: Regional Environment Challenges

with their combined allocations of only 10% of the total. In 2010, Uganda, Tanzania, Rwanda, and Ethiopia agreed to seek larger shares in the proposed Cooperative Framework Agreement, which Egypt has delayed since the 1980s.

Egyptian politicians reacted with shock in 2013 when Ethiopia began diverting the Blue Nile to build the Grand Ethiopian Renaissance Dam near its border with Sudan. The dam will be the largest in Africa and its reservoir will increase evaporation losses. Moreover, filling the reservoir will reduce the flow of the Nile for several years.

Egypt's President Morsi responded that "all options are open," and that he would not allow Egypt's water supply to be endangered. However, beyond economic pressures and encouraging discontent in Ethiopia, there seems little that Egypt can do. More dams will follow, some for irrigation that will divert far more water. An attack on the dams, even if a military success, would isolate Egypt and end U.S. aid. Given the region's expected population growth by 2050, Egypt will find it advantageous to conserve the Nile waters.

Diverting the Euphrates

To the north and east, dams on another river of Biblical fame also threaten violence. The Euphrates springs forth in the high mountains of Turkey, whose rains contribute 80% of its volume but whose rough terrain meant little is used. It flows into Syria and then across Iraq to join the Tigris at the Shatt al-Arab just before emptying into the Persian Gulf. Far larger than the Jordan's, the flow of the Euphrates averages 31 billion cubic meters per year. However, ambitious development plans in the three countries exceed the river's capacity by about 50%. As long ago as 1975 Iraq actually threatened war with Syria over the scanty flow below Syria's Tabaqa Dam.

Upstream diversion of the water to fill dams and supply irrigation essentially caused a crisis, when Turkish engineers reduced the river's flow to fill the lakes behind the Keban and Ataturk dams (see Turkey, economy). The Tabaqa Dam and agricultural development project in Syria also diverted the river's flow. Alternative resources may exist for Iraq, since there is excess flow in the Tigris to the east, but development projects to use it require time and funding.

Even worse, the Euphrates and the Tigris carry a naturally high level of dissolved salts that accumulate in irrigated soils and reduce fertility. Intensive irrigation usually raises the water level in the soil, dissolving even more salts, agricultural chemicals, and fertilizers. Unless drainage ditches are constructed to carry away salty and polluted waters, the land eventually becomes useless. Thus, Iraq

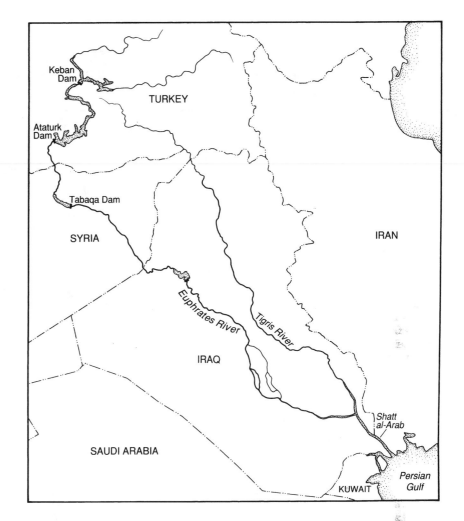

faces not only water shortages, but the danger that water quality in its major rivers will fall to levels unfit for human consumption and harmful for agriculture.

The nations of the Euphrates basin have not yet fought over water, but Syria and Turkey joined the anti-Iraq Coalition in the 1990–1991 Gulf War. However, in the absence of settled water rights, the potential for violence exists, and diplomatic relations remain poor.

Fighting did rage across the lower reaches of the Tigris and the Shatt al-Arab during the Iran–Iraq War of 1980–1988. That dispute had virtually nothing to do with irrigation. Iranian demands for control of the river to mid-stream, as opposed to the traditional Iraqi border on the Iranian shore, contributed to the crisis that produced the war. Control and navigation rights in the Shatt al-Arab remain disputed.

International Cooperation in the Indus Basin

In South Asia, two nations born in hostility faced the challenge of sharing water from the Indus River and its tributaries. By approving a technical solution, India and Pakistan brought prosperity and

greater food production to the Punjab, the fertile region divided by their borders.

The Indus is fed by monsoon rains and snows in the Himalayas of India and Tibet. Carrying more water than the Nile, its annual discharge reaches 97 billion cubic meters, much of it carried across the plains by five important tributaries. During British rule a system of irrigation canals was dug. After partition, India possessed the strategic advantage of controlling the head waters, but lacked economic benefit; its water was remote and difficult to use. Pakistan, in contrast, found itself farming with water from India, but strategically disadvantaged in the event India chose to divert or otherwise interfere with the flow.

In 1951, a mission from the World Bank proposed a rational solution: consider the issue a technical, not a political, problem. In effect, the key was to base water usage on irrigation potential, not nationality. Compensation for one district's use of another country's water could be made elsewhere. Despite two wars, the system has worked. Dams built with World Bank funds, plus a complex system of canals, have enabled the two countries to irrigate the Punjab, breadbasket of the sub-continent. Once

An Uncertain Climate: Regional Environment Challenges

again, however, increasing needs for water and power are currently leading to tension over India's planned Baglihar dam on the Chenab River.

Besides its rivers, the Punjab's other major source of irrigation is groundwater. Unfortunately, that source is rapidly depleting. Intensive agriculture, especially since 1970, has resulted in extremely high demand for irrigation. The result has been that in the last thirty years Punjab has nearly exhausted ground water reserves that had been building for more than a century.

Changes in climate may eventually reduce the flow of the Indus more than most other major Asian rivers. According to the models, increasing global temperatures will melt Himalayan glaciers, initially increasing the river's flow. After the glaciers retreat, however, their runoff will decline in exactly the vital spring and summer periods when irrigation is most needed on the plains of India and Pakistan. Farm output would then fall dramatically, at a loss of crops sufficient to feed perhaps 26 million people.

A boat bridge across the upper Indus

Opposite Extremes

Bangladesh and northeastern India struggle with entirely different difficulties. With as much as 50% of annual rainfall occurring in less than three weeks Bengalis have, for centuries, reconciled their ways of life with the seasonal flooding of the Ganges, Brahmaputra, and other rivers, whose water and silt deposits nourished the soil and produced three crops per year (see Bangladesh). With few possessions and minimal homes, farmers lived knowing that floods could strike, and river channels might be altered by hundreds of yards overnight. Nevertheless, they could hope to escape with their lives and a few possessions to begin farming anew.

Such a fate hardly appealed to modernized city dwellers living in permanent homes. In 1989, Bangladesh embarked on the Flood Action Plan to build embankments to protect cities and to confine rivers to channels. Unfortunately, confining the rivers creates the danger that silt will raise the level of the river, eventually causing them to flow *above* ground-level. If this happens, one of the poorest countries in the world will have to construct and maintain a vast system of dikes for the rivers at an enormous cost, if indeed it can be done, considering frequent devastating hurricanes and monsoons.

Even in this region of great annual flooding, periodic droughts strike during the dry season, and rival irrigation projects highlight the need for water-sharing agreements. A proposal to divert Himalayan river water to South India also looms as a threat to Bangladesh. It shares 50

rivers with India, but only one is covered by an international agreement regarding its flow.

Global warming, by changing mountain snowfall to rain, increases flooding and reduces off-season flow. As in the case of the Indus (but probably not the Ganges), the decline of Himalayan glaciers may eventually diminish spring and summer melt-water in the Brahmaputra basin. One model predicts this could reduce agricultural output by the equivalent of food for 34 million people.

Few countries in the world are as vulnerable to climate change as Bangladesh. As low-lying areas are subsumed by rising sea-levels, millions will be forced to flee inland. By 2050, as much as 17% of the Delta will be permanently submerged. Already, riverbank erosion has displaced up to 200,000 Bengalis. As warmer sea temperatures increase the ferocity (and, in some case, the frequency) of tropical hurricanes, millions of individuals are affected. Accompanying storm surges contribute to heightened soil salinity, further reducing the capacity of the land to sustain its people. Dhaka, the capital city, is one of the fastest growing mega-cities in the world. Climate-induced migration is a real and present problem for Bangladesh and one that may have a broader regional impact in the coming decades.

Amongst a handful of nations at the forefront of efforts to ramp up global responses to the threat of climate change, is the tiny South Asian island nation of the Maldives. For this archipelago of coral

atolls in the Indian Ocean, rising sea levels poses an existential threat. Already, increases in intense rainfall, subsequent flooding, hurricanes, and higher than usual storm surges are providing a foretaste of things to come. Various plans—from abandoning the islands to instigating costly land reclamation projects funded by the lease of land to foreign investors—have been raised, and abandoned. For now, the government is focused on mitigating the worst impacts of climate change, while maintaining hope for global solutions to the crisis.

Consequences of Dams and Large-Scale Irrigation

Large dams that tower hundreds of feet above a valley or stretch miles across a lower river basin represent a triumph, however momentary, of the 20th century. First constructed in the United States and Soviet Union in the 1920s and 1930s, dams proved valuable for flood control, hydroelectric power, recreational use, and irrigation. After World War II, building dams became a worldwide fad, and 95% of all large dams date from this period.

Dams in the hot climates of the Middle East and South Asia have some significant drawbacks. An obvious one is evaporation, largely because the sun's rays strike directly and the desert air carries little of the humidity that would slow evaporation. The loss from Egypt's Lake Nasser to the air is an estimated 10 billion cubic meters a year, one-fifth of Egypt's recognized portion of the Nile's flow.

An Uncertain Climate: Regional Environment Challenges

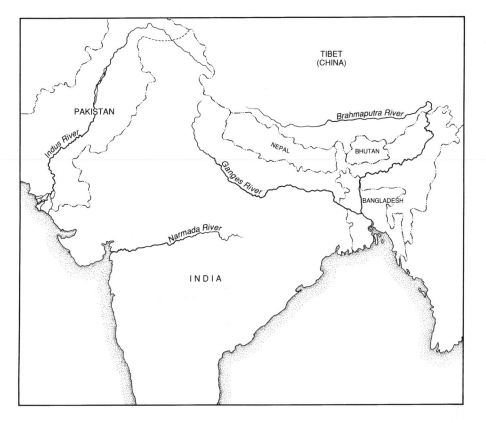

On many rivers, a much more serious problem is the buildup of silt. Engineers only recently recognized how great this problem is in warmer climates. The Ganges-Brahmaputra and Indus each carry roughly 1,700 gallons of silt in each million gallons of water. Rivers drop this sediment in the slow waters of the reservoirs, creating a builup.

At the Tarbela Dam in Pakistan, for example, some 2% of the reservoir fills with soil annually, and hundreds of tons of dirt settle above the Mangla Dam. Because of the silt, the Tarbela Dam may prove useful for only 40 years, a poor investment in view of its life expectancy of 100 years when built. In Sudan, the Roseires Dam on the Blue Nile ceased effective operation when deposits formed an island above the water intakes for the hydroelectric turbines.

Rapid silting not only spreads a dam's huge construction costs over fewer years, it also renders the location permanently useless as a dam. Unfortunately, projects conceived to reduce soil loss, such as planting trees, often proved less effective than projected.

As environmentalists and others have long pointed out, silt plays important roles in nourishing fields and supporting the coastal ecosystem. Deprived of sediments, Egyptian and other farmers spread tons of chemical fertilizers on their soil, polluting the land and rendering drainage water unfit for most use. Coastlines deprived of silt may succumb to the sea, as has happened in Egypt and elsewhere. This is even more problematic when combined with projected sea-level rises.

Silting risks partly forced the scaling-back of the Narmada Valley Development Project in central and western India. Probably the largest single project in the world, its plans included 30 major dams, dozens of smaller ones and thousands of minor ones, constructed over a period of 50 years. The dams will supply irrigation water for millions of acres in the states of Gujarat, Rajasthan and Madhya Pradesh, and generate vast amounts of electricity for homes and industry. However, the new reservoirs also flood large expanses of tropical forest and forced hundreds of thousands of people from their homes. A series of court actions in 2000 finally lowered the maximum permitted height of one major dam, though it permitted construction to resume.

The Environment as Political Risk: Of the 10 most polluted cities in the world, seven are in India and two in Pakistan. Many households in South Asia rely on solid fuels for cooking and heating. Poor industrial regulations and a reliance on vehicular transport in cities with high populations, further contribute to poor air quality. Researchers have warned that air pollution in India represents a public health emergency, leading to 1.2 million premature deaths in 2017. As far back as 2013, the economic cost of India's air pollution was estimated at 8.5% of GDP. However, the government appears little interested in treating the issue as an emergency, providing only band-aid measures in response. Modi's BJP has prioritized economic growth, while critics have accused the government of failing to adequately address a whole range of environmental issues.

In 2017, residents of the Iranian city of Ahvaz, took to the streets in protest, as dust storms, drastically exacerbated by drought and water-mismanagement, caused air pollution to soar far above levels considered safe, impacting industry, shutting schools, and causing widespread power failures. Ahvaz, has long had the distinction of being Iran's most polluted city, a consequence of the petroleum industry's presence in the region.

In recent years, the environment has increasingly been an exacerbating factor in anti-government protests in Iran, drawing new segments of the population into opposition with Tehran. In Isfahan farmers have accused local politicians of diverting water in return for bribes. Water shortages have become acute and, increasingly, rural populations are being forced into towns and cities.

As the government becomes increasingly aware of the potential political costs of decades of poor management of the environment, it is environmentalists who are finding themselves in the firing line. In recent years, a number of environmentalists have been imprisoned in Iran. The head of the Persian Wildlife Heritage Foundation was accused of spying and died, under suspicious circumstances, in prison.

In 2019, deadly floods ravaged much of Iran and neighboring Afghanistan, devastating areas that had suffered years of drought. Many of those who had lambasted authorities for mismanaging water in the 2017–18 protests, now spoke out against the government's poor response to the flooding. In Ahvaz, Sunni Arab citizens—an ethnic and religious minority in Iran—accused the government of protecting oil installations from flood damage, while neglecting to protect local populations.

Across the region, climate change and other environmental challenges pose new and continuing risks to vulnerable populations. However, in some cases, new forms of cooperation are shaping up in response to these risks. Some of this cooperation is occurring at the official level, as states seek new ways to manage finite shared resources. In other cases, cooperation at the grassroots will force governments to respond, as populations that did not share political ground, in the past, find that their interests align against rising threats.

The Rise and Fall of a Modern-Day Caliphate

In mid-2014, the leader of the Islamic State of Iraq and [Greater] Syria (ISIS), Abu Bakr al-Baghdadi, declared the establishment of a Caliphate, an institution that had not been seen since the waning days of the Ottoman Empire, in the aftermath of World War I. The idea of the Caliphate can be traced back to the early Islamic period (see: Historical Background), when great swaths of territory fell under Muslim control. From its birthplace in the Hejaz, Islam expanded dramatically, in a matter of decades, under the leadership of the first Caliphs—the successors of the Prophet Muhammad. It was this golden era of Islamic expansion, a period in which conquering Muslim armies and their message of submission to God transformed the world, that Baghdadi harked back to. As ISIS tore across northern Syria and Iraq, effectively demolishing the boundary that had created the two countries under an imperial treaty negotiated between France and Britain in the early 20th century, their trajectory must have felt not dissimilar to that of the early Muslims. Al-Baghdadi could not have predicted that within four years the Caliphate would be defeated, its thousands of fighters killed, captured, or dispersed, and Baghdadi himself forced into hiding.

Formation of an Islamic State

For a decade after the attacks of September 11, 2001, al-Qaeda dominated the emerging international sphere of *Salafist* jihadism. No group came close to competing with al-Qaeda, either for recruits or as the standard-bearer of Islamist terrorism. Likewise, no single figure approached the status of al-Qaeda's founder and leader, Osama bin Laden, as the personification of terror in the global imagination.

Al-Qaeda had its origins in the Soviet–Afghan war. It found a broad support base and a willing pool of fighters, in the thousands of young (mostly Arab) men who flocked to Afghanistan to support the *mujahideen*, the "holy warriors," who fought against "godless communism" and the imperial encroachments of the Soviet Union. Armed in some cases with U.S. weapons, the mujahideen kept up the fight for almost a decade, eventually pushing the Soviets out of Afghanistan. The victory of the mujahideen and the subsequent collapse of the Soviet Union imparted a lesson that would have devastating repercussions: guerilla tactics and moral convictions rooted in an extreme view that divided the world into Muslims and "infidels" could stand against the might of modern empire. On a more practical level, the dispersal of Afghanistan's foreign fighters created, almost overnight,

a global network of willing and able adherents to bin Laden's violent and fundamentalist vision of Islam.

The death of bin Laden in May 2011, killed in a U.S. special operations raid on his compound in Abbottabad, Pakistan, weakened al-Qaeda. Its cell formation—sometimes described as the al-Qaeda franchise—increasingly, and in the absence of the sort of charismatic leadership the bin Laden had provided, came to resemble fragmentation. As the Arab Spring swept across the Middle East it seemed that the appeal of violent Islamism, as a way of overthrowing authoritarian regimes in the region, might give way to democratic means of reform. Such hope was short-lived.

In removing Saddam and dismantling the Ba'thist institutions that had served him, the U.S. had let loose and, indeed, at times knowingly cultivated, ethnic and sectarian divisions. Suppressed and persecuted under Saddam, Iraq's Shi'a majority seized the chance to reposition themselves within the social hierarchy. Increasingly, the country divided along ethnic and sectarian lines: Kurds in the north, Shi'a in the south, and an embattled Sunni Arab center. As Iraq became a nation at war with itself, the ground was set for the rise of the Islamic State (IS).

The organization that would, in a relatively short space of time, come to take al-Qaeda's position as the leading global terrorist network, had its origins in al-Qaeda in Iraq (AQI). Under the leadership of a Jordanian jihadist Abu Musab al-Zarqawi, AQI found sectarian violence instrumental in mobilizing Sunni Arabs to the cause. In turning their sights on Shi'a and other Muslims, AQI departed from al-Qaeda's vision of an Islamic community united, at least in the short term, against an external enemy. The Salafist orientations of al-Qaeda prioritize a strict, literalist, and puritanical interpretation of Islam. It promotes a return to the practices of the *salaf*, the first three generations of Muslims and place great emphasis on acting in accordance with the *Sunnah*. As such, there is minimal tolerance for so-called innovation in Islam, such as Shi'ism. However, al-Qaeda under bin Laden and his successor, Ayman al-Zawahiri, saw utility in avoiding Muslim deaths, whether Sunni or Shi'a. By way of contrast, the situation in Iraq lent itself to an exacerbation of sectarian violence and the targeting of Muslims including, but not limited to, Shi'a Muslims.

In 2006, the leadership of AQI announced the establishment of the Islamic State of Iraq (ISI). By 2013, it had set its sights on Syria, renaming itself Islamic State in Iraq and [Greater] Syria, and

unilaterally declaring a merger with the Syrian-based *Jabhat al-Nusra*, an al-Qaeda affiliate. Fighting between Jabhat al-Nusra and ISIS led al-Qaeda to renounce ties with the latter in 2014.

From its relative safe-haven in war torn eastern Syria, ISIS overran northern and western Iraq, seizing the city of Mosul and declaring the establishment of a caliphate. At its peak IS controlled almost 40,000 square miles (over 100,000 square kilometers) containing more than 11 million inhabitants. Most of this territory was in Iraq and Syria, although it also held smaller pockets of territory in Afghanistan, Egypt, Libya, and Nigeria.

Gains on the battlefield, combined with extraordinarily sophisticated use of social media for recruitment, played a key role in inspiring thousands of people from across the world to leave their homes and travel to the region to live, fight, and die under the caliphate.

The savagery of IS was unprecedented, in a region that has seen more than its fair share of violence. As IS approached hundreds of thousands fled, pushed out by rumors of ethnic cleansing and by the circulation of IS propaganda videos detailing acts of sadism. Those that remained suffered extreme violations of human rights as IS sought to impose its violent interpretation of *shari'a* and force the submission of local populations. Where ISIS occupied areas with diverse ethnic and religious communities, minorities were killed or forced to assimilate. Women and girls were excluded from public life and subject to regulations outlining what they could wear, with whom they could associate with, and where and whether they could work. Sexual violence and slavery became a hallmark of IS. Extreme punishments included public executions, beheadings, amputations, and whippings.

The battle to liberate Mosul in Iraq, the largest city once held by IS fighters, began in October 2016 and ended in late 2017. With coalition support, the main fighters on the ground were the Iraqi military and Kurdish militias. Likewise, the Islamic State's de facto capital in Syria, Raqqa, was liberated in October 2017. The group to do that was the Syrian Democratic Forces (SDF), an 80,000-strong coalition of Kurdish and Arab fighters. By early 2019, IS territory had been reduced to a single town in Syria's Deir Az Zor province. The Islamic State was in an existential battle. Its territorial defeat seemed certain and by March, the caliphate was defeated.

Although the caliphate, as a territorial entity, was defeated, the ideology that underpinned it was not. On Easter Sunday 2019, just a month after the defeat of IS in Syria, coordinated suicide attacks targeted

The Rise and Fall of a Modern-Day Caliphate

local churchgoers and foreign tourists. IS claimed responsibility, with Baghdadi emerging from hiding just long enough to praise the attackers. Without a state to administer, IS can turn its attention to the propagation of global terror. In doing so, it may have come to accept the al-Qaeda edict: victory against the west and its allies in the region must necessarily precede the establishment of a caliphate.

In addition to its territory in Syria and Iraq, IS declared a number of far-flung provinces or *wilayat*, IS Khorasan (or ISK) was established in early 2015, when militants of Pakistan- and Afghanistan-based groups pledged allegiance to Baghdadi. In 2019, IS declared the establishment of a Wilayat-e Hind and a Wilayat-e Pakistan. The IS province in India is located in Jammu and Kashmir, where tensions between Muslims and Hindus have simmered for seventy years. The strategy of mobilizing around existing conflicts, perfected in the context of the sectarianism that beset Iraq following the U.S. invasion, is clearly emerging as an important modus operandi of IS. Conflict across the Middle East and South Asia may be ripe for exploitation by IS or its successors.

HISTORICAL BACKGROUND

The Emergence of Civilization

In earliest human history people depended, for food, upon hunting wild animals and gathering the edible parts of plants. For warmth, they clothed themselves in animal skins, and they found protection from the weather in caves or temporary shelters. Archaeologists have found evidence for this kind of life on six continents and many islands.

Exactly why humans made the shift from a nomadic lifestyle, to forming settled communities remains a matter of sometimes heated debate. What is known, is that a similar process occurred in a number of different parts of the world at much the same time. The Neolithic, or New Stone Age, was a remarkable period in which the seeds of civilizations that have profoundly shaped the modern world, were planted. Early theories on why this occurred focused on archaeological discoveries in the Middle East and, extrapolating from the evidence uncovered, zeroed in on environmental or climatic reasons. Changes in climate almost certainly shaped how (if not why) early communities formed and developed. As the earth warmed after the last Ice Age, rainy weather retreated northward and to the tropics. A permanent zone of high atmospheric pressure began to dominate Southern Europe and North Africa from the Atlantic to the Middle East, and Southern Asia up to monsoon-soaked India. Under the impact of successive dry, sunny days, deserts formed and nomadic

hunters and gatherers increasingly narrowed their peregrinations to river valleys, watered by rainfall trapped by mountains and highlands often hundreds of miles away.

Beside rivers and streams in Southwest Asia, women (more likely than men) first deliberately planted seed—barley and a variety of wheat—and cultivated land. These events are dated by most historians to around 8,000 B.C. Agriculture is often identified as having flourished at the earliest date in what is known as the Fertile Crescent (modern-day Iraq, Israel, Palestine, Syria, Lebanon, Egypt, and Jordan as well as the southeastern fringe of Turkey and the western fringes of Iran). About the same time, people in the region domesticated animals: cultivation and domestication together formed what is sometimes known as the Agricultural Revolution. While it certainly had (in the long-term) revolutionary impacts, it was a much more gradual process than such terminology might imply.

Some scholars, suggest that rather than acting as the catalyst for the development of settled communities, agriculture was itself a consequence of a new way of organizing social life, borne not out of climatic necessity but changes in human psychology and cognition.

Initially hardly more productive than hunting and gathering, soon farmers were capable of producing a surplus over the minimum requirements of food, clothing, and shelter. Once people had learned how to plant grain crops and raise captive animals, a much more secure supply of food was available. It was no longer necessary for small groups to keep constantly on

the move in search of food. They planted their fields near sources of water, their numbers increased, and village life developed. The sites of the oldest villages so far discovered lie in a zone stretching from southeastern Europe across Asia Minor as far eastward as the region of the middle Tigris River.

The level of technology, combined with the tasks of obtaining food, clothing, safety, and other essentials of existence are likely to have shaped daily activities and society during prehistory. Life was short, even for survivors of infancy and childhood. Food supplies limited the maximum size of the group; hunters and gatherers had to move further to procure food as the group expanded in number. However, high mortality for children and adults—let alone infants—decreed the importance of having many women, all either pregnant or about to become so. Only thus could the existence of a next generation be expected.

Larger communities and more efficient food production allowed—and required—increased specialization of activity; farm lands and permanent buildings required greater property rights. Rulers, warriors, administrators, and priests acted to protect property from invaders, settle disputes, and establish moral codes. By authority, force, and religion, these new, specialized professions appropriated much of the harvest, leaving the farmers who worked the land little beyond the minimum subsistence necessary for life. Not for the last time, therefore, improvements in ability to control nature enriched the few who took advantage of the new circumstances, but left much of society little better off (and

sometimes considerably worse off) than before. Nevertheless, the agricultural surplus made possible a larger population, growing slowly and settling more densely. This, in turn, saw the emergence of cities, trade, writing, metallurgy, and the opportunity to seek beauty and truth through philosophy, the early sciences, and new forms of art.

The discovery of metals, the importance of which is such that historians have named epochs for the metal that predominated at a particular time, began perhaps by accident, when rocks containing copper melted around some cooking fire. Far easier to shape than stone, copper nevertheless suffered grave defects of softness and brittleness that hampered its use in tools and weapons. With the invention of bronze around 3,000 B.C., metal became more than an ornament. So important was bronze that its era lasted until approximately 1200 B.C. in Southwestern Asia.

With the new agricultural wealth concentrated in relatively few hands, trade and the production of luxuries increased. New crafts developed and old ones expanded. Artists improved their skills, notably in sculptures and reliefs, sometimes with impressive use of gold leaf. Jewelry of gold, silver, and semi-precious stones like lapis lazuli and carnelian was used as adornment among the wealthy. For the poor, seashells, colored stone, and beads of painted pottery sufficed. With even greater visual drama, towns developed

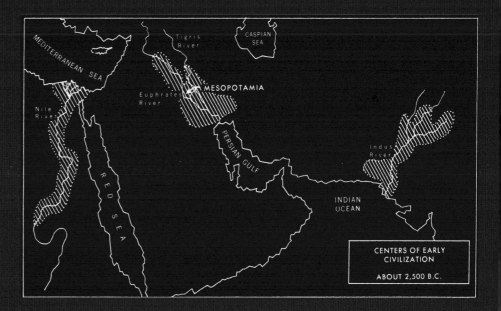

and architects experimented with new techniques for larger and more imposing buildings. Frequently the temple of the city god became the focus of town life, and its structure was often designed as much to impress the beholder as to provide shelter for priests and rituals. Not surprisingly, temples provide some of the earliest examples of monumental architecture.

Other discoveries of the Bronze Age included improved and specialized tools, the wheel (or, more accurately, the fixed axle), and eventually the domestication of the horse. Together the last two made possible the chariot, the greatest weapon of the age. Early horses were too small to be ridden in battle, and without stirrups proved unstable fighting platforms, but a chariot could overwhelm infantrymen. As technology armed the defenders of the river valleys with weapons superior to those of invaders from the hills, steppes, and mountains, the opportunity arose for the three great river valley civilizations—Mesopotamia, Egypt, and the Indus Valley—to develop.

The Spread of Civilization

The development and spread of writing systems during the Bronze Age meant that information about business transactions, deeds of kings, and knowledge about the world could be recorded and preserved, to be read in other places and at later times. Around 3,000 B.C., the first true writing appeared, among the Sumerians of the Tigris-Euphrates Plain. Their wedge-shaped characters, impressed with a reed pen on wet clay tablets, produced a script now called cuneiform. Its pictographic origins pre-dated the Sumerians, and it developed from the needs of business contracts and records in the growing cities. Cuneiform was a cumbersome and inefficient writing system; each symbol could represent any one of several ideas or syllables, and later even sounds.

Cuneiform

Consequently, long years of training were required to become a scribe, capable of distinguishing alternate meanings. Nevertheless, cuneiform spread widely, as illustrated by dramatic and relatively recent archeological discovery. Ebla, in northern Syria, lies hundreds of miles from Sumer. In the 1970s, archaeologists unearthed at Ebla a royal library of some 16,000 clay tablets, in Sumerian and Eblaite, dating from about 2,400 B.C. They provided new knowledge about the Canaanites of Abraham's time and also proof of the extent of Sumer's influence. Indeed, the writing system lingered long after Sumerian died out as a spoken language soon after 2,000 B.C.; cuneiform continued to be used for the Babylonian, Assyrian, Hittite, and other languages, only dying out by the time of Christ.

Evidence suggests that writing began rather suddenly in the Nile Valley shortly after 3,000 B.C. Possibly the idea of writing, but not the system, was borrowed from Sumer. Drawings of gods, people, animals, birds, and inanimate objects represented words, ideas, and sounds. These so-called hieroglyphics were not a very

Hieroglyphics

efficient method of writing, but they were capable of recording information.

It is not surprising that a third system of writing, the alphabet, replaced both cuneiform and hieroglyphics. Around the 12th century B.C., Canaanites living along the eastern shores of the Mediterranean assigned each symbol to represent a sound, rather than a picture, syllable, or idea. Easily applied to Semitic languages, whose words generally were characterized by three root sounds and simple vowels, the new script vastly shortened the task of learning to read and write. The alphabet thus broke the power akin to monopoly the scribes had previously enjoyed over writing. While most people remained illiterate, merchants and officials adopted the idea of the alphabet to keep accounts and records, whatever their language.

Propelled by trade, the alphabet spread both east and west from Canaan and Phoenicia. By the 10th century B.C. it began to replace cuneiform in Babylonia, in the cursive Aramaic script whose descendants include modern Arabic and Hebrew. A century later, the alphabet spread to Greece. The Greeks, in turn, used it in their far-flung trading colonies across Southern Europe, preserving in the process the name of the Phoenician city-state of Byblos, whose trade with Egypt provided Greeks with papyrus. The name remains in the English prefix *biblio* for book, and *Bible*: "The Book."

Using the Canaanite alphabet

Only after the conquest of Egypt by Alexander the Great in 332 B.C., and the rise thereafter of a great center of Hellenistic civilization at Alexandria, did the use of hieroglyphics decline. A modified Greek alphabet was devised for writing the native language, Coptic. Its use continued despite foreign rule by Greeks, Romans, and Byzantines. Although after the Arab conquest, Coptic gradually fell into disuse in daily speech, it remains today in the liturgy of the Egyptian rite of Christianity, the Coptic Church.

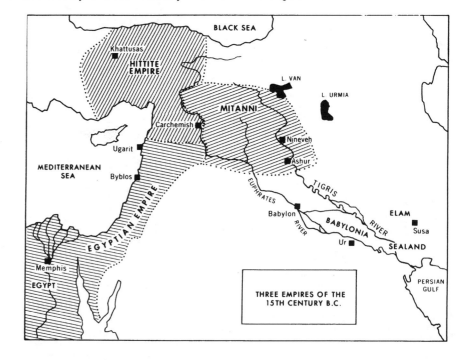

The Rise and Fall of Empires

The sport of an Assyrian king

During the many centuries of civilization's uneven advance, life for ordinary people often proved harsh. Only in the most fortunate times did the countryside and towns enjoy peace. Instead, farmers, merchants, and craftsmen alike suffered interruption of work and safety; civilization had provided the incentive and means for increasingly well-organized warfare.

Sometimes there were disputes over territory between neighboring communities. This led to a new dimension in fighting when one city set out to dominate others and when one small state began to expand and subjugate others. In modern times, mechanized industrial production has permitted populations of entire nations to enjoy lives of relative comfort and convenience. In ancient times, however, production depended on human and animal energy for power and thus luxuries and comforts could be enjoyed only by small, privileged groups—and only through taking wealth from others, both slaves within society, and increasingly by conquest. Thus, the new inventions of civilization encouraged aggressive people, at first individually, then as groups, and finally as nations, to reap personal benefit from the labor of others.

In the Nile Valley, where rival cities and regions had struggled for supremacy, there arose around 2850 B.C. a leader capable of unifying the distinctly separate regions of Upper and Lower Egypt (the Nile Delta). Hardly distinct from associated myths, Menes founded the first of 30 dynasties to rule Egypt. Claiming divine descent, his successors as kings or Pharaohs exerted enormous power over society. By the 26th century B.C., the pyramid age, rulers constructed enormous stone monuments as their tombs. Amazing in size and accuracy as feats of engineering, (the Great Pyramid, for example, contains 2,300,000 blocks and varies only 9 1/2 inches, or 24 centimeters, on a side) they also bear dramatic witness to the organization of society and the Pharaohs' ability to extract labor and resources from the populace. However, one of the Pharaohs' greatest weaknesses was organizational: as local governors passed office to their sons, central authority weakened and the dynasty increasingly risked collapse.

Although Egypt possessed then, as now, relatively secure borders against foreign attack in the form of deserts to the south, east, and west, strong Pharaohs frequently sought conquests abroad. During the Middle Kingdom (2100–1800 B.C.) and the New Kingdom (1550–1085 B.C.), Egyptian armies defeated the Nubians up the Nile and struggled for the wealth and control of Syria against both its inhabitants and powerful kingdoms in Mesopotamia.

In the 15th century, Thutmose III fought seventeen campaigns and crossed the Euphrates; hieroglyphics at the Temple of Karnak in Egypt portrayed his conquests and booty.

The growth of powerful states in Mesopotamia illustrated many features common to Egypt, including the divine origin of rulers. However, geography decreed greater difficulties for those desiring to unify the land. The broader river valleys allowed city states to develop, and peoples to retain separate ethnic identities and languages. Moreover, invaders repeatedly pierced the natural barriers of desert and mountains and established new kingdoms. Thus, for most of the 3rd millennium B.C. the dominant political organization was the city-states of Sumer. In the mid-24th century B.C., however, Sargon, ruler of Akkad to the north, conquered Sumer and proclaimed himself king of Sumer and Akkad. The next centuries, marked by rivalry between the Akkadians and Sumerians as well as invading Amorites, nevertheless witnessed another great achievement of civilization: the promulgation of codes of law. The first recorded law-giver, Ur-Nammu, was followed by the much more famous, though significantly harsher, Code of Hammurabi.

In the struggle for territory and the wealth of civilization, empires and

23

The Rise and Fall of Empires

dynasties rose and fell. Warfare took a new turn when horses were introduced into the civilized area from the northeast about 1600 B.C. Horse-drawn chariots could crash through a line of foot soldiers. The infantry, poorer soldiers who could not afford horses and chariots, lost status in the new military organizations.

The rise of iron-smelting in Asia Minor around 1200 B.C. apparently provided an important strength for the next dominant power of Mesopotamia: the warlike and often cruel Assyrians, with their capital at Assur. Armed with iron weapons and heavy chariots, Assyrian troops proved invincible. They raided as far as the Black Sea and ruled to the Mediterranean, marching into captivity (and often extinction) skilled workers and sometimes entire populations.

Enriched by conquests and the labor of subject peoples, the kings of Assyria adorned palaces and decorated impressive buildings with monuments and stone reliefs of colossal winged animals. The last powerful king of Assyria, Ashurbanipal (668–627 B.C.), personally directed an effort to collect the literature and learning of Mesopotamian civilizations. His royal library at Nineveh, excavated in the 19th century, acquired thousands of cuneiform tablets, including the Epic of Gilgamesh and the Babylonian Creation Epic. This single most important collection of cuneiform tablets provides modern historians with much of their knowledge of the culture and history of the Tigris-Euphrates Plain.

After the collapse of the Assyrian Empire, the center of power and wealth on the Tigris-Euphrates Plain shifted again to the city of Babylon. The neo-Babylonian (or Chaldean) Empire, which extended from the head of the Persian Gulf to the Mediterranean Sea, gathered wealth to give Babylon a final burst of glory before it gradually faded away.

The next great empire had its base in the mountains east of the Tigris River. The Medes were the first Iranian-speaking group to establish an empire. They dominated a large territory to the east and north of Babylonia. About the middle of the 6th century B.C. the empire of the Medes was taken over by their fellow Iranians and former subjects, the Persians. Under the leadership of Cyrus the Great and his successors, most of the civilized world except for East Asia and the defiant city-states of Greece, fell under the sway of the Persian Empire.

Like the Assyrians before them, the Persians did not hesitate to use force if the assigned taxes, or "gifts," were not sent by subject communities when due. On the other hand, many of the Persian rulers tried to gain voluntary submission of

Ninevah: how it may have looked from ruins

their subjects by showing toleration for local cultures and religions.

The vast Persian Empire was united by improved roads, a postal system for official use, uniform laws, and employment of a single language for administrative purposes. The language of administration was not Persian, but Aramaic, which several centuries earlier had become dominant in business in the region between the Euphrates River and the Mediterranean Coast. The empire was divided into provinces, each with a governor *(satrap)* responsible to the Great King. Eventually the personal ambitions of these satraps contributed to the weakening of the empire. Another destructive force within the empire consisted of civil wars led by rival claimants to the throne. Each faction sought to gain power,

receive honor, and control the wealth produced by civilization.

The extension of Persian control over the Indus Valley had significant cultural effects. Interchange of religious and philosophical ideas was one. Another was the spread of the idea of an alphabet into South Asia, apparently in the 5th century B.C. The earliest alphabet used in the Indus-Ganges civilization preserved forms of the Aramaic alphabet used in the Persian Empire. During the period of Persian domination to the west of it, the Ganges Basin was under the control of rival minor kings. The largest of the kingdoms was that of Magadha near the mouth of the Ganges River. Meanwhile, civilization was also developing in the southern part of the Indian Peninsula.

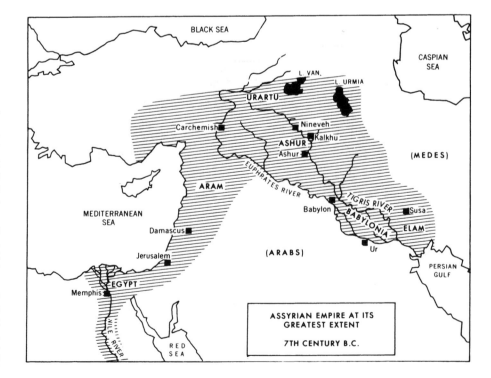

24

Hebrews and Judaeans

the Philistines of the coastal plain and nomadic tribes to the south and east. However, after David succeeded to the throne around 1000 B.C., the small kingdom expanded in size and military prowess, reaching its zenith in peace and prosperity under David's son Solomon (961–922 B.C.), who built the first temple dedicated to Yahweh in Jerusalem. According to the Biblical account (disputed by some scholars), at Solomon's death the state fractured, with the northern tribes establishing a Kingdom of Israel in Samaria. Lacking the great religious center of Jerusalem, and prey both to Canaanite religions and invasion by foreign armies, the Kingdom of Israel lasted until destroyed by the Assyrians in 722 B.C. Under the somewhat more capable kings of the House of David, the southern Kingdom of Judah survived until finally captured by the great neo-Babylonian ruler Nebuchadnezzar in 586 B.C. His troops carried off to exile in Babylon the royal family of Judah, together with many of the upper classes and skilled workers.

After Cyrus the Great captured Babylon in 539 B.C. (in the process bringing to an end over two thousand years of Mesopotamian empires), the liberal religious policies of the new Persian Empire allowed some worshippers of Yahweh to return to the land of their forebears. Others

Lacking the material splendor displayed by the great empires of the river valleys, the Hebrew tribes of the plains and highlands of Canaan can nevertheless be said to have had an almost unparalleled impact on civilization, through the refinement and circulation of the theological concept of monotheism. In sharp contrast to the many gods worshipped by most surrounding societies, Hebrew prophets and scriptures proclaimed that one God, Yahweh (or Jehovah), created all. Descendants of this faith—especially Judaism and Christianity, but also Islam—have influenced European civilization more than any other cultural achievement of the ancient world.

Historical research in the 20th century lends credence to at least some of the accounts given in the Jewish scriptures, which also form the Old Testament of the Bible. The first patriarch, Abraham,

claimed as ancestor by both Jewish and Arab societies, roamed Canaan with his herds, erecting in the midst of polytheism altars to Yahweh. His grandson, Jacob, also known as Israel, is generally regarded as the first Hebrew: from his sons descended the tribes of *B'nai Yisra'el*, the Children of Israel. After settling in Egypt for generations, the Hebrews left Egypt abruptly and on mass around 1400 B.C., to be led into Canaan by Joshua.

Tempted by religions with physical idols that could be worshipped, the ancient Hebrews sometimes seem hardly distinguishable from other Canaanite tribes. They rarely ruled the entire land, and for several centuries lacked political unity even in the central highlands where their population was concentrated, running from north to south between the Mediterranean and the Jordan River. Their first king, Saul, faced invasions from

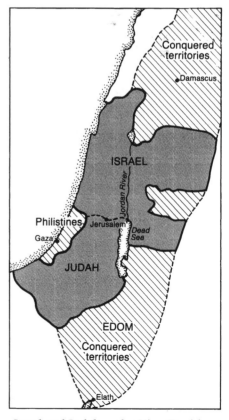

Israel and Judah under King David, c. 1000 B.C.

Hebrews and Judaeans

remained in Persia and Mesopotamia, developing a large and often prosperous center of Judaism. Despite local opposition, those who returned rebuilt the walls of Jerusalem, then the Temple itself, under tolerant Persian rule.

Far greater threats to Judaism followed the next conquerors, the Hellenistic armies of Alexander the Great in 332 B.C. Greek ideas soon came to dominate the Jewish upper classes as they discovered Greek athletics, music, and art as well as the Greek language itself. Religious concepts, like resurrection and angels, deeply appealed to the wealthy and separated them from most Jews, with their more traditional and pious values.

Direct attacks on Jewish religion and customs aroused greater resistance. When the Seleucid rulers of Syria, having captured Palestine, ordered pigs sacrificed to Zeus at the Temple, rebellion broke out. After bitter fighting, Jewish independence briefly flared anew under the Hasmonaeans, also known as the Maccabees (129–63 B.C.). Split by political rivalry, divided by religious factions, and resented by non-Jewish inhabitants, the Jewish territories were easily annexed to Rome by Pompey in 63 B.C. Julius Caesar later appointed a governor named Antipater, an Idumaean from the coastal region previously conquered by the Hasmonaeans and himself possibly a descendant of the Israelites' ancient enemies, the Philistines. Converted to Judaism but opposed by the Hasmonaeans, Antipater and his sons struggled to control Judea. Finally, declared King of Judea by the Roman Senate, and aided by Roman troops, his son Herod succeeded in capturing Jerusalem (37 B.C.).

All accounts portray Herod as hated by his subjects for many reasons. A foreigner himself and a collaborator dependent on Roman rule, he was a tyrant capable (at the very least) of killing his own sons. The Gospel of Matthew records the likely apocryphal story of Herod's execution of all male children two years old and under in the vicinity of Bethlehem.

Despite a blood-thirsty reputation, Herod built cities and established peace. For the non-Jews he provided festivals and Greek arts. For the Jews, he rebuilt the Temple on a grander scale than ever before. His heirs proved less capable, and Caesar Augustus extended direct Roman rule over the area.

Increasing Jewish opposition to Rome broke into open rebellion in A.D. 66, after increasingly intolerant policies of the Emperors Caligula and Nero. Aided by rivalries for the throne in Rome, Judea became independent again, but four years later Titus defeated the Jewish armies and sacked Jerusalem after a lengthy siege. The temple, so recently rebuilt by Herod,

Solomon's Temple was made from timber brought from Tyre

was destroyed, and Jewish zealots holding the fortress of Masada overlooking the Dead Sea finally committed suicide rather than surrender. Again the Jewish population faced persecution and forced exile. After a second failed rebellion in 135 A.D.

Rome made Judea a pagan colony, prohibiting Jews from living there, although believers survived in neighboring Galilee and elsewhere throughout the Roman Empire, as well as flourishing on occasion in Babylonia.

A rabbi reads from the *Torah* in a synagogue.

The Hellenistic Age, Roman Rule and Christianity

Alexander

The sudden and furious conquests of Alexander the Great shattered the dominance of Persian emperors in Asia; a new language and a new civilization began their lengthy domination of Southwest Asia. For centuries the city-states of Greece had learned from the older civilizations to the East. In the decades after 500 B.C. they fought off Persian invasions with difficulty, in battles such as Marathon, Thermopylae, and Salamis. However, in 11 short years after 334 B.C., Alexander the Great, king of Macedonia (although Greek in culture and education), captured the known world as far as India and established the greatest empire then known. This laid the political conditions for a new era of civilization called *Hellenistic*, meaning "Greek-like," in contrast to the previous Greek, or Hellenic civilization.

Although Alexander's empire broke up after his death at the young age of 33, rival kingdoms succeeded him in Egypt (the Ptolemies) and Southwest Asia (the Seleucids). In both kingdoms Greeks and Macedonians—forming the urban upper class of rulers, soldiers, merchants, and artisans—mixed with the local population, in the process creating Hellenistic civilization. Trade flourished, from India and even China in the east, to Italy and North Africa in the west. The growing wealth made possible great libraries at Alexandria and Pergamum as well as new cities and art. Science and learning advanced dramatically: among other achievements, scholars calculated the earth's circumference, founded geometry, and interpreted literature.

After 200 B.C., however, the Hellenistic world began to decline. Never solidly established east of Mesopotamia, the Seleucids retreated from the Iranian plateau and later from Mesopotamia in the face of Parthian invasions. Moreover, within the remaining territories, native populations increasingly rejected Greek beliefs, values, and language. With relative ease, then, the Roman general Pompey captured the remaining Seleucid territories (64 B.C.) and

Egypt finally fell to Octavian (30 B.C.). However, the Romans failed to conquer either Mesopotamia or Persia from the Parthians. Moreover, within those Asian territories it did conquer, Greek rather than Latin remained the language of trade and learning. Significantly, the struggle between Hellenistic and local beliefs and cultures continued.

Into this world was born Jesus of Nazareth. Educated by his mother, rather than Jewish scribes or Hellenistic scholars, in adulthood he preached a message of love and obedience, of humility and enjoyment of the good. As reports of his apparent miracles spread, he rapidly gained a following of Jews and others who hoped for deliverance—divinely aided deliverance—from Rome. Nevertheless, his popularity and message threatened both the Hellenized Sadducees and the carefully traditional Pharisees. Charged by Jewish leadership with claiming to be the Son of God, he seemed to Pontius Pilate, the Roman prefect, just another agitator. Deserted by almost all his followers and those who had desired political revolution, he was crucified. Dying at about the same age as Alexander, Jesus conquered no territories, founded no cities, and overthrew no empires.

To his followers, however, Jesus conquered much more than the world. His crucifixion was said to have made possible the redemption of humankind from sin. His claimed resurrection three days later, and subsequent return to heaven, brought the assurance of a final Judgment followed by a New Earth ruled by God. Passages from the Jewish scriptures—to Christians now the Old Testament—were interpreted to show him as the fulfillment of many prophecies of the Messiah (Greek, *Christ*). Within weeks of his death an active and growing church sprang up in Jerusalem.

Christianity first spread most rapidly among Jewish communities scattered throughout the Roman Empire. Within a generation, however, the preaching and writings of St. Paul rendered Christianity a world religion that promised salvation to all who believed, Jewish or otherwise. Both hindered and helped by occasional persecution, Christianity spread rapidly, especially among the lower classes. By the middle of the 2nd century, the major tenets of the faith had been established, the Canon of Biblical books had been largely selected, and the church had been organized into a hierarchy. When persecution by the Emperor Diocletian failed to destroy the church (303–311), a pivotal moment was reached. Diocletian's successor, Constantine, granted toleration and equality for Christianity while eliminating cults of the state.

In matters beyond religion, Constantine changed the face of the Roman Empire as well. In 330 A.D. he moved the capital from "heathen Rome" to Byzantium on the shores of the Bosporus. During the two centuries that followed, the eastern and western halves of the empire drifted apart, each facing invasion and struggling to maintain order and civilization in the midst of economic decay. Gradually there emerged in the east the Byzantine Empire, ruling over Greece as well as Asia Minor, geographical Syria, and Egypt. Greek in language, and Hellenistic in much of its culture, though still calling itself Rome, the Byzantine Empire mixed Christianity with the grandeur of Oriental potentates. The emperor ruled absolutely, as God's representative on earth, standing as head of the military, government, and church.

For almost a thousand years the Byzantine Empire survived, an enormous accomplishment that contrasts with the total collapse of Roman rule in the West. During those centuries, it witnessed great achievements in law, and it preserved Greek and Roman learning largely lost elsewhere. In art and architecture the stunning beauty created by Byzantine artisans remains at St. Marks in Venice and the Hagia Sophia in Istanbul. As defenders of the faith, the Byzantine military stopped numerous invasions by infidels, and passed Orthodox Christianity and Greek-based alphabets along to Russia and much of Eastern Europe. Nevertheless, bloodshed stains many pages of Byzantine history, and tolerance brightens few. When conflicts in theology and religion followed the same dividing lines as differences in language and culture between Greek rulers and native inhabitants of Egypt and Syria, the consequence was restlessness in those lands and weakened loyalties to the empire. When new armies appeared out of Arabia in the middle of the 7th century, Syrian, Egyptian, and North African possessions were quickly lost.

Zoroastrian, Buddhist and Hindu Cultures

When the Roman legions attempted to press eastward from Syria in the 1st century B.C., they were stopped by another military power, the Parthian Empire. This state had its origins in the 3rd century B.C. when warriors from Parthia, an area in the northeast part of the Iranian Plateau, gained local independence from Hellenistic rulers. Regarding themselves as the heirs of the first Persian Empire, the Parthians eventually expanded their control both east and west, building an empire that stretched from the Euphrates Plain to the Indus River.

Hellenistic culture declined, but was not totally eradicated, within the territory under Parthian rule. Native ideas, architecture, art, and literature developed along independent lines. Although religious activity in Parthian domains is not well known, it seems that Zoroastrianism made great advances. This faith revered the teachings of Zarathustra, who lived during the 7th century B.C. In its developed form, Zoroastrianism stressed the struggle between two principal supernatural beings representing good and evil. The leading position was held by Ahura Mazda, the god of light and goodness.

About 225 A.D. the weakened leadership of the Parthians was replaced by a Persian dynasty descended from a little-known figure named Sassan. Occupying the Parthian capital of Ctesiphon on the Tigris as their own, the Sassanids presented themselves as the restorers of the purity of the first Persian Empire. Zoroastrianism took on its most highly developed form as the established religion of the government. The Sassanids increased the level of civilization in their territories by encouraging the development of cities.

The Sassanids also possessed a strong expansionist urge; this kept them in conflict with their neighbors, such as the Late Roman (Byzantine) Empire to the west, which had similar impulses. For a time in the 6th century and the first decades of the next, the Sassanid Empire was the world's leading power. In a final burst of militancy it captured Damascus and Jerusalem from Byzantium in 614, but lost them a decade and a half later. The Sassanid Empire, exhausted by the wars, succumbed to the attacks of the Muslim Arabs beginning with the fall of Ctesiphon in 637.

The golden age of Buddhism in the Indian Peninsula occurred in the state ruled by the Maurya family. At its height in the 3rd century B.C., the Mauryan Empire controlled the Ganges Basin, the Indus Valley and large regions to the south and northwest. The most illustrious ruler was Asoka (or Ashoka); during his long reign (273–232 B.C.) he turned from bloody wars of expansion to the peaceful teaching of Buddhism.

Gautama Buddha had lived several centuries earlier and it was Asoka's patronage of the Buddha's teachings, which contributed greatly to the spread of Buddhism as a world religion.

Many inscribed pillars, set up on Asoka's orders, have been found in all parts of modern India, in Pakistan, and in southern Afghanistan. These provide scholars with a picture of that early period, including Mauryan knowledge of the Hellenistic world to the west. After the death of Asoka the Great, the empire of the Maurya declined and finally ended in 185 B.C. It was replaced by many small states about which little information is available.

For nearly five centuries during which there was a notable development of trade with the outside world, attempts to build a new empire in the Indian Peninsula failed. Then in the early 4th century A.D., a territory nearly as extensive as that ruled by the Maurya was brought under the control of the Gupta dynasty. The Gupta period from the early 4th to the early 6th century is often described as the golden age of Hindu culture in the Ganges Basin, although the central and southern parts of the peninsula were to achieve their zenith of classical Hindu culture later.

The Gupta Empire reached its height from its capital of Ayodhya on the Ganges River, during the reign of Chandra Gupta II (A.D. 385 to 413). Later, particularly from about A.D. 480 to 490, Hindu civilization was badly mauled by invading Huns, who raided from bases north of the Hindu Kush Mountains. The menace of the Huns and the disturbances caused by various other peoples entering the Indian Peninsula from Central Asia did not subside for nearly a century. By then the region was again divided into a number of warring local kingdoms.

Little is known about events until the early 7th century, when a youth of only 16 years became king of a small state and attempted to build an empire. This king, Harsha, ruled well for 41 years. Not only was he a patron of art and literature, but was himself a poet and playwright. Three of his plays in Sanskrit have survived, including one called "The Pearl Necklace." With Harsha's death the last great Hindu kingdom in the Ganges-Indus region ended, a prelude to later foreign invasion.

Life-size sculpture of Buddha
Courtesy of the Government of India

Muhammad and the Rise of Islam

In the rugged desert landscape of western Arabia, far from civilization's major centers and some six centuries after Christ, the third great monotheistic religion arose with the preaching of Muhammad. This solemn and meditative man warned the citizens of the city of Mecca of a coming great cataclysm to end the earth, followed by a final judgment over all deeds that would grant to the righteous heaven, and to the evil, the fires of hell. From his initial messages of repentance and care of one's fellows, Muhammad's teachings expanded to fill almost all aspects of society. This religious protest first attracted a few followers, and later an entire city. Within a generation the entire Middle East lay conquered by a newly united people, and the Islamic civilization began its often brilliant rise.

Born about 572, probably after his father's death, Muhammad was orphaned as a child when his mother died. Few details of his early life are certain, but he grew up in a society undergoing dramatic social changes.

Prolonged conflict between the Sassanid Persian and Byzantine empires disrupted the traditional Mesopotamian trade route between India and the Mediterranean. One alternative route ran along the mountainous western coast of Arabia. Several Arabian tribes remained neutral in the great clash between Byzantium and Persia that stretched as far south as Yemen, and this encouraged trade. So did the religious customs that brought an annual truce to desert warfare and a pilgrimage to Mecca. Some Arab tribes, particularly Muhammad's own Quraysh, seized the opportunities, and exchanged herds for trade caravans. In the process Arab society itself changed significantly. For wealthy merchants, houses replaced tents, and the family structure strengthened as fathers viewed sons as assistants and successors. However, increasing wealth for some meant greater disparities of wealth, and thus sometimes a decline in loyalty to the clan and tribe. As the family strengthened, other social bonds weakened, and the poor increasingly found charity less common.

Raised by relatives and trained as a merchant, Muhammad had the good fortune to marry Khadija, a rather older widow of substantial wealth. Nevertheless, despite his financial success, he suffered inner distress over social wrongs, and meditated extensively. At the age of 40 he is alleged to have become conscious of a message from the angel Gabriel to praise the one God, Allah, as the Creator, and to care for the unfortunate.

Though living in a pagan culture, Muhammad, as a relatively successful merchant, had presumably had the opportunity to become familiar with Jewish and Christian customs and beliefs. He now identified Allah as the God of their scriptures, recognized many of their prophets, and identified himself as the final Messenger, who revealed words sent from heaven.

Like many religious leaders, Muhammad at first appealed to relatives and friends, as well as the unfortunate. However, he aroused the hostility and anger of the leading merchants and politicians of Mecca by his vision of a dreadful judgment, by his strident demands for greater charity, and even more by his condemnation of pagan idol worship. This struck at the financial foundation of Meccan society, for pilgrimages to Mecca, with its famous black stone *Ka'aba* provided great opportunity for trade, and religion sanctioned an annual truce from raids, valuable to merchants and pilgrims alike.

As pressure became economic embargo and persecution, some followers fled to Ethiopia. By 622 Muhammad himself forsook Mecca for Yathrib, soon renamed Medina, "The City" of the Prophet. Celebrated as the *Hijra*, the event marks the beginning of the Muslim era.

Once in Medina, Muhammad became far more than a religious leader. He had come, by agreement, as the leader of the "Umma" or community: he was the primary secular authority. His Meccan followers abandoned the protection of the

A prayer in Tehran (late 19th century drawing)

Muhammad and the Rise of Islam

tribes of their birth by following him to Medina. Now they formed in effect a new tribe, and Muhammad became responsible for their welfare, and that of the converts in Medina. Certainly, too, the revelations continued, and they included, along with calls to repentance, much practical material for the lawgiver of a new society.

The ten years Muhammad lived in Medina saw established the religion of "Islam," or submission to God. Despite some resistance from Jews and other non-believers resident in Medina, the Muslim ("One who submits") community grew and adopted the distinctive beliefs and practices that continue to the present. The individual Believer had five obligations, now known as the pillars of Islam. He or she must believe, confessing that "There is no God but Allah, and Muhammad is his Messenger" and bow in ritual prayer five times daily. Annually, during the Islamic month of Ramadan, he or she must abstain from food, drink, and sex during the day. If possible, once during his or her lifetime a Muslim should undertake a pilgrimage (*hajj*) to Mecca. Finally, a Muslim must contribute annually a portion of his or her wealth as charity.

Beyond these duties, the Muslim must accept the Quran ("Recitation") as the literal word of God. Other sources of authority include the Hadith (collections of the sayings of the Prophet Muhammad) and the Sunna (accounts of the deeds and behaviors of the Prophet, also sometimes called "traditions"). Muslims believe that the Quran is unchanging and that it only exists in Arabic. Translations of the text into other languages are only considered interpretations of the original. In contrast to the generally unquestioned authenticity of the Quran, however, disagreement does exist about the authenticity of various Sunna and Hadith. These accounts have been reported from generation to generation, sometimes orally and sometimes in print, and the credibility of the "chain" of transmission of these accounts is often a point of contention among scholars of Islam.

Summaries of Islam like the paragraphs above cannot do justice to the combination of religious observances and custom in Islamic societies. The religion deliberately appeals to people of all languages and nations, and promises equality among the believers, who in forming the Umma attempted to have religious boundaries the same as political. For centuries the Umayyad and Abbasid caliphates achieved this in practice, as they fused subjects of varied languages and religions into a Muslim society ruled more

or less within the framework of Islamic law. Despite Muhammad's condemnation of the practices of wealthy Meccans, private property is allowed, and numerous traditions report God's favor towards merchants. Usury is forbidden, paralleling early Jewish and Christian views.

In social aspects, Islam reinforced the position of the husband, allowing up to four wives and divorce on (his) demand, although he was urged to limit himself to one wife if he felt incapable of treating more than that number fairly. Nevertheless, a woman retained the right to property she brought into a marriage, a privilege enjoyed centuries before Western nations granted similar property rights to women. On balance, scholars agree that Muhammad raised the status and condition of women, in part by rigidly punishing adultery as well as condemning the practice of female infanticide.

A Muslim's worship contrasts substantially with certain aspects of Jewish and Christian traditions, yet there are many similarities: sermons, ritual prayers, and reading (or recitation from memory) of the scriptures. However, music played with instruments is remarkable for its absence, as are drawings, paintings, or sculptures of living things, especially prophets. Friday, the day of worship, is not a day of rest, and the believers commonly gather in the mosque in the afternoon, entering without shoes after washing hands and feet. Generally in Islam there is no equivalent of a priesthood: any believer may address the congregation, who stand in rows before the pulpit, with the women meeting separately. The dead await physical resurrection and judgment, and are mourned extensively at the funeral and 40 days thereafter.

Thanks to the media, Westerners are much more familiar with regulations of Muslim law that have roots in the early days of Islam, such as amputation for certain crimes. The Quran strictly forbids wine, and by extension alcoholic drinks of any kind. Pork, carrion, and blood are forbidden, but in great contrast to the many unclean foods of Mosaic Law, Allah is thanked for the abundance of animals created to be eaten. In dress, the veil, often worn by Muslim women, in fact reflects pre-existing regional practice rather than explicit commands in the Quran or sayings of Muhammad. Instead, recognizing the power of temptation in sexual matters, Muslims are directed to dress modestly, an injunction interpreted in some circles as requiring a woman's upper arms and shoulders to be covered. Despite the climate, men's legs are always covered.

Perhaps the Islamic doctrine most perplexing to modern, secular societies is the concept of *Jihad*, occasionally listed as a sixth individual duty. In everyday speech the term admits many meanings such as task or burden, though the word is most correctly translated to English as "struggle." The word Jihad appears in the Quran with both a military meaning—wherein it implies an armed struggle for the faith, to extend the boundaries of Islam or to defend them from invasion by the unbelievers—and as a term for describing the internal striving to be a better Muslim. In the 21st century, the rise of extremist groups such as the Islamic State, has given Jihad a particular notoriety.

Did Islam spread largely by conquest and forced conversions? Outside the Hijaz, only rarely. During the early conquests, Arab Muslims regarded with some suspicion those who wished to adopt the faith of their conquerors. In many places, it may have taken a century or two before the majority of the population accepted Islam. The converts' motives were almost certainly mixed. To some, accepting the new religion removed discriminatory taxes. To others, a new community might bring different laws and personal advantages. To all, Islam offered a form of equality under God's law and a moral code that was both simple and encompassing.

Where missionary activity led to spiritual conviction, it often was the work of Islamic brotherhoods. Organized around a master, who initiated disciples in the ritual and beliefs of the particular brotherhood, these *Sufi* (from "one garbed in wool"; a holy man) orders reached beyond formal Islam into mysticism. They frequently incorporated ideas of existing religions, and this, like the missionary fervor of the members, advanced Islam as a spiritual force. On occasion, linked to Muslim rulers, Sufi brotherhoods also aided Islam as a conquering political force.

Islamic Expansion and Society: The Arab Caliphate

A Mosque near Hofuf; Saudi Arabia combines traditional architecture with modern materials.

The weapon quickly proved useful. Under Muhammad, Muslim raiders reached the fringes of the Byzantine Empire. Under Abu Bakr, Arab columns appeared out of the desert almost simultaneously, attacking Byzantine cities in Palestine and Persian troops in Iraq. The great mobility of their camel transport enabled them to strike far from the defending forces. At one crucial period Khalid ibn al-Walid's troops rapidly crossed the desert from Iraq to defeat the Byzantine army, leaving Palestine open to Muslim conquest.

Proclaimed caliph at Abu Bakr's passing, Umar (ruled 634–644) continued the policy of conquest. In 637 Arab armies defeated the Byzantine emperor at the Battle of Yarmuk, thus adding Syria to Arab conquests. The homeland of Christianity was lost to Christian rule; Jerusalem surrendering in 638. Meanwhile, at Kadisiya in Iraq, the Persian army was routed and Sassanid rule effectively destroyed. Soon afterwards, raiding forces unleashed by Umar on Egypt proved unexpectedly successful, and in 641 its last Byzantine city, Alexandria, surrendered. For the next century, Muslim expansion continued to the east across the Iranian plateau into Central Asia, to the west across North Africa and into Spain and France.

To the European Christian imagination, the Muslim conquests were a matter of religious crusades. Muhammad appeared as the anti-Christ of scripture; his conquering hordes offered captives the choice of conversion or the sword. Certainly religion played a great role in motivating individual soldiers, for death in battle to extend the boundaries of Islam brought God's mercy at the judgment and the promise of greater physical comforts and pleasures in heaven than on earth.

Other reasons for the dramatic rise lay outside the Muslim community. For the previous century in particular, the Byzantine and Sassanid empires had fought long and hard over Syria. Now both empires lay exhausted, separated by buffer states of Arab tribes unlikely to halt armies from Arabia. Under Byzantine rule, the Christian farmers of Syria and Egypt had long suffered heavy taxes, an alien language, and religious persecution over their theological interpretation of Christ. When Arab armies arrived, the vast majority of inhabitants did not resist: the Arabs offered not apostasy or death, but rather lower taxes and greater religious freedom. Likewise, in Iraq the native inhabitants had never become Persian; they too welcomed the Muslims. Only in Asia Minor, with its Hellenic population, were the Arab invasions repulsed. In Iran, the collapse of the Sassanid dynasty enabled a rapid Muslim conquest. Administration of the new empire from Medina proved a difficult task.

For eight often precarious years after the Hijra, Muhammad struggled to maintain the Muslim community in the face of Meccan opposition. After 624, there were raids on Meccan caravans and battles as the Meccans counterattacked, as well as expulsions and massacres of the Jewish tribes of Medina and alliances struck with Bedouin tribes. Finally, in 630, Mecca capitulated, and the entire population converted. Almost all Arabia acknowledged Muhammad as politically supreme, although many tribes were reluctant to embrace Islam. Two years later, however, at the height of his political power, Muhammad died. Although about 60 years of age, and too ill to worship in his last days, he left no messages about the future of Islamic society or its government.

As news spread that the Messenger of God lay dead, Muhammad's closest advisors met hurriedly to select a new leader of the community and thus avoid its disintegration under rival leaders. They settled on Abu Bakr, one of the earliest converts, and the next day the community publicly pledged allegiance to him. His position was imprecise, for Muhammad had been

prophet, chief judge, supreme military commander, and sole legislator. Abu Bakr gained the vague title *Khalifat Rasul Allah:* "Successor to the Messenger of God," generally known in English as the Caliph. No prophet himself, but Commander of the Faithful, Abu Bakr led the Muslim community as Muhammad's secular successor and the sovereign in whose name the Friday prayers were offered.

Although only ruling for two years, Abu Bakr decided many of the crucial issues for the new Islamic state. When tribes admitting only political allegiance to Muhammad himself, denying Islamic authority, attempted to secede, Abu Bakr sent armies under Khalid ibn al-Walid and other generals to conquer all Arabia. Quickly victorious, the Muslim armies established the central control of the Caliph, altering greatly pre-existing Arab patterns of temporary alliances and confederations. Of additional importance, the apostate tribes soon were permitted to join the Muslim armies almost wholesale, thus turning energies long spent in violence between Arabs into a remarkable weapon directed by the Caliph.

Islamic Expansion and Society: The Arab Caliphate

The caliph's share of the booty from the conquest provided great riches, but numerous problems arose. One was membership in the Muslim community, now a lucrative benefit, as the caliph's income from the captured territories was distributed among all Muslims, whose taxes in any case were minimal. Conversion, therefore, brought administrative difficulties: taxpayers became welfare recipients. To discourage them, converts had to be attached to Arab tribes. Despite Muhammad's message to all, regardless of tongue or nation, in some cases converts were not freed of their taxes on becoming Muslims. Later the contrast between religious appeal and fiscal expediency would fester and encourage the violent overthrow of one dynasty of caliphs.

Land ownership was another problem. Had Muslim soldiers received lands upon their conquest, their self-interest would have reduced the drive for further conquests. The issue was resolved in theory at least by keeping agricultural land as public land, the property of the caliph, with taxes on the harvest. Muslim troops were established in barracks cities on the fringes of cultivation, the better to keep them accustomed to a hard life and to separate ruling from ruled.

Where the local populations surrendered willingly, and possessed scriptures, they became *dimmis*—"protected subjects." The exact rights depended on the local surrender terms, but in general, each recognized sect received religious toleration and maintained its own laws of personal status under its chief religious leader, typically a bishop or patriarch. For example, divorce, freely available to Muslim men, remained prohibited in most circumstances in the Christian communities. (A Christian desiring an additional wife, or divorce from his existing one, could usually convert to Islam.) Laws of marriage and inheritance likewise varied by religion.

Islamic toleration, while far greater than the practices in Europe of the period, did not mean freedom or equality, but limited rights mixed with discrimination. Non-Muslim testimony against a Muslim was suspect in the courts. New churches generally could not be built, nor church bells rung often, and any Muslim who adopted Christianity (as unlikely as that was) risked the death penalty for apostasy. Members of the protected sects did avoid military obligations, but paid discriminatory taxes and observed separate codes of dress and behavior.

A devout man, Umar also led his community in religious matters as well as political. Many Muslims had memorized lengthy passages of Muhammad's messages; others had been written on palm-leaves, stones, and other available materials. However, renderings could differ. Therefore Umar began the collection of an authoritative book of Muhammad's recitations: the Quran. Completed and authorized by Umar's successor as Caliph, Uthman (644–656), the original Quran used the Kufic script lacking the dots that distinguish so many Arabic letters from each other today. The result, not surprisingly, was variant readings, sometimes on matters of importance between Islamic groups.

The death of Uthman at the hands of assassins revealed deep rivalries within the Muslim world, rivalries of ideology and power. His rule of a dozen years illustrated the strength of the Quraysh, Muhammad's tribe from Mecca who had nevertheless been his most aggressive adversaries. Uthman appointed many Quraysh to high office, some of them close relatives newly acquainted with Islam. Their rule created consternation among political opponents, who saw the actions undermining Muhammad's goal of a universal Muslim

Pilgrims visiting the Ka'aba, sacred shrine of the Great Mosque in Mecca

Islamic Expansion and Society: The Arab Caliphate

community. Their sentiments found much satisfaction in the selection of Ali as the fourth, and last, of what came to be known as the "rightly guided caliphs."

Muhammad's cousin and son-in-law, Ali nevertheless entered office surrounded by suspicions that he was an accomplice to the assassination of his predecessor, Uthman. After moving his capital from Medina to Iraq, and out-maneuvered by his opponents and facing rebellion within his own supporters over his policies, Ali was murdered in 661. His major opponent, Uthman's cousin Muawiya, became Caliph in Damascus, purchasing the acquiescence of Ali's oldest son, Hasan, and established the Umayyad dynasty of caliphs.

From their capital in Damascus, the Umayyads ruled the entire Muslim world. Attacks on the Byzantine Empire were renewed; Constantinople itself came under siege in 717. In some respects Arab, rather than Muslim, in their approach to administration, the Umayyads first used the existing Coptic, Greek, and Persian administrations, ranging from coinage to provincial officials. Where necessary, as in Iraq, the Umayyads ruthlessly repressed disorder and established calm for the first time in years. Religiously, however, by opposing Ali, and especially by defeating and killing his younger son Husayn at the battle of Karbala, the Umayyads split the Muslim world into two factions. Moreover, when they sought to rule by family descent, they introduced a fatal flaw. Those who had opposed in battle Muhammad's son-in-law and shed the blood of his grandson stirred resentments that in ninety years would overwhelm their descendants.

To the strife between Ali and the Umayyads is commonly traced the origins of the major sectarian divisions in the Muslim world. In particular, as the supporters of Ali broke away to form the Shi'a ("Partisans" of Ali), those accepting Umayyad rule became the Sunni, whose name implied orthodoxy. A number of aspects set Shi'a Islam firmly apart from Sunni practice. Its followers claim that Ali's family had been marked to lead the community from the start. Therefore, even the pious caliphs Abu Bakr and Umar were undeserving, and the Umayyads were clearly illegitimate. More commonly, however, the Shi'a termed those God appointed over them as Imams, or leaders, who possessed special knowledge needed to guide the Muslim community. Shi'ism commonly traces a succession of Imams, beginning with Ali. To the Imams was given authoritative understanding of the Quran, sayings, and traditions.

Beginning as a political and social protest movement among Arabs, and quickly

Arab tribesmen water their horses

spreading to the converts, Shi'ism soon included many different groups with rival interpretations and leaders. According to most Shi'a, however, the twelfth Imam disappeared in 878. While the Imam remains hidden, the law and creed would be interpreted by religious scholars as his agents. Consequently, although Shi'a Islam originally began with stress on the rulership of the family of Ali, it has evolved to allow a greater role in political affairs for the religious establishment than does Sunni Islam. In addition, it awaits the hidden Imam, the Mahdi, who will return to save humanity.

Beyond technical differences with Sunni Islam, the Shi'a bring to religion an emotional fervency unlike the Sunni variety. The agony and death of Husayn at the battle of Karbala are portrayed annually at the anniversary with marches and flagellation. As their own blood streams from self-inflicted wounds, the marchers feel a unity with one who suffered 1300 years ago.

The Shi'a played an important, but not exclusive, role in the overthrow of the Umayyad caliphate. After an extensive propaganda campaign concentrated among converts, in 746 rebellions broke out in the name of Abu al-Abbas, and drew support from many discontented groups in the empire. First Iran, then Iraq, fell to the rebels, and in 750 they defeated and later almost annihilated the Umayyads. The new ruling dynasty, the Abbasids, claimed descent from Muhammad's uncle and the support of Ali's family. It ushered in a religious empire for all Muslims, in sharp contrast to the Arab kingdom of the Umayyads. Symbolizing the change, Abu al-Abbas moved the capital from Damascus to Iraq;

his successor al-Mansur established the new empire along Persian rather than Arab lines, and constructed for it the magnificent capital of Baghdad. Amidst the pomp and titles, the Caliph exchanged the openness of an Arab tribal *sheikh* for an Oriental despot's glory and seclusion, complete with court executioner.

Trade and agricultural prosperity brought enormous wealth to Baghdad and its caliphs, who ruled an area larger than had Alexander the Great. Products from the Indus valley reached the Atlantic coast of Morocco, all without leaving the empire, and banks developed a widespread system of checks and letters of credit. Irrigation and drainage canals in the Tigris-Euphrates valley brought prosperity to the heart of the empire, and new foods, products, and technologies spread across the vast area unified by administration, religion, and increasingly, the use of Arabic. Paper making came from China, sugar from India, and the textile centers like Damascus and Mosul enriched European languages as city names became synonymous with particular qualities of cloth (damask; muslin).

Under Harun al-Rashid, perhaps the most famous Abbasid caliph, toward the end of the 8th century Baghdad became the wealthiest city on earth. It hosted one of civilization's great intellectual flowerings. Scholars from a variety of ethnic backgrounds studied Greek and Hindu authors, advanced the sciences, especially optics and astronomy, adopted "Arabic" numerals from India, and discovered algebra. Historians, geographers, and essayists wrote at length. In religion, Muslim scholars collected traditions attributed to

Islamic Expansion and Society: The Arab Caliphate

Muhammad, and developed schools of law. Meanwhile, theologians disputed at length the role of logic in religion and the appropriate methods of interpreting the Quran.

From the moment they seized the caliphate, the Abbasids faced revolts and challenges to their rule, from disenchanted supporters, Shi'a splinter groups, and opportunists. In such a vast empire, control from the center often weakened along the fringes, where independent Muslim states arose. In Baghdad itself, power fell increasingly into the hands of the vizir, or chief minister, who eventually attempted to make the office hereditary. Generals intervened between rival caliphs to decide succession to the throne, and what little power remained eventually fell into the hands of the Turkish bodyguard. Although caliphs did remain, by the end of the 10th century they ceased to rule even nominally outside Iraq. Two hundred years after the Abbasids seized power, the reinvigorated Iranians and Turks, new to both Islam and the Middle East, came to dominate the Asian lands of Islam.

A European artist's concept of a Umayyad palace in Damascus; European reports of Arab societies often exaggerated the exotic and the sensual

The Barbarian Invasions

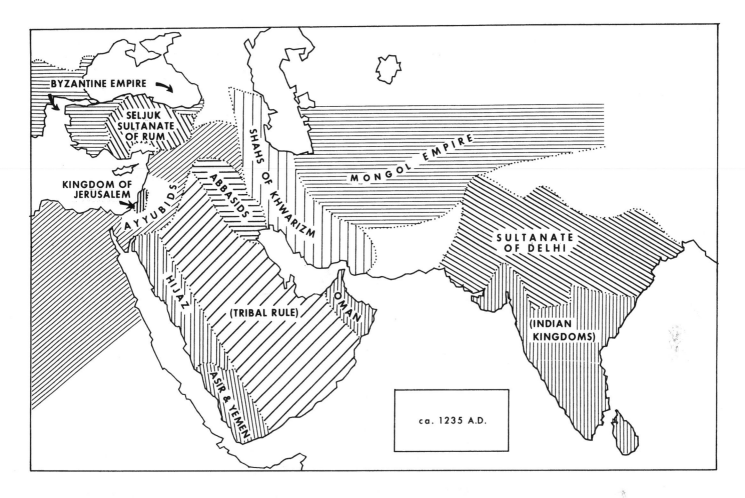

During the Middle Islamic Period (the 10th to 15th centuries A.D.; 4th to 9th centuries by the Muslim calendar) waves of invaders assaulted civilization in Southwest Asia. There was an enormous loss of human life in these invasions, as well as extensive damage to the economy. The Turkish and European inroads in this period were relatively temperate preludes to the far more destructive incursions of the Mongols and their allies.

Adventuring bands of Turks from Central Asia began arriving in Southwest Asia in the 10th century. Soon they started establishing themselves as a kind of military aristocracy, and by the 12th century various regions from Asia Minor to the Ganges River had overlords of Turkish origin. While introducing a new military fierceness into society, the Turkish rulers patronized writers, poets, and learned men, especially Persians. They readily adopted Islam with their own modifications.

The rapid influx of Turks into Iraq in the 11th century led to the establishment of a vast empire stretching from Central Asia to the Syrian coast. This was ruled by Toghril, of the Seljuk (Saljuq) clan, who made himself Sultan in Baghdad in 1055 while reducing the Abbasid Caliph to the status of a spiritual figurehead without

power. A decade and a half later, one of Toghril's nephews, Alp Arslan, defeated the Byzantine army and made the emperor a prisoner. This victory opened Asia Minor to Turkish immigration; in 1078 these newcomers established the Seljuk Sultanate of Rum. (*Rum*, pronounced like "room" in English, was the Asian name for the Byzantine Empire, which was still called Rome).

Seljuk attacks on the Byzantine Empire and interference with European pilgrims to Jerusalem helped inspire the Pope in 1095 to proclaim a Holy War to recapture the Holy Land. The soldiers of the First Crusade had to fight their way through the Seljuk Sultanate of Rum in order to reach Jerusalem and wrest it from the garrison placed there by a Muslim government based in Egypt. These Europeans joined in the turmoil and warfare of the Eastern Mediterranean, inflicting and enduring great loss of life. On capturing Jerusalem in 1099, the Crusaders set about an indiscriminate massacre of Muslims and Jews.

The Latin Kingdom of Jerusalem was established to govern the Holy Land. It lost Jerusalem to the Muslims under the leadership of Salah ad-Din (Saladin) in 1187, but regained it again after his death. The

Crusader kingdom finally lost the Holy City in 1244, but held coastal enclaves until near the end of the century. At times, the Crusaders had Muslim allies against other Muslim armies, so confused were the times and intense the political rivalries.

Seljuk power was not permanent, and rival Turkish leaders displaced them. In Iran, a line of rulers known as the Shahs of Khwarezm (Khwarizm) became prominent in the 12th century, but their power was too fragile to protect the region against new invaders.

Turks also established kingdoms in Buddhist and Hindu lands. Although there had been earlier Muslim raids into the Indus Valley, the main Muslim conquerors in the northern Indian Peninsula were Turks. The rival Hindu *Rajputs* (princes) were unable to provide a unified defense against the Turkish warriors.

In the second half of the 12th century, Turkish warriors led by the Sultan of Ghur wrought great destruction on Indian civilization. Their mounted archers swept down the Ganges Valley. Hindu temples were made into mosques and attempts were made to force people to convert to Islam. Buddhism in its stronghold in Bihar had its monks massacred, its books burned, and its temples destroyed. Buddhism was

35

The Barbarian Invasions

virtually extinguished and Hindu rule was ended in northern India. From that time onward, Muslim ruler and Hindu subject were always aware of belonging to different orders.

Muslim rule in India, established following the conquests by the armies from Ghur, took the form of the Sultanate of Delhi. In 1206 a Turkish general (and legally a slave) seized the opportunity created by the murder of the Sultan of Ghur and proclaimed himself Sultan of Delhi. Although hampered by frequent struggles over the succession, the Sultanate expanded, and reached its greatest extent in the early 14th century, when it ruled nearly all of the Indian Peninsula. In some ways, the Sultanate flourished, for despite severe taxation of the largely Hindu peasantry, great prosperity developed in trade and the production of textiles in Bengal, Lahore, and Kashmir. Nevertheless, decay set in rapidly, and during the late 14th century the Sultanate of Delhi ruled only Northern India.

Southwest Asia began to feel the full force of the Mongol Empire in 1219 when an army of some 100,000 led by Genghis Khan invaded Iran. Seeking vengeance against the Shahs of Khwarezm for their early cruelty against Mongol subjects, the invading Mongols looted, destroyed, and massacred as they advanced. Tens of thousands of people were slaughtered, while only artisans were spared for use as slaves in Mongolia.

Part of Genghis Khan's hordes turned south to ravage the Indus Valley and Punjab. Delhi became a refuge for Muslims escaping from Mongol terror. At the height of this campaign of terror and for reasons that are unclear, the Mongol hordes turned back for the long journey home, laden with the wealth of the devastated lands through which they had passed.

Again, in 1227, the Mongols and their allied hordes returned to plunder. For ten years they could not be withstood by any force in Iran or in the Tigris-Euphrates valley. Of all the great Muslim centers of civilization, only Cairo escaped entirely unscathed and the Mamluk rulers of Egypt gained much prestige for defeating a Mongol force in Palestine. By the middle of the 13th century, much of Southwest Asia was either ruled by Mongols or paying tribute to them. However, the next generation of Mongol rulers adopted Islam. Soon the empire began to break up into small states and the way was open for another empire builder.

Claiming to be a descendant of Genghis Khan, Timur Lang (Tamerlane) looms prominently in the Mongol tradition. He rose to power in the second half of the 14th century, using a dubious devotion to Islam for his political purposes. On the one hand, he may be pictured as a fierce warrior on horseback, wielding a bloody sword as he leads his hordes of Mongols and Turks over civilized areas which have no power to resist. On the other hand, he may also quite accurately be visualized seated in a splendid palace, surrounded by poets and admiring rare works of art, in his capital at Samarkand.

Before his death in 1405, Timur conquered the Tigris-Euphrates Plain and all of Iran. He raided the leading cities of his time, including Damascus, Moscow, and Delhi. Upon the last-mentioned, he poured such destruction that a century was required for it to recover. In the very last years of his life, he defeated the rising Ottoman Empire in battle, took its Sultan prisoner and seized control of Asia Minor. Using the wealth of his vast domains, Timur made Samarkand a center of civilization.

Timur's successors ruled a smaller territory until near the end of the 15th century. They presided over a mixed Turkish-Mongol-Iranian culture, which created many masterpieces of art and literature. With the end of the invasions of Central Asia hordes, a new order could take shape.

Gustave Doré's drawing of the Crusaders storming the walls of Antioch in 1098 on their way to liberate Jerusalem from the Muslims

The Safavid, Ottoman and Mogul Empires

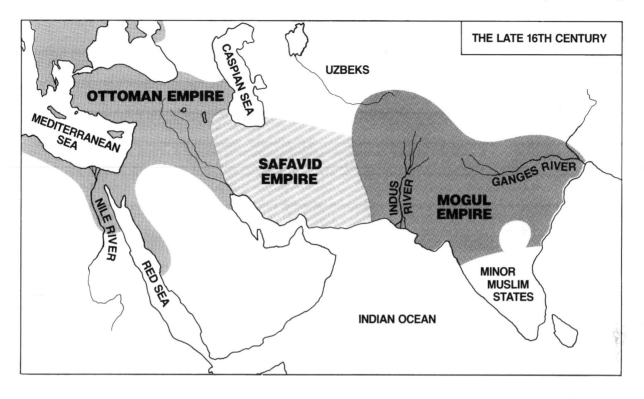

THE LATE 16TH CENTURY

In many ways, Islamic civilization reached its height in the 16th century. Vigorous and ambitious, its religion and rulers dominated southern and western Asia, southeastern Europe, and all North Africa. It also swept south across the Sahara and through the savanna as far as the fringes of the rainforest. The caliphate, by now only an empty title in Cairo, failed to unite the Muslim world, and numerous independent Muslim states existed along the fringes. Nevertheless, the heart of the Muslim world divided into three major Islamic empires, each centers of an important culture.

In the middle, centered on the Iranian Plateau, the Safavid Empire split the Muslim world, for its strongly Shi'a Islam contrasted with the Sunni views both in the Mogul Empire in India and the Safavids' bitter rival to the west, the Ottoman Empire.

The provinces of Iran had witnessed numerous struggles for power after the rapid collapse of Timur's empire, especially among the Turkmen tribes of the north and west. In 1503, Ismail Safavi, a youth merely sixteen years old but hereditary leader of a Shi'a religious order, proclaimed himself shah and Shi'ism the sole religion. Offering all the choice between conversion to Shi'ism or death, Ismail rapidly united the Iranian peasantry, urban classes, and Turkish warriors into a new society and state. In time, Iranian civilians replaced warriors in the administration and central authority replaced mystical adoration of Shah Ismail as the basis of government.

From its very beginning, the Safavid state struggled with the Ottoman Empire to the West, for it appealed to Turkish tribesmen with Shi'a leanings. Nevertheless, in battle the swords, arrows, and light firearms of Shah Ismail's warriors proved no match against Ottoman muskets and artillery. After losing much of Asia Minor, and then Iraq, the Safavids in the 17th century accepted a border between Iran and Iraq that largely remains today.

In retrospect, Shah Ismail attacked the Ottoman Empire during the zenith of its 600-year-long history. It began inconspicuously around 1299, when a Turkish warrior named Osman (Arabic *Uthman;* to Europeans, *Ottoman*) proclaimed himself sultan in northwestern Asia Minor. Welcoming all who would fight Byzantium, he allied his dynasty with Sufi brotherhoods and merchant guilds, and adopted Byzantine administrative techniques. Steadily the Ottoman forces advanced against Christian Byzantium. By the middle of the 14th century, permanent forces had replaced mere raiding groups across the Bosporus, isolating Constantinople. The capital itself lingered for nearly a century, spared by Timur's crushing defeat of the Ottomans in Anatolia (Asia Minor). Finally, in 1453, Sultan Mehmet II massed his armies against the Byzantine capital and captured it, ending a millennium of the city's rule of Eastern Christendom. Under its Turkish name, Istanbul, the city flourished as the Ottoman capital. Sultans and leading officials adorned the city with palaces and mosques, changing

the skyline. Meanwhile, further conquests continued.

The Ottoman Empire drew its strengths from many sources. To the uncommon valor and wisdom of the first ten sultans must be added the willingness to adopt new skills and technology. The *devshirme,* in effect a tax on Christians paid in young boys who were enslaved and educated into Islam, provided both soldiers for a standing army and administrators single-minded in devotion to the Sultan and lacking family loyalty. Financially, conquests in Europe produced great loot and tribute; in turn they enabled further aggression against Christian states. Only after 200 years did the sultans attempt significant conquest of Muslim territories. Then, under Selim I (1512–20), dramatic conquests brought under Ottoman rule much of Anatolia and Iraq, as well as Syria, Palestine, and Egypt. Under Suleyman I ("Suleiman the Magnificent"), known to his subjects as "The Lawgiver," the empire reached the height of its power and grandeur.

By the 17th century the Ottoman Empire illustrated many signs of decay. At first Austria, then Poland and Russia pushed back the Sultan's armies in the Balkans, recapturing Hungary and parts of Yugoslavia. In the Mediterranean, the Ottoman navy had suffered decisive defeat. Within the empire, anarchy spread as local administrators attempted to maintain their positions, and the sale of offices became a regular practice. The devshirme collapsed, and troops garrisoned in many cities rebelled. Although the capable Korprulu

The Safavid, Ottoman and Mogul Empires

"The Golden Horn"—Constantinople in the days of yore

beginning in 1524 Babur invaded northern India. His army, small in size but compact and united, possessed two great advantages: unequalled cavalry and superior cannon from Turkey. In 1526, in a single great battle outside Delhi, he destroyed the enemy military, comprised mostly of Turkish and Afghan foreigners like himself. No national movement resisted his advance, and he found himself master of a personal domain across the plains of northern India as far east as the borders of Bengal.

Plunged into disorder on the early death of Babur, the Mogul Empire finally took shape under his grandson, Akbar. Only thirteen when he came to the throne, Akbar proved a superb general, moving armies rapidly and conquering all but the southern quarter of India. Much more than a soldier, Akbar established stable government that would last a century. He reached beyond mere military power to become the accepted ruler of most of India, most importantly by incorporating the Rajput chiefs, as governors and military commanders. Indeed, he even married a Rajput princess. As a result, the Hindu community largely accepted Akbar's empire as their own. Open-minded in religious matters, he welcomed Zoroastrians and Jesuits to his court, as well as Hindus and Muslims. There was also an attempt to develop an eclectic cult centered on himself.

His successors lacked both his power and his wisdom; the empire inevitably declined. The decay came gradually, and the Moguls sponsored learning through libraries and schools, and in art perfected a distinctive fusion of Persian and Hindu styles in the Taj Mahal. However, the sixth Mogul ruler, Aurangzeb (1658–1707) proved a zealous Muslim whose limited toleration of non-Muslims increased Hindu dissatisfaction and contrasted sharply with the policies of Akbar. A man of battle for much of his long reign, Aurangzeb attempted to unite all India, fighting Muslim states as well as Hindu ones in the south.

By the time of his death, the merchant vanguard of the next wave of foreign invaders of India had appeared, not in the traditional invasion route in the northwest, but in important ports along the coasts. After decades of disorder, British rule would replace Mogul, though the dynasty nominally ruled in Delhi until abolished by the British in 1857.

Until the end of the 15th century, the direct routes from Europe to the East and its lucrative trade were blocked by the Ottoman Empire and Egypt. Europeans finally overcame the obstacle by outflanking the Muslims entirely, sailing around the southern tip of Africa. When

family of vizirs restored administration, the Ottomans increasingly lagged behind Europe in scientific pursuits and modern learning, with unsurprising consequences for military technology. As the center of world trade shifted to the Atlantic following the discovery of the New World and sailing routes to India, the Ottoman Empire increasingly stagnated economically as well. If diplomacy and European rivalries slowed the loss of territory, the descent nevertheless seemed certain to most observers.

A Muslim Empire in India

The Mogul Empire did not rise immediately out of the ruins of the Sultanate of Delhi which had ended with a period of peace, prosperity, and construction of public works, such as new irrigation canals and dams. The last important ruler let authority slip into the hands of local officials. This meant that there was no unified resistance to the hordes led by Timur Lang into the Indus-Ganges basin in 1398. Some 90,000 horse-mounted soldiers killed and looted without restraint, and it is said that when Timur's army returned to Samarkand, there was not a man who did not take at least twenty Indians home as slaves.

So complete was Timur's destruction of the Sultanate of Delhi that another great state did not arise in the area until the Mogul Empire was founded in about 1525. In the interim, a number of kingdoms with Muslim rulers flourished. These sultans,

mainly of Turkish origin, were in general more tolerant of the culture of their Hindu subjects than the sultans of Delhi had been. Learning and the arts developed a distinctive style in this period of Islamic history in the Indian Peninsula.

The only Hindu state during the period was Vijayanagar, a name meaning "City of Victory," located on the southern tip of the Peninsula. For some two centuries after its establishment just before the middle of the 14th century, Vijayanagar defended itself against Muslim encroachment from the north and carried on Hindu cultural and artistic traditions. The combined forces of three Muslim states in the central plateau of the Peninsula finally defeated Vijayanagar in 1565, after its aged ruler was unexpectedly captured in battle and beheaded. The city of Vijayanagar was sacked by Muslim forces, with many Hindus and their temples destroyed. The fall of this state marked the end of Hindu political power.

Just after 1500, a new Islamic state was founded in Afghanistan by Babur, an adventurer from Turkistan far to the north. Barely twenty years old, and a man of taste and letters as well as the power to unite his soldiers, he claimed descent from Timur and thus the right to rule as king. Mongol by proclamation, but Turkish in race, his dynasty nevertheless became known as the Mogul or Mughal. Invited to the plains between the Indus and the Ganges by disaffected local chiefs willing to replace their own king with another,

38

European Expansion into the Indian Ocean

the Portuguese navigator Vasco da Gama reached the Indian Ocean by this route, his tiny fleet opened up a new era. First, only patterns of trade were altered, but in later centuries the total political organization of Southwest Asia was affected. Europeans, possessing increasingly superior weapons and better-trained soldiers, gradually made themselves masters of the vast region.

When the first Portuguese reached the Indian Ocean in 1498, they sought only to monopolize sea trade, not to rule a land empire. By 1509 they had put an end to Arab sea power. Portugal then began building a maritime empire. Alfonso Albuquerque, who had become governor of the Portuguese settlements in India in 1509, carried forward the program of building forts at strategic locations on the coasts of India, Persia, Arabia, and the African continent. His fleet also continued to prevent native ships from carrying items so profitable in European markets. His nation thus gained almost a monopoly on trade in these goods, which required their transport in Portuguese ships, in keeping with the economic theory of mercantilism. Albuquerque on occasion treated with extreme cruelty rebellious subjects or Asian merchants attempting to compete with the Portuguese monopoly.

For over a century the Portuguese remained the chief traders across the Indian Ocean. By concentrating their activities on the sea and a few ports in regions without strong governments, they did not affect significantly the history of the nations of Asia, although colonies in East Africa eventually spread inland. By the end of the 16th century, however, other Europeans, eager for a share of the trade, began forcing their way into the Indian Ocean. Later, in 1650, the Portuguese position further declined after evacuation of the Arabian port of Masqat (Muscat) with accompanying loss of control of the Persian Gulf.

The 17th century belonged predominantly to Dutch merchants and sea power. They left less of a mark on Southwest Asia than had the Portuguese traders, for the Dutch preoccupation was with the spice lands farther east. The 18th century was characterized by rivalry between French and British interests seeking control of India and the approaches to it. In the end, Britain dislodged France from all but a few small enclaves, similar to those retained by Portugal.

The governments of the Netherlands, France, and Britain played only secondary roles in this commercial expansion. Companies chartered by the respective kings were the leading agents. The Dutch East India Company, chartered in 1602, achieved remarkable success. With

fortified trading depots at two places in Sri Lanka (Ceylon) and a number on the coasts of southern India and Southeast Asia, the company flourished during the 17th century. With aid from the strong Dutch fleet, it captured the spice trade from Portugal, despite British and French competition. When the demand for Asian spices fell, it encouraged the production of coffee, tea, and cocoa. Over two hundred years, its annual dividends reportedly averaged 18%.

The British East India Company, chartered in 1600, became even more important, both as one of the first permanent joint-stock companies and in that it received authority to administer government where it operated. Concentrating on India, while the Dutch withdrew to the Spice Islands (Indonesia), the British East India Company established itself first at Surat on the west coast of India, with Mogul permission. Surat rapidly developed

into the most prosperous trading center in the country. Later posts followed at Bombay, Madras, and Calcutta, each to become a center of British influence. The East India Company traded especially in indigo, saltpeter, textiles, and spices, often purchasing goods of greater value from India than it could sell there, and supplying silver to make up the difference.

During the 18th century the French Company of the East Indies (founded 1664) slowly emerged as the chief European rival to the British East India Company in both commerce and political influence. When the two nations fought in Europe, competition between the two companies took on military dimensions in India. The British East India Company won the struggle and limited French influence to several small ports. These French-administered areas only rejoined India after the subcontinent's independence in 1947.

The Creation of the British Raj

George III (1738–1820)

A consistent theme in the history of the Middle East and South Asia from the late 18th century until 1947 was the expansion and strengthening of British colonial rule, often described by the Hindi and Urdu word "Raj", meaning "sway" or "rule." Beginning in Bengal, in eastern India around 1750, its encroachment elsewhere often followed the desire to protect existing possessions and trade routes.

By the mid-18th century, India lay ripe for foreign intervention. In the north, the Mogul Empire had reached a state of advanced decay, both in quality of rule and defeats by Indian and foreign enemies. Particularly threatening were the Marathas, a Hindu people adept at warfare and distinguished by their own language. They lived along the western coast and in central India but spread across the sub-continent. In a series of wars with the Mogul Empire they exhausted its resources, but in the process the Maratha kingdom itself broke up into a loose confederation of states. While they dominated central India, they failed to establish firm central government. Henceforth the Marathas became raiders known for their rapacity and ruthlessness, plundering widely and feared by Hindus as much as by Muslims.

Then, in 1739, the Persian ruler Nadir Shah captured Delhi, plundering the treasury and Peacock Throne, and massacring the city's inhabitants. In a little more than a decade, it was the Afghan army's turn. Finally, in 1761, the Maratha army attempted to stop a renewed Afghan invasion in a battle near Delhi. The decisive defeat of the Marathas and the deaths of many of their leaders appeared to place India within the Afghan king's grasp. At this crucial moment, his troops mutinied. Thus India broke up into many smaller states, divided and lacking in direction, just when Europeans sought control.

Learning from its French rival, by the 1740s, the British East India Company began to strike alliances with Indian rulers. Its weapons included interfering with the succession of Indian princes and bribery. Granting military aid to favorites often proved very effective, for European weapons and techniques increasingly outpaced local ones. With the Company's victory at Plessey in 1757, it effectively conquered Bengal, and British territorial rule began in India.

Circumstances encouraged the British domain to expand. Native attacks on Indian allies led to the retaliation and conquest. War with France in Europe led to conquest in India. Reports of great wealth in the hands of native rulers encouraged Company officials to conquer. However, their harsh treatment of the Indian populations led to interference by Parliament in London, culminating in the India Act of 1784. This placed British rule in India under a governor-general, appointed not by the Company, but by the British government. Ironically, it was Lord Cornwallis, the general who led the British army to defeat in Yorktown, during the last major land battle of the American Revolutionary War, who preserved Britain's colony in India as the new governor-general.

Imperial Rule: The Raj at Its Height—and Fall

Warfare against Napoleon, in Egypt and in Europe, combined with circumstances in India to encourage the last great expansion of British rule. The British conquests were swift. In just over two decades from 1795, large territories fell: Mysore and Hyderabad in the south, the Marathas in the center, and finally the remaining Rajput states in the west. British India more than doubled in size, and unity of the peninsula within its natural boundaries became an appealing goal. Unity would end foreign intrigue and permit British commercial expansion at minimal defense costs. Moreover, ending the virtual state of anarchy in parts of India would bring peace to the inhabitants. The East India Company had traded with Indians for a century and a half before warring with them; for almost another century and a half the British would rule India.

The British Raj brought many advantages, including peace after the ravages of lengthy wars. Physically the country changed with the construction of harbors, railroads, and irrigation projects. Colleges and universities educated an Indian elite in science and medicine, and the administration became more regular and less arbitrary. The British (much like other ruling powers before it) banned the practice of *sati* (or *suttee*; the self-immolation of a Hindu widow on her husband's funeral pyre). In general, though, the British granted religious toleration in areas they ruled directly, and in the many princely states allowed traditional dynasties to continue, whether Muslim or Hindu.

On the other hand, India was exploited economically and its people suffered often considerable hardship under British control. Indian handicrafts suffered from cheap cloth manufactured in England. Each improvement in transportation rendered the competition worse, while British policies retarded the development of Indian industry. High taxes rendered the peasants impoverished tenants, and few schools served the masses. Moreover, in Indian eyes British rule involved westernization to an unsettling degree, and in 1857 the introduction of rifle cartridges greased with animal fat offended Muslim troops (over lard) as well as Hindu (over cows' grease). The Indian Mutiny of 1857–58, at times

The Creation of the British Raj

savage and repressed sternly, brought the attention of London and with it, reforms. The East India Company, long stripped of its trade monopoly, was dissolved. The British Raj now meant authority lay with Parliament and the monarch in England.

Possession of India encouraged further British imperial expansion, for both strategic and commercial purposes. After the defeat of Napoleon in 1815, Britain's great European rival became Tsarist Russia, whose expansion towards both India and the Middle East seemed threatening. Recognizing that the traditional invaders' route to India came from the northwest, British officials extended their rule in that direction, adding the Punjab and Kashmir, then later Baluchistan (bordering Iran), and finally the North-west Frontier Province (1901). By then, only a thin, very mountainous portion of Afghanistan separated Russia from India, but in three different wars the Afghans proved far easier to influence than to conquer. Afghanistan became, in effect, a buffer state for India, as did Bhutan, Sikkim, and (much earlier) Nepal (1816). Another direction of British expansion from India lay to the east, and Burma became a province of India in 1886.

Commercial conquests took place in the west. A naval force from India in 1820 forced Bahrain and rulers in Trucial Oman (now the United Arab Emirates) to recognize British authority. In the latter case, the British strongly desired to end trade in slaves and raids on shipping, in an area that was popularly known as the Pirate Coast. At the other end of the Arabian Peninsula, British forces seized the port of Aden in 1839. Administered by the Government of India, it became an important coaling station for British ships.

Developments in Egypt inspired far greater British attention to the Middle East. The Nile Valley produced fine cotton needed by the mills of Britain, and in Egypt cotton provided government revenues. The ambition and determination of Muhammad Ali (1811–47) so threatened the Ottoman Empire that it required careful European diplomacy, and on occasion Great Power military action to maintain the Ottoman Sultans. Under Muhammad Ali's successors, Egypt also provided an opportunity for European loans, to the ruler as well as to ordinary farmers. Finally, as overlord of the Sudan, Egypt inevitably played an active role in attempts to eliminate the slave trade from Africa.

Each of these reasons for British involvement, however, seems inconsequential beside the construction of the Suez Canal, completed in 1864 on French initiative. Already British passengers to India had reduced the long journey around Africa by using overland transportation across Egypt to the Red Sea. The canal, by

Victoria (1819–1901), First Empress of India

enabling vessels and heavy freight to use the route, quickly became "the lifeline to India." British strategic policy in the region focused on the canal, and the Egyptian shares in the Suez Canal Company were purchased. When Egypt nonetheless went bankrupt and both anti-European riots and a nationalist uprising broke out, British troops landed in 1882 and restored order, defeating nationalist troops. Lightly disguised by diplomatic formalities and the almost total withdrawal of British troops, Egypt became a sphere of British influence, although nominally part of the Ottoman Empire.

Its conquests during World War I brought the British Raj to its greatest extent in the Middle East and South Asia. When the Ottoman Empire entered the war as a German ally, Britain quickly annexed Egypt and Cyprus. Shortly thereafter, troops from India landed in southern Iraq, and despite setbacks began the slow conquest of that land. After repulsing Ottoman Turkish attacks on the Suez Canal, troops from Britiain, Australia, and India moved forward from Egypt into Palestine, capturing Jerusalem in 1917. When Ottoman Turkey appealed for peace in October 1918, these forces and their Arab allies had captured all of Syria as well. The Ottoman Empire, having flourished for 600 years and having wrought extraordinary social and political changes to a region covering not only western Asia, but also north Africa and southeast Europe, collapsed. From the Nile to the Ganges, and between the Mediterranean and China, no power now rivaled British influence. British goals dominated the postwar assignment of mandates of Syria

and Lebanon to France, and Palestine and Iraq to Britain.

Nevertheless, as the Raj reached its greatest extent, the forces of its future downfall became evident. In Egypt the 1919 Nationalist Revolution led to the creation of an autonomous kingdom three years later. Arab nationalism, the ideology of only a handful of inhabitants of the Ottoman provinces in 1912, spread rapidly with the imposition of European mandates by force of arms in Syria and Iraq, as well as Zionist immigration into Palestine. In Iran, popular opposition blocked an attempt to establish a veiled British protectorate, and Afghanistan undertook its War of Independence. In India, nationalism had showed itself a potent force, and its repression at Amritsar produced one thousand dead and wounded. Under the leadership of Mohandas Gandhi, the struggle for self-determination was becoming effective. Nationalism would emerge as a defining feature in a region historically dominated by loyalties to family, tribe, ethnic group, and religious community.

From west to east the British Raj tottered seriously in 1919–20. Twenty-five years later the Second World War left Britain, armed with weapons of greater sophistication than ever before, but too enfeebled to maintain the empire. In 1947, the Raj formally ended for India, although it continued for another generation on the fringes of Arabia, where ironically formal British intervention had always been smaller. When the last Gulf Arab states gained independence in 1971, it marked the official end of the era of European colonialism in the Middle East and South Asia and a new era of independent states, emerging nationalisms, and new forms of identity that sometimes threaten the existing order.

George VI (1895–1952), Last Emperor of India

The Kingdom of Bahrain

Downtown Manama, capital city

Area: 297 square miles (775 square kilometers).

Population: 1.7 million; 65% non-nationals.

Capital City: Manama (141,000 city; 340,000 metro).

Climate: Extremely hot and humid except for a short, moderate winter. There is very little rainfall.

Neighboring Countries: Saudi Arabia (West); Qatar (Southeast).

Time Zone: GMT +3.

Official Language: Arabic.

Other Principal Tongues: English, Farsi (Persian), and Urdu.

Ethnic Background: About 50% Bahraini and other Arab, with South Asians—including Indians, Bangladeshis, and Pakistanis—forming the largest group of foreign workers.

Principal Religion: Islam, approximately 65% Shi'a and 35% Sunni.

Chief Commercial Products: Petroleum products, aluminum, ship repairs, liquid natural gas, financial services, and transportation services.

Major Trading Partners: Saudi Arabia, the United States, China, Japan, Australia, the United Kingdom, Germany, and the United Arab Emirates.

Currency: Bahraini Dinar (1 dinar = 1,000 fils).

Former Colonial Status: British Protectorate (1861–1971).

National Day: December 16, (1961; coronation of the first emir of Bahrain, Isa bin Salman Al-Khalifa).

Chief of State: Hamad bin 'Isa Al-Khalifa, King.

Head of Government: Prince Salman bin Hamad Al-Khalifa, Prime Minister.

National Flag: A serration divides a white band at the pole from the remaining field of solid red.

Gross Domestic Product (GDP): $35.43 billion.

GDP per capita: $23,715.

The land of two seas, as its name implies in Arabic, Bahrain consists of a group of islands located off the coast of Arabia between the Gulf of Bahrain and the Persian Gulf. The main island—some 30 miles (50 kilometers) long and 10 miles (17 kilometers) wide, linked to Saudi Arabia by a 16 mile (25 kilometer) causeway—is largely desert, but springs fed by sources originating on the mainland water some gardens and groves near the northern coast. A 2001 decision of the International Court of Justice, granted the Hawar Islands, located off the coast of Qatar, to Bahrain.

History: Bahrain's long history stretches back as far as Dilmun, a prosperous trading center that flourished some 4,000 years ago. Historically a pivotal part of the Persian Empire, Bahrain was strategically located on the trade route between Iraq and India. As such, Bahrain played an important role in Arab commerce during the Middle Ages. Once a center of Nestorian Christianity, the inhabitants of the region embraced Islam during the Prophet Muhammad's lifetime. Portuguese control of Bahrain lasted for much of the 16th century, before the European power was expelled by the Persians. In 1783, the Arabian Al-Khalifa family, which had earlier established itself at Zubara on the Qatar coast, conquered Bahrain, seeking to gain control of its valuable pearl fishing industry. In a series of treaties beginning in 1820, rulers of this family allied themselves more closely with Britain, on occasion seeking aid against Persian claims and local threats. Subsequently, in 1861 Bahrain became a British protectorate.

Independence came in 1971, when Britain withdrew its forces from all Gulf states, and Bahrain decided not to join the proposed union of Arab emirates. A constitution issued in 1973 created a National Assembly composed of the appointed cabinet and 30 elected members. Two years later, the assembly was dissolved for interfering with government, and for the next quarter century, the ruling Al-Khalifa family exercised power with a disorienting mixture of benevolence and repression. Given the divide between the largely Sunni elite and the poorer Shi'a majority, the police and intelligence services—often employing foreigners—have remained alert for subversive activity.

In 1981 security forces discovered an Islamic plot to overthrow the government. The plot was tied to Iran's long-standing claims to Bahrain and desire of the newly

Bahrain

established Islamic Republic to export its revolution. Unrest continued to fester, and in the late 1980s police foiled a plot directed at oil installations. However, by the 1990s, Iranian sympathy with opposition movements was largely limited to refuge, a relatively small trickle of funds, and propaganda.

Bahrain to the Present Day: Anti-government sentiment has long historical roots in Bahrain. Burgeoning demands for political reform in the early 1990s led to the formation of the Majlis al-Shura—an unelected body of thirty "elite and loyal men" who would advise the Emir. However, resentment over the lack of personal rights and political freedoms continued. In 1994, prominent Sunni and Shi'a Bahrainis petitioned for the reinstatement of the 1973 constitution.

The indefinite postponement of Bahrain's 2020 Formula One Grand Prix over coronavirus fears was greeted by many within the country's pro-democracy movement with a degree of weary cynicism and no small amount of frustration. As the wealthy Gulf states have increasingly sought a role in international sporting events and bodies, activists have sought to leverage sport towards the promotion of improved human rights, pointing, in the process, to what has been called government "sportswashing." In Bahrain, Formula One has emerged as a key field of contention between the Bahraini government and its critics. At least one individual protesting against the race has been shot dead. The 2017 imprisonment Najah Yusuf, a Bahraini civil servant who used a Facebook post to call for the cancellation of Bahrain's Grand Prix, draw furious domestic and international approbation. Her eventual release did little to mitigate criticism of the regime and of Formula One officials. Yusuf has publicly accused the authorities of committing acts of torture, including rape, during her imprisonment.

The government responded firmly, arresting several hundred and deporting Shi'a clerics who preached democracy. Demonstrations alternated with repression, and in 1996, a wave of protests left 30 dead, including police.

Ominously, the discontent became strongest among the Shi'a majority, whose resentment was fueled by their perceptions of poverty, unemployment, lower-class standing, and discrimination. Behind the Shi'a demands, Prime Minister Khalifa bin Salman particularly discerned "outside meddling" (code for Iran, across much of the Arab Gulf). Despite a minor cabinet reshuffle, riots and sabotage continued, along with hundreds of arrests. The regime chose not to concede reforms,

His Majesty Hamad bin Isa Al-Khalifa

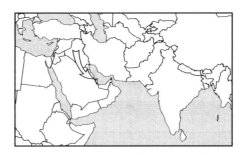

though they might have divided moderate democrats from radical Islamists.

When Sheikh Hamad ascended to power in 1999, hopes rose that calm might be restored. The new ruler released a major opposition figure from prison, and changed policies to increase employment. Under the slogan "Building a New Bahrain," he proposed a referendum on a "National Charter," a proposal to establish limited democracy and constitutional monarchy.

Sheikh Hamad's proposals initially aroused suspicions. The exiled *Bahrain Freedom Movement* considered the proposed parliamentary powers weak and opposed any referendum while hundreds of men and some women remained imprisoned or exiled for political offenses. However, Sheikh Hamad dramatically responded to the criticism by promising real authority for parliament and pardoning approximately 1,000 political prisoners.

In an atmosphere of euphoria, most Bahraini men and women actually voted on the National Charter in 2001, and they granted it overwhelming (98%) support. Soon afterwards, despite his reputation as an opponent of democracy, Prime Minister Sheikh Khalifa suspended the notorious State Security Laws that had permitted detention without trial. The pace of

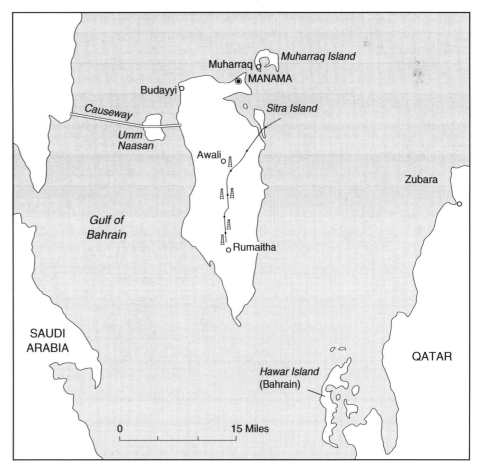

Bahrain

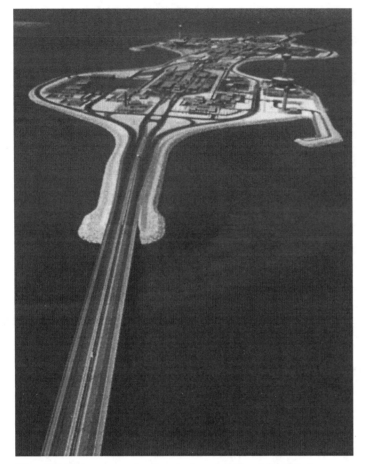

King Fahd Causeway leading to Immigration Island between Saudi Arabia and Bahrain

Courtesy of the Caltex Petroleum Corporation

reforms continued with municipal elections in 2002, in which women were not only able to vote but also to run (unsuccessfully) for office.

Another change that same year promoted Sheikh Hamad from hereditary prince to king. The change brought neither wealth nor additional domestic power to the ruling family, but it distinguished the Kingdom of Bahrain from the emirates around the Gulf, not all of them independent.

For the next decade, politics was dominated by the struggle between Shi'a opposition groups and the ruling family. The regime's critics were not united: some desired an Islamic state or the overthrow of the Al-Khalifa family, while constitutional democrats sought changes like removing parliament's appointed (and powerful) upper house. Other opposition groups concentrated on human rights issues. In response, King Hamad took some conciliatory actions, like dismissing a minister who acted against anti-U.S. protests or appointing an occasional Shi'a activist to the cabinet.

During the 2006 elections, Shi'a opinion shifted in favor of voting, and despite a formal ban on political parties, Sheikh Ali Salman's *al-Wifaq* National Islamic Society emerged as the largest single group, while secular candidates generally lost out. Nevertheless, Shi'a resentment continued over perceived discrimination in government hiring and other prejudicial practices. Activists from the *Haqq* Movement for Liberty and Democracy and the Bahrain Center for Human Rights continued to confront the government.

Small-scale riots in several areas indicated dissatisfaction with the loss of open coastline to development. Allegedly, only 3% of the desert island's coastline remains open to the public. This discontent is heightened by poverty, and by photographs from Google Earth showing the large enclosed estates of the elite, while the lower classes are crowded into far smaller spaces.

Inspired by events in Cairo's Tahrir Square, large protests began in Manama in February 2011. Protestors demanded constitutional changes and the resignation of Prime Minister Khalifa Al-Khalifa, in office since independence in 1971. The demonstrators eventually occupied the Pearl Roundabout, the capital's most prominent traffic circle. The initial government response wavered. Financial handouts and concessions were offered, even as the government sponsored large, pro-regime demonstrations, derided by critics as luxury car parades. On February 17, 2011 the security forces attempted to disperse demonstrators by force, ultimately creating martyrs of slain protesters.

In response to the police attacks, al-Wifaq members resigned from parliament. Supporters of the more radical groups like Haqq chanted for the ruling family to go, and their leaders demanded a republic. As the situation deteriorated, the government blamed Iranian instigators. Other Gulf rulers pressed for action, and the government called in Saudi troops and police from the UAE under agreements of the Gulf Cooperation Council.

Martial law calmed the protests temporarily, and a national dialogue was proposed under the crown prince. However, radical groups, already alienated from compromise, were excluded from the dialogue, and the largest legal opposition society, al-Wifaq, received relatively few seats and almost no time to present its views. It withdrew from the so-called dialogue in July. While the regime enjoys significant support from both Sunnis and wealthier, more secular Shi'a families, the activists and opposition political societies probably represent the feelings of a majority of the Bahraini population.

Western governments found it difficult to respond to the crackdown, which included arrests, prison sentences, and the alleged torture of hospital personnel who treated injured protesters. While sympathetic to demands for reform, the United States valued the kingdom as the home of the U.S. Fifth Fleet and as an ally against the spread of Iranian influence. The U.S. Secretary of Defense did criticize "baby steps" to reform, but did not hint that, like Egypt's President Mubarak, King Hamad should resign.

The continuing clashes, imprisonments, and injustices served to radicalize—and fracture—both the Shi'a opposition and the Sunni community. Some twenty major Shi'a opposition leaders were jailed; one of them, Abdulhadi al-Khawaja, conducted a lengthy hunger strike that aroused wide media attention. Military courts often overlooked expected rights when convicting civilians, among them physicians and nurses. These procedures were condemned by the UN Secretary-general and major human rights organizations. The Bahrain Independent Commission of Investigation into the protests, appointed by King Hamad, concluded that the security agencies had conducted illegal arrests, forced confessions, and systematically used torture.

Angered by their treatment, young Shi'a activists demanded the ouster of the king, far surpassing the call for an elected and governing parliament made by Sheikh Ali Salman, the leader of al-Wifaq. Rarely united, the Shi'a community increasingly fractured, although it was generally supportive of protests against holding the Bahrain Grand Prix, a Formula One race that the regime values as a symbol of normalcy.

Similarly, among Sunnis opinion divided between those who support the king and crown prince in negotiating a compromise settlement, and those backing hardliners, whose slogan became "No dialogue with traitors."

In the fall of 2014 elections were held, but al-Wifaq, sensing no gains from national reconciliation, declared a boycott. In addition, the vote was flawed by the redistribution of electoral constituencies, and critics alleged that the thirteen "general polling stations," where voters from anywhere could cast their ballots, enabled the government to manipulate voting.

Besides achieving Sunni dominance, the elections produced a legislature much more to the government's liking. Only ten of the forty members retained their seats, largely because Islamist groupings lost substantially as voters selected independents generally perceived as practical and less ideological. In a further blow to reconciliation, in 2015 Sheikh Ali Salman, leader of al-Wifaq was jailed for four years for inciting violence. Although acquitted in June 2018 on some charges, in November of the same year he was sentenced to life in prison on the seemingly trumped-up charges of spying for Qatar.

As in many places throughout the region, recent years have seen further crackdowns in Bahrain. In June 2017, for example, Bahrain banned the National Democratic Action Society, Bahrain's largest leftwing political party and an opposition group that has given the king headaches for years. This happened just months after the national parliament approved a constitutional change that enables military courts to try civilians being held on charges related to terrorism. Bahrain argues that military tribunals are better equipped to deal with threats related to irregular war. However, opponents of the move have argued that the step is designed to give the government carte blanche, even calling it akin to the establishment of martial law. Then, in early 2018, parliament approved a bill preventing members of dissolved opposition parties, including the powerful al-Wifaq, from contesting elections. Held in late 2018, Bahrain's general elections were widely criticized as a sham. Marred by boycotts, the 67% turnout claimed by the government is disputed by the opposition, who suggest that no more than 30% of the eligible population voted, with turnout as low as 7% in some districts.

In 2019, Bahrain's courts continue to sentence activists and others associated with the 2011 uprisings. To date, almost 1,000 Bahrainis, including a number of minors, have lost their citizenship under controversial anti-terrorist laws. The loss of citizenship has rendered a number of these individuals stateless.

In March 2020, King Hamad bin Isa Al Khalifa issued a decree granting a pardon to almost 1,000 prisoners, with a further 500 inmates granted leave to serve the remainder of their sentences in rehabilitation and training programs. While the official line is that released prisoners were selected in light of international human rights treaties, in reality almost all Bahrain's political prisoners remain in custody. Most commentators agree that the government's decision was one of pragmatism in light of the outbreak of COVID-19 and the generally poor and crowded prison conditions that make any outbreak of disease among prisoners devastating.

On the foreign policy front, Bahrain is among several Arab countries—the others being Egypt, Saudi Arabia, and the United Arab Emirates—that in early June 2017 cut diplomatic, economic, travel, and other ties with Qatar, accusing the latter of supporting terrorism. Though Qatar has supported extremists in the recent past, it is no different, in this regard, to other countries in the region, perhaps most prominently Saudi Arabia. For years, Qatar has sought to cultivate positive and strong relationships with all of its regional neighbors. That includes Iran, a reality to which the aforementioned countries strongly object. In the case of Bahrain, the worry about support for Iran is acute. Unlike most Arab states (Iraq being the other exception), the majority of Bahrain's citizens are Shi'a. From the perspective of the Sunni minority ruling the country, the less influence Iran has in the region, the better. Two years on, and despite some signs of thawing in relations—including a surprising Ramadan phone call from Bahrain's prime minister to the emir of Qatar—the boycott remains firmly in place.

Culture: The country's first written constitution, made public in 1973, proclaims Bahrain to be an Islamic state. A majority of Bahrainis are Shi'a Muslims, and a minority of Bahrainis, including the ruling family, are Sunni. Opposition groups allege the regime encourages Sunni immigrants to boost that portion of the population. Bahrain's culture includes Persian and Indian influences, but is not radically different than that found in other Arab Gulf states.

The kingdom has a high literacy rate, at some 95%, with universal education for all children. In addition to teacher-training colleges and various institutes, in 2001 the Gulf University was established in Bahrain, sponsored by the smaller states of the Gulf. With facilities larger than its

Bahrain at night
Courtesy of the Royal Embassy of Saudi Arabia

Bahrain

enrollment, it became a refuge for faculty and students from Kuwait who fled the Iraqi occupation.

The civilization of Dilmun left behind on the main island the heaviest concentration of prehistoric burial grounds anywhere on earth, some 80,000 mounds that once covered 5% of the island. Fewer than 6,000 sites remain, but officials hope tourists will be attracted to them, as well as the National Museum, the gold *souq* (market), portrayals of Arab nomadic lifestyle, and water sports along the coast.

Economy: Drillers struck the first successful oil well on the Arab side of the Gulf in 1932, initiating the development of a petrochemical industry and the modern economy. For now, the country's reserves of oil remain relatively small with output around 198,000 barrels per day (compared to some 12.3 million barrels per day in neighboring Saudi Arabia).

In 1996 Saudi Arabia allocated its revenues from a shared off-shore field, and the large oil refinery processes Saudi Arabian crude as well as local production. Oil thus remains vitally important directly, as well for revenues from the important oil refinery.

For decades, recognizing its limited petroleum reserves, Bahrain has attempted to diversify its economy. Government policies encourage companies to invest outside petrochemicals, including low-interest loans, tax waivers, and duty-free imports of raw materials and machinery. Plans call for the expansion of small and medium-sized industries, in part to absorb a rapidly growing workforce. The country is considered one of the most liberal and least regulated in the entire region.

In 2004 Bahrain became the first Gulf state to negotiate a Free Trade Agreement with the United States. Such agreements provide tariff-free access for products of one country in the other, and thus, the agreement should cut the price of U.S. air conditioners in Bahrain and Bahraini aluminum in the United States.

Fishing employs only small numbers, and agriculture faces an uncertain future because irrigation water pumped from the aquifer is turning brackish. Indeed, the availability of fresh water remains a critical issue across the region.

Abundant natural gas provides energy for the region's first large aluminum smelter, Aluminium Bahrain (Alba), which opened in 1972. Later expansion projects increased capacity to 860,000 tons, making it one of the largest in the world, with exports mostly to East Asia. The dominant U.S. producer, Alcoa, negotiated a major stake in the company in 2003.

After years of modest operations, the Arab Shipbuilding and Repair dry-dock began to flourish after the end of the Iran–Iraq war in 1988. Formerly, shipping companies and their insurers had sought to remove damaged tankers as quickly as possible from the zone of conflict.

The construction of the King Fahd causeway connecting Bahrain with Saudi Arabia offers other opportunities for development. Over one million people used the causeway in the first year after its opening in 1986, most of them weekend tourists from Saudi Arabia, coming as families and interested in shopping and amusement parks. These visitors doubled hotel occupancy rates, and the young men among them frequented the island's nightclubs and bars. However, some service jobs thus created in retail, tourism, and entertainment seem undignified to more conservative Bahraini citizens.

Prospects for encouraging tourism from Japan, Europe, and North America improved with the expansion of the airport and with every regional cease-fire in recent decades. However, prospects diminish with regional turmoil and religious-based terrorism. Although Bahrain permits the importation of liquor and taxes it highly, western and East Asian tourists could easily upset conservative Muslims with demonstrations of more liberal lifestyles and entertainment. From a practical standpoint, too, non-Arab tourism also requires simple and rapid immigration procedures and inexpensive air fares, both still lacking. Most of all, of course, tourism requires political stability in the region—something far beyond the control of Bahrain. As global tourism took an unprecedented hit in the context of the coronavirus pandemic, the opportunity for Bahrain to establish itself as a tourist destination was further diminished.

The most important recent developments on the economic front, of course, are all about oil. The dramatic fall in oil prices in 2014 wreaked havoc on Bahrain's economy, pushing the government into debt. A $10 billion aid package pledged by its Gulf allies, is likely to bring some relief. However, Bahrain's budget will remain in deficit for the foreseeable future. Although Bahrain has long recognized its over-reliance on hydrocarbons (which accounted for nearly three quarters of government revenue in 2017), it would be happy to see increased output and higher prices. On the former, the discovery of giant offshore gas and oil reserves is likely to prove a game-changer for Bahrain's economy.

Current Challenges and the Future: The Gulf region has been adversely affected by the coronavirus pandemic. Across the region, hundreds of infections have been recorded, with Bahrain reporting the first coronavirus death amongst the Arab Gulf states. The small kingdom has moved relatively swiftly, calling on thousands of volunteers to help support efforts to combat the emerging health crisis. The government also announced an extraordinary $11.4 billion economic stimulus package, intended to directly support citizens, residents, and businesses in the kingdom. While there is a sense that the kingdom is pulling together to combat a temporary crisis, underlying tensions exacerbated by the sense of injustice felt by many Shi'a are likely to re-emerge in the near future. How the King responds to the existing social, economic, and political inequalities in Bahrain will be critical for the long-term security and prosperity of the country.

Area: 386,873 square miles (1,002,000 square kilometers), of which only about 3.5% of land located in the Nile Valley, the Delta, and a few oases, is arable.

Population: 102 million.

Capital City: Cairo (9.8 million; 20.5 million in the greater Cairo metropolitan area).

Climate: Hot summers, humid along the coast but dry in the south. Winters are cool with some rain along the northern coast, but drier and comfortable inland. Occasional strong winds intensify the winter chill and the summer heat.

Neighboring Countries: Libya (West); Sudan (South); Saudi Arabia (East, across the Red Sea); Israel (Northeast).

Time Zone: GMT +2 (+3 in summer).

Official Language: Arabic.

Ethnic Background: Physical appearances vary, but nearly all consider themselves Arab and Egyptian, except a few Berbers from the western oases.

Principal Religion: Sunni Islam (over 90%) and Coptic Christianity.

Major Trading Partners: The United States, Italy, China, Saudi Arabia, and Germany.

Chief Commercial Products: Tourism, Suez Canal usage, petroleum and refined products, military equipment, cotton yarn and textiles, and light manufactures.

Main Agricultural Products: Cotton, sugar, rice and other grains, tomatoes, watermelons, onions, vegetables, dates, animals, and flowers.

Currency: Egyptian pound (popularly the ghinnayh; 1 pound = 100 piasters).

Former Colonial Status: British control, although still part of the Ottoman Empire (1882–1914), then a "protectorate" of Britain (1914–1922). Britain exercised political influence until the 1952 military coup.

National Day: July 23 (1952; Revolution Day).

Chief of State: Abdul Fattah al-Sisi, President.

Head of Government: Moustafa Madbouly, Prime Minister.

National Flag: Three horizontal stripes of (top to bottom) red, white, and black.

The eagle of Saladin, in gold, is centered on the white stripe.

Gross Domestic Product: $235 billion.

GDP per capita: $2,441.

Strategically located at the junction between Africa and Asia, Egypt holds the rank of the most populous Arab state and the center of Arab culture and entertainment. Most of its territory lies in Africa, forming the northeast corner of the great Sahára Desert. The stark desolation of gravel, sand, and rock is interrupted by the Nile River, which flows from south to north for 750 miles (over 1,200 kilometers) in a valley cut through the desert. Yet for most of its length the valley floor varies in width from a mere few hundred yards to a maximum of 14 miles (22.5 kilometers). Within the valley, agriculture is possible.

About 100 miles (160 kilometers) before reaching the Mediterranean Sea, the Nile divides into branches that spread out over a broad alluvial plain reaching a width of 150 miles (240 kilometers) along the sea coast. Because this triangle of fertility

Egypt

resembles the form of the (capital) letter *delta* in the Greek alphabet, since ancient times it has been called the Delta. The metropolis of Cairo lies at the southern tip of this Delta. At the northwest is the port city of Alexandria, named after Alexander the Great, who founded it following his conquest of the country in 332 B.C. More than a quarter of the people of Egypt live in these two cities. They work as shopkeepers, government employees, in manufacturing, or at the many other jobs associated with urban areas.Most of the remaining three-quarters of the population live in some 4,000 villages and towns scattered in the Delta and up the length of the Nile Valley. Most of them are directly or indirectly connected with agricultural production. A small number of people live in a half dozen remote oases in the desert west of the Nile Valley, while an insignificant and dwindling number of nomads wander with flocks of goats and camels in the desert regions that comprise about 96% of the country. There are no grasslands or forests. The highest point in Egypt, Jabal Katrina (Mt. Catherine) reaches 8,652 feet (2,637 meters) in the Sinai Peninsula, but overlooks barren rock and sands. There is total contrast between the barrenness of the desert (called "the Red Land" by the ancient inhabitants) and the tropical growth of the valley floor and Delta ("the Black Land" of the ancients).

The English name *Egypt* is derived from the ancient Greek name *Aiguptos*, an approximation of *Hikuptah*, one of the names of the ancient capital of Memphis, whose ruins are near modern Cairo. The Arabic name of the country, *Misr,* introduced with the Arabic conquest of the 7th century, originated in an ancient name used in Semitic languages. In the hieroglyphics of antiquity, the country was sometimes called "the Two Lands," referring to Lower Egypt (the Delta) and Upper Egypt (the narrow valley south of Cairo, known as *Sa'id* in Arabic).

History: The shadows of an extremely long early history lie across the modern land of Egypt—of the mighty pharaohs claiming to be gods, of Hellenistic civilization that flourished at Alexandria, and especially of the brilliant Islamic civilization centered on Cairo. Yet the modern state of Egypt cannot be traced back beyond the early 19th century. At that time, it began to take shape under the dynamic rule of Muhammad (Mehmet) Ali, an ambitious Ottoman soldier who was neither Egyptian by birth nor a proponent of (not-yet-existent) Egyptian nationalism.

Pre-Christian civilization in the Nile Valley made enormous contributions to the development of human skills and knowledge. In fact, that civilization is considered the heritage of all humanity. Later ages also influenced the world. Roman Egypt was one of the first fertile grounds for the spread of Christianity, and its thinkers and leaders played important roles in the history of the Christian Church. The Christians of Egypt adopted a modified version of the Greek alphabet to write their language, Coptic, the latest form of the old Egyptian language earlier recorded in hieroglyphics. The Coptic Church still plays an important role in contemporary Egyptian society.

In the early 7th century, Muslim armies from Arabia spread their rule to Egypt, little opposed by the Coptic subjects of the Byzantine Empire (639–642). During the following centuries, both the Arabic language of the new rulers and their Islamic faith were adopted by most Egyptians. When the Abbasid caliphate in Baghdad lost control of distant provinces, Egypt fell under the rule of local governors, and then Turkish dynasties, including the Tulunids, whose mosque remains impressive today.

Further elegant buildings and achievements in the arts and learning followed under the Fatimid caliphs (969–1171), including the founding of the University of al-Azhar, one of the oldest in the world. Claiming descent from Fatima, the Prophet Muhammad's daughter, these caliphs espoused Shi'a Islam but maintained contact with the rest of the Muslim world. Sometimes they ruled much of it, but weak rulers and dependence on foreign slave-warriors eased Egypt's capture by Salah al-Din al-Ayyubi, known to the European Crusaders as Saladin. His Sunni descendants in turn lost authority to the Mamluks (pronounced Mam-luke), warrior slaves often of Turkish or Circassian origins, by the middle of the 13th century.

The most important Mamluk sultan, Baybars, checked the expansion of the destructive Mongol armies in Syria (Ayn Jalut, 1260), and defeated the remaining Crusaders as well. But despite their glories on the battlefield, and their lavish spending on works of art, the Mamluks brought few advantages to the native Egyptians. Generally foreign born, the Mamluks oppressed the Egyptians harshly, and by their intrigues and rivalries brought disorder rather than peace. After the Ottoman Sultan Selim I defeated the Mamluks and conquered Egypt in 1517, the country witnessed frequent struggles between the government in Istanbul and the remaining

Built within Salah al-Din's Citadel, the Mosque of Muhammad Ali dominates Cairo's southern skyline

Mamluks, who dominated Egyptian society.

Napoleon's conquest and the French occupation (1798–1801) proved a vital turning point in the creation of modern Egypt. European ideas spread. More importantly, Muhammad Ali, an Albanian officer in the Ottoman army sent to evict the French, skillfully played off his rivals and seized power for himself while paying lip service to Ottoman rule. In 1806 the Ottoman sultan recognized him as pasha of Egypt.

Despite a barren treasury, Muhammad Ali set about building a modern state. After drastically reorganizing land taxes, he established schools, founded a government press, and attempted to industrialize Egypt with imported equipment, all without borrowing funds abroad. His trade monopoly failed, but he encouraged agricultural improvements and seized vast domains from delinquent taxpayers. Considered the founder of modern Egypt, he separated it from the rest of the Ottoman Empire as a self-governing region.

His successors proved lesser men. His son Sa'id Pasha greatly increased Egypt's strategic status in 1856 when he gave a Frenchman, Ferdinand de Lesseps, a concession to build a canal from the Mediterranean to the Red Sea. The Suez Canal became Britain's "lifeline to India," because it enormously reduced the length of the sea voyage from Britain to the Indian Ocean.

Sa'id's profligate successor, Ismail, borrowed large sums from European bankers for a few good reasons and many poor ones: mostly to finance his high living and elaborate, often unsound, development schemes. Ismail bankrupted the state, and in 1875 he sold Egypt's share in the Suez Canal to Britain and accepted foreign financial advisors. He was finally forced to abdicate.

The British Occupation

After rioters killed several Europeans and others associated with the strict financial administration, in 1882 Britain landed troops in Alexandria. The wealthy, landowning elite, many of them Turkish-speaking, failed to unite and oppose the British, although most Egyptians rallied to support a nationalist colonel, Ahmad Urabi (Arabi). At the battle of Tall al-Kabir, British troops demonstrated an overwhelming supremacy, killing some 10,000 Egyptians while losing fewer than 80 men. The khedive became a British puppet, and the British Consul General, Lord Cromer, became a virtual dictator for over 20 years (1883– 1907), although Egypt formally remained part of the Ottoman Empire until World War I.

Despite Wilson's 14 Points and successful national struggles elsewhere, Britain still sought to dominate Egypt. A long-time nationalist, Sa'd Zaghlul, and his colleagues sought to form a delegation (*wafd*) to attend the 1919 Paris peace conference, but they were arrested instead. An insurrection then spread to all parts of Egypt. Unsuccessful at repression, Britain offered a very restricted "independence" that retained British bases. When Zaghlul and his Wafd Party ensured that no Egyptian would sign such a treaty, Britain simply declared Egypt independent, with conditions, in 1923. Sultan Fu'ad, became king, but proved inept in politics. Raised in Italy, he was scarcely able to speak Arabic.

Under its monarchs (1923-1952), the country saw few positive developments, despite some progress in individual freedom. The government was rent by continuing rivalry by three contending forces: the weak monarch, interfering British officials, and an ineffective parliament dominated by the increasingly corrupt and self-interested Wafd Party. Politicians manipulated the poor for their own ends, but did little to improve their lot. King Farouk, whose reign began in 1937, became a symbol of a system that failed to meet the aspirations of ordinary Egyptians. Opposition to the monarchy mounted after the Egyptian army's loss to Israel in 1949, and the fundamentalist Muslim Brotherhood became increasingly active and engaged in assassinations.

Military Rule and Republic

In 1952, a group of reformist army officers seized control and exiled King Farouk. The self-styled Free Officers sought not merely to change the ruler; they wished to revolutionize the country. Modernists at heart, they believed that an independent, honest, and sincere government could reduce poverty, increase education, strengthen the armed forces and bring dignity to the average Egyptian. In keeping with these aims, they set up the Revolutionary Command Council (RCC) to handle affairs of state. The real leader in the RCC was Colonel Gamal Abdul Nasser (or Jamal Abd al-Nasir), an imposing orator with an interest in ideas. In 1954, he became president in name and fact.

Nasser made an enormous impact upon Egyptians, other Arabs, and people throughout the colonies and newly independent nations of the developing world. The wealthy and ethnic minorities aside, Egyptians loved him. When army officers overthrew monarchies in Iraq, Yemen, and Libya, they modeled revolutionary councils after the one in Cairo. On the world stage, Nasser became a prominent spokesman at conferences of Third World nations, notably in 1955 when he, Nehru of India, and Zhou Enlai of China established the Nonaligned Movement, a coalition of countries neutral in the Cold War struggle between the Soviet Union and the United States.

The idealistic young officers of the RCC aimed to bring progress and greater opportunity for the poor and middle classes through education, public health, and other welfare programs. Lacking experience and finding few advisors, they gradually formulated principles for building a new society, defined as "Arab Socialism." They also desired land reform, to redistribute to the *fellahin* (farmers) the large estates of the rich. As moderate socialists, but not communists, they favored government control of international trade, industry, and banks. Their policies developed some industries, but stagnated much of the economy.

In the 1950s, Egypt dominated the Arab

Monumental architecture started here: the step-pyramid of Pharaoh Djoser

Egypt

world. Its population far exceeded those of other Arab states, it boasted the largest (if not the toughest) military, and its achievements in the arts and culture ranged from universities to movies. Inevitably, once Nasser espoused a pan-Arab policy that blamed Arab weakness on imperialism and dynasties that divided one true Arab nation, Egypt began to champion the interests of Palestinian Arabs and to oppose Israel.

Access to weapons proved crucial. Western allies of Israel who had dominated arms supplies to the region agreed to limit combined Arab armaments to the level possessed by Israel, thus preserving indefinitely Israeli military superiority. In a decisive stroke to escape from Western limitations, in 1955 Egypt purchased arms from communist Czechoslovakia. The move dramatically increased Soviet influence in the Middle East.

When the United States reacted to the arms sale by withholding aid for a proposed high dam at Aswan in southern Egypt, Nasser obtained Soviet assistance for the dam, and then in 1956 seized the Anglo-French Suez Canal Company to pay for the arms and to finance development projects like the dam.

Amid great international furor, Israel, Britain, and France secretly plotted an invasion. Israel hoped to defeat Egypt before the new Soviet arms rendered it strong, and then to force it to sign a peace treaty. In late 1956, Israeli forces opened the Suez War, quickly defeated the Egyptian army, and occupied the Sinai Peninsula. Britain and France then used the fighting as a pretext to take control of the Canal Zone. Public opinion almost everywhere condemned this reversion to power politics, and at the United Nations, a motion demanding a withdrawal won support from the United States and the Soviets alike. Nasser emerged from this episode a hero, although subsequent attempts at unity with Syria (1958-61) and intervention in Yemen (1962) were not successful.

The Six-Day War, June 5–10, 1967

In the spring of 1967, Nasser allied publicly with Syria and eventually with Jordan against Israel. At dispute were water rights in the then Jordanian occupied West Bank. When radicals criticized Egypt for talking tough against Israel, but sheltering behind borders pacified by UN observers, Nasser ordered out the observers and then announced a blockade of the Straits of Tiran. Closing the straits threatened to deprive Israel of all direct trade with East Africa, Southern Asia, and the Far East. Israel publicly considered the action a cause for war, and formed a war cabinet, while Nasser moved troops into the Sinai and delivered bellicose speeches. But with

many troops in Yemen, Egypt otherwise failed to prepare for battle through military incompetence, miscalculating Israeli strength, or presuming the United States would restrain Israel from invasion.

Sudden Israeli attacks on Egyptian and Syrian air bases marked the beginning of the Six-Day War. In a few hours, the Arab air forces effectively ceased to exist. Control of the skies ensured victory on land, as Israeli tanks and infantry swept across the Sinai, reaching the Suez Canal, then turning back to trap retreating Egyptian units in the Sinai passes. Nasser accepted responsibility for the defeat, and dramatically resigned, but emotional demonstrations in Cairo led him to return to power almost immediately. Other consequences of the defeat proved longer-lasting. Egypt lost the Sinai's recently-discovered oil fields and the Suez Canal remained closed, The Israeli occupation of Sinai impoverished Egypt's economy and soon led to a war of attrition, a period of intense shelling and air raids along the Canal.

From Attrition to Peace

When Nasser died unexpectedly in 1970, Egypt's leaders turned to former Vice President Anwar Sadat, one of the few original Free Officers who remained

in public life. As president (1970–1981), he discarded the socialist ideology of the previous decade. Hoping to lure American and other foreign investment, Sadat's government lifted many, but by no means all, restrictions imposed during Nasser's era. Reforms largely failed to spur prosperity, but did contribute to influence peddling and profiteering by politicians, military officers, and their relatives. The perennial problems of unemployment, inefficient industrialization, and overpopulation worsened. While reforms created a wealthy and successful upper class, they also entrenched inequality. In 1977, attempts by the government to remove subsidies on basic food items sparked mass uprisings known as the "bread riots." Dozens were killed and hundreds injured, before Sadat backed down, reversing the most unpopular of the new economic policies.

Initially, Sadat adhered to Nasser's foreign policy, and continued the War of Attrition along the Suez Canal. Despite frequent warlike rhetoric, however, in 1973 Egypt dismissed many Soviet military advisors and other personnel.

Suddenly, in October, the Syrian and Egyptian armies attacked Israeli forces occupying their territory. Egyptian troops successfully crossed the Canal and

Constructed in 1477, the citadel of Qait Bey guarded the harbor of Alexandria for centuries

Photo by Malcolm B. Russell

advanced into the Sinai. There, protected from Israeli bombing by anti-aircraft missiles, they fought monumental tank battles with the Israelis.

Within days, the tide of battle shifted. A U.S. airlift massively resupplied the Israel Defense Forces with sophisticated weapons. In a daring operation, some Israeli units crossed the Canal into Africa, threatening Cairo and encircling large Egyptian armies. Given the risks of warfare, and its enormous human and material costs, Sadat and his advisors concluded that further confrontation with Israel was not only harmful to Egypt but also futile. Egypt accepted a truce.

After the war, Sadat's policies changed dramatically. He restored diplomatic relations with the United States, whose Secretary of State, Henry Kissinger, negotiated the return of both the Suez Canal and Sinai oil wells to Egypt. Domestically, Sadat invoked Egyptian rather than pan-Arab nationalism. Nevertheless, while oil exports and Suez Canal tolls provided foreign exchange, and trade increased, prosperity hardly trickled down to the masses. Likewise, peace remained only a distant hope.

In a dramatic gesture, in 1977 Sadat flew to Jerusalem and addressed the Knesset, offering to accept the legitimacy of Israel in exchange for its withdrawal from territory seized in 1967 from Egypt, Jordan, and Syria. When diplomacy seemed to falter in 1978, President Jimmy Carter invited both Sadat and Israeli Prime Minister Menachem Begin to Camp David, the U.S. presidential retreat in Maryland. Isolated from the press and their domestic political pressures, the two leaders reached the terms of a peace settlement.

The Camp David Accords signed in 1979 fell far short of peace, Sadat's initial goal. Israel retained all the territory captured from Jordan and Syria, and Palestinians received only the promise of distant and vague autonomy. Egypt, however, regained all the Sinai. Diplomatic relations were established in 1980, and Israeli troops withdrew by 1982.

The Camp David agreements aroused widespread Arab condemnation. Without settling the basic problems resulting from Israel's creation in 1948, the agreements established peace between Egypt and Israel, leaving the Jewish state dominant militarily, and the Palestinians adrift. In response, Arab nations broke diplomatic relations with Egypt, and financial aid from oil exporters dwindled. Many Egyptians viewed the accords with misgivings and disliked having diplomatic relations with Israel, especially during periods of bloodshed between Israelis and Palestinians. Nevertheless, given Egypt's poverty and military weakness, the accords seemed necessary.

When Anwar Sadat was assassinated by religious zealots in 1981, there was little spontaneous outpouring of grief such as marked Gamal Abdul Nasser's death. Vice President Muhammad Hosni Mubarak was sworn in as the new head of state. Yet another military officer, he generally pursued the liberalizing economic policies of his predecessor. Major attention was directed toward organizing the economy productively and every effort was made to present an image of stability and moderation. Mubarak also released from prison many (but not all) of Sadat's political opponents, including Islamic fundamentalists. Eventually their places would be filled by Mubarak's own opponents.

Persistent Islamic Opposition

Throughout his presidency, President Mubarak felt most threatened by the same broad movement whose militants had assassinated Anwar Sadat. The revival of Islamic values stretched from peaceful calls of professional groups to adopt Islamic law, the *Shari'a*, through to the Muslim Brotherhood, and beyond, to extremist

51

Egypt

and violent groups such as *al-Gama'a al-Islamiyya* (the Islamic Group).

Because the government effectively banned the Islamists (including the Muslim Brotherhood) from contesting elections, opposition took the form of demonstrations and protests, as well as arson and murder. Feeding on popular dissatisfaction with inflation, food shortages, unemployment, and Israeli actions in the Palestinian territories, militants came to pose a shadowy yet significant threat to the regime. In 1992 alone, some 70 people perished in Islamist violence. Intellectuals, Coptic Christians in Upper Egypt, government officials, and the police themselves suffered fatal assaults. By 1995, terrorist attacks on buses, boats, and trains had left tourists dead and injured; more than 600 Egyptians had been killed. As travelers avoided Egypt or stayed fewer days, the tourist industry's earnings slumped badly.

Some critics feared that the harsh government response to militant Islamic groups might heighten their appeal. Repressive measures by the police and military included widespread arrests and rough treatment of suspects, and allegedly, torture. The government also attempted to take control of all mosques in the country, a task as impossible as it was undemocratic.

To some critics, these desperate measures reflected the government's inability to strike at the poverty, corruption, and social distress that fostered religious extremism. However, the revival of Islamic sentiment reached far beyond the unemployed. Candidates supported by the Muslim Brotherhood captured the leadership of the Bar Association, while Islamic charities won recognition for responding effectively to a Cairo earthquake that killed hundreds and left tens of thousands homeless.

In response, the government struck

Former President Hosni Mubarak

repeatedly at the Muslim Brotherhood. Although technically banned, the Brotherhood had been tolerated for years, while it constructed a network of charities and businesses. Eventually the government attempted to crush all Islamist opposition, with little distinction between non-violent critics and those who attempted to assassinate Mubarak himself. Police detained hundreds of activists. Scores of leaders were sentenced to hard labor for belonging to a banned organization.

Al-Gama'a al-Islamiyya and its offshoots undoubtedly invited repression. Its extremists murdered tourists, including a massive attack in 1997 that killed 62 near Luxor. Weakened by both repression and public revulsion at the bloodshed, the militant organizations apparently lay shattered. Al-Gama'a al-Islamiyya called for a ceasefire, and violence declined even in Upper Egypt. The next year hundreds of imprisoned Islamists were released, and leaders publicly urged a non-violent struggle for their aims. Later attacks seemed the work of small, freelance groups. However, they killed Egyptians and tourists alike—and their very disorganization represented a tremendous challenge to the security forces.

The attitudes of some Islamists contributed to worsening Muslim–Christian relations. In these circumstances, permits for church construction or alterations become more difficult to obtain, and Copts increasingly experienced discrimination in employment. In 2009, the government's brutal attempt to slaughter all of Egypt's pigs (kept only by Christians) on the pretext of protection against the swine flu epidemic also raised protests and resentments, by animal rights advocates as well as Copts working as refuse collectors.

Worse violence came on New Year's Eve in 2010, when a massive explosion killed 21 Coptic worshippers in Alexandria. The police issued conflicting statements about both the source of the explosion and the alleged perpetrators, raising suspicions of government incompetence or worse. Even

Coptic Christians often worship in churches of great antiquity, such as the "Hanging Church" of St. Mary, built in the 600s on the site of an even older church and Roman walls
Photo by Malcolm B. Russell

after the Tahrir Square revolution, many Copts continue to worry about violence as well as discrimination, fears strengthened by the army's apparently unprovoked shooting of Christian demonstrators at Maspero Square in 2011.

Regaining International Prestige

In the late 1980s Egypt emerged from the isolation that had followed its signing of the Camp David Agreements. Symbolically, it returned to the Arab League in 1989, and a high-ranking Egyptian official was elected its Secretary-General in 1991. The greater prominence resulted from Egypt's support for Iraq during its war against Iran and President Mubarak's backing for Yasir Arafat and the Palestine Liberation Organization (PLO). After Iraq's invasion of Kuwait, Egypt joined the anti-Iraqi coalition and dispatched 35,000 troops to defend Saudi Arabia, the third largest foreign force there. President Mubarak came to play a crucial role for the Western-led alliance as an Arab leader who supported the integrity of Kuwait. This weakened Iraqi attempts to portray events as a struggle between nationalist and Muslim Arabs on the one side, and foreigners and their puppet monarchs on the other.

Domestic Economic and Political Stagnation

By the turn of the millennium, the regime seemed to have lost its sense of purpose. Its privatization program faltered, leaving suspicions that favoritism had lined the pockets of some investors in profitable companies, while many money-losing government firms continued to require subsidies. The exchange rate was controlled, then devalued, leading many investors to flee from Egypt. The stock market and economic growth slumped, even before the disastrous impact of the September 11 attacks on Western tourism. Unemployment climbed and probably exceeded 20%. For a variety of reasons, the economy had failed to grow and produce the necessary jobs for the 800,000 new workers annually.

Politics under Mubarak: Under the constitution of 1971, a strong president dominated the Advisory Council and People's Assembly (parliament). Except in 2005, the president was the single nominee of the People's Assembly, who was subsequently approved by a popular referendum.

Political realities tainted elections to the People's Assembly, despite the democratic claims of the constitution. The ruling National Democratic Party (NDP) always won overwhelming victories. Official pressures, from publicity and the use of influence through police intervention to some outright rigging, ensured a majority

so large the legislature served as a mere rubber stamp.

Despite obstacles, opposition parties did exist, some legalized by a parliamentary committee dominated by the NDP, others technically illegal. The small New Wafd Party traced its origins to Zaghlul and the 1919 Wafd. Other minor groups included the small centrist Liberal Party, and several left-wing parties that reflected varying viewpoints. These parties commonly demanded an end to the state of emergency (which banned unapproved meetings of more than five people), a halt to torture, and a new constitution. However, the small parties seemed more suited to permanent opposition than to governing. The Muslim Brotherhood, technically illegal and much more than a party, ran candidates under cover, sometimes from the socialist Labor Party.

The fate of only the third new party legalized in 25 years, *Hizb al-Ghad* (Party of Tomorrow), symbolized the plight of the opposition. Ayman Nour, its founder, was jailed over alleged false signatures on the party's application, although the signatures were not necessary and Nour himself had not gathered them. While in jail awaiting trial, his leadership of the party was challenged, perhaps by government agents, and the party newspaper was refused permission to publish. Released from jail in 2005, Nour ran for president but failed to attract many votes. He was later jailed again, and only released in 2009. A presidential candidate in the election of 2012 that brought Mohammed Morsi to power, Nour fled Egypt after the 2013 coup and remains in exile in Turkey.

When presidential and parliamentary elections approached in 2005, Mubarak reshuffled the cabinet, bringing in a new prime minister and several younger, reform-minded ministers with business experience. Others were known as associates

Handwriting on the wall: Religion to God and the Country for All
Photo by Malcolm B. Russell

of Gamal Mubarak, the president's son, who favored a free economy and was suspected of high political ambitions.

As the election approached, opposition groups formed, were prohibited, and reformed. Students protested the emergency regulations. In response, hundreds of Muslim Brotherhood activists were arrested, but the government also instituted direct presidential elections. For the first time, ordinary Egyptians faced a ballot with more than one presidential candidate. However, with many voters skeptical, changing the process failed to affect the result. Hosni Mubarak won 88% of the vote from the small percentage of the population that actually voted (about 25%).

Reforms, world attention, and careful judges had more effect on parliamentary elections. Held over several weeks, they showed increasing victories for the Muslim Brotherhood, although its members still ran as independents. As the size of their victory increased, so did reports of intimidation, fraud, and violence. Again, the NDP won an overwhelming majority—over 70% of the vote. But the real election news was the Muslim Brotherhood's 88 seats, and the pitiful showing of secular opposition parties.

In 2010, the NDP and its allied independents won 93% of the seats, after opposition voters were sometimes prevented from voting and their parties boycotted the runoff election. The elections were widely considered fraudulent, and dismissing the resulting parliament became a popular demand during the Tahrir Square protests.

Before the 2011 presidential election, Muhammad ElBaradei, the former Director-General of the UN's International Atomic Energy Agency (IAEA), returned to Egypt, willing to contest the presidency as an independent. Several political parties and other groups, including the Muslim Brotherhood, joined him in forming the National Association for Change, a "non-party political movement." While the government press depicted him as out of touch with Egypt, younger citizens relished the prospect of a civilian candidate free of corruption. His supporters turned to Facebook and other social media, a portent of what would follow.

Tahrir 2011: The Downfall of Mubarak

Frustrated by economic stagnation and political repression such as the recent death of Khalid Said, an activist beaten to death by police, and inspired by the ouster of Tunisia's president, the April 6 Youth Movement announced plans to protest in Tahrir Square on January 25, 2011; ironically a national holiday celebrating the police. In a country of aging, often self-interested politicians, the April

Egypt

6 Youth Movement itself was unusual: its three co-founders included two twenty-something activists concerned about the working class. The Youth Movement rapidly became the largest political social media discussion group in the country, with over 70,000 members, most of them also young, democracy-minded, and critical of corruption and economic stagnation.

The activists' messages, like the video by Asmaa Mahfouz, stressed abstract themes like freedom, dignity, and honor, while denouncing corruption. They shamed those who sympathized with their aims but failed to actively participate in overthrowing the government. In Tahrir Square and outside the NDP offices nearby, the slogans included "Down with Mubarak" or simply "GO!" Demonstrations broke out in Alexandria, Suez, and other cities as well.

The government responded by arresting hundreds and blaming the Muslim Brotherhood: who else could organize such numbers? When the protests continued, Mubarak refused to step down himself, but he dismissed his cabinet and for the first time appointed a vice president, Omar Suleiman, the long-serving intelligence chief. Perhaps Mubarak sought to reassure foreign governments who sought stability, but within the country Suleiman's agencies were regarded as instruments of repression and torture.

Its gestures failing, the regime tried brute force. Criminals were released from prison to vandalize homes and businesses in an attempt to discredit the demonstrators. In Tahrir Square, with obvious police consent and support, thugs mounted on horses and camels, and armed with swords and clubs, attacked demonstrators in the legendary "Battle of the Camel." The attacks proved a turning point: despite hundreds of wounded and some deaths, the protesters held their ground, and ordinary Egyptians distinguished between criminals and protesters.

In sharp contrast to the police, when ordered into the square, the army did not attack demonstrations. It protected buildings like the Egyptian Museum and fraternized with activists.

Another crucial event was the dramatic TV interview with Wael Ghonim, a young Google executive who returned to Egypt to participate in the protests. Obviously fatigued and emotional after days blindfolded in police detention, he denied that the demonstrators were traitors and proclaimed that the goal was human rights, not a settling of scores. Ghonim's interview revived the protests by inspiring non-political citizens, many of them never acquainted with Facebook, to support and even participate in the demonstrations.

His financial system tottering, Western support crumbling, the new cabinet of the same old faces discredited, and abandoned by the military, on the 18th day of the protests, Mubarak resigned. The nation rejoiced.

The victory belonged to the protest movements, including those associated with the April 6th Youth Movement.

Social media—especially Facebook and Twitter—provided near-instant communication that overwhelmed the capacities of the secret police. Wael Ghonim argued that without social media the protests likely would have failed.

However, the youthful leaders of the protests also connected with labor movements and the concerns of those too poor to use the internet. They contrasted starkly with traditional politicians interested in perpetual questions such as the role of Islam, fair elections, or seats in the National Assembly. The protesters' focus was ethical and abstract, concerned with human rights, personal dignity, and fairness, combined with a dominant slogan: "The People Want the Fall of the Regime."

Perhaps, too, the protest movements tapped resentment at the web of dishonesty spread by the regime. For example, when four regional leaders walked the red carpet at the White House, the official photo showed the young, President Obama leading his guests, with an aging President Mubarak trailing. But al-Ahram altered the picture to show Mubarak ahead of Obama. When the official media lied in matters so apparently trivial, its statements about so much else, from deaths of individuals in police custody to threats presented by the Muslim Brotherhood, could no longer be trusted.

The traditional political opposition, dominated by the Muslim Brotherhood and a few small middle-class parties, had always failed to take advantage of regime weaknesses to effect change. Mubarak's resignation was not their success.

The Struggle to Shape the New Egypt

Mubarak's resignation proved only the beginning of a revolution, a reshuffling of military rulers forced by public opinion. The Supreme Council of the Armed Forces (SCAF) took control, headed by Mohammad Hussain Tantawi, defense minister and military commander for two decades. The council retained the cabinet, dissolved parliament, suspended the constitution, promised to honor foreign treaties, and pledged to remain in office no longer than six months.

Nevertheless, general intimidation continued. Justice was delayed for victims of police repression: there were almost no convictions. Despite the prominent roles of women in the protests, the army conducted virginity tests on some of those arrested. One general publicly approved the practice, and sexual harassment and groping became nearly universal humiliations. Elections were manipulated: a referendum freer from intimidation than any in decades approved a constitutional amendment. However, the ballot's circle

Protesters like this woman illustrate the success of youthful activists in reaching the general public
Photo courtesy of Jim Neergaard

for "Yes" was printed in bright green and that for "No" in ordinary black.

The military clearly retained control, but with a constitution and elections ahead, other groups sought to influence political decisions. Attention naturally focused on the expected role of the Muslim Brotherhood in a democratic system. Its critics feared the largest and best-organized opposition group to Mubarak would swiftly win elections and impose conservative Islamic values. Given the fractured opinions of Brotherhood members, a variety of worrying quotations were quickly found to substantiate the critics' worst fears.

The Brotherhood initially acted with great caution. It pledged to limit the number of its parliamentary candidates and not to contest presidential elections. However, facing competition from Salafists who campaigned to impose Shari'a law, as well as moderate Islamists, it soon violated both promises. Indeed, it even ran members for non-partisan seats in parliament. With non-Islamists disunited in elections for the People's Council (the lower house of parliament), the Muslim Brotherhood's Freedom and Justice Party swept to victory (36%), followed by the Salafists (24%).

The youthful activists behind the Tahrir protests joined with leaders of some secular political parties to form a second, weakly organized group. Consistently in opposition and unable to unite for the elections, their influence was felt particularly through demonstrations that forced SCAF and others to change policies and bring presidential elections forward.

Many demonstrations passed peacefully, but some activists attacked property, and police and soldiers on occasion assaulted demonstrators, at times clearly shooting to kill. Political violence took a tragic turn at the Port Said soccer stadium, when supporters of the visiting al-Ahly team, known as "Ultras" and recognized for supporting the revolution, were attacked and 70 massacred in the melee while the police watched on.

Judges and officials clearly formed other important centers of power. For example, the Supreme Constitutional Court decreed the parliamentary elections invalid because both the Freedom and Justice and the Salafist al-Nour parties had run candidates for seats reserved for non-party independents. The SCAF immediately dissolved the National Assembly and decreed that new elections must wait for a constitution. Likewise, the presidential election commission disqualified several candidates, most prominently the Salafists' Hazem Abu Ismail (his mother once took out U.S. citizenship) and Khairat al-Shater of the Brotherhood's Freedom and Justice Party (he had a recent criminal conviction).

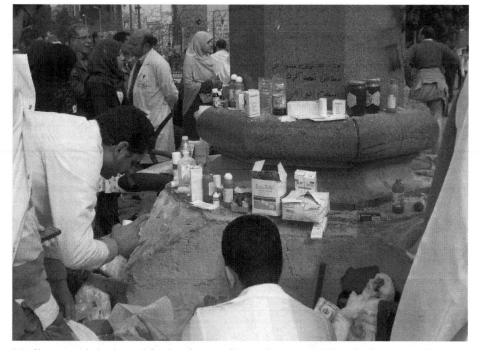

Medics treat injuries with simple supplies; when pro-Mubarak thugs attacked the demonstrators, even simple emergency care became important

Photo courtesy of Jim Neergaard

Given the strong Islamic victory in the parliamentary elections, the results of the first presidential round proved surprising. In a large field, Mohammed Morsi, the replacement candidate of the Freedom and Justice Party, won 24% of the vote. However, Ahmed Shafiq, the former air force commander and briefly Mubarak's prime minister, came in second (23%) on a platform of stability and order. Hamdin Sabbahi, who appealed to Nasserites, leftists, and some centrists, came in third (almost 21%).

Political loyalties thus divided into three distinct groups: loyal Islamists backing Morsi, supporters of Shafiq and his anti-Brotherhood, law-and-order platform, and a rag-tag of pro-democracy forces who backed Sabbahi. But in the second round, dismayed democrats faced the alternative of two disliked candidates.

Morsi won the runoff with nearly 52% of the vote, a narrow yet democratic victory. He took office promising to serve as the president of all Egyptians. He proposed to appoint a cabinet with a Christian and a woman as vice presidents, although eventually installed Mahmoud Mekki, a Muslim man, in the position.

Egypt under Morsi

Mohammed Morsi represented the democratic will of the nation, having narrowly won a contested election. Nevertheless, he took office without a constitution to define his authority or a parliament to draft laws. Facing enormous, often conflicting, demands for rapid change he attempted much, failed often, accomplished little, and antagonized millions. Given the country's revolutionary change, some failures were inevitable, but the direction of the government's policies rightly worried women, the youth movements, civic organizers, the political opposition, and non-Islamists of many varieties.

In some ways a naïve college professor thrust by events into the highest office, Morsi often acted on impulse without recognizing the likely consequences. He promised that during the first 100 days he would tackle the nation's perpetual, but worsening traffic congestion, remove rubbish from the streets, improve security, and overcome shortages of bread and fuel. In fact, these challenges to daily life seemed to worsen. The only realistic improvements would have been rapid imports of flour and fuel, but too few funds were available. Once in power, the Brotherhood's economic policies seemed capitalist, opposing progressive taxation and constraining labor unions.

One particularly ill-conceived action was Morsi's declaration in late 2012 of wide-ranging executive powers. In effect, these powers placed him above any oversight, including the law (or at least the judges).

Morsi's narrow, partisan focus on the Brotherhood's agenda led to flawed actions elsewhere and charges of "creeping Islamization." The constituent assembly appointed to draft the new constitution

Egypt

Serving and waiting: Protesters rest in the shade, ensuring that this tank does not move
Photo courtesy of Jim Neergaard

was stacked with Islamists; a better-balanced membership would have calmed the nation and produced a less-flawed document. Though approved in a low-turnout referendum, the constitution's sections regarding basic freedoms—speech, religion, assembly, and equality—were sometimes vague and contradictory. They worried moderate Muslims; secularists and Christians feared them.

Some of Morsi's decisions that alarmed his critics suggested he cared little for their opinions. He apparently ignored the increasingly violent sectarian strife that included the killing of Copts within their Cairo cathedral. Instead of symbolically addressing Christian suspicions, he declined to attend the enthronement of Coptic Pope Tawadros II, though certainly other Muslim rulers had done so. Morsi also failed to order a serious response to attacks by militants in the Sinai, and initiated better relations with Hamas in Gaza.

One of the most absurd decisions was the appointment of a member of al-Gama'a al-Islamiyya as governor of Luxor. Its members had launched many attacks on foreigners, the bloodiest being the murder of more than 60 (mostly tourists) near Luxor itself in 1997. While the group later renounced violence, the governor's appointment offended the tourist industry, the military, and many others. The minister of tourism resigned.

Despite the frequency of flawed decisions, Morsi could claim credit for some accomplishments. An early move settled relations with the military. It transferred the powers of SCAF to the presidency and thus placed civilian control over the armed forces for the first time in the republic's history. He also forced General Tantawi's resignation and appointed an apparently pious and relatively young officer, Abdul Fattah al-Sisi, as military commander and defense minister.

The government also succeeded in raising some vitally-needed funds abroad. With tourism collapsing, industrial output suffering from strikes and inflation, and demands for fuel that exceeded production, Egypt seriously lacked foreign exchange to finance imports. Fortunately, Qatar lent $3 billion and promised to provide natural gas supplies, badly needed for both households and power plants. However, negotiations with the IMF for a $4.8 billion loan proved inconclusive.

In 2013, Ethiopia announced the start of construction on the Grand Ethiopian Renaissance Dam on the Blue Nile, despite a 1929 treaty that nearly all Egyptians trust to limit upstream diversion of Nile waters. Although the dam's purpose is hydroelectric rather than for irrigation, other dams are planned, and Egypt's military lacks the power to enforce the treaty. Nevertheless, Morsi responded with the threat "all options are open."

When the first anniversary of President Morsi's taking office approached in June 2013, popular agitation swept the country.

A new activist group, *Tamarud*, launched a campaign to gather 15 million signatures calling for Morsi's resignation. The organizers eventually claimed 22 million, more than one quarter of the nation's population.

Tamarud reflected many of the original organizing groups behind the 2011 Tahrir Square demonstrations, including *Kifaya*, the April 6 Movement, the National Salvation Front, and several smaller parties. Ahmad Shafiq, Morsi's unsuccessful rival in the presidential elections, also supported Tamarud, as did, conditionally, the Salafist Nour Party. Thus the movement included most of the country's political spectrum, including former supporters of ex-president Mubarak, excepting, of course, the Muslim Brotherhood.

Whether by pre-arrangement with Tamarud or from a sense of national duty, the military commander, General Abdul Fatah al-Sisi, demanded that, for the good of Egypt, Morsi and his critics should reach a compromise. However, in key televised addresses, Morsi remained defiant. He admitted that he had made mistakes but also accused his opponents of trying to "sabotage" democracy: "The enemies of Egypt have not spared effort in trying to sabotage the democratic experience."

With millions demonstrating for Morsi's ouster, in smaller cities across the country as well as in Cairo, Muslim Brotherhood supporters turned out to support the legally-elected president. Violence occurred, and a crowd attacked and burned the Brotherhood's headquarters. Al-Sisi declared the nation was in danger and imposed a 48-hour deadline for Morsi to share power, or the military would impose a "roadmap for the future." As the crisis worsened, government power slipped from the hands of the president, with state-owned TV channels and newspapers demanding change.

Military Intervention and al-Sisi's Egypt

On July 3, 2013, al-Sisi announced that

Ex-president Mohammed Morsi

the Egyptian people had called on the military for help, "not to hold the reins of power, but rather to uphold its civil responsibility." He suspended the constitution, granted the Chief Justice presidential powers, and pledged an interim government of technocrats until early presidential elections. Mohammed Morsi and other leading members of the Brotherhood and its political wing, the Freedom and Justice Party, were arrested. Its television channel went off the air.

While many foreign governments struggled to respond to the ouster of a legitimately elected president, pro-Morsi demonstrators came under fire by the military, who claimed they had suffered the initial attack. The initial 50 deaths, plus hundreds of injured, strengthened suspicion within the Brotherhood that in Egypt democracy would never offer Islamists a fair opportunity to rule. This verified al-Qaeda's traditional arguments that had been used to condemn the Brotherhood's involvement in politics. However, violence came not only from the military. In reprisal, Islamists attacked Christian churches and schools, some businesses, police stations, museums and other government facilities. For six weeks, Morsi supporters gathered at protest sites, the largest outside the Rabaa al-Adawiyah mosque in Cairo, where militant speeches advocated revolution. The sometimes-violent standoff ended weeks later, when the security services attacked the Islamists and cleared the protest sites. Hundreds were killed; the Brotherhood was banned and eventually termed a terrorist organization. Its leading members were arrested, and numerous charges were brought against Morsi.

While analysts and foreign governments deliberated over the appropriate reaction to the ouster of an elected government and the bloody repression of its supporters, evidence from the streets showed that many Egyptians had tired of Brotherhood rule. For the short-run, most citizens either

The New Egypt: An unmarried Muslim couple enjoys time together, in public   Photo by Malcolm B. Russell

President Abdul Fattah al-Sisi

accepted the law-and-order of a military-backed regime or, if opposing the regime, limited protests to brief affairs.

Against this background, a new constituent assembly re-wrote the Morsi constitution in ways that reflected the interests of the military and its non-Islamist allies. Significantly for a country with millennia of history with strong executive rule, the presidency emerged potentially weaker. Not only can a two-thirds vote of parliament initiate a referendum over holding early elections, but the prime minister appointed by the president must also carry the confidence of parliament. While the president must be a civilian, military influence is secured by the requirement that for the next eight years the defense minister must be an officer approved by SCAF.

Other articles guaranteed freedom of faith, especially belief in the "heavenly religions of Islam, Christianity, and Judaism." The proposals prohibited political parties based on religion, though Islamic law is "the principal" source of legislation. Women's rights were better protected, as were children. Freedom of expression was enshrined, and the ministry of information dissolved. The constitution was approved by a national referendum.

The next step towards a formal return to democracy was the 2014 presidential election. Al-Sisi, whose supporters had apparently used the resources of the "deep state" to popularize him as the

nation's natural leader, resigned as military commander to run as a civilian. The banned Brotherhood urged its supporters to boycott the election; so did some moderates and liberals opposed to a military presidency. Promising expensive projects and a changed society, Al-Sisi won the election with 22 million of the 23 million votes cast, more than had Morsi two years earlier, though critics dismissed the win as relatively meaningless due to low voter turnout. His first cabinet was composed primarily of those who had held positions previously, including Prime Minister Ibrahim Mahlab.

Facing all the problems Mohammed Morsi had on taking office, plus the antagonism of political Islamists, Mahlab recognized great efforts were needed. By 2015 the pattern of al-Sisi's rule became clear. Repression of Brotherhood members continued, and a judge sentenced 188 Brotherhood supporters to hang for the murder of fourteen policemen during the ouster of Morsi. Morsi himself was sentenced to death for participation in a prison outbreak during the 2011 Arab Spring, as well as separately for spying. Other major leaders received similar sentences. Followers also suffered harsh justice: a judge sentenced more than 500 people to death for a single murder. Twice. Mass trials resulted in suspect convictions, some of the most outrageous—such as the sentencing of a toddler to life in prison for murder,

Egypt

attempted murder, and vandalizing government property, in the context of anti-government protests—made a mockery of the justice system. It was increasingly clear that Egypt was slipping back in to autocracy, if indeed, it had ever succeeded in clawing its way free.

At least for the short term, the Brotherhood leadership seemed incapacitated by the arrests of its leaders, and it proved incapable of bringing large numbers of supporters into the streets.

The regime justified the harsh sentences as a necessary response to the terrorism—suicide bombings, assassinations, and beheadings—of the jihadists in the Sinai first known as *Ansar Beit al-Maqdis* (Partisans of Jerusalem), which after pledging allegiance to Islamic State (IS) in 2014, became known as Ansar Sinai (Partisans of the Province of Sinai). Some violent attacks took place in the Egyptian heartland, and IS supporters in Libya executed 21 Coptic workers, most of them Egyptian, merely for their religion. The air force earned public respect for its reprisal bombing of those extremists, rather than criticism for waging war abroad, but some 45,000 Egyptians working in the country fled their homes for safety.

Unfortunately from a human rights perspective, the police and courts also arrested journalists and liberal advocates of democracy. University students were banned from political demonstrations; in fact, all demonstrations were banned that did not possess a rarely-granted license. Meanwhile, many members of the old military regime were rehabilitated. Ex-president Mubarak and his notorious interior (police) minister, Habib al-Adly, were found not guilty of the police brutalities during their last days in power, and their death sentences were revoked.

Recent developments might best be characterized as "more of the same." In March 2018, al-Sisi claimed victory and reelection after official tallies showed that he won 97% of the nationwide vote. It goes without saying that the race was not competitive. On the eve of the election, the president faced one "challenger," a supporter of the president, after all serious opposition had abandoned their campaigns, citing threat and intimidation. Al-Sisi has been further helped by his parliament, where more than 200 members shifted allegiances to form a new political party—Future of the Homeland—which was founded to support al-Sisi. Constitutional changes, approved at referendum in April 2019, will allow al-Sisi to remain in power until at least 2030.

On June 17, 2019, Morsi collapsed and died during a court hearing on charges of espionage. While his death was recorded as being the result of a heart attack, critics of the Egyptian regime blamed the poor conditions under which Morsi was being held in prison. Protests followed Morsi's death, and in September 2019 several thousand Egyptians were arrested during mass uprisings against Sisi's rule. In March 2020, several prominent Egyptians were arrested following calls for the release of prisoners over fears of coronavirus outbreaks in prisons. The Egyptian government responded to the global pandemic by sealing Egypt's notoriously crowded and unhygienic prisons and denying prisoners access to family members or others on the outside. This came amid a broader crackdown on journalists reporting on the spread of Covid-19, including the revoking of foreign press credentials over what the government describes as "bad faith reporting."

In sum, despite the fact that President al-Sisi resigned from his military post before running for office, military rule has

Statue of Umm Kahlthoum, Egypt's great 20th century singer

returned to Egypt. The president is undeniably ruling with an iron first. The cost has been high. Egypt is home to tens of thousands of political prisoners. Forced disappearances, as well as crackdowns on authors, satirists, cartoonists, and other activists, are common. Protestors must seek government permission to protest, and this is usually denied. Anti-terrorism laws that resemble Mubarak's decades-long state of emergency formally legalize what to most outside observers looks like state repression. A recent Human Rights Watch report puts it this way: "President Abd al-Fattah al-Sisi's government continues to preside over the worst human rights crisis in the country in decades."

Culture: Perhaps no other country in the world is so prominent in the popular imagination. Monuments, buildings, ruins and tombs of an ancient civilization all characterize Egypt. Only a few miles separate the incredible traffic jams and skyscrapers of modern Cairo from the great pyramids at Giza on the edge of the desert. Yet the modern culture of the country has little to do with ancient civilization. New religions, crops, and ways of living largely obliterated the customs of ancient times. Even the agricultural cycle for the

Symmetrical and graceful beneath dramatic cliffs, the Temple of Hatshepsut

Egyptian farmer—known as the *fellah*—has weakened, for the Aswan High Dam prevents the Nile from flooding his lands and depositing nourishing silt for the next year's crops.

Islamic values run deep in Egypt, particularly among the impoverished masses, but also among students and some professionals. In contrast, growing numbers of the middle and upper classes, both Muslims and Coptic Christians, blend traditional and western lifestyles, although most remain somewhat faithful to religious customs. The broader culture probably differs from western values most clearly in matters of gender and sexuality.

The most delicate difficulty that tradition presents Egypt's government and society is female circumcision, also known as female genital mutilation (FGM). Defended by conservatives as an Islamic solution to avoid female immorality, the practice is also carried out by many Coptic Christians. It kills girls every year and leaves women maimed, but most Egyptian mothers apparently desire to have their daughters circumcised, despite a (poorly enforced) government ban on it since 1996. According to a recent government report, 92% of Egyptian women aged 15 to 49 have endured the procedure.

Conservative social values create difficulties and obstacles for women in other ways as well. Physical abuse becomes more acceptable when, as survey data indicate, over 80% of young and middle-aged women consider wife-beating justified under certain circumstances. Most women report sexual harassment even when dressed in accordance with Islamic modesty. Despite the efforts of non-governmental organizations, legal equality remains distant. In contrast to fairly rapid divorce procedures when requested by a man, a woman seeking to end a marriage must either spend years in the courts or accept a no-fault divorce that often leaves her without any financial assets from the marriage.

While society frowns strongly on premarital sexual activity, economic change and education increasingly bring single men and women together. Young couples unable or unwilling to have a formal wedding sometimes turn to *urfi* marriages, traditional but unregistered marriages often kept secret even from family. If the arrangement should break down—for example, if the woman becomes pregnant but the man does not wish to be bound by his commitments—the consequences fall most heavily on the woman.

Literary Culture and Education

Although relatively poor, Egypt in many respects remains the cultural center of the Arab World, known for its novelists, short story writers, dramatists, and poets. Indeed, in 1988 Naguib Mahfouz, known best in the English-speaking world for *Midhaq Alley* and *The Beginning and the End,* won the Nobel Prize for Literature. The first Arab writer to receive the honor, international recognition revived domestic (and regional) criticism of his work as blasphemous for portraying irreligious individuals who questioned Islam and his brave condemnation of Ayatollah Khomeini's death sentence on Salman Rushdie. Though in his 80s, after Mahfouz survived an assassination attempt he resumed walking the streets and alleys of his beloved Cairo until his death in 2006.

A generation of young Egyptian authors has likewise won widespread acclaim and even sales. The best known in translation is Alaa Al Aswany's *The Yacoubian Building* (2002), which reveals a society where political corruption, sexual repression, and religious extremism flourish.

Founded in 988, the mosque school of al-Azhar in Cairo is one of the oldest universities in the world. Traditionally its professors sat at the base of one of the mosque's pillars, lecturing to students who came from many lands. There were no official examinations, but when the faculty considered a student proficient in a subject, they issued him a license to teach. Modern changes include formal diplomas, branches in medicine and other non-theological disciplines, and a women's program. The Grand Imam of al-Azhar remains an important spokesman for Sunni Islam, and offers guidance to believers on many theological issues.

For decades education for all remained a dream rather than reality. However, the government built thousands of new schools in the 1990s, for the 90% of young boys and 80% of girls who enroll. Adult literacy climbed from 40% in the 1970s to 60% by the end of the century. That said, with teacher salaries as low as $45 per month, teachers have encouraged the practice of guiding the best learning in private tutoring sessions, and classroom study often decays into rote memorization. Not surprisingly, many children drop out: the law requiring nine years of school cannot be enforced. After just three or four years inside a classroom, many children begin working, often in agriculture and construction, because of family poverty.

Egypt has lost its lead among Arab states in education because of financial limitations and perhaps politically-appointed administrators as well. As in most professions, teachers in Egypt receive pitifully small salaries, so many of the best qualified have been lured to more prosperous countries to work at much higher remuneration. The quality of education at the University of Cairo and the half dozen other universities in Egypt is generally good, although in common with other Less Developed Countries, Egypt turns out an excess of liberal arts graduates, who fill (often needless) government positions or seek work abroad. In contrast, the country needs scientists, and especially skilled manual workers and technicians.

A Cairo street scene

Egypt

Health services in Egypt vary greatly according to family income and education. Although the universities train doctors to world standards, poverty prevents adequate medical services for many. Sanitation is often deplorable. In Cairo, some two million people live in areas without sewers. Preliminary construction of a new sewer system for the city began in early 1985. Years will be required to complete this project which is an urgent matter of public health. The press of millions of poor makes Cairo one of the world's most crowded and noisy cities. Indeed, a survey reported that 60% of Cairenes had used sedatives at least once against the noise and stress.

Popular Culture and Sport

On the popular level, Cairo's constant flow of new films and television dramas makes it the Hollywood of the region. Plots frequently dramatize the sufferings of life, particularly marriage and family problems set against a background of conflict between traditions and modern individuality, as well as the persistent issue of class-consciousness. Difficulties sometimes arise with Islamic conservatives. In one example, a film about Joseph (*Al-Mohager*, "The Emigrant") was banned for showing a prophet on the screen.

Egypt's pre-eminence in Arabic film, television drama and music made the distinctive Cairene accent familiar throughout the Arabic-speaking world. Other Arab countries attempted to develop their own television programming, but the arrival of music videos and satellite TV reinforced Egyptian dominance, as did the construction of Media Palace City (1995), an attempt to create a "Hollywood of the East" production center.

Egyptian musicians also dominate

Camel market in Cairo

Caring for the needy: water pitchers placed for thirsty passersby in Upper Egypt

popular music and videos from Oman to North Africa. The "golden voice" of Umm Kalthoum captivated hearts across the Arab world during a career of six decades, and her recordings continue to sell well. By the 21st century, the country's music scene had developed a wide diversity of styles, from traditional songs and instruments to Arabic Pop, typically a fusion of traditional Arab styles and instruments with Western influences. Even hip-hop and heavy metal have taken off in recent years. Like popular music everywhere, romantic themes dominate, but despite the suggestive clothing of female pop stars, explicit references to sexuality are rare. Overtly political content in music remains relatively rare, but politics is no longer as taboo in music as it once was. Finding protest rap on YouTube is only a click away.

Finally, many Egyptians are passionate about soccer. Indeed, after Egypt lost a World Cup qualifying match to Algeria in 2009, fans stirred by media coverage rioted in Cairo and attacked the Algerian embassy. While rarely successful in World Cup competitions, the Egyptian national team, nicknamed The Pharaohs, won the African Nations Cup in 2010 for an unprecedented third year in succession. Within the country, two teams traditionally vie for championship of the football league: Zamalek and Al-Ahly, the latter with over 40 million fans.

Economy: Although systematic efforts to modernize began two hundred years ago, personal incomes remain low. A rapidly growing population, misfortune in war, misguided government economic policies, and a tradition of government regulation all reduced opportunities in the past 50 years. In addition, natural resources

are few. There is no timber, no coal, and outside the Nile Valley, almost no water. Mineral deposits provide little wealth for a population so large, and are limited to modest oil deposits, natural gas, salt, and manganese.

Visual evidence of the mixture of poverty and progress strikes even the casual tourist, in the form of barefoot children, simple farming methods, and the ever-present unemployed. Also obvious, the gap between the poor and the rich is enormous, the latter receiving incomes some 500 times the former. Though it has fallen from 3% in the 1980s, the population growth rate still requires feeding more than one million additional mouths food every year. Almost all live in the 4% of the country's territory comprising the Nile Valley and Delta. Egypt's population is roughly ten times that of New Jersey but lives in only twice as much territory. Moreover, because one-third of the population is rural, average farms measure only a few acres. This overwhelms the ability of the fertile soil and warm climate to provide either sufficient food or a good standard of living.

Traditionally, agriculture formed the basis of the Egyptian economy. Famous for its desirable long-staple cotton, Egypt also produced and sometimes exported grains such as wheat and rice, as well as sugar, oranges, dates, and tropical mangoes.

Before the 1952 Revolution, much farmland belonged to absentee landowners whose domains included entire villages. Under Gamal Abdul Nasser, the government attempted significant land reform, in part to break the political power of conservative landlords through limiting ownership to a maximum 50 acres in traditional farming areas. Irrigation schemes brought large tracts of desert under cultivation, and the Aswan High Dam provided more areas with successive crops per year.

Unfortunately, government regulations offset much of the progress. Investment in agriculture came low on the list of government priorities, while the new landowners lacked credit ratings to borrow. Additionally, despite the expansion of schools into rural areas, these landowners very often lacked formal education, let alone the technical training required to benefit from scientific advances in agriculture.

Agriculture remains an important sector of the Egyptian economy, contributing to almost one-seventh of GDP and employing a quarter of the labor force. However, production of cereal staples falls well short of domestic consumption needs. Rising food prices have traditionally been the catalyst for social upheaval in Egypt. Deadly bread riots that preceded the Arab Spring, had their origin in disruptions in the supply of subsidized grain. Egyptians are the largest consumers of bread and the country is the largest wheat importer in the world. Any delay or reduction in supply can have catastrophic social and political implications.

Soon after al-Sisi came to power in 2013, Egypt secured a desperately needed $12 billion bailout from the International Monetary Fund (IMF). Funds were provided on the condition that Egypt undertake a significant economic restructuring. Al-Sisi has imposed a series of austerity measures, slashing subsidies across a range of goods, perhaps most significantly, on electricity. While reforms have undeniably boosted the Egyptian economy, they have exacted a heavy toll on the poor and middle class. Inequality in Egypt has not improved and while al-Sisi has kept a tight rein on domestic unrest, the underpinning frustrations that led, first to the Arab Spring and later to widespread frustration and the overthrow of Morsi, have not been dealt with. The government has made a big push in recent years to attract foreign investment. In 2015 Cairo announced a series of large projects funded by foreign companies and governments worth tens of billions of dollars. However, there are question marks over Egypt's ability to attract foreign direct investments. The country has struggled to bring investors on board in the oil and gas industry. A massive effort to create a new government administrative center in the desert, some 30 miles (48 kilometers) east of Cairo, would have eased some of the most pressing social and environmental problems of Egypt's swollen capital city. However, a $20 billion injection of funds from Beijing is no longer on the cards, given disagreements over the respective distribution of revenue to the Egyptian state and the China Fortune Land

Development company. China is clearly an important new player in Egypt and, indeed, in the Middle East more broadly. Al-Sisi has made a number of visits to China, a reflection perhaps of the current, uncertain relationship between the U.S. and Egypt and the perceived need for Egypt to diversify its foreign relations.

Egypt under Nasser trusted the Aswan High Dam to solve poverty and raise farm output by storing the Nile's summer floods in the largest artificial reservoir in the world. The dam would then provide year-round irrigation for many areas and water for thousands of acres of desert. A great technical achievement as well as a foreign-policy success, the dam met these goals at its completion in 1971, and its massive turbines once generated half of Egypt's electricity.

For all its benefits, however, the High Dam also brought problems. Across Egypt, the underground water table rose, threatening historical sites, and year-round irrigation spread bilharzia and other parasitic diseases, as well as obnoxious water hyacinths. Rising soil salinity and the loss of silt that enriched the soil, require expensive drainage systems and chemical fertilizers. Environmental issues pose other, less certain risks to Egyptian agriculture. The low-lying Delta and coastal cities face potential inundation in the context of rising sea levels. Air pollution around Cairo poses a threat to plants and animals, as well as humans.

Industry: Industrial production began modestly in Egypt. After World War I some factories began to process food and cotton textiles, logical industries given the lack of coal and iron ore. The officers that led the 1952 Revolution desired to industrialize the country, motivated by socialist ideas that encouraged national self-sufficiency and equated modernity with heavy industry. However, socialists also loathed foreign investment and discouraged capitalists. As a result, the state nationalized a number of industrial companies, eventually controlling 85% of manufacturing assets. Those that remained suffered paralyzing regulations and red tape that hampered almost all trade and commerce.

Attempts to produce a complete range of manufactured goods within the country, from appliances to cars, provided expensive products of poor quality that required high tariff protection to compete against imports. (In contrast, the rapidly growing countries of East Asia follow the opposite policies, encouraging exports and foreign trade.)

Egypt's leadership in the Arab world also slowed economic growth. Opposing Israel militarily meant five wars (including the War of Attrition) in 25 years

between 1948 and 1973. Besides the human costs of a large military force and several generations of weapons largely destroyed on the battlefield, the damage included Israeli attacks on economic targets and the devastation of cities along the Suez Canal. In addition to untold sums owed the Soviet Union for arms, the country purchased military hardware on credit from the United States, ironically during a period of peace with Israel. In contrast to past military expenses and losses, Egypt today has become a substantial and presumably profitable producer of weapons. Military exports have ranked alongside cotton as a major export.

Four Uncommon Assets in Change

For its past growth and modest prosperity, Egypt relied on four uncommon assets: oil, tourism, the Suez Canal, and remittances from Egyptian workers in other countries. Each provided foreign exchange, vitally important for a country perpetually short of money to purchase goods from other countries. Oil exports and canal revenues also provide alternatives to taxing citizens.

Exports of petroleum products once provided the largest foreign exchange earnings. Although not a member of the Organization of Petroleum Exporting Countries (OPEC), Egypt once exported larger quantities than some OPEC members. However, as fields matured in recent years, oil production fell, despite exploration for new deposits. By 2010, rising domestic demand for oil exceeded supply, and Egypt became an oil importing nation.

Discoveries of natural gas deposits around Suez, in the Nile basin, and in the Western Desert created a surplus, providing both alternatives to petroleum and supplies for export. The first natural gas export pipeline reached Jordan in 2003; the completion of liquefied natural gas "trains" enabled a greater volume to be shipped. However, rising domestic demand for natural gas resulted in legal limits on exports, and by 2013 Egyptian exporters met some obligations by shipping LNG from Qatar.

For two thousand years travelers have marveled at the Pyramids. A century ago, the wealth and beauty of Tutankhamun's tomb rendered a minor Pharaoh a household word. For the present era of mass tourism, Egypt possesses some of the world's most spectacular archaeological treasures and monuments. Other attractions exist as well, often inexpensive and rarely spoiled by rain. They range from sandy beaches along the Mediterranean to relatively unspoiled fishing and diving in the Red Sea. They include Mt. Sinai, where Jews and Christians traditionally believe God gave Moses the Ten Commandments.

Egypt

The Pyramids attract all nationalities

Arabs from oil states often seek culture and entertainment in Cairo, while visitors from West and East seek bargains in the city's *souks* or enjoy luxury cruises on the Nile. Despite attacks by Muslim militants and visits cancelled during times of political unrest, the industry earns billions during prosperous years, and its employees support some one million people.

One unique Egyptian economic benefit comes from the country's location connecting Asia and Africa. Cut through the Isthmus over 10 years, at a cost of perhaps 100,000 lives, the Suez Canal reduces greatly the distance ships must travel between Europe and the Indian Ocean. Tolls from the 18,000 ships that annually make the 15-hour journey through the 120-mile (193 kilometer) long canal exceed $500,000 per trip for the largest vessels able to use the waterway. These tolls provide a very important source of foreign exchange, exceeding $4 billion annually. Further earnings come from the "Sumed," the parallel oil pipeline from Suez to the Mediterranean.

At present, the very largest tankers (Ultra Large Crude Carriers, over 300,000 dead weight tons) are unable to use the waterway. Somewhat smaller vessels would strike bottom when loaded, given its depth of only 58 feet (less than 18 meters). As a result, some loaded tankers sail around Africa to markets in Europe and the United States, but then return, empty, to

the Persian Gulf through the canal. Thanks to this practice, more vessels use the canal going southbound than northbound. Dredging to widen, deepen, and straighten the canal continues, with the goal of eventually permitting passage by any vessel. Many Egyptian nationalists care passionately about the canal's nationalization in 1956, and successful operation since 1975.

No longer the most important source of foreign currency, remittances sent home by more than two million Egyptians working outside the country still play a very important role. Millions of Egyptians—mostly all male, mostly young, and often educated—work abroad, primarily in the Gulf, as teachers, doctors, and other professionals, but some as unskilled laborers.

Reforms and Continuing Challenges

Often appearing piecemeal and half-hearted, the economic reforms of the 1990s created an environment for sustained economic growth. Difficulties like the budget deficit, inflation, and the balance of payments deficit that had plagued the country for decades diminished when the government, hesitantly and slowly, cut subsidies and began to control spending.

The subsidies had distorted prices badly—kerosene, for example, had cost only $.20 per gallon, and legends describe farmers feeding bread to their animals, since it was cheaper than grains. Removing the subsidies encouraged more

efficient use of resources, but Egypt's poor and middle classes found holes in their economic safety-nets. Afraid of popular backlash—in 1977 rioters had chanted at President Sadat, "Hero of the Crossing (of the Suez Canal), Where is our breakfast?"—the cuts were scheduled gradually, and subtly. Rather than raise the price of bread, for example, the government cut the size of the pita-style loaf.

Cutting the government's large payroll and privatizing the companies it owned proved a more difficult task. In 1990, nearly one-third of all employed Egyptians worked for the government and its companies, far more than needed. A major purpose of the privatization drive was to provide jobs for the roughly 800,000 new job-seekers annually, but many legal, political, and practical complications slowed the sale of government firms to private owners.

Some factories proved particularly difficult to privatize, especially textiles, where workers understood that secure lifetime employment, offset low wages. Strikes spread across the Delta's textile industry in 2006–07 over rising prices, lagging wages, and broken promises by management, idling some of the largest factories in the world. Given higher inflation world-wide, living conditions have often declined for industrial workers, resulting in strikes and labor disputes after the breakdown of authoritarianism in 2011.

The Future: Mohammed Morsi seized too much power and failed to deliver government services effectively. But his removal and the subsequent bloody suppression of his supporters will divide Egyptian politics for decades. For almost seventy years, the Muslim Brotherhood was banned, harassed, and often persecuted, but it won the loyalties of millions of Egyptians. The ouster of its legitimately elected president will strengthen extreme Islamists for whom the coup reinforces the position that democracy is not an option and that, therefore, power must be seized by force. Under Abdul Fattah al-Sisi, Egypt has seen a return to veiled military rule, continued corruption, and political stagnation.

This reversion to the status quo has had a demoralizing effect on some. While court rulings sentenced former President Morsi to life in prison on charges of spying for Hamas, Hezbollah, and Iran, and even to death for plotting jailbreaks and plots against police in 2011, his aging predecessor, Hosni Mubarak, was released from jail and returned to his mansion. By all accounts Morsi was particularly harshly treated, even by the often poor standards of rights afforded to political prisoners in Egypt. He was held in solitary confinement for six years, kept in a cell for 23 hours a day with minimal communication. Already suffering ill health, he was reportedly denied medical treatment. On trial for espionage, in 2019 he collapsed in the dock and died, moments after addressing the court.

Like the country's many rulers before him, President al-Sisi's challenges are to restore prosperity and faith in the Egyptian pound, end shortages of petroleum and natural gas, and create productive jobs for the millions of young adults who are unemployed. Foreign investment must provide prosperity across the social stratum, not, as it has done in the past, merely to the already fabulously wealthy upper class.

For states watching Egypt from abroad, the question that al-Sisi poses is familiar. It is one that has characterized so much of Middle East politics for so long. Is the stability that the president seems to preside over real, or is it an illusion? Is Egypt a house of cards built on a foundation of inflation, austerity, and plummeting living standards? Are foreign leaders, including those in the United States, correct to praise al-Sisi and signal that human rights will no longer be part of bilateral relations?

Given endemic corruption and the absence of free debate about politics and government performance, expect Egypt in the short run to retain its long-standing political culture: a public mostly without a voice, dutiful officials, and a powerful ruler.

The Islamic Republic of Iran

Supporters of former President Muhammad Khatami celebrate his victory in 1997; the flowers faded AP/Wide World Photo

Hoping for flowers again: Celebrating the election of Hassan Rouhani, 2013

Area: 636,313 square miles (1,648,043 square kilometers).

Population: 84 million.

Capital City: Tehran (8.7 million, city; over 10 million, metro).

Climate: Arid, except for regions of moderate to heavy rainfall in the northwest. Temperature changes are extreme, from cold winters of the central plateau and northern mountains to the intense heat of the humid southern coast.

Neighboring Countries: Armenia, Azerbaijan, Turkmenistan (North); Afghanistan (East); Pakistan (Southeast); Iraq (West); Turkey (Northwest).

Time Zone: GMT +3 hours, 30 minutes.

Official Language: Farsi (Persian).

Other Principal Tongues: Kurdish, Baluchi, Luri, Armenian, Turkish, Shushtari, Azeri, and Arabic.

Ethnic Background: People are identified mainly according to language (about 80% Persian or Iranian), but also according to tribal group or religion.

Principal Religion: Shi'a Islam (89%), Sunni Islam (10%); other religious groups include Christians (370,000, of which 81% are Armenian), Jews (less than 10,000, most notably in the cities

of Isfahan and Shiraz), and Zoroastrians (approximately 26,000, centered in the city of Yazd). While Christians, Jews, and Zoroastrians are recognized by law and have dedicated seats in parliament, Baha'i (numbering up to 350,000) are not formally recognized and constitute a persecuted minority.

Chief Industrial Products: Petroleum and petroleum products, carpets, iron and steel, light manufactured goods, and vehicle assembly.

Agricultural Produce and Livestock: Wheat, barley, pistachios, rice, sugar beets, sugar cane, potatoes, sheep, goats, cattle, and chickens.

Major Trading Partners: China, Germany, Iraq, France, South Korea, and the United Arab Emirates.

Currency: Rial (10 rials = 1 toman).

Former Colonial Status: Under influence of Russia and Britain (1907–1923); occupied by Soviet and British troops (1941–1945).

National Day: February 11 (1979; Revolution Day).

Chief Executive: Hassan Rouhani, President.

Head of the Government and Supreme Leader: Ayatollah Seyyid Ali Khamenei.

National Flag: Three equal horizontal stripes of (top to bottom) green, white, and red. The edges of the green and red stripes carry 22 repetitions of the words *Allahu Akbar*, "God is Great." A red calligraphic emblem signifying the word God ("Allah") is centered in the white stripe.

Gross Domestic Product: $454 billion.

GDP per capita: $5,628.

Iran is one of the largest countries in the Middle East (second in landmass only to Saudi Arabia). It contains an extraordinary diversity of landscapes, terrains, and climates. It is one of the most mountainous countries in the world. The Zagros range stretches from the border with Armenia in the northwest to the Persian Gulf, and then eastward into Baluchistan.

The Alborz mountain range, narrower than the Zagros but equally forbidding, runs along the southern shore of the Caspian Sea to meet the border ranges of Khorasan to the east. The highest of its volcanic peaks, rising to 18,000 feet (approximately 5,500 meters) is the perennially snow-capped Mount Damavand. Mount Damavand's instantly recognizable

Iran

peak features on Iran's 10,000 rial bank note and as a logo on numerous commercial products.

On the border of Afghanistan, the mountains fall away, to be replaced by barren sand dunes. The arid interior plateau, which extends into Central Asia, is cut by two smaller mountain ranges. Loose stones and sand, gradually merging into fertile soil on the hillsides, covers much of this desert environment, known as *dasht*. Where fresh water can be held, oases have existed, marking ancient caravan routes. The most remarkable feature of the plateau is the Great Salt Desert or *kavir*.

Approximately one-sixth of the total area of Iran is barren desert. Over thousands of years, Iranian peoples have adapted to the harsh climatic conditions. The desert city of Yazd, for example, is known for its *badgirha* (wind towers) used for cooling homes and as a rudimentary form of refrigeration. *Qanats*, have been utilized since ancient time to irrigate arid and semi-arid landscapes, allowing human habitation in areas that would otherwise be unable to support settled communities. However, most of Iran's population is concentrated on the outlying mountains and watered plains, leaving the vast center of the country sparsely populated.

The Caspian Sea, lying 85 feet (26 meters) below sea level, is the largest landlocked body of water in the world. The coastline is a popular tourist destination for Iranians. Its tropical summers and mild winters give rise to lush vegetation and spectacular scenery.

Several million people live in the extreme northwest province of Azerbaijan, a land of mountain forests, cultivated valleys, and good rainfall.

The Persian Gulf is a strategically and economically significant waterway that lies between the Arabian Peninsula and southeast Iran. It has proven a flashpoint for conflict in the region. The southern coast and neighboring areas comprise the hottest parts of Iran. Light rainfall provides poor pasture for livestock, coastal towns are sparse, and poverty is rife. Industry, in the Persian Gulf coast region is largely limited to exploitation of oil and gas reserves.

In the north of the country, Tehran has grown in a matter of two centuries from a village to a huge city and the seat of a highly centralized government. Railroads, roads, and trade center on it; industry is concentrated there. Other major cities include Meshed, Isfahan, Tabriz, and Shiraz.

Geologically, the country sits uneasily atop seismic zones where the Arabian

and Eurasian tectonic plates meet. As the plates press against each other, they generate more earthquakes than in any other country, with small quakes striking daily. Deprived of timber, Iranians construct homes out of concrete block or bricks, and when powerful earthquakes strike, the loss of life is often catastrophic. For example, the relatively small city of Bam in eastern Iran lost more than 25,000 people to an earthquake in December 2003.

History: The name "Iran" means "Land of the Aryans," and its Indo-European peoples formed several of the notable kingdoms of ancient history (see Historical Background). Later invaders added Arab Islam and Turkish warriors to Iranian society. Human history in Iran stretches back many thousands of years and the ruins of earlier civilizations dot the landscape today.

So ancient is the history of Iran, that the modern period began hundreds of years ago with the Safavid dynasty in the 16th century and the widespread adoption of Shi'a Islam. The Safavid Empire reached its greatest power and extent under Shah Abbas (1587–1629), after whose death it declined. By the early 18th century, Persia (as it was then known on the global stage) was threatened by Turkey on the west, Russia on the north, and the Afghans on the east.

After an Afghan invasion ended the Safavid dynasty, Nadir Shah (1736–1747) restored much of the country's unity and conquered additional territory. Famous for his military exploits and adventures, he returned from invading India with incredible wealth and the famous Peacock Throne, but he failed to found a dynasty. The peaceful reign of Karim Khan Zand (1750–1779), from his capital in Shiraz, was followed by the establishment of the Qajar dynasty. Beset with tribal revolts and bloodshed, the sometimes-brutal Qajars maintained power until 1925. Shah Agha Mohammed Khan made Tehran his capital in 1788.

Under Qajar rule, Persia fought unsuccessful wars with Russia, the Ottoman Turks, and the Afghans, and lost territory to each. Under sometimes capricious rulers, domestic politics often stagnated at best, and the country, once a center

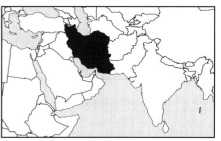

65

Iran

PERSIA NVOVA TAVOLA.

A map of Persia from a 1560 atlas

of learning and philosophy, failed to advance with the times.

Rivalry between the Russian Empire and the British Empire often focused on Persia. Russia sought to expand to the warm water ports of the Persian Gulf, while Britain was concerned primarily with the security of India. Russia enjoyed more influence in Persia, although the British worked hard to gain favor through agents in Tehran. Finally, in 1907 Russia and Britain arrived at an agreement—without any consideration of Persian desires in the matter—providing Russia a "sphere of influence" in the north, and Britain one in the south. A strip of less important territory in the middle was left as a neutral zone.

Dissatisfaction with foreign influence and the ineffectiveness of the monarchy in resisting it grew stronger in the late 19th century, symbolized by disapproval of granting British companies a tobacco monopoly in 1890. This produced protests and a ban from the clergy on using tobacco.

Partly influenced by Western ideas of political freedom, in 1906 groups of merchants, religious leaders, and reformers compelled the shah to grant a constitution and allow a parliament, known as the *Majlis*. Known as the Constitutional Revolution (1905–1911), these changes began an era of numerous struggles between the monarchy and the Majlis over control of the government.

During a decade and a half of struggle, marked by several closures and

re-openings, the Majlis and its reformers had no more success in strengthening the country and reducing foreign influence than had the monarchy. Central authority collapsed almost entirely during World War I, as Ottoman, Russian, and British forces and puppets occupied parts of the country. This set the stage for the rise of a dictator. In 1921 Reza Khan, deputy commander of the Cossack Brigade, joined a coup d'état. After creating a national army to replace various foreign-influenced units, in 1923 Reza compelled the shah to appoint him prime minister. The shah then left for exile, and in 1925 Reza Khan had the Majlis depose the Qajar dynasty. Later that same year he proclaimed himself Reza Shah Pahlavi, taking the ancient name Pahlavi from Persian history and founding a new dynasty.

Reza Shah organized and enlarged the army; then he used it, sometimes harshly, to establish obedience and order in every part of the country. He worked to gain full independence, to make himself the nation's master, and to make it as much like modern Europe as possible. He commanded the construction of roads, and a railroad from the Caspian Sea to the Persian Gulf. He introduced new secular laws and moved away from Islamic religious law. He encouraged modern technical education, forced people to dress more like Europeans, and started factories. By 1942, such factories employed half a million workers. Reza Shah even changed the name by which the country was to be

known in the international arena—from Persia to Iran, tapping into an already significant nationalist sentiment. Moderate but steady income from oil exports produced by the Anglo-Iranian Oil Company financed new projects.

After the German invasion of the Soviet Union in 1941, Soviet and British troops occupied Iran to prevent Reza Shah from allying with Nazi Germany and to secure the country's oil and transportation routes for Allied use. Reza was forced to abdicate. The British, in order to secure his acquiescence agreed to allow the shah's son, Crown Prince Mohammed Reza, to ascend to the throne.

When the Allied troops began to withdraw from Iran after the end of the war, the new shah, young Mohammed Reza faced wide opposition. Factions of many sorts, previously repressed by his determined father, vied to control the government. Great landowners, who paid nearly no taxes, attempted to dominate politics. Nomadic chieftains sought to free themselves and their tribes from central authority. Shi'a religious leaders denounced secular government, and elderly politicians schemed for office. In the streets, the communist-leaning Tudeh Party held sway, and foreign powers courted ethnic minorities.

In these circumstances, the Soviet Union attempted to form an autonomous communist regime in Azerbaijan, the Turkish-speaking northwestern province. However, the United States and Britain stood by the shah, and Soviet troops withdrew in 1946. The Iranian army dealt severely with the separatist leaders.

In response to the dire economic conditions, a seven-year plan won approval from the Majlis in 1949. Because the plan's projected expenses exceeded local taxes, Iranian politicians sought what they considered a fairer share of income from oil exports. When the Anglo-Iranian Oil Company refused higher payments, the Majlis, in 1951, nationalized the entire petroleum industry. The elderly politician who had championed the bill, Mohammed Mossadeq, became prime minister.

The brief Mossadeq era remains one of the most significant turning points in pre-revolutionary Iran. Mossadeq's government implemented a range of social reforms, including substantially bolstered labor laws and the introduction of unemployment compensation. Land reforms sought to force landlords to turn over 20% of their revenues to their tenants. These revenues were to be used for development projects such as public baths, rural housing, and pest control. However, it was the nationalization of the Anglo-Iranian Oil Company for which Mossadeq is best remembered. Refusing further British

66

President Hassan Rouhani

involvement in the industry, Mossadeq clearly appealed to nationalist sentiment. However, Britain would not relinquish its assets easily. Declaring its oil to have been "stolen", the United Kingdom organized international boycotts. Over a period of two years Iran struggled to produce and market oil. As the country's wealth diminished, Mossadeq's enemies saw an opportunity to undermine the prime minister.

By early 1953 U.S. and British intelligence (the CIA and MI6, respectively) had developed plans to overthrow Mossadeq. Operation Ajax (as it was known in the United States; Operation Boot, in the United Kingdom), pivoted on the shah dismissing his prime minister. Mohammed Reza, fearing Mossadeq's popularity, took some time to convince. It was only in August 1953 that the shah finally dismissed Mossadeq. In the event, the prime minister simply refused to leave office. Lacking authority and fearing mobs and riots in Tehran, the shah and his queen fled the country. The operation was very nearly aborted. However President Roosevelt overruled CIA advice that the coup had failed. According to documents released in 2017, some of the most feared mobsters in Tehran were hired by the CIA to stage pro-Shah riots, others were brought into Tehran on buses and trucks, and took over the streets of the city. Several hundred people were killed in the ensuing street fights. Mosaddeq was arrested, tried, and convicted of treason by the Shah's military court. He was initially sentenced to death, a sentence subsequently commuted to three years solitary confinement, followed by house arrest until his death in 1967. The shah returned to Iran, clearly owing his throne to the United States. Indeed, throughout his reign he would never succeed in entirely shaking the perception of him being an imposed ruler and a puppet of outside forces. In the meantime, the United States

had clearly taken the mantle from Britain, of hated foreign power. The seeds of the revolution were planted.

The shah developed several methods of maintaining his authoritarian rule in the post-1953 era. The National Security and Intelligence Organization (SAVAK) was created in 1957 to control political activity and the press. Many of SAVAK's agents—who developed a reputation for brutality—were trained in the United States. SAVAK monitored dissidents, and carried out censorship. Arbitrary arrests, the torture of prisoners, and executions were not uncommon. While effective for a decade at suppressing opponents, including leftists, pro-democratic forces, and the Islamic clergy, SAVAK divided the modernized middle class and left it suspicious of the shah.

To win the support of peasants and moderate reformers, and decrease the appeal of leftist revolutionaries, Mohammed Reza proclaimed a "White Revolution" in 1963. Two aspects of it, land distribution and greater rights for women, aroused the fierce opposition of many Shi'a clergy. They considered that the changes in the role of women threatened family morality, and the distribution of land to the peasants from vast religious foundations endangered the substantial revenues they received as administrators. These reforms turned religious leaders such as Grand Ayatollah Ruhollah Khomeini into irreconcilable enemies.

To support his government, the shah rewarded the upper ranks in the civil service and army with good incomes. Thus, he gained support from a small elite, but the almost ubiquitous bribery and other forms of dishonesty among officials contributed to the hostility of others. Increasingly, the shah proposed grand projects, and emphasized his imperial title. In 1971 he spent millions of dollars celebrating the so-called 2,500th anniversary of the founding of the ancient Persian Empire. A performance clearly aimed at a global audience, the event consolidated domestic opposition to the shah's rule. Amongst the most outspoken critics was the exiled Ayatollah Khomeini.

The shah had forced Khomeini out of the country in 1964, following the cleric's denunciations of the White Revolution. Residing in the Shi'a holy city of Najaf, in Iraq, Khomeini was able to skillfully utilize a network of mosques and religious organizations in order to circulate his lectures and sermons inside Iran.

Although failing to meet the needs and desires of most citizens, the government attempted to assert Iran's role as a regional power with large and well-equipped military forces. This power influenced neighbors. After decades of tension, in 1975 Iran

and Iraq agreed to move their border from the Iranian shore of the Shatt al-Arab to mid-channel. Because the river connects the oil center of Abadan with the Gulf, Iran gained long-sought benefits. In return, Iran halted supplies to Iraq's rebellious Kurds.

Vast increases in oil revenues during the 1970s enabled the government to rush development at home while purchasing the latest U.S. weapons such as the F-15 fighter. The guns-and-butter approach created wealth for many Iranians, but the lower classes gained little prosperity, suffered high inflation, and resented the corruption and westernized lifestyles of the rich. In between, the middle class found few legally-accessible political opportunities.

To prevent opposition in the Majlis and yet maintain a form of representative government, the shah sponsored a royal political party, while other parties were outlawed. With parliamentary opposition stifled, illegal left-wing parties and Islamic groups flourished at the grassroots. Riots in the religious city of Qom and in Tabriz in early 1978 showed deep popular dissatisfaction. In response, the army fired on the mobs, killing many. These deaths triggered further riots, and despite official bans demonstrations spread to Tehran and, eventually, across the country. Massacres by loyal troops ended all pretense of popular support for the shah, and the bloodshed united the rival opposition groups in the single goal of ousting the monarch.

As protests grew, so did the profile and importance of Ayatollah Khomeini. Khomeini very much set the course—and helped maintain the momentum—of the revolution, urging Iranians not to compromise and ordering work stoppages against the regime. During the last few months of his exile, having been forced out of Iraq and living in a suburb on the outskirts of Paris, Khomeini received a constant stream of reporters, and global notables, eager to hear the spiritual leader of the revolution and relay his missives to Iran and the world.

After months of strikes and confusion, with oil production and exports halted and the economy in chaos, Mohammed Reza left the country in early 1979. As a concession, he placed the government under a long-time critic. However, the concessions came too little and too late.

Khomeini flew home to a triumphant welcome in Tehran, and appointed Mehdi Bazargan prime minister. Despite the lavish attention the shah had paid it, the army abandoned its struggle against the revolutionaries. Voters overwhelmingly approved the creation of the Islamic

Iran

Republic of Iran; it became official on April 1, 1980.

The Islamic Republic immediately faced major problems. Restive ethnic minorities, many of them Sunni rather than Shi'a, threatened rebellion. The economy required emergency measures, but was largely ignored. Rival groups and individuals who had united against the monarchy now struggled violently for power. To maintain control, self-appointed "revolutionary courts" began imposing long prison terms or death sentences on former officials, accused wrongdoers, or "sinners." By mid-1979 some 200 executions had been carried out—often within hours of arrest. Opposing groups began political assassinations, and Khomeini ordered the establishment of a special militia for his Islamic Revolutionary Council.

When militants seized the U.S. embassy in Tehran in 1979 and took 63 hostages, they won wide approval in the streets. Demands that the Shah—then undergoing cancer treatment in the United States—be returned to Iran to stand trial for alleged crimes committed during his reign, was at the heart of the hostage crisis. Many political leaders in Iran approved the illegal action, but the Bazargan cabinet resigned almost immediately because it had no effective authority. Khomeini then directed the Islamic Revolutionary Council to take control. International pressures on Iran to release the hostages proved useless, and an American attempt to rescue the hostages in 1980 ended unsuccessfully in the Iranian desert, with eight servicemen killed as a result of a helicopter accident. After the deposed Shah died in Egypt, the hostages were finally released in 1981, on the day of Ronald Reagan's inauguration. This timing is sometimes adduced to argue that the new Islamic Republic feared the strength of the incoming U.S. president, in reality negotiations for the release of the hostages had been months in the making. The exact timing was intended as an insult to Carter, whom Iran despised, rather than indicating a fear of Reagan.

Against this chaotic background, a plebiscite overwhelmingly approved a new constitution. Besides the typical democratic institutions of the elected Majlis (parliament) and president, the Islamic Constitution established two novel centers of power. First, the Supreme Leader (or *faqih*) is the chief theologian, appointed by the 86-member Assembly of Experts. He interprets religious law and acts on behalf of the Hidden Imam, whom many Shi'a believe went into a state of "occultation" in 878. The second unique source of authority is the Council of Guardians, an appointed committee of 12 clergymen charged with ensuring that proposed laws conform to Islam. Given these two innovations, supreme authority lies in Islamic law as interpreted by religious scholars, rather than in the people, and effectively the most important decisions in foreign and domestic affairs are in the hands of the Supreme Leader. The Supreme Leader and Council of Guardians remains the most severe limit to Iranian democracy. During the first decade of revolutionary Iran, Ayatollah Khomeini held the position of Supreme Leader.

The relatively moderate Bani Sadr won the 1980 presidential election, but by 1981, facing impeachment, he fled the country. The clergy's Islamic Republican Party (IRP) then completely dominated government, but faced an uprising by the Islamic socialist *Mujahedin-e Khalq*. The regime suppressed the uprising with great brutality and torture, executing tens of thousands of alleged Mujahedin, who for their part turned to bombings and assassinations, and decimated the IRP leadership in a single blast in August 1981.

The War with Iraq, 1980–1988

Considering Iran to be weakened by a deteriorating economy, political tensions, and international isolation, Iraq invaded Iran's oil-rich southwest in 1980, capturing border cities and driving miles into the country. Within months, however, Iranian troops had reorganized and obtained supplies for its U.S.-made weaponry, some obtained secretly from Israel and financed by oil sales to what Iran has called the "Great Satan," the United States. Revolutionary Guards counterattacked, and largely regained the border by 1982.

Despite major offensives, Iranian forces failed to cross the marshy terrain into southern Iraq. To compensate for Iraq's superior weapons, Iran began human wave attacks with poorly-trained conscripts and young volunteers. However, Iraqi tanks, aircraft, helicopter gunships, and, most distressingly the use of poison gas effectively stalled both conventional attacks and the human wave onslaught.

Notwithstanding high casualties and growing war-weariness, Khomeini rejected any peace that kept the Iraqi president, Saddam Hussein, in office. Desperate, the government secretly worked to release American hostages seized by pro-Iranian groups in Lebanon in exchange for arms and intelligence. Thus equipped, in 1986 troops and the Revolutionary Guards crossed the Shatt al-Arab waterway below Basra and occupied the Faw peninsula, Iran's most successful offensive during eight years of war.

Although Iraq seemed on the verge of collapse, Iranian dominance rapidly faded. Rivalries between the Revolutionary Guards and the military ended their effective cooperation. After the Iran-Contra scandal broke in late 1986, the United States halted vital supplies. In the meantime, Iraq was supported by regional Arab powers and received weapons (including unconventional weapons and dual-use technologies) from a number of European countries and the United States.

Iraq responded to its loss of Faw by widening the conflict. It bombed oil export centers at Kharg Island and tankers hauling Iranian crude oil. When Iranian forces then attacked tankers carrying crude oil from Arab nations, Western nations became more overtly involved and destroyed most of the Iranian navy.

By 1987 defeats followed disasters. Tehran and other cities suffered missile attacks and bombing raids, and Iraqi troops quickly recaptured the Faw peninsula. The Iranian Mujahedin-e Khalq, allied with Saddam's Iraq, "liberated" bits of Iranian territory. Meanwhile, apparent Iranian backing of a Lebanese militant group who hijacked a Kuwaiti airliner isolated Tehran in world affairs. When a U.S. cruiser shot down an Iranian airliner in the summer of 1988, killing all 290 civilian passengers and crew, Iran failed to gain a UN condemnation.

At last, the leadership recognized that continuing the war threatened the Islamic Revolution itself and Iran accepted a ceasefire in August 1988. However, the ceasefire did not bring immediate peace. Disputes remained over the Shatt al-Arab, and repatriation of POWs was soon halted. Some unfortunates lingered in captivity for two decades. The war had a profound and lasting effect on Iranian society. Hundreds of thousands of Iranians had lost their lives and many thousands lived with debilitating injuries, including lasting injuries caused by Iraq's use of chemical weapons. Every village, town,

Ayatollah Ruhollah Khomeini

Iran's Imperial Family in exile, Panama (1980).

suburb, and city could count its war "martyrs," and martyrdom—already a key theme of Shi'a thought and practice—continued to give strength and substance to the revolution.

Domestic Issues under Khomeini

The war with Iraq overshadowed almost eight years of the Islamic Revolution's first decade. After the guns fell silent the next year, debates raged within Iran over the future of the Islamic Revolution. feeling threatened, its leaders lashed out at possible rivals. Thousands of opposition supporters were executed, the savage response by a divided government to opposition viewpoints and to the Mujahedin-e Khalq's invasion. Facing violent insurrection against the Islamic Revolution, the IRP had appealed to religion, ruled by repression, and tortured rivals. Because the IRP opposed any alternative loyalties, the pro-Moscow Tudeh Party joined the Mujahedin as victims. Nevertheless, the often-distorted formalities of a nominally democratic system continued.

Single-party elections to the Majlis brought fewer clergy and other significant changes to its membership. However, the very conservative Council of Guardians repeatedly blocked significant changes, deeming them contrary to Islamic principles. The Council of Guardians also gained a major role in elections through its power to disqualify candidates.

Bitter struggles also deepened within the political elite. "Hardliners," those determined to spread the Islamic Revolution, supported the overthrow of unsympathetic Arab regimes. They also waged a vitriolic struggle against Israel and the United States. By contrast, "pragmatists" wished to use worldwide horror at Iraq's use of chemical weapons to gain closer ties with Western Europe and even the United States, and thus hasten reconstruction.

The scope for rebuilding was vast. At least half a million had died, and tens of thousands were maimed for life. Important cities and industries lay devastated, including one of the largest oil refineries in the world. Contemporary estimates placed the probable cost of reconstruction at $200 billion.

The publication abroad of the novel *The Satanic Verses* strengthened the hardliners. For a variety of reasons, many Muslims found the book offensive. Its author, Salman Rushdie, lightheartedly portrayed the Prophet Muhammad's reference to three idol goddesses as the daughters of Allah as a deliberate attempt to compromise, not a mistaken vision. In addition, Muhammad appears unable to recognize changes his secretary makes to the wording of the angelic message—but to believing Muslims, the Quran is the Word of God, dictated word-by-word to Muhammad and memorized by his followers.

When Ayatollah Khomeini issued a "fatwa," or legal ruling sentencing Rushdie to death—a response likely considered appropriate by many religions before the modern era—he strengthened Iran's hardliners at home. However, the death sentence isolated Iran internationally: any Western sympathy with the anguish of devout Muslims rapidly disappeared in the face of death threats against an author.

In 1989, Ayatollah Ruhollah Khomeini died, just weeks after he disowned his heir-apparent. Nevertheless, succession flowed smoothly. The Assembly of Experts appointed President Ali Khamenei as Supreme Leader. For good measure, given his modest clerical rank, he gained the rank of ayatollah as well. This appointment preserved the unity of mosque and state at the cost of appointing a low-ranking clergyman who had succeeded in politics, to the highest theological position.

Weeks later, with significant rivals blocked from nomination, the speaker of parliament, Ali Akbar Hashemi Rafsanjani, handily won the presidency. The voters also approved constitutional reforms that gave the president control over the cabinet and military.

A shrewd politician, Rafsanjani drew power into his own hands. His priority was reconstruction, and thus an end to Iran's isolation. He negotiated the purchase of Soviet factories and electric generating stations in return for natural gas. He encouraged the release of American hostages in Lebanon and announced that Iran would not export its revolution. He removed several powerful hardliners from the cabinet. However, the regime balanced friendly gestures towards the United States with fiery denunciations of the "Great Satan," and crackdowns on the opposition.

Despite its dramatic impact on politics and the position of women, during the 1990s the revolution remained incomplete. There were successes, especially the roads and electricity that reached many more villages, and higher rural standards of living. Income inequality, having fallen substantially in the immediate aftermath of the revolution, began to creep back up. Khomeini's stated commitment to social justice no longer featured prominently in the revolutionary discourse of the Islamic Republic. Socially and politically, the country stagnated. Despite scheduled elections, the regime limited freedom. It punished journalists and artists whose independent views became too strident. A string of murders and disappearance over a period of a decade cost the lives of over 80 writers, journalists, political activist, and ordinary citizens. The series of car crashes, stabbing, shootings, staged robberies, and drug-induced heart attacks, only came to light in 1998 when five individuals—authors and political activists—were murdered in Tehran over the space of a few weeks. It was "the work of foreign powers," claimed Supreme Leader Ayatollah Khamenei, but the evidence implicated agents from the Intelligence Ministry. The highest-ranked individual to be sentenced for the murders

Iran

committed suicide in prison under circumstances that are considered suspicious. It is widely believed that he was silenced to avoid implicating others.

Hundreds of those who opposed the regime faced charges of drug offenses, many trumped-up or resulting from confessions extracted by torture. Executions continued, often secretly, to frustrate information-gathering by human rights groups, although in some cases public executions occurred. The death penalty was used extensively. It was, and continues to be, imposed for a wide range of often vaguely worded offenses, including political offenses, those relating to freedom of belief, matters of sexual practice or orientation, and for drug-related crimes.

Khatami and the False Dawn of Reform

Against this backdrop, in 1997 Mohammad Khatami, the relatively tolerant Minister of Islamic Guidance in the 1980s, upset analysts' calculations and challenged the leading conservative for the presidency.

Even outwardly, Khatami symbolized changes in society, for he wore both fine European clothes and the black turban that designates descent from the Prophet Muhammad. Khatami was no secularist, his book *Fear of the Wave* proclaimed Islam superior to the West. However, from a study of philosophy, Khatami gained an appreciation of the role of freedom, the benefits of justice, and the importance of civic responsibility. Campaigning on these themes, he attracted wide support: the middle classes, the young who resented personal restrictions, women, and advocates of greater economic freedom. Leftists who desired state control over the economy supported him also, mostly to defeat the conservatives.

The election results were astonishing, particularly in the countryside, where some rural clergy had openly forbidden their followers to vote for Khatami. He won there decisively as well.

Although the conservatives lost the presidency by a landslide, they did not fall from power. The Supreme Leader and other conservatives allied with fundamentalists to block change. Conservatives vetoed reformist nominees to the Assembly of Experts, and several student demonstrators were sentenced to death, without any evidence of a trial. On the streets, fundamentalist street-thugs attacked political rallies organized by moderates.

The most decisive battleground took place in the press. Brash reformist newspapers sprang up and attacked individual officials and narrow-minded policies. For example, *Neshat* questioned the role and authority of the Supreme Leader, Ayatollah Khamenei. Another paper mocked a conservative reappointed to direct the national TV network by publishing a cartoon showing a TV set as a toilet.

The police and conservative judges, beyond President Khatami's control, reacted to the explosion of criticism by arresting editors and closing papers. The leading reformer, Abdollah Nouri, was fined, sentenced to 74 lashes with a braided leather whip, imprisoned for five years, and barred from writing or publishing.

In 1999, police responded violently to student protests, raiding a dormitory at Tehran University, killing one student and injuring many. This provoked student demonstrations in Tehran and Tabriz; when suppressed by police and fundamentalist gangs, the students turned to riots. Although the students had strongly supported Khatami's reform policies, he would not condone the violence, and came out publicly in condemnation of the rioters, causing many of his supporters to turn their backs on him.

Political activity exploded during the Majlis elections of 2000. For the first time, identifiable political parties appeared, rather than factions of the clergy. The most prominent party of the reformist alliance was *Mosharekate* (the Islamic Iran Participation Front) headed by Reza Khatami, the president's brother. Election day provided reformers a two-thirds majority in the Majlis.

However, the reformist victory again aroused conservative militiamen, judges, and other government employees outside the president's authority. With the backing of the Supreme Leader, the police closed every reform newspaper and arrested many journalists. The courts convicted reformers of crimes against Islam that the Majlis could not overturn.

Although his reform program had already failed in many areas, in 2001 Muhammad Khatami won re-election, and once again his victory strengthened the conservatives' determination to enforce strict Islamic rule. Secret trials convicted journalists, old-time nationalists, and even members of parliament for opposing the Islamic Republic. Hardliners attacked peaceful reformist rallies and infiltrated student organizations. Judges sentenced young men to public whippings for drinking alcohol or making social advances at women, heedless of the danger of alienating public opinion, or perhaps knowing that the backlash would fall most heavily upon Khatami.

The reform era effectively ended with the 2004 Majlis elections. The Council of Guardians blocked most reformist candidates, and thus guaranteed conservative victories for nearly half the seats before a single ballot was cast. Along with some other reformist parties, Mosharekate chose to boycott the election. The reformers' defeat left President Khatami an isolated lame duck.

Ahmadinejad's 2005 Victory

The unexpected victor of the 2005 presidential contest was Tehran's relatively inexperienced mayor, Mahmoud Ahmadinejad, a former member of the Revolutionary Guards. A populist, he won the election by appealing to the poor, the unemployed, and others struggling with the weak economy—individuals particularly upset by corruption and possible cuts in subsidies. His other themes, including defiance of Western demands over Iran's nuclear program and opposition to Western culture, also won votes. The appeal of social liberalization seemed, at the time, to be limited to a relatively small, well-off, university-educated class.

In office, Ahmadinejad proved wildly popular with the rural poor, but dangerously incompetent in matters of state. He nominated an oil minister rejected by the conservative Majlis, twice. He proposed admitting women to soccer games, and earned a decisive rejection from religious conservatives worried about allowing women to view male legs and hear the spectators' profanities. He appealed to Iranian nationalism by drawing on popular motifs of the pre-Islamic period, in much the manner of the last shah.

On the streets, yet another crackdown on morality (or, rather, women showing hair and ankles) pleased fundamentalists but angered many university students. Given the president's view of reality, he perhaps feared a cultural "soft revolution" that would weaken the purity of the Islamic Republic. If so, the fear was strengthened by American policy, including $75 million to strengthen democracy in Iran. Several Iranian-American scholars visiting Iran were arrested and released only months later, while a U.S.-born journalist was tried and convicted of spying, but was released. Paranoia became both politics and policy; in this atmosphere Baha'is and others were targeted.

Ahmadinejad's populist economic policies proved particularly bizarre. Benefiting from high international oil prices—oil revenues reached $50 billion in 2006–07—his administration spent even more lavishly, and paid the bill partly by raiding the Oil Stabilization Fund, set aside by law for years of low prices. In addition, the central bank allowed the money supply to grow at 40% per year, stoking inflation.

There were severe consequences: by 2007 housing prices had doubled, and there were shortages of some foods, particularly meat. Inflation reportedly climbed to 30%, but government figures showed less. Gasoline rationing was imposed, despite

Presidents Rafsanjani and Gorbachev in Moscow, June 1989   AP/Wide World Photo

violent protests. During the cold winter of 2008, natural gas and electricity ran short, due in part to unpaid bills for gas imports. The government's responses included contradictory policies like decreeing interest rates below the rate of inflation, and selling shares of government corporations to the poor for a fraction of their value. Politics apparently replaced the laws of economics, at the cost of enormous subsidies.

By 2010, with oil prices at half their 2008 peak, Ahmadinejad struggled with the Majlis to reduce $40 billion of the $100 billion cost of annual energy and food subsidies, with the president arguing, bizarrely, that doing so would cut inflation. Recognizing that such cuts would *raise* inflation and probably ignite social unrest, Parliament hesitated. However, the monthly ration of very cheap gasoline (under U.S. $0.40/gallon) was cut from 20 gallons to 15 per vehicle, saving money on imported gasoline.

Ex-president Mahmoud Ahmadinejad

Foreign Relations: Risking Peace and Prosperity

Republican Iran had historically opposed the West. Ironically, however, the United States and Iran have sometimes shared interests. Both countries faced a common enemy to Iran's east—the Taliban regime in Afghanistan—as well as one to the west, Saddam Hussein's Iraq.

After September 11, 2001, even the hardline Supreme Leader condemned terrorism. The U.S. invasion of Afghanistan in 2001 and Iraq in 2003 benefited Iran enormously. The invasion of Afghanistan ousted the Taliban. This was considered a win in Iran, where concern about the Taliban's treatment of Shi'a minorities, had led Tehran to act as a key supporter of the Northern Alliance against the Afghan regime. Indeed, relationships with the Taliban, strained from the outset, had further deteriorated since 1998, when Taliban forces seized the Iranian consulate in the northern Afghan city of Mazar-i-Sharif and executed Iranian diplomats. On the western border, the U.S. occupation of Iraq brought an end to a hated dictator who had attacked Iran. It halted the persecution of Iraq's non-Sunni majority, and brought Shi'a—believed to be more amenable to Iranian influence on Iraqi politics—to power. However, Iranian policymakers felt threatened by the presence of U.S. ground forces to the east and the west and an American fleet concentrated off the coast. Tehran therefore acted with great caution. Somewhat surprisingly, relations between U.S. occupation authorities and Iran proved workable.

The relationship with the United States took a turn for the worse, however, with the election of Ahmadinejad. He increased the pressure and the tension, out

of conviction as well as to secure popularity among the Iranian masses to whom he appealed. He wrote U.S. President Bush a long meandering letter that was dismissed in Washington as nothing new, but made good propaganda in Iran. The Revolutionary Guards and other organizations armed Lebanon's Hizbullah with the missiles that it showered on northern Israel during their 2006 war. Ahmadinejad repeatedly denied that the Holocaust ever took place. He also promised that Israel would soon disappear (although he claimed to have meant Israel as a political state, rather than the annihilation of its Jewish citizens).

Ambitions for Nuclear Weapons?

Evidence of Iranian duplicity at the nuclear facilities in Arak and Natanz surfaced in 2003, thanks to evidence supplied by an Iranian opposition group. The International Atomic Energy Agency (IAEA) then inspected the facilities. It discovered that in the early 1990s, Iran had launched a secret project to enrich uranium, using Pakistani guidance and equipment from North Korea, China, and elsewhere. The project repeatedly passed uranium hexafluoride gas through centrifuges to concentrate the radioactive U-238.

The Nuclear Non-Proliferation Treaty permits enrichment for peaceful purposes such as low-enriched nuclear fuel (up to 3.5% enriched) and research purposes (up to 20% enriched) but not high-enrichment for nuclear weapons (upwards of 90%). Iranians of all political groups passionately defend their country's right to enrich uranium for fuel. However, nations are obligated to notify the IAEA of enrichment activities, and Iran failed to do this. Moreover, the program hardly seemed peaceful. Its facilities were secret, carefully dispersed, sometimes duplicated, and occasionally built deep underground, obviously to discourage attacks on them. The production of weapons-grade fuel would certainly become a possibility, and Western intelligence analysts speculated that, left undisturbed, Iran could soon complete an atomic bomb.

Facing Western demands to avoid producing weapons-grade uranium, before leaving office President Khatami attempted compromise and diplomacy. Iran halted enrichment during negotiations with European powers, but talks repeatedly floundered. In 2005, President Ahmadinejad authorized resumed enrichment, claiming that Iran gained nothing from negotiations. Soon afterwards, Iran's technicians achieved success with cascading centrifuges, operating some 3,000 simultaneously. They planned for perhaps tens of thousands more. While a 2007 U.S. National Intelligence Estimate concluded

Iran

that Iran had abandoned nuclear weapons production in 2003, many Israelis, Western governments, and Arab states continued to distrust Iran's intentions.

Despite these global anxieties, Ahmadinejad refused to enter serious negotiations. The UN Security Council twice imposed sanctions, eventually overcoming Russian and Chinese reluctance. Concerns grew further in 2009, when reports speculated about advanced work that might produce a warhead small enough to fit inside the existing Sahab-3 missile. Iran declared—tardily—that it had begun work on an additional enrichment plant at Fordo, near Qom. Creative negotiations followed but failed to produce a breakthrough partly because Iran's domestic politics were too weak to reach an international agreement.

As negotiations floundered, Israel's Prime Minister Netanyahu openly threatened a military attack, even though it seems clear that a military strike could only delay a weapon, given a determination to build one. Not to mention that such threats further bolstered any Iranian desire for a nuclear deterrent. A strike would almost certainly plunge the region from Israel to Afghanistan into conflict. Analysts also worried about what political scientists call a "rally around the flag effect," the concern being that a strike would likely unify popular support behind an otherwise unpopular government. In both Israel and the United States, the highest levels of military officials have warned against an attack, although some politicians and interest groups have continued to advocate such action. There are concerns that under the present Trump administration, such interest groups may have found a more sympathetic ear.

The United States, while not ruling out the military option, led other Western powers in applying increasingly stringent economic sanctions, which proved surprisingly effective in both the banking and oil sectors. The sanctions did not halt the economy—their impact was uncomfortable rather than unbearable—but they contributed to a rapid depreciation of the rial, growing inflation, and rising unemployment.

Tehran's determination to continue a suspicious program also led to covert attacks, presumably the work of Israeli and U.S. intelligence agencies. Some physicists disappeared; others were assassinated. Explosions occurred at sensitive military installations. Beyond physical violence, e-warfare attacks included Flame and Stuxnet, the latter an elaborately complex electronic worm designed to target industrial operating systems. Stuxnet in particular will likely hold a unique place in history, it being the first computer virus to cause

The tomb of Darius I, who reigned 521–486 B.C. The ancient kings of Persia had their tombs carved into cliffs so high that they could only be reached by ropes and, thus, could not be easily plundered

significant physical destruction (in this case of nuclear centrifuges).

Against this background, Iran resumed nuclear talks in 2012. With its nuclear negotiator, Saeed Jalili, seeking the presidency, Iran was reluctant to take difficult decisions, however, and did not.

A Stolen Election and Sanctions

The 2009 presidential election campaign witnessed novel political practices, including surprising media freedoms and real one-on-one TV debates. Mir Hossein Mousavi, an early revolutionary who served as prime minister in the 1980s, emerged as the strongest rival to Ahmadinejad's re-election. Mousavi greatly expanded political discourse. He broke tradition by appearing publicly with his wife, Zahra Rahnavard, an accomplished academic, and even demonstrated affection in public by holding her hand. This appealed to women of all ages, and youth were courted by a combination of

Iranian and Islamic themes, including revolutionary-era songs, mixed with internet-based campaigning. Mousavi's campaign platform demanded social reform and changes in the economy.

A high turnout on election day suggested that Mousavi had either won or forced a run-off. However, despite the complication of hand-counting over 40 million paper ballots, Ahmadinejad was declared the winner even before the polls closed. Given his strength in the countryside and among the poor, Ahmadinejad might well have won a fair election. However, the evidence is strong that a group composed of the president's circle, the Revolutionary Guard leadership, and the interior ministry feared a "velvet revolution," one that without violence could reform or even overthrow the Islamic Republic. To defend it, critics alleged they stuffed ballot boxes.

Claims of fraud brought large demonstrations in the streets, often including women, using the color green as a symbol of the opposition. In reprisal, the Basij militia attacked dormitories at Tehran University and protestors on the streets, killing up to 70 people. Gradually, after the Supreme Leader declared the election results were divinely inspired, the Revolutionary Guards and other right-wing Islamic elements of the government re-asserted control, arresting hundreds or even thousands and blocking texting services to disrupt planned demonstrations.

Show trials followed the clampdown, as did reports of the torture, rape, and even the deaths of some prisoners. When later public holidays and the death of Grand Ayatollah Hoseyn Ali Montazeri—a one-time nominated successor of Khomeini and a key critic of the regime—were marked by new demonstrations, some officials made explicit death threats against Mousavi. A decade later, Mousavi and his wife, as well as another opposition candidate who stood for the 2009 elections, Mehdi Karoubi, remain under house arrest.

Ahmadinejad's second term demonstrated the presidency's weakness within the political system. The conservatives who dominated the Majlis generally disrespected the populist and quirky president, who prophesied that Venezuelan President Hugo Chavez will be resurrected alongside Jesus Christ and the hidden imam of Shi'ite Muslims. The Supreme Leader repeatedly intervened to block Ahmadinejad's policies, and publicly forced the resignation of Esfandiar Rahim-Mashaei, whom Ahmadinejad had appointed senior vice president.

Other presidential protégés were arrested on corruption charges. Saeed Mortazavi, a former Tehran prosecutor himself and ally of President Mahmoud Ahmadinejad, was charged as an accessory to the murder of anti-government protesters.

The conservative political establishment clearly acted as part of a deeper struggle for power. The conservative United Front of Principalists won a strong majority over Ahmadinejad's Resistance Front in the 2012 Majlis elections, and its leaders aimed to weaken the president's influence over the 2013 elections. Ayatollah Khamenei eventually intervened in the conflict, ordering the Majlis to stop summoning the president for questioning that might benefit foreign enemies.

As the 2013 presidential elections approached, sanctions imposed by the United States and other Western nations, became increasingly effective. Oil exports fell because of U.S. diplomatic pressure on nations like Japan and India, as well as Europe's own sanctions on imports. The economic warfare continued with prohibitions on insuring cargoes of Iranian oil even to neutral nations, while banking regulations forced banks to choose between obeying U.S. sanctions or risking serious penalties.

The sanctions effectively cut off Iran from the SWIFT system for electronic payments. Money exchangers in Dubai, the transit point for many Iranian imports, became reluctant to trade the rial because American regulations banned payments in them. Some foreign companies ceased operations in the oil fields as Iran struggled to

Nada Sultan, shot dead while joining protests against the 2009 elections

pay for imports, and oil companies found it difficult to pay for Iranian crude oil with international currencies. By some estimates income from oil exports fell over 60%.

The rial slumped in value against the dollar, falling by 90%. Never stable but always growing, the projected budget deficit reached more than $60 billion in late 2012, or 45% of the country's budget.

To keep the economy from slowing severely, the central bank "printed money," thus raising the inflation rate, already under pressure from the much higher costs of imports. Food prices, a politically-sensitive measure, climbed 60% and led to street protests. The expressions of discontent widened, with former president Rafsanjani ruminating, "I don't think the country could have been run worse."

Days before the election, thousands attended the funeral of Ayatollah Jalaluddin Taheri, a dissident cleric. It was the country's biggest anti-government protest for years. Some even dared to chant slogans against the Supreme Leader, calling him a dictator, something that would have previously been unthinkable.

A Centrist Wins, and Then Wins Again

Ahead of the elections, the Guardian Council performed its usual task of removing the most threatening or objectionable candidates from the ballot. This time they disqualified Rafsanjani, all women, a protégé of President Ahmadinejad, and many others. Six candidates remained, four of them hardline conservatives, one reformer, and a long-standing official, Hassan Rouhani, 64, who proclaimed himself a centrist.

Just days before the election, the reformist candidate withdrew on the advice of former president Khatami and threw his support behind Rouhani, the result of reformist surveys that indicated Rouhani was more likely to win. At the same time, Western pundits worried that Saeed Jalili, the inflexible nuclear negotiator and rigid conservative, would likely prove successful. This apparently assured conservatives

Feeroozah bazaar in downtown Tabriz, especially noted for the sale of handwoven rugs
Courtesy of Faranak A. Benz

Iran

that their candidate would win—and among moderates it aroused the reaction "Anyone but Jalili!"

As polls indicated Rouhani's growing strength, many of those intending to boycott the election decided to give even limited democracy another chance. In heavier than expected turnout, Rouhani won just over 50% of the vote, thus avoiding a runoff. Jalili was humiliated, placing third with only 11%.

A cleric with a doctorate from a Scottish university and moderate in both his religion and personal style, Rouhani had been a trusted insider. He once headed the Supreme National Security Council, and he continued as a member. During Khatami's second term, he served as the chief nuclear negotiator, winning respect from European powers and the United States. Nevertheless, as a long-time insider he was distrusted by skeptical foreign commentators who discerned a crafty plot by the conservatives to foist their own safe candidate on the country with the support of gullible moderates and liberals.

Hundreds of thousands of Iranians felt otherwise. They took to the streets on news of the victory, many wearing purple, Rouhani's election color. Others dressed in reformist green. Hopes were raised that Rouhani would oversee the release of those still imprisoned in relation to the 2009 election protests.

President Rouhani symbolized his slogan, "Hope and Prudence," as he addressed the nation's problems. He gained Ayatollah Khamenei's permission to conduct serious negotiations over the nuclear program with Western powers, including the United States, and he promised to resolve the issue within a year. An interim deal, reached quickly, exchanged reduced enrichment activities for a modest decrease in sanctions. Israel called that a "historic mistake," but almost exactly one year after Rouhani's election, diplomats began work on the text of the final accord.

The deal reached in mid-2015 (addressed below) laid the groundwork for a second Rouhani term. In May 2017, the president won re-election in a landslide: with high turnout (more than 70% of Iran's 56 million eligible voters), some 57% cast ballots for Rouhani. For Iran's reformists the scale of this win, constitute a mandate to continue and even expand the moderate policies already in place: opening the Iranian economy to foreign direct investment, gradually expanding personal freedoms, and further opening the political process. The collapse of the nuclear deal, under Trump, has the opposite effect. It is likely to severely cost Rouhani, furthering strengthening the hand of conservative elements and fundamentalists within the Iranian government.

The Iran Nuclear Deal

On July 14, 2015, in Vienna, Austria, the five permanent members of the UN Security Council (Britain, China, France, Russia, The United States) and Germany (the P5+1) signed an agreement with Iran known as the Joint Comprehensive Plan of Action (JCPOA). For Western leaders, the most important text in the document was the last sentence of the first paragraph: "Iran reaffirms that under no circumstances will Iran ever seek, develop or acquire any nuclear weapons."

The issues involved in the talks leading to the agreement were extremely complex, and that an agreement was reached at all represented a triumph over the pessimism of critics around the world—especially within Iran and the United States.

The most important aspect of the deal had to do with what analysts have called "breakout time." Though Iran has always insisted it never sought a nuclear weapon, the 19,000 centrifuges it had amassed in recent decades put the country on a path that would have allowed it to build such weapons if and when the decision were made. Before the agreement, intelligence analysts in the United States estimated that if Iran had decided to go after a bomb, it could have successfully done so—it could have "broken out"—within two to three months.

As part of the JCPOA, Iran agreed to reduce its uranium stockpiles by 98% for a period of 15 years. To that end, it shipped tons of uranium outside of its borders to Russia. Iran also agreed to limit enrichment of the uranium it maintains to 3.67%, well below the medical-grade or research enrichment of 20%. The consequence of all of this, is that Iran's "breakout time" was significantly expanded. After the deal, analysts believed that if Iran were to try to build a bomb, it would take at least a year, with some suggesting it could be considerably longer. Because intelligence experts believed they would be able to detect such action, they were confident this increased breakout time would give the international community time to respond.

In exchange for these concessions, and a host of others, the international community agreed to lift UN, U.S., and EU-imposed sanctions that had crippled Iran's economy in recent years (some estimates suggest that Iran lost more than $160 billion in oil revenue from 2012 to 2015 alone). Iran gained access to more than $100 billion in assets frozen overseas, it was set to again have access to the global financial system, and resumed selling oil on international markets.

In 2018, everything changed. Fulfilling a central campaign promise, on May 9, President Trump pulled the United States out of the JCPOA, overturning Obama's

signature foreign policy achievement while simultaneously alienating some of America's oldest and closest allies, which had urged him not to take that action. Russia and Turkey criticized the U.S. decision, as did Germany and China, which pledged to stay in the accord. Some states—especially in the Middle East—were happy to see the policy reversal. Saudi Arabia, Israel, and the UAE in particular argued that the deal legitimized a bad actor in the region and gave it cover for other nefarious activity. Not incidentally, Iran is a key competitor for regional dominance; any international rehabilitation of Iran's reputation is likely to upset power dynamics in the Middle East. For a year after the United States pulled out of the deal, Iran appeared to be prepared to uphold its end of the bargain, along with the other parties to the agreement. However, secondary sanctions imposed by Washington have made the deal all but unworkable. In June 2019, Iran announced that it would increase enrichment levels to 20% for use in local reactors, but emphasized that Europe still had a chance to save the Obama-era deal. From Iran's perspective, and that of much of the international community, the United States bears responsibility for the failure of a deal that, by all accounts, was working. Today, efforts are underway to revive the nuclear deal, but much of the damage may already be done. Iran has reneged on some of its promises, and with elections looming in the Islamic Republic the opportunity for maneuver on the domestic front has narrowed.

Other Political Issues

From the outbreak of Syria's civil war, Tehran's support for President Assad intensified antagonisms with western nations. However, the rise of Islamic State (IS) united Iranian and U.S. interests in destroying a terrorist group hostile to both Shi'a and non-Muslims.

Although isolated by economic sanctions, Iranian government units (sometimes beyond the control of President Rouhani) played an active role in regional politics. The president and the foreign minister have signaled peaceful interests. The former visited Oman and assured Saudi Arabia and other Gulf Arab states that Iran hoped for good relations. The latter announced a desire for "constructive engagement." However, Iraq and Syria have been the focus of Iranian attempts at regional influence, with military matters at the core.

When the Assad regime seemed close to collapse in 2012, General Qasem Soleimani, commander of the Quds Force (the branch of the Revolutionary Guards that operates outside Iran) was dispatched to Damascus. Iranian assistance to the Syrian regime reportedly included weapons, advisors, and strategy. Soleimani also played an important role in arranging Lebanese Hizbullah fighters and Iraqi Shia militiamen to reinforce the government. Shi'a Afghans, devoid of legal residency status in Iran, were reportedly co-opted into joining the battle for Assad in Syria, often with bribes of money and the promise of citizenship for their families in Iran. In 2015, with the regime again facing defeats on multiple fronts, Iran is said to have dispatched 15,000 Iranian volunteers, something Tehran denies.

When IS seized much of northern Iraq from its Shi'a-dominated government, Iranian advisors and two or three Revolutionary Guard combat battalions were sent to assist the Iraqi army, both on the battlefield and with equipment and training. For many reasons, however, regular army combat troops were not dispatched, although Iran promised volunteers to help defend Shi'a holy places, if necessary.

Tehran's regional role deeply worries the leaders of Arab Sunni states. By 2015, Iran was the most influential foreign power in four Arab capitals—Baghdad, Damascus, Beirut (through Hizbullah), and San'a (after the Shi'a Houthi movement's takeover of the Yemeni capital). Very clearly, Iran (or agencies linked to its government) provided weapons, advisors, and sometimes troops to assist its Arab allies in fights with other Arabs. Sunni concerns were not reduced when an important advisor to Rouhani proclaimed, "All of the Middle East is Iranian." The leading Arab opponent of Iran in the region is Saudi Arabia. The tensions between the two countries have seen the formation of new and sometimes unexpected alliances, some of which are likely to significantly shape the Middle East for years to come.

At home, Rouhani has moved cautiously. He reframed the political debate with the slogan "Moderation is revolutionary, extremism is reactionary." He has spoken at Tehran University about the importance of faculty freedoms and promised the nation that prosperity is the way. Nevertheless, although his opponents within the government and political system are divided, major challenges remain: the release of political prisoners, upholding civil rights, strengthening respect for women, and tackling an economic system bloated by thousands of ex-president Ahmadinejad's appointees.

Moreover, to date, either the president's inclinations or his actual authority have fallen short of achieving what many of his supporters desired. Mir Hossein Mousavi and Mehdi Karroubi, opposition candidates in the 2009 presidential election, remain under arrest. Social reforms have either stagnated entirely or happen at infinitesimally slow rates, leaving Iran's

bulging youth population frustrated. Corruption scandals have rocked all levels of government and the private sector. It has been suggested that as much as $30 billion of $40 billion in national export revenues has been moved out of the country in a one year period over 2018 and 2019. At the same time, the number of Iranians living in absolute poverty has increased steadily.

Culture: More than half the population lives in the 25 largest cities. An increasing number of urban men work in industry and government, a contrast to the past when most were merchants, artisans, or casual laborers. Despite the restrictions placed on them, many women also find employment, and there is even a taxi service in Tehran by women for women. Life in the towns and cities is generally crowded, and wages for the less skilled cover little more than life's necessities.

Most of the rural population lives in small communities, whether peasants who farm in the Elburz and Zagros Mountains, or nomads who live in goat-hair tents that are carried from place to place as they wander in search of pasture for their flocks. These people are as hardy as their life is hard, and generally as hospitable as their environment is inhospitable.

Nearly all Iranians follow the Shi'a sect of Islam, although there are significant Sunni populations, most notably the Kurds of the Zagros Mountains, the Baloch of Sistan and Baluchestan Province on the border with Afghanistan and Pakistan, and the Arabs of Khuzistan, bordering Iraq and the Persian Gulf. Historical and theological differences divide Shi'a Muslims from the orthodox, or Sunni, Muslims who form the great majority in the Islamic world. Relations between Iran and Afghanistan, for instance, are tempered by the fact that most Afghans are Sunni Muslims.

Although Shi'a Muslims make pilgrimages to Mecca as do other Muslims (see Saudi Arabia: Culture), they also have important shrines in Iran, particularly at Meshed, where their eighth Imam, Ali Reza, was buried. Many also journey to Najaf and Karbala in Iraq, holy cities sacred by virtue of the association with Ali, the first Shi'a Imam (and the Sunni's fourth Caliph), and his two sons. The division of Islam between Shi'a and Sunni goes back to a dispute over whether Ali and his sons, or the Umayyad clan were the rightful successors to Muhammad as rulers of the Muslim community (see Historical Background).

A religious hierarchy dominates Shi'a Islam. Simple teachers and the preachers at Friday prayers in rural villages form the bottom rank. Above them are judges of religious law, then mujtahids who interpret

the law, ayatollahs, and grand ayatollahs. At the top, the last (of twelve) Shi'a Imam has remained hidden for nearly a thousand years.

Iran is a country famous for its architectural monuments, some in ruin, like those of the Achaemenid Empire, but some still standing, such as the mosques of Isfahan. Museums have also been established to display antiquities, representing every period of the country's history.

During the 1970s, the monarchy funded a rapid expansion of colleges and universities. However, the quality of education declined, as new institutions struggled to develop traditions, and students valued degrees for job placement rather than learning. Iranian education also suffered widely from a unique defect: students who demanded high grades threatened professors by hinting at connections with SAVAK, the shah's dreaded secret police.

The revolution saw the shutting of some schools, closing of universities, and the banning of women from many teaching positions (and from much of public life in general). However schools have since expanded dramatically in rural areas, the education of girls is expected and encouraged (with female teachers re-employed in girls' schools) and universities were re-opened in the early 1980s (having been ideologically "purged").

The Iranian national school curriculum clearly forms an important part of Islamic socialization. From the earliest grades students are taught religious precepts. History lessons emphasize the role of Islam and the Islamic Revolution, while downplaying or actively disparaging Iran's imperial history. Islamic studies comprises one component of the university entrance exam (*konkur*).

Competition for university places in Iran is fierce, with public universities accepting only 10% of applicants. Furthermore, university education is no guarantee of a job; with the country experiencing record high levels of unemployment, it is estimated that over 40% of university educated Iranians fail to find a position upon graduation.

During the Pahlavi era, many middle- and upper-class Iranians adopted external aspects of Western culture, from stylish clothing to skiing, parties, and rock music. Religious conservatives and the traditional poor opposed and resented these changes; with the Islamic Revolution, such Western customs ended, at least in public. Most obviously, new laws forced women to wear the modest Islamic attire, notably the *chador* (a dark-colored encompassing outer-garb) or at a minimum a headscarf and coat, but a much larger realm of Western culture was suppressed, including magazines and music. Khomeini approved instrumental

Iran

music only just before his death, so symphonic music may now be enjoyed, but many clergy consider rock music or female vocals sinfully enticing. Other regulations prohibit unmarried men and women from walking or dining together in public. While two girls may hitch rides from passing automobiles, unmarried couples ought not ride alone in a car, especially after dark.

Living their entire lives after the revolution, many young people now dislike these strict social controls. Risking heavy penalties if caught by revolutionary committees, some students and other young adults enjoy parties and dancing with members of the opposite sex. Pale lipstick worn by coeds in university classes, colored headscarves, and brightly colored track shoes likewise suggest widening desires for a relaxation of social regulation.

Despite continuing to suffer from controls over the movie industry, Iran's directors still produce impressive films. *Separation*, by Asghar Farhadi, won the Academy Award for best foreign language film in 2012. *Taxi*, by Jafar Panahi, won the 2015 Golden Bear for best film at the Berlin International Film Festival. But regulations prohibited Panahi from travelling abroad to receive his prize.

Advancing technology often presents fundamentalists with additional targets. In the 1980s parliament debated banning video-recorders until it became obvious that leading politicians and clergy found them useful. When a western company began broadcasting TV programs to Iran by satellite in 1995, the government banned satellite dishes, thus placing would-be TV addicts at the mercy of inspectors from the local revolutionary committees. In recent years, Iran has tried to jam satellite broadcasts, and under President Ahmadinejad the government cracked down on illegal dishes. More recently, crackdowns have encompassed new forms of Internet technology and online media. The Iranian government uses speed throttling (limiting available bandwidth) in order to slow internet connections and stymie communication. Tens of thousands of websites are blocked under Iran's strict censorship laws. During times of civil unrest Internet access is often entirely blocked or severely restricted. The Iranian government has attempted, with limited success, to create their own national Internet, thereby limiting Iranian access to the World Wide Web.

Drug Addiction

Probably the most severe and growing social difficulty is the swelling population of drug addicts. The numbers are startling, and on a percentage basis place Iran as the highest in the world. Approximately 20% of all adults and teenagers probably use hashish or narcotics in one

form or another, more than one million of them using opium and heroin. Given its lengthy borders, Iran had a drug problem before the revolution. In the 1980s the problems worsened, with heroin largely replacing opium, and the number of addicts growing rapidly.

As addicts lost the label "miserable persons" and became "enemy infiltrators in society," officials predictably blamed the problem on the American CIA and the Mafia. Possession of more than 30 grams of heroin became a capital offense; hundreds were executed. All addicts were required to register, and many were dispatched to labor camps in distant desert regions to break the habit. Drug-related convictions accounted for 70% of Iranian prisoners. These harsh measures failed, and with an additional 600,000 users each year, three-quarters of them women, a variety of social agencies provide counseling, assistance, and methadone. Drug trafficking remains a capital punishment.

Such large-scale use of narcotics points to more than cheap supplies from Afghanistan. Like the riots that followed World Cup soccer games, narcotics usage indicates a society whose young are unemployed and bored. Lacking jobs and entertainment, many have lost faith in the future, a truly astounding phenomenon for a religious republic.

Population Growth

Traditionally, Iranian families arranged marriages for their teenaged daughters and provided a dowry of furniture for the new household. The *mehr*, a payment from the husband to his wife, that can be released on demand or in the event of divorce, is negotiated between the family.

In the 1980s, reflecting revived Islamic cultural values, the regime's desire for more children, and the circumstances of war, the birth rate approached world record levels and the population grew at 4% annually. However, planners convinced Ayatollah Khomeini of the enormous economic and social pressures such growth would create. He approved family planning shortly before his death, and in 1989 Ayatollah Khamenei declared that birth control was not against Islam. By the mid-1990s all forms of contraception (but not abortion) were available—and free. As a result, the rate of population growth has fallen dramatically to approximately 1%. Indeed, Iran was commonly held up as an example of a country that had implemented successful, non-coercive population policies. In 2012, the government reversed its previous position, and sought to encourage larger families through targeted policy changes. However, shifting attitudes towards women's education and the despair felt by younger Iranians about the future prospects of their country, means that such policy changes will likely meet with limited success.

Even as families shrink in size, the population is set to continue to grow rapidly, a consequence of the 1980s baby boom. Today society faces the challenge of educating, employing, marrying, and otherwise incorporating the children of the 1980s and 1990s into adult society. Young and restless, these adults tend to present challenges to hardline populism and philosophies.

Economy: With a large population and fertile lands, thanks to its abundant and varied mineral deposits Iran possesses

Demonstrators of all ages proclaim that victory belonged to Mousavi, Tehran, June 2009

great industrial potential. It also benefits from large oil resources and natural gas deposits so vast they rank second only to Russia's. The earliest crude oil producer in the region, in recent years it has ranked as the second largest oil exporter in the Middle East, after Saudi Arabia.

Not surprisingly, economic policy in the country revolves around two issues: first, petroleum, the greatest producer of foreign exchange, and second, agriculture.

Agriculture always played an impressive role in Iranian history. The farms vary greatly, from the well-watered lands near the Caspian Sea to plots in the mountains and plateau that depend for irrigation on systems of underground channels.

Generally, life for farmers has meant working another's land. Until Mohammed Reza's land reform program in 1963, some 10,000 of the country's villages had belonged to landlords each owning five or more villages. Indeed, a few families and religious endowments dominated the lives of farmers across the country. While unsuccessful in satisfying the hopes of the peasants, the shah's land reform broke the power of large farming families. It improved the supply of credit, seeds and agricultural techniques. Dams permitted the irrigation of additional lands, and new roads reduced transportation costs. These changes encouraged large-scale commercial agriculture, especially near rivers in the west.

All land reform proposals in Iran face a difficult choice, between equality and economic growth. Because only some 10% of Iran can be farmed, redistributing the land to all existing peasants would create minuscule, inefficient farms. But without redistribution, the great differences in wealth cause political stress, and industry and services are not growing enough to absorb the thousands who leave farms every year.

Although demands for land reform had played a major role in the Islamic Revolution, initial attempts to seize large landholdings were blocked by the Council of Guardians, whose conservative clergy averred that the Quran upheld private property rights. Only 3% of the nation's farmland was distributed during the republic's first decade. However, feeling threatened by calls to seize their lands, the owners of large farms cautiously stopped investing in irrigation and equipment, or even repairing vital irrigation channels.

Predictably, farm output fell. At the same time, the population rose by 3%–4% per year, one of the highest rates in the world. Until 1970, Iran had exported surplus food, but during the last years of the Iran–Iraq war Iran spent over one-third of its oil earnings to *import* food. Millions of refugees from Afghanistan and Iraq added to the shortages.

Fishing is a substantial industry in the Persian Gulf and Arabian Sea. However, it is sturgeon from the Caspian Sea whose eggs (caviar) carry the epithet "black gold." Unfortunately, pollution in the closed sea, combined with legal and illegal overfishing, threatens the long-term future of this delicacy. Despite the annual release of over 20 million young fish, Caspian sturgeon may become extinct in the next decade.

The country's non-petroleum mineral resources include lead, chrome, and turquoise, which are exported, while coal and iron are mined for domestic use, along with some sulfur and salt.

Although handicrafts are losing importance, Isfahan, Tabriz, and other cities remain famous for their metalwork, carpets, ceramics, and textiles. The best carpets come from the Safavid period, but those of recent manufacture deserve fame—and after oil are often the most important export.

Under the Shah's rule, Iran followed a policy of rapid economic expansion and industrialization. It exported vast quantities of oil to pay for large development projects as well as consumer goods and sophisticated weapons. Using its oil revenues on a massive scale, Iran contracted with foreign companies to build and operate entire factories. A number of different cars and trucks were assembled in the country, and dozens of other industries were founded. By 1978, the number of industrial employees reached two million. Iran's first modern steel mill was constructed in Isfahan, with technical assistance and a large loan from the Soviet Union. By the mid-1990s the country actually exported significant quantities of iron and steel.

The policy achieved one of the world's highest rates of economic growth, and the middle class prospered. Unfortunately, other results included inflation and resentment by the unskilled urban poor and landless peasants, who migrated to the cities in search of work.

The Economy after 1979

Despite many hopes, the Islamic Revolution provided little economic progress, though it greatly changed business conditions. It quickly nationalized the oil industry, thirty years after Mossadeq's failed attempt. It also took over many large manufacturing firms, and the entire banking and insurance industries, partly because many owners had fled.

However, because of their divisions over the role of private property, especially in agriculture, the ruling clergy failed to establish the economic rules of the game. Leftist clergy advocated socialism, and blamed inflation and shortages on hoarding by private businessmen. Conservatives claimed that Islam protected private

ownership. The government simply intervened to suit the needs of the moment. Investors, fearing eventual confiscation, avoided long-term projects and favored trade. For those with access to foreign exchange, it became far more profitable to import than to manufacture in Iran. The result was devastating: manufacturing output fell to only 40% of capacity.

Oil policy changed significantly in the Islamic Republic. Initially, the revolutionaries favored only small quantities of exports, thinking that imports implied dependence on Western nations and Japan, and encouraged imitation of their lifestyles. However, the need for revenue for the regime, the military, and economic development reversed that perspective.

One particular difficulty facing the oil industry has been U.S. sanctions, with some in effect for many years. Sanctions block foreign subsidiaries of U.S. oil companies from assisting Iran's industry or providing American technology. They have also penalized any foreign company that spends significant funds to develop Iran's petroleum resources. In step with Iran's nuclear enrichment, the United States increased its sanctions activities, and by 2007 several major projects languished, with foreign companies negotiating for future options but avoiding involvement at the time.

After 2003, world oil prices set new records almost annually, and the country's petroleum industry operated at full capacity. The resulting earnings greatly benefited the budget, and the national economy grew at rates of 5% or more annually, twice the rate of population growth and fast enough to begin to provide jobs for the millions of unemployed. Moreover, the Majlis finally enacted economic reforms. It slashed some business taxes and simplified foreign investment law. Iran also announced a unified foreign exchange rate. As confidence in the economy expanded, wealthy Iranians living overseas invested again in their homeland, even though many fundamental issues remained unsolved. The stock market rose rapidly.

After the election of Mahmoud Ahmadinejad in 2005, smart money feared foreign controls or other difficulties ahead and it flowed out of the country. Economic policies took several drastic turns, including interest rates below the inflation rate. Sanctions spurred by Iran's nuclear program contributed to an already difficult economic situation.

Economic conditions only deteriorated further in Iran over the course of Ahmadinejad's two terms in office. His re-election in 2009 under very contested circumstances put Iran on course to face even stronger sanctions from the international community. By 2012, these were biting

Iran

and the Iranian economy suffered as a result. By 2015, the Europeans, Chinese, and Russians were all on board, doing what it took economically to force Iran to the negotiating table and to eventually secure a deal (the JCPOA).

The Iran nuclear deal changed the economic outlook for the country substantially, which was, in part, what it was designed to do. As noted above, President Obama's hope was that Iranian integration into the international community—including the gradual normalization of economic relations with world powers—would convince Tehran that the benefits of a strong economy and good foreign relations far outweighed those of a nuclear program. European companies in particular poured investment into the new market, and there were signs that ordinary Iranians were beginning to benefit.

In 2018, this trajectory was halted abruptly. U.S. and European companies have largely suspended operations in Iran in order to comply with U.S law. Investment in Iran ceased almost entirely, as foreign companies failed to work around sanctions. EU companies stand to lose significantly more from recent developments than American companies. In 2017, the EU exported some $13 billion in goods to Iran, a 66% increase from 2015, which represented about one hundred times more than U.S. exports to Iran that year.

Reverberations from the collapse of the nuclear deal are playing out in other ways as well—and in fact were doing so even before the announcement. In the months leading up to the withdrawal, with threats and rumors emerging from the White House, Iran's rial lost roughly a quarter of its value against the U.S. dollar. As of mid-2018, inflation in Iran hovered around 8% as the country faced a severe credit crisis. Unemployment was around 11%. The International Monetary Fund predicted Iranian GDP growth of 4.3% before the United States' withdrawal, up from just 1.5% in 2015 when sanctions were in full force, that forecast has been drastically revised, to a loss of 3%.

A year on, there was little to celebrate. Iran has continued to grapple with the pandemic and has had minimal success implementing a vaccination program. Recurrent waves of infections have had a profound social and economic impact and, with elections around the corner, the political implications of the past eighteen mo this remain unclear.

Present and Future Challenges

Throughout 2019 protests simmered across Iran, driven by environmental pressures, economic stagnation, and the social demands of a youthful population led by an aged cleric. However, the spark that ignited the largest protests since the Iranian revolution, was a gasoline price hike that saw prices increase 50% overnight. In the context of severe economic stress, in part a consequence of reimposed sanctions but more broadly a symptom of long-term economic mismanagement, resentments bubbled over. Efforts to paint the protestors as "foreign saboteurs" and "bandits" was largely unsuccessful, and what began as a peaceful act of civil disobedience devolved into violence, as protestors were beaten, shot at, and arrested en masse.

The Iranian authorities have, in recent years, sought to pin anti-government sentiment on a single individual—a US-based Iranian journalist, Masih Alinejad, whose Facebook page is titled "My Stealthy Freedom," emerged as a leader of the Iranian women's rights movement for a new generation. While Alinejad is undoubtedly a significant voice in Iran's broad pro-democracy movement, it is clear that domestic, grassroots opposition to the regime will only continue to expand as economic pressures bite and corruption scandals are exposed.

Although street protests have dissipated with the threat of coronavirus, bitterness about government mismanagement of the crisis may well result in further consolidation of anti-government sentiment over the coming year.

Iran emerged as an early global hotspot of Covid-19. Even as the first cases emerged in the city of Qom, the government downplayed the threat. Sensitive parliamentary elections were looming. In the end, it was not the threat of coronavirus but the barring of reformist candidates and the growing sense that little change could be achieved from within an increasingly corrupt political system that led to wide boycotts of the election. While the Iranian government has denied any coverup of the coronavirus crisis, Iranians have questioned the regime's management of the pandemic. As movement from China was restricted globally, flights between Iran and China remained open. Contradictory statements regarding appropriate quarantine measures created confusion. Iran's generally poor economic situation, a patchy welfare capacity, and a health system suffering under the impost of sanctions, saw failures in processes of testing and efforts to enforce self-isolation. While the government encouraged Iranians to stay home, serious quarantine efforts could not be mounted, given the devastation that sanctions have wreaked on Iran's economy. As the Iranian year drew to a close in late March 2020, war rhetoric was replaced with pleas to lift sanctions as a humanitarian gesture. With thousands of infections, hundreds of deaths, and a cloud of uncertainty hanging over the economic future of the country, Iran's usually festive New Year period was decidedly gloomy.

Iran will face a number of important tests in the near future. Supreme Leader Ayatollah Ali Khamanei is now 80, and his health seems to be deteriorating. His death or incapacity could easily provoke dissent if the process of choosing his successor is not considered legitimate.

Whoever succeeds Khamenei will take control of a country that is deeply fractured. The supreme leader presides over a political system in which Iranians have little faith and upholds an ideology that for large swaths of the population has long lost its appeal.

The relationship between Iran and the United States remains at a low ebb. When Iran's top general, Qasem Soleimani, was assassinated in a US targeted drone strike in Iraq in January 2020, the Middle East—indeed, the entire world—held its breath, anticipating war. A ballistic missile attack on a US base in Iraq generated no casualties (but a number of reported traumatic brain injuries). Several analysts suggested that the lack of casualties was an intentional ploy by Tehran to de-escalate the situation. Hours later—apparently anticipating US strikes on Iranian soil—Iran mistakenly shot down a passenger jet, killing all 176 on board. While some of the war rhetoric has been toned down, as Tehran appeals for the lifting of sanctions in the face of the coronavirus pandemic and with a change of US administration, there is little reason to suppose that relations between Tehran and Washington will thaw in the short term

The Republic of Iraq

In April 1995, Iraqis protested the proposed UN Oil for Food Program. The next year, they celebrated it

Area: 169,235 square miles (438,317 square kilometers).

Population: 40 million.

Capital City: Baghdad (6.7 million).

Climate: Extremely hot in summer, moderately cool in winter; rain is limited, falling in winter. The northern mountains are colder, with snow in winter.

Neighboring Countries: Iran (East); Kuwait (Southeast); Saudi Arabia (South); Jordan (West); Syria (Northwest); Turkey (North).

Time Zone: GMT +3.

Official Language: Arabic (and in northern districts, Kurdish).

Other Principal Tongues: Farsi (Persian).

Ethnic Background: Mixed; mostly Arab (80%) or Kurdish (nearly 20%), plus some Chaldeans and Persians.

Principal Religions: Shi'a Islam (55–65%), Sunni Islam (30–35%), Christianity (less than 3%; mostly Chaldeans and Assyrians), some Yazidis, and a very small number of Mandaeans.

Chief Commercial Products: Petroleum, natural gas, petrochemicals, textiles, and cement.

Main Agricultural Produce and Livestock: Wheat, barley, rice, tomatoes, watermelons, grapes, dates, rice, cotton, sheep, goats, cattle, and chickens.

Major Trading Partners: The United States, South Korea, China, Turkey, and India.

Currency: Iraqi Dinar (1 dinar = 1000 fils, obsolete).

Former Colonial Status: British occupation and Mandate (1918–1932).

National Day: October 3 (1932; independence from Britain); July 14 (1958; Republic Day, overthrow of the Hashemite monarchy).

Chief of State: Barham Salih, President.

Head of Government: Mustafa Al-Kadhimii, Prime Minister.

National Flag: Three equal horizontal stripes of (top to bottom) red, white and black, with *Allahu Akbar*, "God is Great" on the white stripe in Kufic script.

GDP: $197.72 billion.

GDP per capita: $5,114.

Modern-day Iraq stretches across the birthplace of human civilization. Ancient Mesopotamia, the land "of the two rivers," flourished because the Tigris and the Euphrates provided water. Without the rivers, nearly the entire country would be desert. About 12% of the land is arable.

The two rivers flow southeast across an alluvial plain, between the rocky desert of the southwest and the Zagros Mountains along the northern and eastern borders.

Except on the slopes of the mountains there is little annual rainfall, ranging from 6 inches (152 millimeters) in the south to 15 inches (381 millimeters) in the northern plains. Most of the water in the rivers comes from rain or melting snow in the mountains of northern Iraq and southern Turkey.

The people differ as much as the land. A handful of Arab nomads (*badu*) still roam the deserts. In the southern marshes upstream from Basra a few *Ma'dan* remain. They inhabit reed huts, raise water buffalo, and travel by boat. In most of central Iraq farmers live along the rivers, their tributaries and canals, while Kurdish mountain villages dot the heights and valleys in the north.

In recent decades people from all parts of the nation have migrated to Baghdad in search of work. They represent all the linguistic, religious, and social variety of the country. It is this nationwide diversity, and now the absence of Saddam's iron-fisted central authority, which contributes to the difficulty in achieving political agreement.

History: The creation of a single, united government over the region is a modern innovation. In this land of the two rivers, some of the first cities evolved, and

Iraq

writing was invented. Here the caliphs of Islam heard the *Arabian Nights*. After serving as the capital of a vast Islamic empire, Iraq suffered invasions, the most devastating by the Mongols in the 13th century. In 1258, the Mongols swept in from the east. The city of Baghdad was razed and most of its population was killed or forced into exile. Untended irrigation canals silted up; equally seriously, drainage canals that remove salt deposits from the fields disappeared. Today, over two-thirds of the irrigable land lies idle, sparkling in the sunshine but barren because of the high salt content of the soil.

For four centuries the Ottoman Empire ruled the region (1554–1918), and after decades of intermittent warfare, it established the border with Iran. It administered Iraq as the three provinces of Mosul (or Musil), Baghdad, and Basra. Beyond controlling the main towns, the governors attempted to maintain order among the often unruly and usually autonomous tribes. As European nations seized control of trade in the Indian Ocean and the Far East, commerce through Iraq stagnated, and little development took place. Located on the fringe of the empire, the provinces generally received few improvements. Modern schools, hospitals, and newspapers only began to appear around the turn of the 20th century, and steamboats then began regular service on the Tigris.

When the Ottoman Empire entered World War I as a German ally, British Indian troops landed in Basra and slowly moved inland. They found the population generally unsympathetic or even hostile. Politically conscious Arabs, Kurds, Turkmen, and others commonly supported the Ottoman Empire or desired greater autonomy within it. Iraq as a nation—or even as a notion—did not exist. However, a small number of army officers promoted the newly-conceived idea of an independent Arab nation encompassing the Ottoman-ruled areas of Mesopotamia, Syria, and Palestine.

By the end of the war in 1918, British troops occupied most of the country, and shortly afterwards added the province of Mosul, valuing it and the region around Kirkuk because of the presence of oil deposits. The future was uncertain: in the

King Faisal I (1885–1933)

secret Sykes-Picot Agreement of 1916, France had pledged to support British rule over Iraq. However, in exchange for Arab support under the leadership of Sharif Husayn of Mecca, Britain also had promised to recognize the independence of Arab lands, except the Syrian coast and Basra.

After most inhabitants rapidly recognized that Britain meant to rule the territories under the guise of a mandate from the League of Nations, a nationalist, anti-British uprising spread rapidly. To quell the rebellion, Britain sought a political solution as well as military victory, and it successfully supported the claim to the throne of Prince (Amir) Faisal, son of Sharif Husayn and commander of the Arab forces who had fought in Syria.

The new nation adopted the Arabic name for the southern part of the country, al-'Iraq, for the entire state. The state's inhabitants, however, were not solely Arab. Kurdish tribesmen dominated the northern mountains, where Britain desired influence because of oil deposits.

As a Hashemite, King Faisal traced his descent from the Prophet Muhammad through Hasan, son of Ali, the fourth Caliph (and first Shi'a Imam). He therefore brought a semblance of unity to the Arab population with its Shi'a majority but Sunni ruling class. Having learned from the loss of his throne in Syria in battle with the French, Faisal worked to gain

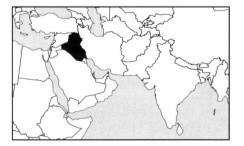

Iraq

independence by compromise with Britain. In 1932, Iraq received its formal independence and became a member of the League of Nations.

Kurdish Rebellions

Even before it received formal independence, Iraq faced rebellion from the Kurds. Hardy and brave, but isolated from commerce and education, Kurdish tribes for centuries had maintained dialects of their Indo-European language. Lacking sea access or rail transport, and little influenced by democracy and nationalism, Kurds populated the eastern lands of the Ottoman Empire as well as western Iran. The Kurds had the misfortune to inhabit the region where three great civilizations (Arab, Persian, and Turkish) came together. Ruled lightly from distant capitals through tribal leaders who often challenged each other, the Kurds received little attention. They were simply Muslim tribesmen in Muslim Empires. After they adopted Sunni Islam, their very names often became Islamic or Arab. Today, the Kurds constitute the largest nation without a state in the world.

Because of Britain's desire to control the oil-possessing regions of Kirkuk and Mosul, after World War I these areas were joined to Iraq, despite their Kurdish majority. Although Turkey and Iran each contained more Kurds than did Iraq, its Kurds formed a large and distinct community that dominated the hills and mountains, with the Arabs centered on the plains.

In every country where they formed a significant group, the Kurds revolted, starting with the British in Iraq in 1923. A major Kurdish uprising lasted from 1930 to 1933, coinciding with Iraq's independence. Its leaders were later confined to non-Kurdish parts of the country, or fled to the Soviet Union. During World War II, a second rebellion was briefly successful. After the war, its leader, Mustafa Barzani, continued the struggle for Kurdish independence by creating, with Soviet sympathy, a republic around the city of Mahabad in Iranian Kurdistan. After years of exile in the Soviet Union, Barzani led later revolts against Iraqi regimes, until supply lines were cut-off by Iran in a concessionary gesture to Iraq's leadership. Shortly after, Barzani along with tens of thousands of his followers crossed the border into Iran. He died in exile. However, his son returned to Iraq and served as the President of the Iraqi Kurdistan region between 2009 and 2017.

Foreign governments often sympathized with Iraq's efforts to transform its Kurdish population into orderly civilians. However, granting Kurdish demands would have threatened oil revenues, and growing nationalism blocked any government in Baghdad from ceding its territory. On the other hand, Iraq generally lacked the military force to control a fierce and individualistic people living in rugged mountains with few roads. Periods of calm and order, therefore, proved the exception.

An Independent State

After the formalities of 1932, many Iraqis recognized that they were not really independent. British military bases remained, British and French companies controlled the Iraq Petroleum Company, and British advisors played very influential roles in government. Restrictions on free elections always seemed to favor those Iraqi politicians closely tied to Britain. On the other hand there was the beginning of a modern school system. Iraqis also gained experience in affairs of state, in politics, administration, and in modern military practices. A modern economy began to develop beside traditional crafts and agriculture, aided significantly by exports of oil after 1934.

Military coup d'état followed attempted coup between 1936 and 1941. The final attempt to seize power was led by Rashid Ali Gailani, a bitter opponent of Britain and a Nazi sympathizer during World War II. With the help of the Arab Legion from Transjordan, Britain quelled the revolt and reinstated friendly officials. The new government declared war on the Axis in 1943 and thereby became a charter member of the United Nations.

Nationalism developed even more during the post-war years with the spread of formal education. During the 1940s and 1950s, a veteran Arab nationalist, Nuri Said, generally controlled parliamentary affairs on behalf of the throne—and in the opinion of many Iraqis, on behalf of the British. The rising popularity of Egyptian President Gamal Abdul Nasser and Arab nationalism isolated Nuri, as did the monarchy's policy of investing oil revenues in long-term projects that favored wealthy landowners.

On July 14, 1958, a day regarded by many Iraqis as their real day of independence, a lightning but bloody revolution by Iraqi army units overthrew the cabinet, the monarchy, and direct foreign influence. King Faisal II and dozens of hated officials, among them Nuri Said, were killed by troops and mobs. The new Republic of Iraq turned sharply neutral in international affairs and renounced treaties with Britain.

The leader of the revolt, General Abd al-Karim Qasim, proclaimed Iraq democratic and united with the Arab world. In reality,

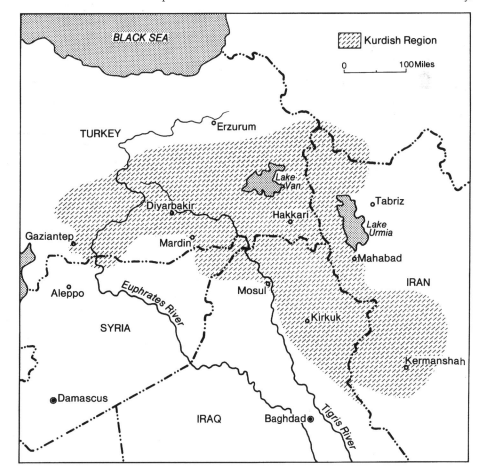

Iraq

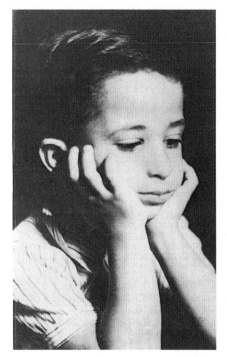

King Faisal II (1935–58)
The six-year-old monarch, 1941

democracy and unity, whether regional or domestic, eluded Iraq under Qasim. A political amnesty allowed exiles to return, including the Kurdish leader Mustafa Barzani. Land reform began. However, Qasim soon clashed with his fellow revolutionaries, especially those who desired rapid unity with Syria and Egypt under Gamal Abdul Nasser. Thus, instead of uniting Iraq with other Arab states, the revolution created new rivalries between it and Egypt.

Faced with assassination attempts and an army mutiny, Qasim turned for help to the Soviet Union and the Communist Party of Iraq. However, Qasim grew isolated, though remaining popular among some of the poor for his spending on housing. He also decreed the equality of women before the law, thus initiating great improvements in women's status.

In 1963 nationalist military officers seized power. To seal their victory, they executed Qasim and displayed his body on television. Nevertheless, his legacy to republican Iraq remained: military rule, government control of the economy, Kurdish rebellion, and claims to Kuwait.

Iraq under the Ba'th

In 1968, one year following the dramatic Israeli military victory that discredited many Arab armies and governments, a nearly bloodless military coup brought the Ba'th Party to power. Its members gained total control over the Revolutionary Command Council (RCC), the chief governing institution. Generally composed of officers, the RCC included a significant young civilian, Saddam Hussein. A former plotter against Qasim, he directed internal security for the party and now the regime.

Socialist and Arab nationalist rather than communist in its philosophy, the Ba'thist government strongly opposed the United States because of its support for Israel. It also regarded pro-American Iran as a prospective enemy, not least because Iran claimed the eastern half of the Shatt al-Arab waterway near Basra.

The new government dealt harshly with individuals and groups remotely capable of rivaling the regime, often discrediting them as alleged agents of foreign countries. Accusations of espionage flowed freely. Among those executed publicly were Jewish leaders, Islamic fundamentalists, and communists. Fierce disputes between the Ba'thists ruling Syria and those in Iraq increased the natural rivalry of the two countries. Nevertheless, in 1973 Iraqi tank units joined Syrian troops fighting Israel on the Golan Heights.

In 1979 Saddam Hussein, for years the real center of power, became simultaneously President, Chairman of the Revolutionary Command Council, and Secretary-General of the Ba'th Party. Saddam considered his clan from Tikrit the only trustworthy group. Some clansmen held high office; others played key roles in the country's several secret police and intelligence services. Rivals within the party were purged (and often murdered), while the public suffered kidnappings and assassinations.

Despite the dictatorship, oil revenues meant economic progress. After decades of production-disrupting disputes with foreign oil companies, Iraq gained total control of its oil production in 1973. Later that year, OPEC raised the price of crude oil four-fold (see Black Gold: The Impact of Oil). Petroleum revenues financed both economic prosperity and military equipment. Living standards rose, education expanded, and new industries and housing multiplied. Young Iraqis flocked to cities for jobs in industry and government offices.

In 1975, a compromise with the Shah of Iran saw the southeastern boundary shifted from the eastern shore to the center of the Shatt al-Arab. In return, Iran ceased supplying weapons to the Iraqi Kurds, who once again had risen in revolt under Mustafa Barzani. The rebellion rapidly collapsed amid deportations and executions.

A second difficulty with the mosaic of Iraq's ethnic groups arose with the Shi'a population, concentrated in the south. Although Arab, and in fact the majority population, they identified strongly with many religious values of Iran. While Iran often lays claim to leadership of the Shi'a world, the most important sites of Shi'a religious significance are located in the Iraqi cities of Karbala and Najaf. The Iraqi Shi'a had never played a political role appropriate to their numbers, even before independence. Thereafter, Sunni officers dominated the

The Mustansiriyah University during the socially more liberal 1970s

army, the focus of political power during both monarchy and republic.

The secular and strongly pan-Arab Ba'th Party evoked particularly little support among the Shi'a. Ba'thist governments, largely military and Sunni, traditionally spurned issues cherished by the Shi'a, and the absence of democracy left the largest community in the country marginalized and often repressed.

Rivalry with Iran brought particular tension for the Shi'a. To oppose the modernizing shah, the Ba'thists accorded refuge to his dedicated enemy, Ayatollah Khomeini. Such support was intended as tactical; the Iraqi regime allowed even less religious influence on politics than did Iran, and dissatisfaction arose among Iraq's Shi'a as well as Iran's. In 1977, demonstrations and riots broke out in the holy cities of Najaf and Karbala. When civil disturbances in Iran threatened an Islamic revolution against the shah, Saddam Hussein expelled Ayatollah Khomeini.

After their Islamic Revolution, Iranian religious leaders, now under the leadership of the charismatic Khomeini, called on the Muslims of Iraq to revolt. Disturbances in Baghdad and elsewhere resulted in stern repression. Ayatollah Muhammad Bakr Sadr, a prominent Shi'a leader, was executed in Baghdad for subversion. Amid such turmoil, controlled elections to the powerless National Assembly meant little.

War with Iran

Angered by Iran's calls for an Islamic revolution, Saddam Hussein sensed an opportunity to weaken a divided and internationally isolated Iran, and in 1980 he invaded. Iraqi troops captured Khorramshahr and pushed into oil-rich regions beyond.

Despite early victories, the president miscalculated. By advancing broadly, Iraqi forces failed to deliver a fatal blow. By 1981, Iraq had lost the initiative and faced the onslaught of religiously-inspired and passionately nationalistic Iranians determined to obliterate the Ba'th regime in Baghdad. Iranian naval and air attacks destroyed tanker facilities on the Gulf near Faw, and Kurdish groups rebelled in the north, supported by Iran.

To defend itself, Iraq drafted almost all able-bodied men. Aid from other Arab governments, fearing that a victorious Iran would export its Islamic Revolution, sustained Iraq's survival. Arab oil states "lent" an estimated $35 billion, and Egypt alone supplied over one million workers. Alone among Arab nations, Ba'thist Syria supported Iran. It halted the flow of Iraqi crude oil through Syrian ports, thus closing the last export route for crude.

Massive Iranian attacks against Basra in 1984 and 1985 inspired Iraqi soldiers with the will to resist. Khomeini's expectation of broad-based support amongst Iraq's Shi'a had been sorely disappointed. The destruction of life and property in Basra, a largely Shi'a city, weakened any residual sympathies of Iraqi Shi'a for Iran.

In an effort to gain traction, Saddam utilized chemical weapons. Illegal under international law, there was little outcry on the part of the international community when repeated attacks were made against Iranian targets. Indeed, Western companies were complicit in the export to Iraq of huge quantities of raw materials, equipment, and small industrial factories to produce poison gases. In the course of the Iran–Iraq war, an estimated one million Iranian military personnel and civilians were exposed to nerve gas and mustard agents, with tens of thousands killed.

Saddam Hussein al-Takriti

Four decades on, almost 100,000 continue to receive treatment for chronic chemical weapons injuries. Largely stalemated on the ground, the war took other forms, including a "Tanker War" when Iran attacked vessels carrying oil from Kuwait and Saudi Arabia. Eventually the United States and other nations sent naval units to escort shipping and clear the Gulf of mines. In 1987, missile and bomb attacks on Tehran and Baghdad caused civilian casualties and created widespread fear.

In 1988, Iraqi forces were finally able to push back on the ground. They recaptured the Faw Peninsula—Iraq's access to the Gulf—and attacked across the border. Internationally isolated and lacking heavy weapons for defense, Iranian resistance was worn down and Tehran finally sued for peace.

On the verge of military victory, Iraq engineered a crime against humanity. Some Kurds had allied with Iran and "liberated" Kurdish territory. The perception from Baghdad was that Kurdish collaboration with invading Iranian soldiers constituted "high treason." In response, the military and police brutally evicted thousands of mountain villagers, demolished their homes, and buried some alive. Survivors were exiled to the deserts. More than 50,000 died, mostly unnoticed by the world press. However, a chemical gas attack on the town of Halabja gained worldwide TV coverage killing 3,000 to 5,000 people and injuring 7,000 to 10,000 more. More than 50,000 Kurds, mostly women and children, then sought refuge across the border in Turkey and Iran.

After the ceasefire, military industrialization remained a priority. Popular generals and other officers were arrested or disappeared. Secrecy cloaked normal public information, such as the budget,

City Street in Karbala　　　Photo by William Parker

trade, and social characteristics. Torture extended to executing children, to persuade their parents to confess.

Believing himself the embodiment of the Ba'thist slogan "One Arab nation with an eternal mission," Saddam Hussein thought himself the liberator of Arabs everywhere from their princes, kings, and presidents. Hence he had ordered massive programs to develop chemical and biological weapons. He recognized that if Arab unity involved conquest, the collapse of the Soviet empire meant it must come quickly It was no coincidence that the first target was ranked among the richest.

War over Kuwait

In 1990, Saddam provoked a diplomatic crisis with Kuwait, demanding that Iraq be absolved of a $14 billion debt incurred during the Iran–Iraq war, seeking border concessions, claiming payment for Iraqi oil allegedly pumped by Kuwaiti wells, and asking for billions in compensation for low world oil prices resulting from Kuwait's production beyond its quota. Negotiations were conducted in poor faith on the Iraqi side and were abandoned without warning. Hours later troops invaded and occupied all Kuwait.

Iraqi rule proved brutal. Officials and troops systematically looted museums, libraries, warehouses, hospitals, and offices to benefit Iraqi hospitals, universities, and government offices. The Central Bank yielded foreign exchange and gold worth billions. Soon Baghdad's civilians could purchase, cheaply, consumer goods long denied them. Sharing in the booty made accomplices of thousands of otherwise innocent civilians.

Responding to the unprovoked aggression, the UN Security Council imposed an economic boycott. The Gulf Cooperation Council enabled Saudi Arabia, protector of Islam's most important Holy Places, to accept a defensive international Coalition force. U.S. and other NATO forces arrived, Egypt and Syria pledged troops, and smaller Gulf states provided bases and token units. Careful diplomacy by U.S. President George H. W. Bush built international support.

Isolated from the Western world, Saddam Hussein apparently believed that Muslim protests and American anti-war emotions would deter any sustained U.S. attacks. He therefore refused to back down. One day after the UN deadline, Coalition aircraft and missiles began massive attacks on military and economic targets. Precision weapons reached their targets with relatively few civilian casualties.

For 38 days and nights, the aerial campaign pounded weapons depots, communication links, bridges and highways, water and sewage treatment plants, refineries

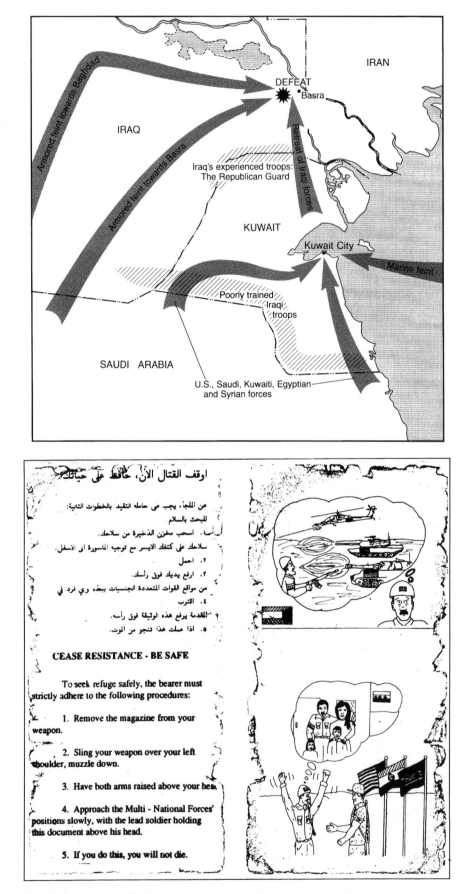

One of thousands of leaflets dropped on Iraqi troops during the Kuwait War

and factories, and the national electric power grid. Military units, especially the better-equipped Republican Guard divisions, suffered intensive bombing by B-52s. To avoid arousing Muslim and anti-war sentiments, the Coalition casualty estimates were kept secret.

To widen the war and thus split the Coalition, Iraq fired Scud missiles at Israeli targets (see Israel: History). Israel did not retaliate, and Baghdad's appeal for a Holy War failed.

Striking swiftly, Coalition ground forces punctured the dreaded Iraqi defenses with surprisingly few casualties. Tanks and airborne units swept around Iraqi defenses from the west, cutting off an Iraqi retreat, while others struck at Republican Guard divisions north of the Iraq–Kuwait border (see map). Egyptian, Syrian, and other Arab troops joined U.S. Marines to push northwards to Kuwait City.

After just 100 hours of ground fighting, President Bush announced a ceasefire. Iraq lost an estimated 10,000–30,000 dead, most of its air force, and some 3,700 tanks. The physical destruction cost scores of billions of dollars. Retreating Iraqi troops systematically set fire to 700 of Kuwait's oil wells, causing unprecedented and long-lasting environmental damage.

The cease-fire did not bring peace. In Basra and other cities, despondent troops and Shi'a militants seized power from officials and the Ba'th Party. The revolt became a bitter civil war in southern Iraq. Kurdish *pesh merga* guerrillas soon revolted in the north. Iraq appeared to be disintegrating along ethnic and religious divisions.

To face the crisis, Saddam Hussein charged Ali Hasan al-Majid, who had earlier "pacified" the Kurds, with restoring control. After the United States refused to intervene, Iraqi troops moved methodically from city to city in the south, pounding rebel areas relentlessly. Mosques were not spared, nor the families of those resisting. Once again, Saddam used chemical weapons. The number of casualties has never been accurately determined.

The rebels lacked an over-all command, and despite fighting desperately, the Islamic revolutionaries lost Basra, the Shi'a holy cities of Najaf and Karbala, and many smaller towns. Some 30,000 died in the fighting. Thousands of others were executed. The displaced flooded into U.S. occupied territory and across the border into Iran.

After subjugating the south, the Iraqi military moved north, and their overwhelming superiority in armor and helicopter gunships defeated the Kurdish fighters who had captured Kirkuk. The resulting flood of Kurdish refugees into Turkey presented a dilemma. Western

states expressed support for Kurdish aspirations for statehood against the interests of Saddam. However, Turkey, already fighting a Kurdish insurgency in the southeast of the country, had little desire to settle tens of thousands of Iraqi Kurds. Nor did it wish to see an independent Kurdish state on its border. Consequently, with UN cooperation, the Coalition forced Iraqi troops to withdraw, and then erected refugee camps *inside* Iraq. A Kurdish alliance took control of northern Iraq, about 10% of the country.

Post-War Difficulties in Arab Iraq

In central and southern Iraq, Saddam Hussein and the Ba'th party retained power, despite military conspiracies and popular dissatisfaction. To ensure the destruction of Saddam's biological, chemical, and nuclear weapons program, the United Nations established economic sanctions. These rapidly took bitter effect. Although they permitted imports of humanitarian goods like food and medicine, they banned the oil exports necessary to pay for them. Moreover, food for civilians was not the government's priority. So effective were the sanctions that the dearth of spare parts and raw materials reduced industrial production to one-tenth of capacity. Dire shortages of insecticides, herbicides, and seeds depressed farm output, and prices rose rapidly.

To shift the blame for inflation, the regime arrested dozens of merchants and executed them for profiteering. Public works projects, from palaces to the "Third River" (designed to drain salty run-off and other pollutants), helped lower unemployment, but popular frustrations rose, as savings disappeared.

Any open expression of discontent, however, risked severe punishment. Few places on earth exhibited official brutality at the Iraqi level. Penalties initially included amputating the limbs of profiteers

or farmers who hoarded their harvest, and removing an ear or tattooing the forehead of military deserters.

Slowly, UN inspectors discovered evidence of a vast prewar operation involving over a dozen factories that might produce, eventually, an atomic bomb. By 1993, Iraqi cooperation replaced confrontation, and the United Nations established a vast monitoring system involving planes, helicopters, ground inspectors, tagged equipment, sensors, and video cameras.

In 1995, biological experts from UNSCOM, the special commission of inspectors, discovered that prewar Iraq had imported vast quantities of growth media for toxic bacteria, far more than necessary to culture and identify hospital germs. Evidence mounted that despite Iraqi denials, a large germ warfare program had existed, aiming to produce anthrax, botulinum toxin, and aflatoxin.

Very possibly, the inspectors' discovery of the project caused the man ultimately responsible for it, Saddam Hussein's son-in-law, Hussein Kamal, to flee to Jordan with his wife, children, and documents. Upstaging any evidence he might give, Baghdad released further evidence of the construction of biological missile warheads and spray containers for pilotless aircraft. However, Iraqi officials claimed that these had been destroyed soon after the Gulf War. For his part, Hussein Kamal returned to Baghdad, where he and his young sons were shot days later.

Despite the inspectors' suspicions of hidden weapons, the Iraqi people's desperation won public sympathy in many countries. Rather than lift the sanctions, the UN Security Council approved a strict "Oil for Food" program. It allowed $2 billion (later, $5.2 billion) in oil exports every six months, to pay for food, medicine, and vital equipment, plus contributions for war victims, weapons inspectors, and the Kurds.

The Highway of Death—The scorched remains of both civilian and military vehicles litter the main highway leading from Kuwait City to Basra and Baghdad. The vehicles were destroyed in allied bombing raids against the retreating Iraqi army.

Iraq

Oil for Food funds did not eliminate poverty, but they did stabilize diet and improve public health. Gradually the death rate of some 6,000 children per month fell. These "silent" deaths, largely unreported by the world's media, occurred because of impure water supplies, open sewage, ongoing malnutrition, and poorly functioning medical facilities. These problems were compounded by government manipulation of the system, that saw the extraction of bribes from some, and the favoring of sympathetic countries and companies.

Amid the general suffering, the country's fortunate few lived well. A new luxury resort opened at an artificial lake near Baghdad in 1999, with nearly every brick carrying Saddam's initials in the manner of Nebuchadnezzar, the ruler of ancient Babylon. New presidential palaces arose across the country, and statues or portraits of the president littered almost every significant intersection.

Kurdish Autonomy in the North

Protected by a U.S. no-fly zone over Northern Iraq, in 1991 effectively three million Kurds found themselves free from Iraq—but short of fuel, food, and the supplies needed to reconstruct hundreds of villages destroyed by the Iraqi army. Kurdish leaders formed their own administration, eventually known as the Kurdistan Regional Government.

Separated by geography, dialect, tribal affiliation, and personal ambitions, the Kurds were divided into two major political groups. Masoud Barzani's Kurdistan Democratic Party (KDP), strongest in northern and western Kurdistan, reflected the spirit of his late father, Mustafa, the legendary hero of the independence struggle. The KDP cooperated with the Islamic Republic of Iran. Jalal Talabani's Patriotic Union of Kurdistan (PUK) drew its strength in southeastern Kurdistan.

Uniting these two parties proved impossible, despite their promises to share public office between themselves. Disputes over taxes, property ownership, and other matters set one party against another. In 1994, the PUK evicted Barzani's followers from Arbil (Erbil), the Kurdish capital, and in 1996 the KDP invited Iraqi troops to capture Arbil from the PUK, in the process discovering sensitive CIA operations. However, aid from Iran enabled the PUK to regain some lost territory, and U.S. and Turkish pressure eventually led to a formal cease-fire. Only the rough rule of Barzani and Talabani limited the zone's descent into anarchy.

Legally part of Iraq, the Kurdish zone traded with the rest of the country and suffered UN sanctions aimed at Saddam's regime. Factories closed for lack of supplies and customers, and trade languished. The major source of taxes and trade was the (sanctions-busting) re-export of Iraqi oil and diesel fuel. Kurdistan also endured sabotage and terrorist attacks by Iraqi agents, and the zone survived largely on sanctions-busting and aid handouts.

The guerrilla war for independence launched by the Kurdistan Workers Party (PKK) against Turkey complicated matters greatly. The PKK sought refuge in Iraqi Kurdistan, and gained some freedom of action by threats to attack trade. In return, Ankara launched major invasions that inevitably destroyed homes and villages but were rarely successful in expelling small PKK units from the mountainous terrain.

In 1998 the two rival parties divided the territory, and formed two administrations. The KDP dominated the capital, Arbil, and the vital road between Iraq and Turkey through Dohuk, with its trucks carrying cheap sanctions-busting oil to Turkey. The PUK capital was Sulaymaniyah, a large and vibrant city despite its location outside the U.S.-imposed no-fly zone.

Despite a legacy of poverty and anarchy, by 2003 new roads crossed the land, satellite TV broadcasts communicated in local dialects, and apartments housed refugees previously living in tents. New universities were established at Dohuk and Sulaymaniyah, in addition to Salahaddin University in Arbil. The United Nations' Oil for Food program deserved much credit for the stability and progress. It distributed Kurdistan's share of oil revenues, and did so quite effectively.

When the United States sought Kurdish assistance against Iraq in 2003, Kurdish leaders feared punishment or genocide if the proposed invasion of Arab Iraq failed. They clearly desired to add the city and oil fields of Kirkuk to the Kurdish zone, but they also recognized that Turkey considered Kurdish control over Kirkuk as a reason to invade. Might they lose autonomy if they were outmaneuvered in the peace settlement?

The Iraq War

Official U.S. policy vis-à-vis Iraq had been regime change since Bill Clinton signed the Iraq Liberation Act of 1998. However, in practice U.S. policy toward Iraq was one of containment. In the aftermath of 9/11, President George W. Bush seized the opportunity to abandon that policy and dislodge the Iraqi dictator through military force. As he made clear at the time, President Bush would have preferred robust support from the international community to remove Saddam, but he was prepared to work with an ad hoc coalition or even alone, if necessary.

Saddam's alleged Weapons of Mass Destruction (WMD) program was generally cited as the primary reason for going to war. In November 2002, after the United States presented intelligence that it had apparently accumulated about a renewed Iraqi WMD program, the UN Security Council drafted and passed UNSC Resolution 1441. This resolution offered Iraq "a final opportunity to comply with its disarmament obligations," lest it face "serious consequences." The United States had hoped to get tougher language in this resolution, language that would spell out the consequences of non-compliance, but this was the strongest text to which all members of the council could agree.

Late that month Iraq did allow UN weapons inspectors on the ground, and they did find minor violations of past agreements (although nothing that represented a casus belli). Inspectors had

School yard in Karbala

Photo by William Parker

86

been looking for evidence of an active WMD program for months, unsuccessfully, when the United States determined in March 2003, that Saddam had run out of time.

After some debate in the White House about the wisdom of returning to the United Nations for a second, more forceful resolution, the administration decided that a second resolution would not be forthcoming. Instead, President Bush announced that diplomacy had failed. He issued a public ultimatum that Saddam leave Iraq, a demand which was, perhaps not surprisingly, rejected by the Iraqi dictator.

On March 20, 2003, the Iraq War began with massive air attacks. There was never any doubt that the global superpower would defeat the ill-paid, badly-equipped, and poorly led Iraqi forces. Unlike the 1991 conflict, no sustained bombing preceded the ground invasion, but intense raids destroyed defensive units. While some units stood and fought—often being destroyed by cluster bombs and other hi-tech weapons—many soldiers simply vanished into the population.

Baghdad fell quickly, just three weeks into the campaign, and Tikrit's surrender soon afterwards marked the end of Saddam's rule. In the north, supported by U.S. bombing, Kurdish fighters seized control of Kirkuk, long desired for its historical connections and oil wealth. At the behest of Turkey, the pesh merga were soon replaced by American forces, but Kurdish families began to return to homes they had fled a decade earlier, sometimes evicting their Arab residents.

From Liberation to Occupation

Contrary to expectations in the United States, there were few scenes of jubilant Iraqis rejoicing at the largely American victory. Iraq's Shi'a apparently remembered the high price they had paid in 1991. The tumbling of one of Saddam's statues in Baghdad reminded foreigners of the fall of the Berlin Wall, but it proved to be a photo op by the U.S. military just outside the media's hotel, stated for a few hundred onlookers. The subsequent occupation cost more American lives—and many, many more Iraqi lives—from terrorism and guerrilla tactics, than had the entire invasion. What went wrong?

First, popular opinion linked the U.S. "liberation" with the looting and destruction of stores, homes, hospitals, oil facilities, electrical generating plants, transmission lines, universities, the national museum, the national library, and much else. Priceless objects were stolen, as well as items of practical value. Some hospital equipment was even seized from the patients using it. Items too large to move were smashed or burned.

The looting, often conducted by gangs, usually occurred after U.S. and British forces had seized a locality. Iraqi security forces would have executed such criminals on the spot. As the occupying power, the Coalition forces were responsible for maintaining public order, yet they did so selectively. For instance, American troops garrisoned the petroleum ministry but ignored pleas for protection from the national museum nearby.

Dismissed in Washington as merely the "untidiness" inevitable at the end of a dictatorship, the looting and lawlessness caused great and serious harm. Professors, hospital workers, private businessmen, and other professionals sympathetic to Western-style democracy witnessed the destruction of their lifework, and sometimes their private property as well. Freed from Saddam's thugs and secret police, they now lived in fear of random arson and violence. Afraid of personal attacks, many women found their freedom curtailed.

There were improvements, notably the religious freedom enjoyed by Shi'a believers to perform ceremonies connected with mourning the death of Husayn ibn 'Ali, grandson of Muhammad. Just days after their liberation, hundreds of thousands walked to Najaf in processions long banned by Ba'thists, who feared the political potential of such gatherings and regarded the displays of emotion and self-flagellation as backward.

Bloodshed in Occupied Iraq

To the world outside, the chief feature of the occupation era was the violence and callous disregard for human life. The insurgency began with selective murders and attacks on U.S. troops, probably by former intelligence agents and demobilized troops. Peace did not follow the destruction of Ba'thist cells, the deaths in battle of Saddam's sons Uday and Qusay, and the capture of Saddam himself. Instead, Islamic extremists and unidentified but sinister groups joined the resistance. The country became a cauldron of anti-American violence that attracted Sunni Islamists and the occasional Shi'a radical from other countries.

In 2005, the Iraqi government estimated the number of insurgents at 40,000 hard-core fighters and perhaps 150,000 supporters and part-timers. A Jordanian linked to al-Qaeda, Abu-Musaib al-Zarqawi, became the symbol of the Islamic resistance. He and his group were specifically blamed for bombings of Shi'a gatherings and the murder of prisoners, often by beheading or the slitting of throats.

In addition to attacks on U.S. troops, the rebels turned to terrorism against soft targets. One suicide bombing destroyed the

UN mission, costing dozens of lives; another, the Red Cross offices. Many Western civilians left the country, or retreated to the fortified "Green Zone," Saddam's former palace area and now the U.S. headquarters. Iraqis employed by the occupation were less fortunate: thousands died, many of them policemen and soldiers. Even in the relatively safe Kurdish zone, the major political parties suffered direct attacks.

Anti-American attitudes and attacks were, until 2007, fiercest in the "Sunni triangle," the region north and west of Baghdad. The resistance there reflected its Ba'thist past and the privileges the region had enjoyed under its native son, Saddam Hussein. The cities of Falluja and Ramadi, in particular, became centers of the insurgency and illustrate the great suffering of the region. Early in the occupation of Falluja, as on occasion elsewhere, U.S. troops mistook rifle fire in celebration of a wedding as an attack. The return fire killed civilians; demonstrations later followed. Gunmen, hidden among protesters, fired at troops, who in turn shot demonstrators.

Following the murder and dismemberment of four U.S. civilian security guards, U.S. Marines besieged the city and attempted to subdue it. After significant casualties on both sides, and widely televised pictures of civilian suffering, a political solution was found: the creation of a "Falluja Protection Force," headed by a former Republican Guard general. The novel arrangement brought temporary peace, but Falluja fell under the control of militant clerics and became a center of the resistance. The Marines renewed the invasion in 2004. Working with mainly-Shi'a units of the new National Guard, they conquered the city, but hundreds died and nearly every building was damaged.

Large-scale Shi'a resistance came in 2004 from the Mahdi Army of Muqtada al-Sadr. The charismatic son of an ayatollah murdered by Saddam's regime, al-Sadr appealed to the poorest sectors of society, and his fiery populism combined anti-American nationalism with Islam and socialism. After he was charged with the murder of a Shi'a cleric and his newspaper was shut down on account of its vitriolic denunciations of the occupation, the Mahdi Army seized parts of Baghdad and the shrine cities of southern Iraq. However, Muqtada's followers wore out their welcome. Pressured by the Shi'a leadership, especially Grand Ayatollah Ali Sistani, al-Sadr accepted a political solution and his fighters were replaced by police.

Photographs of tortured and disgraced prisoners held by American troops for interrogation at Baghdad's infamous Abu Ghuraib prison deeply offended Iraqi

Iraq

sensibilities and drew global condemnation. The United States had, in part, justified the war on the grounds of bringing human rights to a population sorely deprived of such under Saddam. Any moral high-ground it claimed was rapidly diminishing.

Greater Roles for Iraqis

The U.S. Defense Department established the Coalition Provisional Authority (CPA) to govern for several years while attempting to institute a new democratic constitution. The CPA laid ambitious plans for reconstruction and sought a rigidly free-market economy with some of the world's lowest taxes. It quickly spent uncounted billions of U.S. tax dollars and Iraqi oil revenues on contracts to well-connected U.S. companies, some without bids, and on Iraqis, often without receipts. As anti-American violence grew, CPA administrators and military leaders concentrated in the tightly guarded "Green Zone" of western Baghdad.

The CPA reacted slowly to shortages of public services, particularly water, sewage, electricity, and fuel. Power plants, water treatment facilities, and similar installations had not been targets of U.S. bombing, but looting harmed a fragile infrastructure that had suffered 13 years of sanctions. Pumping water and sewers required electricity; this in turn required generating plants that used fuel oil or natural gas. By the summer of 2004, electrical blackouts halted air conditioning and widely depressed morale. Individual acts of good will and reconstruction by U.S. troops and civilians counted for little, against the brutality of war.

Nevertheless, the CPA improved life in significant ways for some. It cut import tariffs from 400% to essentially nothing, enabling merchants to fill the markets, stores, and auto dealerships with new merchandise (even as they destroyed Iraqi competitors). It granted press freedoms, and hundreds of new papers appeared, advocated conflicting viewpoints. It repaired and re-opened schools, and revised school textbooks. It paid veterans, and continued Saddam's massive food distribution policies that meant survival for over half the population. It issued a new currency, and raised wages.

Nevertheless, it was not Iraqi. Popular demands for greater Iraqi decision-making were not satisfied by the appointment of exiles to administrative positions, and resentment of the occupation grew as it endured.

After violence rose sharply, a new Iraqi army was created and the police force expanded, both with American advisors. On June 28, 2004, sovereignty was publicly transferred to the interim government.

History in Iraqi capital: A U.S. soldier watches and Iraqis cheer Wednesday as a 20-foot high statue of Iraqi President Saddam Hussein is pulled down in a central Baghdad square. A U.S. armored vehicle pulled it down.

In Saddam's former Green Zone palace, the largest American embassy anywhere in the world replaced the CPA. It supervised—and subsidized—the country. The new Governing Council selected 'Iyad Allawi, a Shi'a neurologist and businessman, as Prime Minister. While the new leaders thanked the United States for liberating Iraq, they also demanded genuine sovereignty, including the right to demand the withdrawal of occupation forces.

Constitution and Government (2005–06)

Yielding to Shi'a demands for elections, the CPA's transitional laws stipulated elections for a National Assembly that would select a government, draft a new constitution, and hold further national elections, all within a year. Besides this challenging schedule, the CPA prescribed a specific form of democracy: national proportional representation, combined with the requirement that a 2/3 "supermajority" approve the cabinet, thus precluding a Shi'a-only regime.

This approach encouraged politics to focus on religious or ethnic groups. The national electoral district—26 million inhabitants—prohibited local notables from running independently and reduced discussion of local issues. Political parties recognized the importance of a national presence, and as a result, they merged into "lists." In the Shi'a community, the larger religious-based parties, *al-Da'wa* and the Supreme Council of the Islamic Revolution in Iraq (SCIRI) formed the United Iraqi Alliance (UIA) with several smaller groups. Its rival for Shi'a support was the secular Iraqi List of 'Iyad Allawi, the interim prime minister. The major Kurdish parties, the KDP and PUK, set aside their own rivalries to establish the Kurdistan Alliance. However, the largely Sunni insurgency denounced elections, and few Sunni politicians dared to run.

As expected, in the context of heightened ethnic and sectarian divisions, Iraqis voted according to their religious and ethnic identities. The United Iraqi Alliance won 140 of the 275 seats. To gain the required "supermajority" it formed a coalition with the 77 deputies of the Kurdistan Alliance. By contrast, voters decisively rejected Allawi, who gained only 14% of the vote.

However, a system intended to reward communities that voted, backfired in the Sunni provinces. Only small minorities of those eligible cast their ballots, and Sunni Arab candidates, representing a quarter of the population, won only 6% of the seats. Thus the National Assembly failed to include reasonable representation of all Iraqis, a particular challenge when framing the constitution.

Immediately after the elections, the level of violence fell. The voters—58% of those registered—had spoken, and they directly rejected the insurgency. However, the coalition of just two parties took two months to select Jalal Talabani of the PUK as president and three months to form a cabinet under Ibrahim al-Jaafari of al-Da'wa (UIA). Much of that time was consumed by negotiations over the Sunni representatives. Meanwhile, violence returned to higher levels.

Ironically, the United States had sponsored Iraq's most freely contested election in decades—to the benefit of Iranian influence in the country. President Talabani's PUK had often sought military supplies from Iran and had used them to recover lost territory from the KDP in the 1990s. Prime Minister al-Jaafari had lived in exile in Iran and Britain. His party, al-Da'wa, had long contacts with Iran. The deputy Prime Minister, Ahmed Chalabi, had been identified as an Iranian spy just a year earlier. Behind the scenes, other Iranian links included Grand Ayatollah Ali Sistani, who was born in Iran, speaks Arabic with an accent, and heads charitable foundations across the border.

The Jaafari cabinet ruled ineffectively during perilous times. It confronted the insurrection by incorporating Shi'a fighters from the Badr and Mahdi militias into the police. While willing to fight, these militiamen in police uniform reportedly abducted, tortured, and massacred Sunnis. Al-Jaafari's cabinet also earned a reputation for corruption. Oil exports fell, and reconstruction stagnated.

Nevertheless, the cabinet succeeded in two important tasks. It drafted a constitution, and held parliamentary elections that were truly national; they included wide Sunni participation.

The constitutional debate focused on three issues: the role of Islam, the degree of regional autonomy, and control of oil revenues. Article 2 of the draft constitution recognized Islam as the religion of the state, and a "(rather than "the") fundamental source of legislation." It also prohibited any law that contradicted Islam's "undisputed" decisions.

Given the devout population, a formal Islamic role was inevitable, as was a retreat from the relative gender equality imposed by secular Ba'thists. However, some clauses of the constitution left wide room for later disputes. For example, Article 2 prohibited laws contrary to democracy or human rights, and Article 14 granted all Iraqis equality. Elsewhere, women were guaranteed 25% of parliamentary seats.

Demands for regional autonomy proved an even more vexing issue. Sunnis desired a unitary state, ruled from Baghdad, but Kurds insisted on either self-government within Iraq or independence. Some Shi'a leaders also desired autonomous Shi'a regions in the south. Unable to compromise, the National Assembly approved a federal system, but left some details for later decisions.

For good measure, at least to the Kurdish interpretation, the constitution allocated oil revenues from existing fields to the central government, but those from new fields to the regions. Since the major oil deposits lie in Kurdish and Shi'a areas, Sunnis naturally opposed a clause that suggested their future impoverishment.

After a bitter six-week campaign, Iraq's voters ratified the constitution with 78% approval. However, two Sunni provinces (Anbar and Salahuddin) overwhelmingly opposed it. Voters in Nineveh also rejected it, but by only a 55% majority.

Over two hundred parties contested the 2005 elections for a permanent parliament, the Majlis. Sunni groups joined the contest, implicitly recognizing that the opportunity to participate in government outweighed the risk of insurgent opposition. This time, the Shi'a United Iraqi Alliance included Muqtada al-Sadr's organization, but it lacked Ayatollah Sistani's open support.

Once again, the elections proved that voters cherished ethnic and sectarian identity above ideology and political platforms. As expected, the UIA (128 seats) fell short of a simple majority, and with the Kurdistan Alliance still lacked the 2/3 supermajority required to approve a cabinet. Sunni groups gained significant representation, with the Iraqi Accord Front receiving 44 seats. The major losers were secular Shi'a groups. Chalabi's alliance even failed to enter parliament.

Due mostly to rivalries within the UIA, it took five months of bargaining, rising violence, and U.S. pressure before a "supermajority" emerged. Eventually, the UIA proposed Nouri al-Maliki, deputy leader of al-Da'wa, as prime minister. Al-Maliki gained both Kurdish and Sunni approval and formed his cabinet in April 2006.

From any perspective, Prime Minister al-Maliki faced immense challenges. By the time he took office in the spring of 2006, violence had already been raging in Iraq for years. One event of particular importance, however, happened shortly before his rise to power. On February 22, 2006, al-Qaeda militants bombed and destroyed the al-Askari Mosque, known for its Golden Dome and for its importance to Shia Muslims, in the city of Samarra. It was this event that triggered all out civil war. Iraq had been on a cliff, and this event pushed it over.

The United Nations estimated that 34,000 civilians were killed in 2006 alone. Nearly 20% of the population became refugees. Two million wealthy enough to do so moved abroad, millions more were displaced within the country. Their homes were usually looted and then occupied by families from the locally dominant sectarian group. As the professional and business classes began to disappear, hospitals and clinics lost staff. Only the bravest university professors continued to teach: over 200 were assassinated. The Western nations most responsible for the conflict—the United States and Britain—accepted only a few Iraqi refugees, while Syria and Jordan hosted roughly one million each.

Non-Muslim minorities continued to face particular violence. Christian leaders were assassinated, and the laity threatened

Iraq

with death if they did not flee the country. Yazidis (inaccurately) faced charges of worshipping Satan. The Mandaeans, followers of a Gnostic religion pre-dating Islam, feared extinction, because Islamic extremists in Iraq tried to wipe them out through forced conversions, rape, and murder.

In 2006, Saddam Hussein was convicted by an Iraqi court for the killing of 148 Shi'a from the town of Dujail following an assassination attempt. A trial over the Kurdish massacres was also sought, but he and a few aides were rushed to execution. Saddam died at the gallows in December of that year, his execution surreptitiously filmed on a smart phone. That footage quickly made its way to the world's press and was widely broadcast on the Internet and TV.

Despite other successes, such as the death of al-Qaeda in Iraq leader Abu Musaib al-Zarqawi, violence against civilians increased in 2006–07. Suicide bombings, sectarian reprisal killings, improvised chlorine gas bombs, and ambushes of police units proved deadly. Attacks on U.S. troops featured increasingly sophisticated weapons, particularly roadside bombings by "explosively formed projectiles" (EFPs), complex devices that could pierce armored vehicles.

The "Surge" Succeeds

After the Iraq Study Group warned of a slide toward chaos and government collapse, President Bush rejected calls for an American withdrawal. Instead, he ordered an increase in the U.S. military forces in Iraq—an additional five brigades, more than 20,000 soldiers—to provide more troops in zones of conflict. This "surge"

was expected to reduce the violence while politicians in Baghdad reached the compromises necessary to attract Sunnis and radical Shi'a groups.

With more American troops on patrol, American casualties climbed to some of the highest levels of the war. Some of those casualties, inflicted by EFPs supplied by Iranian groups, came from Shi'a militiamen unwilling to accept the limitations of law and order on their ethnic attacks on Sunnis. Nevertheless, the surge gradually reached its military goals; violence declined in Baghdad, temporarily increased in Diyala and other provinces as insurgents found easier targets, then declined there as well. In Anbar province and elsewhere, tribal leaders who had tired of the harsh fanaticism of many insurgents formed tactical alliances with the U.S. military in return for arms and money. Mosul became the last insurgent stronghold.

With the decline in violence, many refugees began to return to Baghdad and elsewhere, in some cases only to find their homes occupied by others. Many returnees were women; like those who had remained, they found conditions worsening for women and girls. Their discouragement over the availability of jobs or fear of violence was expected. However, over three-quarters of those surveyed reported that their daughters were not allowed to attend school, a shocking outlook for the future.

Slow political progress accompanied the security surge. Parliament only tardily addressed legislation crucial to attracting Sunni support, such as reversing aspects of de-Ba'thification, the distribution of oil revenues among the regions, and possible regional units of a federal nation.

Muqtada al-Sadr withdrew his party first from the cabinet, then from the United Iraqi Alliance. However, he proclaimed a cease-fire by his militia, the *Jaish al-Mahdi*, and asserted control over at least some of its rogue elements.

In 2008, Prime Minister al-Maliki suddenly ordered the army and police to crack down on militia activity in Basra some months after the British withdrawal. In practical terms, this meant assaulting al-Sadr's Jaish al-Mahdi. It successfully fought back; hundreds of troops and police deserted; even air support proved insufficient for a clear military victory. The fighting spread to Baghdad, but thanks in part to Iranian counsel, al-Sadr agreed to a cease-fire. Thereafter, police and military patrols and roadblocks gradually asserted law and order. Al-Sadr's followers were not defeated, but stood down.

By 2009, now with a new U.S. president in office, both Basra and Baghdad had become much calmer. On June 30, U.S. troops formally withdrew from Iraqi cities. Hailed by the Iraqi government as a huge victory and celebrated as "National Sovereignty Day," the withdrawal was possible only because of the increased professionalism of Iraqi forces and the war-weariness of the nation. While suicide bombers later managed to devastate government ministries in Baghdad and kill scores elsewhere, the trend of violence was clearly downward, and the attacks did not ignite sectarian reprisals.

The politicians of democratic Iraq move slowly. Legal changes for the 2010 parliamentary elections involved repeated delays, and the elections themselves were postponed briefly without a solution to a major contentious issue, the status of Kirkuk.

When elections were held in March, they confirmed political fractures within sectarian groups as well as between them. The Shi'a religious parties that had united in 2005 as the Iraqi National Alliance fractured when Prime Minister al-Maliki formed the State of Law coalition, clearly hoping to benefit from the improved security. Despite being officially secular and less pro-Iranian, it appealed mostly to Shi'a groups traditionally loyal to the Da'wa Party. The other significant Shi'a parties, including the Iraqi Islamic Supreme Council and the Sadrists, formed the National Iraqi Alliance, and split the votes of conservative, religiously-oriented Shi'a. By contrast, former interim Prime Minister Allawi's *Al-Iraqiyya* (Iraqi National Movement) appealed to Sunnis as well as some Shi'a.

To some surprise, Al-Iraqiyya carried every Sunni Arab province and won 91 seats in the 325-member assembly, two more than the State of Law alliance.

Al-Askari Mosque in Samarra before the 2006 bombing

Despite al-Maliki's charges of voting irregularities and an appeal for a recount in Baghdad, the two-member plurality held. However, with fewer than 30% of the seats, Al-Iraqiyya could not govern alone.

Al-Maliki concentrates power

During Iraq's violent history, compromise often proved dangerous, a lesson learned well by present political leaders. Unable to work together, Allawi and al-Maliki sought allies, particularly after the Federal Court ruled that the largest coalition rather than the largest party should have the first opportunity to propose a government. The ensuring contest established a new world record for the longest time between election day and the formation of a new government, but finally the Sadrists agreed to join al-Maliki's coalition.

By early 2011 many Iraqis already believed government had failed them. Inspired by Arab Spring demonstrators, protestors attempted to publicize their demands for an end to corruption, action on unemployment (estimated at near 30%), improved government services, and transparent security forces rather than perceived repression. Al-Maliki denounced the planned demonstrations as inspired by either the Ba'thists or al-Qaeda. Across the country at least twenty died.

The government maintained unity, and reduced violent attacks, by withstanding pressure from Washington to accept a long-term U.S. military presence of several thousand troops. This rejection publicly humiliated the United States, though it turned out not to be politically damning for President Obama, who had campaigned on withdrawal from Iraq when running for office in 2008.

Although Obama has since been criticized for not maintaining a troop presence, at the time there were many forces pushing in the direction of a U.S exit. After nearly a decade in Iraq, and more time still in Afghanistan, the American public was war weary. Conservatively, the United States had spent hundreds of billions of dollars in Iraq. Thousands of Americans had been killed, and tens of thousands had been wounded. Hundreds of thousands of Iraqis had died. Iraqis themselves wanted a U.S. withdrawal, and the Iraqi parliament refused to extend immunity for U.S. troops in country. Furthermore, as a consequence of the surge, violence in Iraq had reached its lowest levels in years. An important question for critics of the U.S. withdrawal, then, is this: If the United States could not responsibly withdraw from Iraq at the end of 2011, when could it have?

The moment that the last American troops departed their last base, however, political unity fractured publicly. Claiming that the prime minister sought to monopolize power, the al-Iraqiyya bloc walked out of parliament. Days later, its leading official, Vice President Tariq al-Hashimi, was charged with murder. The Vice President fled to the Kurdish zone, then abroad, and was tried in absentia, mostly on evidence supplied by arrested bodyguards.

Though many accused al-Maliki of pursing a sectarian or pro-Iranian agenda, more than anything else he used his second term to consolidate his personal power. He retained personal control of the defense and interior (police) ministries, and reportedly micro-managed them. Court rulings granted him control of previously-independent ministries and confined the ability to propose laws in parliament to the government.

Vindictive by nature, al-Maliki brought charges selectively against those who displeased him. For example, Faraj al-Haidari, who as head of the independent electoral commission rejected al-Maliki's attempt to disqualify some al-Iraqiyya votes, was charged with corruption. The head of the Central Bank was arrested on similar charges. TV stations that broadcasted unflattering news faced temporary closures or worse.

Given these strains, national politics fractured further. To concentrate power, al-Maliki used prosecutors and the courts to harass his opponents. One example was his use of the judiciary to eliminate opponents from running for office. Iraqi law permits the exclusion of candidates who lack a "good reputation." The electoral commission interpreted that as barring individuals convicted of criminal offenses. The ministry of justice, by contrast, selectively blocked candidates for whom arrest warrants had been issued, something it could arrange.

Shi'a rivals attempted, but failed, to displace him with a vote of no confidence in 2012, but the strongest opposition came from Sunnis. The arrest of the Sunni finance minister prompted mass protests in Anbar Province and other Sunni Arab areas; the demonstrators also condemned the general repression of their community's leaders and the arrest of women for the alleged offenses of their husbands and sons. The demonstrations became continuous when a protest camp was established in Ramadi.

Relations between Baghdad and the Kurdish Regional Government (KRG) also deteriorated greatly and in 2012 nearly led to armed clashes over territory. The long-running dispute between Baghdad and the KRG continued over contracts for oil exploration in Kurdish areas and the KRG's agreement with Turkey to pump crude directly to Turkey.

Personal animosities compounded inherent differences, symbolized by the words of Masoud al-Barzani, the Kurdish president: "The F-16 must not reach the hand of this man (al-Maliki)." Barzani, like the fugitive Vice President al-Hashimi, warned that without power-sharing by the Shi'a ruling clique in Baghdad, Iraq might break up.

By 2013, large-scale violence had returned to Iraq. Criminal gangs and terrorists had raised the death toll to nearly 1,000 per month, despite, or because of, al-Maliki's personal responsibility for public security. Iraq's ranking in the corruption index from Transparency International was among the worst in the world.

As parliamentary elections approached in 2014, the political system malfunctioned badly. The president, often abroad, was incapacitated by ill-health. One vice president was a fugitive, charged with murder on evidence from tortured bodyguards. Parliament had failed to vote the budget, and it appeared that al-Maliki's own allies failed to attend a critical vote on it. For their part, many Sunni legislators threatened to resign, while a bitter dispute with the Kurdish Regional Government over its plans to export oil, blocked Shi'a–Kurdish cooperation. Conditions were so poor that reportedly Iran, the prime minister's long-time supporter, sought his replacement.

Prime Minister al-Maliki was more responsible for the dysfunctional government and political system than anyone else: he simply monopolized too much power. Having kept the ministries of defense, interior, and security to himself, he was responsible for the police and military becoming known as Shi'a rather than Iraqi, as well as for their corrupt practices. For example, some 50,000 "ghost soldiers" padded the payrolls of army divisions, their commanders pocketing the salaries.

Even more seriously, al-Maliki strengthened rather than diminished sectarian animosities. He abandoned support for Sunni tribal fighters who had allied with U.S. troops against Islamist terrorists. His government charged Sunni politicians with crimes, though the evidence was weak and sometimes obtained by torture. Increasingly he adopted anti-Sunni positions. In another example of his control over the system, judges disqualified the candidacies of several of al-Maliki's critics because arrest warrants against them made them "criminals," although they had not been tried and convicted.

To some surprise, al-Maliki's fragmented alliance placed first in the voting and actually gained a few seats, though well short of a majority. With the opposition more fragmented than ever, it seemed likely that marathon negotiations could

Iraq

lead to a coalition. However, Grand Ayatollah Ali Sistani called for a government representing all groups, a pointed criticism of al-Maliki's practices. Under the impact of the rapid conquests of the Islamic State, dissatisfied members within his own State of Law alliance defected. This provided the opportunity for Haider al-Abadi, a better-liked legislator from the same alliance, to form a workable coalition.

Islamic State and Beyond

Months before the election, and possibly to enhance his stature, in late 2013, al-Maliki ordered the arrest of a Sunni MP and the closure of the Ramadi protest camp as a "terrorist site." In response, fighters of the extremist Islamic State of Iraq and [Greater] Syria (ISIS or ISIL; later IS) an offshoot of al-Qaeda, struck at police and army units in Ramadi and Falluja, the main urban areas of Anbar province. Despite support from some Anbar tribesmen, government shelling and air attacks were unable to repulse the rebels, whose strength the prime minister blamed partly on missiles and other weapons from Saudi Arabia.

In June 2014, ISIS suddenly launched an unexpected offensive against Mosul, the country's second-largest city. Rather than fight, police and soldiers frequently abandoned their positions; within hours, the city fell. Following accounts of brutality and bloodshed, thousands fled the city for the nearby Kurdish territory. ISIS forces looted millions of dollars from banks: their rebellion seems financed very effectively.

From Mosul the fighting spread further east and south. Joined by discontent Ba'thist sympathizers and others angered by al-Maliki's policies, the rebels isolated and captured Iraqi units that failed to retreat in time, sometimes massacring prisoners of war to enhance Shi'a fears and hatred. The Kurdish pesh merga halted the ISIS advance outside Kirkuk; otherwise nearly all other significant cities and towns in the north and west fell to the group within weeks.

The successes of ISIS horrified Western politicians and their publics, but even more so Iraqis and Syrians who might be the next targets. ISIS used gruesome pictures and videos of executions to boast of its conquests and strike fear into its enemies. By physically destroying border walls and fences between Iraq and Syria, the group struck at the heart of the century-old system of Middle East states, established primarily by Britain and France at the end of World War I. The destruction of parts of that border resonated with many.

As Ramadan began in 2014, Abu Bakr al-Baghdadi, the group's leader, announced a change in name and title. The Islamic State in Iraq and Syria was now simply a contemporary version of a medieval caliphate, The Islamic State (IS), and al-Baghdadi became Caliph Ibrahim, who called for the allegiance of all true Muslims.

Because President Obama deeply opposed sending American ground troops to fight in Iraq and Syria, the United States formed a coalition of Arab and Western countries to carry out an air campaign against IS. While thousands of missions were flown, destroying economic targets, troop convoys, and killing several thousand IS fighters, the air war often had limited effectiveness, with aircraft sometimes returning to base without striking any targets. This resulted largely from great caution over civilian casualties. Perhaps more importantly, the prohibition on U.S. troops participating in the ground war prevented integrating air controllers with the Iraqi military and greatly diminished U.S. ability to identify targets.

Moreover, there was the complication of Iran. A bitter enemy of IS and anxious to support Iraq's largely Shi'a government, it provided advisors, special forces, and reportedly weapons. However, at the time Iran was under strict international sanctions for its nuclear enrichment program, and those included banning arms deals. Tehran also propped up the Syrian regime and aided the Lebanese *Hizbullah* party and militia, a designated terrorist organization. Despite clearly fighting on the same side against IS, it could not be considered a U.S. ally.

Feared on the ground, and cautious about raids from the air, IS jihadists attacked religious minorities in the northern Jabal Sinjar region, massacring several thousand members of the religious Yazidi minority and consigning many of their women to sexual slavery. Assyrian and Chaldean Christians were also attacked and forced to flee. More than lives were lost. The jihadists destroyed cherished religious materials of the present, including churches, shrines to Muslim saints, and Yazidi places of worship. They also smashed irreplaceable works of art created in Mosul and Nineveh by the Assyrian empire over two millennia ago, on the grounds that the statues were idols.

Threats against Baghdad and other Shi'a areas led Shi'a militant groups, including al-Sadr's Jaish al-Mahdi to volunteer alongside the military. These groups became known as the *Hashd*, or Popular Mobilization Forces. Public opinion and U.S. generals regarded them as dedicated and willing to die for the cause, which army soldiers apparently were not. Guided by advisors from the Iranian Revolutionary Guard's Quds Force, they fought to recapture Tikrit. However, their reputations were diminished by allegations of their violence against Sunni civilians.

By early 2016 there was some reason to hope that the tide was turning in Iraq. Cities that had been taken by the militant group (especially Fallujah and Ramadi, both west of Baghdad) were being fiercely contested by the Iraqi army, and many analysts correctly believed that these two cities would soon be returned to the control of Iraqi authorities. That happened by mid-2016, setting the stage for the much

Former Prime Minister Nouri al-Maliki and President Bush   Courtesy of the White House

bigger battle to retake Mosul later that year.

That battle, which some have likened to the worst fighting since World War 2, was horrific. By the end of 2017, two things were true. First, the Iraqi army, working with Shi'a militias and Kurdish forces, and with the support of a U.S.-backed coalition, had cleared the city of IS. Second, the city had been destroyed. Whole streets were razed. People who had lived in Mosul their whole lives were no longer able to recognize neighborhoods. In that sense, the liberation of Mosul was bittersweet. In order to free the city, it had to be destroyed.

Culture: As Muslim Arabs, Iraqis share major cultural features with other peoples of the Middle East, ranging from paternal authority, to food and religious holidays. The family remains the basic social unit, with parents, children, and grandchildren often forming a single household. While their education may postpone it, girls usually marry young, by arrangement between her family and the groom's. Large families have been encouraged by both traditional values and government policies. Consequently, the population has grown rapidly. About half the population is less than 15 years of age.

Before the 1958 Revolution, most Iraqis lived in rural areas, typically in small, mud-brick houses except in the north, where the climate required stone. Agriculture occupied perhaps three-quarters of the population. Living conditions were simple or even harsh, with diets restricted to bread, rice, lentils, beans, onions, occasional mutton, and dates. As oil revenues provided prosperity in the cities, they attracted a great migration, until by 1990 some two-thirds of the nation lived in urban areas, usually in neighborhoods of people from the same rural district. Agriculture, often neglected though still important, proved unable to feed the nation during the UN embargo.

After two decades of war, sanctions, and occupation, these are not ordinary times. Poverty and inadequate food rations discourage parents from having many children. Though the family remains the basic social unit, marriage has become far more difficult. Few men can afford the traditional dowry or furnish a home, while many educated women seeking a successful career prefer to remain single.

Sixty years ago, large Bedouin tribes like the Shammar roamed the deserts. However, the number of tribespeople living a nomadic lifestyle has dwindled to insignificance due to motor transport, resettlement programs, and education.

Modernization most visibly affected the large cities of Iraq, as the government constructed roads, shopping centers, and large buildings. Modern homes and apartment houses in the better suburbs contrast with the narrow streets of older sections. Poor migrants, on the other hand, find temporary shelter on the outskirts of cities, often constructed of reed matting and mud.

Formal culture in Iraq, like most other Arab countries, stresses achievements in poetry and learning, although sculpture, painting, music, and drama are also important.

Few of the older generations of Iraqis formally entered school, but in recent decades the government has vastly extended the educational system. Primary education is compulsory, and schools now dot villages and cities alike. Their renovations are one achievement of the U.S.-led occupation. A modern curriculum with postwar textbooks has become prevalent.

Beyond secondary education, universities in the major cities offer instruction in most disciplines. Until 2003, all schools and universities were coeducational, although this appears subject to change in the political climate of the post-Saddam era. Another threat to higher education comes from the killing of nearly 200 professors and other academics during the first three years of the U.S. occupation of Iraq.

During the Ba'thist era, readership of the press remained low, a function of its predictable propaganda. Today, Iraq boast a relatively vibrant press. Over 100 papers have appeared, with titles like *New Era, Dawn of Baghdad,* and *The New Iraq,* reflecting popular desires for a better future. Daily concerns like insufficient clean water and electricity receive extensive coverage. Some private TV and radio stations compete with the government's broadcasting services and those of the two Kurdish parties.

By the 1980s, many urban men and some women selected Western styles of clothing, although the traditional gowns for men and the voluminous black *abayas* for women remained widely used, and dominated rural areas. Rural Kurds wore distinctive clothing, the men in baggy pants and the women in long gowns over pants.

After 2003, Arab women generally returned to traditional dress and headscarves. For many, this reflected religious conviction, but for others it was a way to avoid harassment.

The Ma'dan

For centuries, the Ma'dan, formed a sharp contrast to the traditional image of Arabs as herders of sheep and goats in a desert landscape. Inaccessible except by canoe, the Ma'dan inhabited a world of water, surrounded by vegetation and living in reed houses with high, arched ceilings. Some homes were even built on artificial islands constructed of reeds. All this was made possible by the flat terrain between the lower Tigris and Euphrates rivers, where the annual flow and flooding of the rivers created an area of permanent and seasonal marshes, lakes, and waterways that stretched across 10,000 square miles (26,000 square kilometers). Invaluable for fish and migrating birds, the marshes also provided an environment for rare species of otter, lizards, wild boar and other animals.

Shi'a by religion, the Ma'dan lived by fishing, herding water buffalo, and weaving reed mats. They preserved several unique customs and, except for limited trade, they mixed little with outsiders. During the war with Iran and later over Kuwait, military deserters sought sanctuary amidst the isolation of the marshes.

In response, the Iraqi government determined to control the region. Because irrigation and dams upstream diminished the flow of the rivers and ended the seasonal floods, some areas became accessible by roads. Later, the "Third River" drainage project diverted water to regions below the marshes. By the mid-1990s, the marshes effectively ceased to exist, and most of the Ma'dan population had fled to refugee camps in Iran. After the fall of Saddam, efforts are now being made, with international support, to restore this unique environment. However, regional drought and dams upstream in Iran, Turkey, and Syria, as well as in Iraq, currently divert too much water to maintain the full scale of the marshes.

Economy: Agriculture and livestock-raising dominated the economy before the construction of a modern oil industry in the 1930s. Iraq once grew 70% of the world's dates, mostly along the rivers and marshes of the south, and wool was a significant export. Today, wheat and barley are the main winter crops of the rain-fed north, while rice and cotton grow in irrigated areas in the south. Sheep, goats, cattle, and water buffalo are raised for meat, milk, and hides.

Agriculture improved markedly between 1958 and the 1980s as a result of irrigation schemes and the introduction of scientific methods. After 1990, failing irrigation pumps and sanctions on pesticides, equipment, and fertilizers combined to reduce output by at least 30%. Because pesticides could not be imported, the date groves became infested with insects, and harvests fell to a small fraction of the 1980s.

The English adjective "muslin" reflects the traditional textiles of Mosul. Present

Iraq

industrial production includes cement, leather, shoes, cotton textiles, and household articles such as matches. Small shop or home manufacturing is still important, especially for homespun woolens, rugs, and reed mats.

Economic sanctions imposed after Iraq invaded Kuwait distorted Iraq's development in almost every regard. UN sanctions after 1991 essentially halted all business investment, but the era of U.S. rule through the CPA witnessed a remarkable reduction in personal and corporate taxes. It also abolished all tariffs and permitted 100% foreign ownership of firms (aside from oil production). Iraqi-owned companies felt unprotected, but this offered foreigners a "capitalist's dream" of purchasing Iraqi land and firms exceptionally cheaply. Should these free-enterprise policies remain when peace and order eventually return, Iraq's business climate will contrast sharply with the rest of the region.

Insurgency, crime, and corruption have greatly slowed recovery from the economic collapse of 2003. Unemployment has neared 40% in certain areas, and for prolonged periods, and the country desperately needs economic growth. Unemployed men in war-torn societies often become desperate, which can lead to violence and a vicious cycle of more desperation and violence. The high hopes generated by the defeat of IS have not always been met. Promises of reconstruction in areas devastated by bitter warfare have foundered on the reality of economic stagnation and corruption.

Petroleum: Since the 1930s, oil exports have provided the major source of government revenue and as much as 95% of foreign exchange earnings. Iraq's proven reserves are vast: over 140 billion barrels, the fifth-largest in the world and about 10% of the global total. Nevertheless, petroleum output has rarely reached a level appropriate to the deposits. Besides wars, friction between the Iraq Petroleum Company and the government often limited exploration and production. Geography was also a major impediment.

Reaching overseas markets from an almost land-locked country proved difficult from the start. The initial oil deposits in the northeast lay almost as far from Iraq's few miles of southern shoreline as from the Mediterranean. Therefore, a pipeline was constructed to Palestine before World War II, but it proved useless when Israel won independence in 1948. Another line to ports in Syria and Lebanon depended on their goodwill and security, and Syria interrupted exports for decades. After the discovery of oil in the south, newer technology permitted offshore loading terminals for the export of southern crude. However, that route depended on freedom to navigate the Gulf and the Strait of Hormuz, and the facilities also lay uncomfortably close to Iran and Kuwait.

Seeking other export routes, in 1977 a new pipeline was completed to the Turkish port of Ceyhan, a new direct access to the Mediterranean that did not cross Syria. Iraq also arranged construction of a pipeline across Saudi Arabia to the Red Sea, capable of raising the export capacity above the country's OPEC quota. However, both the Turkish and Saudi lines were closed after the invasion of Kuwait, and sanctions greatly hampered investment in the industry for over a decade.

While the real role of Iraq's oil in leading the United States to invade is still widely debated, some Washington think-tanks publicly advocated breaking up the government oil monopoly into smaller units that would compete with each other and, in the process, destroy OPEC. After the occupation, Iraqi public opinion strongly opposed doing so, but the country lacked the ability to restore production rapidly. In 2009, Iraq auctioned production contracts for about half the country's oilfields, and Britain's BP and China's CNPC agreed to develop and service the giant Rumaila field in the south.

By 2016 Iraq had become OPEC's second biggest producer, outputting some 4.5 million barrels of oil per day and exporting 3.8 million. In early 2020, Iraq's generally rosy economic outlook was reversed by a calamitous drop in oil prices—precipitated

No cross zone in Karbala

Photo by William Parker

by a price war between Saudi Arabia and Russia on the one hand and a drastic drop in demand driven by the global coronavirus pandemic on the other. Iraq's draft 2020 budget was based on a projected oil price of $56 per barrel. In March 2020, prices had dropped to just $26 per barrel. The implications for Iraq, economically, politically, and socially, are profound.

The Future: While the overwhelming majority of Iraqis wish to put conflict behind them and enjoy peace, prosperity, and freedom to live their lives as they wish,

Iraq's future remains far from secured. Popular discontent, directed at the political establishment that came to power following the US-led invasion, remains high. From October 2019, mass protests rocked the country; rallies drew thousands onto the streets, while violent street battles between young Iraqi men and the security forces erupted after dark. Many hundreds were killed over months of violence, with the US blaming Iranian militia for a string of targeted assassinations.

After protestors stormed and burned down the Iranian consulate in Najaf—in

a sign of anger at Iran's seemingly unfettered interference in Iraqi politics—Prime Minister, Adil Abdul-Mahdi, was forced to tender his resignation.

Anger at spiraling corruption, low wages, limited job opportunities and poor public services, has played out against the backdrop of Iraq's contentious sectarian politics. A solution to the political challenges facing Iraq remains elusive. When and how the deeper challenge of uniting a fractured state and repairing the damage to Iraqi society, wreaked by years of occupation and war, can be achieved is unknown.

The State of Israel מדינת ישראל

Prime Minister David Ben-Gurion signs the independence declaration, May 14, 1948
AP/Wide World Photo

Area: 8,017 square miles (20,700 square kilometers) within the Armistice Demarcation lines effective 1949–67. In addition, since 1967, the West Bank (of the Jordan River), the Gaza Strip, and part of Syria have been under Israeli military occupation and subject to Israeli civilian settlement.

Population: 8.65 million

Capital City: Jerusalem (927,000). Few nations recognize Israeli sovereignty over East Jerusalem (captured in 1967) so most maintain their embassies in the Tel Aviv metropolitan area (460,000).

Climate: Summers are hot and dry, winters mild with moderate rainfall, except in the arid south of the country.

Neighboring Countries: Egypt (Southwest); Jordan (East); Syria (Northeast); Lebanon (North).

Time Zone: GMT +2 (+3 in summer).

Official Languages: Modern Hebrew (until 2018 Arabic was the second official language of Israel).

Other Principal Tongues: Arabic, English, Yiddish, Ladino, Polish, Russian, Persian, German, French, Hungarian, Bulgarian, and Romanian.

Ethnic Background: European, North African, and Asian.

Principal Religions: Judaism, Islam, and Christianity.

Chief Commercial Products: Computer software and high-tech applications, armaments, aircraft and aircraft servicing, military electronics equipment, chemicals, cut and polished diamonds, and agricultural products.

Main Agricultural Produce and Livestock: Oranges and other fruit, vegetables, wheat, potatoes, poultry, sheep, and cattle.

Major Trading Partners: the United States, China, Japan, Germany, the United Kingdom, the Netherlands, and Belgium.

Currency: New Israeli Shekel (1 shekel = 100 agorot).

Former Colonial Status: Britain conquered the territory now controlled by the State of Israel from the Ottoman Empire during 1916–1918 and held it until 1948.

National Day: May 14 (1948; Independence Day, like all holidays, is celebrated according to the Jewish calendar, and thus varies from late April to May).

Chief of State: Reuven Rivlin, President.

Head of Government: Binyamin Netanyahu, Prime Minister.

National Flag: White field with a broad blue horizontal stripes near both the top and bottom; centered between the stripes is a large blue "Shield of David," that is a cut-out six-pointed star.

Gross Domestic Product: $353 billion.

GDP per capita: $42,852.

Lying on the coast of the Mediterranean Sea with the Arabian Desert at its back door, Israel has considerable variety in climate and geography. The north enjoys good rainfall, sometimes as much as 40 inches (1,016 millimeters) in a winter, but the south is arid desert of gravel and rock. Summers can be unpleasantly warm throughout the land. Winters are not severe, although chilly at higher elevations, with possible snowfall.

The Mediterranean seaboard is bordered by a wide coastal plain, broken only by a ridge extending northwest from the West Bank to a promontory just south of Haifa. Much of this plain is under cultivation, as it has been for centuries. A central ridge runs south from the border with Lebanon through Israel and the West Bank, and then fans out in Israel's southern desert. The rainfall caught on the western slopes of these hills allows a variety of fruit trees to flourish, as well as small fields of grain and vegetables. The Hula Plain north of the Sea of Galilee has been partly reclaimed from marshes. A fertile plain lying to the southeast of Haifa has been a source of grains and other foods since ancient times.

Flowing from sources on the slopes of Mt. Hermon and the Golan Heights, the Jordan River provides the major source of fresh water in the region. South of the Sea of Galilee, the Jordan Valley lies entirely below sea level, and at the Dead Sea it reaches the lowest point on earth (1,388 feet—423 meters—below sea level, and falling). South of the Dead Sea, the deep valley rises gently to the Gulf of Aqaba and Israel's southern port, Eilat.

History: Proclaimed independent on May 14, 1948, Israel represents the triumph of modern Zionist dreams for a Jewish state. Its origins reach back many centuries, to the Roman Empire's expulsion of the Jewish population after their revolts in the 1st and 2nd centuries C.E.

Despite ravages of Muslim conquests, Crusaders, the Black Plague, famines, and rival rulers, the Jewish communities survived. They strengthened after 1492 with a rapid influx of Spanish Jews expelled from their homeland, but Ottoman rule (1517) decayed relatively quickly, and many Jews left to avoid the subsequent instability. By 1800 the Jewish presence in Palestine had dwindled to its lowest level in centuries. Events took an unexpected turn a century later. Zionism infused the Jewish world with the idea not merely of Jewish settlements in the Promised Land, but of a Jewish state.

The Birth of Political Zionism

The origins of Zionism lay far from the traditional and pious Jewish settlements in Palestine. Persecutions (including pogroms) in Eastern Europe, especially in Czarist Russia and Poland, led Leo Pinsker to demand a home for oppressed Jews in 1882. By 1900 thousands of Jews fleeing the anti-Semitism of Eastern Europe entered the region to pioneer new settlements with the goal of developing a self-supporting economy based on agriculture. That year, the number of Jews in Palestine increased to an estimated 45,000.

Against this backdrop, the concept of political Zionism arose. It was and remains the belief that Jews across the world constitute a single nation, that their right to liberty and independence—perhaps even their survival—included a return to the Promised Land and the establishment there of the State of Israel. Its best known early advocate was Theodor Herzl, who published *The Jewish State* in 1896 and organized the movement with the first Zionist World Congress, which took place in 1897 in Basel, Switzerland. Against the backdrop of European anti-Jewish persecution and discrimination he envisioned "the establishment for the Jewish people of a home in Palestine."

Only accepted by a handful at first, advocacy for the movement began to grow steadily. Eventually the main ideas of political Zionism included (1) the concept of "a Jewish People," not merely various communities following the religion of Judaism; (2) the inevitable recurrence of anti-Jewish persecution; (3) the impossibility of Jews living full and complete lives outside a distinctive and territorial state; (4) the historic right of "the Jewish People" to *Eretz Yisrael,* the Land of Israel; and (5) the moral obligation of Jews to support the national cause. These ideas formed the ideological foundation for the State of Israel.

Before World War I, the Land of Israel was part of the Ottoman Empire. Most Ottoman authorities did not favor Zionist immigration and land procurement because of local Arab opposition, but they were only partly able to resist external European support for Jewish immigration, as well as internal subterfuges and bribes that provided land to Jewish settlers.

The vigor and ideals of a new generation of Zionist immigrants, known as the Second Aliyah, deeply influenced the founding of modern social institutions. By 1914, they had established newspapers, trade unions, and political parties. Hebrew became the language of Jewish schools, the first secondary school started, and land was purchased for a university. Moreover, the character of Zionist settlement had been formed. The native Jewish settlements were primarily urban, and other Jewish immigrants lacked a clear philosophy of purpose, some producing wines for export using French experts, Arab labor, and Baron Edmond de Rothschild's subsidies. In contrast, socialists within the Zionist organization sought to build a society of collectives where Jews worked together at even the most menial tasks and refused

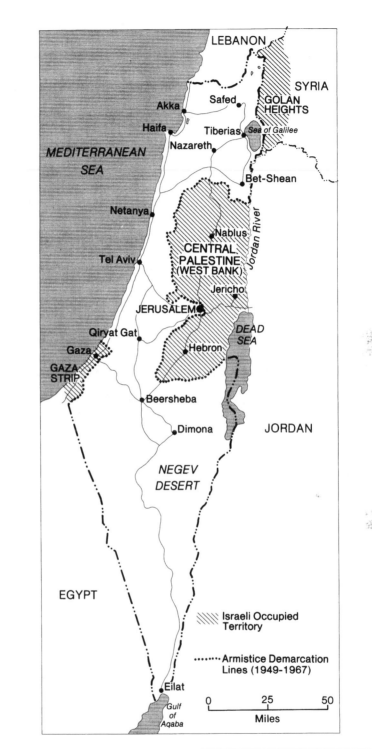

to employ Arab labor. By the beginning of World War I, about 100,000 Jews lived in Palestine, compared to roughly 550,000 Muslims and 70,000 Christians.

World War I proved a major turning point for Zionist hopes when the persuasive influence of a prominent scientist, Dr. Chaim Weizmann, led on November 2, 1917, to the Balfour Declaration. The text of this historically important document is worth quoting at length: "His Majesty's Government view with favor the establishment in

ZIONISM: For centuries, Zionism reflected the yearning of Jews to return to Zion, meaning the citadel at Jerusalem. After increasing nationalism in Europe, Theodor Herzl and others transformed cultural and religious Zionism into a political ideology. It holds that Jews everywhere form one people, whose protection requires a Jewish state in the Holy Land (often called Historic Palestine).

Israel

Palestine of a national home for the Jewish people, and will use their best endeavors to facilitate the achievement of this object, it being clearly understood that nothing shall be done which may prejudice the civil and religious rights of existing non-Jewish communities in Palestine, or the rights and political status enjoyed by Jews in any other country." With these words, the British government went on record with its support for a Jewish state, and it did so in a way that was logically inconsistent. How could a Jewish state be founded in Palestine without prejudicing the rights of existing non-Jewish communities there?

Jewish Achievements during the Mandate

With the end of war and a sympathetic nation (Britain) in control, Jewish immigration rapidly expanded, with predictable Arab reactions. In 1920, serious rioting broke out, as it did frequently during the Mandate. Jewish immigration rose sharply after Hitler gained power in Germany in 1933. By 1939, despite Arab riots and consequent British reductions in permitted immigration, nearly one-third of the population was Jewish. The relative prosperity of Palestine also attracted Arab immigrants, although those numbers are poorly documented. In any case, Zionist leaders planned for the day when Jews formed a majority of the total population. Until then, Jewish organizations bought land, settled it, and established industry.

Jewish land purchases provided a major source of Palestinian resentment. Fertile, watered farmland rarely lay vacant, and it frequently cost far more than similar land in the United States. Cultivation was handicapped by qualities the 20th century would change: the low level of agricultural technology and education, the absence of engine-powered pumps, incursions by Bedouins, expensive animal transportation, and blocked foreign markets.

Against this background, the Jewish National Fund purchased farmland from Arab landlords. The land had rarely been owned by those who farmed it, however. Significant purchases came from absentee landlords residing in Syria, Lebanon, Egypt, and elsewhere.

With the change of ownership, Palestinian tenant farmers became dispossessed. Whether a communally-run *kibbutz* or a *moshav* with private ownership, Jewish settlements stressed the dignity of Jewish labor, with Arab farmers pushed off the land. Moreover, once purchased, the land became the inalienable property of the Jewish community. Superior in education, technical knowledge, machinery, and incentives to the tenant farmers they replaced, Jewish settlers often succeeded in bringing the desert to bloom. Indeed their

Entrance to the Dome of the Rock, a sanctuary erected in the 7th century by Muslims on the site of the Temple of Solomon and the Second Temple, then in ruins. This is one of the most sacred of all Islamic shrines   Photo by Linda Cook

example influenced remaining Arab farmers, whose production increased substantially. Jaffa's oranges won fame as Jewish exports, but Arabs had cultivated them for centuries and still accounted for about half of all orange exports in the 1930s.

The social development of the Jewish community continued apace before World War II. The Hebrew University was founded in 1918, and universal elementary education was achieved in the 1930s. The Jewish Agency was established in 1929 to assist in fostering the immediate goals of immigration and the acquisition of land, as well as the promotion of religion and the use of Hebrew. The Jewish Self-Defense Force, the *Haganah*, developed in secret, eventually constituting a strong organization with significant weapons. The *Irgun* split from Haganah in 1931 and functioned on the principle that every Jews had a right to enter Palestine, only swift and severe retaliation would deter the Palestinian inhabitants of the area, and military action was a necessary precursor to the Jewish state. Jewish paramilitary forces fought alongside the British in quelling the Arab revolt of 1936–39—an uprising sparked by Jewish

1947 UN Recommendation

98

immigration and the growing perception of a demographic and political threat posed by settlers from Europe.

The Jewish community was not entirely united in the Zionist vision. One minority, firmly orthodox, feared that the nationalism of Zionism destroyed the religious basis of Judaism. At another extreme, the Revisionists led by Vladimir Jabotinsky demanded the immediate fulfillment of the Jewish national home on both sides of the Jordan River, including the East Bank or Transjordan.

The War for Independence, 1948–1949

With the Western world aghast at Hitler's Holocaust, after the war skillful Zionist leaders in America, cooperating with David Ben-Gurion, managed simultaneously to uphold U.S. limitations on Jewish immigration and to encourage President Truman to urge it publicly for Palestine. Meanwhile, Britain found the difficulties of ruling Palestine too great and turned the problem over to the newly-established United Nations. The Zionists won a major legal and psychological victory in late 1947 when the General Assembly voted by a narrow margin to recommend the political partition of Palestine. A blow to Palestinian nationalist aspirations, the plan assigned about 60% of the territory to a "Jewish State," although the Jewish settlers comprised only a bare one-third of the population. The Security Council did not endorse this recommendation nor did it provide any enforcement. As Britain had announced its plan to withdraw from Palestine by May 15, 1948, the issue was left open to resolution by force.

Within Palestine, force pitted the Arab majority against the Jewish minority. The latter were organized militarily into three groups. Representing the mainstream Zionist movement, the *Haganah* counted some 60,000 fighters, armed with a few tanks and backed by a supply system that smuggled arms from Europe. In contrast, the Revisionists of the 1920s influenced the two right-wing and smaller groups, the Irgun of Menachem Begin, and the Stern Gang. Sabotage of British military and transport installations already showed their capabilities. The Irgun and Stern Gang in particular adopted methods which see them broadly categorized as terrorist organizations. In one of the most well-known exploits, the Irgun, in 1946, blew up the British headquarters at the King David Hotel, killing 91.

The Palestinians, by contrast, organized no comparable military force, but counted on help from surrounding states. As the British forces withdrew, Syrian volunteers and army officers entered Galilee (January 1948), and an Arab Liberation Army formed, financed and supplied in part by

Egypt and Iraq. By April 1948 full-scale war broke out on many fronts, as both sides fought for as much land as they could obtain, regardless of the UN partition plan. Jewish forces quickly gained the Galilee region and Haifa, according to the partition, part of the Jewish state. In addition, they captured Jaffa and Akka (Acre), allocated to the Arab state.

The fighting involved entire communities, and descended quickly to brutality. The Irgun attacked the Arab village of Deir Yasin, near the vital road to Jerusalem, and massacred some 250 people, many of them women and children. In response, Arabs attacked a convoy headed for the Hebrew University and Hadassah Hospital outside Jerusalem: 77 professors, students, and medical personnel perished. Thereafter, hundreds of thousands of Palestinians fled from villages and cities, as they fell to the Zionists. Known in Arabic as *al-Nakbah* (the Catastrophe), the fighting of 1948 saw the expulsion of 750,000 Palestinians (more than half the pre-war population of Palestine) and the destruction of Palestinian nationalist dreams of an independent state.

As the Mandate drew to a close, on May 14, 1948, in Tel Aviv, David Ben-Gurion proclaimed the establishment of the State of Israel and won immediate recognition from the United States. The next day, backed by resolutions of the Arab League, armies of Egypt, Iraq, Transjordan, Syria, and Lebanon entered the war. The first war between Israel and the Arab states began with the Israelis fighting for their existence as a separate and independent state. The Arabs, on the other hand fought ostensibly for the Palestinians, but in reality had diverse and competing motivations. The Israeli army soon gained the offensive, striking at enemy targets with precision. Poorly coordinated on separate fronts, their equipment often obsolete or defective, the Arab armies failed to evade a UN arms embargo successfully. Like the four major wars that followed, this ended in Israeli victories almost everywhere, although casualties were high, with one Jew of every 100 in Israel killed.

The boundaries of the various armistices of 1949 found Israel much enlarged from the partition plan, with about 70% of the mandate's territory. The highlands of the West Bank remained largely Arab and controlled by the Arab Legion of Transjordan, except for a Jewish sector including part of Jerusalem. The other portion of Palestine not under Israeli rule was the Gaza Strip in the southwest, inhabited mostly by refugees and administered by Egypt.

Building the State of Israel

Independence meant a national government. Chaim Weizmann was elected to the largely honorary position of president in

1948, while the next year elections were held to the *Knesset*, the national parliament, whose majority leader is the prime minister. Israel's electoral system is highly sophisticated, translating preferences for political parties into seats in the legislature with admirable precision. With only one electoral district (the entire country), and proportional representation, each party's number of seats in the 120-member Knesset reflects very closely its percentage of the national vote.

Many parties competed in the elections of 1949. David Ben-Gurion headed the largest, *Mapai* (the core today of the Israel Labor Party), but though it dominated every cabinet until 1977 it never won a majority in the Knesset. Governments in Israel have always been coalitions, in the early years largely between Mapai and the National Religious Party. The need to form a parliamentary majority usually gives small parties disproportionate weight in forming the coalition's policies.

Besides the burden of defense, the government budget faced enormous costs of absorbing Jewish immigration. One of the first enactments of Israel, the Law of the Return, granted citizenship to all Jews who landed in Israel. In the first four years of independence, some 700,000 responded, many of them relatively poor and less-educated from Arab countries such as Morocco, Yemen, and Iraq. In contrast to the Eastern European *Ashkenazi* Jews who had dominated the Zionist movement to date, the new immigrants were overwhelmingly *Sephardic* Jews, with differences significant for Israeli politics and society (see Culture). Another important project was the Israel National Water Carrier, a system of canals and pipelines bringing water from the Jordan River to the coastal plain and then the Negev desert for irrigation.

The Arab Minority

For the Palestinians who remained, Israeli rule brought the second-class citizenship of a discontented and distrusted minority. The symbols of state reminded them that they had lost: the Star of David on an alien flag and an official language they could not speak. Israeli development often removed all traces of previous Arab habitation, including buildings and cemeteries, such that Palestinians witnessed the destruction of the memories of their past. The annual commemoration of Land Day (March 31) protests the confiscation of Palestinian land.

Less educated and relatively impoverished, with a high birthrate, Arab towns often failed to develop municipal services in a country where welfare came from charitable organizations more than from the state. Except for members of the Druze community (see Lebanon: Culture), Arabs

Israel

Theodor Herzl

the Gulf of Aqaba which threatened Israel's maritime route to East Asia. France and Britain had secretly joined the aggression when they then invaded the Suez Canal Zone. However, the United States, the Soviet Union, and most democracies condemned the invasion, President Eisenhower demanded Israel's withdrawal, and the United Nations halted the fighting. A UN Emergency Force took up positions on the Egyptian side of the frontier to prevent incidents, and the Straits of Tiran remained open for Israeli shipping.

Partly a consequence of intense political rivalries, in 1964 the Arab states voted to strengthen their armed forces and divert their major tributaries of the Jordan River. This threatened Israel's major source of fresh water. Palestinian guerrilla raids also increased. Then, in early 1967, President Nasser of Egypt ordered the UN Emergency Force to leave, moved troops into the Sinai, and announced the closure of the Straits of Tiran. In response, Israel demanded that the Straits remain open, world diplomacy sought to relax the tensions, and Jordan and Syria formed a united front with Egypt.

In June, responding at least in part to fiery Arab rhetoric, Israel launched a new war in full force. After a few hours, the Egypt air forces lay destroyed. Israeli tanks again swept across the Sinai to the Suez Canal. Because Jordan and Syria had joined the conflict, by the end of fighting Israel had also occupied the Old City of Jerusalem, the West Bank, and a strip of Syria's Golan Plateau.

Israel's victory translated into significant territorial expansion at a small cost in lives, wounded, and finances. Given prewar Arab belligerency, the United States did not force a return to the 1949 boundaries. The new ceasefire lines stretched fewer miles but encompassed three times the territory of 1949. As important, the Jewish Diaspora again felt its deep attachment to Israel. Thousands came to fight or replace men and women called to battle; funds flowed to aid society and government. Often discouraged and worried about emigration before the war, Israelis found their self-confidence returned with victory.

Diplomatic wrangling delayed the UN Security Council's formal conditions for peace until November 1967. Bland in its wording, Resolution 242 masked strong divisions of interpretation. Israel stressed the need for peace and its right to sovereignty. Thus, Israel interpreted withdrawal "from territories occupied" as withdrawal to secure boundaries. To Arabs, it meant the evacuation of *all* territories occupied. The words "a just settlement" of the refugee problem held no common meaning, and Palestinians resented being classified merely as refugees deprived of a nation.

are relieved of military service and thus of veterans benefits. Nevertheless, their economic progress generally exceeded that of most of the Arab world. Israeli Arabs (many of whom self-identify as Israeli Palestinian or Palestinian citizens of Israel) represent 21% of the population. They enjoy the right to vote in genuine multi-party elections, in contrast to most Arabs' living under dictatorships and authoritarian rulers.

Triumphant Wars: 1956, 1967, and 1973

Armistice agreements—truces between hostile nations—were negotiated with neighboring states in 1949 through UN mediation. Nevertheless, despite the efforts of the UN Truce Supervision Organization,

armed Palestinians launched attacks across the borders, sometimes killing civilians. In the long run, these raids enabled Israel to expand well beyond the 1949 armistice lines through three connected wars.

In 1953 the cabinet adopted a policy of "retaliatory" military responses, raids that destroyed property and inevitably produced civilian casualties on the Arab sides of the demarcation line. Ten times as many Arab civilians died as did Israeli civilians through armistice violations, a pattern that would become common in the ensuing decades. Increasing tensions and rapidly expanding Egyptian armaments led Israel to launch a massive surprise attack across the Sinai Peninsula in October 1956, seizing the Straits of Tiran at the entrance to

Israel moved quickly to incorporate East Jerusalem into Israel itself. Within the Old City lies the Wailing Wall, remaining from the Second Temple and the most sacred Jewish shrine. Greatly complicating the achievement of peace, the Wailing Wall borders the Haram al-Sharif, one of the holiest Muslim shrines, containing the Dome of the Rock and al-Aqsa Mosque. Prohibited from worshiping there during Jordanian rule, the Israelis bulldozed neighboring houses for better access. Reconstruction of the old Jewish quarter commenced, and the city administration of Jewish Jerusalem stretched east.

Unlike events in 1956 and 1967, the third war was not initiated by Israel. While Israel observed *Yom Kippur*, the Day of Atonement, in October 1973, surprise attacks by Egypt and Syria opened the war. Initially successful in crossing the Suez Canal and advancing on the Golan, the Egyptians and Syrians never reached Israel. Rather, they attacked Israeli forces on their own (occupied) national territories.

Mobilizing rapidly, the Israel Defense Force (IDF) counter-attacked, and intense tank battles destroyed perhaps 2,000 tanks and 500 aircraft. Benefiting from advanced arms and technical superiority, units led by General Ariel Sharon crossed the Suez Canal into Egypt itself, encircling an entire Egyptian army and leaving Cairo almost defenseless. The Syrians likewise retreated, but the enormous cost of the war convinced many on both sides of its futility. Henry Kissinger, the American Secretary of State, mediated disengagement agreements that withdrew Israeli troops from the Suez Canal and oil fields used since 1967. The agreement also returned a narrow portion of the Golan Heights to Syria, including the devastated town of Quneitra. Egypt allowed non-military cargoes for Israel to pass through the newly-reopened Canal.

Peace with Egypt and Camp David

When elections approached in 1977, the Labor government disintegrated under charges of mismanagement and corruption. Supported strongly by Sephardic Jews, Likud triumphed and ended Labor's unbroken hold on government. Menachem Begin, who had led Irgun fighters against the British and long opposed returning any occupied territory, formed a coalition of religious and right-wing parties. Rejecting socialism, the government raised taxes, devalued the currency, and reduced subsidies. The labor unions went on strike.

That same year, President Sadat of Egypt offered to visit Jerusalem in quest of genuine peace. For the first time, an Arab ruler publicly met with Israel's prime minister and talked directly to Israelis in their own country. Sadat offered full peace. In exchange, he asked for the principle of withdrawal from the occupied lands and the right of Palestinians to determine their own future.

Sadat's dramatic moves posed a difficult choice for Jerusalem: between territory and peace. After weeks of equivocation, Prime Minister Begin responded that his government could not give up "Judea and Samaria" (to others, the "West Bank"); they formed part of the "historic land of Israel." Instead he offered Palestinians "living in the Land of Israel" civil autonomy under Israeli control.

Attacks by Palestinians and an Israeli invasion of southern Lebanon further jeopardized diplomatic progress, until President Carter invited the Israeli and Egyptian leaders to Camp David. Secluded from the press and political pressures, Menachem Begin and Anwar Sadat negotiated the agreements finally signed at the White House. Israel obtained a major policy goal: peace with Egypt, the most powerful Arab state, at the cost of returning the militarily-valuable Sinai. However, a wider peace was not achieved. Although yielding four Jewish settlements in Egypt, Begin and Likud pledged that no other settlements would ever be removed, effectively ruling out exchanging other occupied territories for peace. Therefore, while Camp David assured Israel's conventional military superiority, it was followed by more conflict.

With Palestinians increasingly restive in the West Bank and Gaza, the Begin cabinet worried about the growing Palestinian military in Lebanon. Under secret plans

---

SPECIAL DOCUMENT

UN Security Council Resolution 242

On November 22, 1967, the Security Council of the United Nations unanimously approved—and has subsequently reaffirmed—a resolution outlining the basis for peace between the State of Israel and the Arab countries with which it is in conflict. The United States, Israel and Egypt, in the Camp David accords of September 1978, specifically endorsed the implementation of this resolution "in all its parts." The following is the text of that resolution:

The Security Council,

Expressing its continuing concern with the grave situation in the Middle East,

Emphasizing the inadmissibility of the acquisition of territory by war and the need to work for a just and lasting peace in which every state in the area can live in security,

Emphasizing further that all member states in their acceptance of the Charter of the United Nations have undertaken a commitment to act in accordance with Article 2 of the Charter,

1. Affirms that the fulfillment of Charter principles requires the establishment of a just and lasting peace in the Middle East which should include the application of both of the following principles: (a) Withdrawal of Israel armed forces from territories occupied in the recent conflict; (b) Termination of all claims or states of belligerency and respect for and acknowledgment of the sovereignty, territorial integrity and political independence of every state in the area and their right to live in peace within secure and recognized boundaries free from threats.

2. Affirms further the necessity: (a) For guaranteeing freedom of navigation through international waterways in the area; (b) For achieving a just settlement of the refugee problem; (c) For guaranteeing the territorial inviolability and political independence of every state in the area, through measures including the establishment of demilitarized zones.

3. Requests the Secretary-General to designate a special representative to proceed to the Middle East to establish and maintain contacts with the states concerned in order to promote agreement and assist efforts to achieve a peaceful and accepted settlement.

4. Requests the Secretary-General to report to the Security Council on the progress of the efforts of the special representative as soon as possible.

Israel

drawn up by Defense Minister Ariel Sharon, in 1982 Israeli forces used a pretext to launch a massive invasion of Lebanon. The IDF eventually reached Beirut's suburbs and linked up with the Maronite Christian enclave. Outside Beirut, Israeli casualties began to mount, eventually making the invasion of Lebanon Israel's most costly foreign war, measured in lives. Moreover, Israeli troops permitted Maronite militiamen to enter captured Palestinian refugee camps, where they massacred over 1,000 men, women, and children. Israeli opinion grew increasingly divided. Many citizens, including some officers, demonstrated for withdrawal from Lebanon; the Peace Now movement reflected such concerns.

Soviet Immigrants Change the Demographics

Jewish immigration from the Soviet Union and the Palestinian *intifada* combined to challenge Israel's occupation, politics and society in the early 1990s. Aided by changes in Soviet society, tens of thousands of Jews and their spouses emigrated from Russia to Israel. This massive population transfer touched the very basis of Zionism. Soviet immigrants boosted the productive population, and they postponed the threatened Arab majority for decades. Further immigrants were airlifted to Israel from Ethiopia in 1991. In time, the immigrants changed Israeli society, with Russian newspapers and even Orthodox churches appearing. Politically, the new immigrants generally opposed withdrawal from the occupied territories, and their politicians initially allied with Likud. They later supported the secular nationalist platform of *Yisrael Beiteinu*, "Israel is our home."

Consideration of a Palestinian State

The first twenty years of Israeli's occupation of the lands captured in 1967 brought few serious challenges. However, the seven years from 1987 to 1994 changed the entire focus of Israeli-Palestinian relations.

The strikes, civil disobedience, rock-throwing, and other violence of the first Palestinian intifada began in late 1987. Coordinated in secret, it took Israeli leaders by surprise. The intifada marked a distinct change from the physical threats posed by Arab armies in past wars. Because the intifada stressed defiance, not attacks on Israel, it contrasted sharply with attacks by Palestinian guerrillas. Indeed, only 15 Israelis died in its first year, compared to more than 360 Palestinians.

Crushing the uprising meant using one of the world's most advanced war machines against teenagers throwing stones and Molotov cocktails. Annual reserve duty was extended, and troops adopted lethal tactics. Nevertheless, military force did not crush the political uprising: rather, the intifada focused world attention on the Palestinians. The United States used "shuttle diplomacy," with high level diplomats traveling throughout the region to meet with relevant leaders. It officially accused Israel of violating human rights and inflicting "many avoidable deaths." Yasir Arafat, Chairman of the PLO, successfully used world concern over the intifada to win UN General Assembly approval of an international peace conference which would grant Palestinians "official observer" status. The Likud resistance to land for peace had lost its foreign support: even American sympathizers and major Jewish groups supported Israel–PLO talks under certain conditions.

Israeli opposition to a Palestinian state includes many strands, most of which relate to the physical and economic security of the state. With Tel Aviv just 32 miles (51 kilometers) from the West Bank as the crow flies, and Jerusalem on the border of the West Bank, Israeli governments have long been concerned at the prospect of an Arab attack originating from the east. If Palestinians were to have a state of their own, even if that state were demilitarized, Israel would no longer be able to prevent the military forces of other states from amassing on its borders. In short, the physical "buffer" that the West Bank represents for Israeli security would be lost. Israel has also expressed concern about the prospect of religious extremists taking control of any Palestinian state. Though this seems far-fetched to many, the Israeli response has been that any skeptics should simply look to Gaza, where Hamas has now held sway for years. Ironically, it was the failure of the secular PLO to achieve an end to Israeli occupation and secure political rights for Palestinians, that saw the rise of Islamist political groups in Palestine.

Other reasons to keep the territories lie in ideology. Revisionist Zionists, from Jabotinsky in the 1920s to ultra-Orthodox Jews today, stress that Israel must occupy the whole of the Biblical Promised Land. Over Jerusalem, the refusal to withdraw becomes almost universal. Arab East Jerusalem physically forms part of a city that Israel has repeatedly promise never to divide. Moreover, Judaism's most sacred shrine, the Wailing Wall, lies within the largely-Arab Old City.

Political reality presents another major hurdle. Decades of construction beyond the 1967 lines have resulted in the settlement of well over 400,000 Jewish settlers in the West Bank and East Jerusalem.Though numbering fewer than 10% of the electorate, these settlers form a major political force with one over-riding issue: "No withdrawal." Finally, there are economic reasons to hold the West Bank, among them the vital water surplus it provides for Israel itself.

Pressures do exist for compromise. One is the difficulty of indefinitely occupying a land and depriving its inhabitants of self-determination. Ruling the restive population requires military control, and increases military influence in public and private life. Moral questions arise, short of ethnic cleansing, the greater Arab birthrate will soon provide more Arabs than Jews living between the sea and the Jordan River.

General Rabin & Negotiation from Strength

Iraq's seizure of Kuwait in 1990 seemed a grave threat to Israel's security, because Saddam Hussein claimed a war over

The West ("Wailing") Wall within Jerusalem where Jews pray. Tradition is that the wall was partially built of materials from Solomon's temple　　Photo by Linda Cook

Kuwait was actually a war for Israel. The government issued gas masks, and hours after coalition forces attacked Iraq in 1991 the first Scud missiles landed in Tel Aviv, destroying and damaging homes in a residential area. Scores of injuries and a few deaths resulted from the attacks. Remarkably, Israel did not retaliate: a general Arab–Israeli conflict would have benefited Iraq, but not the United States or its Arab allies. Patriot missile crews arrived to defend Tel Aviv, and U.S. aid covered missile damage, military expenses, and economic losses such as the decline in tourism.

For the 1991 elections, Labor selected Yitzhak Rabin as its leader. A tough general, he nevertheless favored Palestinian autonomy and peace through concessions. After Labor won a decisive victory, Rabin halted the construction of new settlements in the Occupied Territories. This won U.S. loan guarantees for housing construction within Israel and raised hopes at the peace talks. Rabin's negotiators even conceded a possible withdrawal from the Golan Heights in return for peace with Syria.

The ongoing intifada proved the most pressing and increasingly lethal problem (see Palestine: History). Finally, Rabin closed Israel to the 60,000 workers from the Occupied Territories, thus halting most contacts between Israelis and Palestinians. As calm returned, most Israelis favored a permanent ban. At a deeper level, many believed that the practical separation of the Territories made some later withdrawal more likely.

After secret negotiations in Oslo with the PLO produced a Declaration of Principles for an eventual peace agreement, Prime Minister Rabin and PLO Chairman Yasir Arafat publicly shook hands at the White House in 1993. The declaration stipulated a withdrawal from most of the Gaza Strip and Jericho and the creation of a Palestinian Authority to administer them. It also specified later Israeli administrative and military withdrawals from much of the West Bank.

The Oslo Accords were interim agreements, not a peace agreement. They deliberately left many matters undecided to be resolved within a period of five years. The most difficult issues, such as borders, Palestinian refugees, and East Jerusalem (claimed as the Palestinian capital), remained for the final agreement, to be reached after confidence-building measures provided greater trust between the two sides. Jewish and Arab opponents of peace sought to destroy the peace process through violence that often took the lives of civilians, including children. Each unfortunate case required revenge that in turn incited reprisals that continued the cycle of violence. However, "Oslo" had established a timetable, and after last-minute

Presidents Sadat, Carter and Prime Minister Begin, September 17, 1978, at the White House Courtesy of the Jimmy Carter Library

bickering, in 1994 the Israeli flag was lowered over Gaza and Jericho.

Initial, limited withdrawal brought neither economic bonanza nor safety to Israel. Suicide attacks by Hamas and Islamic Jihad, particularly against buses, killed scores of Israelis. In response, the cabinet again sealed the border with Gaza and the West Bank and halted the agreed release of prisoners. Fearing for the safety of isolated settlements, the cabinet halted further withdrawals.

Despite mixed success with Palestinians, the Oslo Accords brought welcome progress towards peace with some Arab states. Morocco established diplomatic relations. More dramatically, Jordan signed a peace treaty with Israel in 1994, after settling its demands for water rights and a small occupied territory of 145 square miles (375 square kilometers) along the border. Visionaries predicted broad trade and development links, as well as hydroelectric and desalination schemes at the Dead Sea. Peace with Syria proved more difficult, given the domestically hazardous issue of the Golan Heights. Syria continues to demand return of the entire territory. Repeated negotiations have accomplished nothing—but occasionally provided a distraction when a prime minister needs relief from domestic pressures.

In 2019, U.S. President Donald Trump declared that "the United States recognizes that the Golan Heights are part of the State of Israel," making the United States the first and only country to recognize Israeli sovereignty over the annexed region. Other countries have not followed suit.

The Assassination of Yitzhak Rabin

Despite vicious attacks by right-wing extremists, including posters depicting Prime Minister Rabin as a Nazi, in 1995 the cabinet approved a withdrawal from several West Bank cities as a prelude to Palestinian elections. Two months later, after Rabin celebrated at a peace rally in Tel Aviv, a fanatical Orthodox law student shot him in the back. The assassin murdered, he said, because Rabin had negotiated away Israel's God-given land and endangered settlers' lives.

Immediately after Rabin's death, the vast majority of Israelis supported the peace negotiations. Regrettably, suicide attacks, targeted assassinations, and an economic closure weakened advocates of peace on both sides. Israelis buried the dead while elections approached.

Stagnation, not Peace

The forceful and telegenic Binyamin "Bibi" Netanyahu of Likud won the 1996 elections after he accepted Oslo, promising to win a more secure peace in a last-minute gesture that clinched his victory.

In reality, stagnation resulted, not peace. Construction of the Jewish settlement of *Har Homa* on Arab land between East Jerusalem and Bethlehem completed the Jewish encirclement of Arab East Jerusalem. When the bulldozers moved in, Palestinian leaders halted peace negotiations.

Serious fractures appeared within domestic society. Russian and Ethiopian immigrants demanded spending to meet their needs, while many Sephardim (descendants of Middle Eastern Jews) sensed the Ashkenazi (European-descended) elite looked down on them. Students went on strike, demanding lower tuition, and government workers called for higher pay. The divide between religious and secular Jews became a greater issue than peace, and the resulting emotions challenged the integrity of government. When the Supreme Court ended the draft exemption for the Orthodox and allowed farms to operate on the Sabbath, a mass rally attacked the court.

Israel

The "government of national unity," September 1984

Secular Jews objected to the automatic draft deferments for ultra-Orthodox *(Haredim)* students in yeshivas.

Ehud Barak: Worthy Goals Unfulfilled

After Netanyahu's government collapsed, elections brought Labor's new leader, the much-decorated General Ehud Barak, to power with a coalition government.

Against the background of an increasingly harsh culture war between secularists and practicing Orthodox and ultra-Orthodox Jews, the cabinet tackled difficult and divisive issues. Barak moved to end the abuse of draft deferments by ultra-Orthodox men. Yossi Sarid, the minister of education, changed the history curriculum to reinterpret the War of Independence and admit Israeli mistakes. Through its brinkmanship over the budget, the ultra-Orthodox political party Shas retained large subsidies for its badly-run school system.

The difficult work of government reform seemed overshadowed by scandals. President Ezer Weizmann, accused of receiving illegal payments, fell from office, as did the deputy prime minister, over allegations of sexual assault. Binyamin Netanyahu was blamed for corruption and misuse of gifts he received as prime minister, though the charges were dropped. During the next decade, President Katzav was charged with rape, resigned in disgrace, and eventually imprisoned. Further from politics, financial irregularities in some yeshivas vied for

publicity with the national soccer team. Its players lost a match after a pre-game visit to a brothel.

In foreign affairs, Barak sought solutions to all remaining conflicts. He negotiated with Syria and accepted an eventual Palestinian state. Overcoming right-wing criticism, he opened a 27-mile (43 kilometer) route connecting the Gaza Strip with the West Bank. Ten unauthorized Jewish settlements on the West Bank were closed, although dozens remained.

Although Barak often proved a tough defender of Israel's interests, his reputation came to rest on withdrawal from South Lebanon. Unable to negotiate a departure from territory occupied for two decades, the IDF withdrew under pressure in 2000.

Failure at Camp David

In a last ditch effort before departing office, President Clinton summoned both Prime Minister Barak and Chairman Arafat to Camp David in 2000. Removed from the media spotlight, Clinton attempted to resolve the outstanding issues: borders, settlements, refugees, and East Jerusalem. Conceding what no Israeli leader had yielded previously, Barak offered Arafat a Palestinian state with a capital in the Jerusalem suburbs, some local control in Arab districts of the city, and possible international sovereignty over the Muslim Holy Places (the Haram al-Sharif). A small number of refugees would be reunited with families in Israel.

This offer defied the almost universal Israeli desire for a united Jerusalem. It outraged the settlers, Likud, and most religious parties. Vague talk of treason and assassination prompted increased security for the prime minister. But Yasir Arafat rejected the proposal because it failed to meet one minimum Palestinian demand: Arab sovereignty for Arab Jerusalem. This outright rejection was almost certainly a grave misstep, given that immense suffering and thousands of dead since then have failed to produce so favorable an offer. On his return, Barak resigned, forcing an election only for the office of prime minister.

Sharon Dominates Politics; Oslo Collapses

Likud's nominee was the party leader, General Ariel Sharon. Sharon's aggressive career had contributed to the deaths of many Arab civilians, and his recent visit to the Haram al-Sharif, asserting that the Temple Mount was not negotiable, set ablaze already heated passions. A new intifada broke out, this one much more violent. Without a proposed peace agreement, the election failed to offer voters a referendum on peace. Instead, it focused on personalities and approaches. Sharon won in a landslide and formed a government of national unity, including Labor leaders in sensitive positions.

The new intifada brought the Oslo peace process to collapse, and violence escalated on both sides. In response to terror attacks,

Israeli troops surrounded Palestinian-controlled areas, blocked travel and trade, and squeezed them economically. Targeted assassinations killed dozens of alleged terrorist leaders and often innocent bystanders. Palestinian security forces became frequent targets. Yasir Arafat was limited to the city of Ramallah and, after renewed Israeli occupation of much of the West Bank, to two rooms in his headquarters, until Israeli troops withdrew under U.S. pressure.

American, Egyptian, European, and other mediators vainly tried to calm the crisis. but found themselves blocked by the interplay of Palestinian attacks and Israeli intransigence. Sharon's cabinet refused to talk peace during violence and demanded seven days of calm before opening talks or implementing peace proposals. But Sharon excluded from "violence" Israeli assassinations of Palestinian leaders. Historians may well conclude that Prime Minister Sharon bore significant responsibility for the hostilities. Sharon gave Israeli troops great freedom to attack Palestinian suspects, and eyewitnesses claimed the killing of men and boys sleeping or otherwise unarmed.

Sharon had promised peace, but blood flowed in Jewish streets. The economy had nosedived into recession, and 20% of the population lived in poverty. A poll found that most Israelis felt they had never had it so bad. Serious cuts in government services were likely. Media accounts of financial corruption reached all the way up to Sharon himself, accused of past violations of campaign finance laws.

Nevertheless, Sharon and the Likud easily won the 2003 elections, while the left-wing of Israeli politics—*Meretz*, and Labor itself—fell badly, as did Shas. Likud almost doubled its seats in the Knesset. Clearly, Israelis had reacted to the violence by blaming Hamas and other Palestinians. Many Israelis deserted the parties inclined to compromise for peace.

The Roadmap, Gaza, and Kadima

In 2002 the international community aimed to jumpstart the peace process with a "roadmap for peace" developed by the United States, the United Nations, the European Union, and Russia. Backing a two-state solution, the roadmap proposed a provisional Palestinian entity by 2003 and a complete agreement by 2005. The roadmap reflected Israeli and U.S. rejection of Yasir Arafat as a trustworthy Palestinian leader, but it clearly accepted a Palestinian state. This dismayed many settlers, other right-wing Israelis, and their American fundamentalist supporters, some of whom had proposed removing all Palestinians to Jordan. Despite their warnings, President Bush backed the roadmap. Prime Minister Sharon initially refused to accept the plan,

but eventually his cabinet bowed to foreign pressure and did so—by a narrow majority.

The roadmap's first steps included, on the Israeli side, withdrawal from the recently occupied towns and cities, a halt to settlement activity, and the dismantling of illegal and some legal settlements, to permit contiguous Palestinian areas. For their part, the Palestinians needed to achieve political reform (including elections) and end the violence.

Ariel Sharon had always backed Jewish settlements. For decades his vision of a Palestinian state had been Arabs densely packed into several small clusters with municipal self-government but not much else, divided from each other by corridors of Israeli roads and military posts. Sharon's approval of the roadmap was likely a momentary acquiescence to be followed by later obstruction. Certainly, he remained committed to building homes in West Bank settlements, despite U.S. objections.

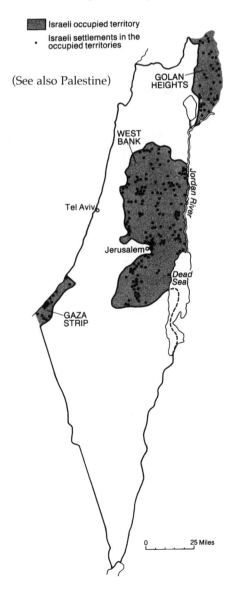

Israeli occupied territory

Israeli settlements in the occupied territories

(See also Palestine)

GOLAN HEIGHTS

WEST BANK

Jordan River

Tel Aviv

Jerusalem

Dead Sea

GAZA STRIP

0   25 Miles

Nevertheless, Sharon's ideology split from the hardliners because he recognized that the Arab population of Gaza was too dense and crowded for Jewish settlements to succeed, and that the price for holding Gaza was continuing casualties.

His solution was to withdraw from the entire Gaza Strip, unilaterally, and for good measure, also from four unofficial West Bank settlements. The roadmap was incidental: other settlements would remain. Most Israelis backed the withdrawal, but the settlement movement bitterly attacked it, and their vigorous campaign led Likud to reject it. The prime minister won cabinet approval for a modified plan, but his coalition frayed.

The Gaza plan represented a one-sided solution to the Israeli-Palestinian conflict. Its logical outcome was not a negotiated permanent peace, but an Israel beyond Palestinian violence, leaving the Palestinians to live in poverty and, if they were inclined, even anarchy. The same philosophy motivated construction of a 300-mile barrier to separate the Arab West Bank from Israel—comfortably encircling major Jewish enclaves at Palestinian expense. It cuts off considerable Arab land (by one estimate this exceeds 40% of the West Bank) and some homes. UN reports condemned it, and the International Court of Justice, in an advisory opinion, decried it as illegal.

To deter any boasts that Israel had been forced out of Gaza, as had been claimed for South Lebanon, IDF raids destroyed the infrastructure and workshops of Hamas and Islamic Jihad. An invasion of the Jabaliya camp in northern Gaza killed more than 100 Palestinians. Success for a unilateral withdrawal also meant the targeted assassination of extremist leaders, most prominently Sheikh Ahmad Yassin, the so-called "spiritual leader" of Hamas and its unifying figure.

On schedule in 2005, Israeli troops removed some 8,500 settlers who clung to the 21 small colonies of Gaza. Building on success, Sharon overturned the political landscape by abandoning Likud and forming a new, centrist party, *Kadima* ("Forward"). A veritable tidal wave of leading politicians, including Shimon Peres, abandoned their parties and joined Kadima, destroying decades-old political and social boundaries. Competitors fumed that Kadima lacked ideology and was dominated by one man.

Months before the 2006 elections, a massive stroke struck the 77-year-old prime minister. The shocked nation compared Sharon's fate with the assassination of Yitzhak Rabin a decade earlier. Once again, a traditionally hawkish leader was struck down on the verge of potentially dramatic actions for peace. Some radical

Israel

THE JERUSALEM POST

SECOND EDITION

VOLUME LXIII, NUMBER 19113 ● SUNDAY, NOVEMBER 5, 1995 ● HESHVAN 12, 5756 ● II JAMAD 12, 1416 ● NIS 4.20 (EILAT NIS 3.60)

RABIN ASSASSINATED

Peres pays tribute to longtime rival, partner

DAVID MAKOVSKY, BATSHEVA TSUR and agencies

AN empty chair draped in black marked Prime Minister Yitzhak Rabin's place at the cabinet table as the nation's leaders met in emergency session and declared a transition government hours after he was assassinated at a peace rally.

Ministers wept while acting Prime Minister Shimon Peres paid tribute to his long-time political rival and partner in forging peace with the Palestinians.

"He was a rare leader in Jewish history...in the last three years as Israeli prime minister he effected a revolution in the positive sense in the Middle East," Peres said in televised remarks.

"I asked myself if this happened to me, what would I want to happen later," Peres

(Continued on Page 12)

A black day for the whole Jewish nation

EDITORIAL

THE shock is·universal. No Israeli, no Jew, no decent human being anywhere can help being shaken to the core, shattered to the depth of his and her soul by the news of the assassination of Prime Minister

Pronounced dead at 11:15 p.m. after being shot

RAINE MARCUS, SARAH HONIG and ALON PINKAS

PRIME Minister Yitzhak Rabin was assassinated last night by a 27-year-old Herzliya law student, who fired three bullets from a pistol at him at point-blank range. Rabin was felled as he was entering his official car at 9:50 p.m. at the conclusion of a massive pro-peace rally in Tel Aviv's Kikar Malchei Yisrael attended by some 100,000 people.

Rabin was pronounced dead at 11:15 p.m. by doctors at Ichilov Hospital, where he had been brought with wounds to his back, abdomen, and chest. He died on the operating table from massive hemorrhaging and heart failure, without regaining consciousness.

The prime minister was not wearing a bullet-proof vest, that he "did not regret his deed," which he said was "planned for some time."

A police source said that Amir had twice before attempted to assassinate Rabin, but no more details were available. In the two previous attempts, said the source, Amir tried to get close to the prime minister and was armed both times.

Amir was apprehended immediately after the shooting by police and pressed up against a cement wall, as dozens of policemen surrounded him.

Eyewitnesses reported seeing Rabin collapse. His bodyguards pushed him into the car and whisked him off to Ichilov Hospital, some 500 meters away. One of Rabin's bodyguards was also wounded by bullets.

Health Minister Ephraim Sneh told reporters at midnight that Rabin sustained bullet wounds in

---

settlers quietly gave God credit for both incidents.

The deputy prime minister, Ehud Olmert, assumed control of both government and party. He maintained Kadima's unity and rallied the nation around Sharon's legacy. The other parties fared less well. The electorate remembered that Likud's nominee, Binyamin Netanyahu, had vacillated over Gaza and had clung to his cabinet post. Labor managed to present a thoughtful campaign, concentrating on domestic issues.

Kadima won 29 seats, and became the Knesset's largest party. Likud tumbled to apparent insignificance, with about 10% of the vote, similar to the Russian émigrés' hardline Yisrael Beiteinu and Shas. Within weeks, Ehud Olmert negotiated a coalition with Labor, Shas, and the Pensioners' Party. However, the press savaged several appointments and the cabinet's lack of military expertise. One opinion poll suggested half the population had misgivings about the new prime minister.

The War with Hizbullah, 2006

Hizbullah guerillas crossed the Lebanese–Israeli border in July 2006, attacked an isolated patrol, and captured two Israeli soldiers. The raid apparently sought hostages for bargaining and to embarrass Israel's newly-formed coalition. The Olmert cabinet, determined to rescue the captives, escalated its response to the raid into a war to destroy Hizbullah. The IDF attacked Hizbullah's military positions and bombed widely. It also targeted Lebanon more broadly, overlooking the important fact that the Lebanese state had little to no control over Hizbullah's actions. Beirut's airport, vital road bridges, gasoline service stations, factories, and road traffic far from battlefields was attacked.

Hizbullah responded by launching missiles—several thousand of them—far deeper into Israel than ever before. They reached Haifa and most of northern Israel. It also fought the poorly-executed Israeli ground assault well enough to boast of divine victory. In any case, Hizbullah was not destroyed. The fighting finally ended when the Security Council established a ceasefire (see Lebanon: History) in a conflict whose human cost was heavy for Israel (40 civilians, 112 military personnel), although heavier still for Hizbullah.

The Israeli public quickly concluded that the war had been bungled by an incompetent cabinet and military. Commissions investigated the failures, and resignations followed. Combined with missile attacks on southern Israeli towns from Gaza, the war led many Israelis to question the very possibility of a two-state solution. After all, Hamas and Islamic Jihad on the southern border, and Hizbullah along the north, rejected Israel's very right to exist.

Olmert Stumbles, Launches Gaza War

A man known to appreciate luxuries, over the years Ehud Olmert had received funds from questionable sources, and had been investigated, but charges were dropped. This time an American businessman testified that he had passed envelopes stuffed with cash for the prime minister's political campaigns. The claims threatened the ruling coalition. Polls indicated that nearly 70% of Israelis desired Olmert to step down, and Labor threatened to withdraw from the cabinet. Olmert agreed to go, but remained in office pending Knesset elections in early 2009. National security issues dominated his last months in office.

After Hamas gunmen gained control of Gaza in 2007, the territory provided a base for missile and other attacks on Israel but lacked a government willing to negotiate with Israel, or one that Israel recognized. The simple, home-made Qassam missiles fired by Hamas and Islamic Jihad at the closest town, Sderot, and the city of Ashkelon did not constitute a strategic threat, but they inflicted casualties. They also posed the eventual risk of longer-range missiles with larger warheads. Ariel Sharon's entire policy of disengagement/unilateral withdrawal collapsed.

In response, the Olmert cabinet declared the Gaza Strip a "hostile entity." In order to force Hamas to halt the attacks, it restricted deliveries of fuel, electricity, and almost all

Former Prime Minister Ehud Olmert

supplies, eventually including food. This effectively crushed the territory's economic life. Virtually the entire population came to subsist on international assistance (see Palestine: history). A truce negotiated in mid-2008 reduced the rocket fire significantly, but the border blockade remained. The truce broke down in response to an Israeli attack on an alleged tunnel from Gaza into Israel.

Striking by surprise in December 2008, the Israeli air force opened the Gaza War when it attacked Gaza, demolishing Hamas militia bases, rocket launching sites, police facilities, and government offices. Civilian locations were also targeted—homes, mosques, hospitals, schools, and others—on grounds they were used by Hamas fighters or stored weapons. After a week of aerial bombardment, the Israeli army invaded the Strip, eventually entering parts of the city of Gaza itself.

After three weeks of fighting, Prime Minister Olmert declared a unilateral ceasefire and promised a withdrawal from the Strip if rocket attacks ended. With the Gaza Strip bisected and most Palestinian population centers surrounded, the major objectives had evidently been achieved. Soon after, Hamas also ended its major hostilities, although in the months following some rockets were fired at Israeli towns.

The Gaza War was planned months before the pretext for launching it, and its major goal was to deter possible future attacks by any enemy, by demonstrating the power and effectiveness of the military's response. Although precision weapons were often used by the Israeli forces, the fighting claimed the lives of hundreds of Hamas combatants as well as many hundreds of civilians. By contrast, just three Israeli civilians and 10 soldiers were killed. Critics claimed that Israel had committed war crimes, including the disproportionate

use of force, and the UN Human Rights Council demanded a credible investigation of charges of war crimes.

Netanyahu's Isolation and the Flotilla Attack

The Gaza invasion was scheduled by politics: it was to end before the inauguration of President Obama in January 2009 but occur close enough to Knesset elections to impress public opinion with the cabinet. Two ministers, Tzipi Livni (foreign affairs, Kadima) and Ehud Barak (defense, Labor), were party candidates for prime minister. The war failed to bring either political victory, although Kadima won the most seats. The greatest beneficiaries of the violence were extreme right-wing parties that opposed any Palestinian state.

With effort, Binyamin Netanyahu of Likud formed a coalition with Yisrael Beiteinu, Shas, smaller right-wing partners, and Labor. The most contentious appointment was the foreign minister, Avigdor Lieberman of Yisrael Beiteinu. His party's electoral slogan, "No loyalty, no citizenship," heightened tensions within the country over the Arab minority. He rejected U.S. calls for a halt to the growth of settlements and his hard line on negotiations created difficulties with the United States and the European Union.

The Prime Minister himself deftly attempted to deflect U.S. demands for a two-state solution by announcing his support for a demilitarized Palestinian state. However, embarrassed by new settlement housing announced during the visit of U.S. Vice President Joe Biden, the U.S. demanded a real halt to settlements, including in East Jerusalem. Netanyahu did halt some new home construction, but he did not apply

the freeze to existing construction or municipal buildings. After the freeze ended in 2010, peace talks collapsed. Most international political leaders believed Netanyahu's cabinet was most responsible for the collapse.

By contrast, a group of former military, security, and intelligence chiefs and officials proposed to restart the talks by offering to recognize a Palestinian state in almost all the captured 1967 lands, with border adjustments to retain the larger settlements. Without such an initiative, one leader warned, Israelis risked the label "peace refuseniks."

Israel's international reputation deteriorated in 2010 when its commandos seized the *Mavi Marmara*, a Turkish ferry used by pro-Palestinian human rights activists who challenged the blockade of Gaza. When they attempted to deliver supplies of cement, paper and water purification tablets, commandoes boarded the vessel in international waters, in the process killing nine Turkish citizens, one of whom was also American.

World opinion overwhelmingly condemned the operation, which brought far more attention to the plight of Gaza than any Palestinian public relations campaign had ever done. Enraged by "state terrorism" against its vessel and the killing of its civilians, the Turkish government halted military cooperation with Israel. The raid thus cost Israel its one alliance with a Muslim state and weakened other relations. Embarrassed by attention to its own blockade of Gaza, Egypt permitted individuals to cross the border. President Obama called the plight of Gaza unsustainable.

With broad Western support, the embargo was initially imposed in 2007 to

Bitterness and frustration: Palestinian youths defy the Israeli army

Israel

block weapons shipments to terrorists. It had also served to pressure the Hamas rulers of Gaza by depriving residents of life's necessities and luxuries. The passing years provided more rationales: it was ostensibly maintained partly to secure Gilad Shalit's release after that soldier's capture in 2006.

The government appointed its own limited inquiry into the *Mavi Marmara* affair, partly to forestall international investigations. More immediately, Israel relaxed the embargo on items such as food, clothing, and toys, and also announced that supplies for UN agencies would be permitted.

The arrival of the "Arab Spring" of 2011 harmed Israel's interests, at least in the short run, and brought with it a period of great uncertainty. Egypt's President Mubarak had cooperated with Israel and the United States for decades, permitting natural gas shipments, adopting a hard line against Hamas and blocking trade with Gaza. His fall led to a modest reopening of the border. Mubarak was ousted, and Jordan's King Abdullah, the other Arab ruler with a treaty with Israel, found himself denounced by demonstrators.

On the ideological level, the Arab Spring awakened waves of protestors who chanted "The People Demand the Fall of the Regime," using Arabic words that emphasized the desire for great change to the system. Although these words generally referred to change of governance within borders, they could also be interpreted to refer to the broader system of international politics in the Middle East. For many conspiracy theorists, Israel was considered to run the system.

The slogans and emotions strengthened a broad international movement to delegitimize Israel as long as it failed to negotiate. The movement argues that the settlements contravene international law; some participants boycott goods from the settlements. Others prefer the benefits gained through supporting the Arab and Muslim worlds rather than by alliance with Israel. Given President Obama's statement of support for the 1967 borders as the starting point for negotiations, Netanyahu's policies failed to maintain the confidence of Israel's closest ally.

Massive middle-class demonstrations shook the country during 2011, complete with protesters' camps. The cause was neither foreign policy nor the culture wars between secular and observant Jews. Rather, it was the high cost of living. Professionals complained that their salaries failed to cover food, housing, child care, and other elements of modern life. The protests diminished during the winter, but suggested rising popular concerns about domestic issues.

Recognizing that his coalition was fraying over disputes on domestic issues, Netanyahu conducted dramatic midnight negotiations with Kadima and established the largest coalition in Knesset history, claiming 94 of the 120 seats. Kadima's presence in the cabinet could restrain the excessive special interest demands by some long-standing coalition partners over issues like subsidies to religious groups and the controversial Tal Law that exempted the ultra-orthodox from military service. The grand alliance also provided Netanyahu the symbolic strength of a unified country as he condemned Iran's nuclear enrichment program at the United Nations. It reduced domestic criticism when he quietly supported Mitt Romney for the U.S. presidency, a surprising instance of interference in U.S. politics.

2013 Elections Strengthen the Center

Lauded in the press as "an authoritative, experienced statesman with no viable replacement," Netanyahu soon switched policies again, calling for elections in January 2013, a year early. He formed an electoral alliance between Likud and Yisrael Beiteinu, the far-right nationalist party headed by Avigdor Lieberman.

Israel

The short, swift election campaign proved that a significant number of Israelis desired domestic change. New faces mattered: nearly half (53) of the members of the new Knesset had not served in the previous one. *Yesh Atid* ("There is a Future"), a new party created by the TV news presenter Yair Lapid, adopted a just-left-of-center platform. It won 14% of the vote and emerged as the second largest party.

Further right, Naftali Bennett, a software multi-millionaire and the new leader of Jewish Home (*HaBayit HaYehudi*) addressed everyday domestic problems—including high prices and the ultra-Orthodox avoidance of military service. Jewish Home placed fourth, with 12 members, some of them settlers.

By contrast, voters abandoned Kadima, that collection of familiar faces recycled from other parties. It fell from 28 seats to just two. The Likud–Beiteinu alliance also fared far worse than expected, losing 11 of its previous 42 seats.

The four right-wing and religious parties had won a bare majority, just 61 seats. Any attempt to form them into a coalition risked immediate failure, because Shas and United Torah Judaism desired privileges over the draft and education that Bennett's Jewish Home would not accept. After weeks of negotiations, Netanyahu formed a coalition of four parties, his Likud–Beiteinu and Jewish Home on the right, and Yesh Atid and Hatnuah (composed mostly of ex-Kadima progressives) on the center-left.

Cooperation between Yair Lapid and Naftali Bennett proved crucial to forming the coalition. The two new leaders advocated a smaller cabinet, budget cuts, work

and military service for ultra-Orthodox men, and curricula in (state-financed) ultra-Orthodox schools that included modern subjects. The stranglehold of the settlers and religious right over cabinet decisions was thus broken. Despite protests by the ultra-Orthodox, in 2014 the Knesset voted to end the draft exemption for students at religious seminaries.

Before the first two years of the Knesset's term had ended, the alliance fractured, and Netanyahu again called early elections.

Wobbly Politics: Early Elections and Shifting Coalitions

The March 2015 elections caught Yair Lapid and his Yesh Atid party at a difficult moment. The public expected that as finance minister Lapid would advance the party agenda of tax cuts and a better quality of life. Instead, he inherited a budget deficit that forced him to cut spending and raise revenues. His party's popularity consequently slumped. Lapid lashed out at Netanyahu and Likud, but polls indicated his party lost its role as kingmaker. Thus, the real electoral challenge to Likud came from the Zionist Union, the electoral alliance of Labor under Isaac Herzog and Tzipi Livni's Hatnuah. Traditionally sympathetic to peace negotiations, its program addressed economic and social issues.

Just weeks before voting day, opinion polls widely indicated the contest between Likud and Herzog's Zionist Union too close to call. Recognizing the possibility of defeat, Netanyahu once again displayed his skills at political infighting. To win Israeli votes, he repudiated the two-state solution to the Palestine problem, and relentlessly urged supporters of right-wing parties to

Former Prime Minister Sharon

vote Likud this time, or risk seeing Herzog and Labor in power. This "relentless cannibalizing" of his past allies' voters succeeded, and reached its height on election day when the prime minister urged Jews to the polls because, he claimed, Arabs were voting "in droves." As the table below shows, while Likud triumphed with a gain of 12 seats, religious and right-wing parties lost a total of 16.

Despite being leader of the largest party, Netanyahu struggled to create a coalition with a Knesset majority. Just hours before the deadline, he reached agreement with Naftali Bennett's Jewish Home and presented President Rivlin an alliance with just 61 of the 120 members, a bare majority. Since most of the smaller parties in the coalition likely lost voters to Likud during the last few days of the campaign, and the more secular *Kulanu* opposed the religious parties' desires for more government assistance to the special interest groups they represented, observers believed the coalition was unlikely to last long.

In fact, the alliance lasted for little more than a year. In May of 2016, Netanyahu surprised many analysts by replacing Defense Minister Moshe Ya'alon with Avigdor Lieberman, a far-right ultranationalist and member of Yisrael Beiteinu. In exchange for his new role as Defense Minister, Lieberman brought his members into Netanyahu's coalition, increasing the number of seats in that alliance from 61 to 67. Internationally, the appointment of Lieberman was met with dismay by those who still hoped that some sort of reconciliation with Palestinians might be possible. Lieberman is known for his blunt rhetoric and has espoused controversial views vis-à-vis Palestinians, publicly advocating the commission of war crimes. In late 2018, Lieberman resigned from his position as Defense

View of the Sea of Galilee　　　　Photo by Eugenia Elseth

Israel

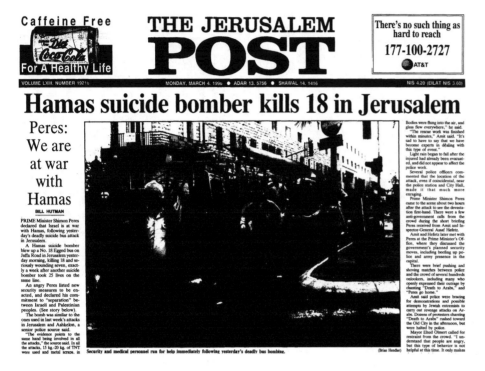

THE JERUSALEM POST

VOLUME LXIII, NUMBER 19216 ● MONDAY, MARCH 4, 1996 ● ADAR 13, 5756 ● SHAWAL 14, 1416 ● NIS 4.20 (EILAT NIS 3.60)

Hamas suicide bomber kills 18 in Jerusalem

Peres: We are at war with Hamas

BILL HUTMAN

PRIME Minister Shimon Peres declared that Israel is at war with Hamas, following yesterday's deadly suicide bus attack in Jerusalem.

A Hamas suicide bomber blew up a No. 18 Egged bus on Jaffa Road in Jerusalem yesterday morning, killing 18 and seriously wounding seven, exactly a week after another suicide bomber took 25 lives on the same line.

An angry Peres listed new security measures to be enacted, and declared his commitment to "separation" between Israeli and Palestinian peoples. (See story below).

The bomb was similar to the ones used in last week's attacks in Jerusalem and Ashkelon, a senior police source said.

"The evidence points to the same hand being involved in all the attacks," the source said. In all the attacks, 15 kg.-20 kg. of TNT were used and metal scraps, in

Bodies were flung into the air, and glass flew everywhere," he said.

"The rescue work was finished within minutes," Amit said. "It's sad to have to say that we have become experts in dealing with this type of event."

Light rain began to fall after the injured had already been evacuated, and did not appear to affect the police work.

Several police officers commented that the location of the attack, even if coincidental, near the police station and City Hall, made it that much more enraging.

Prime Minister Shimon Peres came to the scene about two hours after the attack to see the devastation first-hand. There were a few anti-government calls from the crowd during the short briefing Peres received from Amit and Inspector-General Assaf Hefetz.

Amit and Hefetz later met with Peres at the Prime Minister's Office, where they discussed the government's planned security moves, including beefing up police and army presence in the capital.

There were brief pushing and shoving matches between police and the crowd of several hundreds onlookers, including many who openly expressed their outrage by chanting "Death to Arabs," and "Peres go home."

Amit said police were bracing for demonstrations and possible attempts by Jewish extremists to carry out revenge attacks on Arabs. Dozens of protesters chanting "Death to Arabs" rushed toward the Old City in the afternoon, but were halted by police.

Mayor Ehud Olmert called for restraint from the crowd. "I understand that people are angry, but this type of behavior is not helpful at this time. It only makes

Security and medical personnel run for help immediately following yesterday's deadly bus bombing. (Brian Hendler)

Minister over a ceasefire with Hamas which he decried as "surrendering to terror." The stability of the ruling coalition was further shaken when Naftali Bennet threatened to resign, angered that he had not received the Defense post following Lieberman's departure. Dysfunction continued to plague the government for months, exacerbated by the looming threat of corruption charges to be brought against incumbent Prime Minister Netanyahu. Early elections were called for April 2019.

Once again candidates failed to win an outright majority. President Rivlin designated Netanyahu to form the next governing coalition on the grounds that he had better prospects of forming alliances in parliament, than his competitor Benny Gantz, whose party won the same number of seats. However, Netanyahu failed to do so within the allotted deadline, an unprecedented outcome in the Israeli political system. Subsequently, the parliament voted to dissolve itself, an outcome unprecedented in Israeli politics.

Remarkably, the September elections—conducted amidst claims of vote tampering and bribery at polling stations—failed to bring any clarity on the question of who would lead the country. With Netanyahu failing to form a government within the allotted time, the opportunity to do so was handed over to his political rival, Gantz. Gantz likewise failed to form a coalition, and in December the Knesset once again voted to dissolve. Israelis were to return

to the polls. In March 2020, Israel held its third election within a year. The stakes had never been higher for Netanyahu, who faced indictment on charges of bribery, fraud, and breach of trust. Following the election, it became clear that Gantz had achieved a slim majority. However, it would be an uphill battle to form a governing coalition and dependence on minor Arab parties would leave the government open to attacks from the right. Attempts to form a unity government seemed doomed to failure. However, the Covid-19 crisis encouraged Gantz and Netanyahu to more seriously consider the prospect of governing with some sort of coalition.

On April 20, 2020, Gantz and Netanyahu announced that agreement on a unity government had been reached. The deal would involve both parties sharing power, and Gantz and Netanyahu taking turns being prime minister. Under the terms of the agreement Netanyahu was to be prime minister until October 2021, with Gantz serving as vice prime minister. In December 2020 the unity government collapsed amid bitter infighting, and weary Israelis were once again forced to the polls in March 2021. This time, Netanyahu was banking on the perception of success around the vaccination rollout and the relief of ordinary Israelis at a return to some sort of normality. However, clear victory for Israel's longest-serving prime minister remained elusive. As the deadline for forming a government drew near, an outbreak of deadly violence between Israel and Palestine seemed the possible impetus to bring opposing Israeli factions together. However, when the deadline passed, Rivlin handed over the opportunity to form a government to centrist opposition leader Yair Lapid.

The Stalled Peace Process

One of the most enduring issue of foreign affairs is the Israeli–Palestinian conflict. Given the rightward shift of popular opinion in Israel in recent years, the chances of Jewish Israeli agreement over this issue in the near term seem bleak. The parties on the right basically oppose a two-state solution, and some advocate a goal of one million settlers in Judea and Samaria. Such settler numbers would render any Palestinian state impossible. The core issues of any peace treaty include:

The status of Jerusalem: Israel has proclaimed the undivided city its capital. But Jerusalem—or at least its eastern portion—also remains sacred to Palestinians as their capital and a deeply revered Islamic site.

Borders and settlements: Many and perhaps most Israelis desire to keep major Jewish settlements. Palestinians demand the pre-1967 armistice lines but would accept some land swaps. Israeli settlements in the West Bank have created a series of

Party	Leader	%	Seats	+/–	Alignment
Likud	Binyamin Netanyahu	23.40%	30	12	Right
Kulanu	Moshe Kahlon	7.49%	10	New	Center
The Jewish Home	Naftali Bennett	6.74%	8	-4	Right
Shas	Aryeh Deri	5.73%	7	-4	Populist; religious
United Torah Judaism	Yaakov Litzman	5.03%	6	-1	Ultra-Orthodox
Coalition Total			61		
Zionist Union	Isaac Herzog	18.67%	24	3	Center-left
Yesh Atid	Yair Lapid	8.81%	11	-8	Center-left
Yisrael Beiteinu	Avigdor Lieberman	5.11%	6	-7	Right
Meretz	Zehava Gal-On	3.93%	5	-1	Left-center
Joint List	Ayman Odeh	10.54%	13	2	Arab alliance

Former President Shimon Peres

Prime Minister Binyamin Netanyahu

isolated Palestinian townships. Allowing some form of contiguous or semi-contiguous Palestinian land would seem a necessary starting for the formation of a legitimate, sustainable Palestinian state.

Palestinian refugees: Israel rejects any Palestinian "right of return," but the "Right to Return" is an article of faith in refugee camps.

Security: Palestinians wish their homeland free of any Israeli military or police presence, while many Israelis consider the occupation of strategic locations near the Jordan River essential to security.

Likud and several other parties have publicly stated that they would require Palestinian recognition of Israel as a "Jewish state." In 2018, Israel's Knesset passed the "Nation-Sate Bill" by which , Israel would be defined as the nation state of the Jewish people, and the right to self-determination in Israel would be unique to the Jewish people. Palestinians argue that this severely compromises the citizenship of Muslim and Christian Arabs living in Israel.

The most recent push for Israeli–Palestinian peace was initiated in mid-2017, after President Trump appointed his son-in-law, Jared Kushner, as a special envoy for Middle East Peace. Significantly, Kushner has no experience as a diplomat before coming to this role. Furthermore, the White House has made no effort to appear neutral. In May 2018, the United States moved its embassy from Tel Aviv to Jerusalem, upending decades of American foreign policy in a move that was widely condemned by the international community. President Trump argued that the move represented nothing more than a recognition of the reality that Jerusalem is Israel's capital. Critics responded that it imperiled already-stagnant hopes for peace even further, and that it

abolished any pretense that the United States could be a fair broker if and when the parties return to the table.

On the same day that the U.S. Embassy in Jerusalem opened its doors, Palestinians in Gaza were marching toward Israel, intent on passing through the security fences and walls that line the border between the two lands. It was a large scale protest, one that occurs each year on the anniversary of the creation of the state of Israel. Israeli soldiers opened fire on protestors, killing over 60 and injuring several thousand. The UN Human Rights Council voted 29–2, with 14 abstentions, to condemn "the disproportionate and indiscriminate use of force by the Israeli occupying forces against Palestinian civilians." The United States decried the resolution as shameful, instead placing responsibility for Palestinian fatalities and injuries on those who organized and encouraged the protests, ultimately withdrawing from the UN Human Rights Council citing anti-Israel bias.

A further blow to Arab hopes for a just peace agreement was Trump's recognition of Israeli sovereignty over the Golan Heights. The international community has long condemned the 1967 capture and 1980 annexation of the Golan Heights as an illegal military occupation of Syrian territory by Israel. Syria called the 2019 White House proclamation—fortuitously made just weeks before a critical election at which Binyamin Netanyahu faced possible defeat—a "blatant attack" on its sovereignty and territorial integrity.

In January 2020, the White House revealed the aspects of the plan that dealt with the delineation of borders, the status of Jerusalem, and the prospects of a future Palestinian state. In essence, what was being offered was a proposal that largely met the aspirations of the Israeli government—keeping intact settlements in the West Bank and, crucially, offering a unified Jerusalem as the capital of Israel. In return Israel would only freeze construction of settlements for a mere four years, while Palestinian leaders can decide whether to resume negotiations. The "state" of Palestine would, under the Trump plan, constitute a series of mostly disconnected enclaves.

Culture: As the Zionist settlers of the pre-independence period were mainly Europeans, their culture has tended to dominate, with attempts to Europeanize later waves of immigrants from Persian, Afghani, Kurdish, Yemeni, Iraqi, or North African backgrounds. These Sephardic Jews now outnumber European Jews, and they increasingly assert their own cultural values.

Israel in fact enjoys cultural diversity as great as that found anywhere, because its people have come from across the globe. Long an immigrant society, even today a

quarter of Israelis were born abroad. And they bring a variety of cultures with them.

The non-Jewish minorities are almost entirely Arabic-speaking and comprise about 1.2 million Arab Muslims, 123,000 Christian Arabs and 122,000 Druze (see Lebanon: Culture). In general these minorities suffer lower standards of living and receive less education. One recent study found 52% of Israeli Arab families living below the poverty level, and the high school dropout rate is 12%.

The complex educational system includes both state and private schools, but even the private schools are partly subsidized and controlled by the government. Within the state schools there are three systems: secular, religious, and Arabic-speaking. Secondary schools receive no direct public financing, but the government helps pay the fees for qualified students on the basis of need.

Of the several institutions of higher learning, the oldest and most prestigious is the Hebrew University of Jerusalem. Many faculty members have been educated in Europe or North America, and there is significant interchange with universities on those continents. In terms of its research accomplishments, publications, and student quality, the university outranks all others in the Middle East. However, between 2001 and 2005, the Israeli government cut its funds to higher education by about 15%, leading to student strikes supported by academic administrators who feared that further cuts could cause the system to collapse. Strikes by professors and others marred the 2007–08 academic year.

At independence, Orthodox Judaism became the established religion of the state. Religious holidays and Sabbath observance marked the nation; in Orthodox and ultra-Orthodox areas, stores close and

Israel

public buses cease operating on Saturdays. Until 2012 only Orthodox rabbis were paid by the government, and even now, only Orthodox weddings are legally binding. Secular couples therefore submit to Orthodox rituals many find sexist, or marry elsewhere. Each year, over 10% of Israeli Jewish couples who marry do so outside Israel, often in Cyprus.

Today, a minority of Israeli Jews adheres to this branch of Judaism. Others consider themselves secular, or worship at Reform synagogues, but the fastest growing congregations are the ultra-Orthodox, a term applied to a number of black-clad groups, including the Hasidim of European origin and Sephardim from the Middle East. Collectively they are known in Hebrew as the *Haredim*, "those who tremble before God."

Culture Wars and the Roles of Women

Religious and ideological differences between groups have led to sharp social and political disputes, sometimes labeled "culture wars." At one extreme, secular Jews may define a Jew as anyone who considers himself or herself such, even though an atheist. In contrast, many Orthodox and ultra-Orthodox hold strict expectations of converts, even desiring to exclude converts according to Reform, Conservative, and Reconstructionist Judaism for citizenship under the law of return. Many also consider secular Jews responsible for the loss of Jews through assimilation in other societies. Some are not Zionists, believing that the Messiah's return should precede the establishment of Israel, and a few equate secularism as a loss to Jewry equivalent in numbers to Hitler's exterminations. Ultra-Orthodox vandals recently defaced the Yad Vashem Holocaust memorial in Jerusalem with graffiti denouncing Zionism.

The most perplexing conflicts usually involve the ultra-Orthodox or Haredim.

They formed just a few small communities at independence, when David Ben-Gurion offered them subsidies and exemption from the military draft. In sixty years the Haredim population grew to about one million, initially through immigration, then through early marriages and high birth rates. Although women may be employed outside the home, many Haredim men devote themselves to study of the Torah. Most avoid both military service and work. Their unemployment rate hovers around 60%.

The combination of refusing military service and declining work, while accepting government studies and averaging six children per family, upsets many others in society. They fear that future prosperity will suffer from the rapidly growing, but poorly educated and economically unproductive Haredim population.

The conflict between secular rights and divine commands often leads to bitter language. Rabbi Ovadia Yossef, spiritual leader of the Sephardic party, Shas, claimed in 2006 that God helped soldiers when they "believe and pray" and so they do not get killed. In fact, many observant soldiers had been killed in Lebanon. Some years earlier, a Shas cabinet member called a fellow minister a "Satan to be wiped from the face of the earth."

Perhaps the sharpest disputes revolve around the role of women, their place in society, and their right to be visible in public. Following the Talmud, much as very conservative Muslims follow the sayings of Muhammad and rulings of Shari'a law, Haredim men argue that to preserve the purity of their thoughts women must be covered—and out of the public eye. The resulting restrictions render women second-class citizens when not entirely invisible. For example, the national bus company, Egged, has designated "modesty buses"

that separate the men (in the front) from women (at the rear). Religious extremists spat on an 8-year-old girl, Naama Margolese, as she walked to school, because they considered her clothing immodest. Professor Channa Maayan, receiving a health ministry award for her book on hereditary diseases frequent among Jews, discovered at the awards ceremony that she and her husband would have to sit apart—and that since women were not permitted on stage, a male colleague would receive the award for her.

Separately, many Israelis feel that the character of the nation is at stake. In the first decades of Israeli statehood, citizens bonded together over the shared experiences of persecution, the trauma of the Holocaust, and the experience of winning independence. Zionism unified diverse populations, and socialist ideology minimized differences of wealth and income among the population. Concern with morality delayed the introduction of television to Israel.

As Israeli society matured, individualism played a greater role, and great distinctions grew between economic classes. Today, income inequality in Israel is among the highest in the OECD states.

Given social change and economic disparity, in common with other developed societies, Israel's crime rate has risen in recent years. The more common criminal acts range from fraud and corruption to burglary, and reach from high government officials to youths from the less prosperous Sephardic Jewish and Arab communities. In addition, the occupied territories continue to witness high levels of crime, including murder, often between Israeli settlers and Palestinians.

Economy: During the first two decades of its existence, Israel enjoyed one of the fastest rates of economic growth of any country, despite insignificant oil, natural gas, and coal deposits. Following a basically socialist pattern, the government established new towns for immigrants and subsidized essentials like bread and milk. Extensive medical care and other benefits came through the widespread system of labor unions. Some of the highest taxes in the world accompanied these social advantages, with rates as high as 70% on upper middle class income. Not surprisingly, budget deficits, inflation, and trade deficits accompanied the rapid growth.

During the oil shocks of the 1970s and 1980s, most non-oil economies suffered stagflation—the combination of high inflation and high unemployment. Israel also suffered the heavy burden of defense spending (24% of GDP in 1984) and the marriage between socialism and Zionism that produced a bloated bureaucracy,

Panoramic view of Tel Aviv

Courtesy of the Embassy of Israel

extensive government regulations, and heavy taxation.

International factors and deliberate political choices played major roles in enabling the highly-educated workforce to achieve its present success. Rigid control over the money supply, just as world oil prices declined and then plummeted, broke inflation. Though occurring slowly over a number of years, the privatization of industries, the nation's shipping firm and the national airline, El Al, increased competition and efficiency, as well as inequality.

During the 1990s, three further factors contributed to economic prosperity. First, a million immigrants from the former Soviet Union brought education and skills, and strengthened demands for pro-business legislation.

Simultaneously, the Oslo Accords reduced political tensions. The moves towards peace also weakened the Arab boycott of Israeli goods, and the secondary boycott of companies doing business with Israel.

Finally, a great inflow of foreign investment, particularly in electronics and telecommunication, provided prosperity and foreign exchange. Because scientific and technological research occurs at one of the highest rates in the world, major firms like Microsoft and Intel frequently sought and bought out local startups. This contributed to the prosperity of the banking, acquisitions, and venture capital markets as well. Solar energy, the medical sciences, genetics, and engineering firms also attracted foreign interest.

In 2010 Israel gained recognition as a developed economy when it was admitted to the Organization for Economic Cooperation and Development (OECD). The country generally ranks as one of the top 30 in per capita income and foreign exchange reserves and in recent years has boasted an unemployment rate below the United States and European Union. Despite the prosperity, about 20% of the population lives below the poverty line. Two population groups account for much of the poverty: the ultra-Orthodox Haredim and Arab citizens.

Two international developments in the mid-1990s offered greater opportunities for the Israeli economy. First, the Arab boycott of companies doing business with Israel, a form of secondary boycott illegal in many countries, shuffled towards final collapse when the Gulf States abandoned the boycott. Second, a Free Trade Agreement between the United States and Israel came into full effect in 1995, and included Israeli agricultural products excluded by the Free Trade Agreement with the European Union.

Agricultural output has expanded enormously since 1948. The introduction of new crops, chemical fertilizers and irrigation systems increased production more than 500%. Sparse grazing lands turned into farms, thanks to irrigation from the Jordan River and the most advanced dry-climate agricultural cultivation methods. Israel imports basic foodstuffs, including beef, but it exports high-value and out-of-season fruits and vegetables to Europe and even the United States. Water rights in Israel remain a matter of dispute. The West Bank mountain aquifer and the Sea of Galilee provide Israel about 60% of its fresh water. Israel, and Israeli settlements, take about 80% of the mountain aquifer's flow, leaving the Palestinians with 20%. The right of Israel to the mountain aquifer is not considered a settled matter. With water consumption outstripping supply in both Israel and the Palestinian territories, Palestinians complain they are inevitably the first community to be rationed as reserves run dry, with all the implications for agricultural output and health that this entails.

For a small country, Israel produces a wide variety of industrial products, from simple furniture to cut diamonds to satellites. The armament and related service industries employ over 10% of the national workforce and produce a leading category of exports. These have included guided missiles, artillery, and fighter aircrafts as well as the most famous, the Uzi submachine gun. Customers range from the United States to Taiwan, South Africa, and a number of Latin American nations. Israel typically ranks as one of the world's larger arms exporters, with India the largest customer.

Israel Aircraft Industries had hoped to become a major producer of high-technology fighters, but financing failed. While planes are serviced and executive jets are built, the pride of the aviation industry is missiles. The Arrow missile system, one of the few anywhere that intercepts ballistic missiles, is now operational. The Iron Dome anti-missile system, created with significant financial assistance from the United States, reportedly proved very effective against short-range missiles from Gaza during the 2012 fighting there. Iron Dome batteries were also moved north during the worsening Syrian civil war, amid fears that one side or the other might lob conventional or chemical weapons at Israel's cities.

The recent discovery of major off-shore natural gas deposits about 50 miles from the Mediterranean coast portends a major boon for a land poor in natural resources. Gas started to flow from the Tamar field in early 2013; its output will eventually exceed national needs. The Levant Basin also includes the Leviathan field, farther out and considerably deeper. It was only discovered in 2010 and is also under development. The production companies have suggested exporting the gas as LNG, possibly to Korea, but yielding to consumer pressure, proposed regulations will cap exports at no more than 40% of production, to ensure sufficient supplies for domestic use at low prices.

Another prominent industry in terms of foreign exchange earnings is tourism. Jerusalem contains the holiest shrines for both Jews and Christian pilgrims. It also hosts the third holiest site in Islam. Numerous Biblical and historical sites elsewhere also attract visitors, and there are beaches and other attractions, both scenic and cultural.

The Future: Israel is a fascinating place, and in many ways it has succeeded against all odds. Despite its small size, and despite being surrounded by states and people who have objected to its very existence, Israel has built one of the region's most vibrant economies. Indeed, some call it "Start-Up Nation," a reference to the emergence of a tremendous number of successful Israeli companies. Israel also boasts the region's most technologically advanced military, and is the only country in the Middle East with nuclear weapons (although official government policy is to remain silent on this point).

At the same time, and not unrelated to the points above, Israel has always faced challenges. The most enduring of these is its security situation. A two-state solution acceptable to Israelis and Palestinians continues to elude and the prospect of peace appears to be receding. At present, there is little to suggest that a solution is in the offing. Israel's international reputation is undoubtedly suffering. Most UN member states now recognize Palestine as a state. Israel's blockade of Gaza has drawn widespread criticism. Likewise, the continued building of settlements (and refusal to disband already established settlements and outposts) could be seen as an attempt to create facts on the ground, allowing Israel to effectively annex large parts the West Bank. Indeed, during the 2019 election campaign Netanyahu promised just such action. Furthermore, U.S. recognition of Israeli sovereignty over the Golan Heights may provide an implicit green light for such an outcome. However, it would effectively create Palestinian enclaves in the non-annexed areas, with limited contiguity and no viability as an independent state. Furthermore it would subject Palestinians to permanent, unprecedented Israeli control over movement, with all the associated impacts on health, education, access to employment, and connections to family, that this implies. Such a development would see Israel openly depart from its democratic principles.

The Hashemite Kingdom of Jordan

Carved from the multi-colored sandstone cliff, the Treasury at Petra symbolizes the ancient Nabataean center of trade and wealth. It creates a dramatic impression on visitors emerging from the long, narrow entrance gorge known as the Siq.   Photo by Seth Cantey

National Day: May 25 (1946; Independence Day).

Chief of State: Abdullah II (Abdullah ibn Hussein al-Hashimi), King.

Head of Government: Bisher Al-Khasawneh, Prime Minister.

National Flag: Three horizontal stripes of black, white and green and a red triangle at the pole bearing a white seven-pointed star.

Gross Domestic Product: $40.07 billion
GDP per capita: $4,095.

The borders of Jordan, like those of many other countries drafted by colonial powers, fail to reflect either natural features or differences in populations. In the years immediately following World War I, the boundaries were drawn to suit British policy, and they have been modified little since. The country takes its name from the Jordan River, which with its tributary, the Yarmuk, is the only real river in the area, and provides the only natural boundary.

The Jordan River, deprived of an estimated 95% of its fresh water by diversions, is only a small stream when it empties into the salty Dead Sea, the lowest body of water on earth. Its surface lies more than 1,300 feet (almost 400 meters) below sea level. Because the Jordan's scanty flow falls short of the very rapid evaporation caused by the heat and solar rays in the depression, the Dead Sea is drying up, the water level falling about 3 feet (almost 1 meter) per year. About 50 miles (80 kilometers) long from north to south just a generation ago, as shown on the map, it has lost the southern third. However, the sea will not quickly disappear: its maximum depth reaches about 1,200 feet (roughly 360 meters). The salt concentration is almost ten times that of

Area: 34,495 square miles (89,342 square kilometers).

Population: 10.2 million, including 2.1 million registered Palestinian refugees and 800,000 refugees from elsewhere in the Middle East (primarily Syria, but also Iraq, Yemen, and Sudan).

Capital City: Amman (2.6 million).

Climate: Hot and dry in the summer, but winter can be cold with moderate rain and even snow in the northwest. The Jordan Valley and Aqaba area are warmer. The eastern and southern regions are desert.

Neighboring Countries: Syria (North); Iraq (Northeast); Saudi Arabia (Southeast); Israel and Occupied Territories (West).

Time Zone: GMT +2.

Official Language: Arabic.

Ethnic Background: Arab except for small Circassian communities; approximately half with Palestinian roots.

Principal Religion: Sunni Islam

Chief Commercial Products: Phosphate, olive oil, tomatoes, wheat, barley, figs, lentils, tobacco, sheepskins, hides, cement, salt, and refined petroleum products.

Major Trading Partners: Saudi Arabia, the United States, China, Iraq, Japan, the United Kingdom, Syria, and India.

Currency: Jordanian Dinar (1 dinar = 100 piasters).

Former Colonial Status: Under British control (1918–1946).

A first glimpse at the Treasury in Petra

Jordan

Amman, a city built on seven hills. Against the slope of one is this large Roman amphitheater now restored and being used for performances as it once was almost 2,000 years ago

Syria to the French mandate. Jordan, comprising the southern portion of Syria, nonetheless lay in territory that by Anglo–French agreement fell under British influence. Hence France did not occupy it. Weeks later, Faisal's brother Abdullah arrived in Amman from the Hijaz, hoping to regain all Syria for Arab rule, but only minor raids took place against the French.

Acting on the wishes of Britain and France, the League of Nations granted Britain control over the territory within the Palestine Mandate (the term "Jordan" then referred only to the river and valley). However, conditions contrasted greatly between the two banks of the Jordan River. The western territory had cities and towns, farmland, and villages. The East Bank resembled a frontier society. There were no cities, a mere scattering of towns,

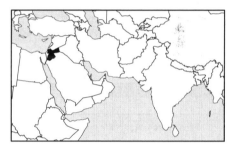

ordinary seawater. This great density allows bathers to float easily. If a swimmer wants to, for example, he or she can float with head, hands, and feet above water.

Immediately east of the Jordan Valley the land rises steeply to the edge of a high plateau. The strip along the edge of the plateau, wider in the north, receives moderate rainfall of about 25 inches (635 millimeters) annually. As the plateau drops in elevation to the east and south, rainfall diminishes rapidly to nothing. Only the hardiest Bedouin nomads wander out into that area in search of a livelihood.

Amman, the capital of the country, lies on the plateau, spread onto the sides of several converging valleys. In 1925 it was only a small Circassian village built among the ruins of ancient Roman Philadelphia. Since then, Amman has grown into a large and relatively modern city.

History: Although the high plateau was farmed extensively during the Roman and Byzantine eras—and Umayyad caliphs built palaces in the desert—for most of the last thousand years, Bedouins dominated the area that forms modern-day Jordan. During the 19th century, settlement increased, as did Ottoman control, and the Hijaz railroad was built through the territory from Damascus to Medina a decade before World War I. During that conflict, the troops and Bedouin allies of the Arab Revolt fought against the Ottoman forces along the railroad, and the port of Aqaba became the first important Arab conquest outside the Hijaz. Under Emir Faisal, and supported by British supplies and advisors such as T.E. Lawrence (Lawrence of Arabia), the Arab forces used their mastery of the desert to outflank the Ottoman

forces, tying down large numbers of them in garrison duties.

After the war, Jordan fell under Arab rule from Damascus, and thus in 1920 part of Faisal's Kingdom of Syria. However, French forces soon marched on Damascus, ousted Faisal, and subjected

Jordan

and only the skeleton of modern government. Tribes of nomads and semi-nomads raided each other and the few settled farmers.

For the practical reason that Abdullah already ruled the area as Faisal's replacement, and as a reward for his family's alliance, Britain formed the Emirate of Transjordan for Abdullah. Claiming descent from the Prophet Muhammad's family, and thus a Hashemite, Abdullah eventually gave his clan name to the state: the Hashemite Kingdom of Jordan.

Aside from settled areas around the towns of al-Karak, al-Salt, Ajlun, and Irbid, nomadism remained the dominant way of life. Abdullah selected Amman as his capital. An impressive city in ancient times, it was located on the Hijaz Railway, and a few Circassian refugees, fleeing Russian expansion in the Caucasus, had settled nearby. During the 1920s Emir Abdullah attempted to establish law and order, protect the frontier, settle nomadic tribes, and undertake the beginnings of modern government.

The military, known as the Arab Legion, became the instrument that brought order to the countryside. Composed of Arab soldiers with British officers, during World War II it also fought for the Allies in Syria and Iraq. As the emir's government showed more competence, the treaty with Britain was revised several times, each revision giving his officials more authority. Finally, negotiations in 1946 led to a treaty recognizing the independence of Transjordan, and Abdullah proclaimed himself king. A mutual defense treaty permitted British troops to remain in the country, and British officers—technically under Abdullah's orders—commanded the Arab Legion.

King Abdullah of Jordan (1882–1951)

When the United Nations voted in late 1947 to partition Palestine between Jews and Palestinians, King Abdullah saw the opportunity to realize one step in his cherished dream of ruling a kingdom of "Greater Syria," including Transjordan, Syria, Lebanon, and Palestine. When Britain's mandate over Palestine expired, he sent the Arab Legion to fight the newly proclaimed state of Israel. Other Arab states acted likewise, but in the War of Israeli Independence (1948–49) Arab armies suffered defeat. Israeli forces occupied areas reserved by the United Nations partition plan for the Palestinian state. The Legion fared better than most Arab forces, capturing the Jewish section of Jerusalem's Old City, but before the final armistice it was forced by Israeli ultimatum to pull back elsewhere.

Most Palestinians recognized that King Abdullah had intervened in Palestine more for dynastic gain, than to repulse the Israelis in support of the Palestinian cause. As the fighting ended, he secretly met Israeli officials to assure them of his limited intentions. Later he convened a congress of Palestinian notables that proclaimed him King of all Palestine. In 1949 he formally annexed the central portion that his troops controlled. Except for Gaza, all Arab Palestine became the West Bank of the Hashemite Kingdom of Jordan, and Abdullah came to rule the holy places in Jerusalem, Bethlehem, and Hebron.

However, Jordan also gained a large and restive population, including several hundred thousand refugees on both sides of the river. They widely opposed Abdullah as an agent of Britain and a traitor to the Palestinian cause. Furthermore, because of their greater achievements in education, larger population, and greater

sophistication, Palestinians considered Transjordan backward. Not surprisingly, tensions arose between the Palestinians and the Transjordanians.

In 1951 a Palestinian assassinated King Abdullah as he walked in Jerusalem. His young grandson, Hussein, then became king, although guided by a regency council until he turned 18 in 1953.

At first, Hussein permitted political activity and allowed parties to organize and govern through parliament. Most politicians were extremely nationalistic and anti-Western, critical of the roles played by Britain, France, and the United States in the creation of Israel. In a showdown in 1957, King Hussein dissolved parliament, arrested the cabinet, ended the Anglo-Jordanian defense treaty and dismissed Glubb Pasha (Lieutenant-General Sir John Bagot Glubb), the long-serving British commander of the Arab Legion.

These events marked the young king's assumption of personal authority. To replace British aid, he sought financial, military, and technical assistance from the United States. Nevertheless, following the Iraqi Revolution in 1958 that overthrew and murdered Hussein's cousin, Faisal II, British troops returned to Jordan to uphold the monarchy.

The late King Hussein of Jordan

The Royal Family of King Abdullah II

The Monastery, Petra

Between War and Peace with Israel

Given Israel's military strength, Jordan recognized the importance of preserving the 1949 armistice agreement with Israel. However, most Palestinians, especially those exiled from homes in Israel, wanted Jordan to join other Arab nations in a military confrontation against the Jewish state. Tensions between several Arab states and Israel, led Egypt's Nasser to deepen the crisis in May 1967. King Hussein was drawn unwillingly into a military treaty with Egypt, and then into war with Israel in June of that year.

In four days of fighting, the vastly superior Israel Defense Forces (IDF) crushed all Jordanian units west of the Jordan River and seized the richest portion of the kingdom. With nearly half the population lost, and economic benefits from the major tourist locations around Jerusalem ended, Jordan faced great economic, political, and social difficulties.

Nearly 400,000 Palestinians fled to Jordan, creating a new wave of refugees, adding to the large communities of displaced Palestinians from 1949 around Amman, at Zarqa, and elsewhere. New camps were set up, with international aid, to provide food and shelter for the floods of people crossing the river. The burden of the refugees stretched Jordan's finances; their numbers swamped the available jobs and created new domestic tensions.

Both old and new camps became fertile recruiting centers for *al-Fatah* and other guerrilla groups linked to the Palestine Liberation Organization (PLO). Claiming they would succeed against Israel where the combined Arab armies failed, these groups launched attacks against Israel and Israeli-occupied areas. Israeli reprisals turned much of the Jordan valley into a zone of sporadic battles, but at Karamah in 1968 the guerrillas held their positions against an Israeli raid, consequently gaining fame and support in the Arab world.

After first permitting the guerrillas to operate in its territory, Jordan feared both their growing power as a "second government" and Israeli reprisals for guerrilla raids. The government therefore attempted to curtail the armed groups. Finally in "Black September" 1970, King Hussein ordered his army to crush the guerrillas. Several thousand people, most of them Palestinian, died in Amman during the fighting; much of the city was heavily damaged. A tank invasion by Syrian-based units of the Palestine Liberation Army met defeat from Jordan's small air force, while troops set free Western passengers hijacked by Palestinian guerillas.

The firm suppression of these armed groups evoked fierce hostility from Palestinians and other Arabs, but by 1971, after sometimes bitter fighting, the military had regained control.

The widespread nationalist uprising *(intifada)* that began in 1987 in the Israeli-occupied territories showed again that the inhabitants of the West Bank considered themselves Palestinians, not Jordanians. The 1974 Arab summit had proclaimed the PLO to be the only representative of the Palestinian people, thus denying Jordan's claim to the West Bank. However, Jordan continued to pay the salaries of some civil servants in Palestine. As the intifada gathered strength, however, such links aroused widespread criticism from Palestinians and other Arabs. Consequently, in 1988 King Hussein recognized the Palestinians' wish to form their own country.

Iraq's invasion of Kuwait in 1990 plunged the Jordanian economy into a major depression. UN sanctions halted the transit trade and Jordan's own exports to its main customer, Iraq. Some 200,000 Jordanian workers returned from the Gulf states, reducing the annual remittances sent to families and raising the unemployment rate to nearly 30%.

In the aftermath of the war, King Hussein ended the martial law imposed in 1967. He issued a "National Charter" that re-established multiparty democracy and secured allegiance to the king. Prime ministers followed in rapid succession, and some 15 political parties, including the Islamic Action Front of the Muslim Brotherhood, contested the 1993 elections. However, the new and sometimes uneven electoral districts weakened parties by allowing voters just one vote even if there were multiple campaigns in the district. This helped independent candidates from traditionally important families, nearly all of them the king's supporters. The largest group, the Islamic Action Front, led the opposition to Arab nationalists and leftists.

In the shadow of the Madrid and Oslo peace processes between Israel and the Palestinians, quiet and symbolic diplomacy tackled and resolved the major disputes with Israel. In 1994, a peace treaty formally ended 46 years of belligerence and regained for Jordan some small parcels of land totaling 145 square miles (376 square kilometers) occupied by Israel, although the *kibbutzim* cultivating them leased some property back. Also importantly, the treaty restored water rights in the Jordan and Yarmuk valleys, and the United States promised to waive repayment on loans of nearly $1 billion. Jordan gained a privileged role at Muslim sites in Jerusalem, though it promised to turn them over to Palestinian authorities once Israel withdrew.

Peace required Jordan to amend its anti-Israeli laws and permit trade with Israel, but popular opposition made this difficult. Some professional associations banned their members from dealing with Israelis. Islamic, leftist, and Pan-Arab parties demanded that the treaty be scrapped. The opposition gained strength because the first visible benefits seemed limited to

Jordan

Wadi Rum drivers taking a break

Photo by Susan L. Thompson

short-term tourists bound for Petra. However, critics failed to anticipate the opportunity for exports of light manufactures to the United States under the accompanying free trade agreement. By 2002 the United States had become Jordan's largest export customer, although the products were largely assembled by Asian temporary workers, not Jordanians.

The last months of King Hussein's rule showed again that real power in the country lay not with parliament but with the royal family. Stricken with cancer, Hussein left his treatment at the Mayo Clinic in 1999, to fly home to Amman, where he very publicly designated his eldest son, Abdullah, as heir, in place of his brother, Hassan, the crown prince since the 1960s. Days later, after final medical efforts at the Mayo Clinic failed, King Hussein returned home to die.

Hussein had ruled Jordan for nearly 47 years, many of them tumultuous, and he had become a much larger figure on the world stage than his country's population and wealth would have suggested. A vast assembly of world leaders gathered for his funeral—the only significant absentee seemed to be Saddam Hussein of Iraq.

Jordan under King Abdullah II

The son of Hussein's British second wife, Abdullah had spent almost his entire life in the military, eventually commanding the special forces. Educated in Britain and the United States, he had long accepted his uncle as the next king. Nevertheless, commentators commended the initiative and energy he displayed as monarch. He quickly visited most Arab rulers and improved relations with political opposites like Syria and Kuwait. During trips to Western capitals, he sought economic concessions, particularly debt relief.

In Amman, Abdullah proved adept at popular symbolic gestures, and over

the years appointed a succession of new prime ministers. However, the cabinets often failed to move as quickly as the king desired, and hopes for substantial change remained unrealized.

Overdue elections in 2003 reestablished parliament, and expanded it, after two years of rule by royal decree. Voters of the newly designed districts overwhelmingly favored independent candidates, a goal of the electoral system. The Islamic Action Front won only 20 seats, and both women and leftists failed to win a single contested seat. However, the introduction of a quota system allowed women to fill nine reserved seats.

Coordinated attacks on three foreign-own hotels in Amman killed dozens of Jordanian wedding guests, and a few foreigners in 2005. King Abdullah rallied public opinion in the shocked nation against Abu Musaib al-Zarqawi, the Jordanian leader of al-Qaeda in Iraq, who claimed responsibility for the attacks. The televised confession of an Iraqi woman whose explosives failed to detonate strengthened the king's claims and increased popular opposition to terrorism. By definition, faithful conservatives supported the king's rule and avoided stringent criticism over the peace treaty with Israel. However, that same conservatism opposed important elements of the king's reform agenda. Apparently unhappy with the failure of parliament to enact desired legislation, in 2009 King Abdullah again dismissed parliament and used the year before the next election to initiate reforms, most prominently economic liberalization. Modest changes in the electoral system reserved six more seats for women, but changed little else.

Even before the Egyptian protests at Tahrir Square, unrest over corruption and unemployment began in Jordan's conservative south—the heartland of the king's

support. Leftists, Islamists, and other traditional opposition groups joined Friday demonstrations, calling for reforms and democracy. Significantly, they did not espouse revolution against the king.

In contrast to other most Arab rulers, King Abdullah initially defused the protests. Very likely, the security services hacked into dissident blogs and closed websites, but the police treated protestors carefully—handing out water bottles rather than beating them. Abdullah met with the Muslim Brotherhood and dismissed the prime minister, who was considered too close to corruption and the IMF.

The king apparently yielded to one of the opposition's chief demands—that democracy meant the people, through parliament, should choose the prime minister. However, Abdullah left plenty of room to retreat, stipulating that a functioning three-party system (left, center, and right) would be necessary, and would take years to become effective. Cynics noted that the monarchy's electoral system, so often modified, is deliberately designed to weaken political parties.

A violent protest by Islamist Salafists in Zarqa reminded the general population

---

The 1989 elections in Jordan demonstrated vividly the deeply-held differences between Muslim fundamentalists and women influenced by Western concepts of equality and women's rights.

In her campaign for parliament, TV personality Toujan al-Faisal raised a number of social issues, including child abuse, polygamy, and wife-beating. For this, she was charged in Islamic court by two Muslim radicals, one a deputy to the Mufti (legal scholar) of the military, on grounds she had "defamed Islam." As punishment, her critics demanded the court declare her legally incompetent, dissolve her marriage, remove her children, and grant immunity to anyone who shed her blood.

The Islamic court dismissed the case, at the urging of the royal palace. Neither al-Faisal nor any other woman won a seat in the elections, but soon after King Hussein did appoint Layla Sharaf the first woman in the Senate.

Al-Faisal later became the first woman elected to parliament, but after she posted an article on the internet that accused the prime minister of corruption, she was imprisoned. She was pardoned by King Abdullah in 2002, but she remains banned from parliament for life.

of the dangers posed by some opposition groups. Waving a sword in front of the media's cameras, the group's leader demanded the release of prisoners, including the mentor of the slain leader of al-Qaeda in Iraq, Abu Musab al-Zarqawi. When police attempted to break up the protest, they were attacked by Salafists wielding swords, clubs, and clubs.

The king later proposed reform measures, and parliament approved them, including a provision that enabled electors to vote for both the local representative and a vote for the 27 nation-wide seats distributed by proportional representation. This modest reform failed to meet opposition expectations, since gerrymandered districts remained, and the powers of the lower house of parliament were limited. It would not be permitted to

choose the prime minister, formulate the budget, or even introduce laws. After protests, parliament postponed consideration of a proposal to criminalize allegations of corruption, but journalists were arrested for reporting that the king had intervened in parliament's investigations.

The small weekly protests by Islamists continued and grew dramatically when the cabinet withdrew subsidies on bottled gas, necessary because of attacks on the pipeline bringing cheaper Egyptian supplies. Some demonstrators even dared to blame the king himself for financial difficulties. Foreign observers worried that the January 2013 election, if boycotted successfully by the Muslim Brotherhood's Islamic Action Front, trade unions, and leftists, could discredit the entire reform project and provoke widespread protests.

On election day in 2012, Jordanians voted at a slightly higher rate than in past elections—at 56%, just over half the electorate. Perhaps conscious of the political and economic difficulties in Egypt, Yemen, and Syria, they chose tribal and business independents sympathetic to the king. After consultation with parliament—for the first time—Abdullah appointed a reformer, Abdullah Ensour, as prime minister.

As the Syrian civil war worsened, Jordan played an increasingly important role as a conduit for supplies and weapons to militias fighting against the Assad regime in southern Syria. Hundreds of thousands of refugees fled in the opposite direction. The fortunate could afford to rent modest apartments in cities; some 120,000 impoverished others crowded into the Zaatari Refugee Camp, becoming, in effect, Jordan's fifth-largest city. The Syrian

King Abdullah II

conflict also led to the temporary posting of American troops and aircrafts.

Two happier events in the summer of 2013 united nearly all Jordanians except the strictest fundamentalists. Mohammed Assaf, a young Palestinian singer from Gaza, won the Arab Idol contest in a gentle assertion of Palestinian identity that won millions of non-Palestinian votes.

On the playing fields, the national women's soccer team, *al-Nashmiyyat* ("The Brave"), representing many of Jordan's ethnic and religious divisions, achieved an unthinkable 21–0 victory over Kuwait to qualify for the Asian Cup for the first time ever. A week later, the men's team, *al-Nashama*, beat Oman 1–0 in a must-win battle to remain a contender for the World Cup. Though Jordan failed to play in Brazil, such events helped, at least temporarily, to unite the nation. Moreover, the population was drawn to the monarchy through the efforts of the president of the football association, King Abdullah's brother Ali.

Sluggish economic growth in the kingdom received a significant boost with the Abdali Project, a joint venture between the government and the Lebanese billionaire and politician, Sa'id Hariri. The project is a mixed-use community envisaged to become Amman's new downtown. Expected to include hotels, retail outlets, offices, and residential apartments totaling over 20 million square feet, the development opened its first major component in 2014 and employed over 5,000 workers.

After forces of the Islamic State in Iraq and Syria (ISIS or IS) captured large areas of northern Iraq including the city of Mosul, Jordan joined the U.S.-led coalition against it. King Abdullah also personally displayed opposition to Islamists, militant

T. E. Lawrence described Wadi Rum as "vast and echoing and God-like"

Photo by Susan L. Thompson

Jordan

or otherwise: he quickly supported the ouster of Egypt's President Morsi and marched in Paris to protest the Charlie Hebdo massacre. A Muslim Brotherhood leader was jailed for criticizing the UAE's crackdown on the group.

These initiatives risked isolating the government from many citizens. Islamists have often enjoyed significant support; a survey about the same time (2014) indicated that 40% of respondents did not consider IS a terrorist group. Islamist activists demonstrated their disapproval when Jordan "took America's side" against fellow Muslims, and even some military retirees opposed Jordan joining the air war.

However, IS overplayed its hand in early 2015 with the capture and brutal execution of a Jordanian pilot. On December 24, 2014, Muath al-Kasasbeh's plane crashed during a mission over IS-held territory near Raqqa, Syria. The Jordanian government claimed mechanical failure was the cause of the crash; IS claimed it had brought the jet down with a heat-seeking missile. Whatever the case, al-Kasasbeh was captured and detained.

The group contacted the Jordanian government, seeking a prisoner exchange: al-Kasasbeh for Sajida al-Rishawi, the woman detained by Jordanian authorities after her suicide vest failed to explode in an attack on a Jordanian wedding in 2005. The government insisted on proof of life before talks could go forward, but in fact al-Kasasbeh had already been burned alive in a cage. On February 3, the group released gruesome footage of that murder, preceded by a coerced confession from the pilot.

The response from the Jordanian government was swift: al-Rishawi was reportedly executed within 12 hours of the release of the video, and further airstrikes against IS began immediately. On state TV, the Jordanian military exclaimed, "This is just the beginning, and you shall know who the Jordanians are." A trained pilot, the king himself took part in airstrikes.

For all of the rage that the execution provoked in Jordan, the initial response seems to have suggested a magnitude of retaliation that was ultimately not forthcoming. Jordan continued to be a critical partner in the fight against IS until the 2019 demise of the Caliphate. The problem of extremism in the Middle East—with or without IS—is sure to be a long-term challenge, including in Jordan.

Culture: Antiquities lie strewn profusely across—and beneath—the landscape of Jordan. Perhaps as many as 500,000 identifiable archeological sites exist, and teams of workers from around the world descend annually to discover remains dated from the Paleolithic to the Ottoman periods. In years of good fortune, they unearth seals, broken pottery, and occasional pieces of jewelry. In the popular imagination, however, foreigners come for gold. As a result, archeological pillaging constitutes a widespread crime.

Although desert palaces of the Umayyads and the Byzantine mosaics at Madaba are priceless treasures, the most impressive ruins date from the Roman era. Now the scene of a cultural festival, the columns, buildings, streets, and amphitheater of Jerash rank as one of the Empire's best preserved cities outside Italy. Semitic Nabateans carved residences and tombs in the nearly vertical limestone cliffs of a narrow gorge. The home of enterprising merchants, Petra flourished for about 200 years after 100 BC. Already in decline by the Arab conquest, it became a lost city, rediscovered only in the 19th century. Tourists today endure sand and sunshine to marvel at the intricately carved columns, the splendor of sunlight on rose-colored

sandstone, and carved channels that brought water from a distant spring.

Universal, compulsory education through six elementary and three preparatory ("junior high") years has almost been attained, partly due to facilities provided for children by the UN Relief and Works Agency for Palestine Refugees. The more recent influx of Syrian refugees, a consequence of that country's civil war, has of course complicated this endeavor. The quality of instruction tends to be good, if traditional, in Arabic language and literature, as well as in mathematics, where Jordanian test scores have recently approached U.S. levels.

The University of Jordan opened on the outskirts of Amman in 1963, and remains the most prestigious in the country. Yarmuk University was established at Irbid in 1976, while the 1980s saw the beginnings of Mu'ta University in the south. In the 1990s, numerous private colleges and universities sprouted across the landscape, often to serve students whose families had lived in the Gulf States.

The modern culture of Jordan is essentially similar to that found in Syria and parts of Lebanon, with stronger nomadic and Saudi influences in the eastern and

Hospitality in a Jordanian family.

southern deserts. Nevertheless, observers often notice differences in Jordan, including greater respect for standing in line and obeying traffic regulations.

For most inhabitants, entertainment means spending time with friends and relatives, typically in segregated circles of men and women, drinking coffee and tea. Entertainment may also mean watching television; some Bedouin tents even boast a set. One key difference from American customs is the relative absence of single men and women mingling together. Romances are rarely conducted openly, and few girls or women would consider going to the movies without a group of relatives or friends. A wide variety of sports attract some enthusiasts. As in other Middle Eastern countries, football (soccer) dominates. However, Jordan has also enjoyed some limited success in international rugby test matches, and basketball is rapidly rising in popularity. At the 2016 Rio Olympics, Jordan won its first official Olympic Games medal, with Ahmad Abu-Ghaush taking gold in Taekwondo.

Economy: A century ago life in Jordan revolved around nomadic and semi-nomadic herding and farming, with a handful of small towns. Today, some herders do remain, and Prince Hasan bin Talal's Badia project attempts to encourage ecologically sound ways of life. Where rainfall and irrigation permit, settled farmers cultivate a variety of crops, ranging from grains and other staples to tomatoes, melons and warm-weather vegetables. Agricultural products account for around one-fifth of total exports, but many foods must be imported. The climate and soil usually ensure that farmers, some of them tenants paying one-third of the crop to the

landlord, achieve only a modest standard of living. After independence the government undertook a series of irrigation projects and other assistance for agriculture, particularly the East Ghor Project, to use water from the Yarmuk River for farms in the Jordan Valley.

Water Shortages

Given the frequent pattern of several consecutive years of low rainfall, Jordan often faces prolonged and devastating droughts. Wheat and other crops that depend on rainfall fail, and many herders lack water for their flocks to drink and stubble for them to eat. Piped water in Amman becomes highly contaminated with bacteria and smells foul. Even parts of the capital city receive tap water only one day per week during the summer.

In the short term, little can alleviate a water shortage shared with neighboring countries. Irrigation-based agriculture, which accounts for 75% of water use, may need to be curtailed. In King Abdullah's words, "Drinking water remains the most essential."

For the longer term, the Wahda Dam project with Syria on the Yarmuk River may provide the expected 50 million cubic meters of water to Amman and to agriculture in the Jordan valley, but it will not satisfy the country's needs. Indeed, small Syrian dams upstream threaten to divert much of the expected flow. The Disi aquifer deep in the southeastern desert has been tapped, but it is a non-renewable resource.

Proposals exist to desalinize seawater in the valley south of the Dead Sea. However, that source of fresh water will be distant, expensive, and possibly nuclear-powered. It will also require international

cooperation. Under the auspices of the World Bank, Jordan, Israel, and the Palestinians signed an agreement in 2013 to construct a desalination plant near Aqaba, partly to supply Israel's city of Eilat. In return, far to the north Israel will transfer water to both the Palestinian territories and Jordan. To test the effects of replenishing the Dead Sea with water from the Red Sea, brine from the desalination plant will be piped to the former.

Unlike its Arab neighbors to the northeast and south, Jordan contains no significant oil deposits. The country plays a modest role as a regional trade and commercial center, partly because its drier, cooler climate contrasts favorably with the Gulf, partly because Westerners find their lifestyles less restricted and Jordanians hospitable.

Besides encouraging trade and tourism, economic development projects have included exploiting the phosphate deposits that account for about 25% of the nation's exports. Ambitious plans also exist to exploit the Dead Sea for potash.

The economy has alternately suffered and prospered because of international events. Disputes with Syria often cut access to the Mediterranean. War with Israel in 1967 inflicted 400,000 new refugees, the collapse of tourism, and the loss of the most highly-developed portion of the kingdom, which accounted for 40% of GNP. Financial aid from other Arab states rewarded Jordan's rejection of the Camp David Agreement (1978), and the economy grew at 10% annually. While many Jordanians (330,000 in 1988) worked abroad, often as skilled professionals in oil-exporting countries, some 200,000 other Arabs filled low-paying jobs in Jordan.

The collapse of world oil prices in 1986 initiated an era of economic retrenchment. Aid from Arab oil exporters fell, and job prospects weakened abroad. Interest and repayment on the foreign debt soared, and foreign exchange reserves fell. The dinar fell steeply against the dollar, losing as much as 50% of its value in one year. Thus, by early 1989 several economic difficulties hit simultaneously: lower aid, debt repayment, precarious reserves, inflation, rising imports, and a budget deficit surpassing 20% of GNP. Clearly Jordanians had lived beyond their means, and they could no longer borrow to do so.

Although the government responded with economically-reasonable measures such as higher indirect taxes, cuts in subsidies, and canceling new weapons purchases, popular resistance led to riots and political change. Friendly Arab nations responded with promises of modest aid, and rescheduled debt repayments. The cabinet cut spending for investment projects and devoted more to debt repayment. In these

Arab hospitality quickly means hot tea   Photo by Michael Russell

Jordan

ways the country survived the immediate crisis, only to suffer lost subsidies and disrupted trade during the Gulf War.

Flooded with hundreds of thousands of new refugees, this time from the Gulf, the economy recovered surprisingly rapidly after 1991. Construction boomed, as former workers in the Gulf invested their savings in homes, offices, and apartments. Foreign exchange reserves rose: the economy briefly grew rapidly (over 5% per year), and yet inflation remained modest.

For the medium-term, however, Jordan lost its major export market, Iraq, to UN sanctions. The lost transit earnings themselves reached billions of dollars. Despite fanfare and hopes, peace with Israel brought no great economic dividend. In the late 1990s the country entered a significant recession. Unfortunately, economic policy could not be used to restore output. Fiscal policy was immobilized: massive budget deficits, covered partly by foreign aid, marked good years as well as bad. Monetary policy was equally ineffective: a rapid increase in the money supply would lead the wealthy to send it abroad before the dinar fell in value. As an importer of natural gas and petroleum, the country suffered again when oil prices rose in 2008, requiring 20% of GDP to pay for energy imports.

With a rapidly-growing workforce, the economy must grow by 5%–7% annually to create the number of jobs needed for those newly seeking work. However, after 1996, the population grew faster than the economy, and by 2002 total unemployment perhaps reached 25% of the labor force, and then remained very high. Again, the recent influx of refugees from Syria's civil war has only exacerbated this problem.

A free trade agreement signed with the United States provides easier access for Jordanian goods, especially textiles produced in Qualified Industrial Zones using some Israeli inputs. In recent years these exports grew rapidly, and the zones employ 35,000 workers. However, many Jordanians lack the skill or the desire to work in textile factories, and about 75% of the employees come from South Asia and China.

The recent discovery of substantial uranium deposits in the desert south of Amman offers the possibility of creating a nuclear industry that could generate electricity, power desalination and irrigation projects, and export nuclear fuel. However, the United States generally opposes the spread of nuclear enrichment facilities, and Israel—the only nuclear power in the region—may also raise objections behind the scenes to the construction of civilian nuclear power plants.

Current Challenges and the Future: A range of recent developments in Jordan have been keeping the king and his ministers busy. From economic challenges at all levels (resulting only in part from the influx of refugees in recent years), to China's increasing influence in the region, to the ever-present Israeli–Palestinian conflict, the Kingdom finds itself even more overwhelmed than usual.

Two recent crises in the Kingdom deserve special mention. The first, of course, is the coronavirus pandemic, which arrived on the back of punishing IMF-led economic reforms, including rollbacks of subsidies for electricity, income tax hikes for Jordanians making more than $11,000 per year, and other tax increases on more than 160 items, many of them staples. That the country also hosts hundreds of thousands of Syrian refugees, along with significant numbers of Palestinian and Iraqi refugees, only exacerbates economic challenges. Rising popular discontent over worsening economic conditions and curbs on public freedoms under emergency laws led to a dissolution of the parliament in September 2020, with the King installing Bisher al-Khasawneh as prime minister.

The second noteworthy crisis occurred in April 2021, when King Abdullah accused the former Crown Prince and now a bitter opponent, Prince Hamzah bin al-Hussein, of leading a "foreign-backed" coup attempt. Critics of the king have pointed to increasingly harsh measures being taken against dissenting figures. They claim the arrest of Prince Hamzah and his subsequent imprisonment and publicly released statement of fealty to the throne is further evidence of the repressive political environment being cultivated in Jordan today.

Despite (or perhaps because of) Jordan's economic woes, the country has a degree of external support, and that support is increasingly coming from China. In 2015, China signed investment agreements of more than $7 billion with Jordan, and many of those investments are under way. China views Jordan as a key pillar of its Belt and Road Initiative (BRI) expansion into the Levant, and Jordan will likely be an important jumping off point for Chinese reconstruction projects in neighboring Syria in the years to come. With investment, China is set to wield increasing political influence in Jordan, and that may put it in direct competition with the United States. Washington has historically been an ally of Jordan. However, King Abdullah has registered his disapproval of the so-called Trump peace plan. Any significant annexation of settlements in the West Bank poses an existential threat to Jordan. While dependent on the economic lifelines provided by Saudi Arabia and Israel respectively, any acquiescence to a deal that undermines Palestinian claims to statehood will be catastrophic for the Jordanian regime and could risk its very survival.

The State of Kuwait

National Flag: Three horizontal stripes of green, white, and red, with a black trapezoid at the pole.
Gross Domestic Product: $120.13 billion.
GDP per capita: $33,545.

Kuwait is a tract of flat desert at the head of the Persian Gulf. There are only a few natural oases in the country and no significant supply of fresh water for the city of Kuwait, which gave its name to the state.

Most of the population lives in the modern suburbs, a dramatic change from the old town of mud houses that existed just decades ago. The wealth produced by oil has attracted hundreds of thousands of immigrants, who with their descendants now account for almost 70% of the population. The Arab world, especially the nations from Egypt to Syria, provides teachers, engineers, doctors, office staff, and skilled workers. Sharing language (but not dialect), culture and usually religion with native Kuwaitis, before 1990 these immigrants formed a majority of the population.

In addition the substantial Iranian community, Indians, Pakistanis, and other Asians fill service jobs, and even build *dhows*, the traditional boats that for generations established Kuwait as a trading center and base for pearl diving. The few European and American expatriates work in the oil industry and hold scattered positions in finance and commerce.

History: Although ancient ruins on Failaka Island show human settlements thousands of years ago, for centuries the inhabitants of the region were essentially nomadic. In 1756, Bani Utbah families of the Aniza tribe from central Arabia, settled and built a fort where the city of Kuwait now stands. In Arabic, Kuwait means "Little Fort," and the small collection of mud huts, benefiting from a natural harbor, grew into a trading outpost and pearl-diving center. The outpost eventually came to possess a defensive wall.

The ruling family of Kuwait descended from the first ruler and carries his name, al-Sabah (pronounced es-sabah). Although formally titled emir (prince), the ruler and other important members commonly use the honorary Arab title of sheikh. Arab custom and a tradition of consultation limited the sheikh's autocratic powers, and senior men in the extended family selected the most appropriate successor. Because the early emirs proved to be long-lived, there was less opportunity for interference by the swiftly-growing Ottoman Empire, which claimed the territory as part of the province of Basra.

At the end of the 19th century, Emir Mubarak faced a critical decision. Fearing the increased capacity of the Ottoman Empire to rule its distant territories, in 1899

Luxury Hotels in Kuwait City

Area: 6,880 square miles (17,819 square kilometers)
Population: 4.3 million, 70% non-nationals.
Capital City: Kuwait City (1.8 million).
Climate: Very hot except for a short comfortable winter, which usually brings a few inches of rain.
Neighboring Countries: Saudi Arabia (South) and Iraq (North).
Time Zone: GMT +3.
Official Language: Arabic.
Other Principal Tongues: Farsi (Persian) and English.
Ethnic Background: Overwhelmingly Arab, with communities of Persians, Indians, and Pakistanis.
Principal Religion: Islam, with small native Christian and Bahá'í communities, in addition to expatriates of various religious backgrounds including Hindu, Buddhist, and Christian.
Chief Commercial Products: Crude oil and refined products.
Major Trading Partners: Japan, China, the United States, South Korea, and India.
Currency: Kuwaiti Dinar (1 Dinar = 1000 fils).
Former Colonial Status: British Protectorate (1914–61).
National Day: February 25 (1950; Sheikh Abdullah al-Salem al-Sabah's ascension to the throne).
Chief of State: Nawaf Al-Ahmad Al-Jaber Al-Sabah, Emir.
Head of Government: Sheikh Sabah Al-Khalid Al-Sabah, Prime Minister.

Kuwait

The late Sheikh Jabir al-Sabah

he negotiated a secret treaty with Britain that placed Kuwait under its protection. Then, when the Ottoman Empire entered World War I in 1914, Britain declared Kuwait a protectorate. The Sabah family retained internal authority over the town, which remained an uninviting and lonely trading center.

On the death of Sheikh Mubarak in 1915, succession passed to each of his sons, Jaber and Salim. This established a pattern of succession, alternating between their two families. Thus, until 2005, a "crown prince" was not the son of the current emir, but rather a cousin who traced his paternal ancestry through a different line (see "Domestic Politics after Liberation" below).

As geologists searched for oil deposits near the Gulf, British and American companies formed the Kuwait Oil Company and received a concession from the emir. The company began drilling for oil in 1936, and soon discovered some of the richest deposits in the world. Exports began after World War II, and oil production and revenues soon made a startling impact on the dusty little town as it began the awkward change into a large, modern city.

Sheikh Abdullah al-Sabah became ruler in 1950. A benevolent monarch, he presided over the early period of economic growth. He initiated the policy of using the oil revenues for the benefit of all through a program of public works. In spite of this, much of the money was squandered.

The British protectorate ended in 1961, when Kuwait gained independence. President Qasim of Iraq immediately claimed the state, threatened to invade, and blocked Kuwait's membership in the United Nations. However, Britain remained an ally,

and its troops returned quickly, until Arab League forces replaced them. After the overthrow of Qasim in 1963, the *Ba'thist* government in Iraq recognized Kuwait's independence, reportedly for a fee. Several treaties followed between the two states. One difficulty remained the boundary. The 1932 demarcation agreement between (British-protected) Kuwait and (British-influenced) Iraq contained neither map nor detailed descriptions, so that Kuwaiti territory began "south of the southernmost palm tree at Safwan."

After independence, Kuwait moved tentatively towards democracy. Elections in 1961 selected twenty men to serve with members of the ruling family in a Constituent Assembly that would draft a constitution. The 1962 Constitution retained the emir as the chief executive of government, assisted by a prime minister and cabinet. An elected National Assembly received the power to make recommendations and serve as a forum of discussion. The electorate, however, extended only to males whose family possessed citizenship in 1920. Additionally, the Constitution prohibited Kuwaiti-born males of a

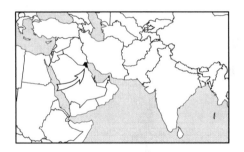

non-Kuwaiti father from voting. As such, only about 10% of the population was eligible to vote.

In its early years the National Assembly worked reasonably well. However, in the late 1960s the ruler faced a series of difficulties—foreign military tensions, the hijacking of Kuwaiti airliners, and terrorist violence. He reacted by suspending the Assembly and imposing press restrictions. This halted inconvenient criticisms from its members, and press censorship discouraged unflattering commentary by journalists. Kuwait reverted to government by decree, in common with the other Arab Gulf states.

During the 1980s, the war between Iran and Iraq pitted two ideological opponents of monarchy against each other: socialist republican Iraq against Islamic republican Iran. Fearing Islamic revolution more than the traditional threats of its large Arab neighbor, Kuwait loaned more than $10 billion to Iraq interest-free, and sold oil on its behalf against promise of repayment. Kuwait also allowed Iraqi military supplies to pass through its territory.

When combatants attacked neutral vessels in the Gulf, Kuwait sought assistance. The United States provided naval protection. After an Iranian missile attack on the main oil terminal in 1987, Kuwait purchased military hardware and sought closer ties with other Arab Gulf states, Egypt, and the United States.

Invasion, Occupation and Liberation

After the 1988 cease-fire between Iran and Iraq, popular protests swelled among Kuwaitis anxious to end censorship and

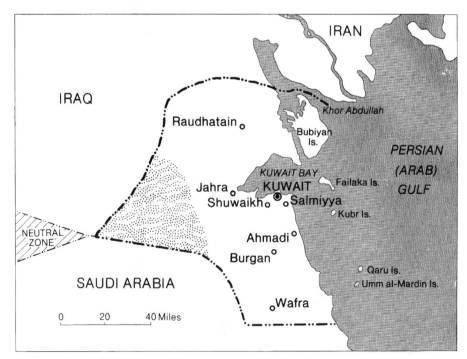

Kuwaiti women weep at the graves of relatives killed by the Iraqi army during the 7-month occupation

AP/Wide World Photo

restore parliament, suspended since 1986. Some politicians even questioned the royal family's role in a stock market crash at this time. The emir, Sheikh Jaber al-Ahmad al-Sabah, balked at these demands, and police used unexpected violence on the wealthiest demonstrators in the world. In 1990 he ordered elections for a *Shura*, a consultative council, rather than the legislature. Members of the former Assembly boycotted the elections, complaining that the *Shura* "lacked teeth," and condemned the arrest of critics.

In July 1990 President Saddam Hussein fiercely denounced Kuwait, warning that "cutting necks is better than cutting the means of living." Iraq complained, first, that Kuwait had exceeded its OPEC quota and thus was complicit in driving down oil prices. After the economic costs of a protracted war with Iran, Iraq could not afford the reduction in oil revenue.

Second, Iraq demanded money: billions in aid, writing off the wartime loans, plus compensation for $2.4 billion worth of Iraqi oil allegedly pumped from the Rumaila field that straddles the Iraq-Kuwait border. Finally, Iraq demanded long-term leases on the islands of Bubiyan and Warba to protect its naval base and retain access to the Gulf.

Hours after Saddam's diplomats suspended negotiations on August 2, Iraqi forces attacked Kuwait. By nightfall, Iraqi troops had crushed all opposition. Sheikh Jaber and the crown prince barely escaped; other members of the ruling family were arrested.

Initially Iraq claimed it had acted to support Kuwaiti revolutionaries. However, courageous Kuwaiti opposition leaders refused to collaborate. Iraq annexed Kuwait six days later.

The Kuwait Investment Office and other resources in London funded the Kuwaiti government-in-exile. The government lent to Kuwaiti banks, preserving them from default, and promised $5 billion to the coalition forces gathering against Iraq. Further billions were pledged to countries suffering severe hardship from the invasion and economic sanctions against Iraq.

To unite Kuwait's citizens, Sheikh Jaber met with opposition figures, and the crown prince pledged trust in the 1962 Constitution and parliament. For its part, the opposition agreed to support the dynasty, in the face of the more pressing threat.

Meanwhile, Iraqi forces plundered Kuwait: gold and foreign currency worth billions, truckloads of consumer goods, cars stolen from the streets. Hospital equipment and library books disappeared. Even traffic lights were stolen, along with cadavers from the medical school. Iraqi university officials apparently divided the academic spoils before shipping them home. The vast booty depressed prices in Baghdad.

Such rampant pillaging inspired resistance by the 200,000 citizens who remained in Kuwait. Government employees stopped work, and at night defiant women shouted "Allahu Akbar" from rooftops. A resistance movement helped subvert Iraqi rules and aided foreigners sought as hostages by the Iraqis. Equally important, it maintained morale and social order.

In response, the Iraqi forces deported thousands; thousands more were executed and buried in mass graves. Several hundred deportees remain unaccounted for, almost three decades after the conflict.

As coalition forces neared victory in the 1991 war to liberate Kuwait, Iraqi forces deliberately sabotaged industry and the environment. Eight million barrels of crude oil were dumped into the Gulf, creating one of the greatest oil slicks in history. Decades later, local coral reefs have still not recovered.

Iraqi units also set fire to 732 of the nation's 950 oil wells. The fires burned up to 6 million barrels of oil daily, about 10% of all petroleum consumed world-wide. The smoke from burning oil wells damaged neighboring countries with soot, acid rain, and other pollution. Led by the legendary Red Adair, teams from nine nations extinguished the fires, an exercise dubbed Operation Desert Hell. While the fires were predicted to burn for several years, the last was extinguished in November 1991. The escaping oil eased underground pressure in the oilfields, thus permanently reducing the Kuwait's oil potential.

Liberated by coalition forces, Kuwaitis rejoiced. However, their euphoria soon

Sheikh Nasser Muhammad Al-Ahmad Al-Sabah, Prime Minister 2006–12
Copyright: Brian McMorrow

yielded to concern. Destroyed water mains and electrical generating plants took time to repair, despite stockpiled equipment and parts. Within days, leaflets condemned the government for the lack of food and utilities, apparently delayed because of bureaucratic fumbling. Critics demanded the ending of martial law, a broader-based cabinet, and restoring the Constitution. In response, Sheikh Jaber promised to restore the National Assembly.

Searching for Security: Foreign Relations

After 1990, Kuwait's search for security surpassed many traditional concerns. The post-war demarcation of the border placed several oil wells, a ship channel, and the major Iraqi naval base within Kuwait. Though approved by Saddam Hussein's rubber-stamp parliament in 1994, international disputes over the new border seem inevitable.

After its liberation and for the good part of a decade, Kuwait spent more per capita on arms than any other country. Defense spending exceeded 20% of the total budget.

Seeking allies from outside the Gulf region, Kuwait signed a defense pact with the United States in 1991 (renewed in 2001) that covers joint training and military exercises, as well as U.S. stockpiles of equipment. Similar arrangements provide French and British support in time of conflict.

In a rare move for an Arab country, during a 1998 crisis over UN inspection in Iraq, Kuwait agreed to let UN forces use its airbases. After U.S. and British bombers used those bases to attack Iraq in 1999, Saddam Hussein denounced Kuwait's sovereignty. However, threatened by a U.S. invasion, in 2002 he softened this stand and even returned some of the seized National Archives.

Alone in the Arab world, Kuwait publicly backed the U.S.-led attack on Iraq

Kuwait

in 2003. Most Kuwaitis delighted in the destruction of Saddam Hussein's regime in Baghdad, but the thousands of foreign troops passing through the emirate presented targets for international terrorists and grounds for Islamic criticism. In 2005, several fatal shoot-outs occurred as security forces attempted to capture Muslim militants, some of them foreigners. Partly in response, the government announced moves to curb militancy by removing intolerant school textbooks and closing unofficial mosques.

The U.S. defeat of Saddam Hussein's Iraq ended the constant threat of an Iraqi invasion but, clearly in retrospect, did not preface international calm. Today, Kuwait faces a bevy of new foreign policy challenges. Three reign over the rest. First, how will Iran's role continue to evolve in the region, and what will be the implications for Kuwait? While Saudi Arabia is an unremitting opponent of Iran and has called for intra-Arab unity on the issue, Kuwait has taken a cautious approach, cooperating closely with Saudi Arabia, while maintaining economic and political relations with Iran. Second, will regional instability—caused by the Iraq war and subsequent developments like the Arab Spring and the rise of ISIS—spill over into the tiny Gulf nation? Domestic politics in the post-Arab Spring era were fractious, at best, however calm seems to have prevailed. Third, when will the GCC crisis between Saudi Arabia, the UAE, Bahrain and (non-GCC member) Egypt, on the one hand, and Qatar, on the other, be resolved? Kuwait has refused to take sides in the spat, preferring to maintain a neutral stance as mediator, but the damage done to relations between these states will inevitably have a broader regional impact. There can be little doubt that Kuwait's leaders spend a great deal of time thinking about all three of these questions.

Domestic Politics after Liberation

The 1992 National Assembly elections proved honest and even festive. Given the few thousand male voters in each two-member district, the numerous candidates met the electorate at *diwaniyas* (see Culture) to chat about politics and society. Lacking political parties, voters could choose between candidates sympathetic to the ruling family or opposition candidates reflecting three broad groupings: the *Democratic Forum* (secular liberals), Islamists, and traditional politicians. During the following years, this "Opposition" proved to be little more than unstructured and shifting alliances. Though it represented a majority on some issues, it could not form the government, and its options were, and remain, limited.

As a result of the system, in practice the Assembly has proved a debating society incapable of effective action. It debated but could not remedy challenges common to many Gulf states: severe budget deficits in years of low oil prices ($5.6 billion in 1994, some 20% of GDP), a bloated bureaucracy, and inefficient government-owned companies. It delayed approving the vote for women until 2005. However, it could attempt a motion of no confidence because free copies of the Quran had been distributed despite a missing verse (Muslims believe the book is the uncreated Word of God, so such an error is more significant than, say, a printer missing a few verses of the Bible).

In 2006, Sheikh Jaber died. The planned succession faltered when the crown prince proved too ill to recite the oath of office. After two weeks of uncertainty, both a family majority and the National Assembly elected Prime Minister Sheikh Sabah, the younger half-brother of Sheikh Jaber, as emir. He in turn chose his brother, Sheikh Nawaf, as crown prince, and his nephew, Sheikh Nasser, as prime minister. These appointments destroyed any

semblance of alternation between the al-Ahmad and the al-Salem branches of the family.

Reformers in the Assembly and Kuwaitis in general welcomed the promise of a more active leadership. However, within months the long-simmering demands for electoral reform suddenly caught the public's attention. Reformers claimed that, in the absence of political parties, the system of 25 two-member electoral districts encouraged corruption, exaggerated tribal influence, and favored local notables—"service politicians," concerned with petty local issues. Both the government and loosely-linked opposition recognized the need for reform. The cabinet favored 10 districts, the opposition just five.

At first sight, the emir's "one-man, one-vote" decree seems reasonable. Indeed, many well-educated Kuwaitis defend it as the sort of practice common in democracies. However, because Kuwait does not have single-member constituencies, the similarities are misleading.

Each of the country's five electoral districts selects 10 members of the National Assembly (or parliament). By allowing voters only one vote in an election for 10 seats, the emir's decree minimizes tactical voting. It also prevents election alliances that resemble political parties. Less evidently, the single vote encourages corruption among the lower tiers of candidates, where an extra million funneled to the right candidate to spend on receptions and posters might mean ninth place instead of eleventh. Then, the single-vote decision gravely harms the development of a functioning democracy.

KUWAIT'S FOUR WOMEN ELECTED TO THE NATIONAL ASSEMBLY IN 2009

Dr. Maasouma Al-Mubarak

Dr. Rola Dashti

Dr. Salwa al-Jassar

Dr. Aseel al-Awadhi

A Kuwaiti oilfield worker kneels for midday prayers near a burning oil well
AP/Wide World Photo

Adopting the slogan "5 for Kuwait," young and educated activists launched a campaign of public protest to demand change. Focusing on just one issue, the activists communicated by text messaging and blogs, and they cut strips of orange cloth for sympathizers to wear. Night-time demonstrations outside the National Assembly surprised the nation. Orange-clad protestors filled the Assembly's visitor galleries. Emboldened, the Assembly demanded, without precedent, to question the prime minister, and opposition members walked out. A constitutional crisis ensued. To defuse it, in 2006 Emir Sabah called early elections. For the first time, women could vote and run for office.

The results disappointed women candidates. Women's issues such as the financial problems of divorcées, widows and children, the unequal treatment of women married to non-Kuwaitis, and health care, received less attention than redistricting and alleged government corruption. Not a single woman won.

Sheikh Nasser, the emir's nephew, again formed a cabinet and accepted the proposed five electoral districts, but within months conciliation failed on other issues. The Assembly's opposition members continued attacks on the government, but the emir and crown prince were constitutionally protected from criticism. Rather than face questions about the economy and corruption, the prime minister resigned again.

The 2009 elections provided a substantially different set of victors. Dr. Maasouma Al-Mubarak, the first woman to hold a cabinet position, received the most votes in the first district, and three other women—all holders of doctorates from U.S. universities—also won seats in the Assembly. Their gains came at the expense of Islamic conservatives.

Denunciations of corruption and mismanagement exploded in 2011 when newspaper accounts alleged payments—apparently bribes—deposited in the bank accounts of some members of parliament. The amounts were substantial: two members reportedly received $92 million between them. Protestors stormed parliament, and its members scheduled a grilling of Sheikh Nasser about the allegations. Recognizing the need for change, the emir appointed another relative as prime minister, Jaber Al-Mubarak Al-Sabah. However, with the opposition sensing instability, his first months in office proved difficult. Once again the emir, Sheikh Sabah, dissolved the legislature.

With corruption and government failure so obvious, the campaign for the 2012 election was filled with invective and hate. The opposition triumphed, winning about two-thirds of the seats. Islamists captured some of the previously Shi'a-held seats and defeated every single woman. Both groups had previously been considered too sympathetic to the ruling family. Islamists then began enacting legislation for their preferred causes: amending the constitution to make the Shari'a the only source of Kuwaiti law, establishing "morality police" to regulate public behavior, and setting death as the maximum penalty for blasphemy.

Within months, the constitutional court ruled the February 2012 elections illegal on a technicality, and restored the previous parliament; however, its members could not establish a quorum, and Sheikh Sabah called new elections for December 2012. In the absence of parliament, he also decreed a single choice for voters "to preserve national unity" (see box).

Angered by the single-vote decree, protests flared. Between 50,000 and 150,000 demonstrators attempted to march on government buildings; police required stun guns and tear gas to block them. The former opposition MP who had received the most votes nationwide, Musallam al-Barrak, warned Sheikh Sabah that he would not be allowed to "take Kuwait into the abyss of autocracy." Opposition leaders decided to boycott the elections; al-Barrak, strongly Islamist in his politics, was later arrested for threatening the emir.

The election results proved about as expected. Due to the boycott, with under 40% of the electorate bothering to vote, Sunni Islamists lost nearly 20 seats. These went to Shi'a lawmakers, women, and independents sympathetic to business. The National Assembly became less contentious. Prices on the stock exchange climbed, buoyed by expectations the cabinet might actually address long-standing financial problems.

Unexpectedly, for the second time within a year, the constitutional court declared the most recent election unconstitutional, and it also confirmed the legality of the emir's "one-man one-vote" ruling. Another election took place during Ramadan/July 2013. It was boycotted by Islamists and liberals but, to some surprise a small majority of the electorate did cast ballots. The new assembly contained many new faces, among them liberals and tribesmen loyal to the regime. Relations improved even before Sheikh Sabah pardoned some of those convicted of insulting him. However, other critics received stiff prison sentences, including Musallam al-Barrak.

In the period since the 2013 legislative elections, Kuwait has enjoyed a period of relative political stability. This does not mean, however, that it is free of domestic and regional challenges. A combination of factors—uncertainty over succession, volatility in oil markets (more specifically, the slump in oil prices), and regional instability, among others—threaten to destabilize what seems to be an island of calm in a sea of turmoil.

There is also reason to believe that Kuwait is facing diplomatic pressure, especially behind the scenes, from the United States and others fighting extremists in the region. As late as 2016, Kuwait had still not criminalized terrorist financing and had not taken steps to shut down Islamic charities connected to terrorism. In the years since then, steps in this regard have been tentative.

Finally, recent years have witnessed a different—but major—problem in the Gulf, one that Kuwait has been hard at work trying to resolve. In mid-2017, several Arab countries—Bahrain, Egypt, Saudi Arabia, and the United Arab Emirates—cut diplomatic, economic, travel, and other ties with Qatar, accusing the latter of supporting terrorism. The rift has deeper roots than alleged support for terrorism (see chapter on Qatar), and in fact it represents the most significant schism in relations between Arab states in recent decades. In addition to the United States, which has sent mixed signals about its leanings in the dispute (with President Trump initially on

Kuwait

record supporting Saudi Arabia, former Secretary of State Rex Tillerson saying the United States remained neutral, and subsequent Secretary of State Mike Pompeo urging Gulf leaders to resolve the crisis), Kuwait has attempted to step in as a mediator. Terms set by the four states in a secret ultimatum to Qatar (which leaked shortly after it was conveyed) were widely understood to be non-starters for the Qatari government. Two years later, a way out of the crisis remains elusive. In 2018, Kuwait's deputy foreign minister noted, "the longer this division the deeper the wound will be in the Gulf body." Kuwait, having managed to steer a delicate path through the conflict, will almost certainly have a role in whatever mediation eventually leads to a resolution.

Culture: Kuwait largely shares the culture of its neighbors. Until the affluence resulting from oil production, its population of less than 100,000 wandered with flocks, engaged in trading in the town, or worked as seamen on the sailing vessels that plied as far as India and East Africa. Its culture was indistinguishable from that of southern Iraq or eastern Saudi Arabia. Some of its inhabitants were the *bidoun*, literally, "those without," nomad whose families wandered across national boundaries in the region. The *bidoun* lacked citizenship because ancestral residence could not be proven. While the *bidoun* are in effect stateless individuals, Kuwait treats them, today, as illegal immigrants. A push for expanded rights for the *bidoun* largely foundered in 2017.

Oil wealth following World War II changed the face of the town and the people. The poverty-stricken *badu* (rural/nomadic) virtually disappeared, as did the Kuwaiti sailors, while poor shopkeepers became wealthy businessmen. Mud huts gave way to air conditioned houses, often of palatial proportions. Kuwaitis often hold the world's top ranking in ownership of many consumer items, from cars to boats to electronics.

Non-Kuwaiti professionals and even workers have benefited from free medical service, educational facilities and other welfare programs. The educational system in Kuwait is among the best financed in the world; students are not only provided free education, including books and other equipment, but are given at least one free meal a day. Secondary school students receive living allowances.

The University of Kuwait, founded in 1966, grew to be one of the best in the region, with the pre-war student body numbering over 10,000. About half of the students came from Kuwait, a quarter from other Gulf states, and the rest from various Asian and African nations. The faculty was drawn from Egypt, Syria, Iraq and other Arab countries. In recent years, a number of private colleges and universities have been established, some with American links.

In recent decades, women have formed a majority of the graduates at the University of Kuwait. This achievement reflects the surprising roles held by women in the country's liberal professions and business community, and it provides the educated women who enable that role to continue. Kuwaiti women drive, shop, and otherwise play a much more public role than women in other Gulf countries, and in 2009 the constitutional court ruled that married women may obtain passports without the consent of their husbands.

In a society without alcohol or nightclubs, and with social restrictions separating men and women, *diwaniyas* play an important role in Kuwaiti society. Held in the relaxed atmosphere of private homes, often with segregation by gender, these evening gatherings bring together the relatively small number of citizens. In recent years they have provided forums to discuss political and social issues, and increasingly they have begun to resemble gatherings of political parties, which are banned.

Economy: Eighty years ago Kuwaitis earned their living by pearling, nomadic herding, and trading with sailing vessels. By 1990, they became the first country in history whose earnings on foreign investments exceeded those of trade. The key to the transformation was petroleum. After reconstruction, it regained its position as the source of almost all (roughly 95%) exports, nearly half (45%) of the GDP, and most government revenue.

Despite its small size—about that of New Jersey—Kuwait sits atop the Burgan field, one of the largest oil fields in the world. The country traditionally ranks fifth in world oil reserves, about 10% of the total, slightly below Iran and the United Arab Emirates.

Oil revenues allow Kuwaitis to live in substantial comfort despite the climate. In a desert land, each Kuwaiti resident consume an average of 22,000 gallons of fresh water annually. While some springs have been tapped, five giant desalination plants provide most of the flow. Brackish water from springs serves for street cleaning, livestock watering, and when mixed with fresh water, for irrigation.

That any agricultural production takes place is surprising, given wealth and climate, and government aid for this purpose is critical. Besides an annual stipend, farmers receive interest-free loans, seeds and other supplies at substantially reduced cost, not to mention subsidies for drilling wells.

After immediate development needs were cared for, in 1966 Kuwait established the Reserve Fund for Future Generations. Its income from oil revenues was to be invested but not consumed until the 21st century. In 1990 its assets approached $60 billion, or over $100,000 per citizen. Additional government funds brought total assets to roughly $100 billion. So large were the accounts that the Kuwait Investment Office (KIO) found it difficult to invest the money abroad without arousing opposition. For example, in 1988 it purchased nearly 22% of the shares of British Petroleum, but it was forced by the Thatcher government to reduce its holding to less than 10%.

Nevertheless, Iraqi occupation in 1990–1991 imposed enormous economic devastation on the small country. Wartime expenses, subsidies to Coalition allies, and the costs of reconstruction amounted to about $50 billion. Deliberate sabotage damaged the entire oil industry, including all three refineries and almost every well. Seeping and burning wells destroyed an estimated $20 billion of crude petroleum. However, reconstruction moved rapidly, and both refining and oil exports resumed in 1991. The pace of reconstruction surprised the experts, and the next year oil production rose to its pre-invasion quota. By 1993, other OPEC nations, which had waived Kuwait's quota, demanded output cuts in an effort to balance world supply and demand.

Revenue from oil sales helped fund reconstruction costs, estimated at $20 billion rather than the initial $60–$100 billion. By 1994, major rebuilding projects had been completed and refinery capacity had climbed to 800,000 barrels per day. However, despite its greater OPEC quota, and oil revenues exceeding $10 billion annually, the government had to borrow massively to fund subsidies, the bureaucracy, and military rearmament.

Recent years have seen new economic challenges, but along with these have come new opportunities. Kuwait was among the first countries to sign a memorandum with China regarding the latter's Belt and Road Initiative, a strategic plan to help connect Asia with Africa and Europe by way of the Middle East. Bilateral trade with China reached some $12 billion in 2017, up 28% from just one year prior. If Chinese investment continues at a similar pace going forward, Kuwait will have a strong foundation of foreign investment as it continues its pursuit of economic diversification away from oil (which still accounts for some 60% of GDP).

Dollar inflows are always welcome, especially in a country where foreigners make up roughly two thirds of the population, but finding the right balance of investment incentives can be tricky. Recently, Kuwait has begun to suffer a real estate crisis, as expat workers have fled the country in large numbers in response to increases in the costs of medical services, electricity, and a range of commodities. Kuwaiti lawmakers would welcome some departures, in hopes of increasing employment opportunities for locals, but the numbers suggest a real problem. In the first four days of May 2019, the total number of expats in Kuwait dropped by 30,000. At present, some 49,000 apartments sit vacant in the tiny country, just as 26,000 more are under construction. Occupancy hovers around 87%, down from 95% just five years ago.

At the same time, rent prices have fallen by more than 13% in a year. New legislation was introduced in March 2019, to increase foreign worker annual leave entitlement and monthly salaries—the first pro-expat law to be debated by the National Assembly in almost a decade.

Current Challenges and the Future: As good as oil has been to Kuwait, the country has long recognized the need for diversification. The world is, undeniably, moving away from a dependence on Middle Eastern oil and toward renewable energy sources. For a country such as Kuwait, the plan has been a gradual reduction of oil dependency, with projects such as the Northern Gulf Gateway, which is intended—in the long term—to replace oil dollars with tourist dollars.

The simultaneous oil price collapse and coronavirus pandemic of 2020 underlined the urgent need for broad economic and social reform in the Gulf state. While these are likely to be temporary challenges, and ones that Kuwait can see its way through, they provide an important warning sign; pointing to the susceptibility of rentier economies to global shocks.

Citizens of Kuwait enjoy a social contract that guarantees jobs, high public service salaries, subsidies across a range of goods and services, and access to generous pensions. Efforts to reform the economy threatens to upset this social contract in ways that could lead to significant unrest.

The Republic of Lebanon

The Souk al-Nasr, a colorful Beirut market, with beautiful materials, sacks of flour, exquisite handicrafts, and fresh vegetables

AP/Wide World Photo

Area: 4,036 square miles (10,452 square kilometers).

Population: 6.9 million. Approximately one quarter of the population consists of refugees, from the Syrian civil war, along with Palestinian refugees, and their descendants.

Capital City: Beirut (1.6 million).

Climate: Summers are hot and humid on the coast, cooler and drier in the mountains. Winters are mild on the coast, but colder and snowy in the high mountains. Rainfall is normally plentiful in winter, but rare in summer.

Neighboring Countries: Syria (North and East); Israel (South).

Time Zone: GMT +2.

Official Language: Arabic.

Other Principal Tongues: French, English, and Armenian.

Ethnic Background: Arab. The largest cultural minority is the Armenians, who comprise about 4% of the population.

Principal Religions: Islam (plurality Shi'a, with an only slightly smaller Sunni population), Christianity (mainly Maronite and Greek Orthodox), and Druze.

Chief Commercial Products: Citrus fruit, apples, olives, vegetable oil, textiles, cement, and chemicals.

Major Trading Partners: The United States, the United Arab Emirates, France, Germany, and Saudi Arabia.

Currency: Lira or pound (1 lira = 100 piastres, obsolete).

Former Colonial Status: French Mandate (1920–43).

Independence Date: November 22 (1943; Independence Day).

Chief of State: Michel Aoun, President.

Head of Government: Saad Hariri, Prime Minister.

National Flag: Three horizontal stripes, with a green cedar tree centered on the wider central white stripe between two red ones.

Gross Domestic Product: $53.58 billion.

GDP per capita: $7,857.

The smallest mainland nation of southwest Asia, Lebanon historically connected the interior of the Fertile Crescent with lands across the Mediterranean Sea. Over the centuries, ideas (including the alphabet), the military (the Persian fleet against Greece), and a variety of products made the journey in one direction or the other. After World War II, Lebanon became an intellectual and commercial center for the entire Arab world, but disputes among

130

its peoples—disputes that involved how closely it should link with the West or East—plunged the nation into a civil war (1975–90) that nearly destroyed it.

Four geographical zones run the length of the country from north to south. First, a narrow plain hugs the coast; the largest cities are all located in this zone. Moving inland, the slopes of Mount Lebanon (a range rather than one mountain), with peaks exceeding 9,000 feet (2,743 meters) above sea level, comprise the second zone.

On the inland side of the Lebanon range lies the third zone, the Biqa' valley, a plain up to 15 miles (24 kilometers) wide. Its rich soil and flat fields provide most of the country's grains and vegetables. The Litani, the only significant river entirely in Lebanon, flows southward through most of the plain before turning sharply to the west to empty into the Mediterranean. The Orontes River begins in the northern part of the Biqa' Plain and flows north into Syria.

The last and easternmost division is the Anti-Lebanon Mountains; these form the border with Syria on the east. Near the southern end of this range is *Jabal al-Sheikh* or Mount Hermon, a snow-capped peak visible in clear weather from the tropical Jordan Valley to the south. Lebanon has no desert.

Winter and early spring constitute the rainy season. Much of the country receives at least 30 inches (762 millimeters) of precipitation annually, some areas much more. Snowfall is often heavy in the higher mountains, making the area suitable for winter sports.

In their physical appearance, culture, and linguistic dialects, the inhabitants resemble those of neighboring Syria. In both cases, the vicissitudes of history have left a variety of traits.

History: Homeland of the ancient Phoenicians, its strategic location made Lebanon a battleground in ancient times. Inscriptions at the Dog River commemorate conquerors ranging from Egyptian pharaohs and Babylonian kings to Roman emperors. The territory fell to the Ottoman Empire in 1516.

Given its rugged terrain, Mount Lebanon traditionally provided a haven for persecuted minorities, who often gained autonomy under their local leaders. Three religious communities dominated the mountains. The Maronite Christians in the north eventually linked with Roman Catholicism. In the center, the secretive Druze split from orthodox Islam in the Middle Ages. Like the Maronites, the Druze were uniquely Lebanese (see Culture). In the south and east, Shi'a Muslim villagers shared religious ideas and practices with fellow Arab Shi'a in Iraq.

During the 17th century the powerful Druze chieftain Fakhr al-Din extended his control beyond Mount Lebanon to parts of Syria and Palestine, but conflict with the Sultan in Istanbul led to his execution. After years of little change, the 19th century witnessed greater trade and missionary activity, especially schools. A decade of Egyptian occupation brought greater rights for Christians as well as (hated) conscription. After communal violence in 1860, to protect the remaining Maronites from further massacres and mistreatment, France landed troops and forced the Ottoman Sultan to grant Mount Lebanon a special legal status under a Christian governor.

As European nations sought zones of influence in the Ottoman Empire, France's traditional protection of Roman Catholic Christians naturally led it to expand its contacts in Lebanon.

When Ottoman Turkey allied with Germany in World War I, its officials seized

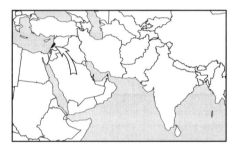

French documents that compromised many leading notables, both Christians and Muslims, and several were executed. As a further punishment, the Ottomans prohibited the transport of grain into Mount Lebanon, and thousands starved to death, particularly after an attack by locusts.

Secret wartime negotiations between Britain and France, formalized as the Sykes-Picot Agreement, assigned the coast and the Syrian interior to France. Thus, soon after British forces liberated the inhabitants from Ottoman troops in 1918, a French detachment landed in Beirut and occupied the coast and Mount Lebanon. However, they did not take control of the Arab-ruled Biqa' valley and the Anti-Lebanon mountains until 1920, when a French invasion defeated the nationalist government in Damascus.

While the League of Nations prepared a mandate for the region, in 1920 the French High Commissioner divided Syrian territory into four districts. "Greater Lebanon" included the coast, Mount Lebanon itself, and the entire Biqa' plain. Nearly twice the size of Ottoman Mount Lebanon, its population was evenly divided between Christians and Muslims. In 1926 France proclaimed this the Republic of Lebanon.

Public opinion divided sharply over the new state. Many Christians favored a separate Lebanon under French protection, thinking it would provide them political power and safety. However, most Muslim

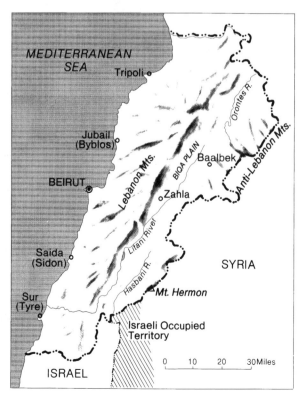

Lebanon

The cedars of Lebanon

Lebanese opposed the mandate. Between 1926 and 1939, occasional outbursts of violence against French rule proved local affairs, discouraged by concentrated French military forces in the country. The Lebanese government received internal autonomy subject to veto by the French High Commissioner, while France continued to control international relations.

After France surrendered to Nazi Germany, British and Free French troops invaded Lebanon and Syria in 1941, and the Free French commander afterwards proclaimed the two countries independent. However, in 1943 the French arrested the elected Lebanese president and his cabinet. This united Christian and Muslim politicians in favor of independence, and pressure from Great Britain and the United States forced France to free the officials and grant independence.

Traditional political leaders began maneuvering for the interests of their communities even before the French withdrew, and formalized the agreement as the National Pact. Broadly revered as the unwritten constitution, this stipulated a Maronite president, a Sunni Muslim prime minister and a Shi'a Muslim speaker of the parliament. Citizens of the various smaller religious groups were thus barred from the highest offices. Unfortunately, Bishara al-Khuri, the first president after independence, manipulated the political system for corrupt ends. He was forced from office.

During the presidency of his successor, Camille Chamoun (1952–1958), Arab nationalist ideas associated with Egypt's President Nasser further stirred tensions in Lebanese society. The champion of conservative Maronites who insisted that the Lebanese were not "Arabs," Chamoun sought support from the U.S. and from monarchial Arab regimes trying to stop Nasser's radical ideology from spreading.

With foreign money, some reportedly from the CIA, Chamoun organized the election of sympathetic candidates in the 1957 elections, filling the Chamber of Deputies with his men. He then proposed to change the constitution so he could have a second six-year term. This would have allowed him to orient Lebanon to the West, strengthen Maronite supremacy, and subdue the opposition.

1958 Disturbances

Dissension caused by the president's actions led to a restrained civil war in 1958. This divided both the country and the capital city into zones controlled by local political bosses and their private armies. Muslims sympathetic with Pan-Arabism and Nasser fought Maronites sympathetic to Chamoun. The national army remained neutral, and used its strength to police danger zones and minimize conflicts.

After a revolution overthrew the pro-Western king of Iraq, at Chamoun's request U.S. Marines landed at Beirut, ostensibly to support Lebanon's independence

from communist threats. Chamoun's attempt to garner further American support for his power play failed, however, and he left office when his term ended.

The crisis of 1958 settled none of the basic issues facing the country. When the Chamber of Deputies met to select a new president, opinion overwhelmingly favored Fu'ad Chehab, the army commander. A neutral and less partisan figure, Chehab's presided over the country's brief golden age of progress and tolerance. However, during the rule of his successors in the late 1960s and early 1970s, dissatisfactions smoldered, factionalism persisted, the gap between the rich and poor widened, and animosities grew. Hampered by a lack of consensus regarding national goals and the virtual monopoly on power held by a few communal leaders, governments rarely acted positively or decisively.

Necessary steps were not taken. Lebanon was unable to impose fair taxation or finance free public education. Attempts to build a strong, unified army were blocked by leaders fearful that such a force might override their individual communities. In time, solutions might have been found, but regional issues forced their way into Lebanon, and its governments could never formulate a widely-accepted policy toward Palestinian activity within Lebanon.

Neutrality

After playing only a nominal role in the 1948 war with Israel, Lebanon's small military avoided the 1956 and 1967 conflicts. Soon afterward, however, the country became the hapless victim of Israeli reprisal raids against Palestinians who launched guerrilla raids into Israel from Lebanon. Both Palestinians and Israelis resorted to tactics directed at civilian targets, including an Israeli raid on Beirut airport that destroyed many of Lebanon's civilian airliners. Concerned about reprisals and national sovereignty, but pressured by Arab states and political opinion among the growing Muslim majority, the government proved unable to assert control over the Palestinians.

By 1975, both society and government exhibited classic signs of failure. Assassinations and small-scale violence erupted between rival groups. Journalists were kidnapped. Armed Palestinian units operated freely in parts of the country, scrutinizing—and sometimes seizing—Lebanese travelers at checkpoints along roads and streets. In this atmosphere of lawlessness and disorder, frustration mounted.

Militia and Proxy Warfare

As tensions rose, Maronite militias trained for battle, and political rallies featured armed supporters. Most Maronite leaders hoped to regain Maronite supremacy, restore order, and rid the country of Palestinians. In early 1975 Maronite militiamen attacked a bus loaded with Palestinians. Palestinian forces retaliated, and for 19 months, war engulfed the country and especially its capital region.

Described abroad as a struggle between Christians and Muslims, the fighting was not purely sectarian. Palestinian and leftist groups joined together, and although overwhelmingly Muslim, they included a few Christians. Nevertheless, many civilians were murdered or maimed solely because of their religious identity, obvious usually from names and certified by national identity cards.

Foreign involvement added further complexity. Weapons, supplies, finances, and advice fueled the conflict. Besides representing a struggle for power in Lebanon, the war served as a battlefield for the Arab struggle with Israel. To accomplish their national aims, first Syrian (1976), then Israeli (1978) troops invaded parts of Lebanon. Syria initially invaded to limit the Palestinians and Lebanese leftists, and to relieve the Maronite forces. Other foreign troops played a peace-making role, including forces from the United Nations

(UNIFIL), in the South and the Arab League.

By the early 1980s violence became more infrequent, crossing the previously-deadly Green Line that divided Muslim and Christian Beirut became more common, and some attention focused on reconstruction.

Israel's War in Lebanon (1982)

Chaos returned when Israel again invaded in 1982, publicly to gain "peace in Galilee" but actually to implement General Ariel Sharon's plans to destroy Palestinian military forces and create a zone of influence in Lebanon. The massive assault occupied the southern half of the country and besieged the capital. Saturation bombing ahead of the Israeli advance kept Israeli casualties to a minimum, but killed over 15,000 civilians. Material devastation was extensive; nearly a quarter of all buildings in Beirut were damaged. However, West Beirut did not fall. As its siege stalemated, international pressures grew on Israel, and negotiations enabled Palestinian forces to evacuate the city rather than surrender.

Through war and occupation, Lebanon's politicians struggled to function. With elections due for a new president, the Chamber of Deputies met, surrounded

by Israeli soldiers and Maronite militiamen. Its members elected Bashir Gemayel, head of the right-wing Phalangist Party as president. Before he could take office, however, a massive bomb killed him at his headquarters, the work of one or more of his many enemies. Parliament then selected Bashir's brother, Amin, as president, though he lacked Bashir's political and military authority.

In response to Bashir's assassination, Israeli forces extended their control around Beirut. Fatefully, they surrounded the Sabra and Shatila (or Chatila) Palestinian refugee camps south of the city and invited pro-Israeli Christian militiamen into the camps. There the militiamen slaughtered between 1,000 and 2,000 civilians. Described as an act of genocide, the apparent complicity of the Israel Defense Forces (IDF) under General Ariel Sharon, generated considerable, if short-lived, soul-searching in Israel. The 1983 Kahan Commission (Commission of Inquiry into the Events at the Refugee Camps in Beirut) found that Israel was "indirectly responsible" for the massacres and Sharon bore "personal responsibility" for ignoring the risks of allowing Israeli-aligned militia to enter the camps.

Beirut "Paris of the Middle East" before the ravaging civil war

Lebanon

Stylish, bustling Beirut in times before invasion and civil war

Credit: National Council of Tourism in Lebanon

It took U.S. and European troops to restore order from the chaos. They maintained public order as Israeli units withdrew; they then helped reorganize the Lebanese army. Soon, however, the army joined the political and sectarian fighting, and the peacekeepers' role became partisan. After a suicide truck bomb killed 241 U.S. Marines in their barracks, the remaining American forces withdrew, and Lebanon returned to its now familiar wartime patterns. The president governed the palace, but the rest of the country fell under control of local militias or foreign troops. Some technical departments still attempted to function.

The worst violence continued in the south, where forces within the Palestinian, Druze, and Shi'a communities fought each other and the Israelis. In central Lebanon, the Lebanese Forces collected taxes and imposed some order and administration on East Beirut and the surrounding countryside, while near-anarchy prevailed in West Beirut.

Final Events of the Civil War

Parliament failed to select a successor to President Gemayel in 1988, and minutes before his term expired, he appointed General Michel Aoun, Commander-in-Chief of the (divided) Lebanese Army, as prime minister. This placed a Christian in the highest office reserved for Sunni

Muslims; the incumbent prime minister and cabinet refused to resign.

Determined to reunite Lebanon and expel all foreign troops, Aoun blockaded small ports used by militias to import military supplies and often to export illegal drugs. He also led his forces into intense battles with Syrian troops, who replied

Civil War Zones, 1983–1990

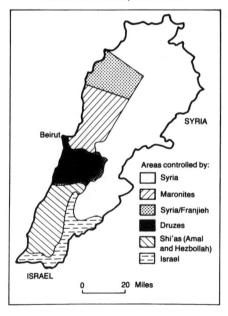

Areas controlled by:

☐	Syria
▨	Maronites
▦	Syria/Franjieh
■	Druzes
▨	Shi'as (Amal and Hezbollah)
▤	Israel

0   20 Miles

with indiscriminate shelling of civilian targets. One million fled, hundreds died, and survivors spent days and nights underground, often without electricity, fuel, or running water. Industry ground to a halt, and most factories were damaged.

Unable to force a Syrian withdrawal, Aoun hoped for foreign pressure to remove them. But no nation intervened when Syrian troops attacked his headquarters in 1990, the last major action of a civil war estimated to have claimed some 250,000 lives.

Under pressure from Saudi Arabia, in 1989 most Lebanese parliamentary deputies met in Taif, Saudi Arabia, and hammered out a new constitutional arrangement. The deputies also accepted the Syrian occupation, at least temporarily.

After their first choice for president was assassinated, the deputies elected Elias Hrawi, a Maronite, to the post. He quickly recognized the prime minister and gained support from important Maronite elements, including the Phalange Party and the Lebanese Forces militia. Hrawi asserted control over East Beirut and began to destroy the many walls dividing Lebanon. Daily life improved, business activity strengthened, funds flowed into the country, and schools reopened.

The army moved to regain control of South Lebanon in 1991. Troops entered Sidon and Tyre to public cheers, and they

134

defeated PLO units that refused to yield their heavy weapons. However, possibly under Syrian influence, the army did not move against Hizbullah units, which continued to attack Israeli troops and the South Lebanon Army (SLA) in what Israel had declared its Security Zone. Israel retaliated. Despite worthy attempts and the release of Western hostages, sovereignty and peace proved elusive. Car bombings occurred even on the American University campus.

Deep controversy arose over elections scheduled for 1992 and, indeed, over many elections that have followed. Until the Syrian withdrawal in 2005, critics—including the Maronite patriarch—faulted elections held under foreign occupation. At a practical level, hundreds of thousands of refugees could not return home safely to vote. True to tradition, political parties did not dominate the results, but Hizbullah consistently proved the strongest party, typically gaining 12 seats of the 128 only because it did not contest more. Its victories reflected Shi'a communal identity, popular appreciation of the party's social welfare programs, and support for its attacks on Israel.

By contrast, in the 20 years that followed, the Maronite community struggled with its loss of primacy and rarely achieved its aspirations. The Maronite leadership fractured, and some Christian seats were captured by pro-Syrian figures elected by Muslims.

Rafiq Hariri was appointed prime minister in 1992, and he would dominate Lebanese politics for the next thirteen years. Born in Sidon to a family of very modest means, like many Lebanese he sought fortune abroad. He found it in construction in Saudi Arabia. Eventually becoming a close friend of the king and a billionaire. Nevertheless, Hariri maintained close ties with Lebanon and provided scholarships to thousands of Lebanese. As a man expected to give Lebanon far more than he might take, his appointment as prime minister won support even from traditional Maronites.

Hariri aimed to fight corruption and cut the bloated bureaucracy. He desired to restore government schools, hospitals, electricity, water utilities, and telephones. He sought foreign aid and extended army control to the Shi'a suburbs south of Beirut. However, Hizbullah retained considerable freedom to strike at Israeli forces and the South Lebanese Army in Israeli-occupied territory.

The prime minister's efforts to build national unity and restore government authority clashed with attempts by Syria, Israel, Iran, and other countries to manipulate events for their own purposes. Thousands of Syrian troops remained. Critics condemned them as occupiers, but to their supporters they were peacekeepers. They assisted Hizbullah, and they provided an excuse for Israel to occupy the south as a "security zone."

Treaties signed in 1991 linked Lebanon to Syria politically and diplomatically. By prohibiting media attacks on Damascus, the treaties clearly violated traditional freedom, exercised by the Lebanese press. The Syrian link alienated most Maronites, who perceived political discrimination in many ways, including selective prosecution of Christians for violent crimes.

Lebanon's recovery from the devastation of nearly two decades of war proved uneven and slow. Annual economic growth rates reached as high as 7%, but although they were impressive as statistics, they failed to bring the expected prosperity to the middle and lower classes. International aid came only in trickles. Tax revenues reached only 50% of expenditures, and exports only about 10% of imports. Government salaries fell behind the comparable private sector, and teachers went on strike.

The focus of Hariri's reconstruction effort was Solidere, a $1.8 billion company given great powers to seize property and rebuild the heart of Beirut. Funds poured into real estate development, and hundreds of buildings were torn down. As the bulldozers moved in, archaeologists found remarkable ruins from almost every era of history, adding another complication to reconstruction.

Rebuilding central Beirut was largely complete by the late 1990s. However, broad-based prosperity still eluded the country, and the political system faltered, unable to select a new president when the incumbent's term ended. Corruption worsened, and critics often blamed Hariri.

The South Liberated

After nearly 20 years of occupation, Hizbullah's attacks on Israel's self-proclaimed security zone and northern Israel sharpened in 1996. Israel responded with large-scale bombardments from land, sea, and air on both military and economic targets, including a water reservoir and an electricity installation in Christian Beirut. Deliberately (the UN finding) or, at best, carelessly, Israeli gunners shelled civilians sheltered at the UN post at Qana, killing over 100 and drawing international condemnation. Tel Aviv and Washington had initially proposed peace terms that disarmed Hizbullah "terrorists." After the slaughter at Qana, to many the term "terrorist" hardly seemed a label for one side alone.

Continuing casualties, sometimes reaching as many as 30 Israeli soldiers killed annually, led Ehud Barak to promise during an election campaign to withdraw from Lebanon. The difficulty, as always, was security: Lebanon and Syria refused to guarantee the safety of northern Israel. While Hizbullah attacks continued, morale declined in the SLA and among Israeli troops. Slowly disintegrating, the SLA retreated from the Christian town of Jezzine in 1999. The collapse of the SLA forced a rapid retreat that saved Israeli lives but meant abandoning supplies and equipment. Abruptly, Israel withdrew from the entire zone in 2000, months ahead of Barak's deadline. Hizbullah was perceived to have forced an Israeli retreat. The war for Lebanon seemed a rare Arab victory in a decades-long struggle.

One significant border dispute remained: the Shabaa farms region on the slopes of Mt. Hermon. Only a few hundred acres, they were claimed by Lebanon historically, but occupied by Syria and captured by Israel in 1967. The UN considers them part of the occupied Golan Heights.

Bleeding Beirut: bomb blast killing 30 people, July 1986   AP/Wide World Photos

Lebanon

The Faraya ski resort—a far cry from the desert heat found in neighboring nations

Despite predictions of a bloodbath for collaborators, when the SLA collapsed completely, its soldiers typically were sentenced to short prison terms. Other former members fled to Israel with their families and South Lebanon remained calm under Hizbullah control. Lebanese administrative control only gradually returned.

Continued Occupation and the Cedar Revolution

Gerrymandering, manipulated regulations, and intimidation marked parliamentary elections held after the Israeli withdrawal in 2000. Nevertheless, in a political system where personalities matter more than parties, voters decisively favored candidates linked to Rafiq Hariri. Despite the personal animosity between the two men, President Lahoud reappointed him.

In fact, campaign rhetoric overshadowed the actual winners. Some candidates openly raised the issue of foreign—meaning Syrian—domination. Walid Jumblatt, the Druze leader long close to Damascus, called for a new relationship between the two countries. Clearly, Lebanese across most of the political spectrum felt that the end of Israeli occupation removed one rationale for the Syrian occupation as well.

In response, Damascus withdrew its troops from Beirut in 2001. However, strong Syrian influence remained, exercised through the Lebanese intelligence services, political manipulation, and some 25,000 troops in the north and east. To counter any sense of declining Syrian prestige, the

security forces (rather than Lebanese police) arrested hundreds of Maronites on flimsy charges. Although most were soon released, several prominent personalities, including international journalists, were charged with treason for communicating with Israel. Such maneuvering further weakened any desires for reconciliation.

Before President Lahoud's six-year term expired in late 2004, Syria summoned the Lebanese cabinet to Damascus. On its return, it proposed a constitutional amendment to extend the president's term by three years. Despite opposition, parliament agreed. However, the UN Security Council, led by the United States and France, voted for the withdrawal of all foreign (i.e., Syrian) troops, the disarming of all militias (Hizbullah; Palestinians in camps), and fair elections. Rafiq Hariri resigned and formed an anti-Syrian alliance with traditional Maronite politicians and the Druze leader Walid Jumblatt, thus uniting three of the country's four sectarian groups.

On Valentine's Day, 2005, a massive suicide bomb killed Hariri and dozens of others. The very sophisticated assassination plunged the country into crisis. Many Maronites and Druze condemned the Syrian intelligence services directly. Others blamed the security forces' failure to protect an obvious target after opposition politicians had warned of death threats against them. In sharp contrast, most Shi'a suspected that Israel or the United States had engineered a murder that would damage Syria's reputation. A leaked UN report later claimed that Syrian President al-Assad had threatened Hariri, that top Syrian intelligence officials were implicated, and that Lebanese authorities had utterly failed to conduct a competent investigation. Everyone but the security services, it seemed, had heard of threats against Hariri. Eventually the UN's report changed, and Hizbullah officials were formally charged.

As protests mounted in central Beirut, political opinion swung strongly against Syria. Perhaps 25% of the country's entire population massed in Beirut's central square on March 14, 2005 to demand justice and the complete withdrawal of Syrian troops. Its participants called this the "Cedar Revolution."

To the surprise of many, Syria responded by withdrawing all its troops from Lebanon. However, many blamed Syrian intelligence and its Lebanese allies for continued bombings in Christian areas and the murders of prominent journalists and politicians critical of Syria.

As Lebanon prepared for elections under a gerrymandered system that most Maronites opposed, the Hariri-Jumblatt-Lebanese Forces alliance took the label

"March 14" forces. The election results showed a starkly divided country. Saad Hariri's alliance carried all of Beirut's seats and did well in the north and east, while the rival Hizbullah-Amal coalition took every seat in the south. In Mount Lebanon, Jumblatt demonstrated his wide support in the Druze community.

Maronite voters, however, sharply rejected Hariri's Lebanese Forces allies in favor of the populist General Aoun, the former ruler during the Civil War who had returned from exile to contest the elections. A decade earlier, Aoun's defiance of Syria had cost the lives of hundreds of soldiers and perhaps thousands of civilians. Now he formed pragmatic alliances with pro-Syrian politicians. The elections thus emphasized the sectarian nature of Lebanese society, with each sectarian group's heartland uniting behind one leader.

Despite his solid majority, Saad Hariri refused office, and his alliance nominated Fouad Siniora as prime minister. Siniora formed a unity cabinet that included pro-Syrian representatives from Hizbullah and Aoun's Free Patriotic Movement.

The Year of Lebanese Turmoil (July 2006–07)

Breaking six years of relative calm along the internationally-recognized Israeli border, in 2006, Hizbullah guerrillas captured two Israeli soldiers and killed several others. Israel's inexperienced cabinet under Ehud Olmert seized the opportunity to turn the border raid into a war, aiming to free its soldiers, crush Hizbullah's military force, and perhaps demonstrate Iran's inability to protect its ally. The IDF launched a missile and bombing blitz of Hizbullah's military in the south, its offices and television station in Beirut, and even the home of Hassan Nasrallah, its leader. Many non-Shi'a Lebanese thought this appropriate retaliation for a reckless provocation, if unfortunate in the civilian casualties.

When Israel held Lebanon directly responsible for the fate of the soldiers, however, it ignored the common Lebanese distinction between Hizbullah's territory and sovereign Lebanon. Long powerless over Hizbullah, Beirut also proved equally powerless when Israel attacked businesses, Beirut's airport, vital road bridges, gasoline service stations, and even individual commercial trucks. A raid on Beirut's generating station created an enormous slick of heavy oil—one of the Mediterranean's worst. An air and sea blockade halted the economy and caused several billion dollars in damages. Hizbullah retaliated by launching missiles far deeper into Israel than ever before, reaching Haifa, then further south. The missiles, supplied by Iran through Syria, killed over 40 civilians and wounded scores more. By contrast,

136

Lebanese civilian casualties from Israeli fire exceeded 1,000 dead, plus thousands injured. Nearly 25% of the population fled their homes.

After weeks of air strikes, the IDF launched ground assaults into South Lebanon. However, by the standards of past Israeli triumphs, Hizbullah fighters inflicted unexpected casualties. The world clamored for a ceasefire but, in hopes that Israel would destroy Hizbullah, the United States obstructed a Security Council decision. After a month of fighting, with no Israeli victory in sight, the Security Council finally voted in favor of Resolution 1701. It called for the return of the two captured soldiers, the disarming of Hizbullah, government control over the Lebanese south, and a strengthened UN presence.

Having battled to perhaps a draw, Hizbullah rapidly won the post-war public relations victory. Its officials poured a "river of green" on Lebanese eager to rebuild their destroyed homes: $12,000 in cash, with virtually no paperwork. *Jihad al-Bina'*, the party's construction arm, quickly cleared ruined apartment blocks. In a play on Hassan Nasrallah's name, the party posted signs proclaiming "Divine Victory;" in Arabic, "*Nasr min Allah*."

By contrast, the widespread attacks on Lebanon weakened the democratic and anti-Syrian Lebanese government. With U.S. diplomatic backing, Israel had devastated a pro-Western country, but it left untouched Syria and Iran, Hizbullah's key suppliers. This strengthened Syrian sympathizers in Lebanon and Islamist extremists world-wide. Hizbullah and its allies left the national unity cabinet, leaving it short of any Shi'a minister, and then declared the government illegal. Whether to block the UN tribunal over Rafiq Hariri's assassination, or to extend its own power, Hizbullah demanded a unity government. It sponsored months of demonstrations in central Beirut, including a protest camp outside Parliament.

The aftermath of the war proved particularly discouraging to the Lebanese, who had long hoped for prosperity and development. Bombings and assassinations targeted anti-Syrian figures, members of parliament and leading journalists.

President Lahoud's extended term expired in 2007 with Parliament immobilized, and the country began a period of anxious uncertainty. Nearly all political groups accepted the military commander, General Michel Suleiman, as a compromise candidate, but the election was held hostage until Hizbullah had gained several wider goals.

After months of crisis, in 2008 the cabinet attempted a show of authority. It dismissed the military commander of Beirut airport and declared Hizbullah's land-line telephone system illegal. Hizbullah's response was firm: its militiamen seized Sunni sections of West Beirut, demonstrating their military superiority over Sunni militias. The military maintained its unity by taking no action, though it threatened to do so if gunmen did not leave the streets.

In Washington, President Bush proclaimed, "The international community will not allow the Iranian and Syrian regimes, via their proxies, to return Lebanon to foreign domination and control." However, the United Stated had no proxies to support its allies. Outmaneuvered, the cabinet backed down. In response, Hizbullah reopened roads and the international airport. Even more important, both government and opposition accepted an invitation backed by the Arab League for talks in Qatar.

With diplomacy and arm-twisting by Sheikh Hamad bin Jassim, the Prime Minister of Qatar, the two sides agreed to a major political compromise. Presidential elections would be held almost immediately. The new cabinet would include a blocking minority from Hizbullah and its allies with the remainder appointed by the new president. Re-drawn parliamentary districts would concentrate sectarian voters, strengthening their ability to elect their own, and no group would be allowed to use arms to settle disputes. Finally, the opposition promised to disband the protests that had paralyzed downtown Beirut for months.

After 19 failed attempts, the Chamber of Deputies met and quickly elected Michael Suleiman president. The next day he took office, and reappointed Prime Minister Siniora.

The Political System in Lebanon

Dating from the French mandate, the Lebanese constitution stipulates a Chamber of Deputies (parliament), and a president elected by it for a single term of six years. The president is the most powerful authority, having the capacity to select and dismiss the prime minister, subject to parliamentary approval.

Representative democracy in Lebanon really means representation of religious groups. The National Pact of 1943, an unwritten amendment to the constitution, reserves the presidency to a Maronite Christian, the premiership to a Sunni Muslim, and the speaker of parliament to a Shi'a Muslim. Similar sectarian restrictions apply elsewhere, so that the army commander must be a Maronite. Christians historically dominated the Chamber of Deputies by a 5:4 ratio, but the 1989 Taif Accord equalized the membership of the 128 deputies. The accord also determined the number of seats for the country's six districts based on political compromise, not the actual number of residents.

In practice, the formal democracy becomes a feudal system based on traditionally important families, sometimes abetted by voting practices that trespass on the secrecy of the ballot. Voters support a local leader, known as a *za'im*, from an important family of their own faith. Once elected, a za'im develops a patron-client relationship, using the political system to obtain benefits for his district and his family, a sometimes foggy distinction. While they cling to privileges for their communities, za'ims recognize the benefits of co-operating with leaders from other sects, who often share their economic wealth. Alliances might even be formed across the sectarian divide against rivals of the same faith.

Thanks to this system, there are no significant national parties. Ideology and typical political issues are diminished, as sons—Chamoun, Jumblatt, Karami, Hariri, and many others—replace fathers in politics and often in parliament. There is never a landslide that "throws the rascals out" no matter how disillusioned the voters.

At one time the size of the Maronite community justified its dominance. But Maronites emigrated more often than Muslims, and as they became wealthier more quickly they preferred fewer children. By the 1970s, Maronites (probably) fell to third place demographically, but they refused to relinquish the presidency and command of the army, for they remembered past Muslim domination and persecution. It is very difficult to know the actual composition of Lebanese demographics today, and thus the extent to which the current system remains representative (or not) in the way initially envisioned, because the last official census was taken in 1932.

Long the country's neglected community, the Shi'a rise to greater recognition followed the replacement of feudal Shi'a za'ims by Hizbullah. Because it supported Palestinian groups that murdered Israeli civilians and maintained links with suspected hijackers and the 1983 Marine barracks bombers, Hizbullah is often derided in the United States as merely a group of terrorists.

But in today's Lebanon, the "Party of God" runs schools, dispensaries, and public works projects. It provides fertilizers and agricultural advice to thousands of farmers, and clean drinking water in slums. Now with 13 representatives in parliament, and its ally Amal with 17, the effectiveness of the organization far exceeds any other political group in the country, possibly including the government bureaucracy. Across the Arab world

Lebanon

Sidon: Temple of Eshmoun. Mosaic of the four seasons.

Courtesy of CNT/Yetenekian

it was hailed for liberating South Lebanon and defeating Israel in 2006. These achievements render Hizbullah too strong for the Lebanese government to challenge, regardless of U.S. desires to freeze the organization's financial assets as a terrorist group and the UN vote to disarm it.

Politics Since 2009

Many Western commentators interpreted the 2009 election of a new parliament in geo-strategic terms, portraying Lebanon's vote as a contest between the pro-American, anti-Syrian March 14 bloc and the pro-Iranian/anti-Israeli/Islamist Hizbullah bloc. Though partly true, that explanation ignored local realities, personal rivalries, and Hizbullah's desire to avoid direct control. It also neglected the powerful role played by fear. After the 2008 fighting in the streets of Beirut, Sunnis felt apprehensive of Shi'a encroachment. Shi'a opinion feared the government's alignment with the West would leave Lebanon weakened in another war with Israel. Many Christians feared becoming insignificant.

In almost any democratic election, Hizbullah could easily win about 40 of the 128 seats in parliament, so strong is its hold on Shi'a loyalties. However, it has consistently avoided such an overwhelming victory. In 2009 it nominated only 11 candidates of its own. In fact, there were no close contests for about 100 of the 128 seats. The remaining seats were mostly Christian, and fear of Hizbullah deterred enough voters from supporting General Aoun that Christian candidates aligned with the March 14 alliance gave it a national majority.

Lebanon's government is a rarity among nations: the political opposition often has insisted that democracy means power-sharing, so the cabinet should reflect all factions of the country without giving the victors too much power. After months of bargaining, Saad Hariri formed a cabinet of 30 members, with 15 for the victors, 10 for the opposition, and five loyal to the president.

The cabinet started to act on the backlog of needed decisions: for example, it voted the first budget in five years. However, Hassan Nasrallah, Hizbullah's leader, denounced the UN's Special Tribunal for Lebanon (STL), which indicted party members for the murder of Rafiq Hariri, and warned the government not to cooperate with the STL, which had been created to bring his father's murderers to justice.

Sensing the rising influence of the Hizbullah/Syrian alliance, Walid Jumblatt, leader of the Druze Progressive Socialist Party, withdrew from the March 14 alliance. Hariri's cabinet then collapsed.

Careful once again to avoid formal responsibility for governing, Hizbullah's March 8 coalition selected Najib Mikati, a Sunni independent, as prime minister. A billionaire and the richest man in Lebanon, Prime Minister Mikati represents a world far from the Shi'a suburbs of Beirut. A graduate of the American University of Beirut, he studied management at both Harvard and INSEAD. While his interest in serving all Lebanese must be considered genuine, it is surprising that the cabinet fails to contain a single woman. Iran and Syria cheered his appointment, while Israel and the United States worried that he might be influenced too heavily by his allies.

The political crisis and bloodshed of the Arab Spring in Syria have time and again brought Lebanon to the verge of an abyss of sectarian conflict. Many clergymen take political sides, even if their own confessions are not directly involved. For example, the Maronite patriarch, Beshara al-Rai, told an interviewer "The closest thing to democracy [in the Arab world] is Syria," because Islam was not the state religion. Often, Lebanese consider fighting for their sectarian allies in Syria more important than obedience to Lebanon's laws and neutrality.

Lebanon

President Michel Aoun

Hizbullah views the conflict as a foreign policy matter: an attempt by the United States., Israel, and their conservative Sunni allies to fracture the Iran–Syria–Hizbullah axis. After all, if the Sunni Syrian rebels win, they will cut off the Lebanese party and its militia from Iran, its military supplier. Sectarian concerns also lead Hizbullah to fight alongside Assad's largely Alawi Syrian military.

By 2013 it was clear that Hizbullah fighters played an increasing and sometimes decisive role in the Syrian regime's successful offensives. They have protected Shi'a shrines in Damascus and they proved pivotal in capturing the strategic town of Qusair from the rebels. Hizbullah units now reportedly fight in other critical battlegrounds in Homs, Damascus, and Aleppo. This intervention arouses bitter criticism by those who feel it will bring the war to Lebanon. By contrast, Hassan Nasrallah claims that by winning in Syria, his militiamen defeat threats to Lebanon.

Militant Sunni fighters, many of them from Tripoli, have also joined various rebel brigades in the civil war and smuggle arms to them. Clearly, Lebanon is failing to enforce its neutrality; inevitably, the sides fighting each other in Syria sporadically battle in Lebanon as well. Clashes have repeatedly broken out in Tripoli between the pro-Assad Alawi district of Jabal Mohsen and the neighboring Sunni quarter of Bab al-Tabbaneh.

In response to Lebanese joining the mayhem of Syria's civil war, both the Syrian government and the Islamist rebels carried the fighting back to Lebanon. Car bombings killed scores at a Sunni mosque; suicide bombers also targeted Shi'a and Hizbullah neighborhoods. Given the porous borders, Lebanese security proved unable to deter all the planned attacks.

The violence imperiled the country because its political system was already overloaded. Prime Minister Mikati resigned in March 2013. Within two weeks Tammam Salam was designated his successor by agreement with the major factions, but he could not form a cabinet until the following February. Meanwhile, parliament proved utterly unable to approve a voting system for the 2013 elections, though the deputies were able to find a majority to vote an extension of their terms for 18 months.

With the legislature tottering, the government frequently failed to accomplish its tasks. Decisions as vital as selecting the new army commander could not be made. The public believed corruption had become worse; beyond the usual tales of public sector squandering, scandals in medicine and food safety went uncorrected. In addition to the many accumulated problems that only government could solve, the presence of one million Syrian refugees gathered in perhaps a thousand informal camps demanded exceptional measures. The government could not act decisively.

When Michel Suleiman's term ended and he vacated the palace in April 2014, the presidency collapsed. Disputes between (and perhaps within) the two major blocs, Hizbullah's March 8 coalition and the March 14 alliance of Sunnis and Christians prevented the Chamber of Deputies from even achieving a quorum to elect his successor. The seat remained empty for more than two years, until Michel Aoun was elected.

Many Lebanese have sought to place the blame for dysfunctional politics on regional powers rather than on the country's own politicians. To quote Nouhad Machnouk, a Sunni politician and cabinet minister, "The presidential election is a regional and international decision and no one from inside [Lebanon] can decide on it."

An exceedingly strange development in late 2017 lent credence to this observation—although it related to the premiership rather than the presidency. In November that year, Prime Minister Hariri boarded a plane for Saudi Arabia and, upon his arrival to Riyadh, went on state TV to resign his position. Hariri, who had long been supported by Saudi Arabia (and who holds Saudi citizenship), cited the influence of Hizbullah in Lebanese politics, and fear for his life, as cause for his departure. Accusations that Hariri had been kidnapped and was being forced to resign by the Saudis immediately emerged, and conventional wisdom continues to be that the resignation was compelled by Saudi Arabia. But why would Saudi Arabia want a Prime Minister over whom it had

influence to resign? For most analysts, the answer is that by removing Hariri Saudi Arabia could make the case that the Lebanese state had no counterweight to balance Hizbullah—that the latter, backed by Iran—had effectively taken over the state. Perhaps that would force the international community to confront the group, and Lebanon more generally, in a way that it otherwise would not. In any case, it would offer a degree of cover for the Saudis if Saudi Arabia ever deemed (military) intervention necessary. The international uproar was dramatic, and Hariri eventually (and awkwardly) rescinded his resignation.

In March 2018, Lebanon held its first parliamentary elections in 9 years, 5 years after they were originally scheduled. Turnout was down compared to the previous election, 49.2% compared to 54%, and the outcome surprised most analysts. Hariri's Future Party lost a third of its seats, from 33 to 21, while Hizbullah gained one to pick up its 14th seat. Hizbullah's close political ally Amal added four seats, moving from 13 to 17. All in all, Hizbullah and its various allies finished with a slight majority in the 128-seat parliament. Forced to resign under pressure from burgeoning street protests, Hariri was replaced by a little-known technocrat, Hassan Diab. Although he enjoyed minimal support among his own Sunni community, Diab had the crucial backing of Hizbullah. Indeed, the group enjoys alliances across the key levers of power in modern Lebanon.

Culture: Resembling the West in many

Hassan Nasrallah, Secretary General of Hizbullah

Lebanon

ways, nevertheless most Lebanese retain their own social values. A more traditional life and dress is found in small towns and villages, especially in those inhabited by Shi'a Muslims. Traditional culture differs very little from that of Syrians and Palestinians.

The Maronite (Arabic *Maruni*) Church is unique to Lebanon. Formed as a distinct group in Syria about the 6th century, the Maronites have preserved many ancient customs in the mountains. Arabic and Syriac are both used in the liturgy. The marriage of priests is permitted, but the Maronite Church has been in communion with the Roman Catholic Church since the First Crusade. In recent centuries, Maronites have been rivals with the Druze for control of the Chouf Mountains overlooking Beirut. In 1860, when Maronites suffered defeats at the hands of their enemies there, French soldiers intervened on behalf of the Christians. Many Maronites, including monks who own some of the best land, still believe that Western Christians have a duty to help the Maronites gain victory over their non-Christian rivals.

Long before the Israelis adopted the argument, Maronites presented themselves as isolated defenders of the "values of Western Civilization" among unruly Arabs. However, some would argue that the continued bloodshed typical between rival Maronite factions indicates a perverse understanding of "western values." For example, in 1988 presidential bodyguards killed two officers of the Lebanese Forces over some petty dispute. Four days later, two of the president's supporters were murdered in retaliation, following the age-old principle of the vendetta.

The Druze (Arabic *Duruz*) form a cohesive community whose origins lie partly in Shi'a Islam. Several Christian ideas and practices have also been incorporated into the sect along with unique beliefs and interpretations belonging only to the initiated. Besides their stronghold in the Chouf southeast of Beirut, they are also found in Jabal al-Druze in southern Syria.

Traditionally inhabiting the southern mountains and the Biqa' valley, the Shi'a often suffered exploitive landowners and received few government services. In the 1970s and 1980s, their towns and villages suffered Palestinian occupation and then Israeli invasions. Less educated, the Shi'a formed the poorest religious community, but after they migrated to Beirut's southern suburbs they gained significant military and political clout, especially with the formation of Hizbullah.

Nearly all Lebanese value education very highly. Thanks to its mixture of state, private, and church-supported schools and universities, the country has long enjoyed the distinction of some of the finest education in the Arab world. The American University of Beirut has attracted students and faculty from around the world; so have other colleges and universities, helping to maintain Beirut's status as an intellectual center. While the government developed a public school system after independence, its teachers and facilities however, often lack the qualities and advantages of the better private schools.

For many years, the highlight of Lebanese cultural activities was the summer Baalbeck Festival. World-class orchestras, pop stars, and theatrical groups performed against the imposing backdrop of some of the greatest Roman-era ruins. A wartime casualty, the festival returned to the hearts of Lebanese when Fairouz, one of the Arab world's most famous singers, returned to the stage in 1998. During the civil war, she had refused to perform anywhere in Lebanon, and although a Christian she had remained a national symbol. Thus her return to Baalbeck represented the return of normalcy.

Younger Arab men and women often prefer the sounds—and gyrations—of the rock stars of music videos, and Lebanon's Nancy Ajram and Haifa Wehbe attract a large following in the region while scandalizing Middle East conservatives. Members of Bahrain's parliament nearly unanimously sought to ban what they imagined would be a sexually provocative concert—despite Wehbe's promise to cover up.

Another cultural challenge is the recovery of antiquities looted from museums or kept privately, contrary to the law. Officials have seized thousands of works, including mosaics and sarcophagi, and recently even regained full control of Beit al-Din, the 18th-century capital and one of the most famous historical sites in the country.

Economy: In the first decades of independence, many Lebanese prospered from their country's role as a center of international banking and trade. Beirut became the natural Middle Eastern headquarters for many companies. Tourism flourished, transit fees on Iraqi and Saudi Arabian oil helped meet the government's budget, and Lebanon visibly achieved the highest Arab standard of living outside the oil states.

Two decades of civil and international war destroyed much of the formal economy. Artillery salvos gutted banks and factories, the transit trade collapsed, and government revenues plummeted as militias collected customs duties for themselves in the many small ports. Once aspiring to a moderately wealthy standard of living, many Lebanese faced destitution.

The collapse of the Lebanese lira symbolized the wider economic catastrophe. The lira initially maintained its value remarkably well. However, sometimes the government printed money to pay its bills, especially after 1986. The resulting inflation drove the exchange rate so low that one lira became worthless. Money, in fact, became cheaper than wallpaper. The human effects of inflation were often disastrous. It wiped out the lifetime savings of many people, and because wages failed to rise equally with prices, it impoverished most others.

The chaos of civil war provided a little-noticed example of the unacceptable face of unregulated capitalism. An Italian company, Jelly War, shipped thousands of barrels of toxic waste to Lebanon, burying the containers in the mountains or near the sea. Complaints led the Italian government to repossess much of the material, but Greenpeace claimed that several thousand barrels remained.

The task of reconstruction was enormous. Wartime destruction and neglect particularly devastated the networks of electric and telephone cables, water pipes, and sewer lines. Enterprising Lebanese often coped by makeshift arrangements that conveniently avoided payment for the erratic services, but massive rebuilding was required. In the late 1990s government reconstruction funds had reached about $20 billion, and a construction boom brought new housing as well as roads and commercial buildings. Most construction workers were not Lebanese, but rather Syrians and other Arabs who formed roughly 20% of the workforce. After 2006, they were needed again, for reconstruction after Israeli attacks.

Protests since late 2019 have exacerbated Lebanon's economic woes. As banks

Lebanese rock star Nancy Ajram

These activists in Beirut say it all

imposed unprecedented restrictions on dollar withdrawals and transfers, in the context of spiraling political chaos, the World Bank warned of impending recession. In March 2020, Lebanon defaulted on its foreign debt. The economic crisis could not have struck at a worse time. While across the Middle East, governments are scrambling to deliver bailouts and stimulus packages in response to the coronavirus crisis, Lebanon, already teetering on the brink of bankruptcy, simply has no room for maneuver.

Current Challenges and the Future: Lebanon and its people have demonstrated extraordinary resilience in the face of civil war, violence, and political instability. Yet in a time of peace, Lebanon's prospects have rarely looked so grim. In late 2019, protests flared across the capital as ordinary citizens demanded the dismantling of the elite political class, an early election, and an end to the sectarian power-sharing system that has institutionalized clientelism and corruption in the country. The ascension to power of political outsider Diab and his cabinet of experts and technocrats might have seemed the perfect panacea to the political instability rocking Lebanon. However, it was not to be. On the evening of August 4, 2020, a massive explosion rocked the capital city. Even in a country that has suffered through decades of civil war, foreign invasion, and terrorist attacks, the sheer scale and force of the explosion was unprecedented. The effects of what turned out to be an industrial accident at a port were felt in countries across the region, and a substantial portion of the city of Beirut was flattened. More than 200 people were killed, and more than were 6,000 injured, with as many as 300,000 Lebanese left homeless. The explosion impacted Lebanon's food supply, as the port had handled around 70 percent of the country's imports. The explosion affected multiple public and private schools and rendered half of Beirut's healthcare centers nonfunctional. Diab was forced to resign days later, although he remained on as interim prime minister. Saad Hariri was nominated the country's prime minister on October 22, 2020, nearly one year after he resigned from the post amid popular protests. Through the tumultuous year, protests have continued, as the people of Lebanon see an already dire situation take a turn for the worse.

The Sultanate of Oman

Small village in the interior of Oman

Area: About 119,500 square miles (309,500 square kilometers).

Population: 5.1 million, 40% non-nationals.

Capital City: Muscat (800,000).

Climate: Extremely hot and dry except for the short winter season which is comfortable in most areas, cool in the mountains. Winter normally brings adequate rainfall at higher elevations.

Neighboring Countries: United Arab Emirates (North); Saudi Arabia (West); Yemen (Southwest).

Time Zone: GMT +4.

Official Language: Arabic.

Other Principal Tongues: Baluchi and languages of the Mahri group.

Ethnic Background: Predominantly Arab, with significant African and Asian inter-marriage. Small communities in Dhofar preserve the remnants of older linguistic and ethnic groups.

Oman

Principal Religion: Islam (approximately 70% Ibadi, 25% Sunni, and 5% Shi'a), other religious communities are comprised almost entirely of expatriate workers.

Chief Commercial Products: Petroleum, dates, dried fish, grain, pomegranates, limes, goats, cattle, and camels.

Major Trading Partners: Japan, the United Arab Emirates, the United States, China, and India.

Currency: Rial (1 rial = 1,000 biaza).

Former Colonial Status: Independent but under British influence, mid-19th to mid-20th centuries.

Chief of State: Haitham bin Tariq Al Said, Sultan.

National Flag: At the pole there is a vertical stripe of bright red bearing the national emblem (crossed swords behind a broad dagger on a belt) at the top; the remainder of the flag consists of three horizontal stripes, white, red and green, top to bottom.

Gross Domestic Product: $70.78 billion.

GDP per capita: $15,170.

One of the hottest and driest countries on earth, Oman lies on the southeast corner of the arid Arabian Peninsula. Facing the Gulf of Oman to the northeast and the Arabian Sea on the south, it extends along 1,000 miles (1,700 kilometers) of coast. It is the oldest independent Arab state.

Stretching from Sur at the eastern tip on the country toward the northwest, the Hajar Mountains form one of the major geographical features of Oman. The highest part of the range, with peaks rising more than 9,000 feet (3,000 meters), is *Jabal Akhdar*, the "Green Mountain." Average annual rainfall on the upper slopes is a modest 20 inches (about 500 millimeters) per year, far exceeding the country's typical precipitation of only 3–4 inches (75–100 millimeters) annually.

Between the Hajar Mountains and the sea from just north of Muscat to the UAE border beyond Sohar lies the Batina Plain. Watered mostly by mountain rainfall that flows underground toward the coast, its inhabitants depend on shallow wells for drinking water and agriculture. Nearly all sedentary Omanis live on the Batina Plain, in Muscat or its twin city Matrah, or on the eastern slopes of the mountains.

The remaining three-quarters of the country is mostly arid steppe, with no standing water. The scant pasturage for goats and camels is found in river valleys. One unusual climatic feature helps a few varieties of wild animals survive in otherwise uninhabitable regions. Sea breezes moving inland bring fog and dew. To survive without streams or drinking holes, animals must lick the moisture off the leaves of plants. In one such area

conservationists are attempting to reintroduce the locally-extinct Arabian oryx with animals bred in captivity in the United States.

In the southwestern corner of the kingdom lies the smaller coastal plain of Dhofar, with the town of Salalah. Rising behind it, the Qara Mountains receive enough moisture during the summer monsoon to support cattle and goats. In ancient times, Dhofar flourished as a supplier of frankincense, the fragrance famed in the Biblical story of the Three Wise Men. In the late 1990s, the moist climate of Salalah began to attract Arab tourists who found vacationing in clouds and rain cheaper and more congenial there than in Europe.

History: Before the 19th century, the history of Oman was largely a series of tribal

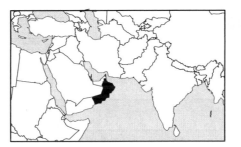

wars, peaceful interludes under powerful rulers, and foreign invasion from other parts of Arabia or Persia. Saif bin Sultan, who died about 1711, extended Omani control over ports of East Africa and Zanzibar, establishing an empire.

The present line of rulers, who belong to the Al Bu Said family, was established about 1744, when the Persian invaders were expelled from Muscat and other coastal towns. The reign of Said the Great (1804–56) saw Oman as the strongest native power in the Indian Ocean. The newly established cloves plantations on Zanzibar and the slave trade—until curtailed by the British—accounted for Said's wealth, along with his active fleet of sailing craft. When he died, his empire was divided between two sons. One took Zanzibar (now a part of Tanzania), where his descendants ruled until deposed in a 1964 revolt. The other received Oman, then of much less international significance. Gradually, Oman came under increasing British influence, although it retained its legal independence.

In 1932, Said came to the throne on his father's abdication. Said took to the job readily, but after two decades of uneventful rule largely hidden from the outside world, he faced two crises. The first was

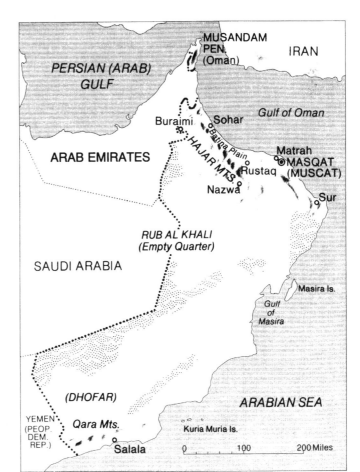

Oman

A young couple in traditional dress

a dispute over the Buraimi Oasis, which Oman shares with Abu Dhabi (see United Arab Emirates). Saudi Arabian soldiers occupied this collection of villages in 1952, and a Saudi governor took up residence. Eventually, after several years of adverse publicity, Sultan Said reoccupied the villages he claimed with the aid of British-trained and British-led soldiers from Trucial Oman (now the United Arab Emirates).

The second major crisis was an armed rebellion (1957–59). Ghalib bin Ali claimed both the religious title of imam and an independent state in the interior, with its capital at Nazwa. Ghalib's followers received weapons and training in neighboring Saudi Arabia. Returning to Oman, they seized control of Nazwa before the Sultan had time to act. The rebellion was suppressed with the aid of British soldiers and aircraft after a few months duration.

A palace coup deposed Sultan Said in 1970. His only son, Qabus (also spelled Qaboos) swiftly seized power and undertook cautious modernization. To symbolize his new policies, he changed the name of the Sultanate from "Muscat and Oman" to simply "Oman."

The scope for social reforms was vast. Committed to preserving the traditional Omani lifestyle, Sultan Said had failed to spend the new revenues from oil exports. The country's sole hospital had 12 beds, and only six miles—10 kilometers—of road had been paved. Fewer than 1,000 students attended primary school; no high school existed. Communications languished, with only 550 telephone subscribers, and the ports, airfields and public

utilities remained primitive. The new sultan's government attempted to develop all these areas, as funds permitted. In addition, he outlawed slavery, although the descendants of slaves in Oman continue to face significant discrimination.

Under Sultan Qabus the country began to emerge from diplomatic isolation. It joined international organizations and allowed foreigners to enter. Oman was admitted to the League of Arab States and the United Nations in 1971. That same year, diplomatic relations were established with Saudi Arabia, the most important neighbor and a past supporter of rebel movements in Oman.

The first six years of Sultan Qabus' reign fell under the shadow of the Marxist-oriented rebellion in Dhofar, which his father had failed to restrain. Supported by the People's Democratic Republic of Yemen, the leaders of the rebellion ultimately aimed to overthrow all the conservative rulers in Arabia and thus control vast oil-producing regions. Advised by British officers and aided by Iranian units supplied by the shah, Omani forces claimed victory in 1976. This freed the government's attention for economic development.

In the 1980s relations between Oman and South Yemen improved, and Oman came to play an important role in the Gulf Cooperation Council, although it frequently follows its own foreign and defense initiatives. Indeed Oman's independent approach to international and regional affairs has caused some angst within the Council and rumors arise periodically of Oman's intention to withdraw. However, it joined the war against Iraq over Kuwait (1991), and supports

U.S. and British forces today. On the other hand, it has refused to be drawn into the conflict in Syria—maintaining communication channels with Assad on contrary to other Gulf Arab states. It has also, notably, maintained strong ties with Tehran, despite Saudi Arabia's disapproval.

Widening its diplomatic contacts substantially, in 1994 Oman hosted Israel's Prime Minister Yitzhak Rabin for discussions, the only known visit by an Israeli leader to a Gulf state. Radical Palestinian groups and Iran strongly condemned the visit. However, Oman cooperated with Iran in developing joint oil and gas fields, and has sent observers to Iranian military exercises. It essentially seeks peaceful relations in the region.

Seeking to modernize the government as well as the economy, Sultan Qabus gradually increased popular participation in political decisions. In the early 1990s he established a Consultative Council (Majlis al-Shura) free of official appointees, and thus more open to citizen viewpoints. Voting was limited to select tribal sheikhs, religious leaders, and businessmen.

In 1996 Sultan Qabus extended the reforms by decreeing a "Basic Law" that created a supreme court and added an upper house, named the Council of Oman. However, Qabus apparently sensed that the political elite seemed more interested in personal success than the national good. In response, he reshuffled the cabinet to involve more reformers, and appointed women to both houses of the Council.

For the first time, all adult Omani citizens held the right to vote in the Council's 2003 elections, and a woman was appointed a cabinet minister. Despite these formal changes, some analysts suggest that many Omanis have felt apathetic towards an advisory group that has done

His former Majesty the Sultan Qabus

relatively little address issues like defense, foreign policy, or other sensitive matters.

A desert country whose scant rainfall falls partly in scattered summer thunderstorms, in 2007 Oman unexpectedly suffered the most severe storm ever recorded to hit the Arabian peninsula. Cyclone Gonu, a category 3 hurricane, passed along the eastern coast, killing over 40 people. It knocked out power in Muscat, and flooded roads, homes, and cars.

The government reacted swiftly and efficiently to the disaster. It evacuated people from flood areas, closed shops ahead of time, and ordered everyone indoors. Repairs to roads and electric systems began almost immediately, and both of Muscat's water desalination plants returned to operation a few days later. Despite economic losses estimated at about $1,500 per inhabitant, Sultan Qabus politely declined offers of aid from Gulf nations and the United States.

Inspired in part by events in Tunisia and Egypt, protests and a sit-in erupted in Oman in the spring of 2011, with some initial violence. The demands were typical: additional jobs, dismissal of corrupt officials, and greater freedoms. Sultan Qabus responded by relaxing limits on the media, promising to involve the Council in decisions, and dismissing 12 cabinet ministers. He raised the minimum wage, initiated unemployment benefits, and pledged to create 50,000 new jobs. Funding for the additional spending came from $10 billion in assistance from the Gulf Cooperation Council.

The protests largely subsided, but some activists continued critical blogs and writings, until a sharp crackdown in 2012 led to the arrests of dozens of critics. However, Sultan Qabus did not follow the stern example of other Gulf rulers and order trials and harsh punishments. Instead, within a year he issued a blanket pardon of his critics, leading to rare praise from Amnesty International for an Arab ruler.

The 2011 protestors demanded an end to corruption, not the region's worst but recognized by Transparency International as significant. At the Sultan's orders, the state auditor and prosecutors investigated contracts and payments; this resulted in criminal convictions of several highly-placed officials. A former minister of commerce, for example, had paid a bribe to win a contract for the airport's expansion, and the CEO of the state oil company received a twenty-year sentence for bribes and money laundering. Prosecutors were reportedly astounded by the extent and scope of the corruption. The level of business investment seemed to falter: no doubt many executives worried about past arrangements as well as what rules would be enforced in the future.

Opportunities for corruption frequently result from conflicts of interest when government officials, including cabinet ministers, legally maintain business interests in firms seeking government contracts. Oman has failed to sign the OECD Anti-Bribery Convention.

In 2014, serious but undisclosed health difficulties led the Sultan to seek medical treatment in Germany. During his absence

of eight months, officials continued to direct the country, and one analyst considered this an opportunity for the country to learn to govern itself without the presence of its absolute ruler.

Culture: Oman has one of the highest percentages of nomads of any country in the world. Approximately half its people spend most or all of the year moving with their herds. The remainder of the population is divided between farmers and townspeople. In the principal ports of Muscat and Matrah, many Baluchis and Indians work respectively as laborers and merchants.

Most Omanis follow the teachings of the Ibadi sect of Islam, the origins of which lie in the *Khawarij*, a faction that disagreed with Ali, the fourth Caliph of Islam. Many traditions and rituals found in Sunni and Shi'a Islam are not followed by the Ibadis, who stress the importance of proper belief, righteous conduct, and the supreme authority of the Quran.

Through much of Ibadi history, a leader called the *imam* led the community in both religious and secular domains. He was selected in theory by all believing males, but in practice by tribal leaders. His duty was to rule the true Muslims, i.e., the Ibadis, and force heretics—Sunni or Shi'a—to follow him. Outside Oman, there are only scattered Ibadi communities in North Africa, India, and Pakistan.

Dhofar is administered separately from Oman itself, and has communities that are distinct from other Arabs. Most important among them are the *Qara* people, who speak their own Semitic language and give their name to the mountains in which they live. The Qara dress distinctly, and follow different social habits from most Arab tribes. They are the only Arabs who depend primarily on cattle rather than on goats and camels for a livelihood. Their cattle are very small, about half the size of usual breeds.

One of the most important developments in Oman has been the expansion of educational facilities. In 1970 there were scarcely half a dozen schools. Today, hundreds of schools, with thousands of foreign teachers, many of them Egyptian, enroll over 300,000 students, more than half of them girls. Evening classes provide learning for adults.

Sultan Qabus University opened in 1986 with a largely Western curriculum. In common with many other Arabs, Omanis find the study of the humanities, Islamic studies, and the behavioral sciences more appealing than technical skills, engineering, and the physical sciences. Around one-half of the university students enroll in the former programs, although the country needs technicians and scientists.

The highway at Matrah

Oman

The expansion of education now includes a university at Nazwa.

Thanks to the classical music tastes of its former sultan, Oman boasts the only professional symphony orchestra of the entire Arabian Peninsula. When the Royal Oman Symphony Orchestra was founded by the sultan's decree in 1986, there were no pianos or violins worth mentioning in the entire country. No Omanis had studied music, and the first high school was only a decade old. British instructors conducted a talent search and identified musically talented children. Now young adults, these Omanis form the national orchestra. Its performances, are considered of high quality by Western critics.

Economy: Unlike the smaller, oil-rich nations of the Arab Gulf, Omanis acquired a strong agricultural tradition over the centuries. This provides a significant focus for economic development. Even with oil revenues, farming, herding, and fishing remain vital parts of the economy; the government, however, no longer depends on taxing produce and livestock to meet its budget.

In 1967, just three years after the discovery of petroleum deposits, Oman began exporting oil and the country entered a new economic era. After Sultan Qabus seized power, development activities increased rapidly. Agricultural projects improved water supplies and crop varieties for farmers. Investment in up-to-date shipping facilities at Matrah and an international airport improved transportation links with the rest of the world, while paved roads and airfields eased travel within the country. Electrical generating plants, housing projects, and radio stations increased the enjoyment of life, while modern hospitals

and public health programs extended the lifespan of the population.

Given these favorable conditions, private businesses also expanded rapidly, in the retail trade, services, and other areas. In 1989 the Stock Exchange opened, with 71 companies, mostly in services such as insurance and transportation. The pace of economic development attracted foreigners as well.

Although income from oil constitutes about 70% of government revenues, known reserves are estimated at a modest 5 billion barrels. As a minor producer, Oman never joined OPEC. By 2006, production had fallen to 630,000 barrels per day due to disappointing declines in output. Recent efforts at steam injection, which heats oil in the rock and facilitates its flow, are among the largest in the world. By combining steam and gas injection methods (known as enhanced recovery) with other improvements, the industry hopes to raise the recoverable portion of oil deposits from 10–20% to nearly 40%. Helped by the first off-shore production, by 2013 output had surpassed 900,000 barrels per day.

Natural gas offers more promise of long-term benefit. In the mid-1990s an ambitious program to develop natural gas resources raised confirmed reserves to 25 trillion cubic feet. The government created Oman LNG, a joint venture with oil companies and private firms to build a multibillion dollar plant to export 6.8 million tons of liquefied natural gas annually. The first shipments took place in 2000.

Recent years have seen the Omani economy take a significant hit and, according to the Sultanate's Ministry of Manpower, the country is now facing its worst jobs crisis in four decades. Unemployment in Oman reached a high of almost 20% in

2000 and today hovers around 16%. The policy response has been one of "Omanization," a reprise of policies enacted in past decades that incentivize the hiring of local workers over expatriates. The government has advised foreign firms that if they cannot or will not nationalize a significant percentage of their employee base, they will lose a range of incentives, from free commercial land to subsidized business loans. Although this may increase job availability for Omanis, which is the objective, the process is already creating a different problem. From 2016 to 2018, some 115,000 foreign workers departed Oman as firms decided not to renew contracts. This has led to a housing crisis, with plummeting rent prices, as well as empty flats and commercial buildings. Finding the right balance will be as challenging as it is imperative.

Current Challenges and the Future: On January 10, 2020, Omanis awoke to the news that their beloved Sultan had passed away. Oman faced a moment of reckoning. During his lifetime, Sultan Qabus has refused to publicly name a successor, and following his death it was feared that the formerly stable Sultanate might be thrown into turmoil. In any event, Haitham bin Tariq al-Said took the throne at the directive of Sultan Qabus's will. Sultan Haitham faces significant challenges as he seeks to secure Oman's future. For years, Oman has prided itself as being a neutral party in a volatile region. It did not break diplomatic ties with Bashar al-Assad when Gulf states and others did and it did not join the Saudi-led coalition to pursue a war in Yemen. It has not followed Saudi Arabia into its embargo of Qatar, and it has long resisted what can

The Qurum Natural Park in the Heart of Muscat

Courtesy of the Royal Embassy of Saudi Arabia

only be understood as efforts by some to turn the Gulf Cooperation Council into an anti-Iran partnership. Additionally, Oman has sought to bridge the divide between Israel and the Arab world.

The luxury of neutrality, however, has become expensive, and Oman needs to find ways out of its various economic crises. The problem for Sultan Haitham lies in the 2020 global collapse of oil prices and the new unwillingness of potential international partners to provide a line of credit at a time of global crisis. In April 2021, the new monarch faced his first serious test as protests broke out across the country. The coronavirus pandemic and rolling lockdowns severely depressed an already struggling economy. Government debt, once 6 percent of Oman's gross domestic product, has increased to 79 percent. Unemployment has skyrocketed, particularly among Omani youth. Going forward, it will be interesting to see how well Oman can balance its priorities and hold true to its vision of its role in the region and the world, while at the same time doing what is necessary to improve the situation of its people.

Like many states in the region, Oman is attempting to diversify its economy away from oil and gas. Industries ripe for scaling include tourism, fishing, mining, and manufacturing. Education reform has also become an important priority as Oman tries to position its people to be competitive in an increasingly global economy.

In the summer of 2018 global temperature records were broken when a coastal town in the north of Oman recorded a 24-hour minimum temperature of 108.68° Fahrenheit (42.6° Celsius). Across the region, climate change will bring new challenges to some of the harshest inhabited environments in the world.

State of Palestine

CAN THIS FRAGMENTED HOMELAND SUCCEED?

Total Palestinian control
Palestinian civil control
Continuing Israeli control
The fate of Jerusalem and surrounding areas awaits negotiation

Sweden recognized the State of Palestine in late 2014. In 2018, 146 UN member states voted to allow the Palestinians to act more like a member state, during 2019 meetings as chair of the G77 (the group of 77 developing nations). Just three member states—Israel, the United States, and Australia—voted against the move. The U.S. ambassador to the UN stated strong opposition to the election of a Palestinian representative to chair the G77. However, the Palestinians hailed the resolution as "a new dawn in the Palestinian quest for statehood."

The Palestinians have seen many false dawns in their long and so far fruitless quest for statehood. After suffering many calamitous events during the 20th century, the Palestinians now reside in four distinct categories:

1. Territory administered by the Palestinian Authority: Gaza (under Hamas) and most (but not all) Arab-dominated areas of the West Bank

Area: Gaza: about 139 square miles (360 square kilometers). West Bank: Palestinian autonomy in Area A (18% of West Bank) and joint-control with Israel (security provided by Israel, civic administration by PA) in Area B (21% of West Bank), as designated in the Oslo peace accords. Areas A and B of the West Bank comprise 227 separate, discontiguous territories, 199 of which are less than 1 square mile (under 2.6 square kilometers) in size. Area C (at least 60% of the West Bank) is solely Israeli administered.

Population: 5.1 million, of which approximately 2 million live in Gaza.

Capital City: Claimed capital: East Jerusalem; Legislative capital: Ramallah (25,000).

Climate: Mild winters; summers hot (Gaza) to very hot (Jericho).

Neighboring Countries: Israel; Jordan (east of the West Bank); and Egypt (west of Gaza).

Time Zone: GMT +2.

Official Language: Arabic.

Other Principal Languages: Hebrew (used by Israeli settlers); English.

Ethnic Background: Arab.

Chief Commercial Products: Citrus (especially oranges), olives, grapes, figs, vegetables, flowers, grain, handcrafted items, and services.

Major Trading Partners: Israel and Arab states (for oil imports).

Palestinians unite around a common Arab-Palestinian culture and a love of their ancestral homeland between the Mediterranean and the Jordan River. More than two decades ago, the Oslo Accords created the Palestinian Authority (PA), intended to be the foundation of an eventual Palestinian state, complete with a legislature and presidential executive. However, sovereignty and the gold standard of international recognition—full membership at the United Nations—still elude the long-suffering Palestinians. The PA has always lacked access to its self-proclaimed capital, Jerusalem. It controls no borders, governs only a fraction of the West Bank territory, and survives on foreign assistance. Yet Palestine boasts a flag, a government, and police. It has also been recognized as a state on a bilateral basis by a majority of the world's countries, and the number of countries that recognize it as such grows almost annually. These

advances toward statehood merit the inclusion of Palestine among the formally independent states of this volume. That said, the nation-state of Palestine is not an accomplished fact. Israel rules over most territory the Palestinians claim in the West Bank and continues to hold enormous influence over Gaza, despite its withdrawal of settlers from that small strip of land in 2005.

Having attempted but failed to obtain UN recognition of Palestine's independence, in 2012 the PA successfully appealed for the General Assembly to raise Palestine from an "observer entity" to the status of a "non-member observer state." Israel rejected what it considered a unilateral attempt to change the status of territory it controls and banned passports issued with the new title "State of Palestine" (as opposed to Palestinian Authority). Western governments continued to use previous designations until

Currency: Israeli New Shekel; a preference for dollar transactions.

Colonial Status: Still subject to Israel; previously under direct Israeli occupation (1967–94; parts have since been re-occupied) and rule by Egypt (Gaza) and Jordan (West Bank) (1948–67). Britain ruled the area under League of Nations Mandate after World War I, until 1948.

Official Holiday: November 15 (1988; commemorating the National Council's declaration of independence of the West Bank and Gaza).

Leader: Mahmud Abbas, President of the PA and PLO chair.

Head of Government: Mohammad Shtayyeh, Prime Minister; the Hamas government in Gaza is led by Ismail Haniyeh and refuses to recognize the legitimacy of the Ramallah-based Palestinian government.

National Flag: Three horizontal stripes of black, white, and green and a red triangle at the pole.

Gross Domestic Product: $14.8 billion.

GDP per capita: $3,054.

2. East Jerusalem and other Israeli-controlled areas

Area: Viewed as an integral part (and capital city) of a future Palestinian state: about 27 square miles (25 square kilometers) annexed to Jerusalem in 1967 (see Disputed Territories). Other Israeli controlled areas are near (Israeli-identified) strategic locations or Jewish settlements. Approximately 82% of the West Bank is under some form of Israeli control.

3. Israeli Arabs (Palestinian citizens of Israel)

Population: 1.9 million (21% of the Israeli population).

4. Refugees and Emigrants Abroad

Population: At a minimum, 5 million, according to the United Nations Relief and Works Agency for Palestinian Refugees in the Near East (UNRWA). Nearly one third (more than 1.5 million) live in 58 recognized refugee camps in Jordan, Lebanon, Syria, Gaza, the West Bank, and East Jerusalem.

Palestinian-administered territory lies in two portions of the ancient Biblical holy land. The smaller but far more densely populated is Gaza, a narrow strip at the southern end of the coastal plain. The larger region, whose boundaries perplex negotiators, is the West Bank, located on the ridge of hills between the Mediterranean Sea and the Jordan River. The western slopes of the hills enjoy substantial rainfall that seeps into important aquifers that extend into Israel. By contrast, the barren eastern slopes and Jordan valley receive little precipitation.

History: Civilization extends back into pre-history in the land between the Jordan and the Mediterranean. Jericho, for example, is one of the oldest continuously-occupied towns in the world. Given the light rainfall, most of the population herded flocks of sheep and goats outside the villages and towns. The Biblical narrative of Abraham and similar accounts in the Quran, suggest a semi-nomadic life under the authority of a family patriarch.

Some 3,000 years ago two new peoples settled among the existing Semitic Canaanites. The *Bnei Israel* (Sons of Israel) crossed the Jordan River and seized the central hill region. Their Semitic language resembled the Canaanites', but religious, intellectual, and tribal matters set them apart. The Philistines, a sea people, landed and occupied the coastal plain. Influenced by the Greeks, the Philistines enjoyed superior iron technology, but their power eventually weakened. Nevertheless, the Philistines contributed their name to the region's Greek and Roman occupiers. Jewish revolts against Roman rule in the century following the death of Jesus of Nazareth led the Romans to expel most Jews from the territory. A vanishingly small contingent remained, such that Jews have—in some capacity—had a continuous presence in the region.

The centuries following the Arab conquest of Palestine (635–638) brought major changes in religion and language. Most of the Christian majority converted to Islam. With the exception of the Crusaders' conquests, the chronological record of Palestine differs little from those of neighboring territories (see Historical Background).

Modernization impacted the region visibly during the 19th century, and the first substantial Jewish immigration took place at its end (see Israel: History). Nevertheless, the population remained largely Muslim and overwhelmingly Arab. Only about 10% of the inhabitants were Jewish when British forces defeated Ottoman armies during World War I and ended Muslim rule.

Arab nationalism grew rapidly during the early 20th century, but Palestinian identity—like other national identities—developed more slowly. In 1919 most Christians and Muslims desired to form part of a united Arab state, as indicated to the King-Crane Commission. Nevertheless, the 1923 San Remo Conference granted Britain a mandate whose terms incorporated a Jewish national home.

Both Muslim and Christian Arabs fared badly under the mandate. Misled by Hajj Amin al-Husayni, the Mufti of Jerusalem, the Palestinians failed to develop pragmatic leaders or quiet methods to influence the government in London. Their leading families considered each other rivals, rather than allies against foreign threats, though the struggle with Zionism did lead them to perceive themselves as distinct from Arabs living in Transjordan or Syria. Arab society lacked funds for investment, and because the mandate deliberately left health and education to the communities, rather than to the government, Arabs fell further behind Zionist settlers.

With a coherent nationalist ideology still in its nascent stages, the Arab population readily realized that if immigration continued Arab Palestinians would eventually become a minority in a Zionist state. In desperation, Palestinians turned to large-scale communal violence in 1929 and a lengthy general strike in 1936. When, in 1937, a British commission proposed the partition of Palestine, virtual civil war broke out, with Arabs fighting the British. The latter were aided by Jewish paramilitary forces organized as the *Haganah* (Defense). Lasting until 1939, the Great Revolt (as it became known), would come to form a decisive factor in the 1948 Palestinian War. It forced the exile of Grand Mufti Mohammad al-Husseini, fractured the Palestinian nationalists, and caused the British to throw their support behind the Zionist project.

Origins of the Refugee Problem

After the mandate ended, with partition voted by the United Nations (1947) and growing violence (see Israel: History), Palestinians began the flight that divided them into four groups. During the 1948–1949 Israeli War for Independence some 700,000 Palestinians fled their homes. Undoubtedly, the actions of the Israeli military incited—perhaps intentionally—panic in the Palestinian population. Massacres decimated Palestinian villages, while bombing attacks in Jerusalem targeted urban residents. Some Arab homes were demolished, and their inhabitants forced out. As Palestinians fled it understandably precipitated further movement. Often, as the fighting drew near, the sight of refugees encouraged other families to seek greater safety while they awaited the verdict of battle. After atrocities such as the massacre of Arab civilians at Deir

Palestine

Palestinian youth protest Israeli occupation in Gaza before Israel's 2005 withdrawal

Yasin, and the reprisal murder of Jewish medical personnel on Mt. Scopus, individuals on both sides of the conflict must have felt their lives were at stake.

The single biggest expulsion of the war was the Lydda Death March—the forced exodus of the residents of Ramla and Lydda (Lod), many of whom were Palestinians already displaced from their homes in the preceding months. The death march followed an unprecedented massacre at Lydda that cost the lives of hundreds of Palestinian civilians. Survivors were forced out at gun-point and were made to walk, in intense summer heat, for three days. Estimates of those who perished along the way range from dozens to over 300.

Palestinians who ended up in refugee camps in neighboring countries were almost universally perceived as a burden. The Arab states, emerging from decades of colonial rule and still in the throes of developing their own national identities, struggled to manage the immediate, pressing needs tens of thousands of displaced Palestinians. Despite shared language and religion, most Arab states discouraged the integration of refugees. Often, Arab regimes did little but police camps and proclaim the refugees' distress as evidence of the moral wrongs inflicted by Zionism.

Many refugees themselves also rejected assimilation. They argued that they should return to their homes in Palestine;

some, indeed, could see their houses and lands across the armistice lines. Resettlement in other Arab countries might weaken their claim for justice. However, Israel consistently rejected any form of repatriation, leaving Palestinians in a state of protracted displacement.

For nearly 70 years, refugees and their descendants have yearned for their day of return. While waiting, they lived first in tents, then crowded into houses of concrete block and galvanized roofs. Many lacked running water, and the buildings proved cold in the winter and hot in the summer. Often unemployed and nearly always poor, the refugee camps remained fertile ground for political agitation. Minimal levels of food and clothing provided by the United Nations Relief and Works Agency (UNRWA) merely ensured that none starved. Ironically, UNRWA schools, employing Palestinian teachers, made the Palestinians among the best-educated Arabs. They have also instilled an intense nationalism in their school children.

The West Bank

In 1949, after his Arab Legion proved at least partly effective against Israel, King Abdullah united the West Bank with his existing state of Transjordan and proclaimed the Hashemite Kingdom of Jordan. For the West Bank Palestinians, the union with Jordan proved difficult. Although Palestinians outnumbered East Bank Jordanians and had achieved higher

PALESTINE: Partition Plan recommended by the UN General Assembly, November 1947

levels of education and political sophistication, East Bankers dominated government and the military.

Palestinians distrusted Abdullah's moderation towards Israel. They interpreted his annexation of the West Bank as an attempt to enrich his dynasty. Abdullah enjoyed his enlarged kingdom only briefly; he was assassinated by a militant Palestinian in 1951. King Hussein, his grandson and successor, continued the royal moderation; Palestinians retained their suspicions. Investment was concentrated in the East Bank, an astute policy in view of the increasing military superiority of Israel, though naturally unpopular on the West Bank.

Conditions were materially worse for the Palestinians in Gaza, a strip about 25 miles (50 kilometers) long and five miles (8 kilometers) wide administered by Egypt but not annexed. The 200,000 refugees overwhelmed the existing population of 70,000, and the dense population limited agricultural development. With its own impoverished millions, Egypt lacked funds to develop Gaza, and in fact Cairo discouraged the refugees from settling in Egypt.

Israel's conquest of the West Bank and Gaza Strip in June 1967 ushered in a new era. East Jerusalem was annexed, and its inhabitants therefore gained the vote. The rest of the West Bank fell under military administration. Absent a peace agreement, its inhabitants officially lived in occupied Jordan, but West Bankers grew increasingly separate from it, despite financial aid and salaries—for some West Bank Palestinians—from Amman.

Although Security Council Resolution 242 called for an Israeli withdrawal from territories occupied during the war, Israel evidently intended to remain. Israelis created "facts on the ground," establishing settlements on Arab lands, particularly around Jerusalem, at strategic points along the Jordan River, and in places where Jewish settlements were determined to have existed before 1948. Within 20 years, the 60,000 settlers came to control about 50% of the West Bank's land, and 34% of that in the crowded Gaza Strip. Settlers also claimed a disproportionate share of water, using almost four times as much per person as Palestinian Arabs. Until 1988 the occupation failed to arouse any significant criticism in Israel or the United States.

Palestinians in Exile

By contrast, Palestinians abroad sensed a surge of hope after 1967. The 1964 Arab Summit Conference established the Palestine Liberation Organization (PLO). Subsequently, the Palestine National Council was formed to reflect Palestinian opinion, and the Palestine National Charter formalized the PLO's goals. These called for a "One State Solution"—replacing Israel with a secular and democratic state where individuals of all religions could live together. Such phrases perhaps seem innocent, but the Charter also called on Palestinians to liberate their land by force and denied Jewish immigrants a place within Palestine. Even without Zionism's emphasis on a special state for Jews, Israelis would hardly accept a solution that expelled most of them from their homes. Also in 1964, Yasir Arafat founded *al-Fatah*, a guerrilla movement that conducted small attacks on Israel from Syria and Jordan, actions that drew Israeli reprisals that in turn led to the June 1967 War.

That war exposed the futility of Arab military goals to defeat Israel, and it discredited virtually every Arab leader. Only the guerrillas "who sacrificed themselves," the *fida'iyin*, remained. When they fought back bravely against an Israeli raid on Karameh in Jordan, they became heroes. Guerrilla groups multiplied: among the many were the Popular Front for the Liberation of Palestine (PFLP), the Popular Democratic Front (PDFLP), and *Saiqa*. The first two groups reflected leftist ideologies, complete with class struggles and the necessity of political and social revolution throughout the Arab world. Others were basically paid agents of particular Arab regimes.

Most Palestinians and their financial backers turned to the straightforward nationalist views of al-Fatah. Its founder, Yasir Arafat, became Chairman of the PLO in 1968 and came to symbolize Palestine as no other leader had. The PLO, in turn, became an umbrella organization for the various fida'iyin, running refugee camps and conducting Palestinian publicity and diplomacy.

Inevitably the guerrillas disturbed Arab governments. Raids into Israel provoked retaliation, against both commando groups and economic targets in the host country. The fida'iyin then sought sophisticated weapons and fortified bases, and became armed units operating within an Arab state, often better paid and more glamorous than the national army. Syria quickly controlled its local guerrillas. Egypt permitted none. For Jordan and Lebanon the experience was bitter, but the refugees themselves suffered the greatest losses in fighting between Palestinians and their reluctant Arab hosts.

Its long border with Israel and large Palestinian population made Jordan a naturally desirable base for the fida'iyin desiring to liberate all Palestine—including freeing the West Bank from Hussein's kingdom. In 1970, the Popular Front hijacked Western jetliners to a desert landing strip in Jordan. In part to free the passengers taken hostage, the Jordanian army fought bitterly against Palestinian guerrillas in Amman. Thousands died, many of them civilians, and the surviving Palestinians called it Black September. Indeed the name "Black September" was later adopted by a secret terrorist group linked to al-Fatah, as a memorial to those lost during the eleven days of battle. King Hussein regained control of his capital, and after further fighting, expelled the fida'iyin from Jordan.

The group moved to Lebanon, a country too weak to limit its activities or prevent Israel from striking at will. Scores of problems developed between the Palestinians and the Lebanese, ranging from unpaid traffic tickets and electric bills, to guerrilla checkpoints and gun battles. Against a background of political wrangling between Lebanon's Muslims and Maronites, in 1975 the ambush of a Palestinian motorcade by Maronite militia marked the beginning of the Lebanese Civil War (see Lebanon: History).

Palestinian losses were significant, and the victims were often civilians. The major refugee camp at Tel al-Za'tar fell to Lebanese Christian forces after a bloody struggle. Thousands of Palestinians and Lebanese alike perished in 1982, when a full-scale conventional attack brought Israeli troops to the suburbs of Beirut (see Israel: History). Still, more civilian deaths resulted when Israeli troops allowed Maronite militiamen to enter Palestinian refugee camps outside Beirut and massacre—unopposed—hundreds of women, children, and old men.

The long years of fighting brought few benefits to Palestinians, and the hopes kindled by Palestinian success at Karameh dissipated. The fida'iyin killed many times more Arabs—Jordanians, Lebanese, Syrians, and others—than Israelis. Likewise, the refugees suffered more deaths from Arab weapons than from Israeli ones. Despite their great popularity in some Arab and Developing World circles, the fida'iyin had by their actions aroused intense disgust in Western public opinion. Fortunately for the Palestinians, world attention turned in 1988 from the exiled Palestinians to those living in the West Bank and Gaza Strip.

Resisting Occupation: The Intifada

The popular rebellion known as the *intifada*—literally, the "shaking off"—began in 1987. To protest Israeli occupation, civilians of the West Bank and Gaza used strikes, civil disobedience, rock-throwing, other small-scale violence, and boycotts of Israeli goods. Rock and bottle-throwing youths damaged thousands of passing cars and buses; firebombs gutted others. However, the violence was usually not intended to be lethal, and the statistics for 1988 firmly established the one-sided nature of fatal violence: 366 Palestinian deaths and 11,000 wounded compared with 15 Israeli deaths and 420 injured. The intifada sought more to defy Israeli rule than to kill Jews.

The youthful activists earned wide television coverage, but the intifada involved many elements of Palestinian society. Middle-aged, middle-class merchants accepted repeated general strikes designed to demonstrate the authority of the resistance movement. Traditional Israeli controls—for example, smashing shutters on closed shops or welding them shut—failed to break the strikes.

Other economic actions included the boycott of Israeli cigarettes and soft-drinks and widespread resistance to taxes. The 140,000 Palestinians who provided the major source of cheap unskilled labor in Israel's construction and other industries obeyed strike calls and disrupted the Israeli economy.

The intifada also inflicted heavy costs on Palestinians. Besides the deaths—many of them avoidable—there were beatings, deportations, and tens of thousands of arrests. Attempting to break the uprising, Israel closed professional associations and charitable groups. It destroyed the homes of families whose teenagers were suspected of throwing gasoline bombs.

The intifada dramatically changed world opinion about Palestinians. They had been refugees first, then terrorists who hijacked airliners, murdered Olympic athletes, and massacred hostages. Such acts provoked outrage and extreme hostility in the Western world. After the intifada, they increasingly were viewed around the world as a defenseless people, beaten and shot by alien soldiers. Even in the United States, the televised suffering of Palestinians eroded the prevailing belief in the moral rightness of the Israeli occupation. Closer to home, witnessing intense nationalism, King Hussein of Jordan withdrew his claims to the West Bank.

These developments enabled Yasir Arafat to take the diplomatic initiative in seeking an independent Palestine limited to the Occupied Territories. When the Palestine National Council met in Algiers in 1988, Arafat's carefully worded policy triumphed. Despite years of condemning it, delegates voted to accept UN Security Council Resolution 242, linking it to the Palestinian right to self-determination. The resolution also implicitly abandoned the PLO's goal of eliminating Israel, and it condemned terrorism of all kinds. The Council balanced these actions by declaring Palestine independent, using words that mirrored Israel's similar declaration in 1948. However, the acceptance of

Palestine

a separate Palestinian state on the West Bank and Gaza—the "Two-State Solution," split the Council into moderate and rejectionist camps. It also failed to win recognition from European nations and the United States, who insisted that accepted territory and boundaries must precede formal recognition.

Soon afterwards, Arafat addressed a special session of the UN General Assembly, held in Geneva because the U.S. considered him a terrorist and refused him a visa. In his speech, he detailed the positions adopted by the National Council and gave away the ultimate Palestinian bargaining chip—recognition of Israel. He hoped, in response, for negotiations that would ultimately free the occupied territories and form a Palestinian state. After more than two years of the intifada, Palestinians had restored their self-respect and unity, and they had gained Western sympathy. But neither the intifada nor Arafat's recognition of Israel had gained an inch of territory or improved the harsh military occupation. Israel's new hardline cabinet under Yitzhak Shamir fundamentally opposed ceding any territory for peace.

Moreover, the facts on the ground worsened. In its last days, the Soviet Union reversed policy and allowed its Jews to emigrate. Some one million Jewish immigrants did, and in doing so they placed a longer fuse on the "demographic time bomb" of an Arab majority between the Jordan and the Mediterranean. Settlement activities also increased in the territories, subsidized by the government despite international condemnation.

Within Palestine, the intifada showed signs of disintegration, as increasingly its targets shifted to alleged "collaborators." Nearly 1,000 Palestinians were killed in intra-communal violence, most on the sometimes spurious charge of having passed information to the occupying power. The intifada, itself a struggle of the weak against the powerful, was creating its own victims. To some extent, the violence between Palestinians resulted from Israeli success in rounding up or eliminating leaders and activists. Some 10% of the population suffered imprisonment, injuries requiring hospital care, or material losses such as destroyed crops or confiscated possessions.

The Price of Backing Saddam

Many Palestinians enthusiastically supported Iraqi President Saddam Hussein in 1990 when he seized Kuwait, because he then demanded a peace settlement involving Israeli-held lands. Yasir Arafat publicly embraced him, the triumph of emotional desperation over reason. Palestinians suffered more from the Gulf War than any nation besides Kuwait and Iraq. The not

The first *intifada* began with protests and stones

insignificant population of Palestinian exiles in Kuwait, although divided in their response to the invasion, suffered collective reprisal. Thousands lost their jobs and life savings. Hostility, revenge, and mass deportations decimated the community. Palestinians in other Gulf countries found themselves under suspicion and unable to renew visas. Losing residence and employment, they became refugees yet again.

In the West Bank and Gaza, support for the invasion cost Gulf Arab support for hospitals, schools, and the intifada, just as Israeli curfews worsened living conditions. Gulf rulers halted aid estimated at $100 million per month to the PLO. The official PLO position swung to "neutrality" over Kuwait, but popular feeling in refugee camps and the Occupied Territories openly supported Saddam Hussein and cheered Scud attacks on Israel. It was undoubtedly a public relations disaster, at a time when international sentiment had been slowly and cautiously shifting towards the Palestinians.

Despite their misfortunes, Palestinians won representation at the 1991 peace negotiations in Madrid because the Jordanian delegation included Palestinian intellectuals outside the PLO. These negotiators won wide respect. Their spokeswoman, Hanan Ashrawi, presented their case to Westerners far more persuasively than Yasir Arafat ever had, and without invoking the hostility that Arafat did. Nevertheless, the discussions produced nothing of substance, not least because Israel intended to yield nothing, as its prime minister later confessed. Meanwhile, led by Hamas and other militant Islamic groups, Arab opposition strengthened against the talks.

After the 1992 Israeli elections, the incoming Labor government halted most new settlements outside Jerusalem. However, when the killings of Israeli soldiers and civilians continued, Prime Minister Rabin refused Palestinians entry to the Occupied Territories, even for work. Immediately unemployment soared to 50% or more in some places. The closed border carried momentous consequences. Israelis realized that they preferred life without Palestinians, and support rose for a break with the Occupied Territories.

Against this background, Israeli and PLO negotiators secretly met in Oslo in 1993, and they agreed to create a Palestinian administration in Jericho and Gaza by April 1994. A now-famous handshake at the White House formalized the Declaration of Principles between two men who had been bitter enemies for decades: Prime Minister Rabin and Chairman Arafat.

Progress towards Palestinian Autonomy

While the Oslo Accords won wide support in the world's press, many Palestinian groups condemned them, both on the left (the Popular Front and the Democratic Front) and the religious right (Islamic Jihad and Hamas). These groups considered two disconnected parcels of land under limited self-rule far too small a reward for ending the struggle to replace Israel with a Palestinian state. Opposition also arose within the Palestinian leadership. Calls grew for democracy, and Hanan Ashrawi chose to serve on a human rights group rather than on the administrative council.

The Oslo Accords envisaged complete agreement in 1993, followed by a phased Israeli withdrawal and elections in 1994.

Palestine

All outstanding issues were to be settled during a five-year interim period. However, each side desired the immediate steps to reflect its vision of the final arrangements. And over the final arrangements there had been no agreement. Officially, Israel still regarded a Palestinian future as up for negotiation, and it sought to protect every Jewish settlement and access route, even those surrounded by tens of thousands of Arabs in Hebron and Gaza. In contrast, Palestinians considered their zones the embryo of an independent state, and sought the trappings of statehood: tariffs and economic regulations, currency (even if only symbolic), passports, stamps, and telephone area codes. From its beginnings, the Oslo process fell behind schedule, and the slow pace of negotiations weakened support for its vision.

Important forces on both sides ultimately sabotaged the peace process. Unwavering in their rejection of the Oslo Accords, Hamas and Islamic Jihad launched raids that ranged from the isolated murder of soldiers to suicide attacks that killed dozens. Yasir Arafat proved unwilling or unable to enforce the security that Israeli leaders saw as the basis of peace. On the other side, Israeli cabinets often pressed tactical demands about negotiations at the cost of setbacks to the strategic goal of peace. Border closures inflicted unemployment and other hardships on Palestinians, that served to create additional recruits for the most militant groups. Targeted assassinations—the selective murder of militants by intelligence agents or missile strikes—often provided the justification for further suicide raids. Targeted killings are widely supported by Israeli society, but a 2011 study found that 40% of victims of such assassinations are Palestinian civilian bystanders, raising important questions around the long-term strategic gains of such a policy.

Against this background, there were moments of achievement. In 1994, Palestinian autonomy took its first steps when the PLO took control of Jericho and Gaza. Middle-aged soldiers from the Palestinian Liberation Army arrived to become policemen; crowds of well-wishers cheered them. The rapid pace of events caught Palestinian leaders unprepared, but the Palestinian flag flew over Gaza and Jericho. After later negotiations, the occupiers departed Ramallah, but two-thirds of the West Bank still remained under Israeli control, including military bases, 128 settlements, and access roads.

Freed from the occupation, in 1996 voters overwhelmingly elected Arafat as *Ra'is*, or president. His supporters likewise won a majority in the Palestine National Council. Arafat then kept a very

significant promise. He summoned the Council to Gaza, where after decades of exile, it met and voted overwhelmingly to delete the Charter's call for the destruction of Israel. Talks began on the final, most difficult issues: East Jerusalem, refugees, water, and settlements.

During the elections that followed the assassination of Yitzhak Rabin by a Jewish extremist, Palestinian suicide bombers demonstrated the insecurity of the peace process, and thus aided the victory of Binyamin Netanyahu, whose Likud Party had opposed the Oslo Accords, and in fact any Palestinian state.

While Netanyahu withdrew troops from part of Hebron, he also permitted the start of a new Jewish settlement, Har Homa (Jabal Abu Ghnaim), in the vital stretch of Arab-inhabited land between Bethlehem and East Jerusalem. The Peace Process continued to disintegrate. Suicide bombings by Hamas in Jerusalem provoked an internal closure on Palestinian areas. This shut down travel and trade between the individual Palestinian towns, a blow far worse than closures Israel had inflicted before the Oslo Accords. Unemployment afflicted half the working population, and many individuals had incomes of under $2.00 per day.

The city of Hebron, the largest Arab community, then with more than 100,000 inhabitants, remained an intense source of conflict and resentment. To protect just 450 Jewish settlers and students, Israel retained 20% of the entire city, including its commercial and religious center. On the outskirts, other settlers used any available pretext to seize Arab farmlands and demolish Palestinian homes that had been built or extended without the almost impossible to obtain Israeli permits.

Near-success, then Diplomatic Collapse

The greatest opportunity for peace occurred in 2000. During the final days of his presidency, President Clinton invited Arafat and then-Prime Minister Ehud Barak to the Camp David presidential retreat. During intense negotiations, Barak conceded a greater Palestinian role in East Jerusalem than any Israeli leader had ever discussed in public, but he would not yield actual control over the Arab parts of the city. Mindful of both political opinion at home and his place in history, Arafat rejected the concession, insisting that "the Arab leader has not been born who will give away Jerusalem."

Months later, General Ariel Sharon's visit to the Haram al-Sharif plunged the two sides into violence. The leader of the opposition Likud party, Sharon had earned a reputation for aggressive behavior towards Arabs (the 1953 Qibya massacre in Jordan; ignoring a cease-fire with

Egypt, in 1973; permitting and encouraging Lebanese militiamen to enter Palestinian camps in Lebanon in 1982). Angry Muslims considered his visit a sacrilege and protested by stone-throwing; the police shot dead some rioters. This marked the beginning of the *al-Aqsa intifada*, a bloody resumption of protests and violence against the occupation.

The Palestinians overwhelmingly suffered the casualties in any outbreak of violence. Under Labor's Prime Minister Barak, troops shot to kill, and huge numbers of casualties came from gunshots to the neck and head. The televised death of Muhammad al-Dura, a twelve-year-old boy shot while huddling with his father, won sympathy (but little else) in Arab countries and the West. Instituting a collective punishment over all the territories, Israel re-imposed its closure system, cutting Gaza into six enclaves and the West Bank into 24. Economic conditions, never prosperous, again became desperate. Families shared what they had, but many survived only on UNRWA food subsidies and aid from abroad (perhaps averaging $500 per person in 2001).

Seeing little progress, Palestinian popular opinion increasingly accepted the militants' argument that the Oslo peace process had created little other than a powerless and undemocratic Authority mismanaged by President Arafat. The Palestinian police even did some of Israel's security work: the occupied provided security for the occupier. Because Israel was unwilling to grant Palestinian demands, reasoned the militants, the intifada must continue until victory.

Yasir Arafat, alternating between his role as president and a manipulator seeking negotiating strength, permitted or (allegedly) encouraged violence if that might strengthen Palestinian interests. By omission or commission, he oversaw the use of terrorism in an attempt to force concessions from Israel. Likud's new Prime Minister Sharon held Arafat personally responsible for the terrorists' bloodshed. In reality, militants had escaped official control, if indeed they had ever been beholden to Arafat and the PA. Religious and secular groups joined the armed struggle. Besides Hamas and Islamic Jihad, they included the al-Aqsa Brigade of Arafat's own Fatah movement. This placed Palestinian security forces in impossible circumstances. Israel and the U.S. demanded that Arafat end terrorism and arrest perpetrators before negotiations could take place. To make those arrests required the police, but widespread public support for these groups sometimes blocked Palestinian police who attempted to arrest alleged militants. The police became targets of Israeli fire in

Palestine

reprisal killings, while also increasingly being viewed as working to Israeli interests and therefore legitimate targets of Palestinian militants.

After an explosion killed 25 elderly Jews gathered for Passover in the spring of 2002, Israeli forces systematically attacked major West Bank cities in an effort to destroy terrorist cells. Over 200 Palestinians died; tens of thousands endured hardships ranging from battle wounds to confinement indoors. Government offices, police offices, and stores suffered vandalism. After a carefully planned ambush in the Jenin refugee camp took the lives of Israeli soldiers, the Israel Defense Forces (IDF) left destruction compared by eyewitnesses to an earthquake zone. Accounts verified by Human Rights Watch state that war crimes occurred, such as the use of civilians as human shields, and the prevention of medical assistance to the camp for five days.

In Ramallah, the Israelis deliberately spared part of Yasir Arafat's headquarters, but they confined him to two rooms and prevented him from attending an Arab summit conference. Released only after pressure from Washington, Arafat later promised reforms and elections, the first

A Palestinian boy throws stones

to the legislature in six years. However, suicide bombings led Israel to seize and hold most Palestinian cities and towns. The elections were postponed. Arafat's popularity, overwhelming while he was besieged, fell rapidly in the face of demands from nearly everyone—Palestinians of all parties, Americans, Israelis—for improved security, a response to corruption, and the implementation of the rule of law.

Fatah Fractures; Hamas Wins

Beyond symbolism, in almost a decade the Palestinian National Authority had achieved little. Israel controlled the electricity, water supply, and telephone lines, and it divided Palestinian islets from one another by roads to the growing settlements. Financially, the PA depended almost completely on foreign aid. Most of its own taxes are collected by Israel on trade, thus enabling Israel to block Palestinian revenue at whim. Arafat's employees felt underpaid, and the Palestinian public resented corruption and the creation of monopolies. The heavy-handed police often acted repressively. When 20 academics and legislators signed a statement attacking the Arafat administration and calling the Oslo peace process a "conspiracy" against the nation, Palestinian security forces arrested half the signatories and detained them without charge.

Arafat's death in 2004 was widely mourned by Palestinians. Long a key symbol of the Palestinian struggle, and a towering figure in the efforts towards Palestinian statehood, his failures as a leader were largely forgotten in an outpouring of grief. In Ramallah crowds scaled the walls of the compound to which he'd been confined by Israel for over two years. Mourners from Gaza were prohibited by Israel from leaving the Strip in order to attend the funeral. Questions were raised about the cause of Arafat's death, although a French inquiry found that it had "not been demonstrated that Mr Yasser Arafat was murdered." In Israeli and American eyes Arafat had been equated with terrorism, his death offered the possibility of a fresh start.

In fact, Arafat's death left a nation so fractured politically that commentators speculated about the possibility of anarchy, or that Islamic militants might seize Gaza and split it from the West Bank. In the presidential race that followed, Fatah united around Mahmud Abbas, a longtime aide to Arafat. Despite his moderation and opposition to the violence of the intifada, Abbas won an overwhelming majority in a light turnout. He adeptly negotiated a ceasefire with Israel that required a halt to Palestinian violence. In return, Israel agreed to withdraw from some

West Bank cities, stop assassinations, and release hundreds of prisoners.

Abbas fared less well with domestic politics. He failed to combat corruption effectively, or to halt the growing anarchy when Fatah's own multiple security forces confronted each other and those of Hamas on the streets of Gaza. Managing, from Ramallah, a territory physically removed from the West Bank was always problematic. However, Abbas did persuade the various armed units to halt suicide operations in 2005, thus paving the way for the Israeli withdrawal from Gaza.

Recalling the Arab sense of victory that followed Israel's withdrawal from Lebanon, the Sharon cabinet sought to erase any doubts about Israeli power before withdrawing from Gaza. The IDF assassinated a number of militants, notably Sheikh Ahmad Yassin, the elderly leader of Hamas who died in his wheelchair. After his successor was assassinated a few weeks later, Hamas kept its leadership secret.

Besides exterminating the militants' leadership, the Israeli military also targeted supply depots and workshops, amongst other sites identified as militarily significant. Its units inflicted such destruction on the Rafah refugee camp that the United States abandoned its usual veto and allowed the UN Security Council to condemn the operation.

Israeli withdrawal from Gaza in 2005 initially brought a great sense of freedom to that strip of land, but within months predictions of anarchy seemed on the verge of being fulfilled. Abbas's own party, Fatah, splintered between the Old Guard around Abbas and supporters of younger militants like Marwan Barghouti, a hero imprisoned for life in Israel for approving attacks on civilians. Without Barghouti, Fatah symbolized a policy blamed by the public for corruption and economic depression. By contrast, Hamas decided to contest legislative elections, and it entered the contest united and disciplined. As a result, Hamas won decisive victories in most locations, the highest share of the national vote, and captured 72 of the 132 legislative seats.

By exercising their democratic right to vote for the party of their choice, even though it refused to recognize Israel, Palestinian voters plunged themselves into difficulties. Hamas found no allies: its prime minister, Ismail Haniya, immediately faced a cut-off of almost all government revenue—taxes collected by Israel, foreign aid from the United States and Europe, and funds from Arab states. On the surface, Israel and the United States refused to contribute funds to a group committed to Israel's destruction. At a deeper level, leaders believed this policy might strangle the Palestinian Authority to financial death and thus also discredit Hamas.

The financial strangulation carried somber consequences. Following a relatively free election, the West punished the Palestinian people for voting out a decrepit and divided party. Arab democracy, it seemed, was desired—but only as long as voters selected winners approved by Israel and the United States.

The results of the financial blockade were as predictable as they were perverse. Unable to pay salaries, the regime floundered. The economy continued in depression. Western nations and organizations therefore funded relief activities and even paid salary support for civil employees. In fact, they actually spent more money on Palestinians during the blockade than they would have without it. Arab government aid, however, could not reach Haniya's legitimately elected government.

Gaza under Hamas

In 2007 King Abdullah of Saudi Arabia pressured Hamas and Fatah to form a cabinet of national unity, in hopes of lifting the blockade and ending the frequent clashes between their militias in Gaza. However, Ismail Haniya remained prime minister, and he continued to refuse to recognize Israel, so the blockade continued. That summer, clashes between the two parties' militiamen in Gaza reached a crisis. Hamas rejected President Abbas's attempts to control security forces and arrested or killed Fatah's fighters in Gaza. In response, Abbas dismissed Haniya's cabinet. Almost immediately, the financial blockade was lifted on Abbas's government. Because Hamas members still formed the parliamentary majority, contrary to standard democratic practices Abbas governed only the West Bank. Gaza remained under Hamas rule.

With Hamas ruling Gaza, Israeli restrictions gradually halted Gaza's economy. The level of goods entering Gaza fell to 10% of the previous level. Construction stopped completely, 90% of private industries shut down, farms became free-fire zones for Israeli tanks, and 80% of the population only survived thanks to food aid. The power generating plant failed to operate well after it was attacked, and Israel cut the levels of electricity and fuel permitted into the Strip. Hospitals fell short of medicines for Palestinians in desperate need, but animal vaccines were rushed into Gaza, to prevent communicable diseases that might spread across the border.

In response, enterprising Gazans and Hamas militants built multiple tunnels where smugglers brought consumer goods—eventually even new cars—and military supplies. Ironically, since Hamas taxed the smugglers, its control over

the economy increased. The group now gained revenue from trade without Israel collecting the taxes.

Soon after the 2005 Israeli withdrawal, sporadic fighting broke out between Islamic militants in Gaza and the Israeli military. A brazen raid by militants over the border into Israel captured 19-year-old Corporal Gilad Shalit, and during 2006, while Israel fought Hizbullah across the northern border, it also launched attacks on militants in the Gaza Strip. The bloodshed proved mostly one-sided. During the year after the withdrawal from Gaza, two Israeli civilians died from the militants' simple rockets. By contrast, according to the human rights group B'Tselem, the retaliatory air strikes and tank invasions killed about 400 Palestinians.

Despite foreign mediation, by 2008 neither side had achieved its desired goals. A truce had committed Israel to permitting increased trade, and Hamas to halting all attacks by all groups on Israel. But the rocket attacks never entirely stopped, and trade never resumed to peace-time levels. After the formal expiration of the cease-fire, Israel launched an intensive bombing campaign followed by a land invasion of Gaza, seeking to destroy the rocket-launching capabilities, reduce or eliminate Hamas as an armed organization, and re-establish respect for its military after the inconclusive war against Hizbullah in southern Lebanon in 2006.

Hamas fought back with tactics borrowed from Hizbullah. Its fighters dispersed among the population to fight

in civilian areas, with weapons stored in homes, mosques, and even schools. Clearly, these tactics did not seek to minimize civilian casualties, and Amnesty International faulted Hamas for endangering Palestinian civilians by firing rockets from residential neighborhoods. It should be noted that the Gaza Strip is one of the most densely populated areas on earth (approximately 13,600 people per square mile or 5,250 per square kilometer) with no options for its civilian population to flee.To avoid air attacks, fighters moved directly between homes, or used tunnels and underground command posts. For their part, Israeli troops rarely entered houses by the door, fearing booby-traps, and they combined the use of precision weaponry with heavy, short-range firing at points of resistance. Inevitably, hundreds of Palestinian civilians were killed, some of them sheltering beside UN compounds or, notably, in a UN school. Thousands more were wounded.

Charges of war crimes quickly arose against both sides. Israel received the most condemnation (e.g., from the United Nations, the Red Cross, and Amnesty International), for its use of white phosphorous bombs, for obstructing access to medical care, and for the "wanton and deliberate" destruction of homes, businesses, and public buildings. Hamas, in turn, was blamed for its rocket attacks on civilians. Israel also claimed that Hamas fighters abandoned uniforms to mix with the population, violated rules on the use of the white flag, sheltered behind civilians,

Palestinian Red Crescent Society offices, directly targeted   Photo by Said Abedwahed

Palestine

A wounded Palestinian being evacuated. Palestinian and Israeli accounts conflict dramatically over the identity of those killed and wounded

and generally fought in ways that endangered civilians.

The three-week war ended when first Israel and then Hamas independently announced cease-fires. It left enormous destruction, including neighborhoods and an industrial area flattened by bulldozers and shells. Along with other infrastructure, damaged sewer and water pipelines would take years to repair. Nevertheless, the fighting had failed to create new rules of the game. Hamas remained in power, the blockade continued, and the world perceived Gazans as the victims, but did little about it. Smugglers quickly resumed their trade through the tunnels, importing weapons as well as consumer goods.

Although the United Nations, the International Committee of the Red Cross, and other organizations long warned about the consequences of the blockade of Gaza, for three years Israel successfully defended it in Western public opinion as a necessity for security against home-made missiles. The gradual release of information about details of the restrictions failed to change perceptions.

However, when Israeli commandos stormed the *Mavi Marmara* in international waters and killed 9 peace activists, world perceptions shifted. The Turkish ferry was part of a flotilla organized to challenge the blockade by attempting to carry humanitarian supplies to Gaza. World. Even the U.S. president recognized that conditions in Gaza had become unsustainable.

Responding to international pressure, the Israeli cabinet reduced the embargo's scope. Food, toys, and kitchen utensils

would be permitted, as well as material from the UN, but sea shipments to Gaza remained prohibited. Given Egyptian cooperation, Israel retained almost total control over imports. The collective punishment of Gaza continued. After the downfall of President Mubarak, Egypt symbolically opened the Rafah crossing, but strict controls remained, with only a fortunate few allowed to cross each day. Since 2013, the border crossing has been opened only sporadically. In late-2017 the Ramallah-based PA took over control of the crossing as part of a deal with

Egypt that would see it opened, provided Hamas were kept from any involvement in its day-to-day operation. The deal has since collapsed and access to the border remains tightly restricted and unevenly applied.

After repeated cross-border attacks by both sides, open warfare resumed between Israel and Gaza in November 2012, beginning with a surgical airstrike that killed Ahmad Jabari, the Hamas military commander. For most of two weeks the two sides conducted an aerial conflict, with Israeli strikes on militants, Hamas's rocket launchers, underground tunnels, storage areas, and other facilities. In turn, Hamas fired some 1500 locally-manufactured short-range missiles and a few Iranian-made Fajr-5 and M75 medium-range missiles at Israeli towns and cities, some reaching the outskirts of Tel Aviv, despite the success of Israel's Iron Dome anti-missile system.

The conflict ended through U.S. and Egyptian mediation. Israel's motives in launching the war were complex and remain murky. Rocket fire from Islamic Jihad and sometimes Hamas often provided a pretext. Two other factors may interest historians. The fighting began a few days before the UN General Assembly was set to debate the appeal of Palestinian President Mahmoud Abbas for "non-member observer state status." A war with Hamas might weaken the appeal. And just like the last war (of 2009) the fighting occurred just a few weeks before Knesset elections, a good time to remind voters of the prime minister's leadership.

Meanwhile, Israeli restrictions continue to make life extraordinarily difficult for Palestinians in the West Bank. Getting to

Israeli missiles score direct hits on Gaza University

156

The late Yasir Arafat, PLO chairman and PA President

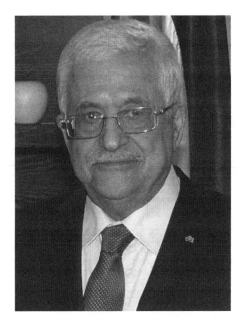

Mahmoud Abbas, President of Palestine

school, work, or hospital is often virtually impossible, and restrictions linked to Israeli settlements deprive many Palestinian farmers of their land. An estimated 50% of the West Bank's population lives in poverty.

Domestic Instability and International Stagnation

Free and open Palestinian elections were extremely unlikely, given the division between Hamas-ruled Gaza and the West Bank under Fatah. Moreover, Fatah is divided between those loyal to Mahmud Abbas and others seeking a new face such as Marwan Barghouti, although he remains imprisoned. Therefore, when the already-extended presidential term neared its end in 2010, the PLO met the difficulty by prolonging once again the terms of the president and parliament. Predictably condemned by Hamas, the decision hardly strengthened popular support for the Palestinian Authority.

The post-Mubarak regime in Egypt mediated an understanding, but after just a few weeks the conflicting needs of each party overwhelmed it. After all, Fatah desired early elections to restore legitimacy to the presidency and legislature, whose terms had expired. But for Hamas, early elections risked unfavorable comparisons between the economic disaster of Gaza and the modest prosperity of the West Bank.

Such domestic political shambles left the PA a poor partner for the indirect "proximity negotiations" widely considered the only route leading to a two-state solution. However, it was Israel that

essentially ruptured the talks. When the Netanyahu cabinet refused to extend the settlement freeze in 2010, the Palestinian Authority halted negotiations, as it had threatened to do.

The Palestinian Authority then sought a distinctly different path to a settlement: a UN vote recognizing independence. Several European governments seemed sympathetic, but the United States threatened a veto in the Security Council, and the matter was sidetracked. Then, in November 2012, with Abbas repeating his acceptance of the 1967 borders, Palestine appealed to the UN General Assembly for recognition as a non-member observer state. It was not recognition of independence, but the United States carries no veto in the General Assembly, and the motion passed, 138 to 9, with 41 abstentions. In retaliation, Israel blocked the transfer of taxes collected on imports to Palestine, financially crippling the Palestinian Authority. Palestine's status in the United Nations was further bolstered when it was granted the 2019 chairmanship of the G77. In order to take on the role, a UN General Assembly resolution was adopted to temporarily grant Palestine additional rights beyond those of its observer state status. The Palestinians plan to launch a new bid for full member status, despite knowing that it will face U.S. veto in the Security Council.

Years after his presidential term expired, Mahmud Abbas continues in office but lacks legitimacy in the eyes of many Palestinians. Parliamentary and presidential elections scheduled for 2021 were postponed following the outbreak of violence centered in East Jerusalem. Unconstitutional and often ineffective, Abbas's rule nonetheless permits far greater freedom than enjoyed in some Arab states. For example, one of the most popular TV programs is "The President," a weekly reality show that features real politicians interviewing ordinary people willing to discuss what they would do if they took office.

Financial difficulties in Gaza, Abbas's need to demonstrate accomplishments, and U.S. pressure for new peace talks spurred moves to end the political dispute between Hamas and Fatah. At least temporarily, the rivals overcame their internal rivalry and, after seven years of separate regimes in Gaza and the West Bank, in 2014 they agreed an independent cabinet supported by both parties.

The agreement to create a unified cabinet aroused intense criticism from the Israeli government. Prime Minister Netanyahu denounced any cabinet supported by Hamas, but in doing so he failed to win much international support, even from some normally pro-Israeli commentators.

As the United States officially commented, Palestinians had formed "an interim technocratic government" that did not include any members of Hamas. Nevertheless, the unity cabinet provided the final obstacle to U.S. peace efforts led by Secretary of State John Kerry.

In summer 2014, increasing violence marked Palestinian–Israeli relations, including the kidnapping and subsequent murder of three Israeli teenagers. By early July, Israeli air raids and Palestinian missile fire reached the intensity of open warfare that lasted until mid-August. Hamas, Fatah, and other Palestinian groups attempted to infiltrate Israel through tunnels, and they fired over 4,000 missiles into Israel. Heavy surveillance and the Iron Dome anti-missile system kept Israeli casualties low. For its part, the IDF attacked suspected missile fabrication centers, launching sites, and tunnels—as well as houses and buildings suspected of protecting fighters. Almost 2,200 Palestinians were killed, more than half of them civilians, compared to 67 Israeli soldiers and six civilians.

Israeli attacks destroyed entire neighborhoods and scores of children were killed after having sought refuge in UN schools. Soldiers later described orders to shoot to kill rather than to use the minimum force necessary.

Several important developments have taken place on the Israeli–Palestinian front since 2014, though few analysts believe Palestine has come any closer to achieving real independence. In early 2017, President Trump and his Ambassador to

Palestine

Gaza University leveled by direct Israeli attacks

the United Nations, Nikki Haley, were explicit about reaffirming U.S. commitments and support to Israel in its dispute with the Palestinians. Although in many respects President Obama supported Israel as much (some say more) than past presidents, there was tension between Obama and Israeli Prime Minister Netanyahu. The Obama administration sought for years to play the role of honest broker in the conflict. Most watchers believe that that policy, and any pretense at U.S. neutrality, has gone out the window, a shift welcomed by Israeli hardliners. The new approach has put distance between the United States and many of its traditional allies, including in the European Union, and has cast doubt on whether any peace plan to come out of Washington—expected in mid-2019—will get off the ground. Indeed, Palestinians are fearful that Trump's "deal of the century" is nothing more than a complete acquiescence to Netanyahu.

One of the clearest manifestation of the new approach has been the United States' decision to move its Israeli embassy from Tel Aviv to Jerusalem (see Israel: The Stalled Peace Process). In the ensuing protests, more than 60 Palestinians were killed, and thousands were wounded. Israel was condemned by the UN Human Rights Council, a resolution that ultimately precipitated the long-threatened withdrawal of the U.S. from the Council.

Another potentially important development in recent years has to do with Hamas, which has long rejected Israel's legitimacy and positioned itself as the implacable foe of the Jewish state. In 2017, the group moderated its rhetoric vis-à-vis Israel. During a public ceremony in Doha, Hamas released a new Document of Principles, which calls for better ties with Egypt, moderates anti-Semitic language, and provisionally (if implicitly) accepts a Palestinian state that could exist alongside Israel. Then, in 2018, Hamas leader Yahya Sinwar gave an interview to al Jazeera that praised 'popular non-violent struggle.' Although the group has not formally recognized Israel, and while Israeli hawks may cast these developments as attempts to win plaudits from the international community without embracing real change, many analysts interpret this as a break from the past. If the group can make the case that it is not as extremist as it once was, its role in the future of Palestinian politics is only likely to grow.

Culture: As Arabs, and predominantly Muslims, Palestinians share many cultural values of the surrounding countries. Customs regarding food, dress, and limitations on young men mixing with young women are similar to those in Jordan. However, the diversity of personal experiences provides a greater variety of cultural experience than in most Arab states.

Heavily influenced by Marxism and other secular ideas, the Palestine Liberation Organization accepted women as professionals, and many of them dressed in Western styles. With the growth of Islamist militancy, however, women in Gaza and other bastions of Hamas increasingly wear at least a head covering, and conservatives clearly consider a woman's significance to come from her husband or family. Islamists in recent years have discouraged concerts of popular music and dancing. There is only one movie house in the entire Palestinian authority.

The most-recognized Palestinian intellectual in the Western world was undoubtedly Edward Said, the eloquent literary critic and author of *Orientalism* (1978), a serious attack on Western writing and thought about the region. Far closer to contemporary passions, the feature film *Paradise Now*, a joint production of Israelis and Palestinians, portrayed the emotions of two young men recruited as suicide bombers. The movie was nominated for an Oscar in 2006 as best foreign film and it won that category at the Golden Globes.

Economic Prospects: Several recent studies attempt to predict economic conditions in the first years of an independent state. Given the high birthrate, and the possible return of some refugees, the population governed by the PA would climb significantly from current levels. Water use for irrigation, industry, and households by such a dense population would place severe pressure on already limited resources and complicate Israeli dependence on West Bank supplies.

Estimates of the cost of establishing a Palestinian state exceed $14 billion, with large investment in housing, business, industry, and infrastructure. Because independence would likely reduce the number of jobs in Israel, it would also require more economic opportunities in the West Bank and Gaza. Companies linked to Israel would need to shift to other export markets or find alternative suppliers. Given such substantial financial burdens, an independent Palestine located between Israel and Jordan can prosper, at least initially, only with large subsidies from Arab states or other external sources.

The Future: Much of Palestinian agony is not about reducing unemployment a few percentage points or raising GDP growth. Instead, the questions are existential. Will

A Palestinian girl in Gaza

a Palestinian state exist between Israel and the Jordan River? Is a two-state solution viable any longer, given Israeli settlements scattered across much of the land? Will changing demographics—specifically, faster population growth among Palestinians than among Israelis—somehow force a solution? What does the future hold for five million Palestinian refugees and is there any prospect for return? How does Israel's status as a Jewish nation affect the rights of Palestinians (including Israeli citizens of Palestinian heritage)?

Beyond the big picture, things are happening on the ground that raises questions for the future—and at breakneck pace. In 2018 the Palestinian Authority joined yet another intergovernmental organization—the Organization for the Prohibition of Chemical Weapons. This followed the group's decision to join other such entities, such as the International Criminal Court (April 2015) and Interpol (September 2017). Mahmoud Abbas has also submitted a letter to the United Nations seeking membership to its Conference on Trade and Development (UNCTAD).

Membership at the ICC has allowed the Palestinian Authority to take a step that it has long sought: in 2018, the organization asked the court to investigate Israeli crimes in the Palestinian territory. According to Palestinian Foreign Minister Riyad al-Malki, the referral addresses issues ranging from settlement expansion and land grabs to the illegal exploitation of natural resources and the targeting of unarmed protestors in Gaza. Israel's own Foreign Minister has responded to the referral by arguing that "The ICC lacks jurisdiction over the Israeli–Palestinian issue, since Israel is not a member of the Court and because the Palestinian Authority is not a state."

Looming over this and every other development related to the Palestinian Authority is the health of President Mahmoud Abbas. In 2018, the 83-year-old was hospitalized in the West Bank for roughly a week with fever and pneumonia. He has not named a deputy or successor, which has raised important questions about the future of Palestinian leadership. The introduction of yet another failed peace plan, under Trump, will almost certainly raise Palestinian frustrations to new heights. Rejection of the plan by the Palestinians and any ensuing violence is likely to play into the hand of Israel's dominant right wing. More than 70 years after the withdrawal of colonial Britain and the establishment of the State of Israel, Palestinian demands for recognition and statehood appear no closer to fulfillment.

The State of Qatar

The Museum of Islamic Art, Doha, designed by I. M. Pei

Area: 4,416 square miles (11,437 square kilometers).

Population: 2.9 million; nearly 90% non-nationals.

Capital City: Doha (1.5 million).

Climate: Extremely hot and humid except for moderate and dry winters.

Neighboring Countries: Saudi Arabia (South); Bahrain (off Northwest coast); United Arab Emirates (Southeast).

Time Zone: GMT +3.

Official Language: Arabic.

Ethnic Background: The Arab majority is less than half Qatari. Much of the workforce is Iranian or Pakistani.

Principal Religion: Islam (68%, predominantly Sunni), other religious communities are composed almost exclusively of expatriates.

Chief Commercial Products: Liquefied natural gas (LNG), petroleum and petrochemicals, iron and steel, urea and ammonia fertilizers, and some vegetables during the winter.

Major Trading Partners: Japan, the United States, Germany, and China.

Currency: Riyal (1 riyal = 100 dirhams).

Former Colonial Status: British Protectorate, 1916–1971.

National Day: December 18 (1878; Founder's Day, commemoration of Qatar's unification).

Chief of State: Sheikh Tamim bin Hamad Al Thani, Emir

Head of Government: Sheikh Hamid bin Khalifa bin Abdul Aziz Al Thani, Prime Minister.

National Flag: An unadorned maroon field with a broad, serrated vertical band of white at the pole.

Gross Domestic Product: $168 billion

GDP per capita: $61,264.

Qatar occupies a peninsula jutting northward into the Persian Gulf from mainland Arabia. It is little more than 100 miles long (160 kilometers) and varies from 35 to 50 miles in width (55 to 80 kilometers). The terrain is almost entirely

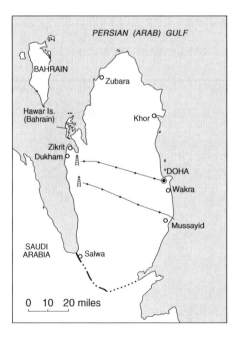

a barren desert of gravel, rock, and sand. Sources of fresh water are extremely scarce. Aside from a few date palms and agricultural experimental stations, the little vegetation is hardy desert scrub.

History: Two fundamentals—dependence on the sea for livelihood and a culture shared with others in the region—have influenced life in Qatar since the Late Stone Age. Given its meager water supplies, Qatar played no significant role in the region's conquests, whether by Alexander the Great's navy, Muslim Arabs nine hundred years later, or occasional Persian rulers. However, archaeological remains from the Abbasid era (9th century) suggest that the inhabitants used their wealth, perhaps from selling pearls, to construct homes and public buildings. When Abbasid prosperity declined in Iraq, so did the population of Qatar. By the 13th century, an Arab geographer considered it just a village.

Safavid Persia claimed the area in the 18th century and taxed coastal communities for their pearling activities. In 1795, Saudi forces captured the important fort of Zubara. The Saudis appointed a governor in 1809, but within a decade the Saudi state collapsed.

Sporadic confusion and disorder marked much of the 19th century. Raids by Gulf towns on each other and on merchant shipping led Britain in 1820 to draft a treaty that committed most Gulf ports to honor a regional truce, but Qatar lacked an acknowledged ruler to sign the document. Fighting later broke out with its traditional rival, Bahrain, whose forces razed the largest town, Doha. Following inconclusive skirmishes, in 1868 Britain negotiated a settlement with Muhammad bin Thani, a leading tribal leader, whose authority gradually spread to the entire peninsula. Before the end of the century, Ottoman Turkish troops had landed, and the population had mostly embraced Wahhabism.

By the early 20th century, four outside powers desired to influence the territory: Bahrain, the Saudis, the Ottoman Empire, and Great Britain. Despite the rivalries, it was at this point that Qatari pearling activities reached their zenith, with hundreds of pearling boats carrying nearly 13,000 crew and divers.

After World War I began, the Ottoman detachment withdrew, and the 1916 Anglo-Qatari treaty ended centuries of legal limbo. It recognized British influence as paramount, gave protection to the pearling fleet, and forbade the slave trade. Qatar was allowed to govern itself under the auspices of the Al Thani family. The country remained almost completely undeveloped in this period, with virtually no medical facilities and only a solitary modern grade school.

The 1930s proved devastating. World demand for jewelry, and thus pearls, fell greatly during the Great Depression. Even worse, the Japanese discovered a method to raise cultured pearls. This created serious competition, leading to sharply falling prices. In 1935 another agreement with Britain granted the Anglo-Persian Oil Company exclusive rights to search for oil. Commercial deposits were discovered in 1939, but World War II postponed

development, and oil exports only began a decade later.

Oil changed Qatari society thoroughly and permanently. The ruling family inevitably squandered some of the new wealth, but oil revenues financed roads, schools, and hospitals. A shortage of local labor led to a steady influx of workers and professionals from other Arab and Muslim nations. Soon Qataris found themselves a minority in their own state.

With British withdrawal from the Gulf on the horizon, Qatar considered federating with Bahrain and the seven sheikhdoms of Trucial Oman (see United Arab Emirates). However, old rivalries stirred distrust, and satisfactory terms could not be negotiated. Qatar then proclaimed its independence and in 1971 it gained membership in the League of Arab States and the United Nations.

As independence neared, the emir approved a basic law for the state. While no charter of democracy, this included a bill of rights and provided a Council of Ministers and an Advisory Council—both appointed by the ruler. Soon after independence, a more cautious and hard-working cousin, Sheikh Khalifa bin Hamad, seized power, blaming his predecessor for squandering financial resources. The ruling family and most Qataris approved the change.

The new emir energetically devoted oil income to economic development, including steel and fertilizer projects. He appointed an advisory council in order to solicit opinions from outside the ruling family. Internationally, he donated generously to Palestinian and other Arab causes.

Given the historically insignificant value of the surrounding uninhabited coral reefs

and expanses of desert, some of Qatar's boundaries had never been demarcated. In 1986 a dispute with Bahrain heated up over Hawar Island, an outcropping of reef whose possession conferred sovereignty over potential oil deposits (see Bahrain). Failing to obtain local mediation, Qatar asked the International Court of Justice to determine its rightful owner. In 2001 the court ruled that Hawar was indeed Bahraini territory, but that the contested town of Zubara belonged to Qatar. Both sides accepted the ruling.

As a member of the Gulf Cooperation Council, Qatar joined the multinational coalition to liberate Kuwait. Its forces fought in the first ground victory of the war, defeating an Iraqi attack on the Saudi city of Khafji.

After years as prime minister, in 1995 Sheikh Hamad overthrew his father Sheikh Khalifa Al-Thani. Much younger than many Gulf rulers, Sheikh Hamad displayed a distinctively independent foreign policy, sometimes labeled "Brand Qatar." The pillars of this approach were: spend wisely; give generously; and keep your name in the public eye. He approved military facilities for U.S. forces, and hosted visits by Israeli officials. He also expressed sympathy with Iran and Iraq.

Sheikh Hamad took initiatives in domestic politics as well. He reduced press censorship and encouraged media discussion of serious issues such as the role of women in public life. Along with greater freedom of speech, he instituted municipal elections. This proved a success with the voters, and five women ran for office, of whom two won.

The constitution issued by Sheikh Hamad and approved in 2003, created a partly-elected advisory parliament and provided a level of democracy surpassed by only Bahrain and Kuwait on the Arab side of the Gulf. Sheikh Hamad has also emphasized the separation of family and state finance.

During the 2003 invasion of Iraq, the United States increasingly used the al-Udaid military base south of Doha. It became a politically safe location because Qatar's small population seemed too rich to protest the bases, whereas many Saudis opposed the presence of U.S. troops on Saudi soil. The U.S. military concentrated its information activities in Doha and installed the latest command facilities at al-Udaid, which became the primary U.S. base in the region.

The combination of growing wealth and Sheikh Hamad's interest in mediating thorny regional problems elevated Qatar's international influence above that expected for its population-size. The emir and his officials successfully mediated between Lebanese factions (2008),

Former Emir Sheikh Hamad and his wife Sheikha Mozah with President and Michelle Obama in 2009. Sheikha Mozah plays a major role in Qatar's culture and education

White House photo

Qatar

An exciting and highly competitive camel race across the desert

Sudan and the Darfur rebels (2011), and the Palestinian rivals Fatah and Hamas (2006). Going beyond the Arab League's call for intervention in Libya in 2011, Qatar dispatched fighter aircraft to police the no-fly zones. It also provided diplomatic support for the Syrian demonstrators and reportedly supplied weapons to Bashar al-Assad's opposition.

In 2013 Sheikh Hamad abdicated in favor of his son, Tamim, then aged 33. By far the youngest ruler in the region, he also enjoyed the first peaceful transition of power in three generations. Educated in Britain, Sheikh Tamim had a passion for sports that led to chairing the organizing committee for the 2006 Asian Games and serving on the International Olympic Committee. He also chaired the Qatar Investment Authority, the state's sovereign investment fund that owns Harrods, the London department store, and has major investments in Western oil and banking companies.

As emir, Sheikh Tamim has broadly supported Qatar's major domestic policies, especially vis-a-vis major infrastructure. However, upon taking office the new ruler quickly enforced modest spending cuts and limits on borrowing by state-owned companies. Some cuts took place in the arts, until then often lavishly funded. One program that has been cut back is the multi-billion dollar Qatar National Food Security Program. As its name implies, its purpose is to produce most of the country's food needs, for the most part using desalinized seawater to support the agricultural sector. While Qatar, similar to other Gulf countries, currently imports at

least 90% of its food requirements, its goal is to meet 60% of domestic food demand from local suppliers by 2024. However, some of the more ambitious goals have been downgraded, as a result of reduced funding.

One of the primary cause of the cutbacks is massive spending for the 2022 FIFA World Cup. Its eight new air-conditioned football (soccer) stadiums and accompanying infrastructure—a rail system, new airport, seaport, and hundreds of miles of expressway—may cost $200 billion, or over $75,000 per resident. Allegations that a former Qatari football official, now disgraced, paid bribes to win votes for Qatar's proposal have cast a shadow over the entire enterprise. More disturbing still are the claims of gross mistreatment of migrant workers engaged in building the World Cup infrastructure. The Nepalese government claims that 1,400 of its 400,000 citizens in Qatar have died on construction sites since 2010, when the Gulf state

Sheikh Tamim bin Hamad Al Thani, Emir of Qatar

won the contract to host the World Cup in 2010. This figure is disputed by the Qatari government, who released a report into the matter in February 2020.

The coronavirus pandemic has again highlighted Qatar's treatment of migrant workers. Human rights activists have raised concerns about the decision of the Qatari government to place Qatar's densely populated and poorly serviced working-class district in lockdown beginning in mid-March.

The new Sheikh is considered more religiously conservative than his father and reportedly sympathizes with Egypt's Muslim Brotherhood. He became emir just as Egypt's President Mohammed Morsi's government was overthrown by General al-Sisi, a setback for one of Qatar's favored causes. Nevertheless, backing for the Brotherhood continued, financially and symbolically. Sermons by Yusuf Qaradawi, a Brotherhood preacher, continued to be broadcast by the Arabic channel of al Jazeera, which is based in Doha. Many of these speeches criticized Arab governments. In response, Saudi Arabia, Kuwait, and the United Arab Emirates withdrew their ambassadors from Qatar in 2014.

The frantic pace of urbanization, economic growth, and pursuit of the consumer culture have imposed significant social costs on native Qataris, as well as on foreign workers engaged in often high-risk construction jobs. In addition to the highest per capita incomes in the world, Qataris enjoy free education, free healthcare, free water, and free electricity. There are job guarantees for those who study;

The ultra-modern Doha Sheraton Hotel

unemployment is the world's lowest. However, financial abundance enables a lifestyle that leaves approximately half of Qataris, adults and children, obese. Perhaps 40% of marriages now end in divorce, and nannies from the Philippines, Nepal, and Indonesia raise most Qatari children. Some believe the family unit, the underpinning social structure of traditional Qatari society, is breaking down.

Culture: Qatar is the only country besides Saudi Arabia with a sizeable Wahhabi community. As most Qataris (but few of its foreign workers) follow Wahhabi practices, strong historical ties link the state with Saudi Arabia.

Like most Arab countries, Qatar's school system provides free education through high school. More than 50,000 children and young people enroll in this twelve-year system. There are also technical schools, a teacher-training school, and a religious institute. The University of Qatar, established in 1973, now has an enrollment of about 8,000, nearly 75% women.

The Qatar Foundation for Education, Science and Community Development opened Education City in 2001, bringing together everything from schools to graduate programs. Six prominent U.S. universities, including Cornell and Carnegie Mellon, and three European universities offer specialized programs on an impressive campus that reflects Qatar's determination to become a leading educational

force in the Middle East. The curricula and textbooks are the same as the home campus, and all instruction is in English.

Qatar's al Jazeera satellite TV station, government-financed but operated independently (at least, relatively so), broadcasts sophisticated critiques, interviews, and debates. The broadcasts occasionally lead some governments to shut down al Jazeera's offices. In 2008, for example, a group of Arab governments attempted to crack down on satellite channels that "offend leaders and religious symbols" of Arab countries, or fail to "protect Arab identity from the harmful effects of globalization." Surveys indicate that audiences across most of the Middle East enjoy its approach, including its persistent political coverage of the region.

Economy: While the traditional Arab lifestyle of nomadic herding existed for centuries, locally the most important industry was pearling. In the relatively shallow waters around the peninsula, mollusks grew thickly enough to permit a flourishing trade involving, at its peak, 13,000 sailors and divers and hundreds of boats. Life aboard pearling vessels was difficult. With no underwater supply of air, most divers sought banks of oysters at depths of about 50 feet (15 meters), descending rapidly and returning to the surface within a minute. The most daring might descend 80 feet (25 meters), but consequent severe health problems were not uncommon.

The international price of pearls climbed rapidly after the 1870s, and an economic system developed to finance pearling expeditions. However, in the 1930s Japanese development of cultured pearls undercut the industry with devastating effect.

After the discovery of oil in Bahrain and Saudi Arabia, it was not surprising that the Anglo-Persian Oil Company (predecessor of today's British Petroleum) found modest quantities of commercial deposits in Qatar. Thanks to its deep port, Umm Said became the center of petroleum operations and industry. Although Qatar today is relatively industrialized in terms of output, industry is concentrated in a small area.

The oil price increases of the 1970s provided enormous wealth. The government bought out the subsidiaries of foreign companies producing in the country, and by 1977 all production came under its Qatar General Petroleum Company.

Recognizing that oil deposits were fairly small, the government adopted a deliberate policy of diversification away from petroleum. By the late 1990s, exports of steel, aluminum, fertilizers, and other petrochemicals based on natural gas partly offset the decline in oil revenues. Qatar is becoming the Middle East's largest producer of ammonia and urea fertilizers, with export markets in India, China, and Japan.

The most important diversification was the development of Liquefied Natural

Qatar

Gas (LNG). Liquefaction is the only practical means of transporting natural gas to markets that lack pipelines to them, but it requires expensive facilities, known as "trains," to convert the gas to a highly explosive liquid at –256° Fahrenheit (–160° Celsius) and only 1/600th the original volume. Specially designed ships then carry the liquid to another "train" near the consumer, which transforms it back to gas.

In 1997, Qatar shipped its first exports of LNG, and East Asia became a major market. However, in 2005 Qatar Petroleum and ExxonMobil began to build the world's largest LNG refinery at a cost of $14 billion. Its two "trains" produce 15 million tons of LNG per year, originally for the U.S. market but now shipped elsewhere since the great increase in U.S. natural gas output due to fracturing shale. Qatar is the greatest LNG producer in the world.

The North Shore gas field below the waters of the Gulf is enormous. Its reserves, estimated at 900 trillion cubic feet, suffice to place the country third in global proven reserves, behind Russia and Iran. Since world demand for LNG is limited mostly to electric generating plants, Qatar seeks additional uses for natural gas. A joint Qatari-South African venture opened a gas-to-liquids refinery in 2006 to produce environmentally cleaner low-sulfur diesel.

However, the process is tremendously expensive. With a competitor's plant expected to cost $18 billion, in 2007 ExxonMobil abandoned a similar project.

With both gas and oil exports immensely profitable in recent years, Qatar's per capita incomes are the highest in the world.

The Blockade Against Qatar and the Future: In June 2017, four Arab states—Bahrain, Egypt, Saudi Arabia, and the UAE—cut diplomatic, economic, travel, and other ties with the peninsula. The main reason cited was Qatari support for terrorism. However, this is only part of the story. Key to understanding the rift between Qatar and the four Arab states, is Qatar's relationship with Iran. In contrast to its primarily Sunni neighbors, Qatar has sought to cultivate its relationship with the Shi'a power, recognizing that the two share the world's largest natural gas field and an important maritime border. The break with Qatar represents a backlash against that policy at a moment when Saudi Arabia and others, newly empowered by assurances from Washington, are competing against Iran on several fronts—militarily, economically, and otherwise.

When the blockade was initially imposed in mid-2017, few analysts had a clear idea of how long the dispute would last or which side would first back down. The ultimatum that Saudi Arabia and the other states delivered to Qatar, a list of more than a dozen non-negotiable demands, was a non-starter in Doha. It was essentially a call for the state to give up any autonomy in its foreign policy. Two years on, Qatar appears to be weathering the storm. Pressure is increasing on Saudi Arabia and the other parties to do more to justify their policy or back down. Whereas in the United States, President Trump initially sided with the Saudi coalition, a year later he was sending Secretary of State Mike Pompeo to Riyadh to push for a resolution.

The crisis has forced the state to implement reforms that, being one of the richest countries in the world in per capita terms, it had previously had little incentive to do. This includes the addition of new trade routes and increased trade with certain partners (especially Turkey and Iran), the relaxation of visa requirements to encourage more visitors and tourism, and substantial investments in infrastructure. Furthermore, just as Saudi Arabia, Bahrain, and the UAE are cracking down on any criticism of the policy, thus limiting freedom of expression even further in those states, Qatar is adopting more tolerant policies. Admittedly, it helps that the population has almost uniformly rallied around the emir and that it does not blame him for the crisis.

None of this is to say that the embargo hasn't been tough on Qatar. The national airline took a substantial loss during the first year of the crisis and continues to lose money. The unprecedented global freeze on international movement, in the light of the 2020 Covid-19 pandemic, had additional significant economic impact on Qatar. As a major transit hub, the airport in Doha saw a precipitous drop in passenger numbers from mid-March. Over a period of just weeks, Qatar Airways saw most of its capacity disappear. As a result, flights were slashed.

The ongoing blockade of Qatar by its neighbors was intensified by a campaign of Twitter disinformation, much of it generated by bots, which blamed the Gulf country for, variously, developing Covid-19, sponsoring its development by China, and intentionally (or negligently) spreading it.

At the end of the day, the biggest rift between GCC states in decades is likely doing more economic harm to Qatar than to the countries that have imposed the embargo, but Qatar seems to be winning in the court of public international opinion. The dispute cannot go on indefinitely, but Qatar continues to be a rich state and shows little inclination to yield to the unreasonable demands of its neighbors.

Qatari woman weaving intricately-designed heavy rugs

Masmak Fortress Riyadh   Courtesy of the Royal Embassy of Saudi Arabia

Saudi Arabia

Area: 830,000 square miles (2,150,000 square kilometers).

Population: 34.9 million, 26% non-nationals (with estimates of several million additional undocumented residents and visa overstayers who don't appear in any official population statistics).

Capital: Riyadh (7.7 million).

Climate: Very hot and dry, but humid on coasts; at higher elevations nights are cool. Rain is negligible except in the southwestern highlands.

Neighboring countries: Jordan (Northwest); Iraq (North); Kuwait (Northeast); Qatar (East); the United Arab Emirates (East); Oman (Southeast); Yemen (South).

Time Zone: GMT +3. Solar time, calculated daily from sunset, is used for religious purposes.

Official Language: Arabic.

Other Principal Tongues: English, in commerce and in some schools.

Ethnic Background: Arab

Religion: Islam (84% Sunni, 10% Shi'a), the remaining 6% is comprised of non-Muslim foreign workers.

Chief Commercial Products: Petroleum, dates, salt, gypsum, cement, wool, grain, hides, fish, chemical fertilizers, plastics, and steel.

Major Trading Partners: The United States, Japan, France, Italy, Germany, and the Netherlands.

Currency: Riyal (1 riyal = 100 halalah).

Former Colonial Status: Ottoman rule in the west; British advisors in the east.

National Day: Only religious holidays are officially observed.

Chief of State: Salman bin Abd al-Aziz Al Saud, King and Prime Minister.

Leading Royal Aide: Mohammad bin Salman Al Saud, Crown Prince.

National Flag: The Islamic creed in ornate Arabic script is written in white on a green field; beneath the writing is a horizontal sword, also in white.

Gross Domestic Product: $687 billion.

GDP per capita: $20,747.

Covering more than two-thirds of the Arabian Peninsula, Saudi Arabia is one of the bleakest desert countries in the world. It has no rivers, no perennial streams, and no lakes. Most of its total surface is rock, gravel, or sand. Less than 1% of the land has enough natural moisture for agriculture of any kind. There are no real forests; only sparse desert plants survive. Nearly one-third of the area is used seasonally as scrub brush grazing land.

From west to east, the country's terrain begins in the Hijaz, with a coastal plain along the Red Sea. A chain of mountains then rises steeply, from Jordan in the north to Yemen in the south. With peaks ranging up to 10,000 feet (3,000 meters), the

mountains in the south catch some precipitation and allow limited agriculture. Further inland, the land slopes down gradually toward the Persian Gulf. The central region, known as *Najd* ("steppe"), receives only two or three inches (five to seven centimeters) of rainfall annually, while much of the southern area receives none at all in most years.

Known as the *Rub' al-Khali,* or "Empty Quarter," the south contains virtually no permanent habitation, but the largest stretch of sand in the world. It is a region of giant, seemingly endless sand dunes, often several hundred feet high and miles in length; eternally shifting, pushed by the hot desert winds. Finally, along the Gulf

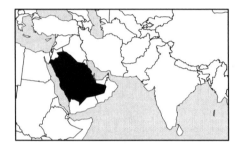

coast stretches the Eastern Province, Hasa, with a hot, humid climate and an abundance of oil.

History: A land of nomadic tribes and scattered oasis settlements, Arabia was never united until Muhammad proclaimed his prophetic messages and established an Islamic government with its capital at Medina (see Historical Background). However, after Ali, the fourth caliph, moved the capital to Iraq, Arabia lost much of its political importance, though Mecca and Medina retained significant religious roles.

When the later caliphs in Damascus and Baghdad lost control of the united Muslim world, most of Arabia returned to tribal rule. Outside influence was greatest in the Hijaz, thanks to the pilgrimage and the general prestige of Islam's origins. Ottoman sovereignty was proclaimed there in the 1500s.

The origins of the Saudi kingdom lie in the 17th century, when Muhammad ibn Saud, a tribal leader in Najd, accepted the teaching of Muhammad ibn Abd al-Wahhab. After study in Damascus and Baghdad, Abd al-Wahhab had become convinced of the need to reform and purify

166

Abd al-Aziz Al-Saud, King of Saudi Arabia, 1932–53

sacrilegious traditions. At the end of 1924 the Ikhwan entered Mecca and within a year took Medina also. In 1926 Abd al-Aziz was proclaimed "King of Hijaz." After repressing a revolt by the Ikhwan, in 1932 he formed his various domains into the Kingdom of Saudi Arabia. Satisfied with his conquests, and blocked from further expansion by Transjordan and Iraq, King Abd al-Aziz turned to consolidating the country he ruled.

Unhampered by a constitution or democracy, his autocracy nevertheless faced limits from the Wahhabi religious leaders and from the ruling family, enlarged by his many marriages to daughters of tribal leaders. Moreover, the kingdom was poor: for many years pilgrims visiting the Hijaz were its economic mainstay.

The discovery of oil in Hasa in 1938 marked the beginning of a new era, but significant petroleum production was delayed by World War II (see Economy). By the late 1940s, oil revenues began to pour into the country, and the aging Abd al-Aziz faced the challenges of corruption common to the arrival of such wealth. His numerous sons and relatives squandered millions of dollars monthly and every transactions often involved payments of suitable bribes to officials.

Reforms under Faisal

Since 1953, Saudi Arabia has been ruled by one of the 37 sons of Abd al-Aziz. The reign of Faisal, the second to rule, witnessed gradual but limited reforms that became the pattern of nearly all subsequent changes. Faisal shared the oil wealth, but limited abuses by family members. He greatly increased budgets for education, medical care and transportation facilities. However, he rejected many aspects of westernization and made little effort to promote social change. He refused to allow free political expression or formal public participation in government. The traditional Saudi social system spread responsibility over a large number of relatives, and politically it provided access to the royal family for even the poorest citizen. Rather than replace these features, Faisal worked to render them more honest and efficient.

In international affairs, Faisal proved a cautious conservative willing to work quietly for his goals. He sought better relations with neighboring states and naturally opposed any communist or other revolutionary influences in the Arab world. Only after Egypt's defeat in the 1967 Arab–Israeli War ended its revolutionary propaganda would Faisal cooperate with it.

Another pivotal Saudi issue was support for Palestinian Arabs. Faisal, and his brothers who ruled after him, considered Jerusalem to be Islam's third holiest city, and he wished to pray there under an Arab and

Muslim society of pagan practices among the Bedouin and philosophical and secular influences in the cities.

Strengthened by the appeal of these teachings, known to Westerners as Wahhabism, during the 18th century Saudi troops and Wahhabi believers conquered large parts of central Arabia and raided north into Syria. During the Napoleonic wars, the Wahhabis conquered the Hijaz, seizing from the Ottoman sultan the holy places of Mecca and Medina that he claimed to protect. However, the Wahhabis had overextended. Muhammad Ali, the ruler of Egypt, defeated the Saudi fighters and even destroyed their capital. Rival Arab rulers encroached on Saudi lands.

By 1902, the heir to leadership was a 28-year-old exile, Abd al-Aziz Al Saud. With only a handful of followers, he undertook a daring mission to restore family fortunes, seizing Riyadh, the capital, from the rival family of Rashid.

With a natural gift for leadership, Abd al-Aziz gradually enlarged the area of his

control by victories over rival tribes. In 1913 he conquered the eastern coastal district of Hasa from the Ottoman Turks, not knowing that years later the oil under its sands would make him one of the world's wealthiest men. During World War I, Abd al-Aziz promised the British that he would not join the Turks against England; for this he was rewarded with $25,000 a year.

Dominant in central Arabia by 1921, Abd al-Aziz turned against his remaining rival, Sharif Husayn (Hussein) of the Hijaz. Supported by Britain during his revolt against the Turks, Husayn was a difficult character, and harbored great ambitions. In pursuit of them, he adopted the imprecise title "King of the Arabs" and hinted at proclaiming himself caliph, thereby outraging Arabs of many different backgrounds.

Abd al-Aziz's followers, the militant *Ikhwan* ("Brotherhood") who relinquished tribal loyalties for Wahhabism, were eager to cleanse the holy cities of Mecca and Medina from what they considered

Saudi Arabia

Islamic flag, rather than a Jewish one. To that end, Saudi Arabia paid funds directly to the Palestinian leadership, to Arab countries partly occupied by Israel in 1967, and to the UN, to care for Palestinian refugees.

Like his father, Faisal worked closely with the United States. However, Saudi Arabia did join the Organization of Petroleum Exporting Countries (OPEC), and during the Arab–Israeli war of October 1973 Faisal proclaimed an embargo on all oil shipments to the energy-short U.S. until he was "able again to pray in Jerusalem under an Arab flag." He ended the embargo in 1974 in exchange for vague assurances concerning Israeli withdrawal from Jerusalem.

While the embargo was not fully effective, it was accompanied by a reported 10% cut in oil exports. Against the background of tight world oil supplies, these Saudi moves enabled OPEC to raise the price of oil about 400%. A flood of oil revenues resulted, and Faisal reaped a great increase in prestige at home and abroad.

Four years after King Faisal was shot fatally by a nephew, the government, royal family, and outside world were stunned in 1979 when Islamic extremists seized the Grand Mosque in Mecca and called for revolution. After crushing the rebellion and executing some participants, the

Saudis responded with reforms, in particular for the Shi'a inhabitants of the eastern province bordering on the Gulf. The mosque's takeover emphasized the importance of maintaining royal links with the *ulama'*, or Muslim scholars, and it also served to warn that social changes should not overtake cultural and religious values.

Invasion and the Gulf War, 1990–91

The 1990 Iraqi seizure of Kuwait placed Saudi Arabia in grave peril. Iraqi forces in Kuwait alone numbered three times the total Saudi military (although the Saudis enjoyed vastly better equipment). Baghdad threatened to attack if its oil exports across Saudi Arabia were halted, as the UN Security Council demanded. Enormously complicated oil installations—wells, pipelines, tank farms, refineries, and ports—lay within range of Iraqi missiles and bombers. Moreover, if he kept Kuwait's oil wealth, Iraq's President Saddam Hussein would control reserves and output rivaling Saudi Arabia's, upsetting the balances of power in both the Arab world and OPEC.

The political threat also seemed substantial. Saddam Hussein's invective against the Kuwaiti ruling family mocked all Gulf dynasties, including the Al Sauds. Demands that Arab oil wealth support all

Arabs stirred popular resentment among poor Arabs everywhere and threatened isolation from the Arab world.

Acceptance of the U.S. offer to defend Saudi Arabia and liberate Kuwait also carried risks. To many Muslims, the "Protector of the Two Holy Places" must not depend on "infidel" troops. Some Arab nationalists condemned an attack by Israel's ally (the United States) against Israel's strongest enemy, Iraq. Domestic opponents could scorn defense by "Jews and women" and religious conservatives would take offense at the display of Western lifestyles ranging from Christmas, to unveiled women actively serving in the military. Hosting foreign troops also risked the presence of foreign politicians and journalists, who could and did circulate unflattering commentary on the lack of Western-style democracy.

Despite these risks, King Fahd and his government quickly requested troops from a coalition force of Arab and western nations. After the United Nations deadline passed for Iraq to evacuate Kuwait on January 15, 1991, Coalition aircraft, often from Saudi bases, largely destroyed Iraq's military and infrastructure. In response, Iraqi Scud missiles targeted Riyadh and along with oil and military installations in the Eastern Province. Damage did occur,

The modern Red Sea port of Jidda

Jidda Tomorrow: The $1 billion Jeddah Tower complex is expected to soar 3,284 feet at completion in 2020

notably to a Muslim religious college in Riyadh and barracks housing Americans in Dhahran. An Iraqi tank column also assaulted the city of Khafji but was repulsed by Saudi and Qatari troops. Rather than undermine the government, the attacks generally served to increase patriotism among Saudi civilians, including the minority Shi'a of the Eastern Province. Saudi ground forces played an important role in the recapture of Kuwait City.

Like many wars, this one, with thousands of foreign soldiers, created expectations of reform. Partly in response, in 1992 King Fahd proposed a formal, written constitution, with a *Majlis al-Shura*, or consultative council, and he appointed the council's 90 members. He gave them no executive powers, however. The country was not becoming a democracy: the king remained commander of the armed forces, chief administrator, and dispenser of the royal treasury.

Terrorism and Counter-terrorism

By 2001, relations with the United States—the country's major ally—showed signs of strain. Most Saudis sympathized with the Palestinians and rightly believed that the Bush cabinet strongly backed Israel. This sentiment led officials to call off high-level military talks in Washington just days before the September 11 terrorist attacks.

News that fifteen of the nineteen 9/11 hijackers came from Saudi Arabia placed the kingdom on the ideological defensive. In addition to repeating long-standing concerns about human rights violations like harsh justice and the treatment of women, critics made three particular allegations.

First, Saudi policy had created a society that encouraged radical fundamentalist religious groups. Extending its long-standing alliance with doctrinaire Wahhabi leaders, in the decades after the Iranian revolution of 1979, the state funded a rapid increase in religious schools. Years later, their graduates, ill-equipped for employment in business or technology, formed a pool of potential extremists.

Second, al-Qaeda and other militant Islamic groups had been funded, knowingly or not, by contributions to various charities. Critics suspected that the regime had reached an unspoken understanding with the religious militants. If they spared the kingdom from their violent attacks, militant organizations could raise funds for various causes.

Third, some U.S. critics claimed the kingdom was not a genuine ally. It refused permission for U.S. bases in the kingdom to launch aircraft against the Taliban and al-Qaeda in Afghanistan. The government also rejected use of its territory for an attack on Iraq, even if the UN approved the invasion.

With limited success, Crown Prince Abdullah and others explained that the West's enemy was not Islam, but rather a few misguided individuals. In addition, they argued that Western nations' support for Israel weakened the position of moderate Arab governments friendly to the United States. Ultimately, the monarchy found itself trapped between U.S. policy and the Islamic and Arab values of its population. It proposed a comprehensive plan for Arab–Israeli peace, but Washington ignored the proposal and some preachers at home condemned it as compromising.

In 2003, the two governments announced the closure of American bases, but regardless within a month simultaneous suicide car-bombers struck three residential complexes for foreigners in Riyadh, killing or wounding scores of Westerners and Saudis. The next year, terrorists struck repeatedly in Riyadh, in Yanbu, and at a luxury business and hotel complex in Khobar. Individual Westerners also became targets, a policy that had the potential to harm the oil industry.

The security situation worsened as militants murdered non-Muslims in cold blood. This shook international confidence in the government's ability to protect foreign workers. In response, Prince Nayef bin Abd al-Aziz, the minister of the interior, launched a vigorous assault on the extremists. Police hunted them in Mecca and fought several pitched battles elsewhere, eventually killing a number and seizing large caches of weapons. Some of those arrested reportedly suffered torture; those convicted of murder were publicly beheaded. By 2005, terrorist attacks had diminished, and most militants known to the government were dead or in captivity.

Nevertheless, the violence confirmed that extremists drew strength and political allure from the country's economic and political malaise. Hundreds of Saudi men a decade earlier had trained with Osama bin Laden in Afghanistan. These "Arab Afghans" maintained loose ties and spread their messages by fax and the web, as well as sermons. Their proclamations advocated replacing corruption with morality, repression with legitimate Islamic government, and weakness with a strong military. This morally pure critique appealed to the young, often unemployable graduates of religious schools.

Pressures for Reform

Confronted by declining standards of living, high unemployment, allegations of corruption, and heavy-handed policies by the justice system and religious police, many Saudi civilians strongly desire change. However, public opinion has been deeply divided about the direction of reform. Advocates of greater personal liberty inevitably clash with preachers blaming lax morality for social decline. Because each side's essential reforms reach deep into personal lives, the pathway to reform remains as dangerous as it is vital.

Often influenced by their higher education in the West, the country's relatively few liberals, advocate greater personal liberty and a softening of the harshest elements of the Shari'a. Some concentrate on economic reforms, such as wider roles for private business and reduced regulation of them. Others desire social changes, including fewer restrictions on women. The first formal elections in the country's history were the municipal elections in 2004–05. However, with political parties banned, religious conservatives won most seats, and at least initially the councils accomplished little.

When King Fahd died in 2005, his half-brother, Crown Prince Abdullah, ascended the throne. Having already served as the de facto ruler for perhaps a decade, Abdullah encouraged several types of reform. He curbed privileges for members of the royal family (such as free water, free electricity, and free tickets on Saudia, the national airline). He also favored the country's successful application to the World Trade Organization, and sought to raise the standard of competition and streamline bureaucracy. In the political realm, he championed elections for half the city councilmen, although these were won by religious conservatives and did not meet often. In 2009, his gradual efforts at reform resulted in the dismissal of both the head of the religious police and the country's most senior judge, who had earlier approved killing the owners of satellite TV channels that offered immoral content. He also appointed a woman as government minister, a first for the country.

King Salman bin Abd al-Aziz

169

Responding to the Arab Spring

Despite protests in the Eastern province among the Shi'a population, and attempts by liberal activists' to use social media to organize demonstrations and demand reforms—such as the implementation of a constitution—the wave of demonstrations that swept the Arab world in 2011 largely missed Saudi Arabia. King Abdullah apparently calmed potential unrest by promising major spending increases. A half-million housing units would be built for low-income families, and a minimum wage was established. Unemployment benefits would begin with a monthly stipend of $250, and some 60,000 new security jobs were promised to reduce youth unemployment. University students received extra grants, while government workers gained two months' extra pay. If those promises were to eventually be delivered, they would cost an estimated $130 billion.

The arrests of peaceful dissidents, including Shi'a protestors, reinforced the powerful image of the near-absolute monarchy. Clearly, the pre-conditions for popular demonstrations like those of the Arab Spring could not be permitted. A blogger who declared May 7 "a day for Saudi liberals" was arrested and charged with apostasy, a capital offense. Among other offenses, he had apparently pressed the "Like" button on a Facebook page for Arab Christians. Although a court later refused to charge him, he remained imprisoned. Similarly, a court dissolved the Saudi Civil and Political Rights Association and sentenced its founders to lengthy prison terms.

The kingdom also moved to calm popular agitation beyond its borders. Grants of $10 billion each were provided Bahrain and Oman, the two neighboring countries with significant protests. Additionally, Saudi security forces entered Bahrain to ensure that demonstrations there did not lead to the downfall of the king. Riyadh often sought to link protests in neighboring countries to Shi'a dissidents and, by extension, to Iran.

If Saudi Arabia holds Iran responsible for the restlessness of Shi'a populations across the region, the origins of Sunni dissent is often pinned on the Muslim Brotherhood. A transnational Sunni Islamist organization founded in Egypt in the early 20th century, the Muslim Brotherhood has long condemned rule by kings as contrary to Islam. As such, the election of Muslim Brother Mohammed Morsi as president of Egypt created a serious rift between the two countries. Riyadh welcomed General al-Sisi's ouster of Morsi in 2013, and together with Kuwait and the United Arab Emirates provided billions of dollars in financing for Egypt.

Courtesy of the Royal Embassy of Saudi Arabia

King Abdullah has played a significant role in international efforts to address the civil war in Syria, that began when regime forces attacked demonstrators who supported the Arab Spring. The kingdom funded opposition groups, including religious extremists, advocated resolutions against Syria at the Arab League and United Nations, and reportedly provided military assistance in the form of light weapons and ammunition to the broader opposition.

Involvement in Syria led to disillusionment both with the Syrian opposition and the kingdom's long-time partner, the

United States. Deprived of the anti-tank and anti-aircraft missiles necessary to defeat the Syrian military, the opposition splintered. Salafist groups such as Jabhat al-Nusra and IS (the Islamic State), both with origins linked to al-Qaeda, proved the most successful on the battlefield. While to an outsider they share many religious similarities with Saudi Wahhabism, in reality these Salafist groups are bitter critics of Gulf rulers.

Saudi foreign policy difficulties increased when IS, with the evident assistance of Sunni tribes, rapidly captured Mosul and large parts of northern and western Iraq in

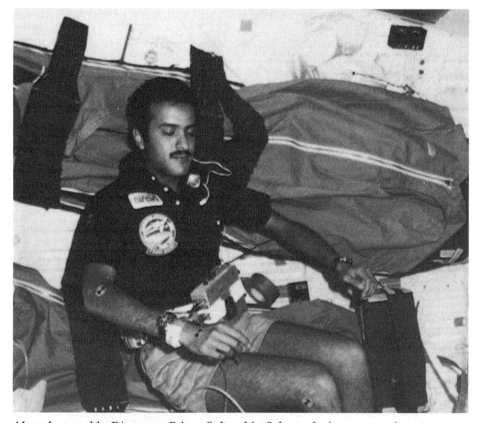

Aboard spaceship *Discovery*: Prince Sultan bin Salman during an experiment.

Courtesy: NASA

2014. Concerned about its own restive Shi'a minority, the Saudi government naturally sympathized with Sunnis in Iraq who had suffered loss of influence and repression during the long rule of Shi'a Prime Minister Nouri al-Maliki. But the Islamic State's self-proclaimed caliphate in Iraq's Sunni Arab territory, also threatened the Islamic legitimacy of Arab monarchies.

Since 2015, Saudi Arabia has led a coalition of forces providing military support to the pro-Saudi Yemeni government, against the Shi'a Houthi rebels. Belonging to the Zaidi sect of Shi'ism, the Houthis emerged as a militant outfit in northern Yemen, against a backdrop of government corruption, economic underdevelopment, and political and social marginalization of Shi'a. As the situation has continued to deteriorate in Yemen, it has becoming increasingly clear that a proxy war between, on the one hand, Saudi Arabia's (mostly) Arab allies backed by the United States, the United Kingdom, and France, and, on the other, Iran, is being fought. Tens of thousands of Yemeni civilians have lost their lives as a direct consequence of the fighting (the vast majority in the context of Saudi bombing campaigns), with almost a quarter of a million more estimated to have died as a result of famine, lack of access to safe drinking water, and disease. In 2019, Yemen remains the most significant extant humanitarian crisis.

Saudi Arabia has long considered Iran its most prominent rival. The Saudis fear that Iran still desires to export the ideology of its Islamic revolution. Iran's very existence as a (Shi'a) Islamic Republic threatens the legitimacy of the Saudi throne and is seen to have the potential to incite the Saudi Shi'a against the monarchy. Saudi leaders fear that the so-called "Shi'a crescent" of Iraq, Alawi-dominated Syria, and Lebanese Hizbullah, may become a "Shi'a full moon," as Sunni Arab states fall under Iran's influence.

Lacking any nuclear weapons program of their own, the kingdom's leaders have strongly criticized Iran's program. The U.S. withdrawal from the Joint Comprehensive Plan of Action (the Iran nuclear deal) under President Trump, has shone new light on the shared regional aims of Washington, Riyadh, and Tel Aviv.

Saudi Arabia also joined Kuwait and the United Arab Emirates in pressuring Qatar to end its support for the Brotherhood, even withdrawing its ambassador from Doha.

In his last years, Abdullah reshuffled his cabinet, replacing several but not all long-serving ministers. He also created a new institution to guide the succession, the Allegiance Committee. Composed of sons and grandsons of Abd al-Aziz, it can reject the king's nominee and thereby force

discussion of other potential heirs. The group approved Abdullah's final appointments, long-time governor of Riyadh, Salman bin Abd al-Aziz, as crown prince and Prince Muqrin, the youngest son of Abd al-Aziz, as his deputy. Abdullah carried his modest reforms further by reviving the Majlis al-Shura and appointing 30 women among its 150 members. Also, for the first time in history women were able to vote in the 2015 municipal elections.

The Ascension of King Salman, 2015

King Abdullah died in early 2015 after a short illness. According to Wahhabi custom, public grieving was restrained and he was buried in an unmarked grave. The royal transition was smooth, and King Salman, 79, immediately confirmed Prince Muqrin as crown prince, as expected. It was the designation of Prince Muhammad bin Nayef, the son of Salman's late full brother, as deputy crown prince that created real excitement. Muhammad bin Nayef became the first grandson of Abd al-Aziz to be listed in the succession, marking the ascension of a new generation to Saudi leadership.

Three months later, Salman showed his real intentions. He removed Prince Muqrin as crown prince, and promoted to the position Muhammad bin Nayef, who at 55 was far younger than his predecessors. Moreover, the king's own thirty-something son, Defense Minister Muhammad bin Salman, became deputy crown prince. This cemented the rule of the "Sudairi faction" of Abd al-Aziz's sons, it seems likely that Salman will be the last son of 'Abd al-Aziz to serve as king.

King Salman's record as governor of Riyadh encouraged those who considered him progressive and likely to accomplish change, but critics considered him reactionary, pointing to his appointment of Muhammad bin Nayef, whose police had shot Shi'a protestors, as proof.

Very likely, King Salman is most concerned about security, external and internal. Jihadist cells were being suppressed just before he became king, so it seemed logical to strengthen the kingdom with the steady hands of Prince Muhammed at the interior ministry, where he had directed the suppression of al-Qaeda a decade earlier. Threatened on the southern border by Yemen's Shi'a Houthi militia, and on the north by the Islamic State expanding across Iraq, Saudi Arabia needed an activist minister of defense. Who better than his own son, Muhammad, who directed the brutal air war against the Houthis?

The Next King

In a royal decree issued in 2017, endorsed by 31 of the 34 members of Saudi Arabia's Allegiance Council (a high-level

advisory body made up of members of the royal family), King Salman promoted his son, Muhammad bin Salman, to the role of Crown Prince. In doing so, he displaced Muhammad bin Nayef from the role, elevated other princes from other branches of the family to signal that they would continue to have prominent roles in Saudi governance, and conditioned the promotion on the inability of Muhammad to eventually appoint one of his own sons as successor. This was a monumental development in Saudi politics. Muhammad bin Salman is poised to take the throne in the next decade and, given his youth, could well lead the country for decades to come.

In late 2017 and early 2018 the crown prince took surprisingly aggressive steps to consolidate his power. In the process he sought to mitigate a serious corruption problem in the kingdom and to pave the way for modernization. His boldest actions involved rounding up and arresting hundreds of members of the Saudi political and economic elite, including 11 members of the royal family. The most important of these individuals were detained for varying lengths of time at the Ritz-Carlton hotel in Riyadh, before eventually being released on the condition that they turn over substantial sums that the crown prince believed (likely correctly) to be ill-gained. The development was pitched to the international community as an effort to rid the kingdom of any corrupt influences that might inhibit foreign investment. The real effect was that it left no question as to who was in control of the country: not the king, but the crown prince.

At the same time, the kingdom has been moving forward with implementation of its strategic "Vision 2030," an ambitious plan that aims to modernize the state in a variety of ways. The most important aspect of Vision 2030 is the plan to diversify Saudi Arabia's economy away from oil dependency. The program toward economic reform incorporates a broad range of social reforms. Recent developments include the reopening of cinemas in Saudi Arabia, the end of a long-standing ban on female drivers (a ban that existed in practice if not technically in law), and the arrest of dozens of extremist clerics. These reforms have raised —hopes that the crown prince can guide his country toward the adoption of a more moderate version of Islam.

The early actions of the crown prince—such as lifting the aforementioned ban on female drivers, passing anti-harassment laws, and taking measures to gradually reduce segregation—were widely celebrated as evidence of a new, positive direction in Saudi society. However, critics of Muhammad bin Salman were skeptical. According to a UN special rapporteur on

171

Saudi Arabia

anti-terrorism, speaking in 2018, "Under Crown Prince Muhammad bin Salman, Saudi Arabia is undergoing the most ruthless crackdown on political dissent that the country has experienced in decades." Notably, in the month prior to the June 2018 lifting of the driving ban, a number of the most prominent campaigners behind the women-to-drive movement were arrested and remain in the detention to the present day.

One of the crown prince's most vociferous critics was Jamal Khashoggi—a dissident journalist living in self-imposed exile in the United States and writing for the Washington Post. Opposed to the crown prince's domestic policies, Khashoggi was also an outspoken opponent of Mohammad bin Salman's military campaign in Yemen. In October 2018, Khashoggi entered the Saudi consulate in Istanbul, where he met what was, by all accounts, a grisly demise. To date, the saga has cost several high profile Saudis their positions and a number of arrests have been made. However, the crown prince, who is widely held to have been behind Khashoggi's murder, appears to have gone unscathed. However, in 2019, a UN special rapporteur revealed new details of the slaying, insisting that there was "credible evidence" to warrant further investigation and financial sanctions against Saudi Crown Prince Mohammed bin Salman. The report is likely to increase pressure on U.S. President Donald Trump, who has been reluctant to sever close ties to the crown prince and the Saudi regime more generally.

In mid-2017, Saudi Arabia and three other Arab states—Bahrain, Egypt, and the UAE—announced the imposition of an embargo against Qatar. Trade was suspended; borders were closed; Qatari nationals were expelled from other Gulf states. Saudi Arabia claimed that the core of the break was Qatar's support for terrorism, but the roots of the problem undoubtedly go deeper. Though it is true that Qatar has provided financial and other support to extremists in recent years—especially in the war against Assad in Syria—Saudi Arabia has done the same. In fact, Qatar and Saudi Arabia have at times supported the same extremist groups.

The deeper reasons are many, but Qatar's relationship with Iran holds a special place in the discussion. In contrast to its primarily Sunni neighbors, Qatar has sought to cultivate positive and enduring relationships with all of its regional neighbors, including the Shi'a power. In a moment when Iran appears to be on the rise, and with growing power across the Middle East, Saudi Arabia is pushing back on all fronts. Kinetic competition in Syria and Yemen has now extended to diplomatic competition in Qatar.

How long the break can hold is unclear, but after two years there are few signs that either side of the dispute is willing to back down. Iran and Turkey have come to Qatar's aid, and the United States and Kuwait continue to try to broker a rapprochement, but the end game in this dispute remains unclear.

Culture: To understand the workings of Saudi Arabia, one must appreciate some aspects of its social structure, such as the unwritten laws relating to kinship. The most important unit is the extended family or clan: all descendants from a common ancestor carry responsibilities to one another. In the era of tribal desert raids, this system protected individuals. Membership in the family system is based on male descent; a person belongs to the same clan as the father's family, but not necessarily the mother's family and clan. The House of Saud, the ruling family in Saudi Arabia, is just such a clan—these relatives have the duty of looking after their collective interests.

Groups of clans that allied together historically and believe they share descent from a common ancestor form a tribe. Until the establishment of the kingdom there was no important group larger than the tribe. They often skirmished with each other despite forming temporary alliances.

As Saudis gain more wealth, travel abroad, and study in universities, traditionally strong family bonds seem to be weakening. Conservative Saudis associate these weaker bonds with lowered ethical and moral standards and even illegal drugs. Naturally, Saudi leaders seek to maintain the strong sense of family loyalty and discipline, considering them an underpinning value of Islam.

The Hajj and the Role of Islam

The Prophet Muhammad lived and recited the words of the Quran in the western province of the Hijaz. All Muslims, and thus about one human in six, regard the land as holy and bear the obligation to perform the Hajj, the pilgrimage to Mecca, at least once in their lifetimes if they have the means. Over two million pilgrims annually perform the *Hajj*. All of them hope to spend the same five days praying at the Grand Mosque, circling the Ka'aba with its black stone, and joining the final ceremonies on Mount Arafat, where Muhammad preached his last sermon. Transported by 10,000 buses from Jeddah to Mecca, most pilgrims sleep in a vast tent city, where they meet fellow-believers from across the globe. They slaughter half a million animals as sacrifices.

Given the size of the crowds, Saudi officials attempt to take careful precautions, screening for communicable diseases and

Saudi Pilgrims congregate near the Ka'aba in Mecca.

providing the services of thousands of medical personnel, guards, food preparers and cleaners. After an inferno killed hundreds in the 1990s, the authorities supplied fireproof tents and carved large water storage tunnels in nearby mountains. They also widened narrow passageways where there was the risk of pilgrims being crushed in the massive crowds. Nevertheless, disasters continue, most notably in 2015, when well over 2000 pilgrims were killed—crushed and suffocated—when a panicked stampede began during the annual Hajj. With almost 500 of those killed Iranian nationals, tensions between Saudi Arabia and Iran ratcheted up.

A day, in Saudi Arabia, was traditionally observed beginning not at midnight, but at sunset. This meant that in spring when the daylight gradually lengthens, a Saudi day takes slightly longer than 24 hours. In the fall, of course, it takes slightly less. For obvious reasons, this system of time is not suitable for international airline schedules and many business purposes, where Arabia Standard Time (GMT +3) is observed. The construction of a giant clock tower opposite the Ka'aba has excited some to propose moving the prime meridian from Greenwich to Mecca, and thus making Mecca Mean Time the world's standard.

Although Islam teaches the brotherhood and equality of all believers, class distinctions have developed. In the old days, some tribes considered themselves more socially important and prestigious than others, and would not intermarry across such tribal boundaries. Modernization reduces class distinctions of these traditional types, for wealth and education are becoming the tokens of status, but family prestige still matters.

Based on Islam and enforced in a traditional fashion, the legal system varies considerably from Western practices. The courts impose one of the highest execution rates in the world, for drug dealing, rape, murder, and witchcraft, while a victim's family may accept blood money in place of other punishment. A woman's testimony carries half the weight of a man's, the practice of non-Islamic religions is forbidden (even to non-Saudi residents), and freedoms of speech and the press are extremely limited. The severity of Saudi sentences is sometimes offset by royal pardons or, again by the substitution of payments to a victim's family.

Foreigners are sometimes surprised by the absolute ban on alcoholic beverages, in accordance with strict Islamic belief. A non-Saudi tourist found with any quantity of alcohol in his or her belongings is normally deported on the next available flight. Penalties for possession of narcotics are also strictly imposed, and importers of narcotics risk the death penalty. On the other hand, tobacco is allowed, and an education program warning against the health hazards of smoking is only now becoming significant.

In 2007, King Abdullah announced major reforms of the judicial system that would create a supreme court, a system of appeals courts, and courts for commercial and labor matters. Besides modernizing the system, the reforms apparently aim to reduce the wide discretion judges have had to impose their own, sometimes unique, interpretations of Shari'a law. Lacking an effective appeals process, it required King Abdullah himself to pardon "the Qatif girl," sentenced, on appeal, to 200 lashes and jail for being alone with an unrelated man when she (along with her male companion) was abducted and raped.

The modern side of Islam is reflected in the style and substance of the "satellite sheikhs," popular preachers like Ahmad al-Shugairi or Amr Khaled who expound religious perspectives over television and the internet, often working the emotions of crowds in ways similar to American televangelists. The emotional, joyful perspectives of such preachers attract the young and relatively secular who find traditional preaching dull and out-of-touch. At the same time, some of the most popular and prolific Twitter users in Saudi Arabia are religious extremists.

Social media has been enthusiastically embraced in Saudi Arabia, providing a space of congregation that simply doesn't exist offline. Activists have utilized social media to mount campaigns against issues as diverse as male guardianship, sexual harassment, government corruption and the introduction of value-added taxation. At the same time, Saudi courts have introduced some of the harshest prison sentences in the world for internet users who run afoul of newly instigated cyber-crime and anti-terrorism laws. Anti-terrorism legislation includes criminal penalties of up to 10 years in prison for portraying the king or crown prince, directly or indirectly, "in a manner that brings religion or justice into disrepute;" and a 15-year prison sentence for those using their "social status or media influence to promote terrorism."

Education's Expansion and Reform

As suggested above, education very rapidly changed life in the kingdom. In 1953 only ten junior and senior high schools offered public instruction, with a total enrollment of 1,315. By 1973, there were 573 schools at these levels with 105,853 students. During the same 20 years, the number of elementary pupils increased from 39,000 to more than half a million. Access to primary education is now virtually universal, with millions of children in gender-segregated schools.

Critics of the country's schools often focus on their educational style. Thanks in part to the conservatism of the country's heavy religious influence, student learning often means rote memorization of facts, which is much safer for teachers than the development of questioning minds that think critically. Both foreign commentators and some Saudi commentators have also faulted the sometimes reactionary comments and interpretations of Islam found in a number of textbooks.

The first full institution of higher education was the King Saud University in Riyadh, dating from the 1950s. The university system expanded with the rise in oil revenues, though at the turn of the millennium only eight public universities served a population of nearly 15 million Saudis. However, after the higher education budget tripled starting in 2004, more than 100 new colleges and universities opened.

The kingdom's education leadership was shocked when the country's three leading universities received low scores—or were not even rated—in the 2006 international rankings. The response was a series of successful efforts to raise quality. Research chairs were endowed, and highly-published foreign scholars recruited. All professors were encouraged to conduct research, collaborate with academics in other countries, and publish in selective journals.

The most impressive new institution is undoubtedly the graduate-level King Abdullah University of Science and Technology, which opened in 2009. Funded by $10 billion of the monarch's personal wealth, its research orientation and goal of educating women and men together are precedent-setting. It offers programs in fields like nanotechnology, water and conservation technology, the biosciences, energy and the environment, and applied computer science. This curricular emphasis is no accident. More than half of Saudi college students major in history, geography, Arabic literature and Islamic studies, but the economy generates fairly few jobs in these areas.

The Slowly Changing Status of Women

Aside from King Abdullah University, education carries the burden of separate schools and other facilities for girls and women. This is part of the struggle to prevent gender mixing. In the cause of maintaining sexual purity, Saudi women must be kept apart from men outside the family. At least to the political and religious leadership of the country—almost exclusively male—this is a matter of modesty and separation rather than inequality. To critics it amounts to "gender apartheid."

To Western critics, regulations of the status of women extend beyond Islamic concerns of morality to a desire to keep women in a "perpetual childhood" that requires male relatives to exercise "guardianship" over them. Saudi women have to obtain permission from male relatives to work, travel, study, receive health care, or even open bank accounts for their children, matters sometimes removed from sexual morality but key elements of the social order. In recent years there have been a number of high profile cases of Saudi women fleeing or attempting to flee the country in order to seek asylum elsewhere. This has drawn increased attention to the guardianship system and to

Reem Asaad, campaigner for women-staffed lingerie stores

Saudi Arabia

the various impositions and restrictions that it places on women.

There is no minimum age of marriage in Saudi Arabia, although a girl must reach puberty before the marriage is consumated. Although the average age of first marriage for Saudi women is just over 20, child marriages are not uncommon. Domestic law in Saudi Arabia is among the strictest in the world. Vice police ensure utmost modesty in dress and brevity in contact. Efforts to repeal some of the harshest restrictions are often divisive, with the result that change is infinitesimally slow. One of Saudi Arabia's most prominent women's rights activists is Loujan al-Hathloul, who was arrested in 2018 and tortured in prison while awaiting trial. Al-Hathloul is a leading figure in the women's right-to-drive campaign and has been a prominent social media activist. In March 2020, her trial was postponed indefinitely due to the COVID-19 outbreak. She was released in February 2021.

Economy: Before the discovery of its oil, most inhabitants of the country's arid lands lived by herding flocks or raised dates and a few other crops in oases. The yearly pilgrimage, or Hajj, to Mecca and Medina employed others, but the traditional camel trade routes of ancient times could not compete with sea freight, especially after the introduction of steam and the construction of the Suez Canal. Then came oil.

It is difficult to over-estimate the impact of oil on Saudi Arabia. It typically funds about 80% of the government budget, directly contributes over 40% of GDP, and provides 90% of exports. In addition, the major industry, petrochemicals, depends on oil as a raw material.

Saudi Oil Policy

Having persuaded King Abd al-Aziz to grant a concession for drilling, prospectors for a group of American oil companies struck commercial quantities of oil in 1938. After World War II, oil production by the Arabian American Oil Company (Aramco) increased by nearly 20% a year. Soon the kingdom ranked with Iran and Iraq as a leading Middle East producer. In the following decades, the search for oil, its production, and its export revenues completely transformed the Saudi economy.

From the late 1950s economic development became a priority. This created challenges, because the industry provided only a few thousand jobs. How could millions of people be transformed from a life of subsistence herding and agriculture to the levels of income and comfort enjoyed by advanced industrial nations? One answer came from Aramco, which built a

The University of Petroleum and Minerals, Dhahran

hospital, clinics, schools and housing. It also provided assistance for agriculture and lent advice for a variety of projects, including the kingdom's railroad.

The cooperation between Aramco and the government contrasted with usually bitter relations in other oil exporting nations. Nevertheless, Saudi Arabia became a founding member of OPEC, where it usually adopted a firm but moderate stance. Given the country's reserves and production, its opinion mattered.

By the early 1970s, with its oil sales rising at 25% per year, the country became the dominant Middle East producer, and Sheikh Ahmad Yamani, the Petroleum Minister, became a leading figure in the cartel. He played a major role in the 1973 oil embargo, and in other agreements that drove the price of oil from roughly $2.50 in 1970 to $32 in 1980. However, high prices encouraged production elsewhere and reduced consumption through conservation. When demand declined for OPEC's exports, Saudi production and oil revenues both plummeted.

During the 1970s, Saudi Aramco invested in additional pipelines to carry crude to the Red Sea, beyond the potential bottleneck of the Strait of Hormuz. Investment also increased oil production capacity to about 10 million barrels per day. During the Gulf War of 1990–91, Saudi Aramco met world oil needs while exports from Iraq and Kuwait were halted. During the next era of tight oil supplies, in 2005–08, Aramco initiated projects to raise

output to over 12 million barrels per day, nearly a 25% increase.

Growth of the National Economy

From the late 1950s to the early 1970s, the government erected public buildings, paved roads and highways, and began to offer education and health services for its citizens. Oil revenues supplied foreign exchange to purchase all manner of imports from cars to cloth and even building materials. Money that found its way into private hands frequently went into large homes, as well as stores and office buildings. Reluctant to have a "Central Bank," with implications of interest payments, the nation established the Saudi Arabian Monetary Authority (SAMA) to provide modern control over national finances.

Following the 1973 spiraling of oil prices, the nation's economic development spurted to higher levels of growth. The government offered tax breaks and subsidies to attract firms in non-oil industries. Factories began to appear, sometimes joint ventures with foreign firms. The early ones typically provided consumer goods or construction materials for the building boom, such as a mill for rolling steel rods. With the decline in oil prices in the mid-1980s, government subsidies diminished.

In general, Saudi industrial projects suffer from a number of common difficulties. Lucrative profits in trade and other services also discourage long-term investment in manufacturing. Once established, local entrepreneurs, managers, and skilled

174

workers are scarce. Until recently, inadequate financial markets made it more convenient for Saudi capitalists to buy shares in foreign companies rather than take ownership of local factories. Finally, for all its famed wealth, the country represents a relatively small market, whose consumers are fewer than those of Belgium or Illinois, and until recently much poorer.

The most impressive industrialization effort is the petrochemical producer, the Saudi Arabian Basic Industries Corporation (SABIC). It rapidly grew to massive size, the only Arab industrial company on the international Fortune 500. By 1988, its major plants had been constructed, and profits soared as the company turned cheap petroleum raw materials into fertilizers, plastics and other products. By 2004, SABIC held 10% of world sales of petrochemicals. It also produced a much larger proportion of specialty products like MTBE (methyl tertiary butyl ether), a gasoline additive that reduces carbon monoxide emissions and replaces lead in enhancing octane. In 2007, SABIC purchased the plastics subsidiary of General Electric.

Saudi Arabia became a major exporter of grains by the end of the 1980s. Fearing an American food embargo in retaliation for the 1973 oil embargo, the government provided extensive subsidies for grain farmers, paying the costs for wells, fertilizers and other supplies. Cultivated acreage increased tenfold, and giant green circles provided bumper crops of wheat. From a mere 3,000 tons in 1976, output climbed to 3 million tons in 1989, three times consumption. Similar subsidies raised the output of eggs, dairy products, and dates, spreading national wealth and slowing migration to the cities by keeping a quarter of the population in agriculture.

The successes were costly, and did not last long. Annual wheat subsidies of $1 billion equaled *eight times* the cost of equivalent imported wheat. By 1996 price supports had been cut 25%, and production fell to half the record of 4 million tons. After later cuts in subsidies, many small family farms collapsed. In 2008, the country again became a net importer of wheat.

Nature has reinforced the financial austerity. About 90% of water supplies come from "fossil" sources trapped far below the soil during a much wetter climatic age. In the 1990s, the nation used 18 billion cubic meters of this fossil water annually, against apparently reliable estimates of only 500 billion cubic meters in the aquifers. Desalinized water, somewhat expensive for household use, becomes exorbitant for wheat farming. Imaginative alternative supplies—from the Nile, Turkey, Iraq, or Antarctic icebergs—are likewise prohibitively costly and uncertain. Despite its wealth, the country's future food production seems limited to drought-tolerant crops, plus fish and shrimp from the sea.

Economic and Budget Policies

When oil prices fall, Saudi Arabia suffers financial distress. If they fall sufficiently, it will face a budget deficit as well. To cover such deficits, the government borrows money, while trying to obey the Islamic prohibition of the payment of interest. Thus it issues "development bonds," whose payment depends in theory on the success of the project. Total indebtedness by 2003 exceeded $130 billion, a much higher level than most developed countries, but with annual oil revenues of about the same amount, it was a trustworthy borrower. Revenues hit $200 billion in 2007 but fell in 2008–09 with the decline in oil prices and the world recession.

Other revenue sources are difficult to find. Only a few acceptable taxes exist, for the wealthy and commoners alike expect government services to be financed by oil. An attempt to impose income taxes on foreign workers created such difficulties that it was withdrawn. Higher tariffs on imports largely breed domestic inflation and are no longer an option since the country joined the World Trade Organization (WTO).

Despite the boom in oil prices during the first eight years of the 2000s, foreign financing is still necessary for major electric, water, and petrochemical projects. Estimates of the funds needed by 2025 are astounding. Development of natural gas reserves will probably cost even more than the $45 billion Aramco is spending, plus the $25 billion initially agreed by several major oil companies. To meet estimated electricity needs in 2025 will require $120 billion in new generating plants and transmission facilities. The six new "economic cities," planned for five million inhabitants by 2020, will cost another $100 billion. These intend to be stepping stones toward a post-petroleum era.

To meet these challenges, the government promised larger roles for private companies. However, international firms capable of billion-dollar projects, delighted to invest in projects that export oil and gas, hesitate to become involved in local utilities, given the unprofitable traditions of nearly-free water and electricity.

The Future: In early March 2020, an agreement between Russia and Saudi Arabia to limit oil extraction broke down. In a gamble, intended to force Russia to slow the supply, Mohammad bin Salman oversaw a precipitous drop in the price of crude. Launching an all-out oil price war puts Saudi Arabia on the offensive in the struggle to retain the global dominance of Middle Eastern oil against the US shale market (in the short term) and the renewable energy sector (in the medium to long term). However, it poses considerable risks to the kingdom. The sudden drop in oil prices forces the government to make cuts to spending, which will increase social tensions and undermine the position of the crown prince. More worryingly, it places at risk the ambitious—and expensive—2030 vision, making it harder for

King Abdulaziz Al-Saud meets with President Franklin D. Roosevelt on board the *USS Quincy* in the Suez Canal's Great Bitter Lake, February 1945

Saudi Arabia

Saudi Arabia to successfully transition the economy away from oil. With an unprecedented downturn in demand generated by the COVID-19 pandemic, the gamble is starting to look more like a misstep.

Internationally, the Arab Middle East lies in shambles, and Sunnis split political loyalties between moderates and Islamists. Although in some respects the Wahhabi doctrine is close to several jihadist strands, the Saudi royal family is the bitter enemy of many, from the Muslim Brotherhood to the Islamic State, because these groups challenge the very legitimacy of an Islamic kingdom.

Another threat comes from Iran, the long-time rival across the Gulf. It benefits from the Fertile Crescent's strife by supporting Shi'a militias across the region and manipulating governments in Baghdad, Damascus, Beirut, and San'a. Recent developments regarding Tehran's nuclear enrichment program—specifically, the Trump administration's decision to withdraw from the Iran nuclear deal—were welcomed by Saudi Arabia but have created more uncertainty, not less.

Reforms in Saudi policies traditionally move at glacial speed, but society itself is changing rapidly. Nearly half of the population is under the age of 25, and their videos, satellite TV, and internet sites typically portray the pleasures of living now more than the blessings of prayer.

Also threatening both the royal and religious establishments are foreign intellectual influences that consider truth to be the outcome of testing conflicting ideas. It follows that individuals will make personal choices rather than accept pronouncements from a traditional leader or book.

King Salman has shown he can move quickly and decisively to replace government officials. His great challenge—or, more accurately, his son's—continues to be reforming quickly enough to satisfy those with modern inclinations, while not alienating the religious establishment and increasing the allure of extremism among the devout.

The Syrian Arab Republic

Desert Protector: This little-known fortress towers above the ruins of Palmyra

Area: 71,498 square miles (185,180 square kilometers).

Population: 17.5 million (a decline from a pre-war population of 22.5 million), 5.6 million Syrians are refugees abroad, and 6.2 million are displaced within Syria.

Capital City: Damascus (3.5 million).

Climate: Summers are generally hot and dry; winters are mild in low areas, cooler with increasing elevation. Winter brings some rain in the western part of the country, but the remainder is arid.

Neighboring Countries: Turkey (North); Iraq (East); Jordan (South); Lebanon (West); Israel (Southwest).

Time Zone: GMT +2 (+3 in summer).

Official Language: Arabic.

Other Tongues: Kurdish and Armenian.

Ethnic Background: Arab.

Principal Religion: Sunni Islam (60%), Shi'a Islam (16%, mostly Alawi), and Christianity (10%); additionally there are communities of Druze, Yezidis, and Jews, including Israeli citizens in the occupied Golan Heights.

Chief Commercial Products: Petroleum, cotton, calcium phosphates, and fruit.

Major Trading Partners: Lebanon, China, Jordan, and Turkey.

Currency: Lira (1 lira = 100 piasters).

Former Colonial Status: French mandate (1920–1946).

National Day: April 17 (1946; Independence Day).

Chief of State: Bashar al-Assad, President.

Head of Government: Hussein Arnous, Prime Minister.

National Flag: The flag consists of three horizontal stripes of (top to bottom) red, white and black; two green, five-pointed stars are aligned on the central white stripe.

Gross Domestic Product: Last recorded at $73.67 billion (2012).

GDP per capita: $1,700 (2012).

Lying at the eastern end of the Mediterranean Sea, Syria consists of two main climate zones. The western region includes the coastal mountains, the Orontes River valley, and a range of interior hills or mountains. On its eastern limits, the western zone includes Damascus and Aleppo and is home to four-fifths of the population.

The eastern zone takes the form of foothills descending from an average elevation of 3,000 feet to the vast, open desert cut by the Euphrates River as it flows across Syria from north to southeast. Its two main tributaries come from the north,

and they also support agriculture along their banks. Arabs invading the region called the area north of the Euphrates *al-Jazira*, "The Island," a cultivated expanse of green surrounded by desert.

Most of Syria has an average rainfall of less than ten inches (254 millimeters) per year, but the western zone enjoys more. The seaward slopes of the coastal range may receive as much as 50 inches (1,270 millimeters) near the crest, which in some places is 5,000 feet (1,524 meters) high. Cities such as Damascus and Homs along the eastern base of the inland range are great

Dome of Sayyidah Zaynab Mosque in the suburbs of Damascus

177

Syria

oases watered by springs and streams fed by the mountain rains.

History: Human civilization extends back as far in time in Syria as anywhere else; indeed, two Syrian cities—Damascus and Aleppo—compete for the title of oldest continuously inhabited city in the world. Many of antiquity's great empires occupied the country, although no Syrian dynasty arose to conquer the region, a reflection perhaps of its diversity of geography and population. For the 2,700 years between Assyrian conquest and Ottoman expulsion, Syria's history is deeply intertwined with the events related in the Historical Background section of this book.

In the 7th and 8th centuries, Syria became home to Umayyads, a Meccan dynasty that ruled from Damascus. The region flourished, with the construction of new cities and palaces. However, the Abbasids overthrew the faltering Umayyad dynasty in 750 and moved the capital to Iraq. As the united Muslim empire disintegrated in the following centuries, Syria's important geographical position attracted invasions from every side except the desert: Seljuk Turks, Egyptian caliphs, European Crusaders, Mongols, Mamluks from Egypt, and finally, the Ottoman Turks.

By the late 19th century, most of the territory now included in Syria formed the two major Ottoman provinces of Aleppo and Damascus. Present international borders

Umayyad Mosque, Damascus

did not exist, even as provincial boundaries. Jordan and parts of Israel and Lebanon reported to Damascus, while Antakya and smaller regions of southern Turkey near the city of Aleppo formed part of Aleppo province.

Around this time, greater education and economic development encouraged the rise of a self-consciousness of being Arab in language and culture. Partly as a result, the politically active upper class of landowners, officials, and Muslim scholars demanded a greater degree of local self-government. Just before World War I broke out, small, secret societies of civilians and officers, *al-Fatat* and *al-Ahd*, formed to struggle for Arab independence from the Empire.

After the Ottoman Empire joined the Central Powers in 1914, these nationalists plotted with Sharif Husayn of Mecca to gain independence. They provided the details for territorial demands he made from Britain in exchange for an uprising against Ottomans. After the Arab Revolt in June 1916, Syrian opinion increasingly favored the Allies.

The great British victory over the Ottoman army in Palestine opened the way to Damascus. British and Arab forces raced for the city—historians still debate who conquered it—and pressed on to capture

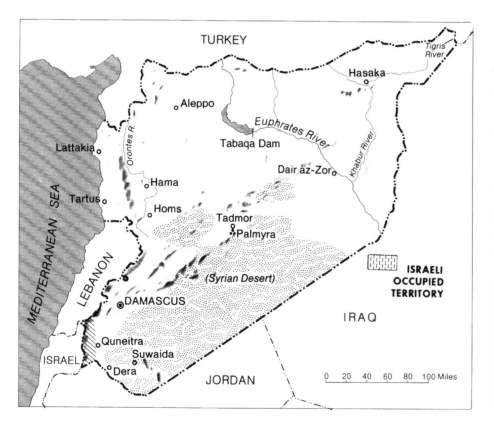

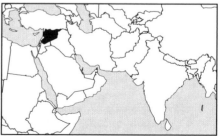

178

Syria

Roman Colosseum in Busra, Syria

Aleppo in the last weeks of the war. Initially the Arab army administered the interior of Syria, and French troops were limited to Mt. Lebanon (to the west) and the coast northward into Turkey.

In 1920, nationalists in Damascus proclaimed the independence of Syria (including Jordan and Lebanon), with Emir Faisal as king. The son of Sharif Husayn, he had led the Arab army into Damascus, but his rule was brief. It ended when France invaded and imposed its rule on Syria. Faisal then moved to Baghdad, where with British support he ruled Iraq from 1921 to 1933.

Although the French mandate provided some modernization and technical progress, the French divided Syria into small regions that emphasized ethnic minorities, such as *Jabal al-Druze* (the Mountain of the Druze) in the southeast and an Alawi state based in Lattakia. The fertile Biqa' Valley was assigned to Lebanon, and Antakya, a region in the far northwest, was transferred to Turkey. This divide-and-conquer approach created social scars that still contribute to political discord today.

The French goal was to weaken the Sunni majority with its nationalist ideas, but it also stirred nationalist fervor. In the mid-1920s a revolt shook much of the country, and French artillery shelled sections of Damascus sympathetic to the rebels. Bullet holes from these strikes can still be seen in the roof of the biggest souk in Damascus (*Souk al-Hamiddiyah*). During the 1930s, protests and general strikes dominated political life. Shortly after the

conclusion of WWII, the French finally withdrew.

Years of Political Instability

Syrian independence came to a country uncertain of its destiny. The generation of nationalists who had opposed the French—and sometimes compromised with them—took power, but rival, more radical ideologies attracted support, especially from students and army officers.

Some sought the borders of geographical Syria; others, a merger with Iraq to counter the Jewish settlement of Palestine. Socialists hoped to weaken the power of the wealthy notable families who formed the top nationalist leadership.

Increasingly, politicians appeared grasping for power. Corruption proved to be one cause among several for the Syria's conclusive defeat by Israel in 1948–49, when the army entered Palestine to attack the new Jewish state.

Against this background, Husni al-Za'im, the Chief of Staff, carried out Syria's first military coup d'état in 1949. He arrested leading politicians, banned political parties, arranged a cease-fire agreement with Israel, and reached a verbal alliance with Iraq. Al-Za'im offered to meet with Israel for peace talks, but was rebuffed. Less than five months after seizing power, another military coup led to his execution. No Syrian leader ever again offered to meet Israel's prime minister.

By ending ineffective, if constitutional government, al-Za'im ushered in a long era of instability. For the next 21 years, Syrian governments proved unstable, suffering more than a dozen military coups, some quite bloody. Elections generally showed popular support for pan-Arab and socialist politicians, whose rivals came from a small group of leading families who exercised great influence through their vast land holdings and wealth.

The Ba'th Party soon proved more influential than other radical ideologies such as the communists. Founded in the early 1940s in Damascus by Michel Aflaq, a Christian, and Salah al-Din al-Bitar, a

Young Syrians performing a traditional dance at a local festival

179

Syria

Syrian Army troops

Photo courtesy of SANA

Sunni Muslim, the party took its name from the Arabic word for renaissance. Highly committed to a nation uniting all Arabs, and thus bringing them self-respect instead of backwardness and defeat, its ideology naturally threatened Arab states created by European agreements. The party's socialist goals included the creation of a classless state, and its radicals threatened a government takeover of industry and trade as well. Though the party's legality was sometimes uncertain, it attracted disillusioned military officers and spread to Jordan, Lebanon, and Iraq.

By the mid-1950s, Syria lurched unsteadily leftward in its domestic politics and had received Soviet military equipment. Given the nationalist appeal of Gamal Abdul Nasser of Egypt, several leading politicians successfully sought a union with Egypt. In 1958, the two countries officially formed the "United Arab Republic," with Nasser as president and the ideological source of all authority.

Economic problems aggravated by drought and friction between Egyptian and Syrian officials enabled conservative groups to organize a revolt which broke the union in 1961. Reformist politicians soon regained power, however, and in 1963, army officers favoring the Ba'th Party seized control in yet another coup. They outlawed all rival political groups, and despite factional struggles within the party, the Ba'thists forced economic and social changes, such as the nationalization of petroleum and other major industries. The wealthy and tradition-minded complained privately about the seizures of property and loss of freedoms, but they could not successfully oppose Ba'thist government.

Clashes with the militarily-powerful state of Israel across the demilitarized zone frequently broke out between 1949 and the 1960s. Occasionally they flared into serious incidents with artillery and aircraft joining the battle. Several clashes followed Syria's attempts to divert headwaters of the Jordan River that flowed to Israel.

Tensions along the Israeli border led to aircraft dogfights in May 1967, and full-scale war in June of that year. After quickly defeating Syria's Egyptian and Jordanian allies, Israeli forces stormed into Syria and up the slopes which rise to the plateau known in Arabic as *Jawlan* (pronounced *Golan* by Israelis), occupying some 1,250 square miles (approximately 3,240 square kilometers). Israeli troops forced nearly all the remaining civilians to leave, and they destroyed or damaged public buildings and homes in the regional capital, Quneitra. Rather than permit the Syrian refugees to return to their farms and villages in accord with a UN resolution, Israel established its own settlements on the farmlands of ousted Syrians.

Hafiz al-Assad, an Alawi, Seizes Power

In 1970, General Hafiz al-Assad seized power from his fellow Ba'thist officers. Unlike its unstable predecessors, his regime succeeded in neutralizing all rivals, by crushing them or winning their support. Al-Assad ("The Lion") was elected president in 1971, as the only candidate on the ballot, and two years later a new constitution provided for an elected legislature, the People's Council. Formal power remained firmly with the president, by law a Muslim, who appoints the vice president, prime minister, and cabinet. But the important decisions in Damascus were been taken in secret, by the president and a close circle of family, relatives, and army officers, rather than by the civilian prime minister and cabinet. In the half century since, that aspect of political authority in Syria has not changed.

Within the tightly-controlled country, al-Assad's government won some public acceptance for its stability, reduced radicalism, and pragmatism. The relaxation

Shi'a pilgrims at a mosque outside of Damascus

The late President Hafiz al-Assad

of doctrinaire socialism encouraged economic growth. Syria was not a democracy, and al-Assad always won the referendum on the presidency with an overwhelming majority. Likewise, elections to the People's Council (parliament) always returned the Ba'th Party to power, though some independents and minor leftist parties held a few seats.

By 1980, many Syrians desired political change and the end of military rule. Like most top officers, Hafiz al-Assad was a member of the Alawi community, a variant of Shi'a Islam that incorporates ideas from several other religions. Patronized by the French, but ignored after independence, the frequently-impoverished Alawis had found few opportunities open to them. As a consequence, their young men sought careers in the military. As Alawi soldiers moved up the ranks, they eventually formed a majority of the officer corps. Ba'thist military rule eventually meant an Alawi-dominated regime, although some Sunnis continued to hold important positions. By embracing Ba'thist socialism and linking with the Communist Party, the officers presented themselves as secular and modernizing.

Since Syria was a police state that prohibited open discussion and independent political parties, opposition to al-Assad's government came largely from the illegal Sunni Muslim Brotherhood, which advocated an Islamic state. Repressed by the regime, the Brotherhood turned to violence, and in 1982 launched a revolt in the conservative city of Hama. In brutal fighting isolated from the news media, the military crushed the rebellion, at a cost of perhaps 20,000 lives. The bloodshed ended most dreams of removing the regime by force.

Syrian domestic affairs traditionally received little foreign attention, in part because the public rarely expressed itself, and the press, firmly controlled by party and government, was bland, propagandistic, and unquestioning. The regime has so far remained in power for four decades by removing possible alternative leaders from influential positions. Those critical of the government have often been arrested and detained. According to the Center for Documentation of Violations in Syria, as of March 2014 the country was holding more than 37,000 political prisoners. It is little surprise, then, that many political activists have sought exile abroad.

International Involvement and Isolation

Despairing of diplomatic efforts to recover their lost territory, the relatively new leaders of Syria and Egypt launched a surprise offensive in 1973 in an effort to drive out Israeli forces. Three weeks of intensive fighting again demonstrated Israeli military superiority but, with aid from Iraq and Jordan, Syrian defenses did not break. U.S. mediation efforts led by Henry Kissinger in 1974 returned a small strip of territory to Syria and established a buffer zone between the two armies.

An important recurring theme in the country's recent history has been its often self-inflicted isolation. Its military intervention during the civil war in Lebanon became brutal, and the subsequent occupation lasted decades. Western nations often felt disturbed by terrorism allegedly masterminded in Damascus by Palestinian and other radical groups. The struggle to regain the Golan inevitably discouraged

amicable relations with Israel's fervent allies, and intelligence services, sometimes perhaps following their own agendas, indulged in murderous exploits. Eventually, the Soviet Union, Syria's strongest ally, refused al-Assad's request for high-tech weapons, because his government could not pay for them, his troops could not use them effectively, and the Syrian army generally could not protect secrets.

Within the Middle East, the revolutionary Ba'thist vision of a single Arab state—"one Arab nation with an eternal mission"—naturally prohibited enduring alliances with monarchies. Al-Assad's uncompromising stand against the Camp David Accords precluded friendship with Egypt or the U.S., and quarrels with Yasir Arafat isolated Syria when the Palestine National Council and the United Nations favored Arafat's diplomatic approach.

Other Middle Eastern disputes also isolated the regime. Most Arab states feared the Iranian Islamic Revolution, and when Iraq invaded Iran in 1980 they supported Iraq. Al-Assad, already embroiled in a bitter party rivalry with Ba'thist Iraq, and as an Alawi more sympathetic to Shi'a than Sunni Islam, uniquely allied with Iran. A decade later, because Iraq's seizure of Kuwait in 1990 threatened to strengthen his long-standing Ba'thist rival, al-Assad supported the posting of American forces in Saudi Arabia and even dispatched 20,000 troops of his own.

Popular opinion accepted such behavior only reluctantly. Syrian troops played only a defensive role and did not invade Kuwait or Iraq. President al-Assad again surprised observers—and upstaged Israel—in

A covered 17th century *souk* (shopping area) in the old part of Damascus

Syria

1991 when he accepted a U.S. invitation to a peace conference on the Middle East. The alternative, a military re-conquest of the Golan was clearly impossible, given the end of Soviet assistance and the destruction of Iraq, a potential ally in this regard.

Negotiations with Israel proved surprisingly hopeful during the Labor government of Yitzhak Rabin. His negotiators conceded the possibility of withdrawing from the Golan. Damascus suggested that if Israel acknowledged Syrian sovereignty, demilitarized zones and agreement over water rights might form part of the peace settlement. But neither the simplicity of the solution nor the advantages of peace brought agreement. Each side demanded conditions the other would obviously reject.

Given its own bloody conflict with Islamic groups in the 1980s, Syria's leadership privately cooperated with the U.S. in the aftermath of September 11. However, with its own Golan Heights occupied, Damascus considered national resistance against Israel "a social, religious, and legal right." It proclaimed some of the most virulent anti-Israeli propaganda of any Arab state, but maintained tight security and calm along the ceasefire line. Instead, Syria used auxiliaries to exert violent pressure against Israel. It openly supported Hizbullah's struggle to free South Lebanon in the 1990s, and (secretly) provided the supply route for missiles used against Israel during the 2006 war. Damascus has also hosted the leadership of Hamas.

Faced in 2003 with President Bush's demand that Damascus "choose the right side in the war on terror," Syria voted for UN Security Council Resolution 1441, which demanded new inspections and threatened "serious consequences" if Iraq did not cooperate. However, Syria strongly condemned the U.S. invasion that followed. It quietly allowed Arab volunteers to pass through Damascus en route to battle. Militants continued to do so even after the fall of Saddam's regime, despite the building of a border barrier and efforts to arrest some Iraqi militants and turn them over to Baghdad.

The U.S. occupation of Iraq threatened the near-encirclement of Syria by rival or enemy states. Moreover, U.S. critics attacked Damascus for supporting anti-Israeli groups and its occupation of Lebanon. Congress passed sanctions that prohibited U.S. companies from trading with Syria. In response, Bashar al-Assad undertook to strengthen relations with Turkey, Europe, and other possible moderating influences on Washington, with limited success.

Hariri's Murder Threatens the Regime

Syria's international position deteriorated in 2005 when an expertly executed explosion killed Rafiq Hariri, a Lebanese business tycoon and twice-former prime minister. Blaming Damascus, massive demonstrations in Beirut demanded an end to the occupation. Isolated diplomatically, Syria withdrew its troops and known intelligence offices to the eastern Biqa' valley and then ended 29 years of occupation with a complete military withdrawal.

Despite patriotic celebrations for the returning troops, Bashar al-Assad's regime had clearly suffered a serious setback. Worse followed. The Syrian interior minister and former chief in Lebanon, Ghazi Kanaan, committed suicide in mysterious circumstances. Days later, the interim UN investigation into Hariri's murder named as suspects both the commander of the Syrian Presidential Guard, Maher al-Assad (Bashar's brother), and the head of military intelligence, Asaf Shawkat (Bashar's brother-in-law). One witness reported that planning for the assassination took place in Shawkat's home.

Admittedly, suspicion is not conviction. By 2011 the veracity of many claims was doubted, and evidence pointed to the involvement of Hizbullah. Syria alternately cooperated with the UN investigation and hampered it by creating its own investigation that kept witnesses from appearing in Beirut.

Domestic Affairs under Bashar al-Assad

After Hafiz al-Assad died in 2000, the legislature nominated his son, Bashar, to the presidency. This succession was expected, but it had not always been planned. Until his older brother's untimely death, the consequence of a car accident in 1994, Bashar was not expected to succeed his father. Constitutionally he was six years too young, however, he won overwhelming (and probably genuine) support in a popular vote.

In his inauguration speech, Bashar called for openness and reform. Hundreds of political prisoners were released, and the infamous Mezze prison was closed. So were the special security courts. Internet access greatly increased. On the foreign scene, relations improved with Jordan, with Yasir Arafat, and even with Iraq, which began exporting oil to Syria after Syria reopened the long-sealed border to trade.

Progress towards democracy and individual freedom encouraged Riad Seif, an independent member of parliament, to form the Friends of Civic Society. For the first time since the 1960s independent newspapers appeared. First there was a satirical paper; this was followed by a business journal. The arts reflected the greater openness, and actors enjoyed the new freedom to express on stage sentiments often felt by people on the street.

Portrait of a Young Man **by noted Syrian artist Fateh Almudarres**

The "Damascus Spring" proved brief. Just one year into Bashar's era, in 2001, Seif was arrested, charged with trying to change Syria's constitution by illegal means, and sentenced to years in prison. Dozens more activists were arrested. Apparently the most sensitive topics were corruption and the wide activities of the intelligence services and secret police. Attacks on these institutions, it was argued, threatened the old guard and perhaps Alawi rule, thereby undermining the very foundations of the regime. Despite its proclaimed socialism, the regime in Damascus felt more comfortable with private banks than with free speech.

For a decade, President Bashar al-Assad hinted at reform, but aside from economic liberalization he changed little. Whether the result of rivalries within the elite or hesitancy by Bashar, the regime played games with activists, arresting those who pressed too hard in sensitive areas, but releasing some prisoners to win public support. After forty years of Ba'thist dictatorship, many Syrian opponents of the regime viewed the vacillating policies, the withdrawal from Lebanon, and the UN investigation as signs of fatal weakness. A long-time vice president fled the country and publicly accused Bashar of having threatened Hariri and further pointed the finger for the murder of the former Lebanese prime minister at Syrian intelligence officials.

The village of Ma'aloula where the Aramaic language of Christ is still spoken

Feeling threatened, the regime asserted its strength by repressing intellectuals and critics, such as those who had issued the "Damascus Declaration for Democratic and National Change" in 2005. That had called for an end to emergency laws, a halt to political repression, and a national conference to move the country from a security state to a civil state. The Declaration united aging secular intellectuals, some Kurdish leaders, and a few Islamists, but most were exiles with little influence.

From Arab Spring to Civil War

The Arab Spring came late to Syria. Only in March, 2011, did the motto "The People Desire the Fall of the Regime" appear as graffiti in Dar'a, a disadvantaged small city in the drought-stricken south. The arrest of the graffiti-writing teenagers, and fatal violence inflicted against protesters in Dar'a, ignited widespread demonstrations that gradually spread to most of the country.

The regime initially responded with apparent concessions. A new cabinet was appointed, and the decades-old emergency laws were formally abolished. But fundamentally, Bashar al-Assad and his ruling circle rejected serious reform. Instead, they trusted a mixture of nationalist appeals, financial favors, fears of sectarian chaos, and a manipulation of public opinion. Rather than dialogue with critics, the official media leveled wild accusations at demonstrators, claiming they were Israeli agents or armed Salafist extremists. Large pro-government rallies took place in Damascus, attended by government employees, middle-class sympathizers who feared chaos, and Christians and Alawis who feared Islamist rule.

Despite its talk of reform, the regime soon clamped down harshly on demonstrations for change. Protestors who gathered after Friday prayers were often shot. By July over 1,400 civilians had died; by July 2012, perhaps 14,000. Given the multiple security services, intelligence agencies, and the dozens, then hundreds of increasingly armed opposition groups, responsibility for particular acts of violence was often difficult to demonstrate. Military units and pro-regime thugs (the heavily Alawi *Shabiha*) also besieged towns where demonstrations had taken place, imposing curfews and conducting house-by-house searches for political activists. Many feared a repeat of Hama's repression in 1982, but social media made it impossible to keep large-scale brutality secret.

Instead, terror was unleashed on neighborhoods and small towns, with dozens killed, and sometimes the bodies burned or removed. Activists and their pictures told a story of unprovoked shootings of demonstrators by the police, soldiers, and the Shabiha militiamen, dressed in black.

The really enormous popular protests occurred in the strongly traditional and Sunni cities of Homs and Hama. As the conflict continued, violence spread to the northwest and Deir al-Zor in the east, where the opposition first seized neighborhoods and than towns.

Soldiers who refused to shoot civilians, or who appeared to aim off-target, were executed. Surviving deserters often joined the Free Syrian Army or one of the many opposition militias. As the violence increased, hundreds of security agents and soldiers were also killed. State media displayed often gruesome pictures of their bodies or funerals as evidence of a violent insurrection, but to maintain morale the government ceased the daily announcements of funerals of security personnel.

Six months after the initial slogans, Syria was a country divided. Damascus and Aleppo, with their favored socio-economic classes and less traditional cultures, provided large crowds of pro-regime supporters. Elsewhere, elite army units used artillery on city neighborhoods considered sympathetic to the opposition. Homs in particular suffered a sustained and brutal shelling of the Baba Amr quarter. However, neither side in the conflict possessed the strength to dominate the country. Syria's sectarian diversity had divided the opposition and enabled al-Assad to arouse sufficient fears of chaos to defy demands for reform.

International attempts to halt the repression and fighting proved ineffective. Turkey's Prime Minister Recep Erdoğan warned al-Assad against repression and permitted refugees to cross the border. Turkey also hosted opposition elements, which formed the Syrian National Council in Istanbul. Qatar and Saudi Arabia publicly urged peaceful dialogue, though behind the scenes they funneled money and weapons to the armed opposition. The Arab League proposed a halt to violence, the army's withdrawal from cities, permission for international media to operate, and government-opposition discussions. The proposal failed in practice, and the League's observer mission was soon withdrawn.

Efforts by the United Nations failed in the Security Council. Russia stoutly blocked any intervention, reasoning that regime change was not the United Nation's responsibility. Kofi Annan was dispatched on a fruitless mission to negotiate a cease-fire, and the Human Rights

Syria

President Bashar al-Assad

Council provided evidence that security forces had committed crimes against humanity. Its chief, Navi Pillay, called for al-Assad to be referred to the International Criminal Court.

A UN monitoring mission, accepted reluctantly by the government, was manipulated. Towns and city neighborhoods where demonstrators openly displayed opposition slogans were later pounded by the army's artillery: the government switched from mass arrests to collective punishment.

UN monitors did confirm that the pro-government Shabiha executed most of the 108 victims of the 2012 Houla massacre, dozens of them children and women. After vehicles of unarmed monitors were blocked and hit by gunfire, the monitors withdrew.

One significant difficulty for sympathetic nations is the fractured Syrian opposition. Ranging from western-style liberals to the Muslim Brotherhood and extremists linked to al-Qaeda, the opposition was led publicly by long-time exiles, often professors, and by members of the Brotherhood. These groups failed to unite effectively under their initial umbrella, the Syrian National Council. Its successor, the more encompassing National Coalition for Syrian Revolutionary and Opposition Forces, proved little more effective despite the quality of its individual leaders. Neither organization controlled the Free Syrian Army, and had only limited links with the demonstrators' organization within the country, the Local Co-Ordination Committees. This gravely weakened the opposition's ability to engage in diplomacy, since the fighters within Syria might reject compromises accepted outside.

Most militias and the political opposition failed to address the concerns of Syria's many minority groups. This gravely weakened the supposedly democratic opposition cause. The problem was complex, and remains so. Most Druze and Christians preferred stability under al-Assad to chaotic change. They feared Islamic extremists who might impose Islamic law and persecute their communities as unbelievers. Gaining control of Raqqa, the *Dawlat al-Islamiyya fi Iraq wa al-Sham,* eventually known in English as the Islamic State (IS) imposed the medieval Islamic head-tax on Christians and reportedly crucified opponents.

Similarly, individual Alawis, members of the largest and most important minority, felt their safely depended on closing ranks to support the regime in a civil war. Blood-curdling threats from some Islamic extremists certainly strengthened such perspectives, but even moderate rebels failed to portray a future where Alawis would remain safe.

Descent into War

Violence was unleashed first by the Syrian state. The opposition then turned to violence in defense of neighborhoods and towns. Rather than a single rebel army, an uncounted number of militias (certainly over 1,000) arose. Some of these groups were relatively moderate, and even secular, but those characteristics have tended to be inversely correlated with influence on the ground. Among many "successes" for more extreme militants, it was militant Islamist groups like *Jabhat al-Nusra,* linked to al-Qaeda that successfully captured much of Aleppo in July 2012.

By late that year, rebel militias controlled much of the north and northeast, including border crossings to Turkey. They also threatened Damascus from the eastern and southern suburbs, and the road to the coast. Despite the military's superiority in heavy weapons and relentless bombing, al-Assad's future seemed grim. Prime Minister Riad Hijab defected and escaped the country.

On its heels, the regime reorganized. It formed a large civilian militia, the National Defense Army, which was trained by Iranian Revolutionary Guards to defend local communities. Shi'a fighters from Iraq, Iran, and Afghanistan reinforced the military. Even more important, Hizbullah, the Lebanese Shi'a militia familiar with guerrilla warfare, dispatched thousands of fighters to recapture Qusayr, a small city near the Lebanese border that threatened overland routes from Damascus to the sea. The rebels' loss of Qusayr cut their supply routes from Lebanon and simultaneously strengthened the regime's hold on a vital transportation route. By summer 2013, government forces had seized the initiative.

Modern Syria

The intensity of the fighting in Syria has shocked the world to numbness. In the first three years of war, more than 160,000 were killed, with massacres, sexual violence, and other despicable acts committed by both sides but mostly by the regime. During the fourth year alone, fatalities surpassed 70,000. Tens of thousands are permanently disabled; both sides have deliberately attacked schools. At least 11 million people—half the population—have been displaced, either internally or to neighboring states and farther. Damage to public infrastructure and other economic losses must surpass $100 billion.

At the start, the Obama administration hoped that humanitarian and non-lethal assistance to the rebels would unite them, form an effective fighting force, defeat the regime, and establish a government of moderation. Those hopes proved false as the rebels increasingly fought each other. In particular, IS sought territory so aggressively that local moderates joined with Jabhat al-Nusra and repulsed it from parts of Aleppo. Given the rebels' disorganization, the rivalries, and the shifting alliances, and rivalry, Western nations fear any sophisticated or heavy arms may end up in the wrong hands. This allows the military to pound civilian areas of Aleppo and other cities with barrel bombs, crude canisters packed with explosives, and shrapnel simply dropped from helicopters.

Chemical Weapons Kill Hundreds

After midnight on August 21, 2013, rockets carrying nerve gases landed in at least two rebel-held suburbs of Damascus. Within hours, dozens of videos documented adults and children suffering from the nausea, disorientation, vomiting, and other symptoms of the nerve gas sarin. The opposition blamed the government for the deaths, their numbers estimated from 588 (the UN estimate) to over 1,400 (U.S.). The Assad regime denied its involvement and claimed the rebels shelled their own suburbs to win world sympathy. However, no evidence has been presented that the rebels possessed either the nerve agents or the missiles used to deliver the gas. By contrast, the Syrian military did possess such missiles, and the angle of flight suggested they were launched from military bases overlooking Damascus.

President Obama had earlier pledged that the use of chemical weapons would cross a red line. Syria—and the world—awaited the U.S. response. Given difficulties in Congress and the dangers of unexpected poisons released by attacks on facilities where chemical weapons might or might not exist, Obama backed down. He accepted a Russian proposal that Syria disarm these weapons under the auspices of the Organization for the Prohibition of Chemical Weapons. Despite delays, declared stockpiles were removed from Syria by June 2014. Removing Syria's weapons was a gain for humanity, but the Assad regime had escaped the threatened punishment. And the United States had failed to intervene even in the face of crimes against humanity.

More confident on the battlefield, the government announced that presidential elections would be held in June 2014 in all areas not held by "terrorists." As expected, Bashar al-Assad won handily (88%). Except for allies such as Iran and Russia, most countries regarded the election as invalid.

Years of War

In 2014 the growing power of IS initiated a new stage in the war. Centered on the Euphrates city of Raqqa, IS jihadists swept into northern Iraq and seized its second city, Mosul. Subsequently, they captured the mostly Kurdish-inhabited towns along the Turkish border, facilitating their illegal export of petroleum, archaeological treasures, and valuables seized from captured towns and cities. At the same time, IS imported chemicals for explosives and other necessities. Thus the border with Turkey served as a vital breathing apparatus to keep the caliphate alive. Among the vital incoming valuables were hundreds, perhaps thousands of foreign volunteers.

Very likely the first critical defeats of IS took place along that border. By late summer in 2014, the city and surrounding area known officially as 'Ayn al-Arab, and by most of its inhabitants as Kobani, remained the only border crossing northeast of Aleppo outside of IS control. When jihadists launched a sustained attack to take the city the Syrian Kurdish militia known as the People's Protection Units

(YPG) and elements of the Free Syrian Army slowed it.

The U.S. air campaign shifted to include battlefield support for these fighters. Further assistance came from more heavily-armed *pesh merga* troops from Iraqi Kurdistan. Working together these forces gradually repelled IS forces and recaptured territory along the border, but the city was largely destroyed.

A second critical defeat was inflicted by the YPG and allied Free Syrian Army in mid-2015, when they captured the border town of Tell Abyad, further east. This cut the shortest route between the IS capital, Raqqa, and the border, and forced trade with Turkey to be routed west of the Euphrates.

Although in early 2015 pundits proclaimed the government "set to stay," by mid-2015 regime forces were in retreat almost everywhere, pushed back by reinvigorated foes in the north, east, and south.

Encouraged by their foreign supporters (including elements from Saudi Arabia, Qatar, and Turkey), a number of militias in the north, including Jabhat al-Nusra, formed *Jaish al-Fatah*, the Army of Conquest. Its fighters won successive victories in the northwestern province of Idlib, and moved towards the coast, threatening the Alawi region and port of Latakia. Meanwhile, fighters of the Southern Front captured parts of the southeast, including the major road crossing from Syria to Jordan. It also seized a major military base and approached Druze-inhabited regions. East of Homs, IS forces attacked and captured the city of Tadmur with its adjacent ruins of Palmyra from the Syrian military without much apparent resistance.

These defeats were accompanied by signs of regime fatigue, including stories of desertions by members of the paramilitary National Defense Army, and of young Alawi men who skipped the country to avoid the draft. Reportedly, several thousand Iranian troops (or Shi'a volunteers from other countries) were dispatched to strengthen the regime. Russia, which earlier in the year declared it had met the objectives it set the previous fall, also stepped forcefully back in the fray to back Assad. That support, as well as increased support from Iran, proved crucial. In retrospect, it may be judged by history as the moment the war turned in Assad's favor and didn't turn back.

Recent Developments in the War

In the past year, Assad has clearly consolidated his hold on Syria, pressing deeply into territory that had long been held by rebel groups. For a regime that as recently as 2015 was staring down the barrel of defeat this is a remarkable

turnaround. Russian air support provided a timely and incalculable intervention, in the Syrian war, definitively swaying the victory towards Assad. Today, active combat has slowed across much of Syria, but peace remains elusive. Troops continue to be deployed, militia are being sent from countries across the region, and millions of displaced Syrians remain in limbo. While ceasefires hold in the northeast and northwest of Syria, they remain fragile at best. An agreement made in March 2020 between Ankara and Moscow to cease hostilities in the Idlib region is holds but with no certainty in the long term.

A more pressing immediate concern is the possibility of Covid-19 spreading rapidly through a population already weakened by years of war. Millions of Syrians lack access to reliable running water, let alone soap or sanitizers. The country's health system has been largely destroyed. In displaced peoples' camps within the country and across the region, Syrians remain a population at high risk.

As for IS, its declared capital in Syria, Raqqa, fell to a group called the Syrian Democratic Forces (SDF) in late 2017. This 80,000-plus strong coalition of Kurds and Sunni-Arabs, supported by Western powers including the United States, was vital to dislodging the group from its stronghold, and in doing so vitiating any claim it had to a physical caliphate. In March 2018, IS was routed out of its last bastion—the Syrian town of Baghouz. This does not mean that that IS will go away—on the contrary, the group or derivatives of it are likely to continue causing significant problems in Syria and beyond for years. In the meantime, the international community struggles with the question of how to manage the thousands of former IS fighters and their families.

Syria has become the field for a proxy war that is unlikely to be forsaken by its main protagonists. Outside actors appear set to stay in Syria for the foreseeable future, sometimes at the invitation of the Syrian government. Lebanon's Prime Minister has indicated that both Hizbullah and Iran will remain in Syria "until its territorial integrity is regained" and until the country is "fully liberated from terrorists." Russia's Vladamir Putin has said that the Russian military will stay in Syria as long as doing so is to Russia's advantage, which could be indefinite. Echoing rhetoric about the fight against terrorism not infrequently used in the United States, Putin has explained, "Thousands of militants left Russia and the countries of Central Asia—with whom we do not have hard borders—and gathered on Syrian soil. It [is] better to deal with them there, liquidate them there, than let them come back [to Russia] with weapons in

Syria

School kids at Citadel

hand." Despite sometimes contradictory statements, the U.S. is likely to remain entangled in Syria for some time. Any confrontation between the United States, its Arab allies, and Israel, on the one hand, and Iran on the other, will have significant reverberations in war-torn Syria.

Culture: Most Syrians live in cities or towns, although significant numbers live in villages or farm communities. The few nomads now form under 1% of the total population. The two principal cities are Damascus and Aleppo (*Halab*); each exceeds two million residents. Most industry is concentrated around those cities and at Homs.

A majority of Syrians are Sunni Muslims. The Arab Christian minority, now smaller than ever as a consequence of the war, is mainly Greek Orthodox. The once-sizable Armenian community has declined due to emigration. Several other groups merit mention, including Druze in the southeast and Alawis along the Mediterranean coast and nearby mountains. Together these minority groups form about 16% of the population.

Developing their beliefs and ritual secretly in the rugged mountains, Alawis for centuries remained something of a mystery. Modern scholars, little better informed, find major Shi'a influences, especially of the Ismaili variant. The Imam Ali, for example, is revered as the incarnation of God. Other beliefs and the liturgy suggest Christian and other religious influences.

While not forming as great a community as in Turkey, Iraq, or Iran, several hundred thousand Kurds live in the northern and eastern border areas. Although Syria has provided sanctuary for Turkey's Kurdish rebels, its own Kurds enjoy no legal rights to organize. They appeared restive in 2004, rioting after a soccer match. Further riots followed the kidnapping and murder of a religious leader in 2005, this time with hints at Kurdish demands for independence rather than simply fair treatment.

The Jewish community of Damascus faces extinction. After thousands of years of vibrant life and two generations of experience surviving the Arab–Israeli dispute, by 2002 it had dwindled to about 50 members worshiping in one surviving synagogue. This decline did not result from direct persecution; rather, legal changes permitted families to emigrate together. As the community dwindled, living outside of Syria has increasingly appealed to the few who remain.

Founded by both Christians and Muslims, the Ba'th Party has no formal religious element. For decades, it favored a distinctly secular society, forbidding head scarves in schools or uniformed soldiers worshiping in mosques. Sectarian differences are not recognized in the government structure as they are in Lebanon, and legal political parties were not formed along religious lines. In spite of the religious differences, until the regime's repression of demonstrators during the Arab Spring there was little strife between communities.

Nevertheless, a growing allegiance to Islam has been evident in recent years, as reflected in women's dress, men's beards, and in other ways. This suggests that at the popular level, secularism and pan-Arabism are being replaced by faith. The variety of expression is broad, ranging from students in Islamic schools to women's Quranic discussion groups.

Like Egypt and Iraq, Syria contains numerous archaeological sites of great historical importance, stretching from recent times back to the earliest village life. The spectacular ruins of the caravan city of Palmyra lie in the middle of the desert beside the modern oasis village of Tadmur. Queen Zenobia once ruled there until defeated by the Romans and carried off to Rome as a royal prisoner. Regrettably, in 2015 IS occupied this ancient city. Among the many atrocities committed there, the group filmed executions of dozens of regime soldiers by children, and it destroyed the Temple of Bel.

At Aleppo, in the northern part of Syria, a great citadel of bygone days arises on a high mound in the middle of a modern city. In Damascus, the National Museum contains one of the finest displays of Islamic art to be found anywhere. In the city center, adjacent to the covered market known as the Souk al-Hamidiya, the Umayyad Mosque preserves gold leaf from the 7th century. Other museums illustrate the lifestyle of wealthy families during the Ottoman period, while in small villages outside Damascus some inhabitants still speak Aramaic, the language used by the Jews of Palestine at the time of Jesus.

Economy: Syria has a more balanced economy than most nations of Southwest Asia. One-third of the population still depends directly on agriculture. Farmers raise cotton in irrigated fields along the Orontes and Euphrates rivers, wheat and other grains on the steppe, or fruits and vegetables in oases like the Ghuta outside Damascus.

In years of abundant rainfall, Syria's farms produce grain for export, but usually the country imports food. There is great scope for improved farming methods, and experimental programs are carried on with the United Nations. Given the high cost of importing food, agricultural development is vitally important. Increases in the area of irrigated land resulting from the Euphrates dam proved much lower than expected.

The largest single industry is still textiles. Domestic cotton from the Euphrates Valley, the Aleppo Plain and elsewhere supply the mills. Raw cotton is also exported, but in lesser quantities as more and more is woven into textiles in Syria. Because of various regulations, and more recently sanctions, the country receives relatively little foreign investment outside tourist projects. Because government funds rarely allow large new development projects, emphasis is being placed on improving production levels in existing projects.

An oil pipeline from the modest deposits in the northeast to a refinery in Homs and the port of Tartus has operated since 1968. Syria's oil exports were a major earner of foreign exchange during the 1970s, but declining exports and lower prices brought a drop in this income. Promising deposits of oil east of Deir al-Zor reached commercial production in 1989, but they have since declined. The search for oil continues as production declines in existing oilfields. However, the country has failed to attract steady exploration activities by foreign firms, and several majors have left the country in recent years. In the near future, it could become a net importer of oil, as local consumption exceeds production.

The Future: As the war in Syria draws to an end, the long-term stability of the state is far from assured. Extremists will continue to reside within its borders, even if not openly in urban centers. Tens of thousands of IS fighters have been rounded up. Almost 50,000 children in the al-Hol refugee camp, in northeast Syria, have at least one parent who was fighting for IS. Many of them have foreign citizenship,

but few countries seem prepared to take them back.

Kurdish fighters, who have sacrificed perhaps more than anyone else to defeat IS in Syria, will expect compensation in some form or another. The tensions and underlying factors that sparked protests in 2011 remain either unchanged, or have been exacerbated by events of the past eight years. The fate of al-Assad's domestic opponents is uncertain. Many hundreds of thousands of Syrian refugees may be reluctant to return to a country where their security and prosperity is far from guaranteed. However, regional or, indeed, global solutions to what may well develop into yet another protracted refugee crisis are unlikely. In neighboring countries, Syrian refugees are increasingly viewed with suspicion and hostility. The permanent resettlement of Syrian refugees in third countries occurs on a minuscule scale, when compared to the breadth of need. Amongst those who fled Syria are the doubly displaced Iraqi and Palestinian refugees. Intergenerational experiences of exile are becoming an increasingly common experience in both the Middle East and South Asia.

Syria will continue to be strategically valuable to Iran and Saudi Arabia, both of

whom will continue to vie for influence. Al-Assad's victory in Syria, is a boost to Iran's regional ambitions. Damascus has prioritized working with Russia and Iran, whose militaries bolstered Syrian forces during the civil war. He is also likely to call on China—a neutral party in the conflict—in order to kickstart Syria's reconstruction.

U.S. policy on Syria remains unclear. Throughout the conflict Washington has pursued multiple and often contradictory objectives. In December 2018, Trump declared the withdrawal of all U.S. troops. However, he later backtracked, suggesting that a small contingent of 400 would remain in order to prevent the reemergence of IS on Syrian territory. In March 2019, this was further raised to 1,000 troops—half of the original number on the ground—presumably in response to the new policy objective of countering Iran's influence in Syria.

Historically, Syria has positioned itself as "an agent of stabilization in the Middle East." At one point the only Arab ally of Iran, Syria was uniquely position to mediate between conflicting parties in the region. However, ten years of war have undermined the capacity, not to mention the credibility, of Damascus to assume such a role.

The Republic of Turkey

Residences near the mouth of the Bosporus in Istanbul survive and, looming above them, the Sultan Ahmet I Mosque—the "blue mosque" Photo by Miller B. Spangler

Head of Government: Binali Yildirim, Prime Minister.

National Flag: Red field containing a large white crescent with a smaller five-pointed star between its points.

Gross Domestic Product: $852 billion.

GDP per capita: $10,498.

During the early 1920s, a new state was born on the historical peninsula of Asia Minor and the adjacent tip of Europe. The Ottoman Empire had ruled a mosaic of Greeks, Armenians, Kurds, and Turks in the territory before World War I but faced dismemberment after its defeat. A former Ottoman general, Kemal Atatürk, led the Turkish community to seize its independence and establish a national state. Although Turkish tribes originated in Central Asia, and only 5% of the new country lay in Europe, Atatürk strove to create a modern, secular, and distinctly European country, to replace the religiously-oriented empire.

Geography: Besides a small European portion around the historic city of Istanbul, modern Turkey covers Asia Minor, also known as Anatolia, and the mountainous region to its east. Although the nation enjoys a long coastline on the Aegean Sea, almost none of the major islands are Turkish. Instead, though often located only a few miles from Asia Minor, they belong to Greece.

Two long, narrow straits divide European from Asian Turkey. The Dardanelles leads from the Aegean Sea into the small Sea of Marmara. Vessels continuing to the Black Sea then sail up the Bosporus. For centuries authority over the straits between the Black Sea and the Mediterranean has been important; whichever power rules the straits, influences the commercial and strategic well-being of other Black Sea states.

Apart from its long seacoasts, Turkey is a country of high elevations: its average altitude is more than 3,500 feet (1,066 meters) above sea level. Asia Minor forms a plateau surrounded, except on the west, by mountain ranges. The highest mountains are in the eastern part of the country. A spectacular peak on the Iranian border, called *Ağri Daği* in Turkish and Mt. Ararat in English, reaches 16,945 feet (5,137 meters). Many other mountains exceed 10,000 feet (3,048 meters), and the plateau itself varies in elevation from 2,500 to 7,000 feet (762 to 2,133 meters).

The heart of Asia Minor is largely desert, because mountains to the north and south block out rain-bearing clouds. In this region Lake Tuz has one of the highest concentrations of salt and minerals of any lake or sea. To the east, Lake Van also contains high levels of dissolved salt and

Area: 300,948 square miles (779,452 square kilometers).

Population: 84 million.

Capital City: Ankara (5.4 million).

Climate: Mostly hot and dry in the summer, though humid along the coasts; winters generally are wet and mild on the coasts, cooler inland and very cold in the eastern mountains.

Neighboring Countries: Greece (West); Bulgaria (Northwest); Georgia, Armenia (Northeast); Azerbaijan (East); Iran (East); Iraq (Southeast); Syria (South).

Time Zone: GMT +2 (+3 in summer).

Official Language: Turkish.

Other Principal Tongues: Kurdish; far fewer speak Arabic, Greek, or Armenian.

Ethnic Background: Turkish and (minority) Kurdish.

Principal Religion: Islam (about 98%, mostly Sunni).

Chief Commercial Products: Automobiles, vehicle parts, iron, and jewelry.

Major Trading Partners: Germany, the United States, Russia, Iraq, France, and the United Kingdom.

Currency: Turkish Lira (1 lira = 100 kurus).

Former Political Status: Heart of the Ottoman Empire; independent.

National Day: October 23 (1923; proclamation of the Republic of Turkey).

Head of State: Recep Tayyip Erdoğan, President.

no visible outlet, although underground channels may connect it to the Tigris or Euphrates. All together, lakes comprise around 3,000 square miles (7,770 square kilometers) of the total area of the country.

Two traditionally useful rivers are the Kizil Irmak and the Sakarya, both draining into the Black Sea. The Seyhan and Ceyhan empty into the Mediterranean, after running through the fertile plain around Adana, where much of Turkey's cotton is grown. The mighty Tigris and Euphrates both originate in Turkey, but they pass through steep mountain gorges, so their usefulness was originally irrigation of the plains of Syria and Iraq. Now they serve as the basis for GAP, the Southeast Anatolia Project for agricultural and industrial development, a massive power and irrigation scheme.

Western Asia Minor generally enjoys good winter rains, as do the southern Taurus Mountains. The Pontus Mountains along the north coast have moderate rains throughout the year, especially in the spring. The eastern highlands receive abundant precipitation, but the elevation and rugged terrain makes them often not suitable for agriculture. Forests grow in these mountains and those of the north, but relatively few trees grow elsewhere.

History: The modern Republic of Turkey rose from the ruins of the Ottoman Empire, which was defeated and dismembered at the close of World War I. Secret agreements during the war divided many areas, with little regard for national feeling, and left only a very small Turkish-ruled area in northern Asia Minor. At the Paris Peace Conference, the Arab parts of

the empire fell prey to Britain and France, and Turkish-speaking provinces seemed destined for partition among Italy, Greece and Armenia as well.

To enforce their colonial claims, Greek troops occupied Izmir and moved inland, while the French sought the region around Adana. Pending a peace treaty, British forces occupied the Sultan's capital, Istanbul, while Armenians and Kurds both appealed to the Peace Conference for their own states. However, in 1920 an energetic and determined army officer, Mustafa Kemal, summoned delegates to Ankara to save the nation. Calling themselves the Grand National Assembly, the delegates elected Kemal as its president. He later adopted the surname Atatürk ("Father of the Turks"). In the next months, they established an independent Turkish nation, with a small railroad town deep in Anatolia—Ankara—as its provisional capital.

To the astonishment of the Allies, Atatürk molded Ottoman troops and volunteers into a fervent and disciplined force. It pushed out the French and retook provinces claimed by Armenia. The Italians withdrew from southwest Asia Minor, and Britain from Istanbul. France recognized the new Turkish regime quickly, hoping to gain national advantage. Peace with Greece followed a bitter war, worsened because in retreat the Greek troops destroyed everything they could and committed outrages upon Turkish villagers. Reflecting military successes, the Treaty of Lausanne gave Turkey full sovereignty over most of the territory it now possesses.

In 1923, the Grand National Assembly proclaimed Turkey a republic, and under Atatürk's leadership the Assembly voted

Kemal Atatürk

deep changes that shook Turkish society. The office of caliph was abolished in 1924, along with religious law courts. The 1924 constitution made Ankara the capital, designated the National Assembly as the center of authority, and guaranteed freedom

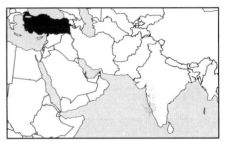

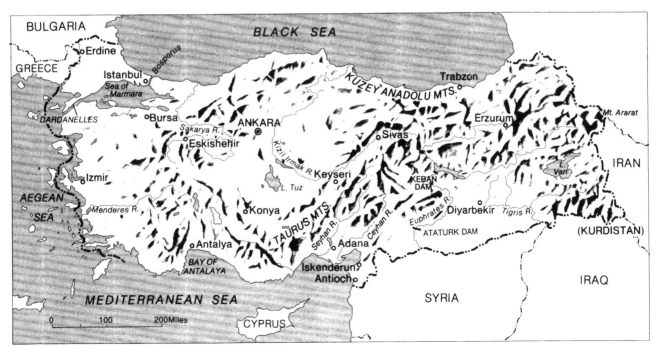

Turkey

Austere, cold and imposing, the Ataturk Mausoleum in Ankara reflects the character of modern Turkey's founder
Photo by Wayne Thompson

of speech, press, and travel. While the document provided for a democratic form of government, in fact Kemal Atatürk ruled as a dictator. Opposition was ruthlessly crushed, particularly that of Kurds in the southeast.

The new government determined to rush Turks towards modernity. It forbade men to wear Muslim-style hats without brims. It forced people to dress like Europeans and, as far as possible, to think and act like them. The government replaced Arabic script with the Latin alphabet, making every book and sign in the country obsolete, a process that helped purify Turkish of Arabic and Persian loanwords. Even names changed, as Mustafa Kemal and the rest of the nation adopted the use of family names. The policy of secularization closed religious schools, abolished the dervish brotherhoods, and eliminated many other aspects of Ottoman culture. The Western calendar replaced the Muslim, polygamy was ended, and women received new status. Codes of law based on European models replaced Ottoman procedures influenced by the Islamic Shari'a. The day of rest was moved from Friday to Sunday.

The pace of change moved rapidly in other social and economic spheres as well. Universal primary education was proclaimed, corruption attacked, and Atatürk committed the military to continuing reform. In subduing Christian Armenians—a population decimated by the genocide of 1914–18—and Greeks, the Turkish army was ruthless. This caused almost all surviving members of these minorities to emigrate.

Economically, Atatürk favored a program of industrialization behind high tariff barriers. When private industry failed to expand sufficiently during the Great Depression of the 1930s, the government created State Economic Enterprises to operate in textiles, metals, banking, and other areas.

Kemal Atatürk died in 1938, recognized as the hero of his nation in his own lifetime. The National Assembly elected his close associate, Ismet Inonu, as the second president. Faced with the difficult task of guiding the nation through World War II, Inonu kept Turkey neutral, but at the end of the war threats from the Soviet Union forced it to seek allies in the West. Beginning in 1947, Turkey received massive U.S. economic and military aid, given to help resist Soviet pressure, and in 1951 it joined the North Atlantic Treaty Organization (NATO). Today it has the second largest military, after the United States, in that alliance.

Turkey moved cautiously toward democracy with competing political parties. The Republican People's Party treasured Atatürk's legacy, but in 1950 the Democratic Party, which appealed to the conservatism of old-fashioned landlords and little-educated peasants, won in a landslide.

Dominant during the 1950s, the Democratic Party became authoritarian. It banned opposition political activities and plunged the country into serious debt. With the nation slipping badly, in 1960 officers seized power, the military considering itself the heir of Atatürk's reforms and, in more than just the conventional sense, guardians of the nation. They arrested

high officials and Democratic Party politicians, executing some, including the former prime minister. The military then oversaw the creation of a new constitution and, after elections, handed power back to the politicians.

Although it returned Turkey to formal democracy and set a precedent for a watchdog role, military intervention did not solve underlying political and economic problems. Indeed, some of the drastic measures taken created bitterness for a whole generation. A decade later, in 1971, student protests, unemployment, and violence by extremist groups shook public confidence. The army forced the prime minister to resign and again took strong measures to restore law and order.

Nevertheless, by the late 1970s, protests and assassinations again shook the country. Extremists on both the Marxist left and Islamic right reinforced old communal rivalries, and in 1978 unrest erupted into mob fighting in Marash, east of Adana. The Shi'a and Alevi communities, generally poorer than the majority Sunni Muslims, suffered more than 100 dead and several hundred injured. Since the Shi'a and Alevi supported the Republican People's Party, and the Sunnis backed the conservative Justice Party, heir to the dissolved Democratic Party, the conflict reflected socio-economic, political, and religious divisions. Despite the imposition of martial law in many regions, the toll from the violence exceeded 5,000.

Surprising almost no one, in 1980 the military seized power again and installed a governing council that took vigorous steps against dissenters on the left and right. It arrested more than 10,000 suspects during the first month. Strict controls were imposed on the press, hundreds of mayors were dismissed, and taxi drivers were ordered to shave daily. Within months, violence declined in the country. However, there were widespread reports of torture and many innocent people languished in prison. In 2014, the only two surviving coup leaders were sentenced to life imprisonment. Both in their 90s they died before the sentence could go to appeal. There are conflicting reports around CIA involvement in the coup.

The Kurdish Insurrection

For millennia, tough mountain tribesmen speaking Kurdish dialects have inhabited the heights and valleys where the borders of Iraq, Iran, and Turkey converge. Outside East and South Asia, these Kurds form the largest ethnic group lacking independence. Kurds have rebelled against each state where they form sizable local majorities.

Many of today's political problems result directly from the breakup of the Ottoman

Empire after World War I. Kurdish leaders claimed eastern Anatolia but failed to influence the peace settlement, and the Treaty of Lausanne brushed aside Kurdish desires for independence.

For decades, Turkey officially classified Kurds as "Mountain Turks," and manipulated their dialectic differences to avoid recognizing them as a separate national group. Kemal Atatürk and his successors rigorously crushed Kurdish revolts and suppressed evidence of Kurdish identity. Regulations prohibited the language from use in personal names, public speeches, and at weddings and social occasions. Until 1991, no books, papers, street signs, or pamphlets legally appeared in the language. Legalizing Kurdish TV broadcasts took another decade. However, the dialects remained alive, even when illegal. Cassettes in Kurdish circulated widely, and in recent years satellite broadcasts enabled programs from Europe to reach viewers.

Most Kurds traditionally lived in mountain villages, divided from others across the mountains by dialect and tribal loyalties. They received little formal education, and what little they did was in Turkish, so for many reasons most Kurds tended to ignore national issues. However, some became successful politicians and advanced to the top of national politics. Indeed, one-quarter of members of parliament have claimed some Kurdish ancestry. At the other extreme, many Kurds passionately desire their own schools and autonomy, including independence.

In the 1980s, violence spread across the southeast and east, fomented by the Kurdish Workers Party (PKK), a Marxist group led by Abdullah Ocalan. Financed and supported by Syria and by Kurds working in Europe, PKK fighters infiltrated into Turkey. The military, a largely conscript army, responded roughly to attacks by the PKK. On occasion it used heavy weapons within towns, and its brutal treatment of civilians often alienated the local population. By the mid-1990s, over 800 villages had been forcibly evacuated to cut off guerrillas from food and shelter.

The violence rose sharply in the 1990s. Despite innovations like winter operations, the military proved unable to crush the insurgency. It mounted large-scale invasions of alleged PKK bases in Iraqi Kurdistan and reported hundreds killed. In fact, alerted by the massive military buildup, most guerrillas had slipped away.

For its part, the PKK attacked civilians, especially Kurds who cooperated with the government. Foreign travelers became targets, even in Istanbul, as the PKK threatened the important tourist industry.

Turkey's laws and methods often seemed designed to provoke resentment.

TURKISH REPUBLIC OF NORTHERN CYPRUS

Area: About 1,295 square miles (3,350 square kilometers).
Population: About 315,000.
Capital City: Turkish sector of Nicosia.
Location: 40 miles from the Turkish coast.
Ethnic Background: Turkish Cypriot, with immigrant mainland Turks.
Chief Commercial Products: Citrus fruits, grain, and light manufactures.
Trading Partner: Turkey.
Former Status: Part of the Republic of Cyprus (1960–1974)
National Day: November 15 (1983; Republic Day).
Chief of State: Mustafa Akıncı, President.
National Flag: A red crescent on a white field between two horizontal red bars.
GDP: About $4,040 billion.
GDP per capita: About $15,100.

Ethnic violence between its Greek and Turkish communities during the early 1960s marred the independence of the small island of Cyprus. A 1974 coup against the Greek Cypriot president enabled Turkey to invade and protect Turkish-inhabited villages and towns, as well as seize Greek ones in the north. The assault captured 38% of the island and divided it along the "Attila Line," to protect the Turkish 18% of the population. The two communities periodically bowed to international pressure and held talks on a settlement, but neither proved willing to compromise.

The Turkish-Cypriot Legislative Assembly proclaimed the independence of the "Turkish Republic of Northern Cyprus" in 1983. Only Turkey recognized this new state, and thus virtually all trade and travel must take place through Turkey. Rauf Denktash, formerly vice president of the entire island, became its president.

Living in Northern Cyprus has required great sacrifices in return for freedom from Greek control. Turkish Nicosia initially possessed no cinema or commercial art gallery and only five public telephones for its 40,000 people. Until recently, per capita incomes averaged about one-third the Greek level. Foreign investment is negligible, especially since European Union courts have allowed Greek owners to sue for their property sold to Europeans. Mainland Turkey provides almost half the zone's budget and funds all major public works. This requires use of the Turkish lira rather than the euro, so common to other European commerce and trade (including in Cyprus). Military forces from mainland Turkey control the local police, and journalists who question such links have been arrested on dubious charges. Moreover, immigrants from Turkey may now outnumber Turkish Cypriots in their own territory.

During three decades of sporadic peace talks, Turkish Cypriots consistently demanded most territory north of the Attila Line, about 30% of the island, and a form of federalism that meant near-complete independence. Greek Cypriot leaders seemed more willing to compromise. However, in a bizarre turn of events, in 2003 many Turkish Cypriots rejected President Denktash's hardline objections and voted to accept UN proposals, while the newly-elected Greek Cypriot president condemned the proposals for granting Turks too much. Thus Greek Cyprus joined the EU on terms constructed to encourage the Turks to compromise, while the Greeks refused the UN compromise themselves.

Mehmet Ali Talat won the 2005 presidential election. He desired reunification and EU membership for the entire island. In 2008, Demetris Christofias of the AKEL Communist Party, who held similar views, won the Cypriot presidency. The two agreed to reopen Ledra Street—the traditional shopping center closed since the 1964 communal troubles—and undertake talks on the many unresolved issues. Both leaders expressed a sense of urgency in supporting a federal republic of two zones and two communities, granting the smaller Turkish community political equality with the Greek one.

Time solved some problems—Cyprus now uses the euro, ending a dispute over the central bank. Grave problems do remain, like the return of refugees, restitution of property, the constitution, and the futures of Famagusta, Turkish settlers, and Turkish troops. Due in part to the lack of progress, Talat's party lost the 2009 legislative elections, and he was defeated the next year by Dervis Eroglu, a separatist. In 2013 voters reversed themselves and made the leftwing Republican Turkish Party the largest, and in 2015 Eroglu's re-election attempt was defeated by Mustafa Akıncı, who like his Greek counterpart, Nicos Anastasiades, desires to solve the forty-year split. The moment seems opportune.

Turkey

Stone heads of gods built for King Antiochus I in southwestern Turkey over 2,000 years ago

For example, Article 8 of the constitution prohibited separatist propaganda in any form, including calls for ethnic autonomy. It was used to convict dozens of journalists, politicians, and labor unionists on charges of sedition.

Turkish courts and the military allowed scant room for peaceful criticism. Kurdish parties faced frequent attempts to ban them from elections. Human rights activists suffered at the hands of the police, who arrested even minor employees. Yasar Kemal, one of Turkey's greatest living writers and the author of the internationally acclaimed *Memed, My Hawk*, received a suspended jail term for merely questioning policy toward the Kurds. Outside the law, a series of unsolved murders decimated journalists and leaders—including over 100 political leaders—sympathetic to Kurdish aspirations.

In 1998 Turkish pressure forced Syria to crack down on PKK activities and expel its leader, Ocalan. This eventually led to his capture in Kenya by Turkish commandos, a tremendous boost to Turkish pride. Britain also closed down a Kurdish satellite channel, Med-TV. Broadcasting across Europe and the Middle East, it had advocating killings in reprisal for the capture of Ocalan.

On trial for his life, Ocalan called the PKK rebellion a "mistake" and ordered his followers to halt violence and adopt a peaceful political struggle. In 2000, a party congress formally adopted Ocalan's political strategy of peacefully promoting the Kurdish community within Turkey. Most PKK fighters withdrew to Iraq, but fighting resumed in 2003 when the PKK demanded an amnesty for all PKK prisoners, including Ocalan, as a condition for a renewed truce.

For decades, the government's modest conciliation efforts have failed to address the underlying problems. One great obstacle to peace remains the uncompromising and strident nationalism common among Turkish officers and officials. This attitude justifies the arbitrary arrests, torture, and bureaucratic heavy-handedness that have long remained the ways of life in Turkey's Southeast. For example, in early 2016 more than 100 fans of a Kurdish soccer team were arrested, and the team's headquarters was raided, after some supporters chanted "Resistance is everywhere" during a game. Around the same time, star player Deniz Naki faced a 12 game suspension for dedicating a team win to Kurds killed during a government crackdown.

Kurdish politicians frequently face legal challenges. The Constitutional Court dissolved political parties because of alleged links with rebels. As many Kurds grew disillusioned by the government's failure to satisfy even modest demands, activists formed the Peace and Democracy Party (BDP) and won 35 seats in the 2011 elections running as independents.

To escape mistreatment, and for better economic opportunity, thousands of Kurds migrate to western Turkey annually. Some have fled to Iraq to join PKK fighters, who launch cross-border raids of increasing severity. The total death toll from the violence exceeds 40,000.

Complying with the human rights provisions of the European Union, Parliament voted major reforms by 2004, including permission for Kurdish schools and radio broadcasts. However, attitudes in the military and government bureaucracy meant that changes came grudgingly and slowly. For example, applicants for licenses to teach Kurdish found themselves blocked by repeated technicalities, and Kurdish broadcasting by the state-owned radio and TV service only began after transmissions of such locally-insignificant languages as Bosnian. Indeed, the 30-minute weekly programs in two Kurdish dialects were not even described as Kurdish.

Following months of negotiations, in 2013 Abdullah Ocalan called for a cease-fire without conditions, arguing, "weapons should be silent and ideas should speak." Soon afterwards, PKK units withdrew to northern Iraq, and in responses to the ceasefire, Prime Minister Erdoğan announced major concessions over language.

Another significant gesture was to propose a lower vote threshold for a party to enter parliament. Kurds comprise about 20% of the nation's population, but the largest Kurdish grouping, the Peace and Democracy Party (BDP), regularly failed

192

to meet the 10% threshold. Erdoğan's target of the bar setting at 5% was more plausible, since BDP candidates received 4% of the vote in the 2014 municipal elections. Regrettably, in July 2015 the nearly two year old ceasefire collapsed. The fighting in Syria between Kurdish militants and Islamic State fighters exacerbated tensions in Turkey.

Political and Economic Stagnation, 1990s

Besides the Kurdish insurrection, the great theme of the 1990s was national stagnation, both economic and political. Rampant inflation, a by-product of successive governments printing easy money to win elections, eroded workers' wages. In response, unions demanded pay increases as high as 300%, and strikes spread in government-owned industries. Accepting the workers' pay demands and those of farmers and civil servants guaranteed even higher inflation, but rejecting them risked provoking serious disorder.

Parliamentary politics continued feverishly through much of the 1990s, with nine governments in as many years, including one headed by Tansu Ciller, the country's first woman to hold the office. Unfortunately, political attention often focused on gaining office rather than on governing well.

This instability resulted from a political culture that fostered aggressive personal ambitions by individual politicians, combined with an electoral system that encouraged parties to splinter. Rather than the "winner-take-all" system of electoral politics, where seats are allocated to the highest vote getters without ensuring representation for minority groups, Turkey adopted a system of "proportional representation" (PR). This kind of system is intended to achieve a legislature whose distribution of seats approximates the parties' share of the votes, even though it risks splitting politics into many, almost ungovernable bits. When adopting PR, Turkey reduced the number of small parties by granting the largest party the additional votes of all parties receiving less than 10% of the total. As a result, parliamentary majorities could be manufactured. For example, in 1987 the Motherland Party won only 36% of the vote but gained a large majority of seats in the National Assembly (292 of 450).

Beyond PR, elections failed to provide good government because political opinion was deeply fractured. In 1996, for example, the Islamic Welfare (*Refah*) Party came in first, though winning only 21% of the vote. On mathematical grounds alone, forming a coalition government became extremely difficult. With the Welfare Party as the largest, stable coalitions became impossible. Islamist in a nation dominated by secularists for 70 years, it seemed guilty, as Tansu Ciller claimed, of "sinking the country into darkness." Six cabinets held office in just three years as civilian and military secularists attempted to keep the Welfare Party from office. However, to avoid possible parliamentary investigations of corruption that might implicate her, Ciller sought the safety of an alliance with her ideological enemy. Welfare's leader, Necmettin Erbakan, became the country's first Islamist prime minister.

Erbakan clearly reoriented foreign policy toward the Islamic world. He visited Iran to sign a major gas deal, and toured Libya. However, his term was brief. When some local officials of the Welfare Party openly contradicted secularist traditions, the military quietly encouraged parliamentary maneuvering that collapsed the coalition in 1997. For good measure, the Constitutional Court later banned the party because it had permitted women to wear head-scarves in public buildings, encouraged Islamic schools, and kept (unproven) links with secret societies. The courts also convicted Erbakan and several other party officials, including the mayor of Istanbul, of making statements deemed too Islamist.

Bulent Ecevit's left-wing but nationalistic Democratic Left Party swept to first place in the 1999 elections. Although the old "bonus" for being the largest party no longer applied, Ecevit succeeded in forming an unlikely alliance with the right-wing Nationalist Action Party. Ecevit now provided stable leadership, waging a war on corruption that landed "big fish" (particularly bankers) as well as petty criminals. The police also discovered that the Turkish paramilitary group *Hizbullah* (not the Lebanese group) had murdered more than 100 secular intellectuals, Marxist Kurds, and other victims. Control over spending brought the rate of inflation below 40%. In 1999 the European Union at last accepted Turkey as a candidate for membership.

That same year, an earthquake devastated seven western provinces—the country's industrial heartland. The civil administration and the military both proved inept at rescue efforts, although better at feeding and sheltering hundreds of thousands left homeless. Despite its location on a major geological fault, Turkey had not developed specialized rescue teams. Television pictures that showed a centuries-old mosque and its slender minaret standing intact beside collapsed apartment buildings illustrated an equally serious failing: for decades, officials had failed to issue and enforce appropriate building codes.

As successor to the long-serving President Suleyman Demirel, the National Assembly elected Ahmet Necdet Sezer, chairman of the Constitutional Court. A legal scholar rather than a politician, Sezer strongly emphasized the rule of law. The changes that Sezer advocated were aimed not so much to please Europe, but to benefit Turks.

Spices in a Turkish souq, Istanbul.

Turkey

When the strong personalities of President Sezer and Prime Minister Ecevit clashed in 2001, stock market investors took flight. Those with money (including, allegedly, the governor of the Central Bank) speculated against the Turkish lira, draining $7 billion from the Central Bank's reserves within hours. Overnight, interest rates reached an annual rate of 5000%, and the country plunged into its worst economic recession since World War II. GDP fell by almost 10%, and nearly a million workers lost their jobs. The rates of suicide, theft, prostitution, and stress-related illness all climbed, and media experts warned of a "social explosion." Another symptom of the misery came from the 1.5 million people who canceled their cell phone contracts. Besides the government's deficit, the banking system lay at the heart of the trouble. Many banks had borrowed funds abroad and lent them for politically-important projects with little chance of business success. Saving such banks required billions of dollars, much of it from the IMF. Turkey became that institution's largest debtor.

Under the stress, Ecevit's coalition fragmented. The Nationalist Action Party opposed human rights proposals like banning capital punishment and allowing Kurdish-language TV broadcasting. Finally, members of Ecevit's own party forced early elections, hoping to catch Islamist political forces disorganized.

Rise of the AKP

After the Welfare Party had been declared illegal, Islamist deputies failed to unite. However, one faction formed the Justice and Development Party (known by its initials AKP), under the country's

President Recep Tayyip Erdoğan

most popular individual politician, Recep Tayyip Erdoğan. A former mayor of Istanbul previously convicted of inciting religious hatred, and banned by the Supreme Court from running for parliament, he claimed that the AKP was not Islamist, but merely Islamic-rooted.

Voting day transformed Turkish politics. Not a single party from the previous parliament managed to win 10% of the national vote, and therefore, all of them, both government and opposition, failed to enter the new parliament. The victor was the AKP, with 34% of the popular vote and nearly two-thirds of the seats. The Republican People's Party captured most of the rest and formed the opposition. Coalition politics had come to an end in Turkey. The large AKP majority soon overturned the law that Erdoğan had been convicted of breaking, rendering him eligible to run for parliament. After a by-election victory, he took office in early 2003.

His initial challenge was the U.S. desire to attack Iraq through Turkey, long regarded in Washington as a special NATO ally, overwhelmingly Muslim but staunchly anti-Communist. However, the Turkish constitution requires parliamentary approval of any foreign troops stationed in the country, and public opinion polls showed that 90% of the population opposed an unprovoked attack on a fellow Muslim country. Business leaders feared the loss of markets and another recession. Strategists and the military worried that Iraqi Kurds might declare independence or seize Kirkuk. Despite promises of substantial U.S. aid, parliament narrowly rejected the U.S. plan.

In his first two years of office, Erdoğan guided a legal revolution in human rights through parliament. After a decade of immobilized coalitions, the AKP's majority enabled it to abolish the death penalty, restrict torture by the police, and increase the media's freedom of expression. A major reform of the penal code raised protections for women and established life sentences for perpetrators of "honor killings."

In the political domain, parliament curbed the military by placing the National Security Council advisory under civilian rather than military leadership. Even military spending was placed under parliamentary control. Political detainees, including some Kurdish militants, were granted amnesty.

Recognizing these long-delayed improvements in human rights, as well as Erdoğan's moderate stand over Cyprus, the EU opened talks on Turkey's admission in 2005. As expected, the talks proved difficult, both for objective reasons like the size, and degree of poverty of Turkey, as well as cultural fears about the designation of 70 million Muslim Turks

as Europeans. One particular stumbling block has been the requirement that Turkey open its ports and airports to all EU members— including Cyprus—though its Greek government refuses trade with the Turkish north.

One unsettled domestic issue—at least for conservative police and prosecutors—is the prohibition on statements that "insult" the nation. For Orhan Pamuk, uttering the words "One million Armenians and 30,000 Kurds were killed in these lands" sufficed to bring criminal charges in 2005. The charges were dismissed, fortunately so, because the next year Pamuk won the Nobel Prize for literature. Three of his novels have been published in English: *The White Castle, My Name is Red,* and *Snow.*

Orhan Pamuk escaped state prosecutors, but in 2007 the deeper intolerance motivated a teenager to assassinate the country's leading Armenian journalist, Hrant Dink. Although Dink had been convicted for claiming that Armenians had suffered genocide during World War I, his murder evoked a surprising outpouring of regret and sympathy from liberal-minded Turks, few of whom will accept the veracity of his claims.

Crises over Presidential Elections, 2007

Political tensions inevitably rose in 2007, when the five-year election cycle of the Grand National Assembly coincided with the seven-year term of the presidency, set to expire in May. Massive demonstrations by secularists reflected fears that the AKP majority in the Assembly would enable it to select the next president. President Sezer warned that the danger of Islamic radicalism was greater than ever. The military chief bluntly stated that a committed secularist was needed in the presidential palace. Symbols matter, and many secularists abhorred the thought of a president's wife wearing a headscarf while hosting a reception in the Çankaya Palace.

Very carefully, party leaders announced their candidate just before the filing deadline, reducing time for public protests. Rather than Prime Minister Erdoğan, the party selected Abdullah Gül, the foreign minister. His nomination lacked a two-thirds majority by a few votes on the initial ballot, but victory seemed assured with the third ballot, when a simple majority would suffice. However, the Constitutional Court insisted, on dubious legal grounds, on a two-thirds quorum for a presidential election. The third ballot did not take place.

In response, Erdoğan called early elections for the National Assembly. Despite the determined opposition of staunch secularists, the AKP won overwhelmingly, capturing nearly half (48%) of all votes

Former President Abdullah Gul

and gaining an absolute majority of seats. The victory also eliminated the legitimacy of any military intervention pretending to "preserve democracy."

Two issues dominated Turkish political life during the following year. First, the National Assembly duly elected Abdullah Gül as president. Second, the AKP formed a tactical alliance with the ultranationalists and amended the constitution to ban the exclusion of students from universities except for reasons stipulated by law. This protection for women wearing scarves met the aspirations of millions of party supporters, but it infuriated secularists. The Constitutional Court soon struck down the amendment.

Democracy itself faced serious threat in 2008 when prosecutors charged that the AKP had sought to undermine secularism and should be banned. Clearly, the party had attempted to abolish universities' prohibitions on wearing headscarves, and it had strengthened religious education. Many commentators expected the Constitutional Court to rule in favor of the prosecutors, but it side-stepped the political chaos that would have followed a ban. Instead, the court decided that since the party had raised human rights standards and had not acted violently, its punishment would be the loss of half its government subsidy.

Long-running investigations of alleged secularist plots have also threatened to provoke military intervention. After a newspaper and a court were attacked in 2006, prosecutors charged that a shadowy group of secular extremists, code-named Ergenekon, had unleashed violence to stoke unrest and provoke an army coup. Dozens of prominent secularists, including university professors, journalists, retired generals, and members of a police special operations unit were arrested. Placing retired military officers on trial in

civilian court for the first time tested Turkish democracy, especially because the alleged conspirators were often prominent critics of the government.

In 2010, hundreds more military officers—including generals and admirals—were charged with participation in the "Sledgehammer Plot." They allegedly conspired to bomb two mosques in Istanbul and provoke Greece into shooting down a Turkish plane, thus creating the circumstances for a military seizure of power. Such trials confirmed the powerlessness of the former secular establishment to protect its prominent members. Generals involved in the 1997 "postmodern coup" that overthrew Prime Minister Necmettin Erbakan were investigated, but perhaps the ultimate symbol of the changed political environment was the trial of General Kenan Evren, who led the 1980 coup d'état and served as president for six years.

As expected, the AKP won a large majority in the 2011 National Assembly elections. Prime Minister Erdoğan had campaigned on both the successful past—the economic prosperity his cabinets had brought the country—and a vision for the future. He promised, for example, a canal around Istanbul, to divert much of the heavy freight and tanker traffic from the Bosporus. He also called on voters to support his quest for a new constitution that would place the military under firm civilian control.

Although Erdoğan won a historic triumph by increasing his party's share of the popular vote in a third successive election, the AKP actually lost seats as fewer citizens "wasted" votes on parties

unlikely to exceed the 10% threshold. By contrast, the major opposition Republican People's Party (CHP) gained additional seats with its new social democratic approach. The nationalists barely survived the 10% threshold.

Foreign Relations: A New Regional Role

For decades, Western nations valued Turkey as a Cold War ally and the eastern bulwark of NATO. More recently it became a military partner of Israel. However, with the Soviet threat removed and the economy developing rapidly, Erdoğan set Turkey's foreign policy on an increasingly independent course. Presenting himself as a Middle Eastern and developing-world leader, he sought to win new markets for the country's industries, as well as to influence the region. He attempted to mediate between Israel and Syria, and offered to process Iran's partially-enriched uranium for research and medical purposes.

The government also supported Turkish Islamist groups participating in the flotilla of vessels that challenged the Israeli blockade of Gaza in 2010. Vociferous criticism followed the Israeli commando raid in international waters on the Turkish vessel *Merve Marmara* that killed nine Turkish citizens. When Israel refused to apologize, diplomatic relations weakened, and the special military alliance collapsed.

During the popular protests of the 2011 Arab Spring, Erdoğan encouraged authoritarian rulers to resign and condemned dictators like Syria's al-Assad and Libya's Gaddafi for using violence against their own people. Turkey accepted refugees

The old Galata Bridge, Istanbul, stretching across the Golden Horn

Turkey

Only the patient and brave (with good lateral vision and quick reflexes) dare to drive Istanbul's Tanlabas Boulevard

Photo by Miller B. Spangler

from Syria and hosted the rebels' political leadership. However, when terrorist explosions killed 46 in the border town of Reyhanli, political critics claimed that Turkey had adopted too great a role.

Erdoğan Tightens His Grip

During the first several years of AKP rule, outside observers pointed to Turkey as a shining example of the compatibility of democracy (in the sense commonly understood in the West) and Islam. To the regret of many, as the 2000s gave way to the 2010s, Turkey became less democratic by the day. By 2013, human rights organizations had criticized Turkey's loss of press freedoms and ranked it first in the world in the number of jailed journalists. Opposition parties and human rights advocates objected to limitations on the sale of alcoholic drinks, and during weekly rallies demonstrators silently protested the justice system over the convictions of so many military officers. Indeed, in an interview in 2016, U.S. President Barack Obama expressed disappointment that President Erdoğan had become authoritarian.

The most publicized protests began in May when a few dozen environmentalists, some of them women and many of

them young and educated, gathered in Istanbul's Gezi Park on the edge of Taksim Square, the heart of modern Istanbul, to oppose plans to replace the park with a shopping center, mosque, and opera house. When police attempted to clear the park, the demonstrators resisted. Other protests formed across the country, joined by activists from the opposition CHP and left-wing labor unions.

In contrast to AKP leaders who apologized for harsh police tactics, the Prime Minister remained critical of the demonstrations and blamed a "treacherous plot" for the affair. After days of protests, he ordered police to clear Taksim Square; they used water cannon, tear gas, and rubber bullets to do so. Other government agencies also attempted to punish the protestors. The health ministry, for example, investigated healthcare professionals at makeshift first aid centers for acting without permission from the ministry.

While Erdoğan removed the protestors, the entire affair weakened him substantially. His authoritarian style and the harsh handling of the protests also delayed membership negotiations with the EU.

More serious crises followed. In December, special police units conducted

spectacular raids on prominent officials and businessmen, arresting more than 50 for offenses ranging from money laundering to bribery in granting construction permits on prohibited sites protected for environmental or cultural preservation. Three cabinet members' sons faced charges of accepting bribes, and the general manager of a large state-owned bank had stashed millions in cash in his home library. The entire scandal pointed to corruption surrounding the Prime Minister.

Clearly taken by surprise, Erdoğan struck back harshly. Discerning a plot by a moderate Islamist group, the Gulen Movement, whose followers he alleged had infiltrated the justice ministry and police, the Prime Minister sacked the top prosecutors and police officials most involved in the investigation and arrests. Thousands of other officers were reshuffled, some to remote rural postings, and new leadership was installed. A later "reform" brought prosecutors and judges under greater control by the justice ministry, clearly attacking their independence.

Very likely, some sort of plot did exist. The Islamic scholar Fethullah Gulen and his *Hizmet* (Service) movement had partnered with the AKP during its rise to power. Its supporters filled many of the new police and judicial appointments and proved a counterweight to the strong secularist traditions within the government. However, from his exile in Pennsylvania, Gulen came to oppose several positions adopted by Erdoğan, including his strong backing of Egypt's Muslim Brotherhood, the widespread arrests of journalists, and police violence against the Gezi Park demonstrators. Then, in November, the education ministry closed down the nation's entrance-exam preparation centers, many of them run profitably by Hizmet.

The Prime Minister became even more biting in his attacks on what he considered the "international conspiracy" against him when an audio recording of a telephone conversation with his son was posted on social media. The voices were apparently genuine and discussed moving millions of euros of cash. The recording suggested wiretapping by his enemies, and Erdoğan ordered Twitter closed (the courts later reversed this decision). Weeks later, a post on Facebook provided a bugged recording of top politicians, military officers, and intelligence experts discussing a possible attack on Syria.

To Turkey's secularists and much of the rest of the world, Erdoğan's political future seemed gravely compromised, and opinion polls charted the public's increasing disapproval. However, public support for Hizmet fell even faster.

Campaign accusations of fraudulent ballots raised fears about the integrity of the 2014 local elections, but most pre-election claims did not prove valid. The national vote tallies proved that AKP had maintained popular support, winning nearly 43% of the vote, almost equaling the combined 44% of the CHP and the right-wing Nationalist Movement Party (MHP).

The great electoral prize of 2014 was the presidency, with a direct popular election for the first time replacing election by parliament. To challenge Erdoğan more effectively, the CHP and MHP selected a joint candidate, Ekmeleddin İhsanoğlu, a widely respected scholar and author. As the former Secretary-General of the Organization of Islamic Cooperation, he was hardly the typical candidate the secular CHP would nominate, but he had the potential to woo religious conservatives who desired change. The AKP, unable to nominate the popular but term-limited Abdullah Gül, accepted Erdoğan's candidacy when he announced it. Against two opponents, he won 52% of the national vote.

Months of campaigning preceded the 2015 parliamentary elections. Very clearly, Erdoğan desired to create a "strong" presidency with executive powers to replace the existing "weak" presidency

constitutionally prohibited from involvement in political party matters. To change the constitution required a two-thirds vote of parliament; achieving this became the AKP's goal. Abandoning the relatively non-partisan role of his predecessors, he threw himself into the election campaign.

Economic and international conditions hardly favored an incumbent. The economic growth rate had fallen because of events both domestic and international (including Syria's civil war). Foreign policy could hardly be portrayed as a success, because bitterness had replaced formerly close relations with Egypt, Israel, Syria, and other countries. The presence of more than one million Syrian refugees provided a daily reminder of an anti-Assad Syrian policy that had failed.

Nevertheless, the CHP and MHP had difficulties attracting voters outside their respective secular and nationalist followers, and the AKP had won three successive elections. In 2015, the crucial factor was the new *Halkların Demokratik Partisi* (HDP), a combination of Kurdish and leftist interests led by Selahattin Demirtaş and his female co-chair, Figen Yüksekdağ. Their crucial decision was whether to contest the elections as a political party, thus needing to achieve 10% of the vote to enter parliament, or for its members to run as independents. If the HDP entered parliament, the AKP was unlikely to achieve its desired majority; if it did not, its votes would be divided among the parties that did, thus boosting the AKP total.

Despite the traditionally rural and conservative Kurdish culture, the HDP ran a remarkably modern campaign. Fifty

percent of its candidates were women, and the list included Muslim minorities, Christians, and other religious groups, as well as the first openly gay parliamentary candidate. Despite sharp attacks from the AKP, election returns provided jubilation for the HDP, which won about 13% of the vote. In a sharp set-back for the AKP, it not only failed to achieve the desired two-thirds majority, but with only 42% of the vote its parliamentary presence was too weak to govern without a coalition or understanding with another party.

More recently, two security-related events from mid-2016 have in many ways dominated Turkish politics. On June 28, 2016, three Islamic State gunmen opened fire at Atatürk International Airport in Istanbul. After killing a number of passengers and airport staff, the attackers detonated suicide vests. At least 45 people were killed; more than 200 others were injured.

This was the third major terrorist attack in Istanbul during the first half of 2016 alone. In January an Islamic State suicide bomber had killed 13 people in Sultanahmet Square, near the historic Blue Mosque. In March another suicide bomber, also from the Islamic State, killed 5 in the city's Beyoglu district. Earlier in June, the Kurdistan Freedom Falcons (TAK), an offshoot of the Kurdistan Workers' Party (PKK), killed 12 and injured more than 50 in a car bomb attack targeting police. These attacks gave President Erdoğan, who had already been tightening his grip on Turkish politics from the presidential palace for years, more reason to embrace the politics of emergency—and more leeway to do so.

A combine harvesting wheat in southern Turkey

Turkey

The second event happened just a month after the airport attack, and it was even more significant. On the night of July 15, when the president was at a seaside resort far from the capital, a faction of the Turkish military attempted to take the reins of state in a military coup. Jets flew low over Ankara in a show of force; tanks were on the streets in major cities; bridges were closed in Istanbul. Helicopters bombed a special forces headquarters of the police outside of the capital.

In the chaos, which lasted into the following day, more than 300 people died, and over 2,000 were injured. When the coup ultimately failed, mass arrests of tens of thousands followed. President Erdoğan immediately blamed Fethullah Gulen, a Turkish dissident who has lived in self-imposed exile in the United States since 1999, and the clandestine movement supporting him within Turkey. In the time since, the Turkish government has continued to demand Gulen's extradition, so far without success, and it has clamped down more firmly on opposition at home. The extent of the response, which has systematically violated human rights, has been difficult to watch for those who once held Turkey in high regard as a shining example of Islamic democracy.

Culture: One cannot think of Turkey without thinking of Istanbul—one of the great historic cities of the world. The ancient Greek colony of Byzantium later became Constantinople, capital of the Eastern Roman Empire. It evolved into the capital and center of the Byzantine world, where ancient Hellenistic culture persisted until its capture in 1453 by the Ottomans under Sultan Mehmet II. The Ottomans renamed it Istanbul and installed their sultan in the Topkapi Saray, the Great Palace overlooking the Bosporus and Golden Horn. The spectacular mosques of Istanbul still remain places of deep reverence.

Although Ankara, located near the nation's center, is the political capital, Istanbul is the modern cultural and economic heart of Turkey. Europe's largest city, with a population above 14 million, it extends for miles along both sides of the Bosporus. Its great variety of people and different ways of living make it one of the world's most interesting cities.

By contrast, Ankara is a very modern city, but it has the unhappy distinction of possessing some of the worst air pollution of any city anywhere. This is not the result of heavy industry, but of geography—the city lies in a natural bowl, trapping smoke and fumes.

Turkish culture today blends strong pride in ethnic heritage with a culture influenced by religion from Arabia and modern arts and ideas from Europe and North America. In many ways, Turkey is a land of many cultures.

From a country long considered overwhelmingly agricultural and rural, between 1970 and 1990 Turkey rapidly changed into a nation of city dwellers. In the cities one hears Western music, and modern young women can meet male friends in a restaurant or dance in nightclubs.

Old ways die hard in rural areas, however. In many villages, for both cultural and Islamic reasons, the feeling is still strong that women should not attend public events with men. Women and girls do not attend the *halkevi*, "people's house," traditionally the center of social life in most villages. Likewise, in remote villages visitors may notice that women dress very conservatively, but in Istanbul, Izmir, and Ankara women work in most positions they hold in Europe or America.

Since the founding of the Republic, educated Turks have often tried to imitate the literature and drama of Europe. There is a state theater performing Western plays (or plays following Western forms), but many

Turks continue to find this alien. Karagoz, the shadow puppet and his friends and enemies are more to Turkish taste. Both fantasy and real-life situations appear in puppet shows. Likewise, the great majority of Turks love their own music. To the accompaniment of three or four instruments, including a lute (bazouki), a drum, and perhaps a violin, a singer's folk songs tell of love, war, heartbreak or death—often drawn-out and high-pitched quavering tones, using minor toned scales.

The traditions of Kemal Atatürk decree secularism, and until recently successive cabinets—if necessary prodded by the military—remained aloof to religion. Nevertheless, today Islam lives as a vital part of the beliefs of most Turks. Religious classes returned to schools after the 1980 military coup, as part of the cultural heritage of the country. Instruction about religion was not intended as indoctrination, though sometimes it had that effect. During the 1980s the Kemalist ban on words of Arabic origin and Islamic connotation was removed, and terms and phrases last used by educated people of the Ottoman

Designing a carpet pattern, Istanbul

World Bank

Turkey

Empire, now reappear in writing and on radio and television.

Education has been a primary concern of the government for decades. Elementary education is completely free and nearly universal. The "middle schools" are similar to three-year junior high schools, while the lycée corresponds to an academic high school and is primarily intended to prepare students for university study. Only higher-ranked graduates of middle schools are able to enter the lycées.

Turkey now has dozens of universities. The oldest is Istanbul University, which traces its founding to Mehmet the Conqueror in 1453. It now enrolls over 30,000 students. The next largest is Ankara University. Another institution in Ankara that offers instruction in English rather than Turkish is Middle East Technical University. Expanded with assistance from the UN, and several foreign nations, it serves other countries of the Middle East as well as Turkey.

Economy: Long famous for carpets, mohair, and dried fruits, Turkey long remained a land of relatively poor traditional farmers who struggled for a living in remote villages. As recently as the 1970s agricultural products amounted to half the nation's exports.

Industry developed slowly, partly because local handicrafts suffered competition from European manufactured goods. The first major thrust of industrialization occurred only in the 1930s, sponsored by the government for political and social reasons as well as economic ones. Protected by high tariffs, regulation and other trade barriers, the factories of the State Economic Enterprises (SEEs) failed to become efficient competitors. High inflation and shortages of foreign exchange frequently halted periods of strong economic growth. The Ottoman Empire had been the political "Sick Man of Europe" in the 19th century, and for most of the 20th century Turkey was the economic "Sick Man of Europe."

In the 1980s, Prime Minister Turgot Özal launched reforms that began to transform the economy. He freed markets, reduced tariffs, eliminated exchange controls, and removed the heavy hand of government trade restrictions. This encouraged investment by both domestic and foreign firms.

Industry seized the opportunity to expand, and the resulting export-led growth transformed the stagnant economy of the late 1970s into one enjoying rapid rates of real GNP growth. Exports rose by 400% between 1980 and 1987, before inflation again damaged their competitiveness.

Özal's free market policies alleviated but failed to eliminate many traditional economic problems. Population growth,

above 2% per year until the mid-1980s, absorbed a major portion of national income growth. Consequently, although many Turks worked abroad, unemployment often hovered around 20%, and incomes reached just 34% of the European Union's average. Public education continued to lag, and social security was minimal (though government employees like teachers retired young). Tax revenues fell far short of requirements, creating a budget deficit regularly exceeding 10% of GNP, and foreign debt required large payments for interest and principal.

Nevertheless, profitable opportunities abounded in many fields. Tourism climbed rapidly in the late 20th century, although hampered by insufficient infrastructure and sanitary facilities as well as fears of terrorism. Given its beautiful scenery, warm climate, exotic customs, and wealth of historic locations, by 2010 the nation attracted some 32 million visitors annually.

A world apart from luxury tourist hotels, the Southeast Anatolia Project (*Güneydoğu Anadolu Projesi*—GAP) offers the possibility of improving some of the country's most impoverished areas. A complex of

Mararias, one of the beautiful summer resorts on the Aegean Sea

199

Turkey

The Keban Dam on the Euphrates River　　　World Bank

20 dams, 19 hydroelectric plants, tunnels, and irrigation canals, the project's expected cost will exceed $32 billion. Besides generating large amounts of electricity from the Atatürk Dam, initially the world's sixth largest, and others on the Euphrates and Tigris Rivers, the project is planned to divert enough water to irrigate some four million acres.

Several problems threaten completion of the project. Declining economic benefits, combined with rising costs, make some dams less profitable than alternative ways of generating electricity, and concerns over soil salinity, chemical pollution, and water quality may limit irrigation. Critics also argue that villagers displaced by the reservoirs are often not compensated significantly, because the land may be owned by rich landlords, and the villagers are conveniently removed. Thus GAP's electrification, roads and farming services may never reach the average farmer in the style of America's TVA, and the local Kurds may lose their heritage without economic gain.

The first two terms of AKP rule (2002–11) witnessed a near-explosion of economic growth. Despite a population increase, per capita incomes more than doubled. Inflation dropped to 4%, while unemployment fell from the traditional 20% to half that. The budget deficit and foreign debt both fell as proportions of GDP, as exports soared across Europe and firms entered new markets. Once a nation of tottering banks, new regulations kept them from risky lending. None failed during the world recession of 2008–09.

Manufacturing also boomed. Shipbuilding came to rank as fourth in the world, automobiles as sixth in Europe, and the country's firms gained a 50% share of the market for European-made color TVs. No longer are exports primarily agricultural. Strongly supported by business interests, Erdoğan personally opened export markets by including executives on his official visits abroad. Transformed from the economic "Sick Man of Europe," Turkey joined the G-20, the club of the world's twenty largest economies.

In 2005, the country celebrated the opening of a pipeline, this one nearly 1,200 miles long from Baku, Azerbaijan. It is valuable to consumers in Europe because it avoids two important difficulties: Russian control (like the other routes out of the Caspian basin), and shipping through the crowded Bosporus. After the 2008 global recession, which hit Turkey hard, the country seemed to recover successfully. However, by the end of 2018 Turkey was once again in recession, with the Turkish lira dropping by 36% against the dollar and the economy declining by 2.4% in the last quarter of the year. By January 2019, unemployment had reached heights of 14.7%, reminiscent of the 2008–09 crisis. In the context of a widening account deficit, skyrocketing inflation, low investor confidence, mounting foreign debt, and the threat of U.S. sanctions, Turkey's economic woes look set to multiply.

The political implications of a slowing economy are clear. In the municipal elections of 2019, Erdoğan's AKP suffered humiliating losses in its traditional heartlands of Ankara and Istanbul. With the party alleging "irregularities," Turkish citizens may be again forced to the polls, in a move critics describe as a further attack on democracy.

On the Bosporus near the Black Sea　　　Photo by Miller B. Spangler

The economy has grown at 5% or better for most of the time since 2010, with 2017 being an especially good year with growth above 7%. Nevertheless, there are reasons for concern. For roughly a year and a half, from February 2017 to June 2018, inflation was in double digits with just a single-month exception. With the exchange rate falling and the economy seemingly overheating, many fear that the Turkish economy could be in for a hard landing.

The Future: Praised by the World Health Organization as an early success story in the management of COVID-19, Turkey ultimately experienced significant infection rates and a relatively high number of deaths. Erdoğan's government has been criticized for lifting restrictions too swiftly, forcing repeated u-turns and losing the goodwill of the Turkish people in the process. In April 2021, Turkey was forced into its first full lockdown in order to combat rising case numbers. As is the case with most economies globally, COVID-19 has had a profound effect on the Turkish economy. With a 70 percent reduction in foreign tourists, Turkey's vital tourism industry has borne a heavy burden.

With recent developments on the domestic political front, Erdoğan appears to have maneuvered himself into a position to lead Turkey for the foreseeable future. Of the many things happening in and around this important country, one to keep an eye on going forward is Turkey's relationship with the United States. In recent years, differences between the NATO allies on Syria have been substantial. U.S. support for the Kurdish dominated YPG in Syria, which Ankara views as a threat to the Turkish state, remains a sore point, as does President Trump's decision to move the U.S. embassy in Israel to Jerusalem. None of this even touches on the continued ire that Erdoğan feels as the result of the United States' refusal to extradite his principal political foe, Fethullah Gulen, from exile in Pennsylvania.

The Battle over Headscarves

In 2008 Turkey's Constitutional Court ruled that parliament's constitutional amendment to permit women to wear headscarves in universities conflicted with the constitutional principle of secularism. Why so great a concern over such modest pieces of fabric?

From one perspective, it is a clear issue of conscience and human rights. If a devout Muslim girl or woman wishes to wear a scarf over her hair, should government interfere? There are surely more pressing national problems to address.

Opponents, some of them practicing Muslims, provide a very different perspective: the scarf, they argue, announces a woman's religious persuasion. By extension, it also proclaims a woman's loyalty to Islamist political parties. Political insignia do not belong in public places such as universities. Even in the individualistic West, they note, France has banned the Burqa in public spaces.

Proponents of headscarves respond that women in scarves intend no criminal conduct. They may vote for any party they please. This is not a return to the brownshirts worn by Hitler's followers in Germany.

After the Islamist-leaning prime minister approved their use in 1998, the courts and military overruled. The election of the Islamist Virtue Party's Merve Kavakci to parliament sharpened the issue. Parliamentary regulations did not explicitly prohibit the scarf, and some reasoned that elected representatives should be entitled to wear whatever they deemed appropriate. Secularists sharply disagreed, regarding the National Assembly as the heart of Atatürk's legacy.

Kavakci appeared wearing a scarf at parliament's opening session in 1999. Accused of violating the republic's basic secular principles, she refused to remove the offending cloth, or leave the chamber. The assembly was forced to adjourn; government came to a halt, even before the new prime minister was designated. Stripped of her Turkish citizenship, Ms. Kavakci now wears her scarf in peace, in U.S. exile.

By some estimates, the country's secular universities dismissed a quarter-million scarf-wearing women in the 1990s and following years. Because their convictions of modesty conflicted with Kemalist conceptions of secularism, these women lost the opportunity for intellectual development and career options. However, most modern societies accept that certain dress standards can be imposed. In 2005, the European Court of Human Rights sided with the ban, justifying it as "protecting the rights and freedoms of others and maintaining public order." It ruled similarly in a French case in 2014.

The United Arab Emirates

The Abu Dhabi business district from a pedestrian crossover

Courtesy of the Caltex Petroleum Corp. (Joe Brignolo, 1995)

Area: 32,000 square miles (83,000 square kilometers).

Population: 9.9 million, 80% non-nationals.

Capital City: Abu Dhabi (585,000).

Climate: Extremely hot except for moderate winters. Precipitation is rare, although some rain falls in the highlands between Ras al-Khayma and Fujayra.

Neighboring Countries: Oman (North, East, and Southeast); Saudi Arabia (South and West).

Time Zone: GMT +4.

Official Language: Arabic.

Other Principal Tongues: English (widely used), Hindi, Urdu, and Farsi (Persian).

Ethnic Background: Arabic-speaking citizens comprise about 20% of the population, while expatriate workers from Pakistan, India, Bangladesh, and Iran compose a majority.

Principal Religion: Islam (55%, mostly Sunni), as well as significant Hindu and Christian minorities amongst the expatriate population.

Chief Commercial Products: Petroleum, liquefied natural gas (LNG), petrochemicals, gold, and diamonds.

Major Trading Partners: Japan, China, the United Kingdom, the United States, Singapore, and South Korea.

Currency: Dirham (1 dirham = 100 fils).

Former Colonial Status: Each sheikhdom accepted British protection and control of foreign affairs but enjoyed domestic autonomy (1892–1971).

National Day: December 2 (1971; Independence Day).

Chief of State: Sheikh Khalifa bin Zayed Al Nahyan (Ruler of Abu Dhabi), President of the Supreme Council of Rulers.

Head of Government: Sheikh Muhammad bin Rashid Al Maktoum (Ruler of Dubai), Vice-President and Prime Minister.

National Flag: Three equal bands of green, white, and black (top to bottom) are flanked at the pole by a vertical red band of the same width.

Gross Domestic Product: $383 billion

GDP per capita: $40,325.

Abu Dhabi and five smaller states south of Qatar and east of Saudi Arabia, plus one on the Gulf of Oman, comprise the federation known as the United Arab Emirates. Most of the land is desert and the climate hot and humid. For centuries, the inhabitants farmed or herded sheep and goats in the interior, or sought a living from fishing and pearling. A further career was piracy, especially in the extremely shallow Gulf, the sandbanks and coral reefs of which protected locals from strangers.

Most of Abu Dhabi is low coastal plain and flat desert. In the south, imperceptibly, these become the Empty Quarter of Saudi Arabia. This topography contrasts greatly with the rugged slopes of the Hajar mountain range that marks the border between Abu Dhabi and Oman and continues to the tip of the "Horn of Arabia." Scattered rainfall in the mountains provides several oases with water for irrigation; the largest is Al-'Ain in eastern Abu Dhabi. While there are no permanent rivers, several dozen dams trap runoff for irrigation or to recharge aquifers.

Each of the seven states bears the name of its capital city and is headed by an *Emir*

("Prince"), who uses the traditional title of *Sheikh*. The territory of Abu Dhabi is about three times as large as the other six states combined. Each state maintains considerable internal autonomy under its hereditary ruler.

Abu Dhabi (3.23 million). Sheikh Zayed bin Sultan Al Nahyan.
Dubai (3.32 million). Sheikh Muhammad bin Rashid Al Maktoum.
Sharja (1.51 million). Sheikh Sultan bin Muhammad al-Qasimi
Ajman (540,000). Sheikh Humaid bin Rashid al-Nuaimi.
Umm al-Qaywayn (80,000). Sheikh Saud bin Rashid al-Mu'alla.
Ras al-Khayma (390,000). Sheikh Saud bin Saqr al-Qasimi.
Fujayra (250,000). Sheikh Hamad bin Muhammad al-Sharqi

In a society developing as rapidly as this, population figures are very rough estimates, and the division of the population is a somewhat delicate issue. What can be stated emphatically is that the population of the UAE has expanded rapidly, from a mere 180,000 at independence in 1971.

Overlapping territorial claims by the various states produced a number of neutral zones, some involving more than two emirates. They are shown darkly shaded on the accompanying map, the lack of clarity reflecting the actual identity of the territories.

History: Recent archeological discoveries show continuous habitation of the coast for the past 7,000 years, and scattered settlements in the *wadis* (desert valleys)

for much of the period. One graveyard excavated in Sharja that dated about 200 B.C. included two horses and 13 camels apparently sacrificed during burial ceremonies. By 2,000 years ago, ports in the region traded as far away as India and China. Perhaps linked to trade, Christianity spread widely, attested by burials, churches, and even a monastery.

The Islamic conquest apparently brought years of substantial prosperity during the Umayyad and early Abbasid dynasties. Later constructions, however, seem to be limited to fortifications. After centuries of Muslim Arab settlement and sporadic Iranian incursions, in the 1500s the Portuguese seized the dominant role in the Gulf. They soon lost it to the Dutch and British, who sought freedom of commerce rather than colonies.

At the turn of the 19th century, *Wahhabi* envoys from Central Arabia incited some local sailors to attack Western commerce, and the area garnered a reputation in Europe as the Pirate Coast. Britain then intervened in local fighting, and beginning in 1820 forced treaties on the states to suppress piracy and prohibit warfare at sea. Thus the terms Trucial States or Trucial Oman came into use, although Arabs generally called it the Oman Coast.

According to treaties signed at midcentury, Britain controlled foreign affairs and defense. Internal matters were left to the rulers, and little development took place. Indeed, major events of world history often had little impact, although competition from cultured pearls drove down profits from pearling and reduced the standard of living. As late as the 1950s disputes over borders or pearling rights led

to skirmishes between desperately poor emirates. One continuing dispute in the 1940s and 1950s concerned rival claims by Saudi Arabia, Oman, and Abu Dhabi to the Buraimi oasis.

The search for petroleum in the emirates began in the 1930s. Later, Sheikh Zayed bin Sultan, served as a guide to one of the first exploration teams. In 1958, commercial deposits were discovered. Oil production began in Abu Dhabi in 1962. Its revenues rapidly transformed the economy and society. Dubai also discovered oil, though relatively small amounts, and it deliberately developed into the region's chief trading center.

Faced with rising anti-colonialism and the high military costs of maintaining the protectorate, Britain withdrew from the Gulf in 1971. It encouraged the emirates to unite. Six formed the UAE, and Ras al-Khayma joined later, but Qatar and Bahrain opted for independence. The federal constitution adopted in 1971 divided responsibility for governance between federal institutions and the individual emirates. The seven sheikhs rule some internal affairs of their own states. They determine oil policy and may even possess their own military. However, responsibility for education, public health and currency belongs to the federation. Given the imposing wealth of Abu Dhabi, other states have tended to cooperate.

At the federal level, authority lies with the Supreme Council of Rulers. It chose as its first president Sheikh Zayed and reelected him for seven consecutive five-year terms. The president appoints the prime minister, typically the ruler of Dubai. Something akin to a legislature

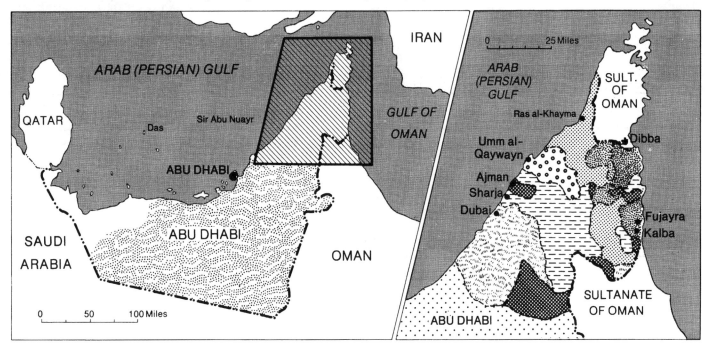

United Arab Emirates

H. H. Sheikh Khalifa bin Zayed Al Nahyan, Ruler of Abu Dhabi and President, UAE

H. H. Sheikh Muhammad bin Rashid Al-Maktoum, Ruler of Dubai and Vice President, UAE

H. H. Sheikh Sultan bin Muhammad al-Qasimi
Ruler of Sharja

H. H. Sheikh Humaid bin Rashid al-Nuaimi, Ruler of Ajman

H. H. Sheikh Saud bin Rashid al-Mu'alla, Ruler of Umm al-Qaywayn

H.H. Sheikh Saud bin Saqr al-Qasimi, Ruler of Ras al-Khayma

exists: the Federal National Council has 40 members represent individual emirates. Half of these individuals are elected by a restricted group of voters.

The 1980s brought two difficulties. Some off-shore oil platforms were attacked during the Iran–Iraq War, disturbing commerce. After the collapse of OPEC's price structure in the mid-1980s, oil revenues fell 40%, and an economic recession struck. By 1990, however, construction cranes again sprouted across the major cities, signaling a return to economic growth. New tourist hotels, shopping centers, commercial buildings and factories suggested that while oil continued to provide the mainstay of the economy, diversification will play an important role in the future. Currently, only 30% of GDP comes from the oil sector.

H. H. Sheikh Hamad bin Muhammad Al-Sharqi, Ruler of Fujayra

To pay for rapid growth in the 1980s, the country allegedly sold more oil than its OPEC quota. Iraq condemned the Emirates as well as Kuwait, and in 1990 the UAE joined the Gulf War coalition to liberate Kuwait. The conflict emphasized the presence of foreign workers in the Emirates, where a law demanding the replacement of all foreign employees of the federal civil service proved impossible to implement.

In 1992 Iran reopened an old dispute over three small but strategic islands in the Gulf: Abu Musa and the two Tunbs. Iran had contested their ownership with Sharja after Britain's withdrawal in 1971, but for two decades a working compromise allowed both countries a role. Iran's unilateral action in 1992, perhaps the hasty result of Tehran politics, aroused Arab fears.

While the UAE desires to settle the matter through the International Court of Justice, Iran has refused and continues to develop the islands. However, Iran is a major trading partner of Dubai, and since Iran has sought friendly relations with some Arab states, the issue lies dormant. Meanwhile, Abu Dhabi remains a major purchaser of modern weaponry, and the country hosts a major biennial arms exposition.

As the 20th century closed, a number of signs suggested that the seven emirates were gradually strengthening their sense of unity. In 1996 a national law replaced individual emirate rules on traffic offenses, and the next year a federal environmental law took effect. Although probably dwarfed by the (undisclosed) Abu Dhabi budget, the federal budget continued to provide funds for the economic and social development of the poorer emirates, and the rivalries of Dubai and Abu Dhabi remained friendly rather than contentious. The sense of unity seems likely to increase: younger inhabitants reportedly feel a greater loyalty to the UAE than do their parents.

After several years of declining health, Sheikh Zayed of Abu Dhabi, died in 2004 at the age of 86. People from all over the Emirates mourned the passing of a leader they considered the generous and wise founder of the country. The succession proved swift and smooth, as Zayed's eldest son Khalifa had been appointed crown prince 35 years earlier.

Dubai's economy suffered particularly hard from the world economic recession of 2008–09, even though the emirate only indirectly depends on oil income. Wealthy expatriates found themselves unable to purchase new properties, speculators pulled out of the market, and real estate prices fell by as much as 40%. The decline in world trade hurt trans-shipment, and aluminum demand fell 30%. As local firms ran short of cash, a massive loan of $10 billion from the UAE central bank cushioned the downturn and provided cash to pay some building costs. Nevertheless, construction on many projects came to a halt. Tens of thousands of expatriates, thrown out of work with construction companies, financial firms, and elsewhere, left for home.

Like other Gulf Cooperation Council governments, the rulers of the UAE are determined to maintain control. One potential source of instability lies in the activities of human rights activists and social media activists. A potentially more violent danger might be the activity of Islamists who reject the moral authority of the government.

In 2013 the Federal Supreme Court tried 94 Islamists with alleged ties to *al-Islah*, a local group linked with the Muslim Brotherhood. The international media was not allowed to observe the trial, and human rights groups condemned the trial as unfair; among other shortcomings, allegations of torture were ignored. Most of the defendants, who include human rights lawyers, professors, and university students were convicted and imprisoned for multi-year terms.

Recent years have seen several important developments related to the UAE, but three merit special attention. First, in 2017 the UAE, along with Saudi Arabia, Bahrain, and Egypt, imposed a blockade on the small but rich state of Qatar, alleging that the latter had grown too close to Iran in its diplomatic relations and that it had supported terrorism in the region. The group also cited a range of other grievances, including al-Jazeera's critical coverage of regional politics (al-Jazeera is based in Doha, Qatar). The diplomatic crisis has now gone on for almost two years and, despite occasional signals of a possible thaw, and increasing pressure from outside powers to resolve the matter, no clear end game has emerged.

In May 2019, Qatar accused the UAE of carrying out "a campaign of violence and hatred" against its citizens. At the International Court of Justice in the Hague the UAE and Qatar traded accusations. Amongst the claims and counter-claims raised, was the suggestion the the Emirates were seeking to use malware to infiltrate Qatar's security and defense systems. The UAE has been an early and enthusiastic adopter of new and emerging cyber-weaponry, not least spyware utilized against it own citizens. Such activity should be understood in the context of what is possibly one of the world's most comprehensive civil surveillance systems. Abu Dhabi's Falcon Eye monitors every person "from the moment they leave their doorstep to the moment they return to it." The purchase of Israeli surveillance technology points to an unprecedented cooperation between the two Middle Eastern states.

The UAE has played an important role in the ongoing civil war in Yemen. In many ways, the UAE has operated in tandem with Saudi Arabia against the Houthi rebels and against Iranian interests in the region, but this alliance has not been without tension. Taking advantage of the chaos on mainland Yemen, in recent years the UAE has increased its presence on the Yemeni island of Socotra—a UNESCO World Heritage Site that has long been coveted by the UAE. In 2018, Saudi Arabia was forced to send troops in order to defuse a stand-off between the nominally allied Emirati and pro-Hadi Yemeni forces. In mid-2019 Yemen again accused the UAE of seeking to seize control of the island, sending up to 100 separatist fighters in an undercover operation.

Finally, the UAE has taken steps towards establishing itself as a nuclear power. The first of four nuclear reactors was completed in December 2018 and is likely to become operational in 2019 or 2020. At that time, the UAE will become the first Arab country to have a viable

Neat as an architect's model: housing in Dubai

Courtesy of the Royal Embassy of Saudi Arabia

United Arab Emirates

civilian nuclear program. Though it may come as a surprise that a country so rich in oil would be interested in nuclear power, many believe there is good reason for what Abu Dhabi is doing. Estimates suggest that the program, which would create large numbers of jobs, could supply up to a quarter of UAE energy consumption going forward, allowing for increased sales of oil to markets abroad, nuclear energy consumption would be cleaner than that of fossil fuels (in a country that is responsible for more pollution per capita at present than almost any other), and extremely high numbers of Emiratis support the program (from 80–90%, depending on how the question is phrased). Two main questions are worth thinking about going forward. First, will the program remain peaceful? Second, how quickly will other Arab states follow suit by establishing their own nuclear programs? Saudi Arabia, for one, has already begun a program and hopes to construct 16 reactors by 2032.

Culture: The culture of the United Arab Emirates is not essentially different from that found in neighboring countries. The majority of the native Arabs, who are Sunni, often retain a sense of their tribal backgrounds and traditions. That said, some parts of the country have a hyper-modern feel. Dubai, discussed in more detail below, comes immediately to mind.

Women in the UAE play a greater role in society than in many conservative Muslim countries. A United Nations Development Programme study from 2018 found that the UAE was the Gulf country that ranked highest for gender equality and had made significant progress in bringing women into the workforce. Although they hold relatively few high-level positions in the private sector, the government employs a significant number of women, especially in education and health care. Indeed, women comprise 66% of the public sector workforce. Not only are girls educated; they hold some 20% of seats in parliament. Modern education arrived relatively recently. At independence, a decade after oil exports began, only 30,000 children attended school. By the mid-1990s, the figure had climbed to 400,000, and enrollments rose even more rapidly in high school. The construction of schools in even the most remote hamlets provides all children with the opportunity to learn; education is now compulsory from the age of six.

Long a particular concern of Sheikh Zayed, who grew up when the Emirates lacked a single modern school, adult education programs have proved so successful that the literacy rate has been reached upwards of 90%. Government policies indicate a concern with the quality of education as well as its extent.

Higher education was traditionally represented by technical colleges, several private institutions, and the Emirates University located in al-'Ain. Founded in 1978, by the early 1990s it graduated its first classes of physicians. Women comprise about two-thirds of the roughly 13,000 students, in part reflecting the greater likelihood that young men will study abroad.

In 2007, Dubai created International Academic City, incorporating Knowledge Village and its 20 foreign higher-education institutions including a branch campus of New York University.

The Federation's Marriage Fund ranks as one of the most unusual features of a society where the state takes responsibility for the welfare of its citizens from cradle to grave. Realizing that marriage to female citizens had become prohibitively expensive for many of its young male citizens, in 1994 the Federation created the Marriage Fund. The fund built special "Wedding Halls" where receptions cost far less than at hotels. The government also urged fathers to accept lower dowries, a major expense for many. It provides up to $19,000 to couples of limited income who wish to marry. In its first year the fund gave or lent nearly $100 million to 3,000 couples. By 2000 this had grown to 44,000 couples, and marriages to foreign women had fallen from 64% of total weddings to 26%.

A major purpose for the Marriage Fund is the need to increase the indigenous population. Nationals are outnumbered about four to one by foreign residents who have found work in the country. Native and immigrant Arabs together constitute no more than 25% of the population, with Indians and Pakistanis comprising major communities.

In addition to popular pastimes like movies and concerts, sports attract great attention. Thoroughbred racing arouses particular passion, and the Dubai World Cup has become the world's richest horserace with a $10 million purse, and the stable of Sheikh Muhammad, Dubai's ruler, often leads the world in victories. Further down the social scale, one finds auto racing and even camel races, held on a special track. The Emirate's powerboat racing team led the world championship in 1995 until an accident killed its most talented driver.

Economy: Despite the relatively late development of its petroleum deposits (exports began in 1962), oil reserves now exceed 97 billion barrels and rank the seventh largest in the world. So vast are the deposits that with present discoveries alone, the UAE can maintain its present level of exports until about the year 2099. Most deposits lie in Abu Dhabi, with very modest output from Dubai and Sharja. Thus it was Abu Dhabi's oil revenues that transformed much of the country. The UAE also possesses the world's seventh largest reserves of natural gas.

Historically, the UAE received a fairly small OPEC quota (e.g., 1.1 million barrels per day, 1989), but partly because of agreements with oil companies it overproduced. The collapse of Iraqi and Kuwaiti exports in 1990 provided opportunity for increased exports, and UAE experts correctly predicted that increasing world demand for oil, plus declining reserves in several OPEC nations, would reduce excess supplies and render quotas relatively unimportant.

Outside the petroleum industry, inhabitants find a variety of ways to earn a living. Agriculture remains an important source of employment, and organic farming has grown considerably in recent years. Currently the Emirates produce roughly half the vegetables that the population consumes—and all the dates. In fact, with over 20 million date palms—approximately five per person, yielding nearly 20 pounds (approximately 9 kilograms) each—the country is one of the world's most important growers.

The Hajar mountain range provides Ras al-Khayma and Fujayra with water for irrigation. Besides dates and other traditional fruits and vegetables, these areas export strawberries, chrysanthemum, tomatoes and other high-value winter crops to Europe. Agricultural research stations attempt to adapt plants and animals to the demanding climate conditions, and seek plants that tolerate saline ground-water.

All the emirates possess stretches of beach, some quite lengthy. Fujayra also enjoys a flourishing tourist trade based on trips to the mountains, including picturesque waterfalls. Sharja and other emirates issue their own stamps, including some of the world's most eye-catching commemorative issues for sale to collectors.

Dubai, Inc.

Dubai ranks as the undisputed commercial center of the nation and the region, and symbols of its brash confidence abound. Its World Trade Center already ranked among the tallest buildings in the Middle East, but the Burj Khalifa, opened in 2010, became the world's tallest at 2,716 feet (830 meters), twice the Empire State Building. The city claims the world's most luxurious hotel, the Burj al-Arab, where the average rate for the Royal Suite comes in at more than $24,000 per night. Still under construction, Dubailand will become the largest entertainment complex in the

Its height of 2,716 feet makes the Burj Khalifa the world's tallest building, an amazing challenge to desert wind, heat, and of course, gravity

Middle East—a family-style Vegas the size of Manhattan, with theme parks, but no gambling, alcohol, or evident illicit sex. The project was announced in 2003 with an estimated budget of $64 billion. Despite significant construction delays as a consequence of the global recession, it is slated to open by 2020.

By 2014 Dubai was attracting more than 13 million tourists per year and had set target growth in the industry at 9% per year going forward. Many facilities already exist to enable the achievement of that goal, including the Gulf's busiest airport, and a $3.7 billion subway system under construction. In 2001 the government-owned airline, Emirates, announced it would spend $15 billion on passenger jets, the largest order ever announced. Today, Emirates is the largest airline in the Middle East, operating more than 3,000 flights out of Dubai weekly.

Aiming to become the home of international jet-setters, but limited by its relatively short waterfront, Dubai has constructed a series of artificial islands. Seen from the air, several take the shape of a palm tree, and their fronds, each over a mile long, extend the emirate's shoreline and provide the setting for communities of luxury homes, each with a view of the beach. Another project created islands in the shape of the world. The really grandiose multi-billion project, known as Dubai Waterfront, was planned to house 400,000 people on an area nearly three times the size of Washington, D.C. The coastlines of the various islands were to stretch 500 miles (800 kilometres) and feature more

exclusive hotels (one, the Atlantis, underwater), more shops, and other entertainment centers. The project largely faltered with the onset of the financial crisis and its success remains uncertain. Dubai's business model is free-trade zones in the desert, where firms with similar interests cluster together and take advantage of capitalism at its least regulated: no taxes, no tariffs, no limits on transferring funds, no visa difficulties for professionals. Media City, Internet City, several villages and parks, and more recently Healthcare City often devote millions of square feet to state-of-the-art industry.

Obviously these projects greatly exceed the needs of Dubai's inhabitants. When planned, they made sense only because the emirate aimed for millions of visitors, and expected the population to reach two million by 2010, as wealthy retirees and business tycoons moved to a land of perpetual sunshine, negligible income taxes and unsurpassed internet service. One challenge in the future may be a struggle against drug use and other forms of hedonism, among both the support staff and the wealthy themselves. Already, gambling, alcoholic drinks, and prostitution are becoming less discrete.

Old-fashioned work also exists. The Jebel Ali Free Trade zone provides warehousing for trans-shipping goods through the world's largest man-made port. Over 1,000 companies use the zone, including Dubai Aluminum's smelter, one of the largest in the world, with a capacity of about 1,000,000 tons in 2009. Its accompanying electric generating plant provides

almost half the city's drinking water through desalination.

Given Dubai's trade, construction almost everywhere, and growth industries like aluminum and liquefied natural gas (LNG), the emirates enjoy increasing economic diversity. In 2006, petroleum accounted for only about one-third of the economy, an exceptionally low proportion given the high per capita incomes. During the years of rapid income growth, the UAE gained the distinction of providing a greater percentage of national income to foreign aid than any country. Much of the funding comes from the Abu Dhabi Fund for Development. Originally established in 1971 to help poorer Arab states, today the Fund had aided some 88 countries in Asia and Africa with loans and grants surpassing $20 billion.

One distinct shadow hanging over the entire construction boom is the treatment of manual workers. Eager to work hard for a few years, then return home to invest those earnings, manual laborers from the Indian subcontinent and elsewhere often find themselves working in health-threatening heat of over 110° Fahrenheit (43° Celsius) at dangerous jobs without insurance or healthcare. Pay checks sometimes come months late, and living conditions may mean 10 men to a room. However, Dubai's rulers have shown some concern: after unofficial demonstrations at the Burj Dubai (renamed Burj Khalifa) project involved 3,000 workers and some violence, in 2006 the government announced that a labor union would be permitted—and even granted a right to strike. In addition,

United Arab Emirates

A view of Dubai. The building in the foreground with the ball on top is the headquarters of the Emirates Telecommunications Corporation

afternoon construction work was banned in the summer.

Another fundamental challenge to the business model was the 2008–09 world recession. It depressed housing prices in Dubai by about 60% as jobs disappeared and thousands of foreign professionals left. There was room to fall: apartments in Burj Khalifa had reportedly sold for $2,700 per square foot. Dubai World, the emirate's investment arm, found itself unable to pay billions of dollars of debt to its banks, and it attempted to restructure $23 billion of debt after being rescued by the government. In the process, banks may have lost up to 50% of the value of their loans. Dubai's total debt as of late 2015 was estimated at over $50 billion.

The Future: At its birth, the United Arab Emirates seemed the façade of a new nation, another alliance of traditional rulers hurriedly patched together by departing colonial officials. Thanks to oil, the pragmatism of Sheikh Zayed, and the dynamic entrepreneurial spirit of Sheikh Maktoum bin Rashid, the UAE enjoyed decades of growth and prosperity. The passing of both those admired rulers failed to dent the high level of economic confidence. One concern for the immediate future is the health of Sheikh Khalifa bin Zayed, who suffered a stroke in early 2014. The day-to-day decision making has passed to Khalifa bin Zayed's half-brother, Sheikh Mohammed bin Zayed.

The astounding scale of Dubai's business model made it the Hong Kong of the last decade. Then, just as its commercial rents ranked among the most expensive in the world, the world recession hit. The property bubble burst. While the 2009 crisis was precipitated by debt, the collapse of demand in the context of the COVID-9 pandemic, along with the drop in oil prices caused by the Saudi-Russia spat, may have a far greater impact on the Gulf economies. Any economic downturn in the UAE will reverberate far beyond the Gulf, given that remittances form a major source of foreign currency income for countries across the Middle East and Asia.

The Republic of Yemen

The old walled city of San'a

Area: 207,286 square miles (536,869 square kilometers).

Population: 29.9 million.

Capital City: San'a; alternatively written as Sanaa (1.4 million).

Climate: Extremely hot and humid on the coastal plain, cooler in the mountains, often cold at night. Rainfall is moderate on the western slopes of the mountains and the highest peaks sometimes have snow.

Neighboring Countries: Saudi Arabia (North); Oman (East).

Time Zone: GMT +3.

Official Language: Arabic.

Other Principle Tongues: Mahri; English in school and international business.

Ethnic Background: Arab.

Principal Religion: Islam. The Zaidi sect of Shi'a Islam dominates the northern mountains; most other Yemenis are Sunnis of the Shafi'i legal school. A small Bahá'í community has been subject to persecution under the rebel government in San'a.

Chief Commercial Products: Crude oil, cotton, coffee, qat, cars, and dried or salted fish.

Major Trading Partners: The United States., China, South Korea, India, and Saudi Arabia.

Currency: Yemeni Rial (1 rial = 100 fils).

Former Colonial Status: Ottoman rule sporadic after the 16th century; British in the South (1839–1967).

National Day: May 22 (1971; Union Day).

Chief of State: Abd-Rabbuh Mansur Hadi, President (currently ruling from the temporary capital of Aden, as Houthi rebels control San'a).

Head of Government: Maeen Abdulmalik Saeed, Prime Minister.

Head of Rebel Government: Mahdi al-Mashat, President Supreme Political Council (Houthi).

National Flag: Three horizontal stripes of red, white and black.

Gross Domestic Product: $31.27 billion

GDP per capita: $1,123.

Located in the southwestern corner of the Arabian Peninsula, Yemen's varied topography contrasts greatly with the flat, stony plains and sand dunes of central and eastern Arabia. In western Yemen, the geography takes the form of zones running from north to south. The first zone, the Tihama plain, lies along the coast of the Red Sea. Level, hot, and arid, the Tihama also inflicts high humidity on its inhabitants.

Some 30 miles (50 kilometers) inland steeply rising slopes mark a scenic mountain range and plateau that run from the Saudi border in the north to the Gulf of Aden. Peaks in the range reach 10,000–12,000 feet (3,000–3,500 meters). By blocking air currents from the sea, they cause summer rains that make the western slopes the wettest region of Arabia, with precipitation averaging 15 inches yearly (380 millimeters), and as much as 30 inches (760 millimeters) in a good year. There are no year-round rivers, but rather seasonal streams in the valleys, known as *wadis*.

San'a, the capital, lies in the interior plateau; its elevation of nearly 7,400 feet (2,255 meters) makes it the seventh highest of any national capital. East of the mountains, the high plateau gradually slopes down to the desert, eventually joining the *Rub al-Khali* or Empty Quarter of Saudi Arabia.

Southern and southeastern Yemen, bordering the Gulf of Aden, endure a harsher geography. This part of the country's lonely, barren landscape of desert plateaus and jagged mountains is broken by two important valleys. In the southwest, the oases around Lahj provide much of the region's limited produce. In the east, the

Yemen

Wadi Hadhramut forms a narrow strip of green. Yemen also rules several islands, including the strategically important Perim Island in the Bab al-Mandab, the strait between Arabia and Africa. Another Yemeni island, Socotra (located just off the horn of Africa) has UNESCO World Heritage status and been described as "the most alien-looking place on Earth."

History: Ancient and civilized kingdoms existed in what is now Yemen long before the time of Christ. One of the most famous was Saba, or Sheba. Near its capital, Marib, a great stone dam captured the runoff from summer rains. Honored in literature and legend, the dam contributed to the reputation of this region as *Arabia Felix* (Fertile Arabia), famous in Roman times for its trade in frankincense and myrrh. However, during the early Christian centuries, rival Jewish and Christian chiefs sought to conquer the region. Foreign armies invaded, the dam failed, and its irrigation system deteriorated. Islam arrived towards the end of Muhammad's lifetime, during the 7th (Christian) century, and spread partly as a reaction against religions linked to foreign powers.

The Zaidi sect of Shi'a Islam became dominant in mountain regions during the 9th century, and its leader, styled an *imam*, became the traditional ruler. The early Islamic period provided security and prosperity. The population increased greatly,

and many terraces on the steep, rain-fed slopes date from that era.

In the 16th century the Ottoman Sultans laid claim to Yemen, but its remoteness and terrain ensured that it was never completely subjugated. Indeed, the Ottomans withdrew in the 17th century and the British gained influence at Mukha (Mocha) where they established a trading station. The interior remained under the Zaidi imams. The Ottomans attempted to regain the coast and more accessible regions after 1849, with limited success, and their rule ended in 1918.

The southern and eastern regions were variously held by feuding tribal chieftains for untold centuries. Britain seized the port of Aden in 1839. It became a valuable coaling station for ships plying the Egypt–India route, but Britain took minimal interest in the interior. Between 1882 and 1914, its sheikhs and other local leaders signed treaties that ceded authority over foreign affairs to Britain in exchange for protection.

After the Ottoman Empire collapsed in 1918, the Zaidi ruler, Imam Yahya, tried to expand Yemen's boundaries. In the south, his expansion was stopped by Britain's defense of Aden and its hinterland. Yahya also claimed sovereignty over Asir, the coastal region to the north. Its ruler then allied with the powerful Saudi monarch, King Abd al-Aziz. After Yahya's forces attacked pro-Saudi tribes, war followed. Saudi forces routed Yahya's poorly equipped tribesmen and captured Hudaida. By the 1934 Taif Agreement, Yahya ceded Asir, although its eastern border remained undefined.

Yahya was assassinated in 1948, and the rule of his son and successor, Ahmad, was severe and ill-informed. Few foreigners were permitted to enter the country; Yemen was as isolated from the world as Tibet. The inhabitants lived much as their ancestors had a thousand years previously.

Soon after Ahmad's death in 1962, army officers inspired by Egypt's revolution against King Farouk seized control of San'a. They declared Yemen a republic, headed by Colonel Abdullah Sallal. Ahmad's son, the imam, attempted to return to power but, even with support from mountain tribesmen, he failed and ultimately fled Yemen. Both the United States and the United Nations recognized the new republic in 1962.

Civil war followed, with bitter fighting in the winter of 1964. The imam was

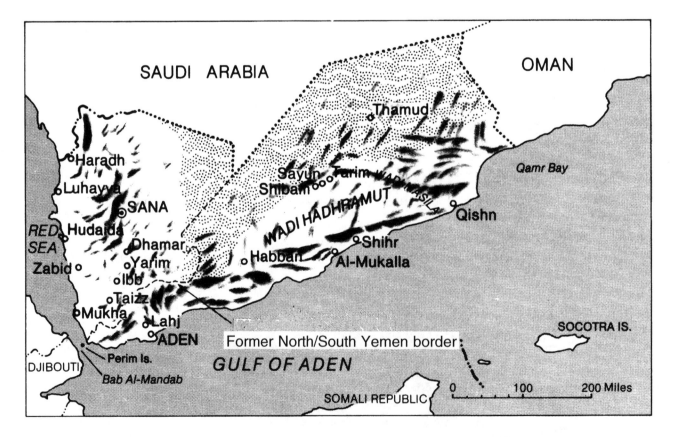

Man on the streets of San'a

supported by the Saudis; the republic, by Egyptian troops and money. Many Yemenis desired modernization and progress under a republic, but disliked Abdullah Sallal. After Egyptian troops began withdrawing during the Arab–Israeli war of 1967, the republicans replaced Sallal with a Zaidi religious leader. Abd al-Rahman Iryani, sought to unite the various republican factions and won the respect of royalist tribes by his religious prestige and political moderation. The civil war ended in 1970.

Aden Colony Becomes South Yemen

Events transpired differently in the south. In 1937 Britain created a crown colony at the city of Aden, while loosely supervising the local rulers of the interior as long as they refrained from violence. After decades of little political development, in 1958 British officials sought to unite the various tribal leaders as a counter to growing Arab nationalism. By 1966, all the local sheikhdoms had joined the Federation of South Arabia.

Spurred by the expansion of British bases, political consciousness developed in Aden, leading to unrest and eventually terrorism. Urban nationalists sensed a British design to govern them through the two dozen tribal rulers of the Federation. After local troops mutinied in 1967, nationalists seized several of the states. Despite conflict between rival rebel groups, one Egyptian-influenced, the other the Marxist National Liberation Front (NLF), the federation collapsed.

In 1967 Britain withdrew from Aden, permitting the NLF to take control. Adopting the title People's Republic of South Yemen, the NLF divided the country into six states to replace the traditional principalities. But the NLF proved incapable of stable government. For the first three years, political alliances shifted almost continuously. In 1969, a strongly communist clique came to power, added "Democratic" to the country's title, and promised an elected People's Supreme Council. However, elections never occurred.

In 1978, the president was overthrown and executed. Thereafter the NLF merged the local communist and Ba'th parties to form the Yemen Socialist Party (YSP), but these factions plunged into open civil war in 1986. Thousands died before the defeated president fled to North Yemen with thousands of armed followers.

In the late 1980s South Yemen permitted non-party candidates in local elections and even allowed opposition parties. In contrast to today, women's rights were among the most advanced in the Arab world. With the Soviet Union collapsing and the economy in shambles, the regime mended links with Arab states and sought closer relations, even unity, with North Yemen.

These were dramatic changes indeed. Most Arab leaders had long felt concern or even hostility toward Aden's radical policies and its sponsorship of Omani rebels. Periodic border clashes with North Yemen occurred in the 1970s, and 1981 saw unfulfilled agreements to unite.

The North Achieves Stability under Salih

Struggles for power also persisted in San'a. A Military Command Council took control of North Yemen in 1975. It established a degree of unity between the various factions and maintained firm central control. More important, it developed good relations with Saudi Arabia, which lent financial assistance. Stability came, unexpectedly, when Colonel Ali Abdullah Salih was elected president of North Yemen by parliament in 1978.

Despite political unrest, assassination attempts, two border wars, and a major earthquake that destroyed 200 villages in the 1980s, Salih established stable government and added democratic features to the military dictatorship. The first general election for the *Majlis al-Shura* (Consultative Council) took place in 1988. It was widely contested, but President Salih's General People's Congress won the most seats. The Muslim Brotherhood and tribal independents also acquired significant representation.

In 1989, the leaders of North and South Yemen again proclaimed plans for a merger. The next year public opinion in both countries surged in favor of rapid union. Both states held referendums, a rarity for the Arabian Peninsula, and trade increased between them as a consequence of greater freedom for private farmers and businessmen. Surprising almost everyone, the two states merged ahead of schedule in 1990, perhaps to out-maneuver domestic and foreign opponents. President al-Attas of the South became Prime Minister of a united Yemen, Ali Abdullah Salih took the new presidency, and a 302-member Council of Deputies included a variety of parties.

Merged, but not United

United Yemen faced grave difficulties, including the legacy of a history littered with failed merger attempts. The South's economy lay in tatters. The North's relative economic success, combined with a population four times that of the South, created fears it would dominate any union. Perhaps surprising, the North's social development lagged significantly behind that of communist-influenced Aden.

Exceptional challenges arose during the first year of union. Linked to Iraq by trade, and Kuwait by aid, Yemen attempted to maintain neutrality after the Iraqi invasion of Kuwait. As the only Arab member of the UN Security Council, however, this was impossible.

Saudi Arabia, already uneasy about miles of frontier with a united Yemen equal in national population, cut all financial aid and expelled roughly one million Yemenis. They returned to face unemployment. Other nations cut development aid, so the central bank printed money and inflation climbed. However, oil discoveries suggested reserves to support greater production.

Despite a background of high inflation and food riots, in 1993 Yemen held the first free multi-party elections of the entire Arabian Peninsula, with some 5,000 candidates for the Council of Deputies. Allegations of vote-buying and favoritism in television coverage aside, the results were considered a broadly accurate reflection of popular opinion. However, they also reflected strong regional differences. Salih's General People's Congress led the Islamic Islah in the north, while the YSP won every southern seat but few elsewhere. Nevertheless, the three parties formed a coalition government.

Personal rivalries and budget conflicts led to increasing hostility between President Salih and Vice President Ali Salem al-Baidh, a southerner. As tensions mounted, clashes broke out between military units and then, in 1994, full-scale civil war. Aided by water shortages in besieged Aden and tribal and Islamist resentments

Yemen

against the YSP, northern troops crushed the rebellion, whose leaders fled.

The war further damaged an already precarious economy. The budget deficit soared, and to meet its bills the state turned again to printing money. Inflation became so great that the government refused to release the figures, though it did devalue the rial by a factor of 10. Salaried professionals found their standard of living destroyed, and Yemeni university professors went on strike because their monthly pay of $140 equaled less than 10% of foreigners' salaries. Subsidies for wheat, flour, and oil products became unbearable burdens, but their reductions doubled prices and triggered riots. Unemployment reached 30%. Further cuts in government subsidies occurred in accordance with an IMF-approved plan in 1996, leading to some foreign aid.

Yemen held the first contested presidential election in the history of Arabia in 1999. Salih won a landslide victory in formally free voting. However, electoral manipulation had occurred earlier. Parliament rejected all opposition nominees as candidates, so the YSP again boycotted the campaign. Islah nominated Salih as its candidate, and to meet the constitution's requirement of two candidates one of Salih's supporters ran against him.

The country boasts well over 10 million firearms, approximately one gun for every two residents. Given Yemen's tumultuous history, men expect they will be called to fight. Law and order therefore remain sporadic. In the 1990s, tribesmen in remote areas discovered a new form of pressure politics: kidnapping foreigners. Tourists, petroleum workers, and even diplomats found themselves seized as

Former President Ali Abdullah Salih
Photo courtesy of the White House

bargaining chips for schools, roads, water projects, and other aid. To protect the oil and tourist industries, officials typically promised to meet some demands, and gained the release of the hostages. Eventually, however, to maintain its authority, the government imposed the death penalty for kidnapping.

In 2000, suicide bombers linked to al-Qaeda unexpectedly maneuvered a small boat filled with explosives alongside the destroyer *U.S.S. Cole* as it refueled in Aden harbor. The subsequent explosion pierced the side of the vessel and killed nearly two dozen sailors. The attack on the *Cole* raised questions about the nature of growing Islamic extremism.

Many Yemenis hold traditional values and regard Western ways with suspicion. The wave of popular Islamic devotion—although not necessarily the violence—is fostered by the separate system of religious schools created by the Islamist Islah party when it ran the education ministry during the 1990s. The party also changed the public schools' curriculum to include a large dose of religious studies, based on books Islah selected. President Salih broke with Islah in 2001 and modified some such policies.

Rumors that the United States might respond to the 9/11 attacks with assaults on Yemen's Islamic extremists prompted an unusually strong crackdown on Islamic militants. Scores of foreign students at Islamic study centers were expelled, and others arrested. Republican Guard and Special Forces units, commanded by the president's son, Ahmad, attempted to extend government authority over tribal areas.

Nevertheless, popular sympathies continue to lie with those who preach Islam, sometimes including militant strains. Tens of thousands of Yemeni veterans of the Afghan war against the Soviets sympathize with al-Qaeda. So do many foreign students attracted to study Islam in Yemen's religious seminaries. Anti-western attacks occasionally take place in the capital and other cities. In 2008 the U.S. embassy ordered out all non-essential staff.

Most militant Islamists come from the country's bare Sunni majority. However, in the distant northern province of Saada, a Zaidi preacher, Hussein al-Houthi, defied the government in the Zaidi tradition that permits rebellion against an unjust regime. When the army attempted to enforce its control in 2004, open warfare broke out involving heavy weapons. Al-Houthi died in the fighting, but his followers continued to resist.

The Houthi rebellion again blazed into the open in 2009 when the Yemeni military launched Operation Scorched Earth, eventually using air raids and heavy weapons

against rebels in the provincial capital, Saada, and elsewhere. When fighting spread into Saudi Arabia, the crisis risked Iranian interference as well. A truce was finally reached in 2010, after attacks on markets, mosques, and residential areas. Hundreds or even thousands of unarmed civilians had died.

A remarkable manipulator, when a financial crisis threatened as the 2006 presidential elections approached, Salih ruled himself out of the race. Heavy subsidies had kept gasoline and diesel fuel cheap for trucks, buses, and irrigation pumps. However, the subsidies became unaffordable, and aid-giving agencies considered them a source of corruption. Two days before the cabinet cut subsidies and tripled the price of diesel fuel, Salih announced that he would not run again.

After the price increases, violent riots shook the country, killing dozens; the army had to patrol the streets. Salih then intervened to raise salaries, cut sales taxes, and order a small cut in fuel prices. Thus, he struck the pose of a caring father of the nation, in contrast to the cabinet. A carefully stage-managed convention of the General People's Congress nominated him for re-election.

In contrast to the staged elections, opposition parties ranging from the secular YSP to the religious Islah set aside other rivalries and united behind the nomination of Faisal Bin Shamlan. A retired economist with an unmatched reputation for honesty, he attacked the country's high level of corruption and attracted wide attention. The battle was uneven—government officialdom knew whom to support and discretely did so. Nonetheless, Shamlan won over 20% of the vote in the first genuinely contested presidential election in the Arab Middle East. His level of support suggested that Ali Abdullah Salih would face popular opposition to his son's automatic succession to the presidency.

Tipping Towards a Failed State

By 2009, multiple crises challenged the government. To fight the Houthi rebellion, the military mobilized extremist Sunni groups influenced by Osama bin Laden. This informal alliance enabled some prisoners convicted of the attack on the *U.S.S. Cole* and other terrorist acts to escape, then to receive pardons for both the escape and the original crimes. However, the alliance was one-sided: the local al-Qaeda cell attacked Korean tourists, other foreigners, and the U.S. embassy. It also renamed itself al-Qaeda in the Arabian Peninsula, (AQAP) suggesting threats to neighboring countries. Now identified as the most active branch of al-Qaeda, some of its local fighters organized as the *Ansar al-Shari'a* (Supports of the Shari'a) and captured

Zinjibar, the provincial capital of Abyan in 2011. Internationally, AQAP is known for a number of attacks. Among others, it was connected to a Nigerian national named Umar Farouk Abdulmutallab (the "underwear bomber"), who attempted to take down an airliner over the continental United States on Christmas day in 2009. It was also connected to Nidal Hassan, who that same year killed 13 people and injured more than 30 others at Fort Hood in Texas.

Meanwhile, retired southern army officers and officials protested their meager pensions and the corrupt acquisition of land and property by northerners, fanning perceptions of discrimination. A loosely-organized, largely civilian Southern Movement emerged, including both former socialists and Islamic militants. Some sympathizers openly demanded succession and independence; perhaps a majority sought a federalist solution with regional autonomy. Protests led to fatalities in several southern locations.

President Salih habitually faced such crises by forming alliances with some rivals against others, while using predictions of disaster to frighten sympathetic countries into increasing foreign aid. However, the failure to keep al-Qaeda fighters in prison poisoned relations with the United States, as well as Saudi Arabia and other oil states. This limited financial aid from abroad.

The underlying socio-economic crisis simultaneously deprived Salih and his government of Yemeni resources. Income from oil exports fell 75% in 2009, and the resulting budget deficit prevented large-scale attempts to reduce unemployment, estimated at 30%. Subsidies to limit unpopular rises in food prices became too expensive. A population growing at 3.7% per year needs social services, but widespread corruption has eroded good intentions, and much of the population lacks access to medical care.

The Arab Spring in Yemen

In the wake of protests in Tunisia and Egypt, in early 2011 demonstrators took to the streets in Yemen. Initially, the demonstrations involved groups from moderate Islamists to leftists and even involved performance art, with music, dancing, skits, and caricatures. The head of Women Journalists without Chains, Tawakkul Karman, eloquently attacked Salih's corrupt rule and his sleazy comments about "ladies" engaging in protests. When released from arrest, she immediately returned to the podium and became a hero. She later received the 2011 Nobel Peace Prize.

Long accustomed to deflecting dissent with promises, this time Salih could not pledge immediate prosperity. Without access to billions of dollars in foreign aid, he initially offered to leave office at the end

of his term in 2013, and not to pass the presidency to his son. Simultaneously, he mobilized supporters for pro-Salih demonstrations. Some opposition leaders were arrested.

After an unprovoked attack in March that killed 45 and injured hundreds, Salih denied his forces had massacred the civilians and declared a state of emergency. It is possible, given the murky world of Yemen's administration, that Salih told the truth: the attack may have been an accident, regime sympathizers may have turned to violence without official orders, or a rival may have actually masterminded the attacks to create an outcry and force Salih from office. Whatever the case, Salih oversaw it all. Demonstrators' deaths in San'a, Taizz, and other cities, and the wide range of human rights violations and abuses, including the detention, torture and killing of children reported by the United Nations led to resignations by some officials and even members of parliament. However, Ahmad Salih, the president's son, commanded the Republican Guard, and it dominated San'a, while nephews and other relatives led other important units. Even the defection of General Ali Mohsen al-Ahmar (Salih's half-brother), commander of an army division, failed to overthrow the president. However, rebellious tribesmen ruptured

Yemeni tribesmen displaying weapons during the Arab Spring

Yemen

the oil export pipeline, halting the major source of government revenue.

The United States and neighboring countries initially supported Salih but encouraged reforms. They feared that al-Qaeda in the Arabian Peninsula and other militant Islamists would use the chaos to organize freely. The president clearly cultivated this fear, and the military resisted feebly when Islamist militants occupied Zinjibar, the capital of Abyan in the south.

Salih's faltering rule and the violence against protesters eventually convinced the United States and Saudi Arabia that stability depended on his departure. The Gulf Cooperation Council (GCC) negotiated with the regime and the Joint Meeting Parties for Salih's resignation, but Salih blocked the deal by refusing to sign it as president.

Badly wounded in an assassination attempt, Salih flew to Saudi Arabia for treatment. He continued to defy demands by opposition parties and demonstrators to transfer power to Vice President Hadi, who was powerless to halt military attacks on the demonstrators and General al-Ahmar's forces.

For months the country teetered on the brink of civil war. Salih eventually signed the GCC's proposal, but he then demanded that parliament grant him and his close appointees amnesty from crimes committed in office. The election for his successor had only one candidate, his vice president, Abd Rabbu Mansur Hadi. He was duly elected, and Salih left office in February, 2012, some 13 months after the protests began.

Hadi Takes Office

Hadi inherited a nation emerging from chaos. In the north, Zaidi tribesmen of the Houthi movement continued their multi-year rebellion. Within the government, Salih's relatives and allies held rival centers of power. The new president dispatched some of these individuals safely abroad, as diplomats. In the south, political activists of the Southern Movement continued to demand autonomy or independence.

More immediate threats came from Islamic extremists of the Ansar al-Shari'a, who defeated the initial military attempts to recapture the southern city of Zinjibar. Within months, however, the military retook the city and much of Abyan and Shabwa provinces, aided by popular disgust at the summary executions and amputations carried out by the extremists. Nevertheless, fighting took a significant toll: in the first half of 2014 nearly 400 security forces personnel were killed.

The military's success was aided by air raids by conventional aircraft as well as drone attacks. Successful assassinations of al-Qaeda leaders were publicly credited to the air force, but it was widely acknowledged in Yemen that attacks on extremists, including some holding U.S. citizenship, were carried out by U.S. drones.

To tackle the demands of the Arab Spring protesters, the GCC's proposal for Salih's resignation included the calling of a National Dialogue Conference. This forum was charged with recommending policy on deep national questions and the direction of the country. These issues were debated by more than 500 representatives of widely differing groups—tribal sheikhs, urban youth activists, established political parties, women's groups, southerners, northern Zaidis, and civil society organizations. The conference completed its work in 2014, and some decisions cut to the fundamental structure of the country. An independent anti-corruption body would be established, and women's rights would be advanced by 30% representation in public office. Child marriages would be banned.

Instead of a unitary state ruled from San'a, the National Dialogue Conference voted a decentralized federal system, but unfortunately if deferred specifying the regions. A presidential committee's decision to create six regions, two of them in the south, brought immediate rejection from southern activists who wished to raise the south's significance. The decision also encouraged fighting in the north, as the Houthi rebels attempted to enlarge the territory designated to them.

The Houthi Rebellion and Yemen's War

The Houthi movement (going by the name, *Ansar Allah*, Supporters of God) clearly desired much more than just additional northern territory before the nation's regions were divided. After negotiations, their fighters entered San'a without combat in September 2014, gradually took it over, and then rapidly captured the port of Hudaida. The United Nations brokered an attempt to form a new government including Houthi representatives, but they withdrew. About this time, at least one boatload of arms from Iran was intercepted; others may have been more successful.

After the Houthis took over San'a, President Hadi offered to resign, but this was rejected by parliament. In February, the rebel command dissolved parliament and declared its Revolutionary Committee led by Mohammed Ali al-Houthi to be the country's acting authority. Although President Hadi escaped his palace and fled to the southern city of Aden, soon Houthi forces attacked that city, assisted by military units loyal to the rebels' new ally, ex-president Salih. Loyalist forces having proved too weak to defend Aden, the president and his vice president fled the country, taking refuge in the Saudi capital, Riyadh.

Militant Islamists have proven to be the most determined domestic opponents of the Houthi conquest. Known for their hatred of the Shi'a, jihadists from AQAP and the Islamic State have fought rebel units and carried out suicide attacks. Coordinated attacks on two Zaidi mosques in San'a during Friday prayers killed 142 worshippers and wounded more than twice that number in 2015.

Fearful of any rebellion on the Arabian Peninsula, and particularly alarmed by an apparent Zaidi Shi'a coup d'état (strengthened by arms and training from Iran), Saudi Arabia and other Arab League nations began airstrikes against Houthi targets in 2015. Hundreds were killed in the first few weeks, and the rebel alliance responded with missile attacks against Saudi Arabia's border regions. Keen to deprive the Houthis of control over Yemen, Saudi policy hoped to destroy the military alliance with Salih.

The civil war and foreign air attacks quickly created a massive humanitarian crisis. Fighting and a sea blockade interrupted the delivery of both food and fuel. By June agencies estimated that some 20 million people desperately required assistance.

Four years on, the war in Yemen continues to rage, its character complex. It is undoubtedly a civil war, pitting Yemeni Sunnis against Yemeni Shi'a; government supporters against Houthi rebels; supporters of the former president, Salih, against supporters of the current president, Hadi; southern separatists against northerners, and Salafist militants against any who stand against them. At the same time it is clearly an international war, with a Saudi-led coalition regularly carrying out bombing campaigns with the support not just of other Gulf states (especially the UAE) but of the United States as well. It is also a proxy war, one where Saudi Arabia and Iran compete, both convinced that limiting the influence of the other justifies the brutal means used to achieve that end. Today, the situation in Yemen comprises the world's worst humanitarian crisis, with more than three million people displaced and some 20 million people—about three-fourths of the population—at risk of starvation. What might have once been called an economy, never strong before the war, lies in tatters. As if the picture were not bleak enough, in early 2018 the International Red Cross pulled 71 workers from the country, citing imminent danger to its staff. At that time, rumors circulated of a likely siege by the Saudi-led coalition, of the crucial port of Houdeidah (through which transits some 70% of international aid). In 2018, fighting around Houdeidah

Yemen

Busy downtown San'a   Courtesy of the Caltex Petroleum Corporation

outside parties has done nothing to alleviate this suffering. Even if the war were to end today, the re-building process will be immense and generations will have been permanently affected.

For the longer term, the growing population requires water for human consumption and agriculture. But the limits of sustainable pumping have been exceeded, and the water table is dropping rapidly around many cities. Yemen has been ranked as the world's most water-challenged country, and the possible solutions require dramatic transformations in lifestyles, including much less agriculture. As long as the war continues, there will be no comprehensive response to Yemen's looming environmental crisis.

Culture: More than 60% of the population of Yemen lives in the traditional style in small towns, villages, or isolated clusters of houses. Until recently, most loyalties were local, mainly to the family, clan, and tribe. A few people are nomads, mainly in the eastern and southern part of the country, while considerably more live in the growing cities, where the alien architecture of new buildings often clashes with the greater dignity and appeal of traditional designs.

Unfortunately many of the mud-brick skyscrapers are in danger of collapse, threatened particularly by running water and burst pipes. Foreign governments have funded a UNESCO campaign to restore San'a, paving streets and restoring portions of the historic *souk* (market place). However, the walled cities of Hadhramut, east of Aden, remain far from tourist routes despite their beauty. Little to no investment means these 500 year old buildings face collapse.

While virtually all Yemenis are Muslims, they form two major sects. In the coastal plain and much of the settled south, inhabitants profess Sunni Islam and provide a center for the Shafi'i school. In the north, the conservative Zaidi sect of Shi'a Islam prevails, and for a thousand years, until the 1962 revolution, Imams ruled the country from the mountains.

In a uniquely Yemeni custom, every afternoon many Yemeni men and many women gather in small social groups to chew leaves of *qat*, a tree cultivated on the terraced mountainsides. Large globs of leaves, when chewed for hours, reportedly produce a mildly narcotic effect that relaxes a person and gives a sense of contentment.

The cultivation and use of qat brings challenges to a country seeking development. For one, it often consumes vast amounts of time, occupying much the afternoon. Producing qat provides employment for thousands of farmers, and it is

intensified. The Saudi-led Operation Golden Victory—the largest battle of the war to date—was an attempt to rout the Houthi rebels from Houdeidah, amid accusations that the port was being used as transit points for the smuggling of weapons from Iran. A localized ceasefire, agreed to in December 2018, was premised on the withdrawal of Houthi rebels from the area. Six month later, the withdrawal began, but sporadic fighting has continued, significantly worsening the humanitarian crisis in Yemen. The notion that the Houdeidah ceasefire would lay the ground for a broader peace deal seems optimistic, at best.

In mid-2019, Houthi rebels stepped up attacks on Saudi Arabia, sending missiles and armed drones across the border. This has coincided with increasing accusations of Iranian militancy and a general ratcheting up of tensions in the Persian Gulf.

However, some analysts have warned that Iran's role in Yemen may be overstated and that the Houthis are in fact "fiercely independent," and allies rather than proxies of the Islamic Republic.

The Yemen war is at the center of a skirmish in Washington between Congress and the Trump administration, which declared a national emergency to get around Congress's objections to selling billions of dollars of arms to Saudi Arabia and the United Arab Emirates. The coalition has repeatedly used American-supplied precision-guided bombs to strike Yemeni civilians. Accusations of Saudi carelessness (at best) and the deliberate targeting of noncombatants (at worst) have not deterred its Western partners.

At the present, the war in Yemen looks no closer to conclusion than it did at the outset. The suffering of the Yemeni population is immense and the involvement of

Yemen

President Abd-Rabbuh Mansur Hadi

a far more profitable crop than coffee or grains. Much of the nation's limited supply of agricultural water goes to the crop.

Qat consumption can also be expensive. Though not physically addictive, it leads to a state of relaxation that discourages hard work. It may cause serious illness, and at least one study of heavy users shows a greatly increased risk of heart attacks. In 1999 President Salih announced that he was giving up the leaves, and he urged the nation to follow his example.

Throughout Yemen, since the fall of the monarchy and the arrival of freedom from colonialism, education has taken great strides among men, although some three quarters of women remain illiterate. There are universities at San'a and Aden, and competition to enroll is fierce. The use of English in education is becoming widespread, since one of Yemen's most valuable assets is the workers which it sends abroad. In turn, they have sent badly needed money back home in the form of remittances.

In their struggle for water, roads, schools, and other projects for a better standard of living, Yemenis often formed "development associations," to pool resources for their goals. Relatively rare elsewhere in the Middle East, these community action groups involve both traditional and modern interests, and reflect a Yemeni sense that combatting poverty requires cooperation rather than simple competition. Unfortunately, the cooperative movement has on several occasions suffered from government attempts to take it over or politicize it.

Economy: In peacetime, agriculture remains the center of the economy, especially in terms of employment. On the coast, one finds date palms and grains suitable to the hot climate. The upper slopes of the mountains, which receive good rainfall, are among the most intensively cultivated in the world. Over the centuries, farmers have built elaborate terraces with stone walls—at some places right up to the crests.

Coffee was traditionally the important cash crop. Shipped from the old port of Mukha, it became renowned as "Mocha coffee." In recent decades, lower world coffee prices have reduced production in Yemen, at the same time as production of qat became more profitable.

Animal herding plays an important role in the economy. Millions of sheep, goats, and humped cattle are raised for milk, meat, and hides. Donkeys and mules are still the most common beasts of burden as camels are not suitable in the rugged mountains, though they are far from unknown in Yemen.

It is possible that mineral deposits in commercial quantities exist in the country, but little surveying has been done thus far. Manufacturing remains in the handicraft stage; while it exhibits a high degree of skill and artistic merit, handmade products cannot supply a comfortable standard of living as can machine-factory production.

Yemen is the poorest country in the Middle East and one of the poorest in the world. Since the 1960s, foreign nations have provided important assistance for development, including roads, health projects and farm programs. During the Cold War, Northern Yemen in particular proved adept at soliciting funds from rival nations, including the Soviet Union, China, the United States, West Germany, and several Arab oil exporters. By contrast, its communist ties prevented South Yemen from receiving Western and Arab aid.

After oil exports commenced in 1988, the role of foreign aid in the Yemeni economy declined somewhat. By 1995 total production reached 400,000 barrels per day, and the country approved a $3 billion project to liquefy natural gas for export. However, only modest quantities of oil have been discovered, and the volume of exports is small, about 5% that of neighboring Saudi Arabia. Consequently, Yemen has not joined OPEC.

Rising oil prices during the mid-2000s disguised the diminishing oil output, but the 75% decline in government oil revenues in 2009 reinforced fears of a possible economic collapse. However, many promising geological formations have failed to yield oil, and the growing violence from al-Qaeda discourages foreign companies. Earnings from exports of liquefied natural gas will only partially replace oil revenues.

The Future: Yemen is a humanitarian disaster, with more than 20 million inhabitants in dire need. At mid-2019 casualties of the war approach 100,000. Approximately 12,000 deaths are the result of direct civilian targeting, the vast majority by the Saudi-led coalition and its allies. Many more civilians have died as a result of famine and cholera caused by the blockade, or as a consequence of attacks

A potter works his trade near Aden

on infrastructure and healthcare facilities, in addition to collateral deaths. When peace does finally come to Yemen the recovery will be slow and almost certainly difficult.

The sectarian aspect of the conflict, mirrors an increasingly familiar pattern of rising tensions across the region. In the long run, the Houthi movement—emerging out of the Zaidi minority—is unlikely to control the nation without Sunni tribal allies. However, in the context of a geopolitical struggle for dominance between Sunni Saudi Arabia and Shi'a Iran, the possibility of such an alliance is vanishingly small.

Even before the war, every socio- economic indicator of long-term success read "dangerous." Yemen has long been the poorest country of the Middle East, lagging well behind its wealthy Gulf neighbors. At present rates of growth, Yemen's population will reach about 60 million by 2050. In such an arid and impoverished land, neither sufficient water nor enough jobs will be available to support that number of people. About 40% of Yemenis suffer inadequate diets, and one-third of children are severely malnourished. The government's crumbling finances limit the opportunities for improvement, and oil exports, formerly the source of 75% of revenue, are dwindling to insignificance. Donor nations have cut foreign aid, as a consequence of widespread corruption and in May 2019, the United Nations threatened to cut off food aid to Yemen as a consequence of the widespread diversion and theft of aid supplies in Houthi-held areas.

Conflict has hampered a timely and effective response to the COVID-9 crisis. Doctors and other medical personnel have been working for months (sometimes years) without pay, if they continue to work at all. Vital medical supplies have been unavailable and vaccines have been limited or difficult to access.

Since neither the Zaidi command nor the exiled Hadi government can assert effective federal authority, the most likely result seems a fragmented nation with regions operating informally on their own. Yemenis should all fear this, because the country's huge social challenges—youth unemployment exceeding 30%, high birth rates, corruption, poverty, budget deficits,

Girl with her father
Courtesy of the World Bank (Tomas Sennett)

and depleted water resources—require national as well as local solutions.

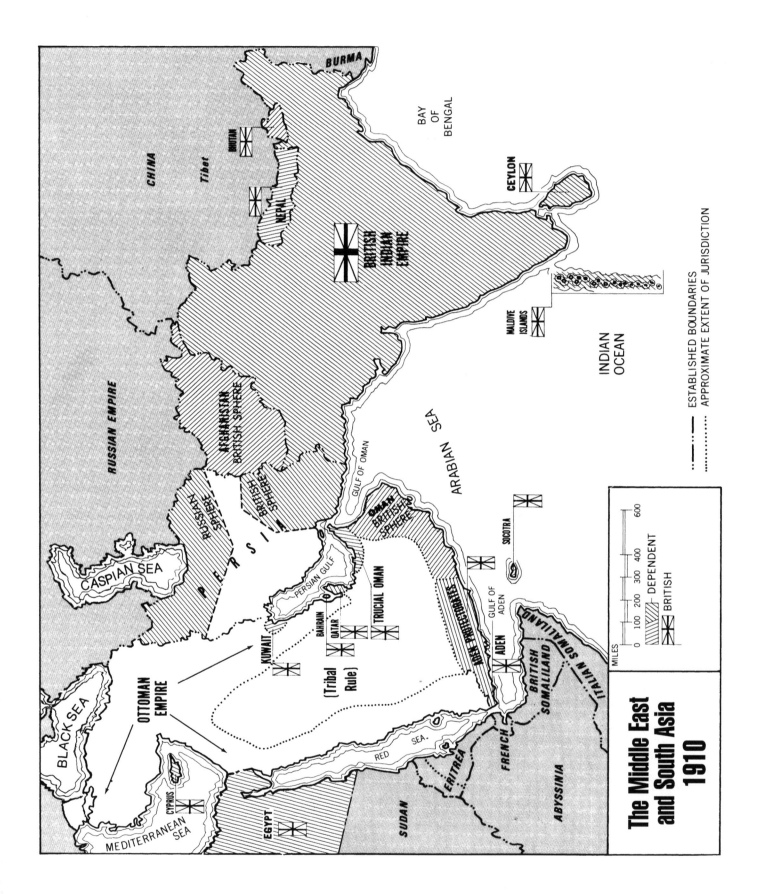

The Middle East and South Asia 1910

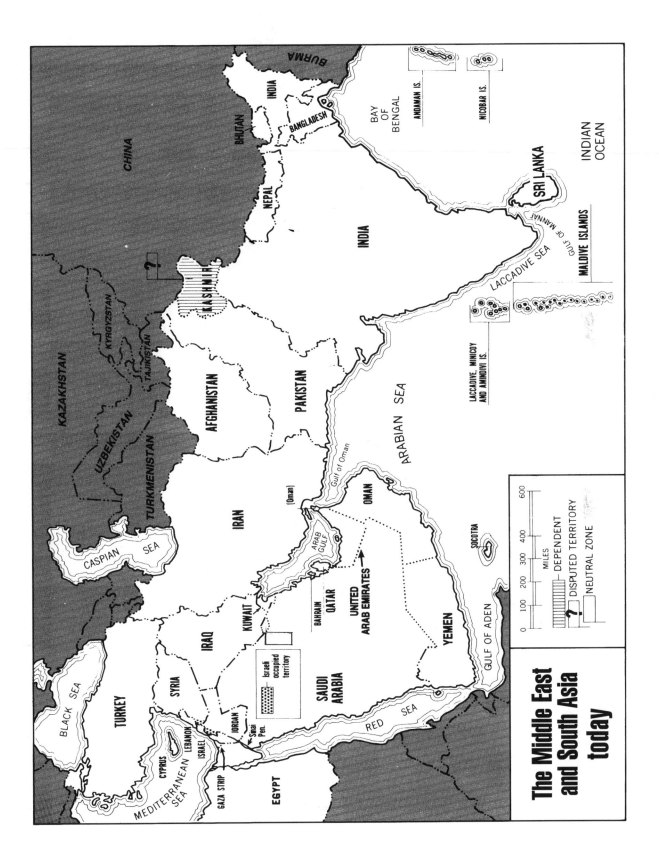

The Middle East and South Asia today

Islamic Republic of Afghanistan

Afghan and international security forces patrol streets during presidential elections in 2014

Afghanistan is also the world's leading producer of hashish, derived from the cannabis plant.

Major Trading Partners: Pakistan, Iran, India, and China.

Currency: Afghani (1 afghani = 100 puls, obsolete).

Former Colonial Status: Under British influence (1837–1919).

National Day: August 19 (1919; relinquishment of protectorate status).

Chief of State: Ashraf Ghani, President.

National Flag: Black, red, and green vertical stripes with a white emblem centered in the red containing a mosque, two flags, and sheaves of wheat (horizontally striped flags are also used).

Gross Domestic Product (GDP): $19.54 billion.

GDP per capita: $538.

Afghanistan's harsh and varied environment is hostile to human comfort and even survival, except for the short spring season when moderate temperatures and green vegetation follow winter rain and snow. Summer temperatures in the low valley of the Amu Darya (Oxus River to the ancient Greeks) often hover at 110° Fahrenheit (43° Celsius). In the winter, blizzards rage in the high mountains, and even at the medium elevations where most people live temperatures may drop below zero for a few weeks. However, in the low valleys agriculture is intensively pursued, and native poplar trees abound to provide wood for rough houses.

The most striking geographical feature of the country is the complex series of mountains extending from the eastern tip for some 600 miles (almost 1,000 km.) southwest before leveling out in the plateau near the border with Iran. Majestic peaks of the central Hindu Kush Mountains tower more than 20,000 feet (over 6,000 meters) above sea level. The rugged terrain has contributed to Afghanistan's relative poverty, its extraordinary ethnic diversity, and its success in withstanding centuries of repeated invasions.

As a landlocked country, Afghanistan depends on transit through neighboring countries for its external trade. Most imports and exports traditionally passed through Pakistan, utilizing the railroad between Karachi and Peshawar, but depending on trucks between Peshawar and points inside the country. Another important trade route runs from Iran to Herat in the northwest. The country's most valuable export, heroin, apparently reaches world markets through Central Asia.

History: The mountains of Afghanistan form a natural divide that separates the Indian subcontinent from Central Asia to the northwest, and Iran to the west.

Area: 251,773 square miles (652,225 square kilometers).

Population: 38.9 million.

Capital City: Kabul (3.1 million).

Climate: Extremely dry, hot summers (but with cool nights); cold winters with moderate rain and snow in the mountains, scanty rain on the plain. Strong winds and dust storms are common.

Neighboring Countries: Pakistan (South and East, including the disputed territory of Kashmir); Iran (West); Turkmenistan, Uzbekistan, Tajikistan (North); China (Northeast).

Time Zone: GMT +4 1/2 hours.

Official Languages: Pashto and Dari (Persian).

Other Principal Tongues: Uzbek, Turkmen, and Baluchi.

Ethnic Background: Pashtun, Tajik, Hazara, Uzbek, Turkmen, Baloch, and others.

Principal Religion: Islam; comprised of Sunni (87%) and Shi'a (12%); small minorities of Sikhs and Hindus (approximately 4,000 in total); the minute Jewish community fled during the Soviet invasion of 1979, leaving a sole caretaker of the Kabul synagogue.

Main Exports: Agricultural products (dried fruit, nuts, lambskins, raw cotton, wool, and grain), carpets, and textiles. Opium production ranks largest in the world, with more than 90% of total output; the trade employs 400,000 Afghans.

220

Afghanistan

Until modern times, the territory did not form a separate political unit. Indeed, its steep mountains and remote valleys usually felt the impact of formal government only lightly. Nevertheless, the land and its people suffered migrations, raids, and conquests as a consequence of its position as the "turnstile of Asia's fate." Iranian languages (a branch of the Indo-European language group) were established in the region more than 3,000 years ago, and related languages have been used ever since by the majority of the population. Often identified as the birthplace of Zarathustra, founder of Zoroastrianism, Islam entered what was then a Buddhist land (the outcome of an alliance between the Greek Seleucid rulers of Afghanistan and the Indian Maurya Empire in 305BC), during the 7th century. By the 10th century Islam was dominant, although other religious practices continued to flourish in small pockets.

From the 14th to the 19th centuries, invaders swept across the mountains and valleys: the Mongols, followed by the plundering hordes of Timur Lang (Tamerlane), and then Babur, a Turkish chief from Central Asia who claimed descent from Timur. Babur established his capital at Kabul in the 16th century; his warriors conquered the Indus and Ganges Valleys, founding the great Mogul Empire. Meanwhile, the Safavid Empire in Iran ruled Herat and sometimes Kandahar.

After two centuries of Mogul and Safavid rule, Pashtu-speaking tribes began to exercise greater local authority, despite frequent internal feuds. These tribes referred to themselves as Pashtun (*Pakhtun* was a dialectic variation), but the Persians called them Afghans, a name that most likely derived from an early tribal group. When Safavid rule proved particularly severe and rapacious, the Afghans of Kandahar revolted and defeated the Persian army in 1711. By mid-century, Ahmad Khan Durani had proclaimed himself shah (or king) in Kandahar and seized the eastern part of the Persian Empire, but his successors proved unable to create an Afghan state.

In the early 19th century, chiefs of a rival family, the Mohammedzai, consolidated their control over the principal centers of the country. Dost Mohammed eventually proclaimed himself Amir of Kabul and ruled as king, although it was decades later before any of his line assumed the title of shah. Dost Mohammed concentrated on controlling a smaller territory rather than overextending his forces as the previous dynasty had done. His last achievement was to drive Persian forces out of Herat.

For the next century, the two main themes in Afghan political history were the struggles between rival leaders and the interference of British Indian officials. Direct descendants of Dost Mohammed remained in power until 1978, but only by repeatedly defeating rivals—often brothers and other close relatives. Most rulers died violent deaths; power passed to brothers or cousins as often as to sons.

Between 1839 and 1919, British Indian troops periodically intervened in Afghanistan, usually in support of a rival claimant to the throne who appeared to be more agreeable to policy in Delhi. They did not always win: the First Afghan War in 1841 (the "Disaster in Afghanistan") ended with the brutal massacre of some 4,500 British and Indian troops and 12,000 camp followers (many of them, women and children, some of Afghan heritage). Caught out in brutal conditions on the rugged mountain passes in the Hindu Kush, many froze to death. Those who survived the conditions were killed in running battles with local Afghan tribes. Only a handful of soldiers made it out alive and a small number of women and children were taken captive.

The major motive for Britain's intervention was the desire to block Russian influence. After a century of expansion toward the Hindu Kush Mountains, by 1875 the Russian Empire nearly reached the Amu Darya—the later border of the Soviet Union. As Russian expansion continued, a new British invasion in 1878 began two years of fighting with the Afghan tribes. In the end, the new ruler, Abdurrahman, was required to put foreign relations in the hands of British authorities. Anglo-Russian rivalry in Afghanistan continued until the Tsar's government acknowledged the country to be an area of British influence.

Although the country remained neutral during World War I, in 1919 Amir Amanullah sought to gain popularity by a half-hearted attack on British India. This war lasted only a month, but ended with Britain recognizing the independence of Afghanistan in foreign as well as internal affairs.

Modernization came very slowly to the country during the first half of the 20th century, and its geographical remoteness, fierce tribal loyalties, and occasionally rigid interpretation of Islam kept foreign influence to a minimum. Amanullah was forced from power after returning from an extended foreign trip and proposing reforms. His successor was assassinated in a blood feud. Family and palace intrigues dominated the first three decades of King Zahir's rule. However, in 1964 the king granted a new constitution that expanded the legal system beyond Islamic religious law and prohibited the king's relatives from serving as minister, chief justice, or as a member of the legislature.

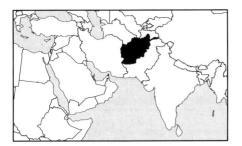

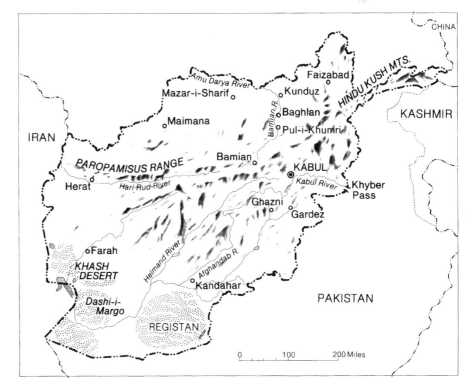

221

Afghanistan

Mujahidin resistance fighters look down on a village after a Soviet aerial attack; at left are terraced crop fields.

As a concession to an educated minority, the king allowed elections in 1965. However, political parties were not permitted, and the king did not grant elected representatives any real law-making power, although the wealthy landowners who dominated the legislature were able protect their interests and block progressive tax laws.

Before the scheduled 1973 elections, an army coup d'etat deposed the king and abolished the constitution. The coup was led by Mohammed Daud Khan, the king's cousin and brother-in-law who had previously served as prime minister. He immediately proclaimed the country a republic and named himself both president and prime minister. Thus, the overthrow of the monarchy actually concentrated power to the ruling member of the Mohammedzai family.

President Daud's dictatorial rule failed to satisfy many people, and there were at least three attempts to overthrow him. To legitimize his rule, he managed his election as president in 1977 by a National Assembly (*loya jirga*), but in 1978 a day-long battle in Kabul between communist sympathizers and loyalists ended with the deaths of thousands, including President Daud. The army officers who led the coup had studied in the Soviet Union, and learned the arts of political subversion along with the art of war.

Under Communist Rule, 1978–89

The victors set up a Revolutionary Council and appointed an elderly poet and journalist as a figurehead president. The new regime rapidly formed close ties with the Soviet Union. Domestically, it adopted a red flag and undertook radical social and economic reforms. Land-holdings were reduced to a maximum 15 acres, Islamic schools were closed, and changes in family law conflicted with traditional Islam.

Not surprisingly, opposition surfaced, and then turned to rebellion, much of it religiously inspired. The government sought Soviet aid to crush the widespread rebellion of the *mujahideen* (meaning "those who undertake jihad"), but the ensuing Soviet presence inflamed both nationalist and Muslim opposition.

Further complicating matters, the Afghan communists were divided into two often hostile factions, *Khalq* ("Masses") and *Parcham* ("Banner"). To avert a likely defeat of communism, in late 1979 a Soviet invasion force suddenly attacked Kabul, attacking and killing the (Khalq) president before installing Babrak Karmal of Parcham as president.

Some 90,000 Soviet troops entered the struggle to defeat the mujahideen. They successfully occupied most of northern Afghanistan and the major cities of Kabul, Herat, and Kandahar, as well as the roads connecting them. However, the mujahideen, although poorly armed and divided into rival groups, operated across much of the country's rugged terrain, and won many small victories. In response, the Soviets adopted a policy of ruthless air and artillery attacks on towns and villages.

The invasion and its indiscriminate bombing and shelling turned the population into refugees. Nearly five million civilians fled the fighting, several million to Iran and more still to Pakistan. Giant refugee camps in Pakistan, funded by Saudi Arabia, other Arab nations, and the United States, became staging bases for the mujahideen.

The Islamic resistance operated most successfully in the mountains near its supply centers in Pakistan. Another stronghold was the Panjsher Valley north of Kabul, not far from the strategic Salang highway linking the capital to northern Afghanistan. There, under a highly regarded Tajik mujahideen commander named Ahmad Shah Masoud, rebels withstood repeated Soviet attacks. In the west and south, other mujahideen groups fought for Herat and Kandahar, and the fighting destroyed large portions of these two historic cities.

Cruelty and inhumanity accompanied much of the fighting. Soviet forces bombed villages and dropped explosives disguised as toys in rebel areas. Soviet and Afghan troops killed hundreds of civilians in reprisal raids and tortured captured mujahideen before executing them. On the other hand, journalists reported that rebel groups often preferred to take no prisoners and executed government supporters in newly-captured towns.

Mid-1980s Soviet policies suffered strong condemnation in the world press, even in many "non-aligned nations" that the Soviet Union had courted for years.

**Ahmad Shah Masoud,
Tajik Mujahidin Leader**

Moscow began to recognize that the Kabul regime remained entirely dependent on Soviet support. The military situation worsened in 1986 after the United States provided some mujahideen with Stinger anti-aircraft missiles and other modern weapons that threatened to neutralize Soviet air power and render difficult the supply of remote outposts.

Recognizing that Babrak Karmal had proved ineffective, in 1986 the Soviet Union forced his resignation "for health reasons." Najib Ahmadzai, then head of security in Kabul and a leading figure in Parcham, took control of government as the General Secretary of the Communist party. In 1987 he was elected president by an assembly dominated by communists but given a smattering of legitimacy by a few tribal leaders and others.

A more flexible politician than his predecessors, Najib restored the Islamic form of his name, Najibullah, and offered political concessions, including a coalition government. However, he won over only a few inconsequential groups. By 1988, after Afghan casualties had surpassed one million dead and millions more wounded or exiled, Soviet leader Mikhail Gorbachev promised to withdraw Soviet troops and let the Afghans decide their future government.

The last Soviet troops departed in 1989 against a background of rocket attacks on Kabul and fierce fighting for several provincial cities. In the capital, crowded by over two million inhabitants, siege conditions appeared, for rebel activity often closed the Salang highway to the north and a Soviet airlift of supplies proved insufficient. Food prices rose sharply, so that the price of a large family's monthly flour—the staple food—exceeded two months' average pay. Malnutrition threatened. However, by summer the guerrillas abandoned their use of mass hunger against the regime and allowed food trucks through. Nevertheless, rocket attacks continued from the surrounding mountains and killed hundreds of people, nearly all of them Muslims and many of them children.

The stalemate in the capital reflected the country at large. The mujahideen fiercely assaulted Jalalabad, between Kabul and the Khyber Pass, but failed despite the highest casualties of the war. Similarly, in Herat, Kandahar and elsewhere the government continued to govern essentially the same cities and territory. Some officials and soldiers defected, but others fought with greater determination, fearing that capture meant death.

Victory eluded the guerrillas largely because they could not unite. Military coordination often proved weak, and separate groups made uncoordinated attacks. Personal antagonisms, ethnic rivalries, and traditional blood-feuds often overshadowed the struggle against the communist regime. In particular, the Pashtun *Hizb-i Islami*, dominant along the Pakistani border, hijacked supplies intended for its northeastern rival, Masoud's largely Tajik *Jamiat-i Islami*. Ambushes and battles broke out between them. Shi'a and Sunni mujahideen differed over their concepts of the state. Moreover the majority Sunni fractured between moderate conservatives and fundamentalists, who tended to follow Gulbuddin Hikmatyar of the Hizb-i Islami. In contrast, only a few mujahideen attacked the departing Soviet troops, and several groups arranged informal cease-fires with Kabul.

The disintegration of the Soviet Union in 1991 disrupted food and fuel supplies for Kabul. New Russian leaders desired to end an adventure that had cost more than $110 billion and countless lives over the course of a decade. The Kabul government tottered, then collapsed when General Abdul Rashid Dostam and his tough, Uzbek militia at Mazar-i-Sharif switched sides and formed an alliance with Ahmad Shah Masoud, who had captured much of the northeast for the mujahideen. Moving quickly southwards, General Dostam's militia and Masoud's Jamiat-i Islami mujahideen cut the Salang highway and captured the Bagram airbase near Kabul. When Gulbuddin Hikmatyar of the Hizb-i Islami sent his forces to infiltrate Kabul, Dostam's militia and Masoud's guerrillas rushed for the city, some flown by air force helicopters. Najibullah attempted to flee but was captured, and the communist regime formally transferred power to an Islamic Afghan regime in April 1992.

Deprived of their prize, Hikmatyar's forces rocketed the city, killing and maiming the first of tens of thousands of Muslims dead by Muslim hands in the Islamic Republic. However, conditions in the capital did not reflect the country. Some areas enjoyed relative calm under the control of local warlords, and several million refugees returned from Pakistan to their often-destroyed towns and villages.

Kabul changed perceptibly under Islamic rule. Women who previously dressed in jeans and T-shirts now covered their hair and wore long black robes, some perhaps for piety; others to avoid molestation. Alcoholic beverages vanished from stores and hotel bars closed. Former officials and agents of Khad, the secret police, disappeared to avoid reprisals. Executions occurred.

Despite the creation of a Leadership Council to guide the country, politics remained confused. Amid accusations of bribery and pressure, a large council elected Burhanuddin Rabbani of the Jamiat-i Islami as president. However, Rabbani failed to win recognition from Hikmatyar and the Hizb-i Islami, and later attempts to bring Hikmatyar into the government also failed, ushering in a four-year struggle to rule Kabul. Rival mujahideen leaders made and broke alliances, all apparently to ensure that no one leader became powerful enough to rule the nation. The most cynical alliance joined Dostam and Hikmatyar, longstanding ideological and ethnic rivals, now united by resentment of Rabbani's rule over Kabul. Blockades on roads ended most travel, and the airport closed. Hundreds of thousands fled. In short, from 1992 to 1996, Afghanistan endured civil war.

The Rise of the Taliban

As the nation collapsed into anarchy, a new political force inspired hope. A protest movement of religious scholars, the *Taliban* (Students) emerged in the southern Pashtun city of Kandahar against the militancy, sexual violence, and corruption of local mujahideen. Desiring to establish Islamic government under the leadership of a recluse named Mullah Muhammad Omar, Taliban fighters ended thievery on the roads and established order.

Most Taliban conquests were relatively bloodless in a nation suffering great war fatigue. The Taliban's superior firepower was reinforced by the mobility of their four-wheel drive pickups and the obvious faults of many corrupt mujaheedin. With relatively little fighting, the Taliban quickly conquered much of the Pashtu-speaking south and advanced on the capital. Briefly repulsed by Rabbani's forces,

Afghanistan

Najibullah

the Taliban conquered Herat in 1995, then launched air and missile attacks against residential areas of Kabul. In 1996 the capital fell, and Najibullah was quickly executed. Aided by Pakistani volunteers and defections among Dostam's officers, in 1998 the Taliban conquered Afghanistan's second largest city, Mazar-i Sharif, and much of the north. The opposition Northern Alliance, led by Dostam and Masoud, controlled only the Panjsher Valley and the far northeast, a region lacking significant cities, plus Shi'a areas in the central mountains.

Taliban rule shocked the world. The group banned television and required beards on all men. Offenders who trimmed their beards too much risked their noses being cut off. To Western and much Muslim opinion, the treatment of women defied human dignity and extended far beyond female modesty in dress. Although several hundred thousand war widows struggled to provide for their families, the Taliban ordered women not to work outside their homes. Later it relented for necessary tasks like nursing (for female patients only), but it demanded extreme measures to keep men from seeing women even at a distance. Even after such precautions were observed, it closed down UN-sponsored bakeries run by women. After closing universities, the Taliban proposed opening them for men only. The group declared that education for girls would stop at the age of eight, and teachers caught schooling girls in homes were arrested and often tortured.

Only three countries, most prominently Pakistan and Saudi Arabia, ever extended diplomatic recognition. The other was the United Arab Emirates. Russia, India, and several Central Asian republics remained critics, sustaining the Northern Alliance and other opposition groups in a bleak existence.

Sanctuary for Osama bin Laden and September 11

The son of a leading Saudi construction magnate from Yemen, as a young man in the 1980s Osama bin Laden accepted militant Islamist ideas and joined the Afghan mujahideen to fight the Soviets. In 1988, he established a loosely-organized society called *al-Qaeda* ("The Base") and became known for criticizing Arab and Western governments. Pressured by Saudi Arabia and the United States, he moved to Sudan in 1992, where his violent diatribes against the United States led Sudan to expel him in 1996. He returned to rural southern Afghanistan, where he established training camps.

In 1998 truck bombs at American embassies in Nairobi, Kenya and Dar es Salaam, Tanzania, killed hundreds and injured thousands. Evidence pointed to al-Qaeda, but Mullah Omar refused U.S. demands to hand over Osama, a "guest." UN sanctions followed in 1999 that banned most flights to the country and grounded the national airline. Al-Qaeda followers attacked the *U.S.S. Cole* in 2000 in Yemen. After the infamous September 11 attacks, evidence again quickly implicated bin Laden and al-Qaeda, and again the Taliban refused to hand over bin Laden.

On October 6, the U.S. aerial offensive began with attacks on air defenses, command centers, and communications facilities. U.S. Special Forces infiltrated Afghanistan to strengthen the Northern Alliance and to mark targets for smart weapons. Fearing that the United States would assist a Northern Alliance attack along the front lines, the Taliban had moved its troops and many Arab and Pakistani volunteers to the northern city of Kunduz before the bombing began. This left other major cities lightly defended.

General Dostam recognized that the capture of Mazar-i Sharif would break the Taliban's supply line and prevent a retreat by troops concentrated in the north. With U.S. air support, Dostam's forces fought bitterly for the city and won. Days later, airpower enabled the largely Tajik forces of the Northern Alliance to break through Taliban defenses outside Kabul and enter the city, almost unopposed. Despite fears that the city might again become a battlefield between rival mujahideen, the population celebrated the Taliban's collapse and, eventually, the legalization of music, kite flying, and education for girls.

In the south, particularly around Mullah Omar's home town of Kandahar, the Taliban faded more slowly. The Pashtun heartland could not be captured by the Northern Alliance. However, local anti-Taliban rivals emerged to provide ground soldiers for the conquest. In the eastern mountains of Paktia province U.S. troops

and Afghan militiamen fought mopping-up operations near Gardez. Large caves in the rugged terrain had provided refuge for the mujahideen fighting the Soviets. Vast weapons stockpiles had passed to the Taliban, and Osama bin Laden himself had frequented the area. However, he eluded his pursuers. He would survive in Pakistan for another decade, until killed by U.S. SEALS at his home in Abbottabad in 2011.

Karzai, Warlords, and Elections

Hamid Karzai, a Pashtun from a notable family, was selected by representatives of several factions at a council in Germany to serve as the provisional national leader after the fall of Kabul in late 2001. Articulate, thoughtful, and distinguished, Karzai persuaded wealthier nations to donate nearly $5 billion in aid. The money was critical: civil servants had not been paid in seven months, and the treasury was bare.

Hundreds of delegates, from all significant population groups and even some (appointed) women, formed a much-anticipated loya jirga in 2002 to select an interim ruler pending a new constitution and elections. After the aged ex-king, Zahir Shah, who reigned from 1933–73, withdrew from consideration, the loya jirga selected Hamid Karzai as president.

Forming his cabinet proved difficult. Tajiks from the Northern Alliance and other militia leaders demanded significant roles, disproportionate to their ethnic groups' shares of the population. Personal rivalries and conflicting political ideologies also complicated matters. The Northern Alliance eventually received the ministries of defense, finance, and foreign affairs, although gradually its members would be forced from office.

His cabinet formed, Karzai faced significant problems in actually ruling. Rather than disarm after victory, the militias remained, and their leaders often controlled their home districts. U.S. forces, initially disinterested in nation-building, worsened the problem by hiring sometimes unsavory warlords as mercenaries against suspected Taliban and al-Qaeda hideouts. For practical reasons—there were fewer American soldiers in Afghanistan than police in New York—the United States could not disarm the militias. In 2003, the UN-sponsored Disarmament, Demobilization and Reintegration Program at last offered militiamen money, clothes, and food vouchers in exchange for weapons.

Lacking supreme authority, Karzai risked becoming little more powerful than the mayor of Kabul, protected by American bodyguards and an international security force. However, militia warlords were not all petty thugs who seized provincial

Then-President Hamid Karzai flanked by vice presidents Mohammed Fahim, a Tajik, and Karim Khalili, a Hazara

capitals and forced Karzai's governors to flee. In Herat, Ismail Khan certainly ignored Kabul's regulations and appropriated customs revenues locally, depriving Kabul of tax revenues. But he ran a fairly effective, if authoritarian, mini-state. Its streets were clean and paved, and opium production was minimal.

Several achievements marked Karzai's early years in office. Three million children entered school, and two million refugees returned. Aid organizations began widespread humanitarian relief.

Committees drafted a new constitution that delicately managed the role of Islam. Business flourished as refugees invested funds previously held abroad, and the economy grew rapidly. The central bank issued a new currency, also called the Afghani, worth 100 times the value of the old one. The new currency conveniently ended the ability of some local rulers to print their own. Reconstruction projects repaired the Salang tunnel and the Kabul–Kandahar highway. Entrepreneurs established mobile phone systems in several cities.

The 2004 presidential election allowed the nation to render its verdict on Hamid Karzai. Karzai picked a Tajik—the brother of Ahmad Shah Masoud—to share the ticket. The voters proved highly enthusiastic about the first free election. Despite Taliban threats, little violence occurred, and Karzai won 55% of the vote. Significantly, Karzai's share of the vote tended to reflect the Pashtun share of the provincial population, from about 90% near Kandahar in the south to only 10% in the Tajik

northeast. In effect, the vote became an ethnic census.

Uniquely for South Asia, the Afghan constitution reserves 25% of the seats in parliament for women. While some elected women were conservative relatives of warlords, even a woman as outspoken as Malalai Joya won a seat. True to her reputation, she addressed the opening session of parliament and attacked the warlords among its members as criminals "with hands stained by the blood of the people."

The Taliban Return

In early 2005 the top U.S. general proclaimed security "exceptionally good." However, when spring returned the Taliban and foreign volunteers launched attacks on isolated troops, murdered aid workers, assassinated officials, harassed candidates, and destroyed schools. Techniques from the Iraqi insurgency, particularly roadside bombs and even suicide bombings, made their appearance. Anti-American activists seized on an alleged desecration of the Quran to stir up deadly riots. Progress in creating a national army, meanwhile, was hampered by low literacy levels, poor pay, and low compensation for soldiers killed in battle.

Trusting local intelligence sources, U.S. forces sometimes struck hard at innocent civilians. An important convoy and several wedding celebrations were bombed, killing dozens of civilians and wounding scores. Informants wishing to settle old scores had suggested that Taliban suspects might be in the area, and Afghans celebrating the joyful occasion by firing

into the air became the targets of missiles. By 2006, the Taliban cynically adopted the tactic of entering a village, attracting U.S. attention, and then withdrawing before air strikes, which inevitably killed innocent civilians. President Karzai protested U.S. policy regarding aerial bombardment, complaints that were repeated with increasing forcefulness and often warranted. More than once, U.S. forces denied causing civilian deaths, only later to admit casualties.

Why, years after the ouster of the Taliban, had casualties climbed to hundreds per month during the summer fighting season? Why did they again dominate parts of Helmand, Zabul, Uruzgan, and Kandahar provinces in the south, while enforcing rules as far north as Kunduz? In one dramatic weekend in 2008, the Taliban freed all the inmates of Kandahar prison and took over villages just a few miles outside of the city. In 2011 they attacked Kandahar again. According to analysis by *The Long War Journal*, by late 2015 nearly 30 of Afghanistan's 398 districts were under Taliban control, and another 36 districts were contested.

Analysts suggest that a number of factors encouraged the resurgence. The United States and its NATO allies initially failed to occupy many rural areas. They left the south's pacification to traditional warlords who failed to impose decisions from Kabul. Over time, these warlords became corrupt as well as inefficient, so much so that NATO commanders demanded the replacement of several of them before replacing U.S. forces there.

Afghanistan

Second, the Taliban retained the sympathy of many traditional Pakistanis, and found refuge in Pakistan's rugged border areas, where its units regroup and rearm. Elements in Pakistani military intelligence have turned more than a blind eye to Taliban fighters seeking refuge. Although publicly an ally in the fight against terrorism, on several occasions Pakistan has responded to U.S. drone attacks and other operations by blocking supply convoys to Afghanistan.

Third, the Afghan government has proven ineffective even in relatively safe regions. Cities desperately need new housing, street repairs, clean water, and sewers that work. An army of the unemployed could provide the labor for much of the work, but between a penniless state and lavish foreign aid spent on experts' salaries and other priorities, reconstruction has proven slow. Polls indicate that a majority feels that foreign aid has not benefitted them.

The poorly trained and poorly paid police have often been corrupt and inefficient. As a result, petty crime is common. Terrorist attacks and suicide bombings occur frequently in Kandahar, and dramatically in Kabul, Mazar-i Sharif, and Herat. These attacks shake confidence. Before the 2009 presidential election, the NATO secretary general publicly blasted "corrupt and inefficient" government.

To no surprise, administrative failures have handicapped the struggle against the Taliban. Some estimates suggested that in 2010 only 25% of the most important areas of the country were secure and supporting the government. The arrival of 30,000 additional U.S. troops in 2009 provided increased firepower, especially in the south. However, even years later the Afghan military remains underpaid, largely illiterate, and poorly trained.

The Taliban movement itself has proven remarkably resilient, spreading quietly across the rural countryside, collecting taxes and attacking girls' schools when powerful enough to do so. Joining nationalist slogans to the religious, the group has depicted Afghan politicians as foreign agents and sought to create a sense of inevitable victory after the foreigners' inevitable departure.

The Challenge of Opium

For the long run, one of the greatest challenges will be the production and trade of opium, because it funds warlords, strengthens the Taliban, and corrupts the government. In 2001 the Taliban had prohibited growing opium poppies. Under Karzai, the absence of authority encouraged many impoverished farmers to resume opium cultivation because opium typically provides the farmer between four and 20 times the income of wheat per acre.

Local scholars of Islam agree that Muslims should not consume it, although they differ as to whether producing opium for use by non-Muslims conflicts with Islamic principles. Regardless of theology, the presence of large quantities of highly addictive drugs has resulted in some one million addicts. Proportionally, this is the highest rate in the world.

To avoid arousing anti-American feelings, U.S. forces initially did not attack opium fields or refining facilities. After rising ten-fold in 2002, opium production doubled again in 2003, almost entirely in the insecure south and west. By 2009, the United Nations estimated that production totaled about 7,000 tons, from 14 of the 34 provinces. Output fell in 2010, due to a plant fungal disease but, in response, prices climbed, encouraging greater cultivation. The next year the value of output rose by 133%. After processing into heroin, the product may be worth half the value of the legal GDP, and the Taliban stronghold of Helmand province produces more opium than the second-largest producing nation, Myanmar.

The opium trade weakens the Kabul government in many ways. It strengthens warlords, who tax or even trade the drug. Corruption flourishes, as payoffs protect certain fields and smugglers. Aerial spraying to destroy the crops upsets aid agencies, who reason that farmers would be driven to desperation if no alternative income was provided, but an internationally-funded program to pay farmers to destroy their opium crops often ended up paying the warlords' supporters instead. Though costing about $1 billion annually, the eradication effort has been a failure in many provinces. Combining broader economic development with stricter legal enforcement may prove the key, but achieving either, let alone both, remains beyond the reach of the government in many southern areas. Meanwhile, the trade continues to enrich the Taliban, who control many producing regions.

An Afghani farmer signs an application for a tractor   World Bank photo

Afghanistan

Afghan vegetable vendor, Kabul   Photo by Jon Markham Morrow

Election Fraud Weakens Karzai

As presidential elections approached in 2009, President Karzai's popularity reached new lows, and American support for him wavered. His 40 election rivals included candidates with many viewpoints, and some with close contact with the United States, a sign of increasing distrust between Kabul and Washington. However, Karzai deftly played several issues. He condemned Washington for casualties from air attacks and demanded the Supreme Court postpone elections from April to August, a delay necessary for both security and administrative reasons.

Few of Karzai's rivals enjoyed national stature of any significance; his most serious rivals enjoyed only limited support. Moreover, Pashtun voters would not likely support a Tajik or other minority candidate, and Karzai reached out to that community by carefully selecting General Mohammed Fahim, a former Tajik militia commander, as a vice presidential nominee. The president's campaign also enlisted the support of tribal leaders, officials, and others.

Although the election transpired peacefully, allegations of mass fraud quickly overwhelmed initial claims of an impressive Karzai victory (55% to 30% for Dr. Abdullah Abdullah, the former foreign minister). Fraud apparently touched the entire process, beginning with voter registration in the absence of an identification system and continuing through bribery and falsified ballots. The results plunged the country into a political and constitutional crisis, and the election commission stripped Karzai of sufficient votes to force

a run-off vote. However, Dr. Abdullah then conceded, claiming that the run-off could not be free and fair.

Despite his waning popularity, Afghans recognized that President Karzai would win a fair contest against a non-Pashtun. His triumph in a corrupt election instead left him weakened internationally and domestically. When he attempted to repay political allies by appointing them to the cabinet, parliament rejected nearly 75% of his nominees. Relations with the United States and other nations declined, as donors threatened to halt aid to ministries run by corrupt politicians.

Fraud likewise dominated the 2010 parliamentary elections. Turnout fell to 40% amid voter cynicism and Taliban intimidation in several regions. Election authorities subsequently invalidated 1.3 million of the 5.6 million votes, and the new parliament included fewer pro-Karzai members.

That same year corruption allegations against Kabul Bank, the largest in the country, led first to a run on the bank, as depositors hurried to withdraw their funds, and then to a massive scandal that on a proportional basis (5% of GDP) was one of history's largest.

Both the communists and the Taliban opposed private banks; when Karzai came to power, the country lacked banks that would take depositors' money and lend to others. At the same time, foreign governments and aid agencies expected to make payments by check. Into the commercial vacuum stepped Sherkhan Farnood, a professional poker player, who established Kabul Bank, with support from well-connected notables—including the

president's brother. Kabul Bank became the government paymaster for its 250,000 employees and teachers. However, it later emerged that the real purpose of the bank was to recycle deposits to just 19 people and companies, who received nearly $1 billion in loans. To hide corruption, some bank records were fraudulent and there were two sets of books indicating what borrowers ostensibly owed, and what they really owed. Most loans left the country and will never be repaid.

International agencies provided the funds to keep the bank in operation, but outside pressure led the Afghan government to bring Farnood and several associates to justice. They were convicted, imprisoned, and their property was seized. Nevertheless, the entire Kabul Bank saga suggests a regime operating to benefit a highly favored elite.

The Withdrawal of Foreign Troops

The scheduled departure of all U.S. and NATO combat troops by the end of 2014 concentrated the minds of military planners, who focused attention on possible consequences. Western military experts initially considered Afghan troops and police incapable of defending the government and society. Afghan units had rarely fought alone, and the Taliban proved able to launch guerrilla attacks in Kabul with some frequency. But in 2013 the Afghan National Army (ANA) carried out successful, large-scale operations that demonstrated effective planning and organization. Coalition casualties dropped dramatically between 2011 and 2013, but ANA casualties rose. Afghans were doing the fighting.

Logistics and military equipment seem the most challenging areas. The ANA will fight with much lower levels of technology, including limited use of air power. Unable to assert its authority over the entire territory, it might be forced to withdraw to the most important provinces that its troop can defend, resulting in the country's informal partition and Taliban rule over the south and east.

Reluctant to see the longest U.S. war result in the collapse of its ally, the United States offered to train and assist the ANA after the withdrawal. Officials from Kabul and Washington negotiated an agreement to establish the roles and conditions for the proposed U.S. training mission. However, on various pretexts Karzai refused to sign the agreement, despite a loya jirga's approval of it, even after the Obama administration threatened that the longer the delay in signing the agreement, the smaller would be the assistance.

Given war-weariness and indications of a military stalemate, both Afghan officials and Western diplomats sought to

Afghanistan

compromise with the Taliban. President Karzai summoned delegates to a special loya jirga to discuss options for peace. However, during a meeting with Taliban representatives, a suicide bomber assassinated Burhanuddin Rabbani, the chief government representative.

At least publicly, the Taliban refuse to negotiate with Kabul as long as foreign troops remain, a policy designed to shame the Karzai government. Likewise, to demonstrate its continuing importance, the Kabul government demands that it take the lead in negotiations with the Taliban.

The United States insists on several "necessary outcomes" in a negotiated peace, including acceptance of the Afghan Constitution (and its promise of women's rights) and a Taliban renunciation of al-Qaeda. Kabul's primary concerns include an end to the fighting.

Fraudulent Elections Again

The scheduled withdrawal of foreign troops coincided with the election of Karzai's successor and the expected first peaceful transfer of power from one elected president to another. Six major candidates emerged from the nomination process, ranging from highly educated professionals to former mujahideen leaders who fought the Soviet occupation. Some nominees worried Western aid donors as well as moderate Afghans. Abdul Rasul Sayyaf, for example, had offered Osama bin Laden sanctuary and campaigned to implement Shari'a. General Abdul Rashid Dostam, the Uzbek warlord and past king-maker, reappeared as a vice presidential candidate. Given terrorists' threats to disrupt the campaigns, each candidate received an armored vehicle and security detail.

In long-established democracies, political parties play the major role in defining platforms and managing campaigns, but in Afghanistan ethnicity, alliances, and patronage networks play crucial roles in winning popular votes. After President Karzai's brother, who had previously displayed little interest in politics, withdrew his candidacy, the experienced Dr. Abdullah Abdullah appeared as the candidate to beat.

Despite terror attacks on foreign observers and the country's election commission, and an assassination attempt on Abdullah, both rounds of the election passed relatively peacefully. The election commission reported double the turnout of 2009 despite the Taliban's intimidation. Moreover, both the top finishers in the first round appeared capable leaders. As expected, Abdullah placed first, with 45%; his rival in the final round was the president of Kabul University, Ashraf Ghani Ahmadzai, a former finance minister and economist with the World Bank. Generally

known by his first two names, he received 32% of the vote.

The second round of voting seemed more suspect. While final round ballots were still being delivered to Kabul and counted, Abdullah publicly rejected any figures that might be announced. He claimed that the counting was fraudulent and the Independent Election Commission partisan. Urging the United Nations to solve the problem, Abdullah withdrew his monitors from the commission's work.

Evidence later confirmed that the commission was anything but independent and neutral. Several thousand employees had been dismissed after the first round, and successors appointed. In some provinces the number of voters in the second round was three times that of the first. Remarkably, the many extra voters rarely spoiled their ballots, and a suspiciously high number of women cast their ballots in traditionally insecure areas. Leaked recordings of telephone conversations captured the voice of a senior election official urging a provincial governor to "bring the sheep stuffed and not empty." He also discussed the response to an army commander's arrest of local election officials after the discovery of stuffed ballot boxes before voting actually began. The Abdullah campaign claimed that only about six million voters actually participated, implying one million fraudulent ballots.

After several months of stalemate and encouragement from the United States, other governments, and the U.N., the two men agreed to a compromise. Ashraf Ghani was declared the winner and became president, though detailed vote counts were not provided. Abdullah Abdullah assumed a new position, chief executive officer, heading a unity government whose cabinet positions were to be shared by the two sides.

President Ghani quickly won high approval ratings from the Afghan population and great respect from foreign experts. He promised to break the corruption and dependence on warlords that marked Karzai's last years. He fired a number of officials, and demanded the retrial of executives from the failed Kabul Bank. Though agreeing to a cabinet that balanced the president's supporters with Dr. Abdullah's took longer than expected, it eventually did happen ultimately included many new faces.

In the wake of new leadership, foreign relations improved, particularly with two crucial nations, the United States and Pakistan. An effective spokesman on the international stage, Ghani thanked Americans for their sacrifices in blood and treasure during the long war against the Taliban, and reached an agreement for U.S. troops to remain in advisory and training roles.

The United States continues to donate billions of dollars annually in military and other government expenses.

The Taliban's leaders and many of its fighters live across the border in Pakistan, and Ghani recognized than an understanding with Pakistan was essential to deprive the Taliban of asylum and support inside Pakistan's frontier districts. He therefore broke Karzai's long tradition of criticizing Pakistan and favoring India, seeking instead a new Afghan orientation that offered the possibility of Pakistani pressure on Taliban leaders to negotiate. Soon after his election, the new president visited Islamabad rather than New Delhi, and courted the new Pakistani army commander, General Raheel Sharif.

Unfortunately, hope in diplomatic circles did not initially translate into battlefield success. In 2015 the Taliban's traditional summer offensive in Helmand province in the south was accompanied by strong attacks in Kunduz, bordering Tajikistan in the north. Coalition politics delayed the appointment of a defense minister for months, and troop strength in the army is declining, hardly a surprise considering that security forces suffered more fatalities in 2014 than the combined international forces had during a decade.

Recent Developments

In 2018, civilian casualties reached a record high of 3,804. Most analysts agree: efforts to stabilize Afghanistan over nearly two decades have mostly failed. The United States has invested approximately $4.7 billion into the country on programs intended to stabilize it and promote demomcarcy. Too often, that money appears to have had the opposite effect. In one of the world's poorest countries, this amount of cash couldn't be spent fast enough. Rather than strengthen existing institutions, it contributed to a climate of corruption. Today, Afghanistan ranks as amongst the most corrupt nations on earth.

In early 2018, President Ashraf Ghani offered a ceasefire to the Taliban, part of which would recognize the group as an official political party. He offered to come to the negotiating table without preconditions and blessed the idea of the Taliban's opening a political office in Afghanistan. He also offered to reverse sanctions against those members of the Taliban who were willing to engage in talks, renounce violence, and integrate into legal Afghan politics. In short, he offered to make extraordinary concessions to the Taliban so that Afghanistan might pull itself out of war.

In March 2019, devastating flash floods hit a country that has now suffered through years of drought. As rivers, already swollen with spring rains, broke their banks, dozens were killed and tens of thousands were displaced, in a country that has experienced far too much tragedy.

Culture: Like many countries, Afghanistan does not possess a culture which is entirely distinct from that of nearby lands. This is true not only of the folkways of a mainly pastoral and agricultural society, but also of religion, art and political organization. One could also say, though, just as accurately, that Afghanistan is not host to a single culture at all. On the contrary, the country reflects a diverse tapestry of ethnicities, tribes, and clans.

The ties of blood and tribe are strong. Loyalty to the extended family, clan and ethnic group often exceeds any sense of nationalism. It is considered not only a duty, but the normal way of doing things to side with relatives or to aid them in time of need, as well as to share in the happy times of weddings, births (especially of sons) and the celebration of holidays. The most firmly implanted of all secular holidays is *No Ruz,* in honor of the first day of spring—March 21st or 22nd.

Most Afghans farm. They live in small villages, often on a slope at the edge of a cultivated valley. Until the civil war, many people had never traveled any distance from their birthplace, and most villages are still fairly isolated. A few nomads move frequently in search of pasturage for their sheep, goats, cattle and (in the case of a few tribes), camels.

Religion is as natural to the people of Afghanistan as the air they breathe. The name of God is invoked on every possible occasion, and political leaders oppose the dominance of religious practices only at their peril. Though many people speak Dari, a form of Persian, most Afghans feel a general distinctness because they are Sunni Muslims, while most Iranians are Shi'a.

Women's Rights in a Patriarchal Society

During the years of Taliban rule, women suffered greater denials of their basic human rights in Afghanistan than in any other nation across the globe. Historically, among some classes and tribes women had been possessions; justice for the rape of a girl might be settled through marriage to her attacker and in order to avoid charges of adultery. Because family honor and the avoidance of shame were—and in many cases remain—higher values than a woman's happiness and safety, female victims often found no protection from the police or relatives. Wives or daughters who attempted to escape abuse by leaving the home generally faced imprisonment, simply for absence from the family.

In the 1990s, the Taliban used the power of the state to enforce its regulations, including the prohibition of girls'

education beyond puberty. In contrast, the Karzai administration improved the practical circumstances and legal rights of women in a number of ways. Where schools for girls could operate safely, they did. Women now serve as members of parliament and are more active in public life. But former President Karzai, perhaps having feared a backlash over granting greater freedom to women, stands accused of making compromises against women's interests. For example, he endorsed a clerical opinion that permitted husbands to beat their wives under certain circumstances.

Surprisingly, a recent poll indicated that only a minority of women fear that the country could become a worse place following the departure of international troops. At least by Western standards, the return of Taliban rule would clearly make conditions far worse for them. To quote one commander, "The rights that Islam has given to a woman, no other religion has— that she sit quietly in her home, veiled. That she take care of food and clothes for her husband."

Artistic and Cultural Expression

Literary expression largely takes the form of poetry, ranging from the intricate, elegant poems of professionals to the more direct, forceful and colorful folk poetry which displays the soul of the people. Poetry often expressed and preserved Pashtun identity and cultural values and the works of two 17th century poets, the warrior Khushhal Khan Khattak and the mystic Rahman Baba, are still popular in a country where only 7% of the population enjoys electricity and poetry readings are large public events.

Especially in Pashtun areas, fundamentalist objections and suspicions often extend to all Western ideas, a view that limits education. The UN Development Report for 2005 ranked the educational system as the worst in the world. In some areas, it has not progressed since then. As few as 14% of the adult population can read and write, while until recently a high school diploma was almost unknown outside the cities and larger towns. Although the new constitution enshrines the right of education for girls, only a few girls' high schools exist, and those who attend them often suffer threats and harassment.

Higher education, backed by the communists, suffered during the civil wars of the 1990s and essentially collapsed under the Taliban. During the following decade, the number of public colleges and universities climbed to 24, while 33 private institutions opened. Their combined enrollment climbed rapidly to 73,000 students—nearly twenty-fold. Since over 50,000 high school students take university entrance

exams, admission is highly competitive, despite often-dilapidated facilities, shortages of faculty, and poor security.

Religion and local traditions combine with poverty and illiteracy to continue to create great hardship for women even though the worst fundamentalist regulations have been removed and women are permitted to seek employment. According to the United Nations, women are often condemned to lives of malnutrition, exclusion from public life, rape, violence and forced marriage. Amnesty International blames feudal customs for women being treated like property—and men suffering no consequences for abusing them. Among the most unfortunate are the tens of thousands of war widows, and young women forced into arranged marriage. Many of these girls are married before the legal age of 18, and many find their conditions desperate. Suicide attempts are on the rise. Cultural change will take longer than a new series of legal edicts.

Despite its poverty, and current cultural attitudes against the visual arts and public presentations by women, Afghanistan historically produced masterworks of art and decoration, variously showing Islamic, Chinese, Indian, and Hellenistic influences. Many such *objets d'art* were already gathered in Kabul's National Museum when the Soviet invasion took place in the lates 1970s. The Bactrian Hoard, some 22,000 pieces dating back 2,000 years and considered the "most important gold treasure ever found in Asia," was discovered about the same time.

One of the most remarkable if unlikely band of heroes during the country's 30 years of conflict was a small group of museum guards and curators who hid and protected the most valuable objects in the National Museum. Some objects were apparently stored in the presidential palace, in a safe that even a notable militia leader could not blast open. Artifacts left in the National Museum suffered rocket attacks, looting, and finally the deliberate destruction of art by Taliban activists. Despite suffering unemployment and cases of torture, those who hid the precious objects succeeded in saving them.

The museum curators could not save from the Taliban two outdoor statues of the Buddha near Bamian. Carved into a cliff over 1,300 years ago, before the Muslim conquest of Afghanistan, the larger of the two statues measured about 150 feet high and ranked as the tallest standing Buddha in the world. Despite an international outcry, troops used artillery to demolish these unique relics.

Economy: The civil war inflicted suffering on some of the world's poorest people and postponed badly-needed reconstruction.

Afghanistan

Poverty stalks the land, and only a few African countries suffer worse conditions. Indeed, since the ouster of the Taliban in 2001, the country has slipped from 117 to 170 in UN rankings of poverty. The child mortality rate exceeds that of every other country. Millions of land mines still threaten. Over 100,000 Afghans, many of them children, have lost limbs.

Agriculture is the livelihood of the country. Yet, only 20% of the country at most can be irrigated, and less than half of that potential farm land is actually cultivated. In good years, the country is self-sufficient in cereal grains, but frequent droughts require grain imports. The high price of cotton on world markets has encouraged its production, though of course the most profitable crop remains opium.

The skins and wool of the Karakul sheep remain important exports in keeping with long tradition. The United States has been one of the principal purchasers, particularly of the skins of the Karakul lambs. While the wool of the mature sheep is coarse, stringy and brown, that of the newborn lambs is tightly curled and a glossy black, highly prized as a material for fur coats.

The northern part of the country has significant deposits of natural gas and a little oil. Natural gas exports to the Soviet Union were halted when the withdrawing Soviets capped the wells, but these may eventually supply Uzbekistan as well as the area around Mazar-i Sharif. Mineral resources, such as iron ore and coal in the Hindu Kush Mountains, have not yet been exploited. These and other mineral resources contributed to Soviet desires to control the country. Soviet data led American geologists to survey the country more intensively, leading to the discovery of the largest known lithium deposits and huge veins of iron, copper, cobalt, gold and other minerals that could make Afghanistan a world mining center.

Developing such resources will prove difficult in a country with minimal roads and a single railroad line of 47 miles, linking Mazar-i Sharif to the Uzbek border. Given these conditions, despite U.S. military involvement and the discovery of resources, western companies often fail to invest. A Chinese company is developing one of the world's largest

A windstorm sweeps down upon an Afghani sheep and camel market

Photo by Jon Markham Morrow

copper mines in Logar province at a cost of $3 billion, and other Chinese investment seems likely.

The Future: For too many years now, Afghanistan has faced a raft of seemingly implacable challenges. Unsurprisingly, many derive from its ongoing war. The deteriorating security situation in recent years has all but eliminated educational gains made between 2002 and 2016. Today in Afghanistan, nearly half of all children from the ages of seven up, are regularly missing or not enrolled in school. The prospects for a more peaceful and prosperous future are grim.

Slightly less hopeful is the situation for Afghanistan's vast diaspora. In the context of the COVID-19 pandemic, refugees and other displaced peoples remain at particularly acute risk. Not only are they considerably more vulnerable to the economic implications of repeated lockdowns and other restrictions, they often have only limited access to appropriate medical care and may lack the capacity to implement basic distancing or hygiene measures. Iran has sought to weaponize its population of more than a million Afghan refugees,

who have remained in the country, preferring the bite of sanctions in Iran to the insecurity of Afghanistan. As Iran faces increasing international pressure, it has threatened to force Afghan refugees out of the country, as a way of destabilizing Afghanistan and the broader region, to the detriment of the U.S. and precipitating a refugee crisis with likely severe implications for Turkey and Europe.

In February 2020, the United States and the Taliban signed a peace agreement titled the Agreement for Bringing Peace to Afghanistan, with provisions including the withdrawal of all regular U.S. and NATO troops from Afghanistan, a Taliban pledge to prevent al-Qaeda from operating in areas under Taliban control, and talks between the Taliban and the Afghan government. The last troops are scheduled to withdraw by September 11, 2021. For many Afghans, the withdrawal of foreign troops marks an important milestone, as further evidence emerges of possible war crimes and sanctioned massacres by U.S., UK, and Australian special forces. Others, however, fear the consequences of a resurgent Taliban.

The People's Republic of Bangladesh

Passengers disembark from a ferry boat in Narayanganj, Bangladesh

WORLD BANK Photo

Area: 57,000 square miles (147,000 square kilometers). Land appears and disappears from the rivers and Bay of Bengal.
Population: 166 million (including at least 1 million Rohingya refugees).
Capital City: Dhaka (18 million, greater metro area; 8.9 million, city).
Climate: Tropical and rain soaked; the country is subject to destructive hurricanes.
Neighboring Countries: Surrounded by India on three sides; a short border with Myanmar lies on the southeast.
Time Zone: GMT +6.
Official Language: Bengali.
Other Principal Tongues: English (in schools and commerce).
Ethnic Background: Over 98% Bengali, except small tribal groups in the Chittagong hills.
Principal Religion: Islam (87%) and Hinduism (11%).
Chief Commercial Products: Garments, textiles, jute, tea, rice, wheat, sugar, and hides.
Major Trading Partners: The United States, India, China, the United Kingdom, and Germany.
Currency: Taka (1 taka = 100 poisha).
Former Colonial Status: Part of British India (1765–1947) then a province of Pakistan under the name East Pakistan (1947–1971).
National Day: 26 March (1971; Independence Day); December 16 (1971; Victory Day).

Chief of State: Mohammad Abdul Hamid, President.
Head of Government: Hasina Wajed, Prime Minister.
National Flag: A green field with a large red circle in the middle.
Gross Domestic Product: $250 billion.
GDP per capita: $1,564.

Most of the land of Bangladesh is flat, wet alluvial plain, formed over scores of centuries by three great river systems depositing silt as they near the Bay of Bengal. These rivers—the Ganges, the Brahmaputra, and the Meghna—lose their identities as their waters become mingled in a maze of waterways and swamps along the southern coast. Much of the country is less than 30 feet (under 10 meters) above sea level.

Four traditional scourges annually threaten life and property in Bangladesh: the rivers flood during the summer monsoons, covering up to half of the land; destructive tropical storms like Cyclone Fani (2019)—equivalent to hurricanes—sweep in from the Bay of Bengal, strengthened by a funnel effect of the shoreline that creates high tides of salt water; diseases are spread by polluted waters; and crops are destroyed by flood leading to widespread famine.

In no other country of South Asia does the environment pose such a pronounced threat to humans. Bacteria flourish in the tropical climate, and the frequent floods multiply the consequences of inadequate sanitation. Dense population in a country with little industry forces landless farmers onto silt islands barely above high tide. Then floods, or even shifting river channels, destroy land and crops. Famine leads to hunger for those who cannot afford to buy food. Beyond individual and local tragedies, statistics of overpopulation paint a grim picture for the future. Although roughly two thirds of its people live by farming, and around one third live in urban areas, the country's population density exceeds 2,900 per square mile (1,100 per square kilometer)—making it one of the most densely populated nations on earth.

In addition to rising global temperatures—resulting in changing sea levels and tropical cyclones of increased ferocity—ecologists blame the worsening floods of recent years on the deforestation of the Himalaya Mountains in India and Nepal, where the great rivers of Bangladesh originate. The loss of forest increases flooding for two reasons. First, soil retains less water, causing faster runoff. Second, rapid runoff carries deposits of silt downstream, raising the level of riverbeds and diverting them. Former president, Hussain Muhammad Ershad declared floods a "man-made curse" and proposed regional cooperation to end them, as well as better control of the rivers in Bangladesh. However, geologists also suspect that the river delta is simply sinking into the ocean.

Where family farms measure a few acres at best, only rice provides subsistence. Two or even three crops per year, tended with much labor and scarcely any machinery, enable the country, in a good year, to almost feed itself.

Unfortunately, another consequence of deforestation is seasonal drought in the west of the country. Essentially, by late winter and spring too little water flows through the region's many rivers. Shipping becomes dangerous, and irrigation canals dry up, just when water is vital for young crops. One solution, the construction of dams to regulate water flow, will require years of study before construction begins. Estimated costs exceed $1 billion.

Geography forces the use of boat and barge for most travel and transportation. There are 3,000 miles (approximately 4,800 kilometers) of navigable rivers, but only about 10,000 miles (roughly 16,000 kilometers) of surfaced roads. The marshy ground and many rivers render road building difficult and costly. Many streams of the delta are not bridged, and ferry services routinely face delays.

A small region southeast of Chittagong—known as the Chittagong Hill Tracts—is located above the deltas and flood plains

Bangladesh

of the rivers. Its hills, valleys, and forests make this the only region in Bangladesh where there is land that has not been cultivated.

History: Bangladesh, and territory to the west, has for many centuries borne the native name *Bangla*. The region was designated by English officials as the presidency, or state, of Bengal in 1699. With the partitioning of British India and independence of India and Pakistan in 1947, the territory became East Pakistan. Although united by the bond of a common religion, East and West Pakistan formed a state that was not contiguous, separated by India. The difficulties in managing such a physically divided state were compounded by ethnic and cultural differences between the two populations. The Bengalis of East Pakistan—a majority in the country—were often unhappy with a political system and governing body dominated by West Pakistan.

Dissatisfaction grew rapidly in the late 1960s with resentment over attempts to promote Urdu, the major language of West Pakistan, and the award of most foreign aid and development projects to West Pakistan. In 1970 the Awami League of Sheikh Mujibur Rahman pledged

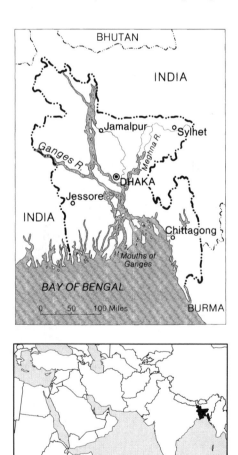

autonomy for East Pakistan and won a majority of seats in elections for the National Assembly. However, General Yahya Khan, the president, prevented the National Assembly from meeting, and hence the Awami League from taking power. Sheikh Mujib was arrested. Uprisings then broke out in the East.

In March 1971, Bangladesh ("The Bengal Nation") proclaimed its independence. A popular rebellion broke out, but was repressed by the Pakistani army for nine months resulting in the deaths of as many as three million Bengalis (a figure disputed by Pakistan). Millions more sought refuge across the border, and in December 1971 India attacked Pakistan. Two weeks later West Pakistan surrendered its claim to the new nation of Bangladesh.

During 1972 the new nation and its government took form. The Indian army withdrew, and massive international aid arrived for the great tasks of aiding refugees and restoring an economy devastated by war. Months were required for the nearly 10 million Bengalis who had fled to India to return to their homeland—often to find that their homes had been destroyed.

Sheikh Mujibur Rahman dominated political life during these years. Still imprisoned in West Pakistan when independence was won, he was immediately declared president of the new nation. Freed in 1972, he received a hero's welcome in Dhaka. His first official acts were to resign as president and take the office of prime minister.

During the first years of independence, political power lay fully in the hands of Sheikh Mujib and loyal members of his Awami League, especially after the 1973 elections gave the party almost all 300 seats in the National Assembly. However, those in power frequently sought personal gain. Much of the international relief sent to alleviate starvation and suffering actually enriched government officials and army officers.

Public feeling eventually, and inevitably, turned against officials over their failure to improve the condition of the poverty-stricken masses. Even Sheikh Mujib's personal popularity melted away amidst the corruption, banditry, and violent disorder. In response, he made himself a virtual dictator and used emergency regulations to censor the press rigorously and jail critics of the administration without trial.

In 1975, a group of military officers murdered Mujib and overthrew his government. They ruled only briefly, 1however, and soon General Ziaur Rahman seized power. The general (popularly known as "Zia") at first chose a retired Supreme Court justice as president before assuming the title himself in 1977.

Although initially a military dictator, President Zia moved toward allowing

Sheikh Hasina Wajed, Prime Minister

political activity by organizing his own Bangladesh National Party (BNP). He won the 1978 presidential election that year, but his assassination during an unsuccessful military coup in 1981 ended an era of relative stability.

Remarkably for a Muslim country (but not unprecedented in South Asia) the two largest parties have been led by women. Sheikh Hasina Wajed, the daughter of Sheikh Mujibur Rahman, inherited his title, a rare occurrence in the Islamic world, and has led the Awami League. Her rival, Khaleda Zia, adopted the Hindu royal title of begum after the death of her husband, Ziaur Rahman. She has headed the more conservative BNP that her husband founded. Both women cooperated in strikes, protests, and boycotts against President Ershad, the military dictator who ruled Bangladesh through the 1980s.

Begum Khaleda Zia

Demonstrations and riots in 1990 followed familiar strike patterns, but this time opposition groups jointly demanded Ershad's immediate resignation and free elections. Riots followed the reported arrests of opposition leaders, and troops fired on crowds killing dozens. When members of Ershad's own Jatiya Party left parliament and senior army officers refused to take control, Ershad resigned.

Bitter Two-Party Rivalry

The parliamentary election campaign of 1991, like most elections since, seemed an often bitter competition between two dead men. The Awami League extolled Mujibur Rahman, while the BNP praised Ziaur Rahman. The results brought Khaleda Zia and the BNP an eventual majority in the 300 elected seats. The newly-elected parliament restored its prime minister to supremacy and rendered the president a figurehead, and Khaleda Zia took office. The Awami League, more socialist in outlook and pro-Indian, led the opposition.

The two women alternated in power for most of the next 16 years, except for several months immediately preceding an election, when the constitution provides for a non-partisan interim administration. Typically, the economy did well at mid-term, but as parliamentary elections approached, there were usually strident accusations of corruption, parliamentary walkouts, frequent general strikes, demonstrations, riots, and travel blockades organized by the party in opposition. These frequently brought the economy to a halt.

For Sheikh Hasina, one contentious issue has remained, bringing to justice the plotters who overthrew and murdered Sheikh Mujib and nearly his entire family. Sheikh Hasina herself escaped death only because she was abroad. Two decades later, as prime minister she ordered the arrest of surviving suspects, despite a promise of immunity issued by military rulers. In 2010, five convicted plotters were hanged for the murders.

General Ziaur Rahman apparently did not participate in the plot, but once in power he sent some of the plotters abroad, and the BNP considered him the real hero of independence. During its years in power, the BNP minimized Sheikh Mujib's role, and Khaleda Zia celebrated her birthday on the day of Sheikh Mujib's death. Symbolically, Sheikh Hasina's government dismantled the pontoon bridge to Ziaur Rahman's island grave, removed his name from the airport, and closed his exhibits in the national museum.

In 2001, the less-secular BNP won an overwhelming victory at the polls, with its allies (including the *Jamaat-i Islami*) capturing two-thirds of parliamentary seats. Khaleda Zia thus gained the ability to move quickly against the public's two greatest concerns: corruption and crime. She failed at both. Repeatedly ranked as the most corrupt nation on earth by Transparency International, Bangladesh proved particularly unable to punish high-level bribe-takers. The anti-corruption bureau operated out of the prime minister's office and never charged prominent members of a ruling party. Popular discontent with crime became so great that during broad daylight mobs lynched nearly a dozen suspected criminals in the capital. Unfortunately, immediate reductions in the crime rate were unlikely; the police were considered the most corrupt institution in the country. Crimes with particularly low rates of punishment included attacks on the Hindu minority. In 2003 the prime minister ordered 40,000 troops into the cities to help police in a massive roundup of suspected criminals. However, crime levels fell only modestly, and public lynching continued despite the military's involvement.

During BNP rule, political violence was disproportionately aimed at the Awami League. The nation was shocked by a grenade and shooting attack on Sheikh Hasina during a political rally that killed nearly twenty people, some of them prominent party leaders.Numbering dozens of publicly identified groups, fundamentalist Islamist movements in the country include both peaceful and violent activists. Secular politicians are not the only victims of the latter: movie theaters, circuses, and other entertainment venues have been attacked.

The extremist *Jamaat-ul-Mujahideen* attacked several courts and assassinated two judges. Since the Jamaat desired to impose Shari'a Islamic law, courts were a particular target. After conviction in court, six Jamaat leaders were executed in 2007.

Demonstrations and general strikes began in 2006 months before the appointment of an interim administration to replace the BNP cabinet. Faulting the outdated and allegedly falsified electoral register, the Awami League determined to boycott the elections and plunged the country into chaos with violence, strikes, and transport blockades. Finally, with the BNP already claiming victory in uncontested races, in 2007 the president declared a state of emergency and appointed Dr. Fakhruddin Ahmad to head an interim government supervised by the military.

A former central banker, Dr. Ahmad was determined to create a voting system worthy of the public's faith. A massive new electoral register was ordered, complete with digital photographs and fingerprints of perhaps 90 million adults, to deter anyone from voting several times. To provide time for the registration, the election was postponed for nearly two years, and the names of 12 million fake voters were removed from the rolls.

In common with his military backers, Dr. Ahmad sought to punish corrupt politicians and halt the destructive rivalry between the two major parties. All political activity was banned. Dozens of former cabinet members and leaders of both parties found themselves under arrest, as did Khaleda Zia's son, Tarique Rahman, and eventually Khaleda herself, charged with corruption. Sheikh Hasina, who was initially abroad, was arrested after her return and charged with extortion.

Despite the military's attempt to reform politics, during the 2009 elections the same two parties made the same promises of cheaper food, tackling corruption, and reducing crime. They were headed by the same two women, both out on bail for corruption charges they considered politically motivated. Sheikh Hasina's Awami League and its allies won an overwhelming victory, gaining 250 of the 300 seats.

Just weeks in office, Sheikh Hasina faced a brutal revolt by troops of the paramilitary border guards, the Bangladesh Rifles, over low pay and the appointment of army officers as their commanders. Scores of officers and civilians were murdered, but the revolt failed. An investigation into its causes was promptly released publicly, and trials followed, allowing Sheikh Hasina to demonstrate the rule of law.

Failed Elections, Recent Crackdowns: In 2013 parliament passed a law that stipulated a non-partisan caretaker cabinet should govern during the campaign season. However, before the 2014 elections the Awami League used its massive majority to overturn the law. Thus, by holding onto power, the Awami League squandered the prospect of effective governance and opened the economy to the inevitably damaging strikes called by the opposition.

As threatened, the BJP and other opposition parties boycotted parliamentary elections in 2014. Only 147 of the 300 seats were contested. The Awami League triumphed, but only 20% of eligible voters participated. While the BJP and its allies predictably condemned the fall of democracy, later opinion polls suggested most citizens were not particularly upset, and the army did not intervene.

In 2010 Sheikh Hasina's government established an International Crimes Tribunal to try those who allegedly committed war crimes during the 1971 War of Independence. The tribunal's title was false advertising: it was not multinational, and its operations did not meet international standards. Instead, it focused narrowly on the largest Islamic party in the country, the Jamaat-i Islami, which had supported

Bangladesh

Pakistan at the time. Eleven of its past and present leaders faced trial.

Death penalties were handed out to a number of party leaders and five have been hanged. The Tribunal has now apparently served its purpose of severely damaging Jamaat, the BJP's political ally, and further executions seem less likely. Jamaat's influence in Bangladesh has waned considerably. Dozens of Jamaat leaders contested the 2018 national elections (under the banner of BNP), but won no seats; the BNP won only eight in total. With infighting over the current direction of Jamaat and the resignation of high-profile leaders over the party's failure to apologize for its support of Pakistan in 1971—and to reform in line with shifting social norms and expectations—Jamaat's star is unlikely to rise in the foreseeable future.

Sheikh Hasina took further actions against the BJP in 2015, as the courts charged Begum Zia with corruption for embezzling charitable donations when she was prime minister. While the BJP attempted to show that it was still significant by launching transport boycotts and a national protest about the 2014 elections, Begum Zia was effectively confined to her office, until granted bail three months later. Other party leaders faced legal difficulties, including Tarique Rahman, Begum Zia's son, who from the safety of London publicly urged the government's overthrow and was accused of treason.

Beyond calling for dialogue, foreign governments did not penalize the nation for either the undemocratic 2014 elections or the justice process. After all, the alternative was not an improvement: the corrupt party leadership of the BJP was allied with sometimes-militant Islamists. So the world muted its complaints, and was reduced to merely hoping that the 2018 elections might see democracy strengthened in Bangladesh.

One significant achievement was an accord between New Delhi and Dhaka to resolve the plight of 50,000 inhabitants of enclaves—150 small "islands" of one nation's sovereignty completely surrounded by the neighboring country. The origins of the enclaves have mostly been lost to history, but since independence, those living in them have rarely received regular government services. Poverty is rampant. The agreement enables the two states to swap territories and grants the inhabitants the choice of remaining in place as citizens of a new nation or transferring to the territory of their long-standing nationality.

Recent years have seen increasing crackdowns on social freedoms in Bangladesh. Critics liken the government's 2018 anti-drug policies to a Duterte-style "drug war" (Duterte is the Philippine president who has overseen the extrajudicial disappearances and killings of thousands in recent years, in an attempt to rid the Philippines of drugs). Over the course of just two weeks in June, for example, security forces and the country's anti-terrorism squad seized nearly 2 million methamphetamine pills and dozens of kilograms of heroin. In the process, well over 100 people were killed and some 9,000 were arrested.

Accusations of extrajudicial killings, forced disappearances, and torture have become increasingly frequent. According to Human Rights Watch, from 2013 to 2018, scores of people have been arrested under section 57 of the Information and Communication Technology Act (ICT Act) for criticizing government officials, often on social media. Like many laws that serve the same purpose throughout the region, this one enables the government to draw on vague and ambiguous language to pursue its opponents. The ICT Act, for example, authorizes prosecution on the basis of publishing material deemed to be fake, obscene, defamatory, or corrupt, where the government determines what these terms mean and whether and how they apply to given behavior. In some cases the language is even more vague: publications that are "aggressive" or "frightening" are also subject to censure, as are those that "ruin communal harmony" or "disturb the law and order situation." In part because of the application of laws like this one, in 2018 Germany's Bertelsmann Foundation labeled Bangladesh (along with Lebanon, Mozambique, Nicaragua, and Uganda) among the "new autocracies." Unsurprisingly, the report has been rejected by the ruling Awami Party, which claims the government is 100% democratic.

Rohingya Refugees in Bangladesh

For decades, the Rohingya Muslims of Myanmar (formerly Burma) have experienced religious persecution and ethnic cleansing within their home country. Hundreds of thousands have fled. A small number have reached western countries, sometimes with the resettlement assistance of the UN refugee agency (UNHCR). Others have made their way to the countries of Southeast Asia, including most prominently Indonesia, Malaysia, and the Philippines. The vast majority, however, have crossed into Bangladesh. Between August and December 2017, alone, more than 720,000 Rohingya entered the country. By the end of 2018, it was estimated that there were 1.1 million Rohingya, mostly unregistered, living in Bangladesh.

For a country that struggles with high levels of poverty, poor infrastructure, and frequent natural disasters, the influx of refugees has created significant strain. Conditions in the refugee camps are poor. Devastating tropical storms and subsequent storm surges, flooding, and landslides in the areas in which camps are located, exacerbate problems of poor sanitation, water-borne diseases, and a lack of access to food. A 2018 repatriation agreement between Bangladesh and Myanmar, which would see all refugees returned home within two years, was unfruitful. No Rohingya refugee has volunteered to return to Myanmar. In March 2019, Bangladesh stated that its border was closed and that it would no longer accept fleeing Rohingya.

The COVID-19 pandemic posed a particularly acute threat to the tens of thousands of Rohingya living in crowded refugee camps in Bangladesh. In 2021, the Bangladeshi government declared its intention to forcibly relocate at least 100,000 refugees to Bhasan Char, an uninhabited silt island in the Bay of Bengal, in order to ease overcrowding in the camps at Cox's Bazar.

Country boats on a Bangladesh river

Bangladesh

The bicycle-rickshaws of bustling Dhaka

Culture: For the two thirds of the population directly involved in farming, plus the small-town merchants, craftsmen, and officials, life revolves around the agricultural seasons. The typical farmer lives with his large family in a simple hut of thatch and mud built on a low mound of earth for protection against monsoon floods. Since the land is extremely fertile, a very small plot can be one man's farm. He sells produce at one of the small towns located on the intersections of waterways. He can afford no modern luxuries; his main entertainment is talking with his family and friends.

Widespread primary education is increasing formerly low literacy rates for both men and women. Roughly 75% of all children in Bangladesh receive some formal education.

Besides vocational and professional institutes, there are several universities, the largest of them the University of Dhaka. Students clashed with police in 1992, after the government approved a law to punish those caught cheating on final exams with five to ten years in prison. Four thousand students were expelled in 2000 for cheating on the English exam required for university graduation.

Despite Bangladesh's staggering population density, it has only a handful of large cities. With the allure of a capital city's opportunities, Metropolitan Dhaka's population has passed the 18 million mark, and it consumes about half the electricity produced in the country. Ringed by rivers, the city was forced to expand upwards rather than outwards and recently experienced a building boom. However, inadequate control of building permits, lax enforcement of standards, and corruption has led to a

number disastrous building collapses and deadly fires. The illegal construction of high rises near the airport in Dhaka have led international aviation authorities to demand their removal.

Numbering over 140 million, the country's Muslims form the world's fourth largest Muslim community, following those of Indonesia, Pakistan, and India. Nevertheless, the Provisional Constitution made the nation a secular state that provides all religions with equal legal standing. Public holidays include Muslim holy days, Christmas, and various Hindu and Buddhist festivals.

The earliest preserved literature in Bangla, dates to the 14th century. Until two centuries ago, it was only verse, intended to be recited or sung. Bangla prose began

in 1800 when a missionary, with the help of native assistants, translated the Bible into that language. The vast literary outpouring of the 19th and 20th centuries included novels and drama. The short stories and poems of Rabindranath Tagore received the Nobel Prize for literature in 1913, one of the first awards for a writer working in a nonEuropean language.

However flourishing, Bangla culture is not the culture of all inhabitants. During the partition of India in 1947, thousands of Muslims from Bihar and elsewhere moved to East Bengal. Loyal to a Muslim state rather than a Bengali one, they tended to support Pakistan during the conflict in 1971. With Pakistan unable or perhaps unwilling to bear the cost of these two-time refugees, about 300,000 of them live destitute in camps in Bangladesh, awaiting some distant solution to their lives of desperation. A high court decision in 2008 granted citizenship to those born in the country after 1950, an important step towards greater rights and economic opportunity.

Other non-Bengalis live in the Chittagong Hills, where some local tribes practice Buddhism, Christianity, or Hinduism. Violence flared in the 1970s after Bengalis moved into the area seeking land. By the mid-1990s, the scattered violence of 20 years had caused over 8,000 deaths, and thousands of tribesmen fled to India and Burma. Following a peace treaty in 1997, some 35,000 refugees returned from India, but slow implementation of the accord leaves some observers fearing renewed violence.

Treatment of Women

The rise of fundamentalist Islamic groups coincided with increasing intolerance within Bengali society. Often those who suffered were women. For example,

Fishing for shrimp and rock lobster

Bangladesh

in the mid 1990s Dhaka University re-imposed the "Sunset Law," a 1922 regulation requiring women students to return to their dormitories before darkness. The restriction, said one faculty member, was "a shield to protect the women's chastity." Outside the university, women's participation in sport has been condemned, and women swimmers were excluded from a swim meet after threats of violence. "Eve teasing," the (often sexual) harassment of women, has become a sport for some young men, who taunt, inflict verbal abuse, and stalk women, especially those not veiled. Fearful of reprisals and shame, victims may not report crimes to the police. Composed of village elders and clerics, village arbitration councils designed to settle property disputes have illegally ordered whippings or even stoning for girls and women charged with sexual immorality. Other women and young girls have been kidnapped and sold into brothels, some abroad.

In the early 2000s there was a spate of acid attacks (mostly against women) in Bangladesh. However, government efforts to address the situation—including imposing the death penalty for perpetrators of such attacks—brought the number of attacks down from as many as 500 in 2002, to less than 50 in 2016.

Death by hanging is the sentence demanded by Islamic militants for Taslima Nasreen and Farida Rahman. The latter, a Member of Parliament, aroused the ire of fundamentalist Muslims when she noted that there would be no harm in allowing women to inherit more than the percentage set by the Qur'an. Nasreen, a feminist whose novel of the plight of Hindus in Bangladesh became a bestseller, denied that she had proposed that the Qur'an be revised to fit the modern world. Charged with blasphemy, she overcame her legal problems but fled the country because of threats on her life.

There are two principal dialects of the Bangla language. The old literary one is much admired but not understood by ordinary Bengalis, while the modern colloquial, understood and used by both the educated and uneducated, is the country's de facto language. It is written in a form of the *Nagari* alphabet, widely used for the languages of India.

Economy: Even today, most Bangladeshis live on farms. Across most of the country, the climate and soil combine to produce good yields of rice, and in years without catastrophes more than 10 million tons are harvested. However, this is not enough to feed the large population, and output falls after devastating floods or cyclones. The government has made valiant efforts to increase food production—for instance by

Thousands of children work as domestic help

digging irrigation canals to water an extra crop in the dry season. Much food must still be imported, and paid for partly by foreign aid.

The country's traditional export crop was jute, the tough plant fiber used to make burlap and rope. When industrial nations turned increasingly to synthetic fibers, world demand for jute declined, and Bangladesh suffered falling profits and cuts in wages and employment. After continuing losses, in 2002 the government closed the Adamjee Jute Mills, at one stroke putting 19,000 workers out of work. For decades the leading source of jobs and exports, the jute industry now employs only a few thousand workers. That may represent the low point in jute's fortunes, because growing environmental concerns encourage the use of jute in packaging, rather than plastic bags, and scientists are discovering uses for the fiber in textiles and carpeting. Annual exports now exceed $1 billion.

The country's poverty results partly from misguided economic policies, past and present. Seeking to raise the standard of living by encouraging industry, early in 1972 the new country took over the businesses, banks and industries owned by West Pakistanis. It then nationalized most other foreign trade, banks and basic industry, leaving only some British tea and jute interests privately owned.

During two decades of mismanagement, few government-owned businesses ever earned a profit. Sectors like telecommunications, electricity and banking still remain inefficient under government ownership. The nationally-owned Biman Bangladesh Airlines managed its fleet of aging aircraft so poorly that it reportedly lost $80,000 on each flight to New York, owed millions of dollars for jet fuel, and could not pay for repairs on several aircraft. The airline cut routes and jobs severely in 2007 to reduce losses.

Privatization and large-scale investment by Japanese and Korean firms once seemed the best hope for economic expansion, but during the 1990s employment grew in an unexpected way. Small and mostly locally-owned factories sprang up to employ growing numbers of workers to produce coats, dresses, and other garments for export. To cut costs, the industry used cramped spaces, low safety standards, and inadequate wiring. Additional floors were often added well beyond the zoning approval. Fires broke out frequently, with employees sometimes trapped by padlocked exits.

Because Bangladeshi garments were not subject to international quotas, output often rose at 10%–20% per year. The industry is vital to exports, providing 80% of all export earnings, valued at nearly $25 billion each year. It has also improved social conditions by providing vital income for women. However, wages have remained abysmal, for some women less than $1 per day.

Touched off by dismissals at one factory, strikes over wages and safety issues broke out in 2006, and some 80 factories were set ablaze before promises were made for higher pay. Workers demanded higher wages again in 2010, up to $72 per month, still among the lowest in the world and about one-sixth the amount necessary to house and feed a family of four. In response, the minimum wage was raised from $20 to $36 per month for a 60–70 hour week. After two years of inflation, in 2012 workers again sought higher pay.

In 2013, the Rana Plaza building collapsed, killing over 1,100 workers and injuring 2,500. It was one of the world's worst industrial disasters and focused global attention on the industry and its safety. The Rana Plaza housed several textile factories and symbolized shortcomings that had long been denounced. For example, the top three floors violated city building codes, and the day before the collapse cracks were visible in the walls.

Although it employed nearly four million workers in 4,500 factories, the industry clearly failed to enforce reasonable

Children fortunate enough to attend school

safety standards. The country's deep levels of corruption left government regulation also ineffective. Months after the Rana Plaza disaster, labor unions and many multinational companies that purchase the exports finally reached a legally-enforceable agreement to inspect the factories that produce their garments.

Because the foreign firms will stand liable for later failures, they have strong reasons to ensure safety. Unfortunately for the factory workers, major U.S. importers such as Wal-Mart, Sears, and The Gap prefer non-binding agreements with smaller roles for labor unions.

For men born to poor families—the vast majority in the country—the route to prosperity has often involved working abroad, particularly in the rich Arab states of the Persian Gulf. Some six million held jobs abroad in 2008, mostly as laborers in construction and domestic service. Unfortunately, the world recession left tens of thousands of migrant workers without jobs, and often still owing substantial debts to middlemen who had arranged their overseas employment.

A decade ago, discoveries of natural gas, both onshore and offshore, offered hopes for potential economic benefits. However, a great dispute arose over the proposal to export gas to India. Foreign companies involved in discovering and developing the fields desired to do so, partly to sell in a more prosperous market. However, nationalists strongly opposed such sales, arguing that with only 20% of homes connected to the electric system there was a huge domestic market for the gas in power plants as well as in producing fertilizer and replacing gasoline in buses and trucks.

Following the unwillingness of the government to permit exports, Shell and Unocal, the largest companies involved, sold their interests to smaller companies more willing to make risky investments. The lack of investment reduced supplies below electric generating needs by 2010, leading to daily limits on air conditioning.

One major nonpolitical issue facing the government is arsenic poison that threatens the water supply of nearly half the population. The arsenic occurs naturally in the soil, and water from deep wells drilled to deliver water with lower bacteria levels frequently carries traces of arsenic. Though not immediately fatal, the arsenic levels often cause tumors and may lead to cancer. Some two million people suffer from arsenic poisoning. In 2006 scientists at Rice University in the U.S. discovered that the arsenic would attach to particles of iron oxide (i.e., rust) about 1/5,000 the width of a human hair. In turn, a simple magnet could remove the iron oxide, but it will take years to provide filters to the

Water, water, everywhere . . . river traffic

25 million people who unknowingly poison themselves by drinking impure water.

Roughly 45 million Bangladeshis exist below the poverty line, and their daily incomes of under $2 mean they often survive on only one meal a day. As always, the poorest are usually women and children. By any standard, Bangladesh remains one of the poorest nations in the world, and public health statistics illustrate the poverty. A majority of children are malnourished and stunted. Sixty percent of the population lacks access to even simple health clinics, and medical challenges abound, including nearly 1,000 deaths per year from rabies.

Nevertheless, there are some success stories. In the mid-1980s, children comprised 40% of the workforce, a rate that officially fell below 10% by the end of the decade. In 2009, estimates suggested that about half of all children aged 6–10 attended school, though only 10% of teenagers enrolled in high school.

One reason that some families could afford to have their children studying rather than working was the Grameen Bank. Founded by Muhammad Yunus in 1976, the bank specializes in making small loans to poor individuals who have productive ideas but lack property to use as security for a loan. In 2006, when he and the bank received the Nobel Peace Prize, Yunus's microcredit program had nearly 7 million customers, the vast majority of them women who repaid their loans on time. Microcredit thus empowered those at the bottom of the social scale and stimulated a revolution of sorts.

By 2009, nearly a dozen organizations, including internationally-recognized agencies like CARE and World Vision, had made loans to some 20 million borrowers. However, the world economic crisis, natural disasters, over-borrowing, and simple bad luck left many borrowers unable to repay without selling their productive investments or removing their

"Two women in Maijpara"

World Bank Photo (Chernush)

Bangladesh

children from school and sending them to work.

Notwithstanding the many challenges that Bangladesh faces, recent years have been positive for the economy. The country's GDP grew by 7.9% in 2018, the third consecutive year with growth above 7%. In this sense, Bangladesh has become something of an unexpected success story in South Asia, but the picture is not uniformly positive. Most of the growth has happened in Dhaka, which has encouraged migration to the capital, producing even more severe overcrowding in a city that has been among the most densely populated globally for years.

The Future: The 2018 elections did nothing to improve the dire state of democracy in Bangladesh. With polling marred by violence that claimed the lives of 26 people, opposition politicians and pro-democracy leader, Kamal Hossain, rejected the results and demanded fresh elections held under a neutral government. The Bangladesh Election Commission said it would investigate reports of vote-rigging, exacerbated by the introduction of electronic voting machines, from across the country. The government of Sheikh Hasina and her Awami League lacks legitimacy in Western opinion. A few months of appointed rather than elected government would have been a small price to pay for elections considered fair.

Unfortunately, history shows that many politicians in Bangladesh have spent more time pursuing the benefits of office than pursue the national interest and development. As a result, operations such as the Grameen Bank will attract unfavorable attention from governments suspicious of rival centers of power. Until such attitudes change, Bangladesh is unlikely to become an Asian Tiger economy, no matter how low its wages.

The country's challenges remain enormous. Half the population lacks access to electricity, and poverty is so vast that many families depend on child labor for regular meals. A fractured political system renders government ineffective, so that critical decisions over the economy are not taken. Bangladesh is already experiencing the impacts of climate change, likely to be further exacerbated in coming years. The country's social and political problems will undermine efforts to mitigate the worst environmental crises.

The Kingdom of Bhutan

Taktsang ("The Tiger's Nest") Monastery, situated high in a cliff near Paro in western Bhutan, was destroyed by fire in April 1998. The King called the incident a national disaster and promised to rebuild it. According to legend, Padma Sambhava—or Guru Rinpoche, as he is also known—flew here on a tiger to meditate when he was introducing Buddhism into Tibet and Bhutan from India in the 8th century A.D. The monastery was built on the site at a later date   Photo by Edwin Bernbaum

National Day: December 17, (1907; coronation of the first king).
Chief of State: Jigme Khesar Namgyal Wangchuck, *Druk Gyalpo* (Dragon King).
Head of Government: Lotay Tshering, Prime Minister.
National Flag: A rectangular field of yellow and vermillion, divided diagonally with a large white dragon in the center.
Gross Domestic Product: $2.5 billion.
GDP per capita: $3,391.

A small nation squeezed between two giants, Bhutan shares much of the culture of Tibet across its Chinese border, while its trade and political alignment lie with India to the south.

Geographically, Bhutan resembles Nepal: both are located on the southern slopes of the Himalayan Mountains. Bhutan's rivers originate in the Great Himalayas in the north and flow southward through intensively-cultivated valleys. The rivers all flow into India and empty into the Brahmaputra River.

This land of rugged natural beauty presents striking contrasts: from its snow-clad northern peaks and wooded mountain slopes to the lush undergrowth of its southern foothills.

History: Few documentary sources provide details of the early history of this land. In the 9th century, Tibetan-speaking peoples entered the rugged mountain valleys. Followers of Mahayana Buddhism, by the 15th century they structured their society around fortified monasteries known as *dzongs*, and maintained links with Tibet. However, there was limited central authority. Raids against the expanding British East India Company ended with a treaty in 1865 that cost Bhutan territory but gained recognition of its autonomy and a British subsidy.

After defeating his rivals in a series of civil wars, Ugyen Wangchuck, *penlop* (governor) of Tongsa, became the dominant power, and in 1907, an assembly of lamas, chiefs, and officials elected him the country's first hereditary *Druk Gyalpo*, or Dragon King. Authority since then has passed from father to son.

Britain recognized Bhutan by the 1910 Treaty of Punakha and in doing so,

Area: 14,812 square miles (38,364 square kilometers).
Population: 772,000.
Capital City: Thimphu (101,000).
Climate: Frigid in the high mountains, temperate with good rainfall in the central valley, and extremely hot and humid with torrential rains in the south.
Neighboring Countries: India (South and East); China (North).
Time Zone: GMT +6.
Official Language: Dzongkha.
Other Principal Tongues: Sarchopkha, a Tibetan dialect, and Nepalese in the south.
Ethnic Background: Ngalop or Bhutanese (60%), Sharchops of Indo-Mongolian origin in the East (20%), Nepalese in

the southwest (15%), and smaller local groups.
Principal Religions: Mahayana Buddhism (75%) and Hinduism (22%), with small minorities practicing other religions, including animism and indigenous folk traditions.
Chief Commercial Products: Hydroelectric power, lumber and wood products, cement, fruit, rice, yaks and other livestock, woven textiles, and other handicrafts.
Major Trading Partner: India.
Currency: Ngultrum (1 ngultrum = 100 chetrum).
Historical Status: Independent, although subject to influence from Britain and India.

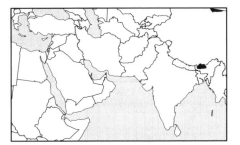

Bhutan

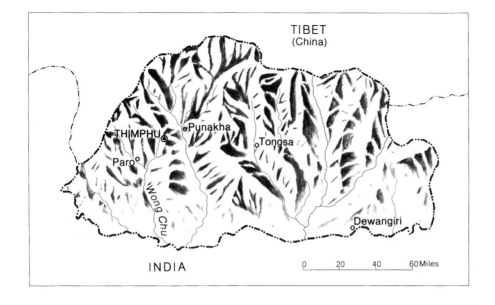

ironically, gained authority over its foreign affairs. Bhutan signed the treaty partly in fear of Chinese claims to its territory, based on alleged Chinese control from Tibet in the 18th century. A new treaty in 1949 with India recognized Bhutan's independence and provided free trade; it was revised in 2007 to provide Bhutan more freedom in military and diplomatic matters. India provides an annual subsidy that accounts for much government revenue.

After China claimed parts of the country in the 1950s, defense relations were strengthened with India. The border with China is not demarcated and remains closed, but Chinese troops allegedly crossed it in 2005 and built roads. The nation's full independence can be marked from 1971, when it joined the United Nations.

Jigme Khesar Namgyal Wangchuck, the Druk Gyalpo or "Dragon King"

Until the mid-20th century, Bhutan imposed rigid isolation upon itself, so that it remained as closed to the world as Tibet. However, when Jigme Dorji Wangchuck became Druk Gyalpo in 1952, he introduced changes. He freed slaves, ended the custom of making his subjects bow down before him with their faces on the floor, set up schools, restricted land ownership, modernized the system of land taxes, and established the Tsongdu, or National Assembly.

When Jigme Dorji Wangchuck died in 1972, his 17-year-old son, Jigme Singye Wangchuck, ascended the throne. Under the new ruler the country continued its slow awakening to the modern world. In 1988, responding to public worries about the succession, the king married publicly the four sisters he previously had wed privately. The celebration distinctly echoed the king's desire to preserve Bhutan's society from outside influences: foreign diplomats were not invited.

Two changes in 1999 brought the population into direct contact with the world outside: Bhutan inaugurated internet service and lifted its ban on television, previously decried as a corrupting influence. The government wanted a single channel to present national arts and culture, rather than rebroadcast Hollywood or Indian programs. However, many viewers preferred to connect to cable. When a wrestling channel and American music channels enticed too many Bhutanese, the government blocked them.

Ethnic tensions represent a continuing challenge to the country. Many ethnic Bhutanese have feared a cultural encroachment by the Lhotsampa, a Nepali-speaking minority in the lowlands. In the past, the Bhutanese government has not been adverse to stoking such fears, linking the Lhotsampa

to illegal Indian and Nepalese migrants and suggesting they pose a demographic threat. The monarchy classified them as aliens and vastly reduced the official estimate of their population. As part of educational reforms, the required teaching of Nepali in schools was dropped.

In 1990, riots and demonstrations broke out in southern Bhutan. Police and troops repressed the disturbances, and over 100,000 people sought refuge in Nepal along with several thousand who fled to India. At least some of those who fled were forced out under an edict that gave them just two weeks to leave their homes. As regional tensions mounted, and events in Bhutan were compared to more prominent incidences of ethnic cleansing, globally, the king took steps to reduce tensions. Some schools were reopened and several officials of Lhotsampa ethnicity were appointed. However, the Lhotsampa continue to be described, incorrectly, as "immigrants" and in some cases denied citizen rights. The United States offered to accept over half of the refugees, whose camps many believed had been infiltrated by extremists.

In 2004, Bhutan became the only country to ban the sale of cigarettes and chewing tobacco, although smoking itself is not illegal. Bhutan's first ruler banned the use of tobacco in government buildings, but modern arguments for the ban revolved around economics. The government pays medical care, it argued, and could ill-afford to subsidize unhealthy habits. Health authorities also fear another social danger. The stresses and opportunities of modernization have encouraged abuse of alcohol. Per capita consumption of alcohol is significantly higher than the world average (8.47 liters annually, compared to the 6.2 liter global average), and Bhutanese police reports show that some 70% of domestic violence happens when perpetrators are under the influence.

King Jigme Singye Wangchuck unexpectedly abdicated in 2006 in favor of his eldest son, Jigme Khesar Namgyal Wangchuck. Young and educated in the United States and Britain, he had won respect in the kingdom and popularity on official trips abroad. His coronation in 2008 proved a lavish affair by local standards, with thousands of foreign dignitaries and media personality. In 2011 he married a commoner, Jetsun Pema, in an elegant ceremony.

Politics: By tradition an absolute ruler, King Jigme Singye Wangchuck yielded additional powers in 1998 and extended democratic reforms with the 2005 constitution, which retains the monarch as the symbol of the state but provides that he or she must retire at age 65.

240

A fascinating mixture of tradition and modernity, the constitution was released on the web to facilitate discussion. It stresses spiritual heritage as well as the government's responsibility to protect biodiversity and maintain a minimum forest cover of 60%. Legislative authority resides in a parliament of two houses: the elected National Assembly and the non-partisan National Council. The National Assembly includes two, and only two, political parties. The leader of the larger serves as prime minister.

The 2018 elections in Bhutan represented something of a minor upset in Bhutan's short democratic history, when the ruling party—the People's Democratic Party (PDP), closely linked to the queen mother—was knocked out of the race at the first round. In the second round of voting, a formerly unrepresented party—*Druk Nyamrup Tshopga* (DPT, Bhutan United Party)—gained an impressive 30 of the 47 seats in the National Assembly. Lotay Tshering, the leader of the DPT, is a highly regarded surgeon and, by some accounts, continues to practice surgery when his prime ministerial duties allow. He was elected on a platform of "nation building," in the context of high foreign debt, youth employment, rising crime, and rural poverty. While the previous government was prepared to borrow heavily in order to fund infrastructure projects (primarily hydroelectric dams), the DPT is much more cautious about incurring further debt to India.

The role of media in politics has also taken on increasing importance in recent years. In 2006, the government passed an Information Communications and Media Act, which established a media regulatory body with the authority to punish a wide array of ambiguous offenses, like fostering misunderstanding or hostility between the government and the people. Consequently, over the past decade and more there is a sense that many journalists

Prime Minister Lotay Tshering

in Bhutan are self-censoring, reluctant to question government policies or to criticize those in charge. The recent approval of a law in 2017, one that criminalizes defamation, has driven several journalists into exile. Not surprisingly, then, although Bhutan arguably continues to have the best working environment for media among the South Asian Association of Regional Cooperation (SAARC) countries, its press freedom ranking fell by 10 places in 2018. Reporters without Borders ranked it 94 among 180 countries in the annual World Press Freedom Index.

Culture: The population is comprised mostly of hardy tillers of the soil and herders. They live in small communities scattered in the fertile valleys cut deeply into the rugged mountains of the central and southern part of the country. No one lives permanently in the high mountains of the north, while those who live in the narrow tropical fringe along the southern border lead a way of life quite different from the rest of Bhutan.

Apart from the capital, Thimphu, few urban centers exist. Communities tend to cluster around a dzong, found in every major valley and settled region. A dzong was originally a great fort built on a strategic spot commanding a river. In times of war, people from surrounding areas sought refuge there. After warlords passed from the scene, dzongs came to serve as administrative centers, monasteries, or even warehouses. Many of them have prayer halls with elaborately carved interiors, walls covered with religious paintings, statues of Buddha, and quarters for officials, lamas, and guilds.

Thimphu has been constructed beside the great Tashi Chho Dzong, once the headquarters of powerful penlops. The city reflects the country's determination to modernize in its own fashion. All buildings must be constructed in the traditional style, and the only traffic light was removed. However, the government provides TV broadcasts, and the newspaper, originally a public relations sheet, appears in Dzongkha, English, and Nepali.

Economy: Unlike most of the world, where Gross Domestic Product (GDP) is considered the chief measure of well-being, the government of Bhutan in recent years has promoted an even less precise measure: Gross National Happiness (GNH). This stresses inner peace and satisfaction, in accordance with the prevailing Buddhist philosophy, rather than material wealth.

Government policy encourages people to remain on the land, essentially as small-scale farmers and herdsmen who nevertheless enjoy access to electricity, simple medical care, and education. While this preserves the culture and therefore GNH, small, inefficient farms cannot compete in price with imported grains and meat. To protect small farmers, Bhutan has not joined the World Trade Organization.

Given the topography, the small country produces a surprisingly wide range of foods, ranging from rice and tropical fruits through citrus and temperate-climate vegetables. The mountain slopes provide abundant pasturage for livestock. Cattle are common up to more than 12,000 feet (almost 4000 meters) above sea level in summer, and yaks graze at even higher elevations.

Since 1961 a series of five-year plans have encouraged development, and usually stressed investment in roads, education, agriculture, health, minerals, and hydroelectric power. Exports of electricity to

Capital with a difference: Thimphu has no traffic lights

Bhutan

India now provide government revenues and foreign exchange. Recent policy favored privatizing the ownership of corporations, including cement and insurance companies. The goal of privatization was to encourage a modern middle class, because unlike government-run corporations in most countries, these were profitable monopolies.

After building two hotels to provide lodging for foreign dignitaries attending the King's coronation in 1974, Bhutan cautiously permitted a small tourist industry to develop, and two five-star hotels were opened in 2005. Travelers may enter by one of only two ways: a difficult land route, or by regularly scheduled air service to Paro by Druk Air.

In deference to local sensitivities, temples and other holy places were closed to tourists in 1988, but the dzongs are still accessible. In addition to cultural tours through dzongs, town, and villages, there are also organized treks along steep mountain trails to isolated mountain valleys. In addition to concern about tourism's sometimes corrosive effects on culture, traditions, and values, there is added concern about environmental damage.

To preserve its natural resources, Bhutan has banned hunting wildlife, prohibited lumbering, and provided a special route for migrating elephants. The government has even warned against the cutting of young trees for use as poles for Buddhist prayer flags believed to guide the dead. However, reports of erosion and polluted water in some locations suggest that population pressure may strain Bhutanese resources, just as it has in India and Nepal.

In 2018, Bhutan graduated to developing country status, from least developed country status, as defined by the United Nations. Several metrics are used to assign states to these categories, including gross national income, the proportion of the population that is undernourished at any given time, child mortality rates, and adult literacy rates. The substantial uptick in tourism, even if absolute numbers remain low (the 55,000 people who visited Bhutan in 2016 represented an increase of 24% since 2012) was one sign of increased development.

Nevertheless, when it comes to the metric for which Bhutan is perhaps best known—gross national happiness—the country doesn't stack up as well as many would expect. In 2018 the country came in at number 97, according to the United Nations. For perspective, Norway topped the list and the United States came in at 14. Several factors are likely contributors to the relatively low ranking, among them youth unemployment, increasing income and wealth inequality, and environmental degradation as the country develops. Recent reports indicate the Bhutan is also grappling with a depression crisis, likely related to the tension between tradition and change felt throughout much of the nation.

The Future: Bhutan features one of the last national contests between the preservation of tradition and modernization. In most societies, tradition has lost out, as television, videos, and even education corrode long-established values. In Bhutan's case, materialistic pursuits clash strongly with the personal inner peace so important to the philosophy of the country.

It will be interesting to see, going forward, how Bhutan continues to grapple with its tentative steps toward development, modernization, and democracy. The extension of full citizenship rights to the Lhotsampa, including voting rights and the capacity to organize politically will be an important step in consolidating recent democratic gains. Among the most important questions the country will face, is the nature of its relationships with neighboring China and India. What will be the balance between accepting not just aid, but foreign investment, given that both of these often come with strings attached? Will Bhutan's nascent tourism industry be able to recover from the impacts of COVID-19? The country's remarkable success at rolling out a vaccine program in a matter of weeks is cause for hope, but the threats not just to health but to the economy remain real and present.

Farm buildings in Bhutan　　　　　　Photo by Richard Harrington

The Taj Mahal at Agra

The Republic of India

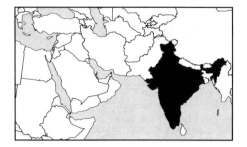

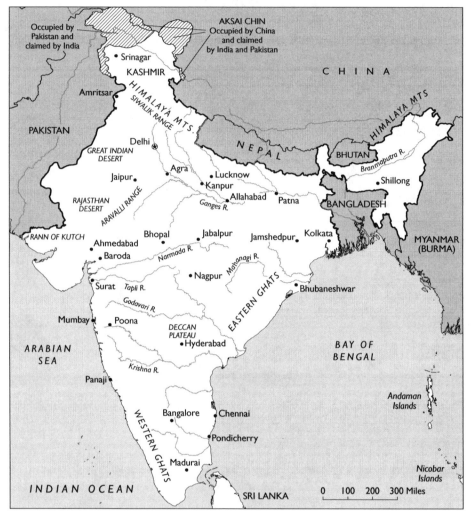

Area: 1.27 million square miles (3.29 million square kilometers), including the Indian sector of Jammu and Kashmir.

Population: 1.4 billion.

Capital City: Delhi (14.2 million).

Climate: Tropical except for the northern mountains. The three seasons are rainy (June to October), cool (November to February), and hot (March to May).

Neighboring Countries: Pakistan (Northwest); China, Nepal, Bhutan (North); Myanmar (East), Bangladesh (East); Sri Lanka (off the southern coast).

Time Zone: GMT +5 1/2 hours.

Official Languages: Hindi and English. Seventeen languages have regional status, including Assamese, Bengali, Gujarati, Kannada, Kashmiri, Malayalam, Marathi, Oriya, Punjabi, Sanskrit, Tamil, Telugu, and Urdu.

Other Principal Tongues: Newspapers within India are reportedly published in at least 49 languages.

Ethnic Background: Communities are differentiated primarily on the basis of language and religion; differences in physical characteristics do not generally correspond with these communal distinctions.

Principal Religions: Hinduism (approximately 80%), Islam (over 14%), Christianity (over 2%), Sikhism (1.7%), and Buddhism (0.7%). Other significant minority religions include Jainism and Zoroastrianism.

Chief Commercial Products: Textiles, clothing, gems and jewelry, steel, cement, automobiles, machinery, computer software, motorcycles, processed food, consumer appliances, coal, chemicals, and various metals.

Main Agricultural Produce and Livestock: Rice, wheat, barley, potatoes, corn (maize), cassava, bananas, coconuts, beans, mangoes, tea, coffee, tobacco, pepper, sugar cane, cattle, goats, buffalo, sheep, pigs, and poultry.

Major Trading Partners: The United States, the United Kingdom, China, and Saudi Arabia.

Currency: Rupee (1 rupee = 100 paisa).

Former Colonial Status: British Indian Empire (1858–1947).

National Day: January 26, Republic Day (1950; first republic in the British Commonwealth of Nations).

Chief of State: Ram Nath Kovind, President.

Head of Government: Narendra Modi, Prime Minister.

National Flag: A tricolor with equal horizontal bands of deep saffron, white, and dark green. Centered on the white stripe is the wheel of Asoka in navy blue.

Gross Domestic Product: $2.51 trillion.

GDP per capita: $1,980.

Second only to China in population, India occupies most of the South Asian subcontinent and ranks seventh among the world's countries in area. The size of its population, combined with its historical and cultural heritage, developed over thousands of years, often overwhelm the imagination and make comparisons difficult. India's population exceeds that of all the other countries in this volume combined. Indeed, the annual growth in the number of India's citizens exceeds the population of many countries in this volume. A land of stunning contrasts in geography, as well as in the quality of human life, India represents a major cultural force in the modern world. In areas as diverse as religion, food, and computer software engineering, India's influence greatly exceeds its boundaries.

Three major topographical regions divide the subcontinent. On the northern borderlands tower the Himalayas, the perpetual snow and ice of their summits overlooking lesser peaks and foothills at their base. Rivers and streams from the mountains flow south to the great plain that provides a home for much of the country's population. Centered on the Ganges River, the plain is also watered by the Indus on the west and the Brahmaputra on the east. The third region is the peninsula that juts out into the ocean, a triangle of plateaus, valleys, and mountains. The coastal plains around this region are moist and tropical, particularly in the narrow plain between the Arabian Sea and the Western Ghat Mountains, as well as densely populated.

India

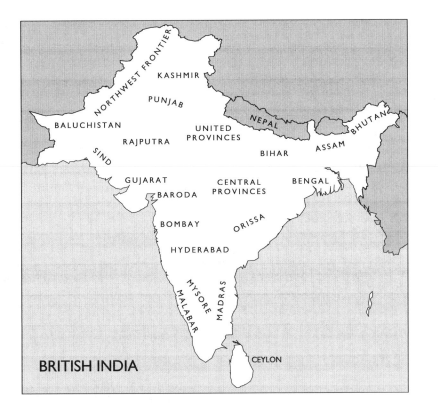

BRITISH INDIA

Extreme variations in rainfall and temperatures have produced great variations in vegetation. On average only a few inches fall annually in the western desert of Rajasthan, but the record in one village of Assam approached an extraordinary 40 feet (over 12,000 millimeters) of rainfall in a year. The northeast is typically the wettest region; it and the ocean side of the Western Ghats generally receive more than 100 inches (over 2,500 millimeters) of precipitation annually. Most of the rain falls during the summer, brought by the southwest monsoon. The Ganges Plain,

the northwest, and the coast of Tamil Nadu also receive varying amounts of winter rainfall.

The land and the climate show great contrasts—and so do the people. Religious practices vary greatly within the Hindu majority, and there are also followers of a multitude of other religions. Folkways differ considerably in various parts of the country, or even between communities in the same city. Sometimes allegiances to language, religion, and ethnic group threaten the unity of India. However, a generally functioning democracy

and economic integration reinforce the national unity forged in the independence struggle against the British.

History: While India possesses a cultural tradition that extends back for several thousand years, the formation of the present nation began only with the British conquest some 250 years ago. By bringing many small states and petty princes under its rule, Britain laid the foundation for both the Republic of India and other nations in the region.

As regions fell under East India Company rule, they desperately needed reform. India was overtaxed and undereducated, with crime rampant and the arts in decay.

Several Indian practices offended British opinion, from the burnings of widows (*sati* or *suttee*) and other ritual murders to values expressed by idol worship. However, British reforms and the seizure of several Indian states aroused both Muslim and Hindu opinion by the 1850s, especially in the north, and led directly to the so-called Indian Mutiny of 1857. Surprising the British in both its extent and its ferocity, the Mutiny drew strength from traditional groups outside the army, as well as native troops from both Hindu and Muslim backgrounds. Although the rebellion was crushed, Parliament ended the East India Company's rule and replaced it with British colonial administration.

The Mutiny produced major changes. Ethnic groups loyal to the British thereafter played greater roles in the army, and close contact between British officers and Indian troops built traditions that remain today. Because princes had generally remained loyal, the policy of replacing their rule in conquered territories was abandoned in favor of close contacts with them. Land reform was set aside, and the upper classes conciliated.

The Mutiny encouraged Britain to abandon the goal of Europeanizing Indians, and the emphasis turned instead to public works to make the land more productive within the empire. The spirit of imperial grandeur led the government to proclaim Queen Victoria Empress of India, in 1877.

Two trends in India during imperial rule deserve mention. First, colonial laws and officials provided unity for a vast region previously divided by ethnic and religious groups. A single administrative and judicial system, roads, railways, and postal communications aided the physical unification. Western-style education provided a new professional class with a common language—English—and greatly contributed to a sense of unity.

Second, and not unrelated, a national consciousness distinct from religious or social feelings arose against foreign rule. Among its first outward signs was the

Making friends in an Indian Village

India

A dairy farmer in Rajasthan

formation in 1885 of the Indian National Congress, which reflected the aspirations of the new professional class. In its early years, it failed to persuade colonial rulers to recognize its demands, and it also proved unable to raise the illiterate masses, especially villagers, to any kind of action.

Although it continued to develop among the tiny minority of Indians educated in English, nationalism had no visible effect otherwise until World War I. Then a man with rare gifts of leadership, Mohandas Karamchand Gandhi, later called *Mahatma* (Great Soul), returned to India from South Africa. An attorney and experienced political activist, Gandhi's insight and ability to translate nationalist ideas into terms that had meaning for the uneducated masses of Hindus, enabled him to capture the leadership of the Indian National Congress by 1920.

Unrest and occasional outbursts of violence were already occurring when Gandhi's public work in India began. His methods appealed to the religious nature of Hindus. Rejecting violence, the weapon he used was passive resistance, a policy of non-cooperation with colonial rule. This became something that the British could not seem to effectively oppose. Slowly, the Congress demands won concessions. Indians were allowed into the Indian civil service and were granted limited local self-government.

Although the Congress was not intended as a Hindu party, Gandhi was not able to bridge the gap between Hindus and Muslims in India, and tensions between the two communities increased. The leading Islamic party was the All-Muslim League led by Muhammad Ali Jinnah. Strongly focused on the interests of the Muslim community, Jinnah and his party led the move to partition India, although recent scholarship shows the crucial role played in this decision by rebuffs from Jawaharlal Nehru, president of the Congress Party, in 1946.

Independence and Partition

India gained independence as a dominion in August 1947, with the British agreeing to the simultaneous creation of a separate Muslim nation (Pakistan). The precise borders between India and Pakistan remained a British secret, lest the inevitable violence following their announcement spoil the festivities. In fact, this lack of clarity has been the cause of much violence since. Jawaharlal Nehru, Gandhi's chief lieutenant in the Congress Party, became the country's first prime minister.

Strife between Hindus and Muslims plagued the partition. In many frontier areas the population was mixed, making it impossible to divide Muslims from Hindus and others. In the end, the British chairman of the boundary commission had to rule on the borders. The most problematic regions were the Punjab in the northwest and Bengal in the east.

In the Punjab, fighting erupted between the two religious communities. Fearful of strife and of becoming a minority, Hindus on the Pakistani side of the border fled toward India while Muslims on the Indian side fled toward Pakistan. Nearly four million people took part in this two-way flight. It was the biggest human migration in history. Hundreds of thousands were massacred on both sides. To avert further bloodshed, Gandhi toured the country, preaching peace and cooperation between the two religious groups, an activity credited with averting similar massacres in Bengal. However, Hindu extremists hostile to his moderation assassinated Gandhi in 1948.

Government and Politics

A new constitution in 1950 made India a fully independent republic and broke the last formal ties to Britain. The presidency is a largely ceremonial post; real power lies with the prime minister and the lower house of the legislature, known as the *Lok Sabha* or House of the People. In contrast, the relatively powerless members of the upper house (*Rajya Sabha* or Council of States) reflect the state governments that select them. The Prime Minister governs with the support of Parliament. However, maintaining a majority in the Lok Sabha has often proved difficult, with the rise of regional parties preventing any one party from winning a majority.

A major challenge at independence was the formation of a modern administration. Britain had often maintained the existing rulers' authority as dependents of the British Crown, and in 1947 Britain restored the rights that the rulers had lost generations earlier. Thus, the Indian government faced some 562 "princely states" ranging in size from Hyderabad (82,000 square miles—over 200,000 square kilometers—and having 16 million subjects) to tiny states of a few square miles and a few thousand inhabitants.

To retain the rights of all these rulers meant chaos. By 1949, through persuasion, threats, and promises of pensions (withdrawn some 20 years later), India had been reorganized into 30 states and territories. Two cases proved especially difficult. The Muslim ruler of Hyderabad, which had a large Hindu majority, sought independence, but unrest and the alleged abuse of Hindus provided an opportunity for the central government to send in troops. His authority thus undermined, the ruler ceded Hyderabad to the central government in 1949.

The other case was a dispute with tribesmen and Pakistan over the large princely state of Jammu and Kashmir, where the population was predominantly Muslim but the ruling family was Hindu. The status of Kashmir remains unresolved well over half a century later.

Boundaries in British India, often drawn by historical circumstances, frequently

India

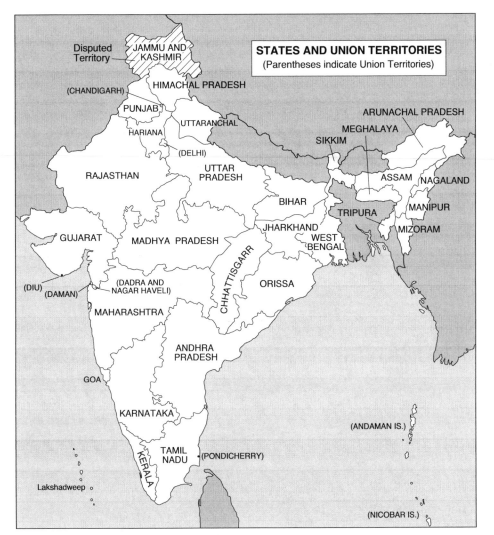

STATES AND UNION TERRITORIES
(Parentheses indicate Union Territories)

subside in a conflict that claimed about 20,000 lives.

Three distinctive regions received statehood in 2000, each one reflecting separate cultures or local resentments. Mineral-rich Jharkhand, formed from districts of Bihar, holds major deposits of mica, coal, iron, and copper. However, after decades of Bihar's corrupt politics and exploitation by government-owned mining and steel companies, the region is littered with the remains of dying industries. Like the tribal state of Chhattisgarh created at the same time, Jharkhand faces rebellions and violence from radical groups. Lying just west of Nepal, Uttaranchal shares with it the Himalayan foothills and mountains. Its population desired statehood to address their particular problems, including land prices forced up when rich city folk purchased vacation homes in the cooler mountains.

State governments are sometimes vast, matching their populations. The people of Uttar Pradesh, for example, outnumber any two countries of the European Union. In each state, the chief minister runs the executive and is responsible to the state legislature. When a state lacks a stable government or fails to maintain calm, the president may place the state under presidential rule, usually until order is restored. Presidential rule occasionally serves to the benefit of the party ruling in New Delhi.

Nehru Sets the Country's Direction

Well before Gandhi's death, Jawaharlal Nehru had emerged as a national figure in his own right and Gandhi's successor to lead the Congress Party from the 1940s to the 1960s. Although of an aristocrat background, Nehru appeared the modern, secular socialist needed to lead India into the future. Young leftists idolized him for his patriotism and his integrity. He won the hearts of the masses, including women and the lowest castes. Energetic and determined, he emerged victorious from three general elections. In the words of one historian, he had a freer hand in molding policy than anyone since the Great Moguls (see Historical Background).

In domestic matters, Nehru focused on economic and social improvements, and he set the broad outlines of national policy for the next forty years. He created an Indian socialism that allowed some private enterprise but kept government ownership of heavy industry, transport, and other key sectors. A series of five-year economic plans attempted to focus on national goals. With foreign assistance, personal incomes rose despite rapid population growth. However, the richest 10% of the country enjoyed most of the benefits of economic growth: they received 40% of personal income, and enjoyed a

separated people speaking the same language. Despite occasional ethnic violence, the government altered the political map of India. Many states disappeared, and new states were created out of parts of the old. For example, Andhra Pradesh, largely Telugu-speaking, emerged from what had been Hyderabad and Madras despite desires of some for a separate Telangana state in the interior. After a campaign of fifty years, the new state of some 35 million people was finally created in 2014.

The creation of ethnic states faced difficulties in the northeast, near the borders of Tibet and Burma, where many tribes in remote areas speak their own languages and are less influenced by Hindu culture. Several small ethnic groups there desired their own states, or even independence, and sometimes adopted guerrilla warfare to achieve it. The first ethnic state, Nagaland, was created in 1961. In the 1970s and 1980s, more states followed, all among India's smallest in population. Arunachal Pradesh faces an unusual difficulty: China claimed almost the entire

state, based on an interpretation of Tibet's one-time borders.

Communal conflict also occurred in the Punjab between Hindus and Sikhs, who desired their own state. The country's breadbasket, it was divided in 1966, right down to the capital, Chandigarh, between the Sikh Punjab and a Hindi-speaking state of Haryana. Nevertheless, Sikh militants demanded the creation of an independent "Khalistan." In 1983 they occupied the Golden Temple in Amritsar, the focus of Sikh religious life. When Indira Gandhi ordered the army to assault the temple, many Sikhs, not all of them militants, resisted the invasion of their shrine, and heavy casualties resulted. The heavy-handedness of the government cost India Gandhi her life, assassinated by her Sikh bodyguards. Thousands of Sikhs were killed in retaliatory violence. Sikh separatism remained acute for a decade complicated by Sikh rivalries, government repression, and unfulfilled promises of justice. Only after the return of civilian rule in the 1990s did violence

India

Prime Minister Nehru with Lord Mountbatten   Courtesy of the Government of India

comfortable standard of living. In contrast, most Indians remained desperately poor, some only employed at planting and harvest.

Social policy stressed equality. The constitution of the Republic abolished untouchability, and prohibited its practice. Caste distinctions in general were discouraged, and the privileged of all types—from the former princes of Indian states to rural tax collectors—came under attack. Landlords, especially powerful in an overpopulated agricultural society, found their lands distributed to farmers by land reform. New laws provided women with equal property inheritance and alimony

for divorce. Education expanded considerably, but as in many other developing countries it grew too much at the top (university) and too little at the bottom (mass literacy and skills).

Nehru created an international reputation as a prominent leader of the non-aligned nations, those officially neutral in the Cold War, who sought independence for European colonies. He was often suspicious of the motives of Western nations and sympathized with the Soviet Union. Such sympathy, however, carried practical benefits, because the rivalry of both communist and Western nations for influence in India meant that both sides provided economic aid.

India's major foreign policy concern, then as now, was Pakistan. Deep suspicions remained after the 1949 war over Kashmir, and an arms race began: Soviet weapons for India, American jets and tanks to Pakistan. Relations worsened when Indian irrigation projects threatened to divert rivers flowing into Pakistan and used for irrigation there. The international community solved this problem by a technical solution: the World Bank provided funds to Pakistan so it could utilize other rivers instead. Tension flared over Kashmir in 1965. Pakistan infiltrated irregulars first, then plunged into conventional war by an armored attack. Indian forces halted the invaders, and the Soviet Union sponsored negotiations that ended the fighting. Each side withdrew to the 1949 boundaries.

India initially welcomed the Chinese communist revolution, but the Chinese conquest of Tibet in 1950 brought together the world's two most populous nations along a lengthy border. After the Dalai Lama fled to India to lead a moral struggle for his people, his supporters sought supplies and weapons to continue

the fight. Tension increased when China constructed a road across the desolate but strategic Aksai Chin Plateau; India claimed the Plateau as part of Kashmir. In 1962 a border war broke out, and Chinese troops defeated Indian units before withdrawing. The border dispute soured relations between the two countries for the next 25 years, and it encouraged China to ally with Pakistan. Before his death in 1964, Nehru was faulted for the failure of his policy toward China, but nonetheless the nation deeply mourned his passing.

Indira: Emergency Rule

In 1966 Congress Party leaders selected Indira Gandhi as party leader and prime minister. Nehru's daughter and thus long acquainted with political issues, she inherited a stumbling economy and a weakened party. Gandhi increasingly adopted socialist economic policies, and she nationalized the banks in 1969. The masses adored her and provided a landslide victory in 1971. Further nationalizations followed. Gandhi also led India into the successful war with Pakistan in 1971 that created Bangladesh. The country conducted its first nuclear test in 1974.

By the mid-1970s, Gandhi's programs proved less popular, and after a state court found her guilty of earlier election violations, she declared a "National Emergency" that invoked extraordinary powers to jail several thousand opposition leaders, some of whom were tortured in custody. Civil liberties were curtailed, the press was censored, and drastic economic reforms were implemented. One of the most shocking policies of the emergency period was the implementation of a population planning program, under the auspices of Indira Gandhi's son, Sanjay, which involved the often involuntary or coerced sterilization of poor or rural Indians. Lasting almost two years, the emergency was India's closest brush with authoritarian rule, and the voters disapproved. Congress lost the next election, but in another major feature of Indian politics, a coalition of small parties failed to rule successfully. Elections returned Gandhi to power and the challenge of communal unrest. She was assassinated by bodyguards angered by the military attack on Sikh insurgents in the Golden Temple at Amritsar in 1984.

Disaster of a different sort struck Bhopal, the capital of Madhya Pradesh, that same year. Poisonous gas used to make the agricultural pesticide Sevin leaked into the atmosphere from a chemical plant owned by the Indian subsidiary of Union Carbide. The gas killed more than 6,500 people, and injured perhaps 200,000, many of them doomed to early deaths. Legal wrangles delayed settlement until 1989, when Union Carbide agreed to an

Mahatma Gandhi

Militant Hindu revival groups such as the *Vishwa Hindu Parishad* and its political ally, the *Bharatiya Janata Party* (BJP), sought to destroy the mosque and rebuild the temple. Initially, national and state governments took extraordinary precautions to prevent violence, arresting the BJP leader, Lal Krishna Advani, and some 100,000 others. However, in late 1992 political maneuvering gave way to direct action. Under cover of ceremonies to construct a Hindu temple, well-organized militants attacked the dome and walls of the mosque. Ordered by the state's BJP government not to fire, the police stood by and in a few hours the mosque lay destroyed, replaced by a makeshift temple.

Within hours, fighting between Muslims and Hindus spread from Ayodhya across India in the worst communal strife since independence. Days of violence claimed some 1,200 lives; thousands more were injured, most of them Muslim and many the result of police bullets. The violence and curfews halted normal business, and losses amounted to billions of rupees. The BJP's parliamentary leader, Advani, was arrested, and the government banned several militant Hindu organizations, including the *Rashtriya Swayam Sevak Sangh* (the RSS) and the Vishwa Hindu Parishad, as well as two Muslim groups. Calm returned, but only slowly. Further anti-Muslim rioting in Bombay, the commercial capital, cost hundreds more lives.

After 400 sittings, 48 extensions, and 17 years in preparation, in 2009 the report of the Liberhan Commission on events at Ayodhya confirmed that the destruction of the mosque involved painstaking, premeditated preparations. It blamed both BJP leaders and local officials.

Violence in Kashmir and Bihar

Sectarian violence flared for different reasons in Kashmir. Kashmir enjoyed a special status, with separate laws and land ownership restricted to Kashmiris, but years of political manipulation and election-rigging—most notably in 1987—destroyed any legitimacy of the state government. Its overwhelming Muslim majority desired an end to Indian rule, though it was divided between favoring independence or unity with Pakistan. Only force and direct control from New Delhi retained Kashmir within India. Economic development languished, and a state with some of the greatest potential for hydroelectric power actually imported most of its electricity.

In the early 1990s, Muslim protests demanded freedom from India. Armed militants took and occasionally murdered hostages, while the often non-Kashmiri police killed dozens of protestors and militants. The leading Muslim activist,

Indira Gandhi signs the Visitor's Book at the White House, July 1982

Indian court's settlement of $470 million. In 1990 the government began paying the minimal compensation of $12 per month to each of the injured, and in 2004 the courts ordered payment of all remaining funds.

Religious Tensions and Economic Reform

Immediately after Indira's death, key cabinet members selected her second son, Rajiv, as prime minister. Heir to the Nehru tradition of leadership, yet in many ways a fresh face, Rajiv seized the moment of sympathy over his mother's death and called fresh elections. Congress emerged triumphant, winning the largest margin of victory since independence, more than 50% of the popular vote and 400 of the 542 seats in the Lok Sabha.

As prime minister, Rajiv began reducing the vast web of government regulations and encouraged international trade. However, Rajiv had been Indira's "non-political" son, a pilot who enjoyed a lavish lifestyle and found governance boring. Two failures marked his rule. First, his attempt to bring peace to Sri Lanka's Tamil rebellion failed when the leading rebel force, the Tamil Tigers, turned against Indian troops sent to maintain peace. Second, Swedish investigators discovered secret payments to Rajiv's friends linked to the sale of Bofors field artillery to India. "Bofors" became synonymous with corruption, and the scandal brought down his government and initiated a brief period of rule by a coalition of other parties. A Tamil Tiger suicide bomber assassinated Rajiv during the 1991 elections.

Destruction of the Ayodhya Mosque

Controversy over the Babri mosque at Ayodhya in Uttar Pradesh dominated Indian politics in the early 1990s. Built by the Mogul emperor Babur, the Babri mosque was holy to Muslims, but Hindus regarded it as the sacred birthplace of the god Ram and sought to rebuild the Hindu temple they believe preceded the mosque.

India

Maulvi Mohammad Farooq, was assassinated, and by 1996 the death toll had reached about 20,000.

The violence was often financed and supplied by Pakistan. In 1999 Islamic fighters and Pakistani troops secretly crossed the Line of Control dividing Kashmir and established positions high on peaks overlooking Kargil on the vital highway to Leh, near the Tibetan border. To repulse the invaders, Indian troops advanced up steep slopes with little cover. It took ten weeks of determined battle, significant casualties, and world opinion to persuade Pakistan to withdraw the remaining infiltrators. For the first time, two nuclear powers had fought significant land battles. This surprised many political scientists who believed nuclear weapons should have deterred such fighting. Others pointed to these same weapons to explain why the conflict did not escalate further.

Jammu and Kashmir held state elections in 2002. This was not the exercise of civic responsibility. Pakistan-based militants murdered moderates, and the All-Party Hurriyat Conference, a loose confederation of 23 separatist groups, boycotted the vote, as they have continued to do so in subsequent elections. But, the elections were sufficiently free and honest to defeat the National Conference, the pro-Indian party that traditionally won corrupt elections. A new coalition government released some militants and promised to relieve harsher regulations and police actions.

Confidence-building progress between Pakistan and India in the mid-2000s brought further hopes for improvements in Kashmir. Bus service between Srinagar, the capital of India's portion, and Muzaffarabad permitted relatives to see each other after nearly sixty years. Moreover, Kashmiris on each side of the Line of Control began to visualize new types of solutions. Moderate opposition groups even traveled on the bus and held a conference that increased the popularity of nonviolent solutions. Though a settlement eluded Kashmir, the level of violence declined. Regrettably, it surged again in 2010–11 amid accusations of harsh treatment by the security forces. In the intervening years intermittent violence has seen accusations exchanged between the two hostile neighboring nations. Human rights organizations have faulted the Indian military for killings of suspects without trial, and Pakistan for backing armed militants. In 2019, tensions between India–Pakistan are considerably heightened, following a suicide car bombing in February that cost the lives of 40 Indian security personnel. Border skirmishes have resulted, with both countries conducting airstrikes, to the great concern of the international community.

Violence of a different nature swept portions of rural Bihar during the 1990s. Again the initial causes were political, social, and economic. The Bihar state government had failed to provide security—or schools, clinics, roads, and electricity. The chief minister, Laloo Prasad Yadav of a cow-herding caste, used state jobs and contracts as sources of patronage for his supporters. Corruption charges finally forced him from office in 1997, but his wife replaced him when their party won state elections. Without economic reform and foreign investment, the level of poverty increased yearly. Signs of improvement only followed the election of a new state government in 2006, whose policies and spending on infrastructure brought signs of growth through road construction and other projects.

Political Corruption and BJP Victories

Financial scandals in the late 1990s finally ended Congress's role as the ruling party. Before the 1996 elections, investigators revealed illegal payments on an immense scale to many prominent politicians and officials. For example, a former cabinet minister kept over 36 million rupees in cash at home. The resulting public uproar forced the resignation of the prime minister, cabinet members and the BJP leader. In subsequent elections the electorate resoundingly rejected Congress and selected new groups like the caste-based *Samajwadi* and *Bahujan Samaj* parties, the right-wing (Hindu nationalist) BJP, or leftist alliances like the *Janata Dal*.

In 1998 the BJP's moderate leader, Atal Bihari Vajpayee, dropped extreme planks of his party's platform such as laws to prohibit Muslims from practicing polygamy and successfully formed a coalition. His coalition's most remembered achievement, however, was a series of nuclear explosions in Rajasthan that stunned the world and delighted most Indians. The tests changed India's rank from "nuclear-capable" to "nuclear power." Despite Pakistan's answering nuclear tests, in the subsequent elections Vajpayee's coalition won a solid majority. It used its powers to enact economic reforms, such as cutting fuel subsidies, and to purchase expensive weaponry: T-90 tanks, an aircraft carrier, and jet fighters from Russia; jet trainers from Britain; a submarine or two from France; and locally-produced missiles and nuclear weapons.

Closer Relations with the U.S.

The September 11 attacks deepened the growing friendship between the United States and India. Officially and popularly, India sympathized with victims of Islamic extremists, having been a victim itself in Kashmir and elsewhere. However, because Pakistan shared information with the United States and allowed U.S. access to Afghanistan, India did not win unconditional American support.

Kashmiri guerrillas launched a deadly attack on the Indian Parliament in late 2001. Prime Minister Vajpayee responded by demanding that Pakistan ban the two groups allegedly involved, *Jaish-i Muhammad* and *Laskar-i Toiba,* and generally clamp down on extremists. The army prepared for battle, and moved to the border. Fearful of the first real war between nuclear-armed antagonists, the United States and other nations counseled Pakistan to yield, and it did. However, brutal attacks again took place on the Indian military and non-Muslim civilians of Kashmir.

Conflict between religious communities broke out again in 2002, when a trainload of Hindu militants returning to Gujarat from Ayodhya was allegedly attacked by Muslim extremists, leaving nearly 60 dead. (A later inquiry blamed the deaths on disputes and a riot, not a terrorist attack.) For days thereafter, well-organized Hindu mobs conducted a pogrom of the Muslim districts of Ahmedabad, the state capital. The mobs slaughtered about 1,500, vandalized businesses and homes, and caused many thousands to flee to refugee camps. The police failed to protect them even there.

Significantly, Gujarat was one of the few states ruled by the BJP. Horror at

Former Prime Minister Manmohan Singh

the violence led coalition parties in the national government to demand the dismissal of Gujarat's chief minister. However, nothing happened, and the coalition did not fracture. Moreover, the BJP easily returned to power in Gujarat's state elections. Hindu militants therefore saw the religious-nationalist ideology of "Hindutva" as the key to power.

Hoping instead for victory based on the country's prosperity, Prime Minister Vajpayee called elections for 2004. A moderate, he adopted the electoral slogan "Shining India," a vague phrase intended to tap "feel good" sentiments after several years of rapid economic growth. BJP advertising showed smiling children at school and well-dressed families relaxing. Sophisticated technology showed in campaign methods, too, with recordings from the prime minister sent to all cell-phones.

By contrast, Congress failed to present a slick message, and its leader, Italian-born Sonia Gandhi (the wife of assassinated former prime minister, Rajiv Gandhi), found herself targeted as a foreigner. However, she traveled tirelessly to speak to crowds about the many who had been left behind by "Shining India," including women, youth, and farmers.

Congress Returns to Power

The nation was stunned by an upset victory for Congress. It replaced the BJP as the largest party in parliament and successfully sought a coalition with minor parties and a common understanding with communist and left-wing parties. Sonia Gandhi surprised the country, again, by refusing to become prime minister. Her party then nominated Manmohan Singh, the "father of economic reforms" responsible for India's rapid growth back in the 1990s. The stock market rebounded. A fitting, if unintended symbol of Congress's greater toleration for non-Hindus, Singh became the first Sikh prime minister just before the twentieth anniversary of the battle for the Golden Temple in Amritsar. By coincidence, the president was not a Hindu either, but a Muslim who won fame as a rocket scientist linked to India's nuclear weapons program.

Determined to spread the nation's prosperity to rural areas, Singh's alliance created the National Rural Employment Guarantee Scheme. Rather than cash welfare payments, it promoted "Growth with a Human Face" through providing a minimum of 100 days employment per unemployed household per year, often in local self-help projects that pay little over $1 per day. The scheme achieved modest results in its first year, but the cabinet deemed it effective enough, and it was extended to the entire country in 2008. Its advocates see the project providing many

good things: increased economic security through higher farm wages, slower migration to the overcrowded cities, the creation of productive infrastructure, and greater independence of women. Critics have pointed to problems of corruption within the system and the siphoning off of a considerable portion of funding to middlemen.

Less successfully, the government proposed to raise quotas in higher education for the socially disadvantaged castes from 22.5% to 49.5%. The better Indian universities already turn away many applicants; however, extending the quota would exclude many middle-class students. Demonstrations against the proposal spread across the country, and even doctors and medical students went on strike against it. Nevertheless, the ruling coalition remained stable, partly because there was no alternative majority. The proposal was delayed by the courts.

With national elections approaching, Singh's Communist allies in the Left Front deserted the coalition over a nuclear technology deal with the United States. To help develop India's energy resources, Singh had negotiated an agreement that separated India's military and civilian nuclear programs and then granted India access to civilian nuclear technology and fuel—both previously denied because India had developed indigenous nuclear weapons. The Communist Party of India (Marxist) and its allies launched popular protests against it. However, they failed to bring Singh down with a vote of no confidence.

In late 2008 a group of gunmen came ashore in Mumbai and launched attacks on the Taj Mahal and Oberoi luxury hotels, a popular restaurant, a Jewish center, a hospital, and a train station, shocking the nation and the world. Anti-terrorism police responded slowly, and nearly 200 civilians died in the suicide raid. Evidence, partly from a surviving attacker, quickly implicated the Pakistani extremist group Laskar-i Toiba in the attack. This group has long been suspected of working closely with Pakistani military intelligence. India demanded that Pakistan ban the group and arrest its leaders and other terrorists; the new civilian government in Pakistan moved slowly in that direction.

The Mumbai attacks apparently did not influence the 2009 Lok Sabha election campaign, although the BJP attempted to cast Prime Minister Singh as weak and ineffective, and controlled by Sonia Gandhi. Abandoned by its former leftist allies, Congress promised to spread prosperity to the poor and ran on a record of economic growth and domestic peace. It nominated Singh (aged 78) for another term against the BJP's equally aged Lal Krishna Advani

India

(aged 81). Analysts widely predicted that neither major party would emerge with enough seats to create a strong coalition; some believed a third group of leftist and caste-based parties might even emerge strongest. Given the massive electorate of 714 million voters and over 800,000 voting centers, voting took place regionally, spread over four weeks. Congress emerged with a remarkable and unexpected win, the greatest by a single party in two decades.

The Naxalite-Maoist Insurgency

In the words of the newly-elected prime minister, the Maoist insurgency had become India's greatest internal security threat. Since the 1960s, Naxalite (Maoist) revolutionaries have considered rural India's strong caste divisions, tribal populations, and great inequality of wealth fertile conditions for class warfare. Operating across state borders, they have organized bands comprised of tribal peoples and Dalits for actions against police and landowners. The armed wing of the Naxalite-Maoists, the People's Liberation Guerrilla Army (PLGA), is estimated to have up to 10,000 fighters.

Active particularly in forested rural districts of West Bengal, Chattisgarh, Bihar and Jharkhand, and Orissa, the Naxalites provided a voice to tribal complaints that their lands were sold to outsiders for development projects such as bauxite and iron mines while they remained landless and poor, lacking in the schools, roads, and investment essential for prosperity. As violence escalated in 2009–10, PLGA militants hijacked one train and derailed an intercity express. For its part, the government launched a massive paramilitary operation to clear large sections of forest, denying the guerrilla group cover. The struggle has claimed up to 13,000 lives over almost four decades.

Corruption Scandals Discredit Politicians

Midway through its term, corruption scandals threatened to engulf Prime Minister Singh's government. The telecommunications minister, Andimuthu Raja, a member of the coalition party *Dravida Munnetra Kazhagam* (DMK), was accused of accepting bribes to sell mobile phone licenses directly, rather than by auction. In the process, the treasury lost some $40 billion in revenues. The scandal led to the trial of Raja and several officials from cell phone companies.

India has long tolerated small gifts in return for official favors. However, these figures are large, and the telecoms scandal was quickly followed by other major allegations involving government funding or approval. Sleaze and shoddy construction

practices marked Delhi's 2010 Commonwealth Games. Several top officials were arrested for corruption, including the organizing committee's director, a Congress Party official.

Corruption extended to both national parties and many regional ones. Indeed, venality seemed rife at the state level. In Tamil Nadu, the DMK lost state elections badly, despite having distributed 15 million small TV sets (a significant gift in a country where millions live on less than a dollar per day). The chief minister of Karnataka, who led the state BJP, conducted a scam involving iron ore mines that cost more than $3 billion in revenues over five years.

Another scandal involved the transformation of a modest building for war widows in Mumbai into a 31-story complex with apartments for retired officers, officials, and relatives of the state's chief minister. Yet another former chief minister of Maharashtra was fined by the Supreme Court for intervening to block legal complaints against a state legislator and his family who had allegedly tortured farmers who fell behind on loans. However, he initially remained in Singh's federal cabinet as industries minister.

The Rise of Hindu Nationalism: Modi and the BJP

Months before the 2014 parliamentary elections, economic indicators declined. Growth fell in 2013 to little more than half its levels during the previous decade. Scores of major infrastructure projects and other government investments stalled,

and the rupee lost value on the foreign exchange market. Apparent good news—a claim that the number of people living in extreme poverty had fallen from 37% of the population to 22%—proved misleading. Meanwhile, inflation rose to its highest level in 20 years, harming the poor and middle classes.

As optimism about prosperity faded, public dissatisfaction with corruption increased. Social activists seized national attention with demonstrations and a series of public fasts to protest corruption. The new *Aam Aadmi Party* (Common Man's Party) placed second in Delhi's territorial elections and briefly took power. Despite bad losses in those elections, Congress failed to heed popular dissatisfaction. When the Supreme Court ruled that convicted lawmakers must be removed from office, the cabinet proposed an executive order designed to block the ruling. Congress again displayed an inability to focus on critical matters when it failed to select its prime ministerial candidate. Manmohan Singh announced he was stepping down, and although Rahul Gandhi managed the election campaign he was not nominated for office.

By contrast, the BJP demonstrated its strong desire to win. Setting aside elderly leaders and the traditional Hindu religious concerns of its core activists, the party nominated Narendra Modi for prime minister, promising the nation rapid economic progress like the success of Gujarat under his leadership. This campaign for prosperity rather than for the BJP's traditional sectarian causes

---

The World's Sixth Nuclear Power

Indian interest in atomic power began before independence, when the industrial Tata Company set up a research program. In the 1950s, the United States, Canada, and Britain all provided nuclear facilities, hoping to encourage research and generate cheap electricity. However, despite its public stand against nuclear weapons, India never signed the Comprehensive Test Ban Treaty, and it undertook the design and construction of nuclear reactors free from inspection by the International Atomic Energy Agency.

After China exploded its first atomic bomb in 1964, scientists at the Indian Atomic Energy Commission secretly began accumulating enriched uranium for possible atomic bombs. In 1974, an explosion in Rajasthan proclaimed that the country was the world's sixth nuclear power. New Delhi proclaimed that its program was peaceful, although it now had the ability to explode weapons.

By the 1990s, politicians desired further nuclear tests to illustrate the country's ability and no doubt to enhance their own reputations. In 1998 Prime Minister Vajpayee publicly promised that India would not test weapons, but then authorized the five explosions that set off the South Asian nuclear arms race with Pakistan.

Military strategists who accept the legitimacy of some nuclear weapons frequently condemn India's acquisition of them. The 1974 explosion, many believe, led Pakistan to create its own bomb. Within both countries, the creation of weapons raced far ahead of designing strategies for their use. Serious consideration of a hot line between the two countries only surfaced in 2004. The resulting arms races for both nuclear and conventional weapons impose unnecessary suffering on populations.

successfully deflected concerns about his role in the 2002 Ahmedabad sectarian riots. Regional, leftist, and caste-based parties continued their traditional appeals.

Again setting a world record for the number of eligible voters (814 million), the 2014 elections delivered much more than had been forecast. The BJP won an astounding victory: 31% of the national vote transformed into 282 of the 543 seats in the Lok Sabha, only the second time in history that a party had won an absolute majority. By contrast, Congress earned only 19% of the popular vote. It lost 162 seats and retained only 44 MPs, making 2014 its worst defeat by far. For the smaller parties, small changes in shares of the popular vote could make great differences. For example, All India Anna Dravida Munnetra Kazhagam (AIADMK)—led by the Tamil film star, Jayalalithaa—won 28 seats from its 1.6% increase in the popular vote, while rival DMK lost 0.1% of the national vote. and every one of its previous eighteen members of parliament.

Cultivating the image of a dynamic and strong leader, in his first year Prime Minister Modi set about invigorating the vast government bureaucracy. A pragmatic modernizer rather than a free-market reformer, he attacked corruption and sloth. One novel idea was to encourage the use of India's biometric database (the world's largest) to monitor whether civil servants had shown up for work and posting the result online. A less intrusive initiative is the attempt to encourage millions of families to establish bank accounts. Some 40% of the population does not possess them. If they did, social programs could be targeted to the poor, replacing wasteful subsidies on food and other items. Millions signed up for new accounts, but many had no funds to deposit.

On the world stage, the prime minister conducted highly-publicized visits abroad, to Japan, the United States, Brazil, Germany, and other countries. The visits encouraged a media frenzy, built understanding, and projected a greater role for India in the world.

Relations with two important neighbors stagnated. Perhaps due to a local commander's miscalculation, Chinese troops in Tibet crossed the frontier and established themselves in Indian territory during a state visit by Xi Jinping, the Chinese president. Prime Minister Modi was humiliated and later signed an American document pledging support for free navigation in the South China Sea, large parts of which China claims as its own. The Modi government has also been more demanding of Pakistan, and fighting across the Kashmir line of control flared in recent years.

After victories in legislative elections in Maharashtra and Haryana, the BJP was expected to do well in the 2015 Delhi assembly elections. However, the capital's citizens handed the nation's ruling party a stinging defeat when the AAP led by Arvind Kejriwal won 67 of the 70 seats. The BJP had maintained its same share of the ballots (about one-third); the difference was that Congress loyalists, members of other parties, and those already disenchanted or fearful of Narendra Modi united behind the AAP.

Disenchantment grew from two distinctly different roots. At his inauguration, Kejriwal pledged to end the "VIP culture" that privileged politicians' vehicles above buses taken by ordinary people. Given the vast publicity about the new prime minister, many ordinary people came to see him an example of privilege. This perception was strengthened by the man himself, who wore a suit with his name embroidered in golden thread when he welcomed U.S. President Barack Obama to India.

The second cause of disenchantment was growing fear among secular citizens and religious minorities that the modernizing and business-like prime minister also shared the values of militant Hindu groups that long provided the backbone of the BJP, particularly the RSS. While talk of welcoming non-Hindus "back home" to their ancestral faith may be understandable in some religious circles, for a junior minister to call non-Hindus "bastards" and then remain in office implied permission for bigotry or worse.

The equating of Hindu Nationalism with Indian Nationalism now appears a taken-for-granted position in India. However, it is a position that sidelines significant minority communities. While Muslims in India comprise less than 15% of the population, in numerical terms it is the second largest Muslim community in the world (only Indonesia has a greater number of Muslims than India). A national security narrative has positioned BJP's main electoral rivals, the secular Congress, as weak on Pakistan and engaging in "Muslim appeasement."

The 2019 election saw the return of Modi, helped to power by renewed conflict on the Kashmiri border. Modi has used the coronavirus pandemic to further bolster his Hindu nationalist credentials, to the detriment of India's Muslim minority. Muslims were blamed for spreading the virus, seemingly to distract from government mismanagement.

Culture: India does not have an official religion; it is a land of many religions. At the same time, it is primarily a Hindu nation. About 80% of the population is Hindu, but there may be as many as 200 million Muslims and about 20 million Christians, the third largest group. There are also many

Prime Minister Narendra Modi

Buddhists in the land where, in the 6th century B.C. Buddha lived and preached a message which emphasized the sanctity of life in all forms.

Hinduism is not merely part of a culture; it *is* a culture—not simply a religion in the Western sense. One example of its all-embracing nature is its rigid social order, dominated by the concept of caste. Hundreds of castes exist; all Hindus belong to one of them. Caste membership comes by birth and remains for life. Social contacts overwhelmingly occur within the caste, and marriages rarely cross caste boundaries.

Each caste traditionally involved a particular occupation, and with some exceptions members of the upper castes have also represented the upper economic classes. The distinctions are far more than economic, however, and include dietary restrictions as well as social discrimination. For example, many Brahmins will not eat food if the shadow of an "untouchable" has passed over it.

Traditionally castes fell into four broad groups. At the top, the Brahmins (priest-intellectuals), kshatriyas (warrior-nobles), and vaishyas (businessmen) compose over one-sixth of India's population. The shudras (peasants and laborers), politically described as the backward castes, amount to 44%.

Below all of these are the "Scheduled Castes," now called Dalits. Comprising over 15% of the population, before independence they faced the discrimination their title "untouchable" proclaimed, while carrying out essential but dirty and dangerous occupations like street sweeping, slaughtering animals, and disposing of corpses and human waste. Indeed,

India

demonstrators in 2010 claimed that one million impoverished Dalits clean non-flush toilets daily, despite laws banning the practice for impossibly low wages.

The Indian constitution removed legal discrimination against the Scheduled Castes, and government programs have provided assistance. Nevertheless, upper class Hindus will not drink from a Dalit's glass or patronize the same barbershop. Despite constitutional protection, in practice Dalits are often banned from temples, cremation grounds, and bathing spots along riverbanks. Dalits who converted to some Christian churches found that they faced similar obstacles: they were shunned from particular pews or even churches by other Christians.

Rituals and ceremonies are prominent in Hinduism, and these are closely related to the family, for the rites are often performed at home. The major rituals relate to birth, marriage, and death. The dead are cremated with as much decorum as the family can afford in keeping with its position on the social scale. Other features of Hinduism include the rejection of worldly pleasure, belief in the soul's transmigration after death to another form of life, the sanctity of the cow, and the belief in many gods.

One Hindu celebration, the *Kumbh Mela*, brings together more people than any other single event worldwide. The "pitcher fair" is named after drops of the elixir of immortality that fell to earth during a struggle between gods and demons. Every 12 years the alignment of the stars makes washing away the sins of the body particularly effective at the city of Prayagraj (formerly Allahabad), the confluence of the Ganges, the Yamuna, and the mythical (but sacred) Sasaswathi. Millions converge on Prayagraj, often taking weeks to walk there. About 100 million pilgrims attended the 2013 ceremony, which was marred by a stampede, as millions of bathers pressed to take trains home in an overcrowded station. In 2019, the *Ardh Kumbh* (a smaller festival that falls halfway through the 12 year cycle) brought over 120 million pilgrims to the city over a seven-week period, with as many as 40 million dipping in the water on a single day in February. To put these numbers in some perspective, the annual Hajj in Saudi Arabia, by any measure a considerable undertaking, involves 2.4 million pilgrims.

Holidays and festivals are associated with each cultural community. There are three important Hindu holidays. *Diwali*, the festival of lights, is a happy celebration commemorating the homecoming of the legendary hero Rama after he defeated the demon king Ravana. The family performs special ritual prayers in the home on this occasion. *Dussehra* has varied

meanings in different parts of the country and is celebrated in various ways: in some places with great happiness, in others with more somber religious ritual. *Holi* is an occasion in March for noise and fun; usually folk songs are sung at gatherings around bonfires.

Muslims celebrate the same holidays as in predominantly Muslim countries but with local variations. In addition to religious holidays, three secular festivals are promoted: Republic Day is celebrated on January 26, Independence Day on August 15, and *Gandhi Jayanti* (Gandhi's birthday) on October 2.

Challenges in the Treatment of Women

The brutal gang-rape and murder of a 23-year-old paramedic student riding on a bus in late 2012 heightened already considerable concern about the treatment of Indian women. Regrettably, popular culture has continued a long tradition of male superiority that often devalues women. For example, the Delhi city police commissioner, facing concerns about growing numbers of rapes, responded that men were not safe either. "Their pockets were picked," he noted, thus implying some sort of equivalence between the crimes. Studies have found that 80% of Indian women have experienced some form of sexual harassment or molestation, known euphemistically as "Eve-teasing"; the vast majority of cases go unreported.

Certainly, some women reach the top in India—in politics (a president, a prime minister, and several party leaders), business, and the professions. However, these are mostly exceptions in a country where many fail to consider a woman's life equal to a man's. The problems are worse in

northern India, where entrenched patriarchal traditions, disrespect for law, and police insensitivity increase the disrespect of women.

Problems begin before birth with (illegal) sex-selective abortion of unwanted girls. Difficulties continue through childhood. With nearly 30% of all Indian children malnourished, girls almost invariably receive less food than boys. On average, they study fewer years than boys, and as they mature, the need to provide funds for a dowry can place considerable financial strain on families, leading in the worst cases to violence, abuse, and forced prostitution.

Adolescence and maturity bring little relief. Girls very often marry young: although the legal age is 18, nearly half (44%) of all brides wed sooner. Women rarely enjoy a healthy diet: in poor families mothers and sisters often forego food to give more to husbands and sons. Some 60% of Indian women are anemic. Serious domestic crimes such as child abuse, bride burnings, honor killings, and marital rape, continue to impact women in India, with the law often lagging behind expectations for reform.

A 2017 global survey found that Delhi was the fourth most dangerous city in the world for women and the worst city in the world for women when it came to sexual violence, rape, and harassment. Protests have shone light on an issue that was often treated as a matter of shame (for the victim and the victim's family), and an important national conversation has begun. Months after the Delhi bus rape, parliament legislated tougher punishment of sex crimes, and expanded the definition of both rape and sexual harassment. Similarly, in 2018, following a number of

Tibetan woman sells her wares in Kalimpong   Photo courtesy of Karla Allen

254

high-profile cases, the government introduced capital punishment for the rape of a minor.

Literature and the Arts

Hindi and certain other Indian languages are descended from ancient Sanskrit. Most of the ancient literature of India was written in that language, including the early religious text, the *Rigveda*. Later, several dramas appeared in Sanskrit. The playwright Kalidasa is among the most famous. India's long literary history has been enriched by contributions from Persia and, more recently, Western ideas and forms. Literature flourishes in a number of the native languages, but there are also poems, novels, and other works in English.

It is only natural when one thinks of the culture of India to think of the Taj Mahal at Agra—not an isolated example of architectural opulence in this land. There are rock-cut temples and architectural monuments from as early as the time of Emperor Asoka in the 3d century B.C. The most admired buildings come from the era of the Hindu–Islamic synthesis beginning in the 8th century A.D. and continuing up until a few centuries ago. The Kurb Minar at Delhi and the Adina Masjid at Ahmedabad come from early in this period. The Taj Mahal, Agra Fort, and Akbar's Mausoleum, the latter at Sikandra, come from later during the rule of the Moguls (15th–16th centuries). After independence, conscious attempts to create a new national architectural style achieved success in combining elements of the past and present, particularly at Chandigarh.

Painting and sculpture, especially the latter, have an ancient history in India. The stone model for the lion of the State Seal, for instance, dates from the 3rd century B.C. But the new generation of artists is not being limited to any single tradition or time; it is boldly experimenting.

Dance, music, and drama are three arts that in India often belong together. Traditionally, plays are acted in dance to the accompaniment of music. Dancing also exists separately and is a highly developed art with elaborate symbolism.

Modern cultural forms play an important role. The movie industry produces more full length films every year (about 1,000) than does any other country. Because studios in Mumbai (formerly known as Bombay) traditionally dominated the industry, it became known as "Bollywood." That said, most movies today come from producers in southern India, in languages like Telegu and Tamil. Most Indian movies attract the entire family: they feature little violence, frequent music and dance, and exaggerated emotional attractions. There is limited overt sexual activity, and the finish is typically "happily ever-after." Stars in the industry draw huge followings, and some transfer their talents—and popular appeal—to the political stage.

Exported for many years across Asia and Africa as an alternative to the culture of Hollywood, the movie industry drew additional strength from the rapid growth of cable TV in India and satellite TV around the world. Because costs of production are relatively low, foreign distribution rights alone can sometimes meet costs. However, until more broad-appeal Indian movies are filmed in English, their audience in English-speaking countries will typically be limited to expatriate Indians.

Television, long stagnant under a government monopoly, broke wide open with the growth of (unregulated) cable TV. Now both Indian and Western programs reach remote villages, brought by some 30,000–70,000 cable companies to 30 million customers, who pay a modest fee (typically $2.50–$4.00 per month) for up to 75 channels.

Education: Independence in 1947 divides the history of education in India. Under British rule, there was no mass education. Thereafter, the government gradually instituted free and universal education through eight years of "basic school." These elementary years provide instruction in crafts along with reading and writing. After a rapid increase in schooling during the last two decades, nearly all children now complete those grades. In 2011, the government finally funded universal access to high school, although poverty and other difficulties discourage millions from attending. Nevertheless, nearly 25% of the population remains illiterate; the rate for women is higher.

Achievements in higher education have been comparable. There were 17 universities in 1947; by 2010 there were some 370 universities and over 7,000 colleges.

Dalits "untouchables" polishing shoes

However, only 12% of the 18–24 year population was enrolled, compared to over 30% in most developed economies. A panel of experts called for 1,500 universities by 2015, but government spending on education did not increase rapidly enough to meet that goal. One alternative, previously blocked by government regulations, would be to allow branch campuses of European and American institutions.

While the Indian Institutes of Technology rank with the world's best in computer sciences, elsewhere the system of education requires reform. In 2007 Prime Minister Singh claimed that two thirds of the universities and 90% of the colleges were rated "below average" (by "average"

Bombay: The Movie

A Tamil film about love against the background of the Ayodhya riots nearly caused disturbances of its own in 1995. In the interests of peace, one of India's best known producers, Mani Ratnam, portrayed a love story between a Hindu man and Muslim woman. Regrettably, the strongest passion he aroused was anger, not love.

For the sake of communal harmony, Mr. Ratnam edited portions at the request of Mr. Bal Thackeray, leader of the militant Hindu party *Shiv Sena* that attacked Muslim areas during the riots. The producer also cut portions in sympathy with Muslim sensitivities, showing newspaper headlines of the attack on the mosque, rather than the attack itself.

Despite passing India's censors, the final version of the film aroused Muslim anger by implying a similar aggressiveness between Muslim and Hindu mobs. Muslim threats of disturbances halted showings for a week in Bombay. However, Mr. Thackeray, who boasted of his control over the newly-elected chief minister of Maharashtra, insisted that threats should not prevent its opening. Under tight security, the film was released.

Regardless of its portrayal of mobs and politicians, the movie risked Muslim resentment from the start. In Islamic law, a married woman joins her husband's community. When a Muslim man marries a non-Muslim, he thereby adds to the community, an honorable action that provided a Christian wife for more than one caliph. But when a Muslim woman marries outside her faith, she effectively leaves it, which in some cases is considered apostasy.

India

he apparently meant "reasonable quality" rather than the mathematical mean). In Singh's words, "We need better facilities, more and better teachers, a flexible approach to curriculum development, and more-meaningful evaluation systems." Nevertheless, it takes an act of parliament to create a university, and the lack of an accreditation process means that quality often remains murky. For example, over half of all college teachers lack a graduate degree, and 25% of university positions are vacant. Salaries are far too low to attract the vast numbers of Indian academics working abroad.

India educates only one-seventh of its young adults, but still has the largest number of unemployed graduates in the world. The unemployed alumni often studied disciplines that are uncompetitive in today's job market, but desire the high salaries of computer scientists, engineers, and finance majors. Unfortunately, in some programs widespread cheating enabled poorly-skilled students to graduate, although not necessarily to practice their professions.

Economy: With 650,000 villages and scores of bustling cities, the economy of India is marked by contrasts greater than any other nation. It is home to humanity's greatest collection of the poor—some 300 million people, one-third of all those worldwide who are so impoverished that they subsist on less than $25 per month. Nevertheless, the middle class numbers about 550 million, and India has amongst the highest number of very wealthy (U.S. dollar multi-millionaires and billionaires) in the world. The rapid economic growth of recent decades has transformed parts of the country, while leaving others virtually untouched (or further disadvantaged). Today, India's richest 1% hold over 50% of the country's total wealth and its wealthiest 10% hold over three-quarters of the national wealth.

Poverty is not inevitable. The land possesses good soil that is easily irrigated and large deposits of coal, iron ore, and other minerals. Regrettably, human decisions are responsible for much of the poverty seen in India today. Among many factors, culture and regulation have kept poverty in place when economic growth could have alleviated it. Regular rainfall, good soil, and tropical warmth encouraged a very large and dense population in the plains and river valleys. Norms often prevented the lower strata of society from escaping poverty, while some members of the nobility enjoyed vast riches. In the traditional world of religious belief and caste divisions, the mixture of poverty and riches seemed natural and inevitable. Fate, or *karma*, dictated life's difficulties.

Accepting it might lead to rebirth in better circumstances.

British conquest brought some public works, along with tariff-free imports. Factory-made textiles, machinery, and consumer goods flooded India, undercutting local craftsmen and hindering indigenous attempts to industrialize. Famine in British-ruled India cost the lives of millions. Inequality of distribution, the promotion of export agriculture, and the diversion of profits to British interests (such as military ventures in Afghanistan), exacerbated problems caused by unfavorable climatic conditions. At independence, roughly 200 million people, half the population, lived below the poverty line.

In the first 40 years of independence, the number of impoverished grew to exceed 300 million, and some economists used the term "Hindu Rate of Growth" to refer to the economy's performance. However, relatively slow growth resulted not from religious culture, but from bad regulation, poor planning, and high tariffs.

Public health and other statistics give some sense of the desperate poverty of many inhabitants. Both bubonic and pneumonic plague broke out in 1994, striking initially at slums on the outskirts of cities like Surat and Mumbai, where crowded immigrants live without clean water or sanitation. By official estimates, some 30,000 tons of waste remain uncollected daily, and in rural areas only 10% of homes have a toilet or outhouse. Over 600 million people lack access to a latrine. Government efforts for better sanitation have had little impact, but the recent publicity campaign "No Toilet, No

Bride" links toilets to courtship and thus may bring comfort and sanitation to those above abject poverty.

Surveys in the 1990s revealed that over 300 million people lived in households so poor no one could afford a watch, and utter poverty condemned 30% of the population to fewer than two meals per day. By 2012 the number in poverty was estimated at 363 million.

After drastic food shortages in the 1960s, great efforts were made to increase the country's grain production. The Green Revolution—selecting strains of rice and wheat that produce well with fertilizers and irrigation—enabled the country to

From 12th century bronze . . .

. . . to advanced rocketry. India's spacecraft reached the moon in 2008.

feed itself in 1971 for the first time since independence. In the contest between better farming and more mouths, freeing markets in the 1990s led to still greater harvests.

For years, the seas around India abounded in fish that an efficient industry could exploit, but the lack of processing and storage facilities, as well as poor transportation, did not allow this to develop. By the late 1980s, however, India had improved the industry and ranked eighth in the world in annual fishing catch. Now the Indian Ocean is suffering from overfishing, particularly near the shores.

A diamond-finishing industry began in India in the 1960s when it was discovered that low wages made it profitable to work imported diamonds that were discarded by the South African syndicate. An estimated 350,000 craftsmen in India now work in sweatshops where they are paid by the piece. A socio-religious group, the *Palanpuri Jains* (from the former princely state of Palanpur), have established a worldwide network to market gems cut in India. India has become the leading exporter of cut and polished diamonds.

Seeking Rapid Economic Growth

The modern Indian economy "took off" in the 1990s, when Manmohan Singh, the finance minister, reduced regulation, encouraged investment by foreigners, and ended most of the industrial licensing that had cobbled Indian industry. Singh also attempted to sell state businesses, simplify taxes, and reduce them for the rich. The opposition charged that the International Monetary Fund wrote the budget, but India started, somewhat timidly, to follow the East Asian model of export-led economic prosperity.

With lower inflation, higher exports, and lower tax rates, Indian and foreign companies expanded. By mid-decade, newly-permitted foreign companies expanded telephone links and constructed power plants. Spurred partly by advertising on many new TV channels, consumers sought appliances and household items. Investment by foreign companies soared, freeing Indian funds for other purposes. Exports doubled. As the growth rate of GDP reached 7%, some commentators considered India the next Asian Tiger.

These years of rapid economic growth produced two Indias, one sometimes quite rich, the other usually oppressively poor. Economic growth failed to bring much relief to those living in poverty, especially the rural poor. At the same time, the middle and upper classes began to grow rapidly. This trend is set to continue: between 2018 and 2022, it is estimated that India will add 70 new U.S. dollar millionaires per day.

Praying in the Ganges at Varanasi, one of Hinduism's holiest places

Photo courtesy of Karla Allen

Certain states managed to capture most of the economic prosperity, particularly Gujarat, Maharashtra, and Karnataka in the west and south. By contrast, the vast Ganges plain across Uttar Pradesh, Bihar, and West Bengal experienced virtually no improvement in personal incomes. Relatively rapid population growth also reduced the economic growth rate per capita.

While conventional development approaches have prioritized high GDP growth rates, the state of Kerala in India's southwest has taken a different approach. Despite relatively low incomes, Kerala has high rates of literacy, life expectancy, and political awareness. These achievements, when held up against the experiences of India more broadly, were sufficiently impressive to attract the attention of economists and development strategists worldwide. The Kerala model has been widely studies in an effort to replicate its successes. Underpinning it is a human development approach; radical reform and redistribution, led by those most affected, has produced better outcomes than the pursuit of endless economic growth.

Success in Computer Services and Autos

The success of Indian-owned firms in the computer software industry, such as Hotmail in the U.S. and Infosys Limited in India, illustrate the potential of the country's millions of engineers, scientists, and other well-trained professionals. Software exports grew at the astounding rate of 40%–50% *per year* in the late 1990s, but rates fell after 2007. The industry employed nearly three million people in 2012 and exported products worth $70 billion,

Shanty town on a Calcutta street

India

more than the country's entire exports in 2000. As many American consumers know, India also became the world hub for call centers and other back-office procedures such as the transcription of medical records. Local firms began these industries, but in recent years multinationals have entered. In 2006, IBM announced plans for investment worth $6 billion, so the growth of these sectors seems limited mostly by the numbers of qualified employees and the supporting infrastructure.

Until the 1980s, policy favored public transportation over private, and Indian Railways carried millions of passengers daily. So few cars were produced annually that prospective customers had to sign up and sometimes wait years for delivery of a locally-made copy of a 1950s-era European car. A joint venture with Suzuki began to produce the Maruti in the 1980s. After Asian, European, and U.S. firms set up production in the 1990s, car sales initially climbed 20%–50% per year. By 2005 sales reached one million, growing at 10%–12% per year. There seems much room for growth: car ownership in 2016 was 20 cars per 100 people, but analysts have recently predicted that that number could grow to 175 by 2040 (a 775% increase).

Automobile production in India mixes modern engineering and traditional construction. There is more unskilled labor, because low labor costs make it profitable to do by hand what elsewhere is done by machine. The product mix, too, reflects the mixture of wealth and modest incomes. BMW and Mercedes now produce expensive luxury autos, while Tata Motors, a local firm, unveiled its rear-engined 33-horsepower Nano in 2008. At a cost of around $2,000, it is the world's least expensive car.

The Indian Institute of Science symbolizes Bangalore's long tradition of excellence in science, technology, and the arts. Today, the city's industrial skills have earned it a reputation as the Silicon Valley of India
Photo by Miller B. Spangler

As the number of cars on the roads doubled, they quickly overwhelmed the streets and highways. Even national highways are often pot-holed, crowded, and narrow. Aside from toll roads, few truckers can drive more than 250 miles per day. The ambitious target for new roads announced in 2010 is to complete 12 miles of road per day, 4,200 miles per year, an enormous task priced at $50 billion, with urban streets costing even more. Again, besides success in software, the dominant theme in the Indian economy for the next decade will be infrastructure development, with projected spending of at least $200 billion per year.

Current Challenges and the Future: In May 2021, India faced a dire situation in which the government had seemingly lost any capacity to manage the novel coronavirus. Infection rates are astronomical and India's health system has bent and, in part, collapsed under the weight of the health crisis. Hospitals lack sufficient supplies, and desperately ill patients are being turned away, many to die at home. While the heartbreaking statistics had started to shift downward by early June, the social, economic, and political implications of the disaster are likely to be felt into the future.

Beyond the COVID crisis, two critical challenges that India faces going forward are climate change and inequality. One recent report suggests that climate change could cost India as much as 10% of its GDP by 2050. Many of the consequences are likely to hit women the hardest; in part because nearly three quarters of working Indian women have jobs connected to agriculture. As for inequality, it is more difficult to climb the socioeconomic ladder in India than in almost any other developing country. India's government exacerbates inequality by consistently underfunding public services, such as healthcare and education, while failing to clamp down on tax-avoidance by corporations and the wealthy. In India's financial center of Mumbai, lavish residential skyscrapers, complete with multi-storey car parking for luxury vehicles and chandeliered ballrooms, loom over slums. Where such obscene disparities of wealth exist, the health of a nation's democracy is called into question. Whether India can forge a prosperous future for all its citizens, remain to be seen.

Smog in Mumbai

The Republic of the Maldives

Typical Maldivian boats known as Dhonis wait for passengers, Malé

Area: 115 square miles (about 300 square kilometers) of land, amid 34,500 square miles (90,000 square kilometers) of ocean.

Population: 540,500.

Capital City: Malé (104,000).

Climate: Warm and humid. Annual rainfall is about 75 inches (1,905 millimeters), mostly from May to October.

Neighboring Countries: The Maldives is located in the Indian Ocean to the southwest of India and Sri Lanka.

Time Zone: GMT +5.

Official Language: Dhivehi (or Divehi; similar to Sinhala of Sri Lanka).

Other Principal Tongues: Arabic and English.

Ethnic Background: Sinhalese, Indo-European, Arab, and Sub-Saharan African.

Principal Religion: Islam.

Chief Commercial Products: Fish (canned, dried, and frozen).

Major Trading Partners: Thailand, France, the United States, Sri Lanka, and Singapore.

Currency: Rufiaa (1 rufiaa = 100 laari).

Former Colonial Status: Controlled by Britain (1796–1965).

National Day: Rabi' al-awwal 1 (1st day of the third month in the Islamic Calendar, in 2019 this falls on October 29; celebrates the end of the brief Portuguese colonial rule in 1573); Independence Day, July 26 (1965; end of British rule).

Chief of State: Ibrahim Mohamed Solih, President.

National Flag: A green rectangle bearing a white crescent is centered on a red field.

Gross Domestic Product: $4.87 billion.

GDP per capita: $9,802.

Long known to Arab sailors as "Islands of the Moon," the Maldives are a string of 26 coral atolls scattered 550 miles (almost 900 kilometers) along the top of a submarine ridge in the Indian Ocean. These atolls contain altogether more than 1,000 picturesque islets. About 200 of the larger ones are inhabited, but few of them extend even a mile. Islands rarely reach more than six feet (just under two meters) above high tide; neither hills nor rivers exist. However, there are abundant coconut palms, white sandy beaches, and crystal clear lagoons formed by coral reefs. With hundreds of species of tropical fish and many varieties of shells and coral, the islands rank as a diver's paradise.

Located close to the equator, the Maldives experience two monsoons each year and average about 75 inches (1,905 millimeters) of rain annually. Between April and October the southwest monsoon brings rain, but the dry winds of the northeast monsoon of "winter" originate in Asia and bring fair weather from December to March.

History: Straddling the sailing route between the Red Sea and East Asia, the islands were mentioned by voyagers from Rome, Egypt, and China, but scholars dispute when the first settlers arrived in the islands. Discoveries by the explorer Thor Heyerdahl suggest that early inhabitants traded with ancient Egypt and Mesopotamia. Nearly nothing is known of those inhabitants, but about 2,500 years ago settlers arrived from Sri Lanka and India. Buddhism came to dominate religious life, and over the centuries sailors from Africa and Arabia joined the ethnic mix. Besides

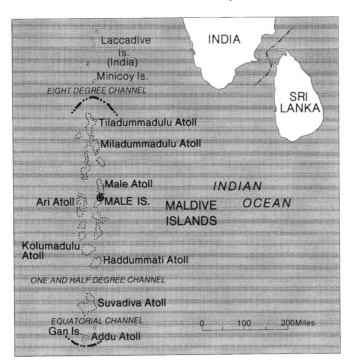

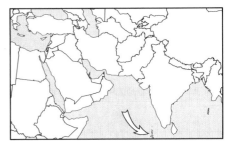

Maldives

President Ibrahim Solih

supplying vessels passing through, the Maldives exported vast quantities of cowrie shells, which became currency in parts of Africa. From this trade, the islands earned the title "the money islands." In 1153 King Dovemi Kalaminja adopted Islam, a crucial event in the island's culture, and thereafter the kings became known as sultans.

During the following centuries, the islanders developed a unique unwritten constitution and fought off invaders, including the Portuguese in the 1500s.

Muhammad Thakurufaanu won recognition as "The Great" for liberating his country, for improving administration, and for introducing the Thaana script to write Dhivehi. Nevertheless, under most sultans the islands remained relatively weak.

After Britain gained control of India and then Sri Lanka (1796), the dangers of invasion receded, as Britain seemed uninterested in the remote, malaria-infested islands whose chief product at the time was dried fish. However, fearing the growing power of Indian merchants, in 1887 the sultan sought British protection. Aside from control over foreign affairs and defense, Britain left the islanders largely to their own ways, not even posting a resident in Malé.

With the proclamation of a republic in 1953, the Maldivians symbolically entered their modern era. Although this First Republic lasted only one year, its president, Muhammad Ameen Didi, won respect for reviving Dhivehi and its literature.

He reformed the system of education, improved the position of women, opened government stores to undercut foreign merchants, and also introduced strict Islamic laws. Partly to reduce the drain on foreign exchange, he banned the importation and smoking of cigarettes. Thus the

Maldives became the first country to ban tobacco in the modern era, but popular dislike of such laws, as well as Didi's increasingly autocratic rule, led to his ouster and the collapse of the republic.

In 1965 a treaty with Britain provided full independence, though Britain retained—and paid for—use of an airfield and a radio communications station on Gan Island in the southernmost atoll. That same year, the Maldives became the smallest nation to receive full membership at the UN. Britain formally returned Gan Island in 1976.

A constitutional change in 1968 again established a republic. The sultan retired. His prime minister, Amir Ibrahim Nasir, won the presidency, but facing deep popular dissatisfaction he resigned in 1978. The *Majlis* (parliament) nominated Maumoon Abdul Gayoom, a previous cabinet minister, and a referendum approved him as president. The president serves a five-year term, and Gayoom's policies of harbor development, women's rights, and limited high-end tourism helped him win reelection every five years as the only candidate proposed by the Majlis.

Tamil mercenaries hired by disaffected Maldivians attempted a military takeover in late 1988, the first invasion in four centuries. The Maldives has no army or navy, but the small National Security Service offered sufficient resistance for President Gayoom to escape his palace and request aid from friendly countries. Within hours, Indian paratroops landed. Outgunned, the mercenaries eventually surrendered. The fighting awoke the nation to the need for modern defense, from radar and a trained fighting force to patrol vessels.

A prison riot of uncertain causes in 2003, led to apparently spontaneous mob attacks on parliament, the election commission, and other official buildings. More than a case of idle youths letting off steam, the riots followed Amnesty International's accusations that the government had taken political prisoners and resorted to torture, a claim the government denied. They also preceded, by just days, parliament's selection of the nominee for the presidential referendum. Despite the mob's furor, the unanimous choice was a sixth term for President Gayoom, already Asia's longest-serving ruler.

In the aftermath of the violence, security forces arrested hundreds, including anyone who had been identified in pictures of the rioters. The firm hand of government blocked access to the web site of the only opposition party, the Maldivian Democratic Party (MDP). Although Gayoom publicly accepted reforms, the special assembly he created to consider constitutional revisions made little progress—it was twice the size of the parliament.

The 2004 tsunami centered off Indonesia wreaked vast damage to the small country: its capital city, Airport Island, and 47 other inhabited islets were flooded, and over 20 of the 87 resort islands were put out of operation. Eighty-two people were killed and 24 reported missing (presumed dead), a fatality figure surprisingly low compared to seacoasts with higher land. Apparently the reefs around the islands absorbed much of the waves' power and the sea wall around Malé broke their force there.

With world attention focused on the tsunami and its aftermath, the government

Muliaage, formerly the official residence of the president

had little alternative but reform. It released prisoners, and held elections for the Majlis. While not exactly fair—rallies, speeches, and political parties were still prohibited, while the media directly or indirectly remained in government hands—the elections were free enough for candidates supported by the MDP (from exile) to win 18 of the 42 seats. Gayoom congratulated even the MDP victors and encouraged the new Majlis to enact reforms. At least on paper, this established multi-party democracy, and widened press freedoms; eventually they produced a democratic constitution that Gayoom ratified in 2008.

Presidential elections were due in 2008, and Gayoom sought a seventh term, promising the voters "dynamic years" under his trustworthy leadership. Four rivals attacked his lavish lifestyle and nepotism. Strongly supported in the more traditional outer islands, Gayoom won 50% more votes than his nearest challenger but was forced to a run-off. Supporters of the losing candidates then switched to Mohamed Nasheed of the MDP, and the former prisoner won the presidency. In doing so, he became the first democratically elected president of the country.

Nasheed moved out of the presidential mansion and planned to sell the multimillion dollar presidential yacht. He also planned to privatize government-owned media, reform education, and restructure government. With a flair for communication, he publicized the threat of rising sea levels—a global problem that will impact the Maldives earlier and more severely than many other parts of the world—by conducting the world's first underwater cabinet meeting with 11 colleagues, who dove to their chairs about 12 feet (more than 3.5 meters) below the surface. Nasheed expressed a desire to buy a new Maldivian homeland if and when rising sea levels resulting from climate change flood the islands, and also promised carbon neutrality by 2020, with electricity from solar power and virtually no use of fossil fuel. Although the Maldives was never a high carbon emitter, these commitments showed how serious and pressing an issue climate change is for low-lying island nations like the Maldives and attempted to shame the big-emitters into action.

Although Nasheed had won the presidency and global respect as a spokesman against anthropogenic global warming, his domestic political strength was weak. His cabinet fractured as members from other coalition parties resigned. Although winning the most votes, the MDP gained only one quarter of the seats in the 2009 parliamentary elections. Gayoom's supporters in the Dhivehi Rayyithunge Party (DRP) and their allies obstructed Nasheed's legislative goals so successfully that loyal ministers resigned in protest.

A strong unsettling force was the growing rhetoric of militant Islamism. Its sympathizers protested airline links to Israel, as well as alcohol and pork being served to tourists at resorts. The government eventually banned the links, the drinks, and the food, but did not act to enforce these new prohibitions. The bans did not prevent a leading member of an opposition party from claiming that Nasheed was under the influence of Jews and Christian priests in undermining Islam. On the streets, the DRP encouraged demonstrations blaming the president for corruption and high prices following the depreciation of the currency. For its part, the government blamed higher world prices.

Maldivian politics took a serious turn in February 2012 when President Nasheed resigned his office. The resignation followed weeks of opposition street protests, which eventually included strong contingents from the country's military and police. Nasheed would later say that he resigned at gun point, a claim security forces have denied despite the now-conventional wisdom that the resignation did come under some form of duress.

Upon Nasheed's resignation, Mohammed Waheed Hassan rose to the presidency. Waheed, a onetime political appointee of Gayoom, sought allies among parties critical of Mohamed Nasheed, even reaching out to the radical Islamic Adhaalath Party, which claims that music and singing are *haram* (prohibited) by shari'a and supports the death sentence for abortion. (It was also allegedly involved in a mob's destruction of the National Museum's entire collection of Hindu and Buddhist artifacts.) Waheed rationalized that it was better to work with such parties than to exclude them. This approach alienated the more secular and liberal citizens, and it also failed to win support from traditionalists. Waheed proved an unpopular president, winning only 5% of the vote in the first round of presidential elections in 2013, and he subsequently withdrew from the contest.

Confusion and interventions marked the 2013 presidential elections demanded by Nasheed's MDP and the international community. With the country clearly split between supporters and opponents of Nasheed, campaigning was sometimes bitter, with strong Islamist accusations against Nasheed. The police and the Supreme Court both interfered with the election commission. One ballot was annulled and, after Mohamed Nasheed won the first round with 46% of the vote, the run-off was postponed to provide Abdulla Yameen, who had placed second, time to forge alliances. In the end, Yameen was

No mountains, no traffic, and short distances. Bicycles abound in Malé

successful. The half-brother of former president Maumoon Abdul Gayoom and candidate of his Progressive Party of the Maldives (PPM) won a narrow majority of 51%. In an act of statesmanship, Nasheed conceded the election.

Parliamentary elections in early 2014 confirmed the old guard's dominance of politics. The PPM emerged with 38 seats in the 85-member assembly; the MDP only 25. Yameen shifted strategy on rising sea levels, abandoning the 2020 carbon neutrality deadline, in favor of mass tourism, and the leasing of islands to foreign investors. Prioritizing development over environmental concerns, the administration claimed that the greatly expanded tourism industry—virtually incompatible with a low-carbon vision—would, in fact, give the country the funds needed to adapt to a changing climate.

Under President Yameen and the PPM, the Maldives experienced a serious backsliding of democracy. Harassment of journalists, activists, human rights advocates, and others—perhaps the most famous being blogger Yameen Rashid, who was killed in mysterious circumstances outside of his apartment in April 2017—became commonplace, culminating in a state of emergency declared by the government in February of 2018. That declaration came on the heels of the country's Supreme Court overturning convictions of nine members of the opposition, including Nasheed, who escaped a 13-year prison sentence by being granted asylum in Britain in 2016.

Foreign observers feared that the 2018 elections would be rigged in Yameen's favor. However, in the event, MDP candidate, Ibrahim Mohamed Solih, won a convincing victory with 58.4% of the vote. After leaving office, Yameen was charged with theft, money laundering, and giving false statements to police.

Former president Mohamed Nasheed returned to the Maldives in late 2018 after two years in exile. In the 2019 parliamentary elections, the MDP won 65 of the 87 seats in the Majlis. Nasheed became the first former Maldivian president to be elected to parliament and was nominated

Maldives

as speaker of the Majlis. He has vowed to use his party's dominant position to usher in a "new era of stability and democracy in the Maldives."

Culture: All Maldivians are at least nominally Muslim and often bear Arab names as a result. Their lives center around fishing, tourism, agriculture, and a few light handicrafts. To a large extent the islanders follow strict Islamic standards of behavior, and laws prohibit drinking alcohol, Western-style dancing, possessing pornography, and extra-marital sex.

Despite its remoteness, few resources, and relative poverty, at over 98%, the Maldives boast the highest literacy rate for women aged 10–45 in the region. This achievement becomes even greater considering that the modern Maldivian school systems only dates to the last decades of the 20th century and instruction occurs in English. Not until 1979 did the government establish primary schools in every atoll, but by the late 1990s it had achieved virtually universal primary education.

For older generations, basic education took place not in a formal school, but in a Kiyavaage, a private home where children studied Dhivehi, arithmetic, and the Qur'an. Thereafter they could enter a Makthab or Madrasa, schools adapted from Islamic models. Maldives National University, the country's first university, was inaugurated in 2011. Its predecessor, Maldives College of Higher Education, was established in 1973 as the Allied Health Services Training Center.

Strengthened by their education, women occupy a distinctive role in Maldivian society. Important even as rulers before Islam, in law they enjoy equal opportunities in employment, remuneration, and cultural activities. However, a 2013 government report concluded that in practice women do not enjoy gender equality. Participation in the workforce is limited to traditional fields such as education, health, and agriculture, and few enjoy opportunities for advancement. Women in particular suffer a very high unemployment rate (40%).

The minimum legal age to marry is 15, and most women who do not study abroad marry as teenagers. Negotiations establish the "bride price" the groom must pay, and this is retained by the woman in the event the marriage breaks down. In theory, respecting the stipulations of Islamic law regarding inheritance, Maldivian practice has allowed a woman to apply for a divorce even against her husband's desires. The divorce rate (nearly 11 divorces per 1,000 inhabitants per year) is the highest in the world. One consequence is that women head 47 percent of households in the Maldives, likewise among the highest rates in the world.

The Domestic Violence Act of 2012 attempted to remedy high levels of abuse and violence. Although the rates already seem high (12% report sexual abuse before turning 15, and 30% of women have suffered from violence), much of the harm is inflicted by partners or within the family and not reported. When sexual morality is broken, it is generally women who suffer at the hands of the law. Women are flogged; men often go free.

In recent decades, competition from foreign goods and modern factories closed some employment opportunities in traditional women's crafts (mat weaving and rope making, plus agriculture and fish processing). Today, women make important contributions in tourism, business, and light industry; they manage companies, and practice law.

Although modernized and expanded upwards and outwards onto reclaimed land, the capital city of Malé retains a number of unusual features. Its population of about 150,000 has no buses and no dogs (dogs are banned in the Maldives, except for policing purposes). Its people enjoy socializing outdoors in the evening and weekends at the beach, where the women retain their modesty fully clothed. The relatively few tourists in Malé linger to enjoy the absence of hassle and a pleasant, laid-back atmosphere with the ocean always a few blocks away.

Economy: Lacking agricultural land, for centuries Maldivians turned to the ocean for fish and commerce. Until very recently, fishing was the principal livelihood for men, and shipments of dried and smoked tuna ("Maldive Fish") accounted for more than 90% of exports. Until the 1970s, fishing craft were small sailing boats, but a government program aided the fleet's conversion to diesel power. Modernization also took place in fish processing, with frozen and canned exports now accounting for over four-fifths of the total.

Many coconut palms and a few species of other fruit trees dot the islands, but agriculture is limited by the few areas of fertile soil on the tiny coral islets. The government is eager to encourage light industry, but there are few natural resources.

Tourists began arriving in significant numbers in the 1970s, attracted by the natural beauty and cheap living. However, the islanders gained little economic benefit, and the spread of drugs, nudity, and alcohol offended local society.

After President Gayoom took office in 1978, the country radically changed its approach to tourism. The jet airport opened in 1981, bringing tourists on package tours seeking relaxation, sunshine, and water sports. Far different from the backpacking crowd of the 1970s, these visitors stayed at self-contained resorts on "uninhabited islands" that were taxed significantly and required to provide increasing levels of luxury. Other regulations reduced pollution, protected reefs and marine animals, and generally preserved the pristine underwater beauty for those willing and able to pay for it.

One difficulty facing the Maldives is an adequate supply of clean fresh water despite the heavy annual rainfall. The rains do soak to fresh water aquifers underlying most islands, but unfortunately improper sewage facilities often pollute them. The islands' geography offers no convenient reservoirs or storage areas for potable water, and consequently Malé uses reverse osmosis from sea water.

Current Challenges and the Future: Moving forward, the Maldives faces a range of challenges. In the immediate future, the Maldives must grapple with the implications of the COVID-19 pandemic on its heavily tourist-dependent economy. Having escaped the worst of the health crisis in the early months, the wave of infections that swamped India in April and May 2021 have seriously threatened the small island nation. The Maldives, despite being a highly vaccinated country, has the grim distinction of having one of the highest death rates globally per 100,000 of the population.

The Maldives has been caught in a battle for influence between India and China, the latter having invested millions of dollars, as part of its Belt and Road plan, during Yameen's rule. The MDP has sought to reorient foreign policy towards India and the West. President Solih claims that 80% of foreign debt is owed to China, a situation that he has vowed to investigate as part of broader corruption probes into the former administration. However, China's role in the region is only likely to grow in coming decades—a situation future governments will need to manage.

One single overarching issue threatens not only future prosperity, but the very existence of the Maldives: climate change. While rising sea levels pose the clearest danger to the low-lying atolls, with most islands likely to be submerged or severely impacted by saltwater incursions, in the event of even a small rise, there are other associated threats for a nation heavily reliant on fishing and reef tourism. Coral reefs are susceptible to catastrophic damage in warming oceans and global fish stocks are predicted to plummet in the coming decades. As a nation, the Maldives can have only a very limited impact on redressing climate change. However, the mounting environmental challenges faced by the country should, ideally, spur global action.

Federal Democratic Republic of Nepal

Downtown Kathmandu

Area: 56,827 square miles (147,181 square kilometers).

Population: 29 million.

Capital City: Kathmandu (1 million).

Climate: Very hot on the southern plains; cooler in the hills, and frigid in the high mountains on the northern border. The plains and lower slopes have heavy rainfall during the summer monsoon.

Neighboring Countries: China (North); India (East, South, and West).

Time Zone: GMT +5 hours 45 minutes.

Official Language: Nepali (also called Gurkhali).

Other Principal Tongues: Gubhajius (Newari), Gurungkura, Hindi, Kiranti, Limbukura (Limbuani), Magarkura, and Tibetan.

Ethnic Background: A mixture of Mongolian, Indian, and Tibetan, who identify as distinct communities based on language and traditions.

Principal Religions: Hinduism (about 85%), Buddhism (9%), and Islam (4.5%).

Chief Commercial Products: Woven carpets, textiles, rice, wheat, corn, millet, jute, oilseeds, cane, sugar, timber, and hides.

Major Trading Partners: India (more than 50%), Japan, Germany, the United States, and Bangladesh.

Currency: Nepali Rupee (1 rupee = 100 paisa).

Former Colonial Status: Limited British control, 1816–1923.

National Day: December 21 (1923; independence from Britain).

Chief of State: Bidhya Devi Bhandari, President.

Head of Government: Khadga Prasad Oli, Prime Minister.

National Flag: Two red triangular pennants, one above the other, each bordered in blue. In the field of the upper is a symbolic moon, while the lower bears a symbolic sun.

Gross Domestic Product: $24.88 billion.

GDP per capita: $900.

Because its northern border runs along the crest of the Himalayas and its southern frontier lies on the tropical Ganges Plain, Nepal enjoys as great a geographical diversity as can be found in any small country. From an elevation of about 600 feet (183 meters) in the southeast to majestic Mt. Everest's 29,028 feet (8,847 meters) is a distance of little more than 100 miles (roughly 160 kilometers) by air. The entire length of Nepal from east to west is about 500 miles (about 805 kilometers); at no point is it wider than 140 miles (225 kilometers).

The strip of hot, marshy plain, averaging 30 miles (48 kilometers) wide along the southern border is called the *Tarai*. It is famed for its jungles and wildlife, though parts have been cleared. Its population and agriculture reflect those found in adjacent areas of India. While least typical of Nepal, its agriculture is the most productive.

The slopes north of the Tarai, known as the Hills, are inhabited to an elevation of about 8,000 feet (almost 2,500 meters) and in summer are used for grazing herds to about 13,000 feet (almost 4000 meters). The Hills, in turn, become the high mountains called the Snows. Some parcels of Nepali territory lie on the northern side of the crest of the Himalayas. Tibetans live there with their yaks and dzos (hybrids of yaks and ordinary cattle).

Another notable characteristic of the land is the pattern of rivers and streams flowing south from the High Himalayas to the Ganges Plain. These rivers carved out valleys with strips of relatively flat land. Surrounded by high mountains, the capital, Kathmandu, lies in the Valley of Nepal, the intensively cultivated bed of an old lake lying at an elevation of 4,500 feet (1,372 meters) and occupying about 300 square miles (about 780 square kilometers). The Valley of Nepal gives its name to the whole country.

History: Until the 18th century, individual cities and towns formed the basic political units. Their ruling families often descended from Hindu aristocrats who had fled from Muslim rule in India during the 14th century. They and their retainers subjugated the mainly Mongol-Tibetan population and subsequently mixed with it.

Nepal's unity began when Prithwi Narayan rose to power in the town of Gurkha and in the 1760s completed conquest of the Valley of Nepal. Prithwi Narayan's successors, the kings of the Shah dynasty, attempted to expand their rule. However, they were blocked by a large Chinese army in Tibet and ultimately defeated by the British (1815), who then controlled most of the Ganges Plain. A British resident was posted in Kathmandu, and only gradually did Nepal win recognition as lying outside India rather than forming one of many Indian kingdoms.

After a period of instability, factional strife, and massacre under weak kings, a capable noble, Jang Bahadur, seized effective control. He retained the king—many Hindus revered him as a god—but kept him only as a symbol while ruling in his name. His family, the Rana, became hereditary possessors of the office of prime minister. The Rana remained in power until the revolution of 1950–51.

An astute manipulator, Jang Bahadur balanced China and British India against each other for the benefit of Nepal. During the Indian Mutiny of 1857, he supplied Gurkha troops to fight against the rebels. The Gurkhas' courage and loyalty won British respect, and the tradition of recruiting Gurkhas for the British Empire began. Britain henceforth considered Nepal as a friendly ally and favored protected state, granting it formal independence in 1923.

India's independence in 1947 spread new ideas of nationalism and liberalism. Politically sophisticated activists from leading families who detested the Ranas' dictatorial methods formed the Nepali Congress Party. Influenced by the Indian

Nepal

party of the same name, they advocated democracy under the king.

As political tensions rose, King Tribhuvan was dismissed by the Rana prime minister and fled to India. Supporting the king, the Nepali Congress launched a revolution and gained control of parts of the country. In 1951 the alliance between King and Congress successfully removed the Rana family from government, and the party leader became prime minister. India and Nepal formed a special relationship that granted their citizens common rights of residence and land ownership, and promised military cooperation against any external threat.

In 1959, the Nepali Congress won absolute control of parliament and Bishweshwar Prasad Koirala became prime minister of Nepal's first elected government. However, when King Tribhuvan died, his son, King Mahendra, moved to rule with an iron fist. He dismissed Koirala, arrested him, suspended parliament, and charged Congress politicians with corruption. All political activity was banned. For the next 30 years, Nepal's kings ruled autocratically, sometimes with non-political elections of local councilors. This suited traditionalists, who regarded the king as the incarnation of the Hindu god Vishnu. In 1989 India blocked most trade across the border, on the pretext of fighting smuggling, but probably to punish Nepal's purchase of Chinese weapons. The people of Nepal suffered greatly, finding themselves desperately short of gasoline, cooking fuel, medicine, and other essentials. The weakness displayed by the royal government encouraged the Congress Party to join the communist-influenced United Left Front in protests.

When police violently repressed demonstrators, killing many, the shocked nation responded with strikes by almost all groups, even newspaper hawkers and health workers. Unsupported even by the elite, King Birendra called for a new constitution and appointed a coalition cabinet of the Congress Party, the United Left Front and royal nominees. The constitution of 1990 established multiparty democracy and an independent judiciary. It thus ended absolute rule by the Shah dynasty.

Congress won an absolute majority in the subsequent elections. The party dominated politics for the next 12 years, but it failed to maintain internal discipline. Two aging veterans of the struggle for democracy in 1950, Girija Prasad Koirala and Sher Bahadur Deuba, manipulated party rules and alliances to gain office or oust each other. Certainly, Congress could win elections: it came in second only once, defeated by the Communist Party of Man Mohan Adhikari in 1995. However, it could not provide stable government.

Cabinets changed about yearly; politics centered on chasing office.

The parliamentary leftists failed to provide a viable alternative. A social democrat rather than a communist (despite the party's name), their leader Man Mohan Adhikari sought free elementary education, more funds for local governments, and tax reforms. However, his party never won a majority in parliament, and in opposition it suffered defections.

In such circumstances, politics became the rapid search for the rewards of office rather than an opportunity to serve the public good. Corruption was so rampant that cynics claimed, "Governing Nepal is the art of appropriating foreign aid for personal use without getting caught." International aid agencies and donor nations became disillusioned.

Throughout the 1990s, economic growth often stagnated, and the distribution of income became more unequal. For example, the poorest 20% of the population received less than 4% of national income, while the top 12% owned 70% of the wealth. Disillusionment with democracy spread widely.

A stubborn Maoist rebellion broke out in poor western districts in 1996. Partly because politicians failed to address the causes of popular distress, and partly because the police lacked the training, resources, and ideas to combat a guerrilla movement, the Communist Party of

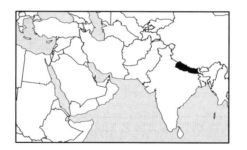

Prachanda, Former Prime Minister and Chairman of the Communist Party of Nepal

Nepal gradually grew in power and destructiveness. It proved particularly adept at interfering with schools and colleges, whether by presenting programs, holding students for indoctrination sessions, or closing campuses during political strikes.

Last Years of the Monarchy

In 2001 the murders of King Birendra, his wife, and several relatives shook the nation. Crown Prince Dipendra, surviving in a coma, was declared king, but he died within hours. Prince Gyanendra, Birendra's brother and perhaps the country's richest industrialist, then assumed the throne, the third king in four days. Official accounts blamed a drunken Prince Dipendra for the murders, but there were many

A solitary spot to pray at Boudnath Temple, Kathmandu   Photo courtesy of Karla Allan

conspiracy theories. The nation hesitantly accepted King Gyanendra.

Gyanendra soon dissolved parliament and appointed his prime minister. Democracy formally ended in 2002. Few Nepalis except the politicians themselves initially seemed to care, and the king promised elections after defeating the Maoists. To crush the rebellion, he declared a state of emergency and ordered the army into combat. However, the rebellion spread, and sympathetic strikes shut down the capital itself. Negotiations between the monarchy and the Maoists failed, because the latter desired a republican constitution, a demand the king rejected.

The Maoists seemed particularly inept at public relations; even China condemned them. Bombing the Coca Cola plant in Kathmandu won grudging support from nationalists who criticized expensive foreign drinks, but it discouraged foreign investment. Needing money, the Maoists extorted it from virtually every possible source, including tourist backpackers (asking modest amounts) and hotel owners (demanding much more). Unable to sustain military units with volunteers, the government turned to conscription. In response, hundreds of schools closed and thousands of teenagers fled to India.

However, Chairman Prachanda and his party stood for more than brutality and bloodshed. In a country with high illiteracy and more than 30% of the population below the poverty line, he demanded education for all children (girls included) and an end to feudal land holding. Many of the fighters were female, and women's organizations pressed for greater rights.

The government also demanded a ban on alcohol, which it considered a serious social problem leading to violence within the home.

Failing to appoint a prime minister acceptable to the political parties, in 2005 the king dismissed the cabinet and took direct power. He ended freedom of the press, arrested many politicians, and tried those alleged of corruption without normal court procedures. Like the Maoists, the military and its vigilante groups committed human rights abuses. International donors withheld aid and demanded the restoration of democracy.

As public resentment rose, the Maoists declared a unilateral ceasefire and agreed to cooperate with the two major political parties, Congress and the Communist Party (UML), for an end to "tyrannical monarchy." The political parties then initiated nationwide protests against the king's direct rule

While the king enjoyed his lakeside retreat near Pokhara, demands for a republic strengthened. Thousands of demonstrators defied prohibitions on public meetings and attempted to march on Kathmandu. Royal officials failed to halt the protests and strikes, even with the bloodshed of shoot-on-sight curfews. After losing support among the military and even within his cabinet, Gyanendra capitulated. He recalled parliament, but the political parties, not the king, named Girija Prasad Koirala as the new prime minister. At Koirala's request, the Maoists lifted their blockade of Kathmandu.

Parliament moved rapidly to eradicate the political roles of the king. It abolished

the title "His Majesty's Government." and removed his title as commander-in-chief. It stripped his image from the designs for coins and paper money, ended his freedom from taxation, and took away his veto power. Nepal had been a Hindu kingdom. With the fate of the monarchy unresolved, the state was declared secular.

The Maoist cease-fire had made the protests possible, and large Maoist demonstrations in Kathmandu prompted the cabinet to negotiate. Prachanda and Prime Minister Koirala agreed to major changes in a Comprehensive Peace Accord in 2006. The Maoists entered parliament (mostly represented by women and minorities) and joined the cabinet. To reduce the danger of violent confrontation, the army was ordered to its barracks, and the rebels to camps, where the UN monitored their surrender of weapons. After perhaps 13,000 deaths from the rebellion, peaceful change seemed possible but not certain.

Ethnic conflicts rapidly replaced warfare over ideology. Speaking Indian languages rather than Gurkhali, many Madhesis of the southeastern plains felt distressed by their low level of government employment and virtual absence from the army. Protests led to riots against Maoist activists, killing many; the police seemed to disappear.

As expected, elections to the vital constitutional assembly involved some intimidation and even violence. The Maoist Young Communist League (YCL) received particular condemnation. Its 300,000 members, led by former fighters, were accused of threatening rivals, demanding payments from businesses, and forming a sort of parallel police force. The danger seemed real that Prachanda and his party leaders had unleashed a force they could not control.

Nevertheless, imperfect elections were widely preferred to strife in determining the country's future. Sensing this, the Maoists left the cabinet and threatened an election boycott if two key demands were not met—proportional representation with quotas for women and under-represented groups, and the abolition of the monarchy before the elections, rather than afterwards. The other major parties eventually yielded, and parliament approved a "federal democratic republican state" by an overwhelming majority.

The 2008 elections passed remarkably peacefully, and the results shocked many. The Maoists captured 220 of the 601 seats, more than the combined totals of Congress (110) and the UML (103). The monarchy's doom was certified by the near-total defeat of royalists, and ex-king Gyanendra left the palace. Until recently a Maoist rebel, Prachanda became prime minister.

He recognized that he faced three tasks, the first to guide the Constituent Assembly in drafting a new constitution by 2010.

Nepal

Ex-King Gynendra, deposed in 2008

Second, the economy needed relief. Third, most pressing of all, the 20,000 Maoist fighters idling in their special camps needed to be integrated into the National (formerly Royal) Army. The military command fiercely opposed the latter, even threatening to boycott athletic events that mixed soldiers and former rebels. When the president vetoed his removal of the army chief, Prachanda resigned before completing his first year in office.

The UML subsequently formed a coalition of 22 parties, including Congress. With the Maoists in opposition and boycotting the Constituent Assembly, fierce disagreements prevented the coalition from meeting its 2010 deadline to complete a constitution. Though the assembly's authority was extended, a fundamental gap remained between politicians who valued law and government institutions and who saw the military as an instrument. After the 22-party coalition floundered, the UML and Maoists formed a new government, likewise considered temporary.

The new government did integrate some 9,000 former rebels into the military, and dismissed more from camps with promises of compensation. Nevertheless, popular anger and frustration with politicians grew when they failed to meet the extended deadline for a constitution in 2011. Thousands demonstrated, and even the UN expressed concern.

At the last minute, the assembly approved a fourth year's extension of the deadline and agreed that the job would be completed. However, the Constituent Assembly could not overcome deep divisions among its members over the creation of ethnically-based states. Feeling he had no alternative, the Maoist prime minister, Baburam Bhattarai, dismissed the Constituent Assembly and called for elections in November 2012.

Strong opposition by other parties to an election held with a Maoist in power led them to reject the November date. Agreement on a new caretaker government led by the well-respected Chief Justice finally enabled elections to be held in late 2013.

By that time, the country lived in a formal political vacuum: it had no constitution, no elected government, no parliament, and no elected local bodies.

The election results upset the Maoists' dominance. They fell to third place, and initially alleged fraud, but local and international observers proclaimed the integrity of the vote. Voters restored the Congress and Communist Party of Nepal (Marxist-Leninist) (UML) to their traditional ranks of first and second largest parties in the Constituent Assembly. After attempts to establish a unity government failed, Congress and the UML supported the appointment of Congress leader Sushil Koirala as Prime Minister. A long-time political activist, aged seventy-five, Koirala came from a notable family: three cousins had served as prime minister. Nevertheless, he was known for living a simple life. Koirala promised local elections in six months and a new constitution within a year.

The years since have been somewhat rocky in Nepal, only in part as a consequence of the new constitution—which turned out to be controversial—that Koirala promised. In September 2015, India imposed a five-month blockade against the Kingdom, a major trading partner, citing the political and economic marginalization of the Madhesi (a people in the southern region of Nepal, near the border of India, also known as the Terai). India had supported Madhesi protests in the run-up to the new document's establishment, but to no avail. The blockade created deep antipathy toward New Delhi throughout much of the country, the effect of which continues to linger.

In recent years the two countries—or, more specifically, their two leaders—have sought to mend the rift. Indian Prime Minister Modi had visited Nepal four times while in office. At a meeting in New

Former Prime Minister Sushil Koirala

Delhi, days after the 2019 re-election of Modi, Prime Minister Oli invited the Indian prime minister to again visit Nepal, with both leaders emphasizing the importance of strengthening bilateral ties and advancing cooperation. For India, ensuring that relations with Nepal are on the right footing is crucial to balancing the rise of Chinese power in the region. One way that Modi has done this is by emphasizing historical and cultural ties between the countries, not just the commercial and economic ties that many see as the basis of Chinese interest in Nepal.

Culture: Though considering themselves Nepalis, most inhabitants retain a strong loyalty to their tribe. Groups such as the Magar, Newar, or Gurkha have distinctive languages and customs; little social contact or intermarriage takes place between them. The Gurkha have enjoyed the most prestige, forming the military caste. During the political ferment in 2005–07, minority groups, whether the indigenous Janjatis or the Madhesis of the southeastern plains, pressed for greater rights.

Nepali school boys meet at Hindu Temple

Although in the hills and mountains the predominant physical characteristic is Mongolian, suggesting the population's origins from the north and east, religion and customs often belong to the south and west. Hinduism has traditionally functioned as the official (and majority) religion. Some Buddhists claim that they comprise a larger proportion of the population than population statistics suggest. The constitution previously required that the king be a Hindu and "Aryan," but in 2006 parliament declared the state to be secular.

Dancing and singing are the principal forms of popular entertainment. Men and women usually hold such celebrations separately; it is not uncommon for young men to dress in women's clothing for the performance of certain dances. Except for simple flutes played by herdsmen, Nepalis of noble tribes usually eschew musical instruments. The Damais provide musicians for celebrations.

Most Nepalis are superstitious. Traditionally, women were often confined away from the house and others for 10 days after the birth of a child (and during menstruation). Although outlawed by Nepal's Supreme Court in 2005, the practice persists in parts of the country. Ghosts, witches, and evil spirits form part of the social landscape, and exorcisms are performed. After a person has died, various rites are used to drive the spirit out of the house. Many superstitions relate to animals, such as the belief that keeping three cows is unlucky. If a farmer has four cows and one dies, he must either sell one or obtain another. Some Nepalis take astrology so seriously that astrologists were jailed for suggesting that the king's fate was "under bad stars."

Isolated and impoverished by its mountains, Nepal only slowly developed modern health and educational systems. Although most boys and half the girls receive a primary education, only about 60% of adults are literate. The leading center of higher education is Tribhuvan University, established in 1959.

Economy: An agricultural country whose inhabitants live close to the subsistence level, Nepal is among the poorest countries in the world. Its per capita income of little more than $2,000 (PPP) per year reflects low levels of agricultural productivity and little industry. Manufacturing concentrates on processing local produce and simple consumer goods. The leading sectors are cotton textiles, pulp and paper, and construction.

The most productive farming region is the low-lying Tarai, where farmers raise two successive crops in a year. Rice is grown in the wet monsoon, other grains in the drier seasons. Level land in valleys as high as 5,000 feet (over 1,500 meters) above sea level is also farmed with the help of irrigation. The uplands are used extensively for grazing livestock.

Nepal's new highways, sometimes blocked by landslides as they run through the mountainous terrain, have attracted concentrations of population along them. As the main source of energy for cooking and heating is firewood, the mountains have become denuded of trees several miles on either side of these roads. The result is massive erosion, and more landslides. Women who carry the firewood in heavy baskets must climb higher and higher on the slopes to obtain their fuel.

Tourism developed at a modest rate in the 1980s but surged in the 1990s, partly because of lower airfares for European and American visitors. Before the Maoist rebellion and political upheavals, the income from tourism exceeded twice the amount earned from the traditional, but declining, service of Gurkhas in the British army. Today, tourism has bounced-back, so much so that fears are being expressed about the environmental impact of hundreds of thousands of tourists and the dangers posed to those lured to the mountains. As this volume goes to press in mid-2019, 11 trekkers have lost their lives on Mount Everest since the beginning of the year, a horror season by any account. In April 2019, Nepal launched an ambitious clean-up campaign, aimed at retrieving trash left by tourists on their trek to the world's highest peak. Over six weeks, 10 tonnes of solid waste was carried of the mountain.

Remittances account for nearly 10% of Nepal's GDP. Nepalis works are employed in the Gulf Arab states, Malaysia, Israel, and South Korea. With the coronavirus seeing economies contract globally and the capacity for migration significantly hampered, remittances have dropped drastically.

Domestically, the next order of business is development of Nepal's hydroelectric power potential, optimistically estimated to exceed 83,000 megawatts. Less than 1% has been exploited, insufficient to supply the present needs of industry and homes. The government has proposed projects worth billions of dollars to foreign firms, but funding proved relatively difficult to obtain, not only because of environmental concerns. The electricity would be needed: in Nepal itself 85% of the population lack access to it, and neighboring India has tens of millions of potential consumers.

Current Challenges and the Future: Nepal has made important strides in consolidating democracy at the political level. Much, however, is still to be done to improve the lives of ordinary Nepalis.

During the country's decade-long conflict at least 13,000 people were killed, and hundreds disappeared. Nepal's Truth and Reconciliation Commission (TRC) and Commission of Investigation on Enforced Disappeared Persons (CIEDP) are generally considered not to meet international standards. Perpetrators who face credible allegations of war crimes remain in positions of power.

The slow pace of reconstruction efforts following the devastating 2015 earthquakes, that left 3.5 million homeless, was exacerbated by corruption. A good portion of aid money that flowed into the country at the time, has yet to be distributed, with many of those impacted by the earthquakes now having now lived through several monsoons and winters in inadequate or temporary housing.

Much more needs to be done to support and protects the more than 2 million Nepalis who work abroad. The government has largely failed to protect migrant workers from abusive recruitment agencies.

Managing the multi-million dollar tourism industry may need a careful reorientation of priorities, from short-term economic gains to a longer-term consideration of the industry's sustainability in the context of growing safety and environmental concerns.

Elderly postal delivery man in Kathmandu　　Courtesy of Mary M. Hill Forida

The Islamic Republic of Pakistan

Monumental shrine in Karachi dedicated to Mohammad Ali Jinnah, regarded as the founder of Pakistan   Photo by Ray L. Cleveland

Area: Some 307,374 square miles (796,095 square kilometers), plus 32,323 square miles (83,716 square kilometers) of Kashmir (see Disputed Territories: Kashmir).

Population: 221 million.

Capital City: Islamabad (1 million).

Climate: Generally dry, except for the mountains of the northeast; hot except for mountainous areas which receive snow in winter.

Neighboring Countries: India (Southeast); Iran (West); Afghanistan (Northwest); China (Northeast).

Time Zone: GMT +5.

Official Languages: Urdu, English.

Other Principal Tongues: Punjabi, Sindhi, Pashtu, Baluchi, Jatki, and Kashmiri.

Ethnic Background: Communities are distinguished by language and religion, but these divisions do not correspond to physical features. Nearly half the population is identified as Punjabi. Other ethnic groups include Pahtuns, Sindhis, Siddis, Saraikis, Baluchis, and others.

Principal Religion: Islam (about 95%), principally Sunni, with a significant Shi'a minority. Hinduism and Christianity each represent less than 2% of the population.

Chief Commercial Products: Textiles, rice, leather products, cotton products, tobacco, and sugar.

Major Trading Partners: China, the European Union, the United Arab Emirates, Saudi Arabia, and the United States.

Currency: Pakistani Rupee (1 rupee = 100 paisa).

Former Colonial Status: Part of British India (up until 1947).

National Day: August 14 (1947; independence from Britain and creation of the Dominion of Pakistan); March 23 (1940; passing of the Lahore Resolution and— on the same day in 1956—establishment of the Islamic Republic of Pakistan).

Chief of State: Arif-ur-Rehman Alvi, President.

Head of Government: Imran Ahmed Khan Niazi, Prime Minister.

National Flag: A large Islamic crescent and a five-pointed star in white lie within a field of green; at the pole there is a broad, vertical white stripe.

Pakistan

Gross Domestic Product: $305 billion
GDP per capita: $1,467.

Geographically, the heart of Pakistan is the Indus River. Tumbling from the Himalayas, the river and its tributaries traverse a vast plain stretching from the Punjab to the coast near Karachi. Irrigation from the rivers and the system of connecting canals supports intensive farming.

Southeast of the Indus Valley, the Thar Desert extends into India. This arid stretch of sand and gravel receives less than 10 inches of rain per year and supports scattered camel-breeding tribes. West of the Indus Valley, desert conditions prevail in Baluchistan, a dry mountainous region with elevations up to 11,000 feet (approximately 3,350 meters). This thinly populated area has some irrigation and farming, but most inhabitants are Baluchi nomads who call the region Makran. The north and northwest are mountainous, including the world's second-highest peak, K-2.

History: Before British rule in the 19th century, the territory that now comprises Pakistan had never formed a distinct political unit. Instead, various states and kingdoms ruled parts of it. When the Indian independence movement raised the possibility of the end of British rule, Muslim leaders like Muhammad Ali Jinnah dreaded the prospect of becoming a religious minority in an India dominated by its Hindu majority. The Muslim League of India publicly endorsed the goal of establishing a separate state for the subcontinent's Muslims in 1940. Staunchly opposed to Hindu rule separatist Muslims likely did not foresee the extent of problems that partition would create.

In 1947 Britain approved partition: the creation of two dominions, Hindu and Muslim. However, many Muslims lived in Hindu areas outside any possible Muslim state. Moreover, while Britain administered areas like Punjab and Bengal, and could divide them on the basis of religion, it granted the rulers of the princely states the choice of which nation to join—if either. From the partition emerged the new nation of Pakistan, the "Land of the Pure," composed of West Pakistan and East Pakistan—two areas separated physically by India (see map of India; Bangladesh was formerly East Pakistan). Ethnically fractured, and held together only by religion, Pakistan would rarely achieve national consensus over any significant secular issue.

Ethnic divisions ran deep within West Pakistan. More than half the population lived in Punjab, but Baluchistan and the North West Frontier Province contained sometimes-restless populations. Several

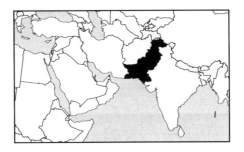

rugged Pakhtun (or Pashtun) inhabited regions bordering Afghanistan formed semi-autonomous areas subject to tribal, not national, law. Tribal leaders made decisions, sometimes under the influence of government officials posted as political agents. In these areas in particular, participation in national political activities was prevented, and women only received the vote in the 1990s. Human rights were often ignored by practices such as collective punishment and detention without trial.

With the British withdrawal rapidly nearing, Muslim leaders hastily improvised a government in Karachi, a port city near the mouth of the Indus River. Muslims elected in 1946 to the Indian constitutional convention now sat in

Karachi as the Constituent Assembly and legislature for Pakistan. Government offices had to be built from practically nothing. Civil servants proved scarce, although soldiers were plentiful; Hindus had dominated the bureaucracy under British rule, just as Muslims had often led in the army.

Unfortunately, the new state soon lost its guiding personalities. Muhammad Ali Jinnah, the Muslim League leader who so strongly demanded partition based on religion, became the first governor-general, but he died shortly after independence. Liaqat Ali Khan, the first prime minister, was assassinated by a fanatic in 1951. The loss of these two key figures set a precedent, whereby political instability would become a norm in Pakistan.

A massive two-way flight of Hindus and Muslims marked the actual partition. Whilst the British had insisted that once partition was accepted in principle there would be no communal violence, the reality, was one of chaotic and sometime involuntary population transfers, costing the lives of millions of individuals. Contemporary accounts describe it as "a slaughterhouse," a damning indictment of how the partition was managed. Pakistan lost many merchants and clerks

269

Pakistan

Quality control workers inspect carpets when they come off the looms and trim excess wool
Courtesy of the Caltex Petroleum Corporation

opposite direction. In total, eight million people moved from one country to another, an almost unfathomable population movement and one that has had lasting effects.

Many Indian politicians resented the separation of Pakistan, and strained relations between the two nations have proven a recurring feature until the present. A dispute over currency exchange (1949–51) disrupted trade. Conflicts also arose over three eastern tributaries of the Indus used for irrigation in India. In a rare diplomatic achievement, this dispute was settled by treaty in 1961.

Pakistan gained United States military aid in 1954, although for different reasons than Washington recognized publicly. While the United States sought to recruit and strengthen an ally against the spread of communism, Pakistan (which had dismissed its civilian government not long before) valued arms for possible war with its neighbors. Pakistan became a member first of the Southeast Asia Treaty Organization and then also of the Baghdad Pact. By contrast, India played a key role in the Non-Aligned Movement (NAM).

From independence to the 1990s, constitutional disputes regularly marked politics. Pakistan produced few political geniuses, but many bitter rivals. The Constituent Assembly failed to determine such practical matters as whether Urdu or Bengali should be the official language. The voting strength of the Bengali (i.e., East-Pakistani) members of the Assembly countered the governor-general who was from West Pakistan. After the Muslim League lost public support in East Pakistan in 1954, the governor-general dissolved the Assembly. Pakistani politicians and military rulers adopted many devices to manipulate the electorate and avoid the will of the people. Simultaneously, economic problems continued to mount, causing widespread dissatisfaction with the government.

A constitution instituted in 1956 established the Islamic Republic of Pakistan. However, elections were never held under that constitution: after just two years, a military coup d'état brought an end to a fledgling attempt at democracy. The army commander, General Ayub Khan, took the presidency for a decade, during which time Pakistan began an inconclusive conventional war with India over Kashmir (1965).

Pakistan Falls Apart

Riots and political unrest in the late 1960s led Ayub Khan to resign, but the same political and economic problems festered under his successor, General Yahya Khan. In 1970 voters for yet another constituent assembly gave the Awami League

while gaining large numbers of poor peasants. While Mohandas Gandhi almost miraculously averted strife in Bengal, in the Punjab, militants on each side massacred hundreds of thousands. A Hindu prince of Muslim-majority Jammu and Kashmir cast his lot with India, against the general expectation that Muslim majority areas would join Pakistan. The ensuing dispute led to conventional war (see Disputed Territory: Kashmir). About 1.5 million Hindus fled East Pakistan (now Bangladesh) in 1950 for West Bengal in India, while some one million Muslims went in the of East Pakistan an absolute majority. Bengalis sensed a legal means to correct the economic and political discrimination that they believed West Pakistani governments had inflicted on them. However, Yahya Khan postponed the assembly and arrested Mujibur Rahman, the Awami League's leader. This triggered an outpouring of long-suppressed feeling in East Pakistan and resulted in its declaration of independence in 1971 as Bangladesh.

Yahya Khan's attempt to use the army to hold the two Pakistans together resulted in the destruction of whole Bengali villages and the massacre of their inhabitants. India intervened; its army defeated the Pakistani forces, and the independence of Bangladesh was secured.

Alternate Military and Civilian Rule

Discredited by the defeat, Yahya Khan resigned. Zulfikar Ali Bhutto, an experienced opposition leader, became president and, like many Pakistani leaders, he won wide initial popularity. This dissipated, however, when economic decisions and ideological differences alienated significant groups. Business leaders particularly disliked Bhutto's socialist reforms, including the nationalizing of private businesses.

Despite political leanings that brought Pakistan closer to China, Bhutto himself came from a landowning aristocracy of Sindh, and he dominated the Sindhi-based Pakistan People's Party (PPP). The PPP won the 1977 elections, but the opposition accused Bhutto's government of fraud in vote counting. Riots and demonstrations led to martial law, and within weeks General Muhammad Zia ul-Haq led a military coup. He arrested Bhutto and other politicians "to save democracy for the nation."

Despite the promise of democracy, Zia canceled elections and banned political activity. His military regime ruled firmly, controlled the press tightly, and executed Bhutto. To foster his regime's popularity, in 1984 Zia proposed the incorporation of further Islamic features into the constitution and a ban on political parties. A national referendum endorsed these changes.

The Soviet Union's military occupation of neighboring Afghanistan rescued Zia's regime politically and internationally. Refugees from the brutal fighting in Afghanistan flooded into Pakistan's border areas, straining the provision of social services. The U.S. and conservative Arab regimes considered Pakistan a bulwark between Soviet troops and the Indian Ocean. In an effort to counter the Soviet Union, weapons and funds were provided to refugees and to Zia's military regime.

After President Zia was killed in a suspicious plane crash in 1988, military rule collapsed. Benazir Bhutto, daughter of the executed Zulfikar, had already led agitation for democracy. Now the PPP quickly became the major national party, and it struck alliances with several regional parties. By contrast, the conservative Muslim League dominated the heavily-populated Punjab. Led by Nawaz Sharif, an industrialist, it became the fierce rival of the PPP.

Alternating Rule by Bhutto and Sharif

For the next 11 years, power alternated between Bhutto and Sharif. Three years in office proved long enough for each to commit enough mistakes to justify dismissal. Both Bhutto and Sharif won elections to come to power, but neither ever completed a term, their effectiveness disintegrating by the third year in office.

To generalize, Bhutto won fame and good relations in the West, but she often proved ineffective in domestic politics. More troubling, her husband, Asif Ali Zardari, allegedly amassed wealth from corrupt dealings and earned a reputation as "Mr. 10%." Open disputes flared between Bhutto, various presidents, and leading generals.

By contrast, Nawaz Sharif broke the tradition that reserved office for wealthy landowners from Sindh. Among other reforms, he promoted some degree of economic freedom, attempted to establish Shari'a as high law, and adopted the death penalty for blasphemy against the Prophet Muhammad. Under the guise of fighting corruption, political opponents were arrested, most prominently Benazir Bhutto's husband.

Neither Bhutto nor Sharif brought peace to Karachi, the largest city if no longer the capital (which moved to Islamabad in 1967). Violence escalated there between the native Sindhis and the Muhajirs; it became an urban battle zone. The police acted brutally but failed to contain the violence, and fatalities reached 800 in 1994 alone. After violence claimed 600 lives in 1998, Sharif ordered military courts to render swift justice: three days maximum for trial, another three days for appeal, then execution. The carnage did decline, but civilian courts declared the special courts unconstitutional.

After India's nuclear tests in 1998, intense domestic pressure built to display Pakistan's nuclear capability. Despite strong foreign warnings and threats of sanctions, Sharif ordered tests in response. Their success propelled Pakistan into the small group of nuclear powers and won Sharif great public praise inside the country. The blasts, however, deepened the discord with India and brought economic punishment by foreign nations.

Perhaps reasoning that nuclear weapons provided a sufficient deterrent against conventional Indian attack, in 1999 Sharif and the military secretly sent Pakistani troops into Indian Kashmir to occupy and fortify positions at Kargil, overlooking India's vital road to Leh. The invaders inflicted heavy casualties on the first Indian troops sent to evict them. However, the invasion turned to fiasco when Indian successes on the battlefield and public condemnation by world leaders forced Sharif to withdraw the troops without even a face-saving gesture.

Following withdrawal from Kashmir, Sharif proved particularly incapable. Rampant corruption flourished, and insensitive appointments antagonized public opinion. To intimidate the press, a respected journalist was beaten up. When Sharif attempted to dismiss the chief of staff in 1999, General Pervez Musharraf led a bloodless coup d'état. He proclaimed a state of emergency, suspended the constitution, dissolved parliament, and became chief executive. He promised to attack corrupt officials and make wealthy defaulters repay their loans. The public cheered, and the courts granted him three years to reform society.

Although powerful, Musharraf faced opposition. The attack on corruption moved very slowly. It also appeared mainly designed to control politicians, ensnaring only a few. Conservative Islamists halted a proposal to reform the blasphemy law, and a strike by shopkeepers forced the government to dilute tax reforms. Suspicions mounted that the military intelligence service (the ISI) really ran the country.

Joining the War on Terror

After the September 11 attacks on the U.S., the government faced a dilemma. The Taliban regime that hosted Osama bin Laden in Afghanistan was partly (perhaps even primarily) a Pakistani creation. Musharraf could either acquiesce in an American attack on Islamic Afghanistan, or defy U.S. efforts and lose any remaining international standing.

Risking assassination from disgruntled Islamists and others inside Pakistan, Musharraf joined the war on terrorism. He permitted U.S. military flights across the country, and allowed U.S. troops to cross the border in hot pursuit. However, many Pakistanis opposed U.S. policies, and therefore Musharraf. The leaders of two Muslim parties, the *Jamaat-i Islami* and the *Jamiat Ulema-e-Islam*, called the regime illegal. After two assassination attempts in 2003, Musharraf reshuffled the high command and retired the ISI director who was sympathetic to the Taliban. The government also ordered 20,000 Islamic schools to stop all fundamentalist indoctrination.

Yielding to U.S. pressure, the government publicly ordered the military to root

Pakistan

General Muhammad Zia ul-Haq

out Taliban and al-Qaeda fighters along the border with Afghanistan. However, the critical border regions had long enjoyed autonomy as tribal agencies. In several of the Federally Administered Tribal Areas and in the North West Frontier Province, attempts to establish military authority resulted in bitter skirmishes, costing the lives of hundreds of soldiers in battle against fighters who knew the terrain and enjoyed local support.

The struggle against militant Islamists in this area proved difficult because of deep popular passions about local autonomy, opposition to Indian rule in Kashmir, and resentment over injustices against Muslims in Palestine and elsewhere. For years, military agencies and intelligence services had stirred up these passions and supported militants. Popular magazines extolled the virtues of jihad as armed struggle. Groups outlawed because of foreign pressure often reorganized quickly under new names.

The war against terrorism did bring some benefits. Musharraf's role led many in the West to forget that he overthrew an elected government. The U.S. dropped the sanctions imposed after the nuclear tests and provided new aid. Both the Karachi stock exchange and the Pakistani rupee surged in value.

Searching for Political Stability

Musharraf's later years in office became dominated by desires to ensure control of politics. To overcome the Supreme Court's three-year limit for military rule, in 2002 a referendum was held to extend his presidential term by five years. Lavishly-funded propaganda favored the proposal, and despite a boycott by the major political parties, the result was 97.5% "Yes." This figure was discredited by low turnout, allegations of irregularities, and

a common sense position that exceedingly few issues ever generate such consensus. Nonetheless, the manipulation was probably unnecessary: the poor often liked the general, while the middle class and more secular-minded citizens despaired of politicians and desired an end to the violence.

Musharraf restored the president's power to dismiss parliament (but not, at least directly, the prime minister). He established a National Security Council of elected politicians and top military officers to review government actions. By involving the military in government, he argued, he would render the army less likely to overthrow democracy.

Before the 2002 National Assembly elections, the regime weakened opposition political parties by banning any candidate who had served two terms from taking office again. Moreover, threats of prosecution kept the most famous politicians, Benazir Bhutto and Nawaz Sharif, out of the country. While the PPP remained loyal to Bhutto, the Pakistan Muslim League split. Most of its supporters formed the PML *Quaid-i Azam* (PML-Q) that accepted General Musharraf's plans. Several Islamic parties united to form the *Muttahida Majlis-i Amal* (MMA) and concentrated their campaign against Pakistan's anti-terrorist alliance with the U.S. That group placed third in the National Assembly and gained control of the border provinces of Baluchistan and the North West Frontier Province, where it began to institute Shari'a-influenced laws.

In 2005, open fighting in Baluchistan, on the border with Iran and Afghanistan, drew attention to a region impacted by drought and mired in poverty. Even today, less than 5% of the population enjoys

running water, and society retains many traditional values. Baluchis list multiple grievances, including the exploitation of the region's natural gas and other resources with few benefits for the locals. They also fear an influx of non-Baluchis and dislike the military's presence in the area. Nawab Akbar Bugti, a rebel leader, died fighting in 2006, which hurt the leadership behind the revolt, but not its basic causes.

Despite its sometimes inept politics, the Musharraf administration earned respect for improved relations with India. However, an attack by Kashmiri militants on India's parliament in 2001 brought the two nations close to war. Ultimately, Musharraf was able to take the steps to avoid a potentially catastrophic outcome of two nuclear powers at war. He yielded to New Delhi's demands and promised to halt infiltration across the Line of Control. He banned two extremist groups and the police arrested thousands of militants (though many soon reappeared on the streets). The ISI had sponsored militants; now it at least ostensibly encouraged them to disband.

With relations warming, despite extremists' threats, a bus service began between Srinagar in Indian Kashmir and Muzaffarabad, the capital of Pakistan's portion, in 2005. Train travel followed, to Lahore.

Years of Challenge, 2007–10

When parliamentary elections and the presidential selection both fell due in 2007, political tensions rose dramatically. At least in retrospect, Musharraf repeatedly made decisions that cost him good will among the public. Seeking a new term as president after ruling for eight years, he schemed for the outgoing parliament to select the president because his supporters formed the majority. To overcome legal roadblocks to this unusual approach, the president dismissed Chief Justice Iftikhar Muhammad Chaudhry for abuse of office.

A visionary for constitutional rule, Chaudhry turned the dismissal into a campaign for an independent judiciary. Thousands of lawyers and judges demonstrated on his behalf, but in Karachi dozens were killed when supporters were attacked after the police vanished. These events weakened Musharraf's support among the middle class.

About the same time, Musharraf's support plummeted among conservative Muslims when, at a cost of 100 lives, the military crushed the Islamic extremists who had seized the Lal Masjid, the Red Mosque of Islamabad, and used it as a base to attack brothels and kidnap a group of Chinese workers. Isolated by events and public opinion, Musharraf restored the Chief Justice and promised to

General Pervez Musharraf

resign from the military if he were elected president. Parliament duly selected him, but the Supreme Court delayed recognizing the decision on grounds that it had not yet ruled on the eligibility of a presidential candidacy by the military commander.

Seeking a natural ally opposed to the militants and religious parties in approaching parliamentary elections, Musharraf sought an accommodation with Benazir Bhutto, the PPP leader exiled over corruption charges. After the president granted amnesty to leading politicians with pending corruption cases, she, her husband, and Nawaz Sharif returned to Pakistan. Bhutto's triumphal tour of the country drew large crowds but was marred by bombings in Karachi that killed scores of PPP supporters.

Still fearful the Supreme Court would void his presidential election, Musharraf declared a state of emergency in late 2007. He suspended the constitution, banned political rallies, curbed the media, and dismissed Supreme Court justices. His newly-appointed judges faithfully approved his election, and Musharraf handed over command of the army to General Ashfaq Kayani, a widely respected career soldier. Musharraf then ended emergency rule. Nevertheless, by this time he was widely disliked, and his manipulation of the state of emergency strengthened his opponents.

Benazir Bhutto's Assassination and Musharraf's Fall

As she left a political rally in Lahore in December 2007, Benazir Bhutto was assassinated. Some branch of military intelligence was likely complicit, and the police at least negligent, partly because Bhutto had earlier alerted Musharraf to the fact that extremist suicide squads and a group of senior politicians and intelligence officials were plotting to kill her. Officially the attack was blamed on Islamic militants, but Bhutto's security was clearly inadequate, and the shoddy police investigation—the scene was hosed down immediately—also pointed to government failure if not complicity.

Responding quickly to the death of its leader, the PPP transferred power to her husband, Asif Zardari. The PPP triumphed in subsequent parliamentary elections, winning the most seats of any party (a total of 87). Its leaders formed a coalition with Nawaz Sharif, whose PML-N emerged the second largest party after campaigning over unemployment, inflation, and the reinstating of Supreme Court justices. The PPP's Yusuf Raza Gillani, a man of character who had served five years in jail, likely on trumped-up charges, became prime minister.

The new cabinet addressed many issues. It revised education policy, published the military budget, and righted past wrongs. The most compelling demands for change involved the fight with militants, and the restoration of Supreme Court judges.

Because both the PPP and the PML-N had supported restoration of the Supreme Court, an agreement on doing so seemed within reach. However, the two parties failed to settle the matter, because their goals differed. Nawaz Sharif clearly desired Musharraf's ouster, so he hoped a restored Supreme Court would void the presidential election. By contrast, Asif Zardari preferred that Musharraf remain president, because a Supreme Court decision dismissing the presidential election might also void his own pardon from corruption charges.

The crisis over the Supreme Court reached its conclusion in 2008. Just days before his impeachment on charges of violating the constitution, Pervez Musharraf resigned the presidency. It was a landmark moment for Pakistan: the ouster of a former military ruler by orderly political process. The National Assembly subsequently elected Asif Ali Zardari president.

Multiple crises soon tested the new regime, including a bitter dispute over demands to reinstate the Supreme Court Chief Justice. In response to forceful demonstrations and a threatened march on Islamabad, Zardari's government arrested hundreds of opposition activists but eventually gave way and reinstated the full Supreme Court.

Predictably, the court addressed the pardon that Musharraf had granted Zardari and some 8,000 politicians, administrators, and other members of the country's elite. When the court proclaimed the legislation illegal, it plunged those amnestied into legal limbo. While as president Zardari enjoyed immunity from prosecution, his popularity slumped as the nation's media became consumed with one topic: how Zardari would be replaced or sacked.

While clinging to office, Zardari accepted major changes that weakened the role of the president. He turned over control of nuclear weapons to the prime minister, and signed major constitutional changes that ceded power to appoint military chiefs, judges, and the chief election commissioner. He lost the long-disputed power to dissolve parliament and to impose emergency rule on a province. The presidency became largely symbolic.

Still Struggling against Terrorism

In 2007, suicide bombers killed nearly 1,000 Pakistanis; after Iraq and Afghanistan, Pakistan had suffered more casualties in the Global War on Terror than any other country. Soldiers had also died in border regions where the Afghan Taliban had gained local support. Additional casualties, militants as well as civilians, resulted from American missile strikes in those regions. Tired of the struggle, many politicians argued in favor of negotiations with militants rather than direct combat. For its part, the Pakistan Taliban Movement (Tehrek-i Taliban Pakistan, TTP—a militant group distinct from the Afghan Taliban) argued that its struggle was with America.

In 2009 the provincial government of Khyber Pakhtunkhwa (the renamed North West Frontier Province) negotiated a truce for Swat, a beautiful, rugged region not far from Islamabad, where insurgents had fought the military to a standstill. In return for a cease-fire, the agreement released militant leaders and imposed Shari'a law in Swat and adjoining regions. Human rights organizations and the international community were horrified at the possibility of punishments such as the amputation of limbs, whipping, and execution by stoning for adultery. One 11 year old girl, Malala Yousafzai began writing about her experiences in Taliban-controlled Swat. Her observations, drawing attention to the everyday indignities for girls and young women, gained international attention. Politicians hoped that concessions over Swat and other regions would halt the extremist violence. No doubt also some intelligence and military officers preferred to see the army defend Kashmir rather than attack tribal areas.

The truce quickly failed when militant fighters appeared even closer to the capital. Open warfare resumed between the military and TTP fighters. Hundreds of thousands fled the conflict, but at least in Swat the army regained formal control, and refugees began to return to their homes.

However, terrorist strikes have continued across the country, including an attack on the visiting Sri Lankan cricket team, a massive bombing of the police emergency response headquarters in Lahore, bombings of military training centers, and suicide bombings in the streets. Malala Yousafzai was shot in the head by Taliban militants, surviving to become "the world's most famous teenager" and recipient of the Nobel Peace Prize. Furthermore, the insurgency threatened to spread. Impoverished areas of southern Punjab seem likely to support groups committed to violence. The region's poverty, high illiteracy, and feudal system provide conditions where such militancy often flourishes.

Temporarily successful in South Waziristan and some other tribal areas, the army and civilian government have not yet formulated a counter-insurgency strategy. Even when the army has controlled an area, the government has failed to reconstruct homes, businesses, schools, and

Pakistan

Pakistanis abroad hail SC verdict

NEW YORK, May 26: Pakistani immigrants hailed as historic the Supreme Court judgment reinstating the National Assembly and Prime Minister Nawaz Sharif, saying they were proud of the contribution of the country's judiciary to strengthening the democratic process, reports APP's special correspondent.

They said that the Nawaz Sharif government had worked for the betterment of the country and that it had achieved definite progress.

In the name of Allah, Most Gracious, Most Merciful

FOUNDED BY QUAID-I-AZAM MOHAMMAD ALI JINNAH

THE PAKISTAN TIMES

National English Daily with the largest circulation — Published simultaneously from Islamabad & Lahore

Regd. No. R-1 Vol. XLVII No. 108 — Islamabad, Thursday, May 27, 1993 — Zilhaj 4, 1413 A.H. — Tele: No. 825893, 825766, Reporters 829297; Telex 54672 44811 (Times PK). Fax: 823467. Price **Rs. 4.00**

PM lauds role of Press

ISLAMABAD, May 26: Prime Minister Muhammad Nawaz Sharif has lauded Press for its outstanding commitment to democracy from the day of dissolution of the National Assembly till its restoration.

He was addressing a news conference at the Prime Minister Secretariat this evening.

Muhammad Nawaz Sharif thanked the Press for making his (Nawaz) cause its own cause.—PPI

Supreme Court declares Presidential Order as *ultra vires* in a historic verdict

National Assembly, Nawaz Govt. restored

Court also dismisses review petition

By Muhammad Ilyas

ISLAMABAD, May 26: The Supreme Court of Pakistan, in a historic decision, today restored the National Assembly, the Prime Minister and his Cabinet with immediate effect.

The Court also outrightly dismissed the request on behalf of the President for suspension of the restoration order pending decision on the Review Petition which would be filed against the Court's order on Mr. Nawaz Sharif's constitutional petition.

As soon as the Court's decision became known, the corridors and vaults of the under-construction building of Supreme Court resounded with slogans of "Nawaz Sharif Zindabad" which were chanted by a large number of his supporters thronging the premises. Mr. Shahbaz Sharif MNA, younger brother of Prime Minister Nawaz Sharif was among those present in the Courtroom when Chief Justice Dr. Nasim Hassan Shah announced the keenly awaited judgement.

(Text of SC verdict)
(See Page 5)

The National Assembly, elected in October 1990, is the 7th Assembly of Pakistan and, thanks to the Supreme Court's verdict, is the first one to be revived. Only two other Assemblies — one elected in 1962 and the other in 1970 — had their culmination under constitutional dispensation. Six Assemblies met with unnatural demise unsung and unredeemed.

Chief Justice Mr. Justice Nasim Hasan Shah of the Supreme Court along with 10 other judges in Islamabad on Wednesday. **(More pictures on Pages 3,5,12)**

Pledge to work within legal framework: Cooperation of political forces sought

Nawaz vows to pursue policies with new vigour

By Maqbool Malik

ISLAMABAD, May 26: Describing the decision of the Supreme Court as historic, Prime Minister Muhammad Nawaz Sharif has vowed to work within the legal and constitutional framework and pursue his programmes with renewed vigour to propel the country out of the setbacks it had suffered in the wake of the dissolution of the National Assembly.

Addressing a crowded press conference at the Prime Minister Secretariat here Wednesday evening after the restoration of the National Assembly and his government by the Supreme Court, he observed that Pakistan suffered heavily in terms of rapid progress, foreign investment and its international image.

He asserted that his government would endeavour to bring about a new political order in the country which would be free of hypocrisy, unscrupulousness and blackmail. tronic media.

The Prime Minister went on to say that the character assassination campaign unleashed against him by the caretaker government died down in the eyes of the public as the caretaker government could not find any valid material against his government. "Had they any valid material against us, why did they not go to the courts to prove it, he questioned.

He asserted that masses did not heed the character assassination campaign launched against "me and my friends, rather they were depressed and unhappy, mourning the dissolution of the National Assembly and dismissal of my gov-

Continued on page 5 col. 2

Gen. Waheed, Admiral Saeed meet Nawaz

ISLAMABAD, May 26: Chief ...

---

offices destroyed in the conflict. It also has failed to develop civil society. Consequently, militancy and terrorism reappear given the opportunity.

Rather than occupy North Waziristan, the military has largely ceded it to Gul Bahadur, the autonomous local Taliban leader, who has proclaimed that his focus is liberating Afghanistan, not Pakistan. Pakistan thus allows refuge for Chechen, Arab, Kashmiri, and Central Asian fighters. It also provides a sanctuary for Jalaluddin Haqqani, the Afghan militant. Given this coalition of al-Qaeda allies, the majority of drone missile strikes by U.S. forces in Pakistan were aimed at North Waziristan.

In times of crisis, the deciding element is often unplanned. Pakistani public opinion about militant Islam changed perceptibly after a two-minute video showed militants flogging a screaming young girl. Interviewed later on television, Taliban leaders awoke national concern by condemning schools, music, most entertainments, alcohol, democracy, and much else, not just in Swat, but anywhere in the country.

Other unplanned events later drove public opinion in the opposite direction. An American security contractor, Ray Davis, shot dead two young men in Lahore traffic and was subsequently identified as a CIA operative. Pakistan denied he held diplomatic immunity, and tried him for murder. "Blood money" paid to the victims' families resulted in his release, but did little for the rehabilitation of U.S. prestige in the country.

Greater consternation within the military and among the public followed the airborne raid by U.S. SEALS that killed Osama bin Laden in Abbottabad, just a mile from the Pakistan Military Academy. The successful raid, publicly acknowledge as undertaken without the military's permission or even knowledge, raised troubling questions in both countries. Pakistani was already critical of the CIA's drone attacks in border areas and questioned the right of U.S. troops to attack a civilian residence deep inside the country without permission. Americans wondered aloud how the world's most sought terrorist could live so safely, for so long, without covert military or intelligence assistance. Many analysts have concluded that there must have been at least some degree of Pakistani complicity in bin Laden's presence in the country.

The tenuous alliance between the two nations frayed further when U.S. aircraft in Afghanistan hit a Pakistani base across the border and killed 24 soldiers. Angered by both the loss of life and the reluctance of the U.S. military to apologize, Pakistan closed its borders to supplies for U.S. and NATO forces in Afghanistan. This forced supplies by land to be shipped through Central Asia.

The Turf War between the Court and the PPP

The final months of the Pakistan People's Party government were marked by deep struggles with the Supreme Court, agitation by militant Islamists, and tension with the military. Chief Justice Iftikhar Chaudhry had returned to the Supreme Court determined to charge politicians for their alleged misdeeds. The court began at the top: it demanded that Prime Minister Gillani ask Swiss authorities to reopen a closed investigation of Asif Ali Zardari for corruption.

Gillani reasoned that as president, Zardari possessed legal immunity. When he therefore refused to act, the Supreme Court dismissed him from office,

Imran Khan

plunging the country into political crisis. His replacement, Raja Ashraf, was the PPP's second, last-minute nominee. Six months later, the court ordered his arrest over alleged corruption when he directed the ministry of water and power. However, the evidence proved inconclusive and he remained in office until a caretaker cabinet formed to supervise the elections.

In 2013, Nawaz Sharif's Pakistan Muslim League swept to an overwhelming victory in Punjab and gained enough seats

President Arif Alvi

to govern without a coalition, supported by friendly independents. Imran Khan's *Pakistan Tehreek-e-Insaf* (PTI) or Movement for Justice broke through to significance with its program of tax fairness and anti-corruption, becoming the third largest party, although not accomplishing the tsunami of reforms he predicted would wash away all the "corrupt politicians and plunderers." The PPP, barely escaping third place, had accomplished what no Pakistani party had ever previously done: govern for its full term of office.

On taking office, Prime Minister Sharif encouraged great expectations that he would tackle the nation's pressing problems, especially terrorism and the economy. However, the first year of his term was more remarkable for its failures than any success in bringing Pakistan back from the brink of disaster. His administration failed so badly that in a symbolic move the state-owned electric utility cut power to his office for unpaid bills. That literal darkness was quickly remedied, but Sharif's attempts to remove the dark cloud of terrorism brought no immediate peace.

A vicious TTP attack on a military school in Peshawar in late 2014 killed 141, including over 130 schoolchildren. Prime Minister Sharif proclaimed that the tragedy "changed Pakistan," and that there would be "no place for terrorism, extremism, sectarianism and intolerance." Henceforth, at least officially, all terrorism was unacceptable; terrorism had previously been classified as "good" (aimed at Indian Kashmir and Afghanistan) or "bad" (targeting other Pakistanis). The extent to which any real change has resulted from this proclamation remains an open question at best.

The fight against terrorism allowed the government to extend its powers in ways that sometimes impacted severely on ordinary Pakistanis and invariably alarmed political opponents, and human rights activists. Special military courts were established to try accused terrorists, because civil court procedures identified witnesses and security personnel, but here too individuals feared reprisals if they testified, thus making it difficult for prosecutors to provide evidence.

The government also lifted the temporary ban on capital punishment, in place for several years. With some 8,000 prisoners on death row, capital punishment was deemed a deterrent to terrorism, and Pakistan quickly reestablished itself as one of the leading countries in the world in terms of rates executions. Human rights groups were furious over the executions of men in their mid-twenties convicted for murders committed during their teen years on evidence extracted by torture.

The decline in global petroleum prices and greater foreign confidence in Pakistan after the clampdown on terrorism provided a small boost to the economy and morale. However, it would not be enough to save Sharif. The release of the Panama Papers in 2016 revealed an extraordinary web of corruption linked to the Sharif family. In mid-2017, a court disqualified the now-disgraced Sharif from holding public office. In 2018, he was sentenced ten years in prison, a sentence that was later suspended. Later in the same year, fresh corruption charges were brought, resulting in a seven-year prison sentence, an ignominious end to a giant of Pakistani politics.

At general elections in 2018, Imran Khan's PTI gained 115 seats, forming a minority government

Culture: Rural Pakistan is characterized by villages, where traditional landowners often dominate society and government. Karachi, Lahore, and Islamabad best represent urban society. With nearly 23 million inhabitants in its greater metro area (16 million in the city), Karachi dominates the nation's business as the major port and industrial center. It is hot, noisy, crowded, and dusty. Lahore is a more traditional city of just over 7 million. Like most urban areas, both cities are crowded with picturesque but tiny stores and workshops, where handicrafts are sold directly by the artists. By contrast, Islamabad, the capital and smaller at just 1.5 million inhabitants, was planned along modern lines in the early 1960s.

Life in the irrigated valley of the Indus and its tributaries differs greatly that in the Thar Desert or the mountains to the northwest. In the deserts and near-deserts, camel and goatherds move continuously in search of sparse vegetation.

Though Islam has a role in nearly all life in Pakistan, society is deeply divided between a small class of wealthy landowners and millions of impoverished farm workers and others, some bonded laborers who will never escape their debts. Though laws do not recognize a special status for the landowners, thanks to their political influence they often pay few taxes, while the urban middle classes are taxed heavily to compensate. Land reforms and the spread of education are very slowly reducing these distinctions.

For those with leisure time, soccer and cricket are popular sports. One unique local festival is Basant, the spring kite-flying festival in Lahore. Though a picturesque sight, Basant's kite-flying competitions could be a hazardous pastime. In an effort to cut loose opponents' kites, competitors' strings were sometimes coated with glass particles, with lethal consequences for

Pakistan

Busy intersection in Karachi   Photo by Ray L. Cleveland

motorcyclists and bicyclists unfortunate enough to ride into the strings of falling kites. Banned for safety reasons in recent years, the festival was revived in 2007 with glass strings banned.

Female participation in outdoor sports has been targeted by Islamic militants and sometimes prohibited. When women were permitted to participate in a recent one kilometer road race in Lahore, some wore the long, traditional *shalwar kameez* (shirt plus pants).

The Role of Islam and Human Rights

Although it was created as a state for Muslims, Pakistan's early leaders avoided direct involvement in religion. However, in the mid-1970s a trend began toward enforcing Islamic practices, possibly to gain political support. Zulfikar Ali Bhutto banned alcohol and introduced Friday as the weekly day of rest, replacing—until it was changed back in 1997—Sunday (a tradition brought by Britain). For his part, General Zia ordered historically Islamic punishments: flogging criminals in public and amputating the hands of convicted thieves.

Sunni militants have gunned down hundreds of Shi'a worshippers in mosques or travelling to religious festivals. In the troubled province of Baluchistan the Hazara Shi'a have suffered in particular. In early 2013, the banned *Lashkar-e Jhangvi* group carried out a double bombing that killed 89 in Quetta, most of them Shi'a. Just one month earlier a bombing in the provincial capital killed at least 92 and led to the ouster of the chief minister.

Blasphemy laws, introduced in the mid-1980s, continues to incarcerate and

even kill. Up until 2018, over 1,500 individuals had been charged under the laws, about half of those were Muslims (Shi'a or Sunni), followed closely by Ahmadiyya (followers of a minority Islamic sect). More than 200 Pakistani Christians have been accused of crimes of blasphemy. While the courts have rarely condemned citizens to death for the crime (and no court-ordered executions have taken place), in a number of cases frenzied mobs have taken it upon themselves to lynch the accused. In recent decades, at least 75 people have been victims of extra-judicial killings following accusations of blasphemy.

The Ahmadiyya offshoot of Islam, considered heretical by many because it regards its 19th century founder as a prophet, face particular animosity. In the 1970s they were declared non-Muslims, and in the 1980s they were banned from calling their places of worship mosques and from preaching their faith. Many members of the community fled the country, but a number of worshippers were massacred in an attack in 2005.

Several factors enhance popular concern over morality and a desire to uphold an Islamic society. Widespread corruption intensifies the appeal of fundamentalist demands for Islamic purity and justice. The struggle against Indian rule in Kashmir also strengthens the appeal of political Islam. However, rival Islamic groups often manipulate the sympathies of the population. Iran and Saudi Arabia, for example, apparently subsidize Shi'a and Sunni schools (respectively) that sometimes become centers for violence within Pakistan as well as across its borders.

Ignorance strengthens the appeal of groups that preach hatred based on ethnic and religious differences. In some areas, only a small minority of adults can read, and given the size of its population, Pakistan spends relatively little on education. As recently as the 1980s, children averaged only 1.9 years of schooling, compared with 2.4 in India. As always, boys

Mangla Dam powerhouse   Courtesy of the World Bank (Tomas Sennett)

A rural scene in the Sindh area, Pakistan Courtesy of the World Bank

attend on average rather more; girls, very much less.

In 1998, soldiers visited every government school in Punjab. They discovered that many schools existed only on paper. Everything from teachers to exams, even repairs and sports results, had been faked. A government report showed that nearly half (40%) of all teachers turned up at work only once per month, to collect their pay. In many cases, the pay hardly provides subsistence living.

The most important private system begins with rural schools and culminates in the Aga Khan University hospital and medical school. The spiritual leader of millions of *Ismaili* Muslims scattered through some 25 countries of Asia and Africa, the Aga Khan sponsors a variety of charitable works. The Ismailis form one Shi'a portion of Islam and accept Ismail, an 8th-century descendant of the prophet, as the seventh and last Imam.

Higher education replicates the pattern, with some private colleges and universities earning strong reputations. By contrast, many state institutions face budgetary problems and their graduates lack respect because of widespread cheating scandals.

Economy: After its creation in 1947, Pakistan made progress from an exclusively agricultural economy, but farm products still account for much of the national income. Besides the fertile soil of the Indus basin, few natural resources exist. Only minor oil reserves have been found, though substantial natural gas deposits exist in Baluchistan. Industrialization

developed around local farm products, particularly cotton textiles.

The valley of the Indus forms the largest canal-irrigated area in the world. Further development is being carried forward by the Indus Basin Development Fund Agreement, supported by the World Bank and several western nations. The largest irrigation projects have been the huge Mangla Dam on the Jhelum tributary and the even larger Tarbela Dam. These dams greatly increased the land under irrigation, and they supply large amounts of electricity. However, because forests in the watersheds above the dams are being stripped away, river waters have become clogged with mud. At the present rate of silting, the Tarbela Dam will be useful for only about 50 years.

Reacting against the dominance of industry by an alleged elite of "22 Families," Zulfikar Ali Bhutto—himself a wealthy landlord—nationalized most large private firms. By 1990 the government owned some 80% of industry. Ironically, when she won power, his daughter, Benazir Bhutto, attempted to privatize some of the same firms. The process proved both difficult and slow. Pakistani businessmen know the virtue of keeping wealth hidden, and the stock market is too small and erratic to absorb large blocks of shares. Sales to foreign investors can provide foreign exchange and managerial skills, but they risk political condemnation. Most of all, though, corruption has plagued all privatization attempts.

The Bhuttos owned land. By contrast, as a businessman, Nawaz Sharif favored a flourishing private economy. His

government sold a few inefficient firms, opened the stock markets to foreign capital, and loosened restrictions on foreign exchange. It reduced regulations over new machinery and factories to encourage private companies to invest.

Nevertheless, the country presents many obstacles to business. The costs of borrowing are very high, and the local market frequently proves too small for an efficient scale of production. Heavy indirect taxation of industry, to compensate for the almost complete absence of taxes on the farming and retail sectors means high-priced supplies, and the low level of education accounts for much of the low productivity per worker.

To provide the two or three million additional jobs annually for new workers requires steady economic growth. In Pakistan's case, this is threatened by poor educational achievements, a decrepit infrastructure, growing pollution, and an investment climate marred by ethnic violence. On the other hand, massive investments in banking and Karachi real estate by companies in Dubai offers hope that foreign funds may someday spark faster economic growth. The problems of spreading resultant wealth equitably, will likely prove as difficult for Pakistan as it has for neighboring India.

For years, under Dr. Abdul Qadeer Khan, Pakistan's nuclear industry secretly worked hard, with stolen plans, to construct the centrifuges necessary to enrich uranium for nuclear weapons. The broad outlines of the industry were suspected well before the first test explosions in 1997.

Farmer inspecting a new tractor Courtesy of the World Bank

Pakistan

However, six years later the discovery of tubes for centrifuges on a vessel bound for Libya enabled investigators from the U.S. and other countries to sketch the outline of a Pakistani "cash for bombs" network. Plans, supplies, and perhaps vital materials were shipped to Libya, Iran, and North Korea. For the moment, at least, world attention has halted that export business.

The Future: When Imran Khan came to office in 2018, it was on the back of claims that he was an outsider who could deal with towering corruption. Certainly, an unusual window of opportunity has opened up, giving Pakistan a rare chance to leave behind the problems that plagued the Bhutto and Sharif administrations. In other respects, however, it represents a continuation of business as usual. For all his populist posturing, few dispute that the true power behind Imran Khan is the military. For the time being, this may mean a period of relative political stability. However, such stability too often comes at a cost to democracy. On the other hand, Imran Khan's anti-militant push may place him on a trajectory to conflict with Pakistan's top generals. For now, the prime minister claims that he has the support of the army and the intelligence services in seeking to dismantle the militant groups that have flourished, particularly in the border areas with Afghanistan. But the ISI has played an active role in creating and nurturing many of these groups over the past four decades and is unlikely to relinquish them willingly. What is clear, is that Pakistan cannot hope to tackle endemic poverty as long as it continues to cultivate domestic and regional instability. With its currency having lost more than a quarter of its value over the past year, a yawning current account deficit, and galloping inflation, the challenges facing Pakistan are enormous.

The Democratic Socialist Republic of Sri Lanka

The way home from school on a rainy afternoon

Area: 25,332 square miles (65,610 square kilometers).

Population: 21.4 million.

Capital City: Colombo (750,000 in the city; 5.6 million in the metropolitan area); Parliament meets in Sri Jayawardene-pura Kotte.

Climate: Warm throughout the year, except for comfortably cool temperatures in the higher mountains. It rains almost continuously from May to August in the Wet Zone of the southwest; elsewhere rainfall varies unpredictably.

Neighboring Countries: At its closest, India lies some 33 miles (about 53 kilometers) away across the Palk Strait.

Time Zone: GMT +6.

Official Languages: Sinhala; Tamil (majority in the north).

Other Principal Tongue: English (among the educated).

Ethnic Background: The main communities identified by language and tradition are Sinhalese (73%), Tamil (19%), Moor (7%), Eurasian Burgher, and Malay.

Principal Religions: Buddhism (70%), Hinduism (13%), Islam (10%), and Christianity (mostly Catholicism; 7%).

Chief Commercial Products: Textiles and clothing, tea, rubber, rice, consumer goods, petroleum products, spices, coconuts, sugarcane, manioc, and gemstones.

Major Trading Partners: India, China, the United States, Singapore, the United Arab Emirates, and the United Kingdom.

Currency: Rupee (1 rupee = 100 cents).

Former Colonial Status: British Crown Colony (1802–1928); self-governing British Colony (1928–48).

National Days: February 4 (1948; independence from British rule).

Chief of State: Gotabaya Rajapaksa, President.

Head of Government: Mahinda Rajapaksa, Prime Minister.

National Flag: Centered on a dark crimson field with gold borders is a large gold lion in profile facing the pole and holding a sword in its right paw. At the pole are two vertical stripes, one green and one saffron, framed together in a gold border.

Gross Domestic Product: $87.17 billion.

GDP per capita: $3,842.

The pear-shaped island of Sri Lanka, or Ceylon as it was first known in English, lies at the southeastern tip of India. Its climate and people resemble those of the nearby regions of India, but under the influence of Buddhism it developed a distinctive culture. Until weakened by civil war in recent decades, Sri Lanka offered the possibility of social development—good health and education—despite relatively low incomes. Today the country is recovering from the scars of that war, which claimed the lives of an estimated 80,000 to 100,000 people, and managing a new terrorism threat posed by globally-connected militant Islamists.

Most of Sri Lanka, including all the northern half of the island and a coastal belt around the south end, is low, flat country. The remaining one-fifth, lies above 2,000 feet (over 600 meters) in elevation, with mountains rising to peaks above 8,000 feet (over 2,400 meters). These highlands force the humid summer monsoon winds from the southwest to rise, producing heavy rainfall in the southwestern quarter of the island and earning it the title "the wet zone" in recognition of its annual precipitation of 100–200 inches (2,500–5,000 millimeters).

The rest of the island forms the dry zone, although its rainfall would be considered sufficient in cooler climates. Rain in the dry zone is unpredictable; it may be quite sudden and heavy, causing

Sri Lanka

**Former Prime Minister
Ratnasiri Wickremanayake**

damaging floods that dump precious water into the ocean. Precipitation in the dry zone also comes from the northeast winter monsoon. Ground water can be raised for irrigation in most of the dry zone, from Jaffna to Batticaloa. Given the tropical climate, agriculture revolves around patterns of rainfall rather than temperature. Wet and dry seasons replace the familiar summer and winter of temperate climates.

The two major population groups inhabit distinctly different climate zones. The Sinhalese majority is concentrated in the wet zone, while the Sri Lankan Tamils live almost exclusively in the northern and northeastern limits of the dry zone—principally on or around the Jaffna Peninsula.

History: Civilization, cities, and governments began in the dry zone of the island's north, and early ethnic conflicts remain today. Sinhalese kings had already established their capital at Anuradhapura in the 3rd century B.C. when Buddhism gradually spread over the island and absorbed many existing religious practices. Sinhalese society skillfully designed irrigation systems and storage reservoirs to make maximum use of the dry zone's scarce water, and an impressive civilization developed.

Attracted by the prosperity of the kingdom, adventurers from India occasionally tried to seize the island, but they never succeeded in retaining it. With some interruptions, Anuradhapura remained the capital for over 1,300 years. In the 14th century a Dravidian ruler from South India succeeded in establishing a Tamil

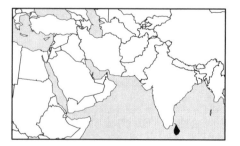

kingdom on the northern end of the island. Meanwhile, aided by improved technology, Sinhalese society had moved south into the wet zone, which had apparently remained dense jungle. By the 16th century, Sinhalese kings ruled from Kotte, near modern Colombo.

The first European sailing vessels came from Portugal and reached Colombo Harbor in 1505. Searching for spices, the Portuguese soon built forts and, by the end of the 16th century, laid claim to all Ceylon. However, the highland kingdom of Kandy maintained its independence.

Superior in both business and warfare, the Dutch East India Company contested Portuguese domination of Ceylon's trade in the 17th century. The Dutch captured Colombo in 1656 and soon controlled Ceylon's trade by holding all the ports. The Kandyan kings, who had hoped the Dutch would recognize them as rulers of the entire island, remained in control of only the interior. The last Sinhalese king of Kandy was captured and exiled in 1815 by the British.

Dutch domination noticeably influenced the island's communities. Many settlers arrived from Holland and other European countries; their descendants became known as Burghers. From their Indonesian colonies the Dutch brought soldiers and workers. Their descendants remained

Muslim: the Malay are still distinct from the earlier Muslim communities who are known as Moors. In a few cases the Dutch rulers moved either Tamil or Sinhalese communities to other parts of the island.

When Holland allied with France during the Napoleonic wars in the 1790s, British forces captured Ceylon and declared it a Crown Colony in 1802. It proved a success. Plantations to raise coconuts, cotton, coffee, sugar, indigo, and opium flourished by the mid-19th century. When a plant disease ruined the coffee industry, tea began to replace the coffee bean. When a shortage of plantation workers developed, laborers were imported from southern India, most of them Tamils. Their descendants formed a separate community known as the Indian Tamils, and they made a strong impact on the wet zone Sinhalese regions where tea plantations were located.

In the late 19th century, a cultural reaction developed against European culture and rule. Interest in Buddhism and Hinduism revived and strengthened in the 20th century. Renewed interest also arose in ancient arts and literature. These movements all encouraged national feeling by restoring attachment to the period before European domination.

British officials very slowly permitted representative government on the island. In 1931 all adults received voting rights,

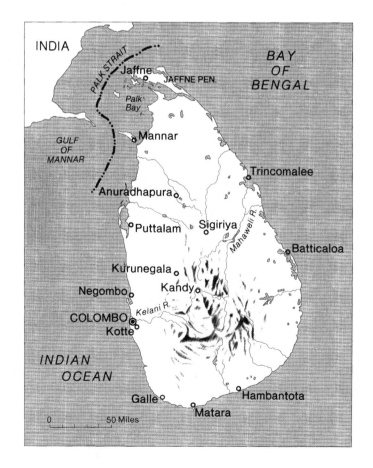

Fishermen at sea with their catamarans

within British rule. The constitution of 1946, with provisions to protect the Tamils and other minorities, established the legislative system. Independence came peacefully in 1948, and two political parties have dominated Sinhalese politics ever since.

Representing the Sinhala elite, the United National Party (UNP) formed the first post-independence government. Its great rival, the more nationalistic Sri Lanka Freedom Party led by Solomon Bandaranaike took power in 1956 and enacted a number of reforms. The new government stripped English of its official status and adopted Sinhala as the only official language. Tamil was permitted "reasonable use." Violence immediately broke out in many Tamil areas. After Mr. Bandaranaike was murdered in 1959, the party was held together by his widow. She led the party to victory at the polls and became the first female prime minister of any country.

Besides differing over Tamil rights, the two major parties clashed over economic issues, with the Freedom Party typically advocating for socialist reform. Mrs. Bandaranaike again won power in 1970 but soon faced a guerrilla uprising led by the People's Liberation Front, known by its Sinhala initials JVP. At the time a communist group whose doctrines attracted many educated but unemployed young people, the JVP capitalized on the lack of economic development, and its Maoist-influenced uprising became violent. With foreign military aid, Mrs. Bandaranaike's government suppressed the JVP.

She also undertook several radical changes. Although a member of a well-to-do and influential family, she adopted socialist policies such as supplying free rice, but this led to economic recession and shortages. Symbolically, a 1972 Constitution ended the nation's ties to the British Crown and changed Ceylon's name to the Socialist Republic of Sri Lanka. The presidency became largely ceremonial, while Mrs. Bandaranaike continued as prime minister.

These decisions and her style of ruling provoked opposition. Continued high unemployment and a declining economy, coupled with charges of mismanagement and corruption, led to her electoral defeat by the UNP in 1977.

From Ethnic Strife to War

The worst communal violence since independence swept the country in 1983, after rebels of the Liberation Tigers of Tamil Eelam ambushed troops near Jaffna. Seeking revenge, Sinhalese mobs (and sometimes security forces) attacked Tamils in Colombo, Kandy, and elsewhere. Altogether some 2,000 Tamils died, while arson left 50,000 homeless, mainly in Colombo. Calm was not restored for more than a week. Most Tamils suspected that the country's leadership was behind the riots, and this strengthened the appeal of the Tamil Tigers.

Parliament catered to Sinhalese nationalism by banning any party that advocated separatism or even autonomy. This move ended any effective Tamil representation in parliament. While Sinhalese leaders did attempt to reduce tensions and violence when convenient, the ethnic rift had become too wide to bridge with minor reforms.

As Tamil guerrilla activity increased, their terrorist acts were matched by massacres perpetrated by the largely Sinhalese army. By 1985 the dispute had plunged Sri Lanka into open civil war. Sinhalese leaders intended to reassert (Sinhalese) government rule over a united country, but to protect their cultural identity many Tamils demanded an independent state of their own.

During the first stage of the war, Tamil guerrillas attacked the police, army units, and Sinhalese civilians in the north and east. Headed by Velupillai Prabhakaran, the Tiger leadership developed a disciplined ferocity among their followers, including a willingness to die for the cause. Their fanaticism—along with refuge, training, and arms from the Indian state of Tamil Nadu—enabled the Tamil Tigers to defeat other Tamil militias and take control of the Jaffna Peninsula. In response, the Sinhala army and police tended to treat all Tamils as rebels. This had the effect of extinguishing moderate political viewpoints.

In 1987, Prime Minister Rajiv Gandhi of India sought to intervene. He pressured the two sides to accept a ceasefire and a small force of Indian peacekeepers to maintain order while disarming the Tamil militias. After peace was achieved, Sri Lanka would unite the northern (Tamil) province with the Eastern province, where Tamils, Muslims, and Sinhalese lived in similar numbers.

The agreement aroused wide Sinhalese hostility. Moreover, the Tigers soon stopped surrendering heavy weapons, apparently never intending to keep Gandhi's agreement. They attacked other Tamil groups and massacred hundreds of Sinhalese civilians living in the east. Facing Sinhalese accusations that India failed to defend innocent civilians, the Indian military mounted a major offensive against the Tigers in Jaffna. Although the Indian force rose to 50,000 troops, far outnumbering the entire Sri Lankan army of 32,000, victory proved elusive. The second stage of the war ended inconclusively, but the army replaced Indian troops in Jaffna. Rajiv Gandhi was later assassinated by a Tamil Tiger suicide bomber.

The Tamil Tigers launched another offensive in 1990 that forced the army to abandon Jaffna and most of the peninsula. The Tigers attempted to offset the military's superior numbers and equipment with daring attacks, and increasingly depended on teenagers who entered battle

Sri Lanka

Village girl with a basket of mangoes

with cyanide capsules, ready to prevent capture by committing suicide. In the Sinhalese heartland, the Tigers assassinated military commanders and politicians. A suicide bomber on a bicycle even killed President Premadasa.

Elections in 1994 brought Chandrika Kumaratunga of the Freedom Party to power. She negotiated an extended ceasefire with the Tigers, which they again used for military purposes, this time infiltrating down the east coast as far south as Batticaloa. They then broke the cease-fire suddenly. War resumed.

Once better-equipped, the troops recaptured Jaffna and much of the peninsula. The Tigers responded with human wave attacks and truck bombs that devastated economic targets in Colombo, including the Central Bank and the port. Another

bomb exploded in Kandy, at a venerated shrine housing one of the Buddha's teeth. It missed the precious relic but disrupted celebrations of the island's 50 years of independence.

Anticipating a truce, in 2000 the military relaxed. Again, the Tamil Tigers struck, concentrating on the southern tip of the Jaffna peninsula. The army's large base at Elephant Pass dominated the causeway linking the peninsula with the mainland. Using long-range artillery, the Tigers shelled the camp, and then advanced to capture its water supply. When the direct assault came, garrison troops vastly outnumbered the attackers, but the fort fell quickly. It was the greatest battlefield victory of the war until 2008–09. At the height of their power, the Tamil Tigers controlled about one-third of the country.

With secure access to the peninsula, the Tigers moved steadily towards Jaffna and the vital airstrip nearby. Sri Lanka appealed to India, Israel, and other nations for immediate military assistance to avert the city's fall and the defeat of some 35,000 troops. Reinforced and rearmed with advanced weapons, the military halted the Tigers' advance just outside Jaffna.

A dramatic suicide raid on Colombo's international airport and military airbase in 2001 significantly changed the military, economic, and political realities. The loss of eight military aircraft gutted the air force, and the army proved unable to reply with a similarly devastating attack on the Tigers.

President Kumaratunga's coalition disintegrated. The opposition UNP won the elections that followed. and formed a cabinet under Ranil Wickremesinghe. Taking the initiative, Wickremesinghe quickly met many Tiger demands. After the Tigers announced a ceasefire, he restored trade with the north and ended an embargo that had kept even food and medicine out of the area. Norwegian mediation arranged a "permanent" ceasefire, with detailed agreements to treat many expected problems. The government lifted restrictions on travel that had long been used to harass Tamil civilians. The Tigers in turn opened highway A9, the route north to Jaffna, for the first time in a decade.

The "Permanent" Ceasefire

In retrospect, it seems the ceasefire was only possible because the Tigers sought a respite from warfare. Besides the evident difficulties of drafting additional troops, concern over public relations also played a role. Britain and Canada had declared the group a terrorist organization and, like the United States, froze many of its off shore accounts. In response, talk of self-determination and a Tamil homeland began to replace calls for independence. Velupillai Prabhakaran apologized for mistreating Muslims and expelling them from Jaffna.

Harsh living conditions within the Tigers' area of influence also encouraged the search for peace. Although perhaps 200,000 civilians had emigrated, similar numbers remained as impoverished refugees. Mines often littered roads and abandoned farmland. Many buildings damaged in the fighting had not been repaired, and some schools lacked roofs, windows, and books. Lighting usually came from kerosene lamps: an entire generation grew up without electricity. Unfortunately, the Tigers themselves inflicted further suffering after the ceasefire, particularly by abducting children to serve in their military.

The rapid progress of negotiations noticeably improved the living conditions of ordinary people. However, the Tigers refused to disarm, and they demanded the immediate creation of an autonomous zone in the north and east. The Sea Tigers (the naval wing of the Tamil Tigers) broke the terms of the ceasefire, while forced enlistment of children did the same on land. In 2003, negotiations collapsed, although fighting did not resume immediately. The Indonesian tsunami of 2004 hit both Tamil and Sinhalese coastal areas with great force. It killed over 30,000 and rendered hundreds of thousands homeless and jobless. The fishing and tourist industries suffered severe damage, even on the southwestern coast. International aid poured into the island, but a critical question arose concerning who would distribute it. The Tigers desired to distribute relief supplies themselves in Tamil areas, rather than permit aid agencies to operate, presumably to avert any other focus of popular loyalty. However, without government approval, the agencies could not turn over supplies to a rebel movement. Negotiations failed over this, too.

Sinhalese Politics and Strife

In amazing feats for a nation drenched in ethnic bloodshed and sometimes facing terrorist campaigns, Sri Lanka held provincial, presidential, and parliamentary elections throughout the civil war era. The two major parties, the United National Party and the Freedom Party alternated in office, but they rarely won an absolute majority in parliament. This frequently forced unstable coalitions.

National reconciliation proved elusive even within the Sinhalese community. In the late 1980s and early 1990s violence

**Former President
Chandrika Kumaratunga**

struck within the majority community. The communist JVP that had launched a guerrilla war in the 1970s now adopted the cause of militant Sinhalese nationalism and launched a bloody revolt in the south. Members of the ruling UNP, among others, were assassinated. Although the JVP ultimately failed, the cost of victory had been high. Up to 60,000 people had died, many at the hands of death squads. Most victims were innocent, secretly denounced by rivals or opponents.

After a vicious parliamentary campaign, in 2001 the UNP won an unexpectedly decisive victory. Following a brief constitutional crisis, the UNP and its allies formed a cabinet under Ranil Wickremesinghe. Chandrika Kumaratunga held the presidency. The daughter of Sirimavo Bandaranaike, Kumaratunga led the Freedom Party, which formed the parliamentary opposition.

Although Prime Minister Wickremesinghe showed notable sympathy with many Tamil demands, President Kumaratunga proved far more suspicious of the Tigers. Other groups that were wary of Tamil separatism, even within a federal Sri Lanka, included the often mistreated Muslims, Buddhist clergy, and the militantly nationalist JVP. In 2004, Kumaratunga called early elections.

The UNP lost the elections. Wickremesinghe took credit for the ceasefire and promised voters that the emerging prosperity was the first reward of peace, but many voters felt that prosperity had reached only the rich and considered the UNP corrupt. Some Sinhalese voters thought the Tigers had gained too much from the ceasefire; instead of supporting the UNP, Tamil voters chose the Tamil National Alliance, a front for the Tigers. A plurality favored the president's Freedom Party/JVP alliance and gave it 105 of the parliament's 225 seats. Another party, led by militant Buddhist clergy, opposed concessions to the Tamils. It too gained seats.

President Kumaratunga's successor as Freedom Party leader, Mahinda Rajapaksa, won a narrow victory in the 2005 presidential elections, partly because Tamils had to vote outside Tiger-controlled areas. On the crucial issue of the day, the civil war, Rajapaksa represented the uncompromising wing of the party and the Sinhala community. He allied with the JVP and the Buddhist monks' party, rejecting a federal state as a compromise solution. The president and the defense minister, his brother Gotabaya Rajapaksa, determined to crush the Tigers rather than compromise over their demands.

The Tigers' leader, Velupillai Prabhakaran, played into their hands. In 2006 the group broke the ceasefire with assassinations and attacks. The Tigers even

bombed the country's major airbase with their small air force of prop-driven planes.

After narrowly escaping a suicide attack that left fragments near his heart, the military commander, General Sarath Fonseka, joined the Rajapaksa brothers in his commitment to defeat the Tigers permanently. Strengthened by arms from China, Pakistan, and Russia, he doubled the size of the army and adopted aggressive tactics at sea, destroying the Tigers' supply vessels far offshore. With new jets and helicopters, the air force attacked suspected Tiger positions ruthlessly, and on land commandos struck key defensive points.

The army then took advantage of its much larger forces to launch multiple attacks from different directions and squeeze the Tigers out of the northern third of the island. From the northwestern coast and from the south, troops advanced on Kilinochchi, the Tigers' administrative center. That city fell at the end of 2008; a few days later Elephant Pass did as well. For the first time in decades, the government controlled the entire length of the A-9 highway up the center of the island to Jaffna. Unable to obtain a ceasefire, and determined not to surrender, the Tigers made their last stand north of Mullaitivu on the northeast coast.

It seems clear that Prabhakaran and the Tigers' leadership considered Tamil civilians their ultimate trump card. Throughout the fighting in 2008 and 2009, the quarter-million civilians under their control were forced to retreat with rebel units. Those seeking to flee were often shot. Hoping to win international pressure for a ceasefire, the Tigers claimed that the military had inflicted large numbers of civilian casualties, many from heavy artillery even in a "No Fire" zone that the army had pledged to honor. The military denied these claims, and both sides kept away independent reporters, so the truth itself became a casualty.

In May 2009, the Tigers collapsed, with most of their leaders killed in the final days. As many as 10,000 Tamils, most of them civilians, had died during the desperate final weeks of the battle.

Victory left the Sri Lankan government triumphant and politically supreme, but burdened with countless refugees, most of them ill-fed and ill-housed in strictly-controlled camps. One crucial challenge facing the government was to free and rehabilitate the refugees without providing new opportunities for any revived Tiger activities. A year after victory, many had returned to their often-destroyed homes and farms. However, some 80,000 still remained incarcerated.

Translating military victory into political dominance, in 2010 President Rajapaksa called presidential elections nearly

Sri Lanka

two years early. Campaigning as the architect of victory over insurgency, he solidly defeated the opposition candidate, Sarath Fonseka. The general who masterminded the military's final assault, Fonseka later accused Defense Minister Gotabhaya Rajapaksa, the president's brother, of ordering the execution of Tiger leaders as they surrendered. Weeks later, the brothers' Sri Lanka Freedom Alliance achieved an overwhelming victory in parliamentary elections, gaining nearly two-thirds of all seats. Human rights observers noted, however, that the media had been intimidated, and that government resources had assisted Freedom Alliance candidates.

Events in the following months confirmed that the Rajapaksa brothers intended to rule forcefully, extend the president's powers, and disregard press freedoms. Few symbolic gestures of healing were offered to the Tamils; instead, Tamil youths were pressed into singing the national anthem in Sinhala. General Fonseka was arrested on charges of conspiracy.

Given Sinhalese pride in the Tamil Tigers' defeat, President Rajapaksa enjoyed great domestic popularity. Parliament readily passed anti-terrorist legislation that ignored human rights, and the Sinhalese public supported statements that aggressively attacked critics of government policies. One cabinet member, for example, threatened to "break the limbs" of those who "betrayed" the country. Less fortunate critics seemed to disappear.

Upset by court rulings, the government moved to impeach Chief Justice Shirani Bandaranayake on corruption charges just one year after she was appointed. Despite rulings by two different courts that the process was irregular and illegal, parliament convicted her. At least initially, many of the nation's lawyers supported the chief justice and opposed the appointment of a former attorney general as her successor.

After the War

By 2012 the country had progressed significantly after the war. Foreign assistance aided in the construction of new roads and ports, and the economy grew fairly rapidly, with GDP per capita rising by 18% between 2010 and 2012. Symbolic of the progress, the Menik Farm refugee camp, which had housed about 300,000 Tamils at the end of the war, closed. In another achievement, partly because of its efforts to trace children missing from the war, the country was removed from the UN's blacklist of nations providing inadequately for child welfare.

Nevertheless, Sri Lanka remained on the defensive in several international forums. The British documentary "Sri Lanka's Killing Fields" showed apparent executions of Tamil men and the corpses of sexually assaulted women. The UN's special investigator considered the video footage authentic and evidence of human rights violations. Gradually the Rajapaksa brothers shifted the government's position. Instead of claiming that the military had not killed civilians, Gotabhaya Rajapaksa admitted that some soldiers may not have withstood the pressures of war. While admitting that perhaps 10,000 civilians had died, he strongly denied that genocide had occurred. Nevertheless, in 2013 the UN's Human Rights Council passed a highly critical resolution that encouraged an "independent and credible investigation" into alleged war crimes.

Mahinda Rajapaksa called presidential elections for January 2015, two years before the end of his term. Conditions seemed auspicious: new highways, an impressive new port and airport, and rapid economic growth pointed to satisfied voters. The opposition was weak and fragmented. However, just weeks before the election, Rajapaksa's Minister of Health, Maithripala Sirisena, bolted the government and declared his own candidacy. Despite having served as general secretary of the Rajapaksa's SLFP, Sirisena soon formed a coalition of almost all opposition parties, from the conservative United National Party to the leftist JVP.

It seemed logical that Rajapaksa, who led the country to victory over the Tamil Tigers, could count on massive support from the Sinhalese majority. To persuade voters of the need for change, Sirisena campaigned against corruption and the "nepotistic Rajapaksa regime." In fact, the president's brothers did hold major government positions: one was minister of defense, another directed economic development, and a third served as speaker of parliament. Sirisena also condemned recent constitutional changes that had removed the president's two-term limit, alleging the president had "acted like an emperor."

Sirisena's ability to unite disparate groups with grievances against the

Bodhisattva Avalokiteshvara, 8th–9th century A.D., gilt, bronze and crystal in the National Museum, Colombo

Rajapaksas—Muslims, Christians, Tamils, the Buddhist monks' party, and others—proved as vital to the campaign as did electioneering slogans. A farmer by background and training, Sirisena also appealed to ordinary Sinhalese as one of them. In a tightly-fought (and occasionally violent) election campaign, Sirisena won a narrow but clear victory with more than 51% of the vote. Fearing that the election might be stolen, he took the presidential oath the next day, and appointed Ranil Wickremesinghe prime minister.

Advocates of expanded democracy hailed constitutional amendments overseen by Sirisena, that set presidential term limits and restored a semblance of balance between presidential and legislative power. However, in 2018 Sirisena plunged Sri Lanka into political crisis, when he appointed former president Mahinda Rajapaksa to the role of prime minister, dismissing the incumbent Wickremesinghe. Wickremesinghe, the majority of the parliament, and opposition parties refused to acknowledge the appointment of Rajapaksa, stating that Sirisena's move was unconstitutional. After Sirisena dissolved parliament the Supreme Court overturned the decision.

About 3 million Sri Lankans form a scattered global diaspora. Thousands of Sri Lankan Tamils continue to seek asylum—predominantly in Western countries and often with limited success—claiming persecution and ongoing human rights abuses.

Minorities in Sri Lanka often find themselves at the receiving end of Sinhalese mob violence, a clear remnant of decades of civil war. In February 2018, simmering tensions between Sinhalese Buddhists and minority Muslims erupted into violence. Mosques and Muslim businesses were attacked.

In 2019, the island was once again rocked by violence. Not unfamiliar with terrorist attacks, the Easter Day bombings of churches, luxury hotels, and other sites across the city of Colombo, was nonetheless shocking, in a country that has made steady progress towards peace. A total of 253 people were killed in the coordinated suicide attacks, with at least 500 more injured. The targets were predominantly Sri Lankan Christians and foreign nationals.

Islamist terrorism is a phenomenon previously unheard of in a country where traditionally the main fault-line falls between the (overwhelmingly Buddhist) Sinhalese and those of Tamil ethnicity (mostly Hindu, with a significant Christian minority; Tamil-speaking Muslims are considered a separate ethnic group). It has become clear, since, that Muslims are now the subject of considerable persecution. Hardline Sinhalese Buddhist groups have targeted Muslims as an "existential threat." The government has used the COVID-19 crisis to implement discriminatory policies, such as forcible cremation against the religious beliefs and sensibilities of Sri Lankan Muslims.

Culture: Culturally, modern Sri Lanka looks in two directions for its inspiration. Extremists may try to exclude one or the other of the two elements, but most people look both to ancient culture and to the technical advantages of modern industrial civilization. For example, some contemporary Sri Lankan artists reflect the influence of Europe, but their works still convey the uniqueness of a native tradition.

The oldest and most famous paintings in Sri Lanka are wall frescoes of maidens at Sigiriya, the palace of a 5th century king, Kasyapa I. The palace itself lies below a rock summit, and for decades it served as a monument to Sinhalese achievements. In the 1990s, archeologists discovered the full extent of the palace gardens, the largest and most complex in Asia. Given the dry climate, the gardens required a complex system of cisterns and irrigation tunnels to maintain fountains, streams, and a water garden some 300 feet (approximately 90 meters) long.

Much earlier architectural monuments from the past impress the visitor at Anuradhapura, for a millennium the Buddhist capital in the dry zone. Enormous domes known as stupas preserved relics, while temples and shrines were filled with stone carvings. The city's skillful engineers were masters of designing complexes of buildings complete with large bathing pools. To provide water in the dry zone, the planners laid out a series of reservoirs and aqueducts to supply not only the capital but also villages along the way. In recent years some of these water systems have been restored and put back into service with new irrigation and hydro-electric projects belonging fully to the 20th century.

Sculpture was another ancient means of artistic expression of beauty and religious feeling, as was Sinhala poetry. Literature took the form of grammatical studies and philosophy. Ancient literary pieces were all written in the Sinhala language, but modern literature also appears in Tamil. There are newspapers circulating in both languages and in English.

Economy: During British rule, Ceylon tea became world-famous, and other plantations produced crops like rubber for export. These provided the income and foreign exchange to pay for imports of rice, other foods and manufactured goods. After independence, socialist politicians who distrusted international markets attempted to make the economy less dependent on foreign sales of tea and rubber. Farmers were encouraged to raise food crops for the local market, especially rice, which for some years was distributed free to all.

Today the country remains among the world's top five largest exporters of tea. In this context, many of the Indian Tamils who formed the industry's workforce were gradually repatriated, and by the late 1990s plantations provided only one-third of the crop. The rest came from 500,000 small farms that sold the green leaves to processors. In the 1990s, difficulties in two large export markets, Iraq and Russia, reduced sales and profits. Although the government removed the tea export tax in 1993, many processors and farmers faced serious losses, given low world prices.

Replacing tea as the greatest export are garments and other textiles. Beginning with an investment promotion zone established beside the international airport in 1978, textile manufacturing has spread across the southern part of the country. Low wages and a literate, mostly female workforce have attracted foreign firms and joint ventures to the industry. Other factories now manufacture electronics components for export as well. However, in the mid-1990s workers demanded higher pay and better conditions, and many went on strike. Militants even held a manager hostage. This apparently surprised companies that expected little union activity. In the words of one foreign owner, "We want the government to keep industrial peace and discipline."

President Maithripala Sirisena

Sri Lanka

Tea pickers on a plantation near Colombo

Hundreds of thousands of Sri Lankan women also work abroad, chiefly as maids in Kuwait and the United Arab Emirates. When Iraq invaded Kuwait, some 100,000 Sri Lankans, the vast majority of them women, lost their employment and returned home.

Sri Lanka's largest single development project, in the northeast, consisted of a series of dams on the Mahaweli River, the country's largest. However, the project has been widely criticized for a design that produced hydroelectric power instead of irrigation for the (Tamil-populated) countryside and for construction flaws that may reduce the long-term potential of the project.

With great natural beauty, a warm climate, and a variety of appealing sights for visitors, tourism developed rapidly in the early 1980s, bringing in about 15% of foreign earnings. However, the JVP attacked tourist centers, and the twenty-six year war with the Tigers discouraged foreigners from visiting. In addition, the 2004 tsunami destroyed many hotels. The 2019 Colombo bombings hit a tourist industry that has made great strides in recent years. In the month following the attacks visits were down a massive 70%.

Notwithstanding civil war, Sri Lanka showed one way to a relatively high quality of life without high incomes or large per-capita use of energy and natural resources. Compared to surrounding countries, the nation is well educated, and its citizens enjoy average life expectancy rates of over 75 years. They also enjoy over 100 non-working days a year, likely the world record. Birth rates and death rates both rank low, the courts and democracy muddle through, and potential seems to exist for a quality of life which, although not rich, allows the simple pleasures to be enjoyed in relative security.

The Future: As a democracy, Sri Lanka stands at an important crossroads. The democratic removal of the Rajapaksa brothers from positions of power in politics and the military marked a hopeful reversal of the worst encroachments of authoritarianism in the post-civil war era. However, it was short lived. Back in power, Gotabaya Rajapaksa moved to consolidate his control, cracking down on dissent and pushing through constitutional amendments that give the president extraordinary powers over the parliament and various bureaucratic arms..

The United Nations has criticized Sri Lanka for slow progress in addressing war crimes and human rights abuses. Failure to face up to some of the military's worst excesses in the final days and weeks of the civil war risks exacerbating underlying tensions. Given the likely complicity of the Rajapaksa family in these alleged war crimes, it is unlikely that they will be aired in the near future.

Nonetheless, there is reason to be optimistic that Sri Lanka can pull itself out of its troubled past. A long history of elections, even during the worst years of conflict, creates a firm foundation for Sri Lankan democracy. Although the government largely denies the existence of an ethnic crisis in the country, instead framing it as an issue of terrorism, local-level reconciliation efforts continue.

A fisherman's catch

Abu Musa (Gap Sabzu) and the Greater and Lesser Tunbs

Area: Abu Musa, 4.9 square miles (12.8 square kilometers) land mass; Greater and Lesser Tunbs, 3.98 and 0.77 square miles (10.3 and 2 square kilometers) respectively.

Population: Abu Musa, 2,200, primarily of *Bandari* (Arab) ethnicity; Greater and Lesser Tunbs, at most a few hundred inhabitants.

Although the territory is insignificant in size, and the population is vanishingly small, current tensions in the region and the strategic importance of the narrow Strait of Hormuz at the entrance of the Persian Gulf, make worthy of attention the long running dispute between Iran and the United Arab Emirates over the sovereignty of the three islands.

The islands of Abu Musa, Greater Tunbs, and Lesser Tunbs are hot and humid. Abu Musa has been mined for red iron oxide for over a century and is rich in offshore oil and natural gas. Historically, the inhabitants relied on fishing, along with farming of subsistence crops.

The islands, previously part of various Persian empires, were seized by the British Empire in 1921 and placed under the administrative control of the Emirate of Sharjah. In 1971, just prior to the British withdrawal and the formation of the United Arab Emirates, Iran and Sharjah signed a Memorandum of Understanding, allowing joint control and shared petroleum revenues. Just a day after signing the agreement, Iran occupied the islands, taking full control, against the muted resistance of a small Arab police force stationed there. One policeman was killed and there is disagreement about whether an Arab civilian population on Greater Tunb was forcibly deported.

In 1980, the United Arab Emirates, considering the islands to be "occupied" by Iran, took its claim to the United Nations, but it was rejected by the UN Security Council and the case was closed.

During the Iran–Iraq war, Iran used the islands to fire missiles at Iraqi and Kuwaiti ships, and as a base for soldiers of the Islamic Revolutionary Guard Corp (IRGC).

In the decade following, disputes arose over Sharjah's efforts to develop part of the island of Abu Musa and to populate it with non-native Arabs. Iran consistently refused referral of the matter to the International Court of Justice (ICJ) or any other form of third-party arbitration.

Tensions ratcheted up when Iran's president, Mahmoud Ahmadinejad, made a high-profile visit to Abu Musa in 2012. This was viewed by the United Arab Emirates and much of the international community as a "deliberate provocation." However, in Iran, it was well received. Ahmadinejad's performance fitted a pattern of populist appeals to Iranian nationalism, coupled with belligerent posturing on the global stage.

If used militarily, the islands of Abu Musa, Greater Tunb, and Lesser Tunb could control the traffic of the Gulf and virtually control world oil supplies, making them amongst the most strategically significant disputed territories in the world.

British Indian Ocean Territory (the Chagos Archipelago)

Area: 21,000 square miles (54,000 square kilometers) total; 22 square miles (57 square kilometers) of land.

Population: U.S. and UK military and support personnel.

The British Indian Ocean Territory (BIOT) consists of the Chagos Archipelago, a collection of more than 60 islands situated midway between East Africa and Indonesia, and the surrounding waters. The archipelago consists of the wettest coral isles in the Indian Ocean, with some 145 inches (3,683 millimeters) of rain a year.

The territory, which consists of well over 1,000 islands and islets in all, was initially claimed by Britain in 1814, but it was formally (i.e., officially) established as a territory of Britain in 1965. The reason for this annexation was the territory's strategic value, not just to Britain but also and perhaps more importantly to its ally the United States.

Britain first considered the use of Aldabra for a military base, but these islands, among the last places on earth almost entirely unaffected by human settlement, contain rare birds and giant tortoises, as well as unique species of invertebrates. A determined "Save Aldabra" campaign led by the Royal Society of Britain, the U.S. National Academy of Sciences, and the Smithsonian Institution resulted rather in the leasing of Aldabra to the Royal Society as a wildlife sanctuary. Control of these three island groups was returned to the Seychelles at its independence in 1976.

Instead, in 1966 the United States and Britain signed a 50-year agreement for the use of Diego Garcia, the largest atoll in the Chagos group, as a joint base. That lease has since been extended to 2036. Between 1967 and 1973, Britain forcibly relocated the entire population of the island (at that time, 1,500-1,800 people) to Mauritius and the Seychelles to make way for U.S. military installations.

In 1971 the U.S. Navy constructed a jet landing strip and a communications center. Later, the lagoon was dredged for use as an anchorage, and the runway was lengthened. By 1988 Diego Garcia had become a major permanent U.S. base, the only one between Italy and the Philippines.

The island has been strategically important to the United States for a variety of reasons, primarily because it is has served as a crucial forward operating base. Military installations on Diego Garcia allow the United States to preposition assets in the region (jets, bombers, aircraft carriers, submarines, other ships), and they serve as space to repair and refuel vessels. The island has two runways that can accommodate long-range aircraft. From here, the United States can conduct return operations from Afghanistan to North Africa, and from the Persian Gulf to Taiwan. Over the decades, the United States has poured billions of dollars into the island and its facilities. It has been important to U.S. war efforts in Afghanistan, Iraq, and the broader "War on Terror." However, the long-term future of U.S. interest on the archipelago is far from certain.

After three decades of life in Mauritius and elsewhere, in 2000 the Chagos islanders won an appeal to the High Court in Britain. Arguing that they had not adapted successfully to living in other locations, and suffered widespread poverty and distress, the islanders insisted on the right of return to Diego Garcia itself. Though the court ruled against the islanders' claimed right of return in 2008, recent years have repeatedly seen the issue come to the fore in ways that suggest global public opinion is with the Chagossians. On June 22, 2017, for example, the UN General Assembly voted 94–15 (with 65 abstentions) to support a resolution seeking an advisory opinion from the ICJ at the Hague on the status of the Chagos islands and those who claim those islands as their home. Numerous EU countries—including Belgium, Denmark, Estonia, Finland, France, Germany, Greece, Latvia,

Disputed Territories

the Netherlands, and Spain—did not support Britain's position on the matter, despite close ties to the United Kingdom.

In February 2019, the case came before the ICJ. In the court's non-binding advisory opinion, the occupation of the Indian Ocean archipelago was illegal. The UK was urged to return the Chagos Islands to Mauritius "as rapidly as possible." Months later, the UN General Assembly passed a resolution demanding Britain relinquish control "within six months." The UK insists that the ICJ exceeded its jurisdiction, as it had not consented to arbitration in what it considered a bilateral dispute. It argues that it will cede the territory only when it is no longer needed for defense purposes. The United States

has strongly backed Britain's position, even as support in the General Assembly dropped to a handful of countries. Efforts by the United States to lobby possible allies in the matter were largely unsuccessful. While the United Kingdom faces the embarrassment of losing one of its few remaining colonial holdings (a clear rebuke to lingering British imperialism) the U.S. confronts the possible loss of one of its most important military assets in the world.

The Chagos contain the world's largest coral atoll. The environments of the Chagos Archipelago provide rich biodiversity. Fish, whales, and turtles swim in the waters surrounding the islands. There are significant breeding colonies of

seabirds in the area and a population of impressively large coconut crabs inhabit the islands.

In 2010 the British government announced the establishment of the world's largest marine reserve, in the Chagos Archipelago a 210,000 square mile (approximately 550,000 square kilometer) area, twice the size of Britain. Leaked diplomatic cables showed the United States and Britain saw the establishment of a marine reserve as "the most effective long-term way to prevent any of the Chagos Islands' former inhabitants or their descendants from resettling." Mauritius disputed the legality of the marine reserve. This position was upheld by the Permanent Court of Arbitration in 2015.

The Occupied Territories

Territories occupied by Israel in contravention of international law (the Occupied Territories) include East Jerusalem, Gaza, the Golan Heights, and the West Bank. While Gaza and the West Bank, as Palestinian territories, have been adequately covered in the chapter on the State of Palestine, East Jerusalem deserves special mention, as does the Israeli occupied Syrian territory of Golan (Arabic *Jawlan*).

East Jerusalem

Area: 68 square miles (175 square kilometers) form the proposed international zone recommended by the UN in 1947.
Population: 550,000. The number of Israelis living in East Jerusalem has grown significantly in recent years, reaching some 200,000 by 2017. The city also includes some 320,000 Palestinians as of 2018, the overwhelming majority of whom are Muslim.

The status of the city of Jerusalem is one of the underpinning aspects of broader conflict in the Holy Land. Old Jerusalem, with its numerous shrines, archaic buildings, narrow streets, and picturesque walls, many of which were last rebuilt in the Ottoman Period, has special significance to Jews, Christians, and Muslims. Because of the city's sanctity, observers sometimes overlook the non-religious political and economic considerations involved in the present contest for control of the city.

After many generations (indeed centuries) of relatively little alteration, the 20th century brought massive changes to the city. As the British administrative center of Palestine under a League of Nations

Mandate, Jerusalem to the west and north of the walled old city. The new city, mostly developed for Jewish immigrants, also had modern Arab areas. In the plan for partition of Palestine recommended by the General Assembly of the UN in November 1947, Jerusalem was given separate status. The plan proposed an internationally administered zone of 68 square miles, including all of Jerusalem, the town of Bethlehem to the south, and a number of nearby Arab villages. This plan, however, was not adopted by the UN Security Council.

After the Israeli War of Independence (1948–49), the new State of Israel held the western part of the city, from which thousands of Muslim and Christian Palestinians had been forced to flee, while the Kingdom of Jordan held the remainder, including Old Jerusalem, from which several hundred Jews had been safely removed under the auspices of the International Red Cross. The proposed Jerusalem International Zone was ignored, except by foreign governments as a diplomatic nicety.

Besides forcing both Jews and Arabs from their homes, the armistice divided the city and deprived Jews of all nationalities visiting privileges to their holy places in the Jordanian sector. Two separate cities came into de facto existence, each with its own character and economy. Jordanian-ruled Jerusalem (Arabic *al-Quds*) was conservative and Arab in character; Israeli Jerusalem was essentially modern with significant European influence. Psychologically and socially the two cities could have been more than a thousand miles apart.

As a result of the war between Israel and neighboring Arab states in 1967, Israeli military occupation was imposed on

Arab Jerusalem. East Jerusalem, as it came to be known, was joined to the municipality of Israeli "West" Jerusalem. Israeli authorities worked systematically to absorb the former Jordanian sector into the city, disregarding entirely UN demands that Israel refrain from annexation of East Jerusalem.

Since its conquest of East Jerusalem, Israel has rapidly moved ahead to develop the city as part of its national territory. Homes for Israelis have been built on land seized for development, private buildings have been torn down to make way for public projects, and Arab Jerusalemites who fled in 1967 have not been permitted to return to their homes. A number of prominent Arabs accused of resisting the Israeli administration have been deported to Jordan, including at least one former mayor of Arab Jerusalem.

Israel has declared emphatically that the "reunification" of Jerusalem will never be reversed, and that the city will remain the eternal and undivided capital of the State of Israel. The decision of the United States to move its embassy from Tel Aviv to Jerusalem in 2018 (see chapters on Palestine and Israel) lends some credence to this notion. Many Arabs and Muslims elsewhere, in contrast, are determined that Old Jerusalem will be restored to Arab control.

Israel has consistently neglected and under-funded East Jerusalem. Despite paying municipal taxes, Palestinian citizens are provided limited services. In 2018, a five year economic plan was to see a drastic improvement in the economic status of East Jerusalem, with parallel expansion of Israeli sovereignty.

The Golan Heights (Jawlan)

Area: About 700 square miles (1,800 square kilometers)

Population: 20,000 Syrians, most of them Druze, plus 22,000 Israeli settlers.

During the 1967 Arab–Israeli War, Israel seized the southwestern portion of Syria, including its administrative center, Quneitra (or Qunaytra). For two decades, the plateau had provided tactical military advantages for the Syrian military, who had on occasion shelled Israeli settlements from the heights overlooking the Jordan Valley and Lake Tiberias. Specifically, it offered (and continues to offer) strategic high ground with broad views of both Israel and Syria. As Syrian troops retreated, Israeli forces rapidly occupied the Quneitra district, which became known as the Golan Heights, the Hebrew term parallel to the Arabic *Jawlan*. Today, Israel occupies roughly two-thirds of the area, while Syria controls the other third.

The area has good rainfall, especially in the north, near the high mountains. Much of it is satisfactory agricultural land, although broken and stony, especially to the north, where the terrain is suitable for little more than pasturage. In addition to the Semitic tribes which had grazed their flocks here since late Roman Empire times, Shi'a and Druze villagers had established themselves on the flanks of Jabal as-Shaykh (Mount Hermon) by modern times. The main town of Quneitra was largely deserted through the first part of the 19th century, but it was revived beginning in 1873 by Chechen and Circassian refugees from the Caucasus Mountains after the Russian Empire imposed its rule on their homeland.

In the population mosaic of the Golan—typical of many parts of Syria in 1967—there were Druze, Shi'a, Circassian and Arab tribes, Turkomans, Kurds, and other scattered minorities. All used Arabic in education and outside their own communities. In the fury of the Israeli invasion, thousands of these peaceful Syrian citizens fled battle scenes. Others were expelled by Israeli troops.

For reasons presumably related to Druze loyalty in Israel, the Israelis permitted only Druze villagers to resume life in the occupied zone. The Circassian, Arab, and other inhabitants of the district became displaced persons, mostly around Damascus. During the 1973 October War, Syrian tank and infantry units pushed into the zone but were eventually repelled, and Israeli forces advanced close to Damascus. The greatest destruction to the town of Quneitra occurred not during warfare, but when the Israel military deliberately ransacked and destroyed buildings, including mosques and a church, before returning them to Syria according to ceasefire agreements.

By 1988 more than a score of Israeli settlements, most of them kibbutzim, had been founded in the area on lands owned by displaced Syrians. Some settlements are right on the narrow buffer zone, patrolled by UN observers, separating Israeli and Syrian troops.

Israeli officials who allowed the Druze to remain in the area may have been surprised to discover that many Druze identified themselves as Syrian Arabs and would not docilely cooperate with Israeli policies. They have protested Israeli economic measures, including high taxation without corresponding benefits. They have also protested restrictions on their freedom of movement from village to village. In an attempt to disrupt them, the Israeli army has at times imposed long curfews to prevent them from carrying out their work; at other times demonstrations were forcefully broken up in confrontations. When they were told they must have Israeli identity cards in order to leave their villages for any purpose, they refused, as this would have been recognition of the permanency of the occupation.

In 1981 Israeli law was extended over occupied Golan, and the area was added as a sub-district to the Northern District, one of the six administrative units into which the State of Israel is divided. This act, tantamount to an annexation, was denounced by the United Nations, most clearly in UN Security Council Resolution 497 (1981), which reads, "The Israeli decision to impose its laws, jurisdiction and administration in the occupied Syrian Golan Heights is null and void and without international legal effect." This resolution, along with resolutions 242 (1967) and 338 (1973) make clear that Israeli occupation of the Golan Heights is illegal under international law. Successive attempts to negotiate peace between Israel and Syria have floundered over Syria's demand for a complete Israeli withdrawal and Israel's refusal to do so.

In May of 2018, the Israeli military announced that it had attacked dozens of Iranian targets in Syria in response to a spate of 20 rockets fired by Iran into Israeli territory from the Syrian-held portion of the Golan Heights. According to anonymous sources within the Israeli military, these attacks, the largest Israeli strikes against Syria since the 1973 war (known to Israelis as the Yom Kippur War and to Arabs as the Ramadan War), targeted weapons storage, logistical sites, and intelligence centers used by Iran in Syria. Commenting on the strikes, Israeli Defense Minister Avigdor Lieberman explained that Israel did not seek escalation, but that it would not allow Iran to turn Syria into a forward base against Israel. Perhaps most interesting about this exchange was that it represented the first time, at least as far as is publicly known, that Iran and Israel have engaged each other directly and militarily. Historically, although tensions between Israel and Iran have been high since the advent of the Islamic Republic, these states have fought through proxies (e.g., Hezbollah) or intelligence channels (e.g., Mossad). It will be interesting to see, going forward, whether events on the Golan Heights were precursors for more direct confrontation.

A further development in 2019, was the recognition of Israel's claim over the Golan Heights by U.S. President Trump. The European Union has unanimously declared that it does not recognize Israeli sovereignty of the Golan. Clearly a symbolic (rather than legal) gesture, U.S. recognition may lend credence to Israel's annexation policy. Furthermore, it undermines any claims of Washington to act as an honest broker in the conflict-riven region.

Disputed Territories

Jammu and Kashmir

Area: 84,471 square miles (218,670 square kilometers). Of this area, 53,665 square miles (138,992 square kilometers) are controlled by India; 32,358 square miles (83,806 square kilometers) are under the control of Pakistan.

Population: About 12.5 million in the Indian zone; 2.6 million in the Pakistani zone.

The disputed territory of Jammu and Kashmir was ruled by a Hindu Maharaja, Sir Hari Singh, at the time of the partition of British India in 1947. The territory consisted of the districts of Jammu, Kashmir, Ladakh, Gilgit, and several smaller areas, all in the northernmost part of British India. The Valley of Kashmir is one of the most beautiful parts of the entire region geographically.

Unrest swept the region when British India was partitioned and the nation of Pakistan was created. The Maharaja suppressed his Muslim subjects in one area, and soon bands of plundering Muslim tribesmen were streaming toward the capital of Srinagar in Kashmir province. He fled to the city of Jammu and there signed a document on October 26, 1947 incorporating his domains into the Republic of India, although about 75% of the population was Muslim.

Indian troops were flown to Srinagar to save it from the tribesmen and to impose control. Troops from Pakistan were drawn into the war, which took place in the winter of 1947–48. Under UN auspices, an agreement to stop shooting was negotiated and took effect on January 1, 1949. The cease-fire line, which ran through the provinces of Jammu and Kashmir and then into the icy wastes of Ladakh, left India in occupation of about three-fifths of the disputed area.

Although the cease-fire halted open warfare, it did not bring peace, and the future of the contested region remained undecided. Pakistan demanded a plebiscite carried out by the United Nations, but India held local elections and claimed that they served the purpose of a plebiscite. The territory was not on the ballot, and many Muslims boycotted the elections.

It was also around this time that India began calling Kashmir an "integral part" of its territory. Outright violence was not serious until August, 1965, when Pakistan sent armed infiltrators across the Line of Control (LOC) to commit acts of sabotage. Indian troops later crossed the LOC in three places. Since Pakistani public opinion strongly supported the fighting, its military launched a conventional invasion of Jammu with tanks and other heavy equipment in September that year. India responded by invading West Pakistan, near Lahore, and then farther south toward Karachi. Pakistan struck at India with attacks into Punjab and Rajasthan.

After the fighting reached a stalemate, the UN Security Council demanded a cease-fire, a decision simplified because both the Soviet Union and the United States opposed the war. The combatants complied, partly because they could not replenish military supplies from the major powers. However, each side suspected the other of seeking further advantage and refused to withdraw forces from positions captured during the fighting.

In 1966 the Soviet Union invited Pakistani President Ayub Khan and Prime Minister Shastri of India to Tashkent in the southern Soviet Union. There they were persuaded to sign an agreement for complete withdrawal behind their own borders and the 1949 LOC. Despite the withdrawal, the causes of the dispute remained.

After roughly two decades of relative calm, in 1989 a small separatist insurgency emerged in Kashmir, ushering in what might be considered the modern era of the conflict. Since then, violence has ebbed and flowed, ceasefires have taken effect in name and occasionally in practice (including a 2003 ceasefire that technically remains in effect but is routinely ignored), and some 70,000 people have died in the fighting. Violence reached a peak in the late 1990s—culminating in a brief war between India and Pakistan (the Kargil War) from May to July of 1999—but in recent years it has been on the uptick again. Fatalities surged from 117 in 2012 to 358 in 2017. By early May of 2018, 132 deaths had already been recorded, and that toll continued to climb.

In this context, in 2018 India declared a ceasefire for the Muslim holy month of Ramadan for the first time in 18 years, hoping that this might ease tensions and perhaps reinvigorate efforts to jumpstart a peace process. Critics argued that the ceasefire would only give militants the opportunity to rearm and regroup, and in any case by the end of Ramadan fighting continued apace again. According to some monitors, the aforementioned 2003 ceasefire, still technically in effect, had been violated more than a thousand times during the first half of 2018.

At the end of the day, the persistence of the conflict in Jammu and Kashmir comes down to a difference of perspective, by the governments and peoples in India and Pakistan alike, about the core problem in the contested area. Indians tend to see the conflict as one where Indian troops are fighting a small but resilient Islamist terrorist insurgency to preserve Indian territorial integrity. Most of the residents of Kashmir, who are Muslim, believe that New Delhi has no interest in a negotiated political solution short of one that would grant India the entirety of the region. Thus India has taken controversial and sometimes brutal steps to crush the insurgency, and in the process has further alienated the local population. Unfortunately, there seems little reason to believe this dynamic will change in the near future.

Gulf Cooperation Council

The rulers of Saudi Arabia, Kuwait, Qatar, the United Arab Emirates, Bahrain, and Oman formed the Gulf Cooperation Council in 1981 to further their common interests, especially vis-à-vis security and defense. Alarmed by the revolution in Iran and Soviet invasion of Afghanistan, the six autocracies sought to protect themselves through cooperation. While closer military contacts began, the GCC's first practical step was the formation of an Arabian free trade area through the elimination of customs barriers. In 1983, the council abolished tariffs on agricultural, manufactured, and animal products originating in member states. Professionals were allowed freedom to move between member states to work. Other joint projects related to uniformity of educational systems and expansion of educational opportunities through exchange programs across the region.

By 1990, the GCC showed some signs of achievement and maturity. It had shifted attention from the distant problems of Israel and Lebanon to closer matters, including peace between Iran and Iraq. The organization also formed a brigade-strength joint defense force, stationed in Saudi Arabia. Although the GCC failed to deter Iraqi aggression against Kuwait, the majority of its members supported the U.S.-led coalition against Iraq during the first Gulf War.

Until 2011, economic issues appeared most prominent. GCC countries would benefit from a common industrial policy (to avoid duplicating expensive projects), a unified external tariff, and a similarity of subsidies and other benefits to businesses. Upset by the decision to locate the central bank in Saudi Arabia, the UAE withdrew from the proposed monetary union in 2009. Kuwait later delayed (indefinitely) the issuance of a euro-style single currency by the remaining members.

When anti-regime protests shook the Arab world in 2011, the focus of GCC members returned to national security, particularly the internal danger of regime change. Saudi Arabia and the UAE denounced protestors in Bahrain—many of them Shi'a—as Iranian proxies, agitating on behalf of the Islamic Republic. They therefore dispatched military and police forces to help the Sunni Bahrain monarch to crush the demonstrations.

Recent years have seen a number of important developments related to the GCC. In 2011, the GCC summit conference welcomed applications to join the GCC from Jordan and Morocco, the two Sunni monarchies outside the Gulf, but many years later discussions about accession continue.

More importantly, 2017 saw the beginning of an ongoing diplomatic crisis between several states in the union. In June of that year, Saudi Arabia, the United Arab Emirates, Bahrain, and (non-GCC member) Egypt (along with a number of smaller Arab states) imposed a blockade on the small but rich state of Qatar, alleging that Doha was supporting terrorism in the region. Chief grievances included Qatar's apparent toleration (and implicit backing) of the Muslim Brotherhood, as well as the country's willingness to retain ties with Iran. Also cited was al Jazeera's critical coverage of regional politics (al Jazeera is based in Doha).

The diplomatic crisis has continued for two years and, despite occasional signals of a possible thaw, and increasing pressure from outside powers to resolve the matter, no clear end game has emerged. The consequences for the parties involved have been serious, in both negative and positive ways.

The blockade has spurred a range of reforms in Qatar that may ultimately be beneficial. Prior to the blockade, 60% of Qatar's imports were estimated to have come through the countries now boycotting it, particularly its food supplies, so the government had to act fast to secure alternative supply routes through Turkey and Iran. The country moved quickly to ramp up domestic production and has focused on economic diversification (an attempt to rely less on revenues from oil and gas), attracting foreign investment, and establishing new trade relationships and tighter trade ties with existing partners. Labor reforms include granting permanent residency to the children of Qatari mothers and foreign fathers and the proposed end to the sponsorship system of labor employment, whereby foreign nationals require sponsorship from Qataris to work in the country.

The Qatari government has been largely successful in insulating ordinary citizens from the economic effects of the GCC crisis. The average Qatari household income has actually increased since 2017, undercutting efforts by the blockading countries to foment internal political unrest through financial hardship. Municipal elections in 2019, were conducted without drama and with relatively low voter turnout, suggesting that the Qatari population is not, at the present, likely to turn against the emir. With resource revenues expected to reach more than $150,000 per citizen in 2019, the government of Qatar has the capacity to withstand the economic pressures imposed on it for some time to come. A resolution to the crisis may not be on the horizon.

The diplomatic crisis has played out not just in the Middle East, but also in Africa and China, where GCC members find themselves competing for influence. Growing economic ties with Africa have been the foundation of diplomatic relations between GCC states and the continent both individually and as a union. As several commentators have pointed out, what GCC member states have in oil and gas, they lack in water and arable land. With imports accounting for some 80–90% of the food that rapidly-growing GCC populations consume, finding a suitable breadbasket has never been more important. Mali, Mauritania, Mozambique, Sudan, and Tanzania are among the African countries that have received the most attention from the GCC over the past decade. Indeed, GCC member states have invested some $30 billion into African companies during that time.

As for most states in the world, GCC relations with China have also been important, and of late these have been centered on the latter's Belt and Road Initiative (BRI), a development strategy that aims to increase connectivity and cooperation between China and countries from Asia to Europe to Africa. Access to secure energy resource underpins BRI activities in the Gulf. For China, the GCC is an especially attractive union, because it represents states where infrastructure (ports, airports, roads, etc.) and trade routes already exist. The area further serves as a remote manufacturing hub that connects Chinese businesses directly to their customer base.

Regional Organizations

The League of Arab States

Representatives of all independent or self-governing Arab countries in the heart of the Arab world met to form the League of Arab States in 1945. The League initially included seven members, aside from Egypt all of them in Southwest Asia:

1. Egypt
2. Iraq
3. Jordan (then Transjordan)
4. Lebanon
5. Saudi Arabia
6. Syria
7. Yemen (Republic of Yemen)

Later, other nations which considered themselves at least in part Arab joined the League upon attaining political independence or soon thereafter (listed with year of adherence and, for those countries not described in this book, location):

8. Libya (1953), North Africa
9. Sudan (1956), Northeast Africa.
10. Morocco (1958), Northwest Africa.
11. Tunisia (1958), North Africa.
12. Kuwait (1961).
13. Algeria (1962), North Africa.
14. Bahrain (1971).
15. Oman (1971).
16. Qatar (1971).
17. United Arab Emirates (1971).
18. Mauritania (1973), Northwest Africa.
19. Somali Republic (1974), East Africa.
20. Palestine (1976).
21. Djibouti (1977), East Africa.
22. Comoros (1993), East Africa.

Palestine was admitted to membership by a unanimous vote in September 1976, although the Palestinian Liberation Organization then controlled no territory.

Until 1979, the League's was headquartered in Cairo on the east bank of the Nile. When Egypt signed a peace treaty with Israel considered unsatisfactory by other members, Egypt was expelled from the organization and the headquarters was moved to Tunis. Egypt rejoined the League in 1989. The League's majority condemned the invasion of Kuwait, but the sharply divided organization lost its Secretary General and returned its headquarters to Cairo thereafter. An Egyptian diplomat, Ismat Abd al-Majid, became Secretary General.

Through efforts of the League, Arabic became the sixth official and working language of the UN beginning January 1, 1983. This decision was reached by the Security Council and followed a practice already common in the General Assembly.

At a summit in 2002, the League adopted the Arab Peace Initiative, a Saudi-inspired peace plan for the Arab–Israeli conflict. The initiative offered full normalization of Arab relations with Israel, in exchange for withdrawal from all occupied territories, including the Golan Heights, recognition of Palestinian independence in the West Bank and the Gaza Strip, with East Jerusalem as a Palestinian capital, as well as a vaguely defined "just solution" for Palestinian refugees. The Israeli government rejected the initiative, on the grounds that it would result in the return of a large number of Palestinians into Israel. However, the Bush government expressed initial enthusiasm. Between 2007 and 2009, some efforts to reach an agreement based on the Arab Peace Initiative were made. In 2013, The League re-endorsed the Arab Peace Initiative, with the updated terms that Israeli-Palestinian peace agreement should be based on the two-state solution on the basis of the 1967 line, with the possibility of comparable and mutually agreed minor swaps of the land between Israel and Palestine.

In 2011, Syria was expelled from the League, following Assad's crackdown on pro-democracy demonstrators. There has been no consensus within the League regarding the return of Syria to the organization.

The South Asian Association for Regional Cooperation (SAARC)

In 1985, the heads of government from seven regional nations met in Dhaka and voted to establish the South Asian Association for Regional Cooperation (SAARC). The founding states—Bangladesh, Bhutan, India, the Maldives, Nepal, Pakistan, and Sri Lanka—were joined by Afghanistan in 2007, which completed the composition of the union as it currently stands. SAARC now occupies a land area and represents more people (22% of the global population) than both the European Union (EU) and the Association of Southeast Asian Nations (ASEAN). Although it boasts a number of populous states, including Bangladesh and Pakistan, it is dominated by the local giant, India, which shares land and maritime boundaries with every other country (with the possible exception of Afghanistan, where the border—in the Kashmir region—remains in dispute with Pakistan).

As with many regional unions, the original aspirations of the organization were as broad as they were grand: member states sought to promote economic prosperity by cooperating on common problems like the poor state of regional infrastructure and development, poverty, and low intra-regional trade. Through cooperation, states sought peace and, ultimately, social justice. Regrettably, after more than three decades and a total of just 18 summits, it would be difficult to make a case for the success of the organization. South Asia remains one of the least integrated regions in the world, and intra-SAARC trade stands at just 5% of South Asia's total trade. A range of problems have contributed to this reality, but two stand out above the others: 1) the structure and decision making rules of the organization, and 2) the rivalry between India and Pakistan.

From the founding of the organization, two principals have hindered SAARC's ability to address the region's most pressing challenges. First, as the group's charter explains, "Decisions at all levels shall be taken on the basis of unanimity." This means that any member state has the ability to veto any proposal raised by another state, just as any emerging decision is also subject to the veto. In a region with more than one famous rivalry, this requirement has proven to be a recipe for stagnation. Second, the charter contends that "Bilateral and contentious issues shall be excluded from the deliberations." The region's most difficult problems, however, are necessarily contentious, and perhaps the most salient of these involves a bilateral relationship.

As outlined in the chapters on India and Pakistan, the relationship between these states has been complex, and the animosity between them high, since independence from Britain in 1947. SAARC's inability to integrate South Asia has been both a cause and an effect of this tension. Perhaps the principal challenge to the Indo-Pakistani relationship has centered on the contested territory of Jammu and Kashmir (see section on Jammu and Kashmir), where Pakistan has insisted that the parties reach a settlement on this issue before talks about normalization of relations with India—and thus greater regional cooperation—can occur. For this reason, Pakistan has lobbied for an amendment to SAARC's charter, one that would allow for the discussion of bilateral and contentious issues. India would rather avoid discussion of this topic in a regional forum and has thus opposed such amendments. Because of the veto power and the aforementioned principle of unanimity, as long as India keeps this position, revising the charter cannot take place.

The 19th SAARC Summit was originally scheduled to be held in Islamabad, Pakistan in November of 2016, but when India, Afghanistan, Bangladesh, and Bhutan withdrew from the summit it was postponed indefinitely. Pakistan has sought assistance from Nepal and Sri Lanka to reinstate the summit, but thus far these efforts have been to no avail. At present and going forward, there is little reason to be optimistic that SAARC member states will be able to resolve their differences in a way that would facilitate the union's pursuit of its original goals. If that continues to be the case, then the organization may continue to exist in theory but be essentially defunct in practice.

Selected Bibliography of Key English Language Sources

WEB SITES
Useful General Sites
www.ceip.org (Carnegie Endowment for International Peace, using a fully integrated Web-database system)

www.cia.gov/index.html (Central Intelligence Agency)

http://europa.eu.int (EU server site)

www.loc.gov (Library of Congress with coverage of over 100 countries)

www.odci.gov/cia (Includes useful CIA publications, such as *The World Factbook* and maps)

www.oecd.org/daf/cmis/fdi/statist.htm (OECD site)

www.osce.org (Site of OSCE)

www.state.gov/www/ind.html (U.S. Department of State, including country reports)

www.un.org (Web site for United Nations. Many links.)

www.unsystem.or (Official UN website)

http://usinfo.state.gov (U.S. Department of State)

www.worldbank.org/html/Welcome.html (World Bank news, publications with links to other financial institutions)

www.wto.org (World Trade Organization site)

www.embassy.org/embassies (A site with links to all embassy web sites in Washington D.C.)

www.psr.keele.ac.uk\official.htm (Collective site for governments and international organizations)

Newspapers, Journals and Television with good coverage on international affairs
www.chicagotribune.com (Named best overall US newspaper online service for newspapers with circulation over 100,000.)

www.csmonitor.com (Respected U.S. newspaper, *Christian Science Monitor*. Named best overall US newspaper online service for newspapers with circulation under 100,000.)

www.economist.com (British weekly news magazine)

www.nytimes.com (Respected U.S. newspaper, *The New York Times*)

www.washingtonpost.com (Good international coverage)

www.foreignaffairs.org (One of best-known international affairs journal)

www.cnn.com (Latest news with external links)

www.news.BBC.co.uk (British Broadcasting Corporation site)

www.c-span.org (Includes C-SPAN International)

Regional resources for news and current affairs
www.aljazeera.com (International news and analysis, with a focus on the Middle East. Based in Qatar)

www.aninews.com (India-based new syndicate with a South Asia focus)

www.asiatimes.com (English language online media company, covers news from an Asian perspective with a solid South Asia section. Based in Hong Kong)

www.dawn.com (long-running English language newspaper group, based in Pakistan. It offers a Pakistani perspective on regional and global affairs)

www.haaretz.com (English language version of the moderate Israeli daily. The print version is printed and sold with the *International New York Times*)

www.jpost.com (*The Jerusalem Post*; internet edition of long-running Israeli broadsheet, takes a center-right editorial position against the center-left perspective offered by *Haaretz*)

www.mideastweb.org (Operated by a nonprofit organization operating out of Israel with a focus on Israeli–Palestinian dialogue and regional peace initiatives)

www.palestinemonitor.org (founded in the West Bank as a "counterweight to the bias against Palestine found in many international news sources." News and analysis from a team of international journalists)

BOOKS
Middle East—general
Abi-Aad, Naji and Michel Grenon. *Instability and Conflict in the Middle East: People, Petroleum, and Security Threats*. New York: Saint Martin's Press, 1997.

Aburish, Said K. *A Brutal Friendship: the West and the Arab Elite*. New York: Saint Martin's Press, 1998.

Andersen, Roy R., et al. *Politics and Change in the Middle East: Sources of Conflict and Accommodation*. Upper Saddle River, NJ: Prentice Hall, 5th ed. 1997.

Anderson, Ewan E., et al. *The Middle East: Geography and Geopolitics*. 8th ed. New York: Routledge, 2000.

Bates, Daniel G., et al. *Peoples and Cultures of the Middle East*. Upper Saddle River, NJ: Prentice Hall, 2001.

Bensahel, Nora and Daniel L. Byman, eds. *The Future Security Environment in the Middle East*. Santa Monica, CA: Rand, 2003.

Choueiri, Youseff. *Arab Nationalism*. Malden, MA: Blackwell Publishers, 2001.

Cleveland, William L. and Martin Burton. *A History of the Modern Middle East*. Boulder, CO: Westview Press, 2008.

Dalrymple, William. *From the Holy Mountain: Journey among the Christians of the Middle East*. New York: Henry Holt & Company, 1998.

Deshen, Shlomo and Walter P. Zenner, eds. *Jews among Muslims: Communities in the Precolonial Middle East*. New York: New York University Press, 1996.

Dorraj, Manochehr, ed. *Middle East at the Crossroads: the Changing Political Dynamics and the Foreign Policy*. Lanham, MD: University Press of America, 1999.

Doubato, Eleanor A. and Marsha Posusney, eds. *Women and Globalization in the Arab Middle East: Gender, Economy, and Society*. Boulder, CO: Lynne Rienner, 2003.

Eickelman, Dale F. *Middle East and Central Asia*. Upper Saddle River, NJ: Prentice Hall, 1997.

Feldman, Shai. *Nuclear Weapons and Arms Control in the Middle East*. Cambridge, MA: MIT Press, 1997.

Fernea, Elizabeth W. and Robert A. Fernea. *The Arab World: Forty Years of Change*. New York: Doubleday, rev. ed. 1997.

Fisk, Robert. *The Great War for Civilisation: The Conquest of the Middle East*. New York: Vintage, 2007.

Freeman-Grenville, G.S. *Historical Atlas of the Middle East*. New York: Simon & Schuster, 1993.

Gerner, Deborah J., ed. *Understanding the Contemporary Middle East*. Boulder, CO: Lynne Reiner, 2000.

Gher, Leo A. *Civic Discourse and Digital Age Communications in the Middle East*. Westport, CT: Greenwood Publishing Group, 2000.

Gilbar, Gad G. *The Middle East Oil Decade and Beyond*. Portland, OR: International Specialized Book Services, 1997.

Gilbar, Gad G. *Population Dilemmas in the Middle East*. Portland, OR: International Specialized Book Services, 1997.

Gilsenan, Michael. *Recognizing Islam: Religion and Society in the Modern Middle East*. New York: I.B. Tauris & Company, 2000.

Glasser, Bradley L. *Economic Development and Political Reform: the Impact of External Capital on the Middle East*. Northampton, MA: Edward Elgar Publishing, 2000.

Guazzone, Laura. *Middle East Global Change: the Politics and Economics of Interdependence Versus Fragmentation*. New York: Saint Martin's Press, 1997.

Halliday, Fred. *Nation and Religion in the Middle East*. Boulder, CO: Lynne Rienner Publishers, 2000.

Hansen, Birthe. *Unipolarity and the Middle East*. New York: Saint Martin's Press, 2001.

Herb, Michael. *All in the Family: Absolutism, Revolution, and Democratic Prospects in the Middle Eastern Monarchies*. Albany, NY: State University of New York Press, 1999.

Hinnebusch, Raymond and A. Ehteshami, eds. *The Foreign Policies of the Middle East States*. Boulder, CO: Lynne Rienner, 2002.

Hiro, Dilip. *A Dictionary of the Middle East*. New York: Saint Martin's Press, 1996.

Hiro, Dilip. *The Middle East*. Phoenix, AZ: Oryx Press, 1996.

Issawi, Charles P. *The Middle East Economy: Decline and Recovery*. Princeton, NJ: Markus Wiener Publishers, rev. ed. 1996.

Jabar, Faleh A., ed. *Post-Marxism and the Middle East*. Portland, OR: International Specialized Book Services, 1997.

Kamalipour, Yahya R. *The U.S. Media and the Middle East: Image and Perception*. Westport, CT: Greenwood Publishing, 1995.

Kaufman, Burton I. *Arab Middle East and the United States*. Old Tappan, NJ: Macmillan Library Reference, 1996.

Kemp, Geoffrey and Robert E. Harkavy. *Strategic Geography and the Changing Middle East*. Washington, DC: Carnegie Endowment for International Peace, 1997.

Lewis, Bernard. *The Middle East: a Brief History of the Last 2,000 Years*. New York: Simon & Schuster, 1996.

Lewis, Bernard. *Multiple Identities of the Middle East*. New York: Schocken Books, 1999.

Lindholm, Charles. *The Islamic Middle East: an Historical Anthropology*. Malden, MA: Blackwell Publishers, 1996.

Link, P.S., ed. *Middle East Imbroglio: Status and Prospects*. Commack, NY: Nova Science Publishers, 1996.

Long, David E. and Bernard Reich. *The Government and Politics of the Middle East and North Africa*. 4th ed. Boulder, CO: Westview, 2002.

Maddy-Weitzman, Bruce, ed. *Middle East Contemporary Survey*. Boulder, CO: Westview Press, 2000.

Maoz, Moshe and Ilan Pappe, eds. *Middle Eastern Politics and Ideas: a History from Within*. New York: Saint Martin's Press, 1998.

Maoz, Zeev. *Regional Security in the Middle East: Past, Present, Future*. Portland, OR: International Specialized Book Services, 1997.

McKale, Donald M. *War by Revolution: Germany and Great Britain in the Middle East in the Era of World War I*. Kent, OH: Kent State University Press, 1998.

Moghadam, Valentine M. *Modernization Women: Gender and Social change in the Middle East*, 2d ed. Boulder, CO: Lynne Rienner, 2003.

Murden, Simon W. *Islam, The Middle East, and the New Global Hegemony*. Boulder, CO: Lynne Rienner, 2002.

Nawawy, Mohammed el and Adel Iskandar. *Al-Jazeera. How the Free Arab News Network Scooped the World and Changed the Middle East*. Boulder, CO: Westview, 2003.

Niblock, Tim. *"Pariah States" and Sanctions in the Middle East: Iraq, Libya, Sudan*. Boulder, CO: Lynne Rienner, 2002.

Norton, Augustus R. *Civil Society in the Middle East*. Boston, MA: Brill Academic Publishers, 1994.

Ochsenwald, William L. and Sydney Nettleton Fisher. *The Middle East: a History*. New York: McGraw-Hill, 7th. ed. 2010.

Ovendale, Ritchie. *Britain, the U.S., and the Transfer of Power in the Middle East 1945–1962*. Herndon, VA: Books International, 1996.

Owen, Edward R. *A History of Middle East Economies in the Twentieth Century*. Cambridge, MA: Harvard University Press, 1999.

Owen, Roger. *State Power and Politics in Making of the Modern Middle East*. New York: Routledge, 2000.

Peleg, Ilan, ed. *The Middle East Peace Process: Interdisciplinary Perspectives*. Albany, NY: State University of New York Press, 1997.

Pervin, David J. and Steven L. Spiegel. *Practical Peacemaking in the Middle East, Vol. 1: Arms Control and Regional Security*. New York: Garland Publishing, 1995.

Pervin, David J. and Steven L. Spiegel. *Practical Peacemaking in the Middle East, Vol 2: The Environment, Water, Refugees, and Economic Cooperation and Development*. New York: Garland Publishing, 1995.

Richards, Alan and John Waterbury. *A Political Economy of the Middle East*. Boulder, CO: Westview Press, 1996.

Rogan, Eugene. *The Arabs: A History*. New York: Basic Books, 2009.

Rubin, Barry, et al., eds. *From War to Peace: Arab-Israeli Relations, 1973–1993*. New York: New York University Press, 1994.

Saikal, Amin and Albrecht Schnabel, eds. *Democratization in the Middle East*. Washington D.C.: Brookings, 2003.

Savir, Uri. *The Process: 1,100 Days That Changed the Middle East*. New York: Random House, 1998.

Schwedler, Jillian and Deborah J. Gerner. *Understanding the Contemporary Middle East*. Boulder, CO: Lynne Rienner Publishers, 2008.

Soffer, Arnon. Translated by Mory Rosovesky. *Rivers of Fire: the Conflict over Water in the Middle East*. Lanham, MD: Rowman & Littlefield Publishers, 1999.

Tal, David, ed. *The 1956 War: Collusion and Rivalry in the Middle East*. Portland, OR: Frank Cass Publishers, 2000.

Tamini, Sargon. *Islam and Secularism in the Middle East*. New York: New York University Press, 2000.

Vatikiotis, P.J. *Middle East: from the End of Empire to the End of the Cold War*. New York: Routledge, 1997.

Viorst, Milton. *Sandcastles: the Arabs in Search of the Modern World*. New York: Random House, 1994.

Williams, Mary E. *The Middle East: Opposing Viewpoints*. San Diego, CA: Greenhaven Press, 2000.

South Asia—general

Babb, Lawrence A. and Susan S. Wadley, eds. *Media and the Transformation of Religion in South Asia*. Philadelphia, PA: University of Pennsylvania Press, 1995.

Bahri, Deepika and Mary Vasudeva, eds. *Between the Lines: South Asians and Postcoloniality*. Philadelphia, PA: Temple University Press, 1996.

Baxter, Craig, et al. *Government and Politics in South Asia*. 5th ed. Boulder, CO: Westview, 2001.

Bose, Sugata and Ayesha Jalal. *Modern South Asia: History, Culture and Political Economy*. New York: Routledge, 1998.

Breton, Roland J. *Atlas of the Languages and Ethnic Communities of South Asia*. Thousand Oaks, CA: Sage Publications, 1997.

Dixit, J.N. *India-Pakistan in War and Peace*. NY: Routledge, 2002.

Ganguly, Sumit and Ted Greenwood, eds. *Mending Fences: Confidence and Security-Building Measures in South Asia*. Boulder, CO: Westview Press, 1996.

Hewitt, Vernon. *The New International Politics of South Asia*. New York: Saint Martin's Press, 1997.

Hossain, Moazzem. *South Asian Economic Development: Transformation, Opportunities and Challenges*. New York: Routledge, 1999.

Krepan, Michael L., ed. *Conflict Prevention, Confidence Building, and Reconciliation in South Asia*. New York: Saint Martin's Press, 1995.

Ludden, David. *An Agrarian History of South Asia*. New York: Cambridge University Press, 1999.

Mitra, Subrata K. And R. Alison Lewis, eds. *Subnational Movements in South Asia*. Boulder, CO: Westview Press, 1996.

Pasha, Mustapha K. *South Asia: Civil Society, State, and Politics*. Boulder, CO: Westview Press, 1996.

Peimani, Hooman. *Nuclear Proliferation in the Indian Subcontinent: the Self-Exhausting "Superpowers" and Emerging Alliances*: Westport, CT: Greenwood Publishing Group, 2000.

Schmidt, Karl J. *An Atlas and Survey of South Asian History*. Armonk, NY: M.E. Sharpe, 1995.

Schwartzberg, Joseph E. *A Historical Atlas of South Asia, 2nd Impression with Additional Material*. New York: Oxford University Press, 1993.

Synnott, Hilary. *The Causes and Consequences of South Asia's Nuclear Tests*. New York: Oxford University Press, 1999.

Tambiah, Stanely J. *Leveling Crowds: Ethno-Nationalist Conflicts and Collective Violence in South Asia*. Berkeley, CA: University of California Press, 1997.

Islam

Allison, Robert J. *The Crescent Obscured: the United States and Muslim World,*

Bibliography

1776–1815. New York: Oxford University Press, 1995.

Arkoun, Mohammed. *Rethinking Islam: Common Questions, Uncommon Answers.* Boulder, CO: Westview Press, 1994.

Armstrong, Karen. *Islam: a Short History.* New York: Modern Library, 2000.

Braswell, George W. Jr. *Islam: Its Prophet, Peoples, Politics, and Power.* Nashville, TN: Broadman & Holman, 1996.

Brown, L. Carl. *Religion and State: the Muslim Approach to Politics.* New York: Columbia University Press, 2000.

Butterworth, Charles E. and I. William Zartman, eds. *Between the State and Islam.* New York: Cambridge University Press, 2000.

Chebel, Malek. *Symbols of Islam.* New York: Saint Martin's Press, 1997.

Davidson, Lawrence. *Islamic Fundamentalism.* Westport, CT: Greenwood Publishing Group, 1998.

———. *Encyclopedia of Islam.* Boston, MA: Brill Academic Publishers, 1997.

Eickelman, Dale F. and James Piscatori. *Muslim Politics.* Princeton: Princeton University Press, 1996.

Esposito, John L., ed. *The Oxford History of Islam.* New York: Oxford University Press, 2000.

Esposito, John L. *Political Islam: Revolution, Radicalism, or Reform.* Boulder, CO: Lynne Rienner, 1997.

Feldman, Noah. *The Fall and Rise of the Islamic State.* Princeton, NJ: Princeton University Press, 2008

Halliday, Fred. *Nation and Religion in the Middle East.* Boulder, CO: Lynne Rienner, 2000.

Hathout, Hassan. *Reading the Muslim Mind.* Plainfield, IN: American Trust Publications, 1994.

Hawting, G.R. *The Idea of Idolatry and the Emergence of Islam: from Polemic to History.* New York: Cambridge University Press, 2000.

Huband, Mark. *Warriors of the Prophet: the Struggle for Islam.* Boulder, CO: Westview Press, 1999.

Khan, Muhammad Z., translator. *The Quran.* Northampton, MA: Interlink Publishing Group, 1997.

Kramer, Martin, ed. *The Islamic Debate.* Syracuse, NY: Syracuse University Press, 1997.

Marshall, Paul, and Nina Shea. *Silenced: How Apostasy and Blasphemy Codes Are Choking Freedom Worldwide.* New York: Oxford University Press, 2011.

Memon, Ali N. *The Islamic Nation: Status and Future of Muslims in the New World Order.* Beltsville, MD: Writer's, Inc., 1995.

Moussalli, Amhad. *Historical Dictionary of Islamic Fundamentalist Movements in the Arab World, Iran and Turkey.* Lanham, MD: Scarecrow Press, 1999.

Nagel, Tilman and Bernard Lewis, eds. *The History of Islamic Theology: from Muhammad to the Present.* Princeton, NJ: Markus Weiner Publishers, 1999.

Nomani, Asra Q. *Tantrika: Traveling the Road of Divine Love.* San Francisco: Harpers, 2003. (Explores women's boundaries within Islam)

Noreng, Ystein. *Oil and Islam: Social and Economic Issues.* New York: John Wiley & Sons, 1997.

Palmer, Monte and Princess Palmer. *Islamic Extremism: Causes, Diversity, and Challenges.* Lanham, MD: Rowman & Littlefield, 2007.

Piscatori, James P. *Islam in a World of Nation-States.* New York: Cambridge University Press, 1986.

Renard, John. *Seven Doors to Islam: Spirituality and the Religious Life of Muslims.* Berkeley, CA: University of California Press, 1996.

Roy, Olivier. *Globalized Islam: The Search for a New Ummah.* New York: Columbia University Press, 2006.

Van Donzel, E.J., ed. *Islamic Desk Reference.* Boston, MA: Brill Academic Publishers, 1994.

Viorst, Milton. *In the Shadow of the Prophet: the Struggle for the Soul of Islam.* Boulder, CO: Westview Press, 2001.

Zepp, Ira G., Jr. *A Muslim Primer: Beginner's Guide to Islam.* Fayetteville, AR: University of Arkansas Press, 2000.

Democracy

Azimi, Fakhreddin. *The Quest for Democracy in Iran: A Century of Struggle against Authoritarian Rule.* Cambridge: Harvard University Press, 2008.

Brown, Nathan J. and Emad El-Din Shahin. *The Struggle over Democracy in the Middle East.* New York: Routledge, 2010.

Chadda, Maya. *Building Democracy in South Asia: India, Nepal, Pakistan.* Boulder, CO: Lynne Rienner, 2000.

Cook, Steven A. *False Dawn: Protest, Democracy, and Violence in the New Middle East.* New York: Oxford University Press, 2017.

Frankel, Francine R., et al., eds. *Transforming India: Social and Political Dynamics of Democracy.* New York: Oxford University Press, 2000.

Hangen, Susan I. *The Rise of Ethnic Politics in Nepal: Democracy in the Margins.* New York: Routledge, 2010.

Hawthorne, Amy W. *Democracy Deficit. U.S. Democracy Promotion Efforts in the Arab World.* Washington D.C.: Brookings, 2003.

Jalel, Ayesha. *Democracy and Authoritarianism in South Asia: a Comparative and Historical Perspective.* New York: Cambridge University Press, 1995.

Oil

Askari, Hossein. *Middle East Oil Exporters: What Happened to Economic Development?* Northampton MA: Edward Elgar, 2006.

Crystal, Jill. *Oil and Politics in the Gulf: Rulers and Merchants in Kuwait and Qatar.* New York: Cambridge University Press, 1995.

Heiss, Mary Ann. *Empire and Nationhood: the United States, Great Britain, and Iranian Oil, 1950–1954.* New York: Columbia University Press, 1997.

Herb, Michael. *The Wages of Oil: Parliaments and Economic Development in Kuwait and the UAE.* New York: Cornell University Press, 2014.

Hess, Andrew C. *Oil and Money: a Global Study of the Middle East in the Oil Era.* Chicago: Firtzroy Dearborn Publishers, 1999.

Morton, Michael Quentin. *Empires and Anarchies: A History of Oil in the Middle East.* London: Reaktion Books, 2017.

Noreng, Ystein. *Oil and Islam: Social and Economic Issues.* New York: John Wiley & Sons, 1997.

Selvik, Kjetil and Bjørn Olav Utvik, eds. *Oil States in the New Middle East: Uprisings and Stability.* New York; Routledge, 2016.

Regional Environmental Issues

Cahan, Jean Axelrad. *Water Security in the Middle East: Essays in Scientific and Social Cooperation.* New York: Anthem Press, 2017.

Momtaz, Salim and Masud Iqbal MD Shameem. *Experiencing Climate Change in Bangladesh: Vulnerability and Adaptation in Coastal Regions.* San Diego CA: Academic Press, 2016.

Pervin, David J. and Steven L. Spiegel. *Practical Peacemaking in the Middle East, Vol 2: The Environment, Water, Refugees, and Economic Cooperation and Development.* New York: Rasid, Harun and Bimal Paul. *Climate Change in Bangladesh: Confronting Impending Disasters.* Lanham MD: Lexington, 2014.

Selby, Jan. *Water, Power and Politics in the Middle East: The Other Israeli–Palestinian Conflict.* New York: IB Tauris, 2003.

Swain, Ashok and Anders Jägerskog. *Emerging Security Threats in the Middle East.* Lanham MD: Rowman & Littlefield, 2016.

Ward, Christopher and Sandra Ruckstuhl. *Water Scarcity, Climate Change and Conflict in the Middle East.* New York: IB Tauris, 2017.

Warrick, Richard A. and Q. K. Ahmad, eds. *The Implications of Climate and Sea-Level Change for Bangladesh.* Norwell, MA: Kluwer Academic Publishers, 1996.

The Islamic State (IS)

Atwan, Abdel Bari. *Islamic State: The Digital Caliphate.* Oakland CA: University of California Press, 2015.

Gerges, Fawaz A. *ISIS: A History.* Princeton NJ: Princeton University Press, 2016.

Manne, Robert. *The Mind of the Islamic State: Milestones along the Road to Hell.* Carlton, VIC, Australia: Redback Quarterly, 2016.

Roy, Olivier. *Jihad and Death: The Global Appeal of Islamic State.* London: C. Hurst & Co., 2017.

Afghanistan

Adamec, Ludwig W. *Dictionary of Afghan Wars, Revolutions, and Insurgencies.* Lanham, MD: Scarecrow Press, 1996.

———. *Historical Dictionary of Afghanistan.* Lanham, MD: Scarecrow Press, 1997.

Barfield, Thomas J. *Afghanistan: A Cultural and Political History.* Princeton NJ: Princeton University Press, 2010.

Coburn, Noah. *Losing Afghanistan: An Obituary for the Intervention.* Stanford CA: Stanford University Press, 2016.

Cordovez, Diego. *Out of Afghanistan: the Inside Story of the Soviet Withdrawal.* New York: Oxford University Press, 1995.

Galeotti, Mark. *Afghanistan: the Soviet Union's Last War.* Portland, OR: Frank Cass & Company, 1995.

Grasselli, Gabriella. *British and American Responses to the Soviet Invasion of Afghanistan.* Brookfield, VT: Ashgate Publishing Company, 1996.

Kakar, M. Hassan. *Afghanistan: the Soviet Invasion and the Afghan Response.* Berkeley, CA: University of California Press, 1995.

Magnus, Ralph H. and Eden Naby. *Afghanistan: Marx, Mullah and Mujahid.* rev. ed. Boulder, CO: Westview Press, 2002.

Margolis, Eric. *War at the Top of the World: the Struggle for Afghanistan, Kashmir and Tibet.* New York: Routledge, 2000.

Pedersen, Gorm. *Afghan Nomads in Transition.* New York: Thames & Hudson, 1995.

Rais, Rasul Bakhsh. *Recovering the Frontier State: War, Ethnicity, and the State in Afghanistan.* Lanham, MD: Rowman & Littlefield, 2009

Rubin, Barnett, R. *The Search for Peace in Afghanistan: from Buffer State to Failed State.* New Haven, CT: Yale University Press, 1996.

Saikal, Amin. *Zone of Crisis: Afghanistan, Pakistan, Iraq and Iran.* New York: IB Tauris, 2014.

Yousafzai, Asim. *Afghanistan: From Cold War to Gold War.* Washingto DC: Ace Publishing, 2013.

Bahrain

Joyce, Miriam. *Bahrain from the Twentieth Century to the Arab Spring.* New York: Palgrave Macmillan, 2012.

Khuri, Fuad Ishaq. *Tribe and State in Bahrain: the Transformation of Social and Political Authority in an Arab State.* Chicago: University of Chicago Press, 1980.

Lawson, Fred Haley. *Bahrain: the Modernization of Autocracy.* Boulder, CO: Westview Press, 1989.

Nakhleh, Emile. *Bahrain: Political Development in a Modernizing Society.* Lanham, MD: Lexington Books, 2011.

Bangladesh

Basu, Ipshita, Joe Devine, and Geof Wood, eds. Politics and Governance in Bangladesh: Uncertain Landscapes. New York: Routledge, 2018.

Baxter, Craig. *Historical Dictionary of Bangladesh.* Lanham, MD: Scarecrow Press, 1996.

Choudhury, Dilara. *Constitutional Development in Bangladesh: Stresses and Strains.* New York: Oxford University Press, 1997.

Heitzman, James and Robert L. Worden, eds. *Bangladesh: a Country Study.* Washington, DC: U.S. GPO, 2nd ed. 1989.

Hossain, Akhtar. *Macroeconomic Issues and Policies: the Case for Bangladesh.* Thousand Oaks, CA: Sage Publications, 1996.

Mohsin, Amena. *The Chittagong Hill Tracts, Bangladesh: On the Difficult Road to Peace.* Boulder, CO: Lynne Rienner, 2003.

Pokrant, Bob. *Bangladesh.* Santa Barbara, CA: ABC-CLIO, 2000.

Rasid, Harun and Bimal Paul. *Climate Change in Bangladesh: Confronting Impending Disasters.* Lanham MD: Lexington, 2014.

Sawada, Yasuyuki, Minhaj Mahmud, and Naohiro Kitano. *Economic and Social Development of Bangladesh: Miracle and Challenges.* New York: Palgrave Macmillan, 2017.

Sisson, Richard. *War and Secession: Pakistan, India, and the Creation of Bangladesh.* Berkeley, CA: University of California Press, 1990.

Warrick, Richard A. and Q. K. Ahmad, eds. *The Implications of Climate and Sea-Level Change for Bangladesh.* Norwell, MA: Kluwer Academic Publishers, 1996.

Wood, Geoffrey D. and Iffath A. Shariff. *Who Needs Credit? Poverty and Finance in Bangladesh.* New York: Saint Martin's Press, 1998.

Bhutan

Apte, Robert Z. *Three Kingdoms on the Roof of the World: Bhutan, Nepal, and Ladakh.* Berkeley, CA: Parallax Press, 1990.

Phuntsho, Karma. *The History of Bhutan.* London: Haus Publishing, 2014.

Pulla, Venkat. *The Lhotsampa People of Bhutan: Resilience and Survival.* New York: Palgrave Macmillan, 2016.

Savada, Andrea Matles, ed. *Nepal and Bhutan: Country Studies.* Washington, DC: U.S. GPO, 1993.

Zeppa, Jamie. *Beyond the Sky and the Earth: a Journey into Bhutan.* New York: Putnam Publishing Group, 1999.

Egypt

Beattie, Kirk J. *Egyptian Politics during Sadat's Presidency.* New York: Saint Martin's Press, 2000.

Boutros-Ghali, Boutros. *Egypt's Road to Jerusalem: a Diplomat's Story of the Struggle for Peace in the Middle East.* New York: Random House, 1997.

Cromer, Evelyn Baring. *Modern Egypt.* New York: Routledge, 2000.

Gershoni, Israel. *Redefining the Egyptian Nation, 1930–1945.* New York: Cambridge University Press, 1995.

Gorst, Anthony and Lewis Johnman. *The Suez Crisis.* New York: Routledge, 1997.

Holland, Matthew F. *America and Egypt: from Roosevelt to Eisenhower.* Westport, CT: Greenwood Publishing Group, 1996.

Ikram, Khalid. *The Political Economy of Reforms in Egypt: Issues and Policymaking since 1952.* Cairo: The American University in Cairo Press, 2018.

Ketchley, Neil. *Egypt in a Time of Revolution: Contentious Politics and the Arab Spring.* Chelsea, MI: Sheridan Books, 2017

Lucas, Scott. *Britain and the Suez Crisis: the Lion's Last Roar.* New York: Saint Martin's Press, 1996.

Meital, Yoram. *Egypt's Last Struggle for Peace: Continuity and Change, 1967–1971.* Gainesville, FL: University Press of Florida, 1997.

Metz, Helen Chapin, ed. *Egypt: a Country Study.* Washington, DC: U.S. GPO, 5th ed. 1991.

Nagi, Saad Z. *Poverty in Egypt: Human Needs and Institutional Capacities.* Lanham, MD: Lexington Books, 2000.

Sullivan, Denis J. and Sana Abed-Kotob. *Islam in Contemporary Egypt: Civil Society vs. the State.* Boulder, CO: Lynne Rienner Publishers, 1999.

Trager, Eric. *Arab Fall: How the Muslim Brotherhood Won and Lost Egypt in 891 Days.* Washington, DC: Georgetown University Press, 2016.

Weaver, Mary Anne. *A Portrait of Egypt: a Journey through the World of Militant Islam.* New York: Farrar, Straus & Giroux, 2000.

Woodward, Peter N. *Nasser.* White Plains, NY: Longman Publishing Group, 1991.

India

Bayly, Susan. *Caste, Society and Politics in India from the 18th Century to the Modern Age.* New York: Cambridge University Press, 2001.

Bouton, Marshall M. and Philip Oldenburg, eds. *India Briefing: a Transformative 50 Years.* Armonk, NY: M.E. Sharpe, 1999.

Burke, Samuel M. and Salim Al-Din Quraishi. *The British Raj in India: an Historical Review.* New York: Oxford University Press, 1995.

Bibliography

Chadda, Maya. *Ethnicity, Security and Separatism in India.* New York: Columbia University Press, 1997.

Chary, M. Srinivas. *The Eagle and the Peacock: U.S. Foreign Policy toward India since Independence.* Westport, CT: Greenwood Publishing Group, 1995.

Chatterjee, Partha, ed. *State and Politics in India.* New York: Oxford University Press, 2000.

Cohn, Bernard S. *Colonialism and Its Forms of Knowledge: the British in India.* Princeton, NJ: Princeton University Press, 1996.

Dantwala, M.L., et al., eds. *Dilemmas of Growth: the Indian Experience.* Thousand Oaks, CA: Sage Publications, 1996.

Derbyshire, Ian D. *India.* Santa Barbara, CA: ABC-CLIO, rev. ed. 1995.

Edney, Matthew H. *Mapping the Empire: the Geographical Construction of British India.* Chicago: University of Chicago Press, 1997.

Flåten, Lars Tore. *Hindu Nationalism, History and Identity in India: Narrating a Hindu Past under the BJP.* New York: Routledge, 2016.

Frankel, Francine R., et al., eds. *Transforming India: Social and Political Dynamics of Democracy.* New York: Oxford University Press, 2000.

Hansen, Thomas Blom. *Saffron Wave: Democracy and Hindu Nationalism in Modern India.* Princeton, NJ: Princeton University Press, 1999.

Harrison, Selig S., et al., eds. *India and Pakistan: the First Fifty Years.* New York: Cambridge University Press, 1998

Heitzman, James and Robert L. Worden, eds. *India: a Country Study.* Washington, DC: U.S. GPO, 5th ed. 1996. James, Lawrence. *RAJ: the Making and Unmaking of British India.* New York: Thomas Dunne Books, 1998.

Jayal, Niraja G. *Democracy and the State: Welfare, Secularism, and Development in Contemporary India.* New York: Oxford University Press, 1999.

Jenkins, Rob. *Democratic Politics and Economic Reform in India.* New York: Cambridge University Press, 1999.

Johnson, Gordon. *Cultural Atlas of India.* New York: Facts on File, 1996.

Keay, John. *India: a History.* New York: Grove/Atlantic, 2000.

Khan, Yasmin. *The Great Partition: The Making of India and Pakistan.* New Haven: Yale University Press, 2007.

Kulke, Herman and Dietmar Rothermund. *History of India.* New York: Routledge, 1998.

Maitra, Priyatosh. *The Globalization of Capitalism and Its Impact on Third World Countries: India as a Case Study.* Westport, CT: Greenwood Publishing Group, 1996.

Mansingh, Surjit. *Historical Dictionary of India.* Lanham, MD: Scarecrow Press, 1996.

Mehta, Gita. *Snakes and Ladders: Glimpses of Modern India.* New York: Doubleday, 1997.

Moorhouse, Geoffrey. *India Britannica: a Vivid Introduction to the History of British India.* Chicago: Academy Chicago Publishers, 1999.

Paz, Octavio. *In Light of India: Essays.* San Diego, CA: Harcourt Brace & Company, 1997.

Rao, C. Hanumantha and Hans Linnemann, eds. *Economic Reforms and Poverty Alleviation in India.* Thousand Oaks, CA: Sage Publications, 1996.

Read, Anthony. *The Proudest Day: Indian's Long Road to Independence.* New York: W.W. Norton & Company, 1998.

Royle, Trevor. *The Last Days of the Raj.* North Pomfret, VT: Trafalgar Square, 1998.

Saberwal, Satish. *Roots of Crisis: Interpreting Contemporary Indian Society.* Thousand Oaks, CA: Sage Publications, s1996.

Sachs, Jeffrey D., et al., eds. *India in the Era of Economic Reforms.* New York: Oxford University Press, 2000.

Sanguly, Sumit and Neil DeVotta, eds. *Understanding Contemporary India.* Boulder, CO: Lynne Rienner, 2003.

Sekhon, Joti. *Modern India.* New York: McGraw-Hill, 1999.

Sidhu, Waheguru and Jing-dong Yuan. *China and India: Cooperation or Conflict?* Boulder, CO: Lynne Rienner, 2003.

Srinivasan, T.N. and Suresh D. Tendulkar. *India in the World Economy.* Washington, DC: Institute for International Economics, 2001.

Sugata, Bose. *Nationalism, Democracy, and Development: State and Politics in India.* New York: Oxford University Press, 1999.

Tharoor, Shashi. *India: from Midnight to the Millennium.* New York: Arcade Publishing, 1997.

Thomas, Raju G. *Democracy, Security, and Development in India.* New York: Saint Martin's Press, 1996.

Tomlinson, B.R. *The Economy of Modern India, 1860–1970.* New York: Cambridge University Press, 1993.

Vanaik, Achin. *The Furies of Indian Communalism: Religion, Modernity and Secularization.* New York: Verso, 1997.

Vohra, Ranbir. *The Making of India: a Historical Survey.* Armonk, NY: M.E. Sharpe, 2000.

Wolpert, Stanley A. *A New History of India.* New York: Oxford University Press, 3rd ed. 1989.

Wolpert, Stanley A. *Nehru: a Tryst with Destiny.* New York: Oxford University Press, 1996.

Iran

Abrahamian, Ervand. *Khomeinism: Essays on the Islamic Republic.* Berkeley, CA: University of California Press, 1993.

Adelkhah, Fariba. *Being Modern in Iran.* New York: Columbia University Press, 2000.

Amanat, Abbas. *Iran: A Modern History.* New Haven CT: Yale University Press, 2018.

Amuzegar, Jahangir. *Iran's Economy under the Islamic Republic.* New York: Saint Martin's Press, 1994.

Azimi, Fakhreddin. *The Quest for Democracy in Iran: A Century of Struggle against Authoritarian Rule.* Cambridge: Harvard University Press, 2008.

Baktiari, Bahman. *Parliamentary Politics in Revolutionary Iran: the Institutionalization of Factional Politics.* Gainesville, FL: University Press of Florida, 1996.

Bayandor, Darioush. *Iran and the CIA: The Fall of Mossadeq Revisited.* New York: Palgrave Macmillan, 2010.

Cordesman, Anthony H. *Iran's Military Forces in Transition.* Westport, CT: Greenwood Publishing Group, 1999.

Cordesman, Anthony H. and Ahmed S. Hashim. *Iran: Dilemmas of Dual Containment.* Boulder, CO: Westview Press, 1997.

Cordesman, Anthony H., Adam Mausner, and Aram Nerguizian. *U.S. and Iranian Strategic Competition.* Washington D.C.: Center for Strategic and International Studies, 2012.

Daneshar, Parviz. *Revolution in Iran.* New York: Saint Martin's Press, 1996.

Farmanfarmaian, Manucher and Roxane Farmanfarmaian. *Blood and Oil: Memoirs of a Persian Prince.* New York: Random House, 1997.

Gheissari, Ali. *Contemporary Iran: Economy, Society, Politics.* New York: Oxford University Press, 2009.

Gieling, Saskia M. *Religion and War in Revolutionary Iran.* London: I.B. Tauris, 1999.

Goode, James F. *United States and Iran: in the Shadow of Musaddiq.* New York: Saint Martin's Press, 1997.

Hashemi, Nader and Danny Postel. *The People Reloaded: The Green Movement and the Struggle for Iran's Future.* Brooklyn NY: Melville House, 2011.

Heiss, Mary Ann. *Empire and Nationhood: the United States, Great Britain, and Iranian Oil, 1950–1954.* New York: Columbia University Press, 1997.

Keddie, Nikki R. *Iran and Muslim World: Resistance and Revolution.* New York: New York University Press, 1995.

Mackey, Sandra. *The Iranians.* New York: NAL/Dutton, 1998.

Metz, Helen Chapin, ed. *Iran: a Country Study.* Washington, DC: U.S. GPO, 4th ed. 1989.

Moses, Russell L. *Freeing the Hostages: Reexamining U.S.-Iranian Negotiations and Soviet Policy.* Pittsburgh, PA: University of Pittsburgh Press, 1996.

Nafisi, Azar, *Reading Lolita in Tehran*. New York: Random House, 2003.

Mousavian, Seyed Hossein. *The Iranian Nuclear Crisis: A Memoir*. Washington D.C.: Carnegie Endowment for International Peace, 2012.

Peimani, Hooman. *Iran and the United States: the Rise of the West Asian Regional Grouping*. Westport, CT: Greenwood Publishing Group, 1999.

Riesebrodt, Martin. *Pious Passion: the Emergence of Modern Fundamentalism in the United States and Iran*. Berkeley, CA: University of California Press, 1993.

Ritter, Scott. *Dealbreaker: Donald Trump and the Unmaking of the Iran Nuclear Agreement*. Gardena CA: SCB Distributors, 2018.

Sciolino, Elaine. *Persian Mirrors: the Elusive Face of Iran*. New York: The Free Press, 2000.

Walsh, Lawrence E. *Firewall: the Iran-Contra Conspiracy and Cover-Up*. New York: W.W. Norton & Company, 1997.

Wehrey, Frederic. *The Rise of the Pasdaran: Assessing the Domestic Roles of Iran's Islamic Revolutionary Guards Corps*. Santa Monica: RAND Corporation, 2009.

Wright, Robin B. *The Last Great Revolution: Turmoil and Transformation in Iran*. New York: Alfred A. Knopf, 2000.

Iraq

Al-Hawaheri, Yasmin Husein. *Women in Iraq: The Gender Impact of International Sanctions*. Boulder, CO: Lynne Rienner Publishers, 2008.

Al-Khalil, Samir. *Republic of Fear: the Inside Story of Saddam's Iraq*. Collingdale, PA: DIANE Publishing Company, 2000.

Arnove, Anthony, ed. *Iraq under Siege: the Deadly Impact of Sanctions and War*. Cambridge, MA: South End Press, 2000.

Baram, Amatzia and Barry Rubin, eds. *Iraq's Road to War*. New York: Saint Martin's Press, 1994.

Bhatia, Shyam and Dan McGrory. *Brighter than the Baghdad Sun: Saddam Hussein's Nuclear Threat to the United States*. Washington, DC: Regnery Publishing, 2000.

Braude, Joseph. *The New Iraq*. Boulder, CO: Westview, 2003.

Clawson, Patrick, ed. *How to Build a New Iraq after Saddam*. Washington D.C.: Brookings, 2002.

Cockburn, Andrew. *Out of the Ashes: the Resurrection of Saddam Hussein*. New York: HarperCollins, 2000.

Cordesman, Anthony H. and Ahmed S. Hashim. *Iraq: Sanctions and Beyond*. Boulder, CO: Westview Press, 1997.

Danspeckgruber, Wolfgang F. and Charles R. Tripp, eds. *The Iraqi Aggression against Kuwait: Strategic Lessons and Implications for Europe*. Boulder, CO: Westview Press, 1996.

Elliot, Matthew. *Independent Iraq: British Influence from 1941–1958*. New York: Saint Martin's Press, 1996.

Eriksson, Jacob and Ahmed Khaleel. *Iraq after ISIS: The Challenges of Post-War Recovery*. New York: Palgrave Macmillan, 2019.

Fawn, Rick and Raymond Hinnebusch, eds. *The Iraq War: Causes and Consequences*. Boulder, CO: Lynne Rienner Publishers, 2006.

Grossman, Mark, ed. *Encyclopedia of the Persian Gulf War*. Santa Barbara, CA: ABC-CLIO, 1995.

Haj, Samira. *The Making of Iraq, 1900–1963: Capital, Power and Ideology*. Albany, NY: State University of New York Press, 1997.

Haselkorn, Avigdor. *The Continuing Storm: Iraq, Poisonous Weapons, and Deterrence*. New Haven, CT: Yale University Press, 1998.

Lukitz, Liora. *Iraq: the Search for National Identity*. Portland, OR: Frank Cass & Company, 1995.

Marr, Phebe. *Modern History of Iraq*. 2d ed. Boulder, CO: Westview, 2003.

Metz, Helen Chapin, ed. *Iraq: a Country Study*. Washington, DC: U.S. GPO, 4th ed. 1990.

Mockaitis, Thomas R. *The Iraq War: A Documentary and Reference Guide*. Santa Barbara CA: Greenwood, 2012.

Mohamedou, Mohammad-Mahmoud. *Iraq and the Second Gulf War: State Building and Regime Security*. Bethesda, MD: Austin & Winfield Publishers, 1997.

Musallam, Musallam A. *Iraqi Invasion of Kuwait: Saddam Hussein, His State and International Power Politics*. New York: Saint Martin's Press, 1996.

Nakash, Yitzhak. *The Shiis of Iraq*. Princeton, NJ: Princeton University Press, 1994.

Rahaee, Farhang, ed. *The Iran-Iraq War: the Politics of Aggression*. Gainesville, FL: University Press of Florida, 1993.

Shadid, Anthony. *Night Draws Near: Iraq's People in the Shadow of America's War*. New York: Henry Holt and Company, 2006

Simons, G.L. *Iraq: from Sumer to Saddam*. New York: Saint Martin's Press, 1994.

Stansfield, Gareth and Robert Lowe, eds. *The Kurdish Policy Imperative*. Washington: Brookings, 2009

Stiglitz, Joseph E. and Linda J. Bilmes. *The Three Trillion Dollar War: The True Cost of the Iraq Conflict*. New York: W.W. Norton, 2008

Israel

Arain, Asher. *The Second Republic: Politics in Israel*. Chatham, NJ: Chatham House Publishers, 1997.

Avruch, Kevin and Walter P. Zenner, eds. *Critical Essays on Israeli Society, Religion, and Government: Books on Israel*. Albany, NY: State University of New York Press, 1996.

Barkai, Haim. *The Lessons of Israel's Great Inflation*. Westport, CT: Greenwood Pub-lishing Group, 1995.

Barnett, Michael N., ed. *Israel in Comparative Perspective: Challenging the Conventional Wisdom*. Albany, NY: State University of New York Press, 1996.

Bar-On, Mordechai. *In Pursuit of Peace: a History of the Israeli Peace Movement*. Washington, DC: United States Institute of Peace Press, 1996.

Barzilai, Gad. *Wars, Internal Conflicts, and Political Order: a Jewish Democracy in the Middle East*. Albany, NY: State University of New York Press, 1996.

Ben-Ari, Eyal, ed. *Grasping Land: Space and Place in Contemporary Israeli Discourse and Experience*. State University of New York Press, 1997.

Ben Meir, Yehuda. *Civil-Military Relations in Israel*. New York: Columbia University Press, 1995.

Benson, Michael T. *Harry S. Truman and the Founding of Israel*. Westport, CT: Greenwood Publishing Group, 1997.

Bickerton, Ian J. and Carla L. Klausner. *A Concise History of the Arab-Israeli Conflict*. Upper Saddle River, NJ: Prentice Hall, 1997.

Boyarin, Jonathan. *Palestine and Jewish History: Criticism at the Borders of Ethnography*. Minneapolis, MN: University of Minnesota Press, 1996.

Bregman, Ahron. *Israel's Wars, 1947–1993*. New York: Routledge, 2000.

Buchanan, Andrew S. *Peace with Justice: a History of the Israeli-Palestinian Declaration*. New York: Saint Martin's Press, 2000.

Chesin, Amir S., et al. *Separate but Unequal*. Cambridge, MA: Harvard University Press, 1999.

Cohen, Asher. *Israel and the Politics of Jewish Identity: the Secular-Religious Impasse*. Baltimore, MD: Johns Hopkins University Press, 2000.

Cohen, Avner. *Israel and the Bomb*. New York: Columbia University Press, 1998.

Cohen, Stuart A. *Democratic Societies and Their Armed Forces: Israel in Comparative Context*. Portland, OR: Frank Cass Publishers, 2000.

Cordesman, Anthony H. *Perilous Prospects: the Peace Process and the Arab-Israeli Military Balance*. Portland, OR: Frank Cass & Company, 1996.

Corzine, Phyllis. *The Palestinian-Israeli Accord*. San Diego, CA: Lucent Books, 1996.

Dumper, Michael. *The Politics of Jerusalem since 1967*. New York: Columbia University Press, 1996.

Eban, Abba S. *Diplomacy for the Next Century*. New Haven, CT: Yale University Press, 1998.

Bibliography

Edelheit, Hershel and Abraham J. Edelheit. *Israel and the Jewish World, 1948–1993: A Chronology.* Westport, CT: Greenwood Publishing Group, 1995.

Evron, Boas. *Jewish State or Israeli Nation?* Bloomington, IN: Indiana University Press, 1995.

Ezrahi, Yaron. *Rubber Bullets: Power and Conscience in Modern Israel.* New York: Farrar, Straus & Giroux, 1996.

Freeman, Robert Owen, ed. *Israel's First Fifty Years.* Gainesville, FL: University Press of Florida, 2000.

Garfinkle, Adam. *Politics and Society in Modern Israel: Myths and Realities.* Armonk, NY: M.E. Sharpe, 1997.

Gilbert, Martin. *Israel: a History.* New York: William Morrow & Company, 1998.

Gilbert, Martin. *Jerusalem in the Twentieth Century.* New York: John Wiley & Sons, 1996.

Goldscheider, Calvin. *Israel's Changing Society. Population, Ethnicity, and Development.* 2d. ed. Boulder, CO: Westview, 2002.

Gordon, Haim. *Quicksand: Israel, the Intifada, and the Rise of Political Evil.* East Lansing, MI: Michigan State University, 1995.

Hartman, David. *Israelis and the Jewish Tradition: an Ancient People Debating Its Future.* New Haven, CT: Yale University Press, 2000.

Hazony, Yoram. *Jewish State.* New York: Basic Books, 2000.

Hohenberg, John. *Israel at 50.* Syracuse, NY: Syracuse University Press, 1998.

Horovitz, David, ed. *Shalom, Friend: the Life and Legacy of Yitzhak Rabin.* New York: Newmarket Press, 1996.

Ilan, Amitzur. *The Origin of the Arab–Israeli Arms Race: Arms, Embargo, Military Power and Decision in the 1948 Palestine War.* Albany, NY: New York University Press, 1996.

Indyk, Martin. *Innocent Abroad: An Intimate History of American Peace Diplomacy in the Middle East.* New York: Simon & Schuster, 2009

Isserlin, Ben. *The Israelites.* New York: Thames & Hudson, 1998.

Karpin, Michael and Ina Friedman. *Murder in the Name of God: the Plot to Kill Yitzhak Rabin.* New York: Henry Holt & Company, 1998.

Karsh, Efraim, ed. *Between War and Peace: Dilemmas of Israeli Security.* Portland, OR: Frank Cass & Company, 1996.

Karsh, Efraim, ed. *From Rabin to Netanyahu: Israel's Troubled Agenda.* Portland, OR: Frank Cass & Company, 1997.

Khatchadourian, Haig. *The Quest for Peace between Israel and the Palestinians.* New York: Peter Lang Publishing, 2000.

Kop, Yaakov and Robert E. Litan. *Sticking Together. The Israeli Experiment in Pluralism.* Washington D.C.: Brookings, 2002.

Lawless, Richard I. *The Arab-Israeli Conflict: an Encyclopedia.* Santa Barbara, CA: ABC-CLIO, 2001.

Lazin, Frederick A. and Gregory S. Mahler, eds. *Israel in the Nineties: Development and Conflict.* Gainesville, FL: University Press of Florida, 1996.

Levey, Zach. *Israel and the Western Powers, 1952–1960.* Chapel Hill, NC: University Press of North Carolina, 1997.

Levran, Aharon. *Israel after the Storm: Strategic Lessons from the Second Gulf War.* Portland, OR: Frank Cass & Company, 1997.

Levy, Yagil. *Trial and Error: Israel's Route from War to De-Escalation.* Albany, NY: State University of New York Press, 1997.

Linn, Ruth. *Conscience at War: The Israeli Soldier as a Moral Critic.* Albany, NY: State University of New York Press, 1996.

Litwin, Howard. *Uprooted in Old Age: Russian Jews and Their Social Networks in Israel.* Westport, CT: Greenwood Publishing Group, 1995.

Lomsky-Feder, Edna and Eyal Ben-Ari, eds. *The Military and Militarism in Israeli Society.* Albany, NY: State University of New York Press, 2000.

Makovsky, David. *Making Peace with the PLO: the Rabin Government's Road to the Oslo Accord.* Boulder, CO: Westview Press, 1995.

Metz, Helen Chapin, ed. *Israel: a Country Study.* Washington, DC: U.S. GPO, 3rd ed. 1990.

Mitchell, Thomas G. *Israel/Palestine and the Politics of a Two-State Solution.* Jefferson NC: McFarland, 2013.

Netanyahu, Benjamin. *A Place among the Nations: Israel and the World.* New York: Bantam Books, 1993.

Peres, Shimon. *Battling for Peace: a Memoir.* New York: Random House, 1995.

Peres, Shimon. *For the Future of Israel.* Baltimore, MD: Johns Hopkins University Press, 1998.

Peretz, Don. *The Arab–Israeli Dispute.* New York: Facts on File, 1996.

Peri, Yoram, ed. *The Assassination of Yitzhak Rabin.* Stanford, CA: Stanford University Press, 2000.

Plessner, Yakir. *The Political Economy of Israel: from Ideology to Stagnation.* Albany, NY: State University of New York Press, 1993.

Quandt, William B. *Peace Process: American Diplomacy and the Arab-Israeli Conflict since 1967.* Washington D.C.: Brookings, 2005.

Rabin, Leah. *Rabin: Our Life, His Legacy.* New York: The Putnam Publishing Group, 1997.

Rabinovich, Itamar. *The Brink of Peace: the Israeli-Syrian Negotiations.* Princeton, NJ: Princeton University Press, 1998.

Reich, Bernard. *Historical Dictionary of Israel.* Lanham, MD: Scarecrow Press, 1992.Reich, Bernard and David H. Goldberg. *Political Dictionary of Israel.* Lanham, MD: Scarecrow Press, 2000.

Reich, Bernard. *Securing the Covenant: United States-Israeli Relations after the Cold War.* Westport, CT: Greenwood Publishing Group, 1995.

Reinharz, Jehuda. *Chaim Weizmann: the Making of a Statesman.* New York: Oxford University Press, 1993.

Rouhana, Nadim W. *Palestinian Citizens in an Ethnic Jewish State: Identities in Conflict.* New Haven, CT: Yale University Press, 1997.

Rubin, Barry, et al., eds. *From War to Peace: Arab-Israeli Relations, 1973–1993.* New York: New York University Press, 1994.

Said, Edward W. *The End of the Peace Process; Oslo and After.* New York: Pantheon Books, 2000.

Sela, Avraham. *The Decline of the Arab-Israeli Conflict: Middle East Politics and the Quest for Regional Order.* Albany, NY: State University of New York Press, 1997.

Shafir, Gershon, ed. *New Israel.* New York: HarperCollins, 2000.

Sharkansky, Ira. *Policy Making in Israel: Routines for Simple Problems and Coping with the Complex.* Pittsburgh, PA: University of Pittsburgh Press, 1997.

Sheffer, Gabriel, ed. *U.S.-Israeli Relations at the Crossroads.* Portland, OR: Frank Cass & Company, 1997.

Shindler, Colin. *Israel, Likud, and the Zionist Dream: Power, Politics, and Ideology from Begin to Netanyahu.* New York: Saint Martin's Press, 1995.

Shlain, Avi. *The Iron Wall: Israel and the Arab World.* New York: W.W. Norton & Company, 2000.

Sternhell, Zeev. Translated by David Maisel. *The Founding Myths of Israel: Nationalism, Socialism and the Making of the Jewish State.* Princeton, NJ: Princeton University Press, 1998.

Thomas, Baylis. *The Dark Side of Zionism: The Quest for Security through Dominance.* Lanham, MD: Rowan & Littlefield, 2009

Troen, S. Ilan and Noah Lucas, eds. *Israel: the First Decade of Independence.* Albany, NY: State University of New York Press, 1995.

Van Creveld, Martin. *The Sword and the Olive: a Critical History of the Israeli Defense Force.* New York: Public Affairs, 1998.

Wheatcroft, Geoffrey. *The Controversy of Zion: Jewish Nationalism, the Jewish State, and the Unresolved Jewish Dilemma.* Reading, MA: Addison Wesley Longman, 1996.

Yiftachel, Oren, ed. *Ethnic Frontiers and Peripheries: Perspectives on Development and*

Inequality in Israel. Boulder, CO: Westview Press, 1998.

Jordan

Brand, Laurie A. *Jordan's Inter-Arab Relations: the Political Economy of Alliance Making.* New York: Columbia University Press, 1995.

Fischbach, Michael R. *State, Society and Land in Jordan.* Boston, MA: Brill Academic Publishers, 2000.

Lukacs, Yehuda. *Israel, Jordan, and the Peace Process.* Syracuse, NY: Syracuse University Press, 1996.

Metz, Helen Chapin, ed. *Jordan: a Country Study.* Washington, DC: U.S. GPO, 4th ed. 1991.

Piro, Timothy J. *The Political Economy of Market Reform in Jordan.* Lanham, MD: Rowman & Littlefield, 1998.

Ryan, Curtis R. *Jordan in Transition: From Hussein to Abdullah.* Boulder, CO: Lynne Rienner Publishers.

Salibi, Kamal. *A Modern History of Jordan.* New York: Saint Martin's Press, 1998.

Satloff, Robert B. *From Abdullah to Hussein: Jordan in Transition.* New York: Oxford University Press, 1994.

Kuwait

Al-Nakib, Farah. *Kuwait Transformed: A History of Oil and Urban Life.* Stanford CA: Stanford University Press, 2016.

Anscombe, Frederick F. *The Ottoman Gulf: the Creation of Kuwait, Saudi Arabia, and Qatar, 1870–1914.* New York: Columbia University Press, 1997.

Clements, Frank A. *Kuwait.* Santa Barbara, CA: ABC-CLIO, rev. ed. 1996.

Cordesman, Anthony H. *Kuwait: Recovery and Security after the Gulf War.* Boulder, CO: Westview Press, 1997.

Longva, Anh Nga. *Walls Built in Sand: Migration, Exclusion and Society in Kuwait.* Boulder, CO: Westview Press, 1997.

Smith, Simon C. *Kuwait, 1950–1965: Britain, the Al-Sabah, and Oil.* New York: Oxford University Press, 1999.

Tetreault, Mary Ann. *Stories of Democracy: Politics and Society in Contemporary Kuwait.* New York: Columbia University Press, 1999.

Lebanon

Abraham, A.J. *The Lebanon War.* Westport, CT: Greenwood Publishing Group, 1996.

Abukhalil, Asad. *Historical Dictionary of Lebanon.* Lanham, MD: Scarecrow Press, 1998.

Bleaney, C.H. *Lebanon.* Santa Barbara, CA: ABC-CLIO, 1992.

Colello, Thomas, ed. *Lebanon: a Country Study.* Washington, DC: U.S. GPO, 3rd ed. 1989.

El-Solh, Raghid. *Lebanon and Arabism.* New York: Saint Martin's Press, 1999.

Harris, William. *Faces of Lebanon: Sects, Wars and Global Expansion.* Princeton, NJ: Markus Wiener Publishers, 1997.

——. *Lebanon: A History 600–2011.* New York: Oxford University Press, 2012.

Kalawoun, Nasser M. *The Struggle for Lebanon: a Modern History of Lebanese-Egyptian Relations.* New York: I.B. Tauris & Company, 2000.

Maasri, Zeina. *Off the Wall–Political Posters of the Lebanese Civil War.* London: I.B. Tauris,

Malik, Habib C. *Between Damascus and Jerusalem: Lebanon and the Middle East Peace Process.* Washington, DC: The Washington Institute for Near East Policy, 2000.

Phares, Walid. *Lebanese Christian Nationalism: the Rise and Fall of an Ethnic Resistance.* Boulder, CO: Lynne Rienner Publishers, 1994.

Picard, Elizabeth. Translated by Franklin Philip. *Lebanon: a Shattered Country* New York: Holmes & Meier Publishers, 2001.

Ranstorp, Magnus. *Hizb'allah in Lebanon: the Politics of the Western Hostage Crisis.* New York: Saint Martin's Press, 1997.

Schulze, Kirsten E. *Intervention, Israeli Covert Diplomacy and the Maronites.* New York: Saint Martin's Press, 1997.

Shehadi, Nadim and Dana Haffar-Mills, eds. *Lebanon: a History of Conflict and Consensus.* New York: Saint Martin's Press, 1993.

Winslow, Charles. *Lebanon.* New York: Routledge, 1996.

Zamir, Meir. *Lebanon's Quest, 1929–1939.* New York: Saint Martin's Press, 1998.

Zisser, Eyal. *Lebanon: the Challenge of Independence.* New York: I.B. Tauris & Company, 2000.

The Maldives

Metz, Helen Chapin, ed. *Indian Ocean: Five Island Countries.* Washington, DC: U.S. GPO, 3rd ed. 1995.

Robinson, J.J. *The Maldives: Islamic Republic, Tropical Autocracy.* London: Hurst, 2015.

Nepal

Cameron, Mary M. *On the Edge of the Auspicious: Gender and Caste in Nepal.* Champaign, IL: University of Illinois Press, 1998.

Gellner, David, et al., eds. *Nationalism and Ethnicity in a Hindu Kingdom: the Politics and Culture of Contemporary Nepal.* Newark, NJ: Gordon & Breach Publishing Group, 1997.

Hangen, Susan I. *The Rise of Ethnic Politics in Nepal: Democracy in the Margins.* New York: Routledge, 2010.

Savada, Andrea Matles, ed. *Nepal and Bhutan: Country Studies.* Washington, DC: U.S. GPO, 3rd ed. 1993.

Oman

El-Solh, Rahbih, ed. *Oman and the South-Eastern Shore of Arabia.* Milford, CT: LPC/InBook, 1997.Jones, Jeremy and Nicholas Ridout. *Oman, Culture and Diplomacy.* Edinburgh, Edinburgh University Press, 2012.

Joyce, Miriam. *The Sultanate of Oman a Twentieth Century History.* Westport, CT: Greenwood Publishing Group, 1995.

Kechichian, Joseph A. *Oman and the World: the Emergence of an Independent Foreign Policy.* Santa Monica, CA: The Rand Corporation, 1995.

Pakistan

Ahmad, Ishtiaq and Adnan Rafiq, eds. *Pakistan's Democratic Transition: Change and Persistence.* New York: Routledge, 2017.

Ahmed, Samania and David Cortright, eds. *Pakistan and the Bomb: Public Opinion and Nuclear Options.* Notre Dame, IN: University of Notre Dame Press, 1998.

Blood, Peter R., ed. *Pakistan: a Country Study.* Washington, DC: U.S. GPO, 6th ed. 1995.

Burki, Shahid Javed. *Historical Dictionary of Pakistan.* Lanham, MD: Scarecrow Press, 1999.

Fair, C. Christine. *The Madrassah Challenge: Militancy and Religious Education in Pakistan.* Washington: US Institute of Peace Press, 2008

Haqqani, Husain. *Pakistan: Between Mosque and Military.* Washington: Carnegie Endowment for International Peace, 2005

Harrison, Selig S., et al., eds. *India and Pakistan: the First Fifty Years.* New York: Cambridge University Press, 1998.

Husain, Ishrat. *Pakistan: the Economy of an Elitist State.* New York: Oxford University Press, 1999.

Hussain, Jane. *A History of the People of Pakistan: Toward Independence.* New York: Oxford University Press, 1998.

Looney, Robert E. *The Pakistani Economy: Economic Growth and Structural Reform.* Westport, CT: Greenwood Publishing Group, 1997.

McGrath, Allen. *The Destruction of Pakistan's Democracy.* New York: Oxford University Press, 1999.

Raza, Rafi, ed. *Pakistan in Perspective, 1947–1997.* New York: Oxford University Press, 1998.

Raza, Rafi. *Zulfikar Ali Bhutto and Pakistan 1967–1977.* New York: Oxford University Press, 1997.

Rizvi, Hasan Askari. *Military, State and Society in Pakistan.* New York: Saint Martin's Press, 2000.

Samad, Yunas. *A Nation in Turmoil: Nationalism and Ethnicity in Pakistan, 1937–1958.* Thousand Oaks, CA: Sage Publications, 1995.

Bibliography

Sattar, Babar. *The Non-Proliferation Regime and Pakistan: the Comprehensive Test Ban Treaty as a Case Study.* New York: Oxford University Press, 2000.

Shafqat, Saeed. *Civil-Military Relations in Pakistan: from Zulfikar Ali Bhutto to Benazir Bhutto.* Westport, CT: Westview Press, 1997.

Shah, Mehtab A. *The Foreign Policy of Pakistan: Ethnic Impacts on Diplomacy, 1971–1994.* New York: Saint Martin's Press, 1997.

Siddiqa, Ayesha. *Military Inc.: Inside Pakistan's Military Economy.* London: Pluto Press, 2007.

Talbot, Ian. *Pakistan: a Modern History.* New York: Saint Martin's Press, 1999.

Wirsing, Robert G. *India, Pakistan and the Kashmir Dispute: on Regional Conflict and Its Resolution.* New York: Saint Martin's Press, 1994.

Zaidi, S. Akbar. *Issues in Pakistan's Economy.* New York: Oxford University Press, 2000.

Ziring, Lawrence. *Pakistan in the Twentieth Century: a Political History.* New York: Oxford University Press, 1998.

Palestine

Abu-Nimer, Mohammed. *Dialogue, Conflict Resolution, and Change: Arab-Jewish Encounters in Israel.* Albany, NY: State University of New York Press, 1999.

Arnon, Arie and Jimmy Weinblatt. *The Palestinian Economy: between Imposed Integration and Voluntary Separation.* Boston, MA: Brill Academic Publishers, 1997.

Ciment, James. *Palestine Israel: the Long Conflict.* New York: Facts on File, 1997.

Cragg, Kenneth. *Palestine: the Prize and Price of Zion.* Herndon, VA: Cassell Academic, 1997.

Dannreuther, Roland. *Soviet Union and Palestine Resistance.* New York: Saint Martin's Press, 1998.

Diwan, Ishac and Radwan A. Shaban. *Development under Adversity: the Palestinian Economy in Transition.* Washington, DC: The World Bank, 1999.

Farsoun, Samih K. and Christina E. Zacharia. *Palestine and the Palestinians: a Stateless Nation.* Boulder, CO: Westview Press, 1997.

Holliday, Laurel. *Children of Israel, Children of Palestine.* New York: Pocket Books, 1998.

Inbari, Pinhas. *The Palestinians between Terrorism and Statehood.* Portland, OR: International Specialized Book Services, 1998.

Jabar, Hala. *Hezbollah: Born with a Vengeance.* New York: Columbia University Press, 1997.

Kass, Ilana and Bard O'Neill. *The Deadly Embrace: the Impact of Israel and Palestinian Rejectionism on the Peace Process.* Lanham, MD: University Press of America, 1996.

Khalidi, Rashid. *Palestinian Identity.* New York: Columbia University Press, 1997.

Kimmerling, Baruch. *Palestinians: the Making of a People.* New York: The Free Press, 1993.

Klieman, Aharon. *Compromising Palestine: a Guide to Final Status Negotiations.* New York: Columbia University Press, 1999.

Mattar, Philip. *Encyclopedia of the Palestinians.* New York: Facts on File, 1999.

Nazzal, Nafez and Laila A. Nazzal. *Historical Dictionary of Palestine.* Lanham, MD: Scarecrow Press, 1997.

Peleg, Ilan. *Human Rights in the West Bank and Gaza.* Syracuse, NY: Syracuse University Press, 1995.

Robinson, Glenn E. *Building a Palestinian State: the Incomplete Revolution.* Bloomington, IN: Indiana University Press, 1997.

Rouhana, Nadim N. *Palestinians in an Ethnic Jewish State: Identities in Conflict.* New Haven, CT: Yale University Press, 1997.

Shemesh, Moshe. *The Palestinian Entity, 1959–1974: Arab Politics and the PLO.* Portland, OR: International Specialized Book Services, rev. ed. 1996.

Swedenburg, Ted. *Memories of Revolt: the 1936–39 Rebellion and the Palestinian National Past.* Minneapolis, MN: University of Minnesota Press, 1995.

Toubbeh, Jamil I. *Day of the Long Night: a Palestinian Refugee Remembers the Nakba.* Jefferson, NC: McFarland & Company, 1997.

Turner, Mandy and Omar Shweiki. *Decolonizing Palestinian Political Economy: De-development and Beyond.* New York: Palgrave Macmillan, 2014.

Qatar

Anscombe, Frederick F. *The Ottoman Gulf: the Creation of Kuwait, Saudi Arabia, and Qatar, 1870–1914.* New York: Columbia University Press, 1997.

Fromherz, Allen J. *Qatar: Rise to Power and Influence.* New York: IB Tauris, 2017.

Reich, Bernard and Steven Dorr. *Qatar.* Westport, CT: Westview Press, 1996.

Saudi Arabia

Cordesman, Anthony H. *Saudi Arabia: Guarding the Desert Kingdom.* Westport, CT: Westview Press, 1997.

Elliott House, Karen. *On Saudi Arabia: Its People, Past, Religion, Fault Line—And Future.* New York: Vintage Books, 2013.

Fancy, Mamoun. *Saudi Arabia and the Politics of Dissent.* New York: Saint Martin's Press, 1999.

Hart, Parker T. *Saudi Arabia and the United States: Birth of a Security Partnership.* Bloomington, IN: Indiana University Press, 1998.

Kostiner, Joseph. *The Making of Saudi Arabia, 1916–1936: from Chieftaincy to Monarchical State.* New York: Oxford University Press, 1993.

Long, David E. *The Kingdom of Saudi Arabia.* Gainesville, FL: University Press of Florida, 1997.

Mabon, Simon. *Saudi Arabia and Iran: Power and Rivalry in the Middle East.* New York: IB Tauris, 2013.

Pampanini, Andrea H. *Cities from the Arabian Desert: the Building of Jubail and Yanbu in Saudi Arabia.* Westport, CT: Greenwood Publishing Group, 1997.

Partrick, Neil, ed. *Saudi Arabian Foreign Policy: Conflict and Cooperation.* New York: IB Tauris, 2016.

Peterson, J.E. *Historical Dictionary of Saudi Arabia.* Lanham, MD: Scarecrow Press, 1993.

Vassiliev, Alexei. *The History of Saudi Arabia.* New York: New York University Press, 2000.

Yizraeli, Sarah. *The Remaking of Saudi Arabia: the Struggle between King Sa'ud and Crown Prince Faysal, 1953–1962.* Syracuse, NY: Syracuse University Press, 1998.

Sri Lanka

Athukorala, Prema-Chandra and Sarath Rajapatirana. *Liberalization and Industrial Transformation: Sri Lanka in International Perspective.* New York: Oxford University Press, 2000.

Bartholomeusz, Tessa J. and Chandra R. De Silva, eds. *Buddhist Fundamentalism and Minority Identities in Sri Lanka.* Albany, NY: State University Press of New York Press, 1998.

De Silva, K.M. *Regional Powers and Small State Security: India and Sri Lanka, 1977–1990.* Baltimore, MD: Johns Hopkins University Press, 1995.

Keethaponcalan, S.I. *Post War Dilemmas of Sri Lanka: Democracy and Reconciliation.* New York: Routledge, 2019.

Perera, Nihal. *Society and Space: Colonialism, Nationalism and Postcolonial Identity in Sri Lanka.* Boulder, CO: Westview Press, 1998.

Ross, Russell R. and Andrea Matles Savada, eds. *Sri Lanka: a Country Study.* Washington, DC: U.S. GPO, 2nd ed. 1990.

Samarasinghe, S.W. and Vidyamali Samarasinghe. *Historical Dictionary of Sri Lanka.* Lanham, MD: Scarecrow Press, 1997.

Wickramasingh, Nira, *Sri Lanka in the Modern Age: A History.* New York: Oxford University Press, 2014.

Wilson, A. Jeyaratnam. *Sri Lankan Tamil Nationalism: Its Origins and Development in the Nineteenth and Twentieth Centuries.* Vancouver, BC: UBC Press, 1999.

Bibliography

Syria

Agha, Hussein J. and Ahmad S. Khalidi. *Syria and Iran: Rivalry and Co-Operation.* New York: Council on Foreign Relations, 1995.

Commins, David. *Historical Dictionary of Syria.* Lanham, MD: Scarecrow Press, 1996.

Gelvin, James L. *Divided Loyalties: Nationalism and Mass Politics in Syria at the Close of Empire.* Berkeley, CA: University of California Press, 1998.

Hinnebusch, Raymond. *The State and the Political Economy of Reform in Syria.* Boulder, CO: Lynne Rienner Publishers, 2008.

Kienle, Eberhard, ed. *Contemporary Syria: Liberalization between Cold War and Peace.* New York: Saint Martin's Press, 1997.

Lawson, Fred H. *Why Syria Goes to War: Thirty Years of Confrontation.* New York: Cornell University Press, 1996.

Perthes, Volker. *Political Economy of Syria under Asad.* New York: Saint Martin's Press, 1997.

Phillips, Christopher. The Battle for Syria: International Rivalry in the New Middle East. New Haven CT: Yale University Press, 2016.

Quilliam, Neil. *Syria and the New World Order.* Lowell, MA: Ithaca Press, 1999.

Rabinovich, Itamar. *The Brink of Peace: the Israel-Syrian Negotiations.* Princeton, NJ: Princeton University Press, 1998.

Saunders, Bonnie F. *The United States and Arab Nationalism: the Syrian Case.* Westport, CT: Greenwood Publishing Group, 1996.

Seale, Patrick. *Asad: The Struggle for the Middle East.* Berkeley, CA: University of California Press, 1988.

Sorenson, David S. *Syria in Ruins: The Dynamics of the Syrian Civil War.* Santa Barbara CA: Praeger, 2016.

Yassin-Kassab, Robin and Leila Al-Shami. *Burning Country: Syrians in Revolution and War.* London: Pluto Press, 2016.

Turkey

Adaman, Fikret and Murat Arsel. *Environmentalism in Turkey: Between Democracy and Development?* New York: Routledge, 2016.

Ahmad, Feroz. *The Making of Modern Turkey.* New York: Routledge, 1993.

Abramowitz, Morton, ed. *The United States and Turkey. Allies in Need.* Washington, D.C.: Brookings, 2003.

Altunisik, Meliha Benli and Ozlem Tur Kavli. *Turkey.* NY: Routledge, 2002.

Balim, Cigdem, et al., eds. *Turkey: Political, Social and Economic Challenges in the 1990s.* Boston, MA: Brill Academic Publishers, 1995.

Balkir, Canan and Allan M. Williams, eds. *Turkey and Europe.* New York: Saint Martin's Press, 1993.

Barkey, Henri J. and Graham E. Fuller. *Turkey's Kurdish Question.* Lanham, MD: Rowman & Littlefield, 1997.

Bugra, Ayse. *State and Business in Modern Turkey: a Comparative Study.* Albany, NY: State University of New York Press, 1994.

Cagaptay, Soner. *The New Sultan: Erdogan and the Crisis of Modern Turkey.* New York: IB Tauris, 2017.

Dadrian, Vahakn N. *Warrant for Genocide: Key Elements of Turko-Armenian Conflict.* Piscataway, NJ: Transaction Publishers, 1998.

Davison, Andrew. *Secularism and Revivalism in Turkey: a Hermeneutic Reconsideration.* New Haven, CT: Yale University Press, 1998.

Fuller, Graham E. *Turkey as a Pivotal State in the Muslim World.* Washington: U.S. Institute for Peace Press, 2007.

Gunter, Michael M. *Kurds and Future of Turkey.* New York: Saint Martin's Press, 1997.

Heper, Metin, et al., eds. *Turkey and the West: Images of a New Political Culture.* New York: New York: Saint Martin's Press, 1993.

Howe, Marvine. *Turkey Today. A National Divided over Islam's Revival.* Boulder, CO: Westview, 2000.

Kahveci, Erol, et al., eds. *Work and Occupation in Modern Turkey.* Herndon, VA: Cassell Academic, 1996.

Kasaba, Resat and Sibel Bozdogan, eds. *Rethinking Modernity and National Identity in Turkey.* Seattle, WA: University of Washington Press, 1997.

Kedourie, Sylvia. *Seventy-Five Years of the Turkish Republic.* Portland, OR: Frank Cass & Company, 2000.

Kedourie, Sylvia, ed. *Turkey: Identity, Democracy, Politics.* Portland, OR: Frank Cass & Company, 1998.

Kramer, Heinz. *Changing Turkey: Challenges to Europe and the United States.* Washington, DC: Brookings Institution Press, 1999.

Larrabee, F. Stephen and Ian O. Lesser. *Turkish Foreign Policy in an Age of Uncertainty.* Santa Monica, CA: Rand, 2002.

Mango, Andrew. *Turkey: the Challenge of a New Role.* Westport, CT: Greenwood Publishing Group, 1994.

Mastny, Vojtech and Craig Nation, eds. *Turkey between East and West: New Challenges for a Rising Regional Power.* Boulder, CO: Westview Press, 1997.

McDonagh, Bernard. *Turkey.* New York: W.W. Norton & Company, 2000.

Muftuler-Bac, Meltem. *Turkey's Relations with a Changing Europe.* New York: Saint Martin's Press, 1997.

Olsen, Robert, ed. *The Kurdish Nationalist Movement and Its Impact on Turkey in the 1990's.* Lexington, KY: University Press of Kentucky, 1996.

Pitman, Paul M., III, ed. *Turkey: a Country Study.* Washington, DC: U.S. GPO, 4th ed. 1988.

Pope, Hugh and Nicole Pope. *Turkey Unveiled: a History of Modern Turkey.* New York: Overlook Press, 1998.

Rittenberg, Libby, ed. *The Political Economy of Turkey in the Post-Soviet Era: Going West and Looking East?* Westport, CT: Greenwood Publishing Group, 1998.

Togan, S. and V.N. Balasubramanyam, eds. *The Economy of Turkey since Liberalization.* New York: Saint Martin's Press, 1996.

Yilmaz, Bahri. *Challenges to Turkey: the New Role of Turkey in International Politics since the Dissolution of the Soviet Union.* New York: Saint Martin's Press, 1999.

Zürcher, Erik J. *Turkey: a Modern History.* London: I.B. Tauris, 1994.

United Arab Emirates

Al-Fahim, Mohammed. *From Rags to Riches: a Story of Abu Dhabi.* New York: Saint Martin's Press, 1998.

Camarapix Staff. *Spectrum Guide to the United Arab Emirates.* Northampton, MA: Interlink Publishing Group, 1998.

Clements, Frank A. *United Arab Emirates.* Santa Barbara, CA: ABC-CLIO, rev. ed. 1998.

Ulrichsen, Kristian Coates. *The United Arab Emirates: Power, Politics, and Policymaking.* New York: Routledge, 2017.

Yemen

Al-Madhaqi, Ahmed Nomen. *Yemen and the U.S.A.: a Super-Power and a Small-State Relationship.* New York: Saint Martin's Press, 1996.

Auchterlonie, Paul. *Yemen.* Santa Barbara, CA: ABC-CLIO, rev. ed, 1998.

Blumi, Isa. *Destroying Yemen: What Chaos in Arabia tells us about the World.* Oakland CA: University of California Press, 2018.

Brandt, Marieke. *Tribes and Politics in Yemen: A History of the Houthi Conflict.* New York: Oxford University Press.

Burrowes, Robert D. *Historical Dictionary of Yemen.* Lanham, MD: Scarecrow Press, 1995.

Dresch, Paul. *Tribes, Government, and History in Yemen.* New York: Oxford University Press, 1994.

Abu Musa and the Greater and Lesser Tunbs

Ahmadi, Kourosh. *Islands and International Politics in the Persian Gulf.* New York, Routledge, 2008.

Mojtahed-Zadeh, Pirouz. *Maritime Political Geography: The Persian Gulf Islands of Tunbs and Abu Musa.* Boca Raton FL: Universal-Publishers, 2015.

Bibliography

British Indian Ocean Territory (Chagos)
Allen, Stephen. *The Chagos Islanders and International Law*. Portland OR: Hart Publishing, 2014.
Evers, Sandra J.T.M. and Marry Kooy. *Eviction from the Chagos Islands: Displacement and Struggle for Identity against Two World Powers*. Leiden: Brill, 2011.

The Occupied Territories
Alayan, Samira. *Education in East Jerusalem: Occupation, Political Power, and Struggle*. New York: Routledge, 2019.
Asali Nuseibeh, Rawan. *Political Conflict and Exclusion in Jerusalem: The Provision of Education and Social Services*. New York: Routledge, 2016.
Bregman, Ahron. *Cursed Victory: A History of Israel and the Occupied Territories*. London: Penguin Books, 2014.

Pappe, Ilan. *The Biggest Prison on Earth: A History of the Occupied Territories*. London: Oneworld Publications, 2017.

Jammu and Kashmir
Bose, Sumantra. *Kashmir, Roots of Conflict, Paths to Peace*. Cambridge MA: Harvard University Press, 2003.
Zutshi, Chitralekha, ed. *Kashmir: History, Politics, Representation*. New York: Cambridge University Press, 2018.